Practical Insights for Fraud Professionals

Lifting the veil on the dark art

Practical Insights for Fraud Professionals

Lifting the veil on the dark art

Craig Bristow

JUTA

Practical Insights for Fraud Professionals – Lifting the veil on the dark art

First published 2018

1st Floor, Sunclare Building,
21 Dreyer Street, Claremont, 7708, Cape Town

ISBN: 978 1 48512 030 8

Production Co-ordinator: Valencia Wyngaard-Arenz
Cover design: Matthew Bubear-Craemer
Typeset: Elinye Ithuba DTP & Print Solutions (Pty) Ltd
Typeset in Franklin Gothic Book Condensed 10pt on 12pt
Editor: Sarah Johnston
Proofreader: Elisma Roets
Indexer: Lexinfo
Printed and bound:

FOREWORD

Managing fraud and corruption risk is a global challenge which has become even more difficult in recent years as criminals have become more sophisticated and have embraced technology in order to penetrate vulnerable organisations and access the finances of unwitting victims. In order to ensure that we are able to withstand the challenge, we as anti-fraud professionals need to collaborate, network and ensure that we share our many skills and experiences with each other to build a strong body of anti-fraud knowledge from which to draw as a united front.

Practical Insights for Fraud Professionals: Lifting the veil on the dark art, offers end-to-end practical guidance, commencing with strategic fraud risk management, through the structuring of investigations (including conducting interviews, performing lifestyle audits and data analytics) to the subsequent actions we embark on (pressing criminal charges, conducting labour cases, making recoveries and civil claims, bolstering internal controls and reporting structural deficiencies and strategic fraud risks).

The text is well-supported by actual examples often absent in more traditional theoretical books, and the writing style is easy to follow. The book offers insights for novices and seasoned professionals alike.

High-profile cases continue to dominate our headlines. Anti-fraud professionals always seem to be playing catch-up. *Practical Insights for Fraud Professionals* provides quick and tested insights for preventing and responding to fraud, and is a welcome addition to the field.

Steven Powell
Cape Town
November 2018

PREFACE

Seasoned fraud investigators are, in some ways, reminiscent of lazy lions basking in the African sun. They prance around boasting about the size of their latest trophies, but are unwilling to share their hunting secrets with young and aspiring cubs. While this ensures the territorial advantage for the alpha lions, it can be very demoralising for young guns.

It is likely that many people will have a sudden and sobering landing into the world of fraud investigation. Whether by default or by career choice, a first investigation can creep up onto a person unannounced. Invariably a loss has been sustained and the aggrieved party (client or employer) is looking for quick and decisive retribution. This leaves very little time for learning and the inexperienced investigator may be left feeling like a deer caught in the headlights of an oncoming vehicle.

While a 'baptism by fire' may ensure that a person grows up quickly and will get a person to stand on their own two feet without too much ceremony, it is not always desirable. The potential for error is high and no one wants to make a mistake. After all, this is the classic story of 'good versus evil' and all super sleuth literature tells us that 'good' must triumph.

At the end of the day there is no substitute for sound basic training. Good training can allow a person to revert to honed instincts even before having been exposed to actual situations. This assertion may be likened to a highly trained marine or reconnaissance soldier who was never exposed to an actual conflict situation during basic training, but who reacts without thinking once dropped into a conflict zone. In short this is what this book is about: broad, basic training.

So how do we decide what basic training encompasses? Let us imagine that you, as a new inexperienced graduate, were at the retirement party of a highly experienced fraud investigator that you are replacing. If that person was to put their arm around you and take you one side to give you a few pointers, what would those pointers be? What would they tell you to do and what would they tell you to avoid? What templates would they give you to make your transition into the world of fraud investigation easier? This book attempts to capture those things that I imagine the retiring fraud investigator would have passed on. While I am not planning to retire in the medium-term, I can hopefully provide you with guidance a little sooner in your career.

This book is not designed to be a technical guideline. It is designed to give sound practical guidelines on matters that may be of value to any fraud investigator. The practical guidelines are supported by established theory (albeit indirectly through my experience) as far as possible. The guidelines are applicable to new investigators as well as seasoned practitioners who are looking to improve specific elements of their skill set. The book is designed to read as if someone is giving you on-the-job training. It is a conversation and not a lecture. So, if you think it is a little too informal, then you have missed the point.

If not already, before long, you too will have enough experiences to fill multiple books. My only desire is that you will be willing to share these with your colleagues. The more we share our skills and experiences, the stronger the body of knowledge in the field will become and the greater the chances of success we will all have.

I learn something new in this field almost daily, and I am sure that you have a similar experience. Let us combine our skills and knowledge to fight fraud through the establishment of a strong anti-fraud learning community.

All the Best

Craig Bristow
Cape Town
October 2018

ABOUT THE AUTHOR

Craig Bristow has worked and studied over the last thirty years in the fields of Governance, Risk Management, Internal Audit, IT Audit and Fraud Risk Management.

Craig is currently a Head of Internal Audit. He has worked for more than six national and international organisations and his experience covers the fields of life assurance and medical aids, retail and pharmaceutical distribution, construction and paint manufacturing, cooperative wine growing, professional services, oil and gas, shipping, logistics and freight forwarding. Craig has been a Head of Internal Audit in three of these organisations.

Craig's qualifications and certifications include:

Cape Peninsula University of Technology (CPUT - RSA):
National Diploma Internal Auditing (1986 - 1988)
National Higher Diploma Cost Accountancy (1989)
National Higher Diploma Management Practice (1991 - 1992)
National Masters Diploma Management Practice (1992 - 1996)
Institute of Internal Auditors (IIA - USA):
Certified Internal Auditor (CIA) (1997 - 1998)
Certification in Risk Management Assurance (CRMA) (2013)
Information Systems Audit and Control Association (ISACA - USA):
Certified Information Systems Auditor (CISA) (2000)
Certified in Risk and Information Systems Control (CRISC) (2011)
Association of Fraud Examiners (ACFE - USA):
Certified Fraud Examiner (CFE) (2011)

ACKNOWLEDGEMENTS

Where do I begin? How far back do I go? Who do I thank and who do I offend by omission?

I must commence by thanking God, without whom I am nothing.

Next, I must thank my wife, whom I have known, at the time of writing this, for more than 28 years. She is my rock.

Then to the many colleagues and friends who have contributed in some manner to my body of fraud investigation knowledge. It is because you took the time to help me that I am now in a situation to extend this help to others. I have referred to some of you directly in this book. Please note however, that this does not by any means diminish the contributions made by all the other people.

Thank you all.

BOOK OVERVIEW

The philosophy of this book is a practical guide to fraud risk management. The chapters of the book can be divided into the following five broad sections:

SECTION A - INTRODUCTION

Section A provides some general insights into the need for such a book. The aim of this section is to inspire you to learn and to share your learnings with the broader fraud learning community.

SECTION B - FRAUD RISK MANAGEMENT

When talking about fraud there is a natural inclination to oscillate towards cases and detailed investigations. This is however only a portion of the tremendous value that can be added by fraud risk officers to the management of fraud. To limit our development to detailed case investigations would be tantamount to concentrating on only 50% of the total fraud gambit.

A suitable metaphor may be like trying to understand the Earth from the ground up, when what we really need to do is to commence by surveying Earth from a rocket ship before focusing on the continents, countries, cultures, languages, customs and diversity.

Section B is a very exciting section, as it completes the 'fraud' picture for us. It is a great starting point, as it gives us the overview of fraud risk management (the proverbial 'globe' view), by recognising that there is a proactive and a reactive side to fraud risk management.

It provides a practical understanding of what fraud is, what fraud risks are and how to manage them in advance and once materialised.

SECTION C – INVESTIGATION TOOLS

The proactive side of fraud risk management is covered in a fair amount of detail in section B. The reactive side of fraud risk management is a sizeable body of knowledge. It therefore serves it well to separate the reactive side of fraud risk management into its own dedicated section.

Section C sets about describing what is required in a typical fraud investigation from the origin at the stage of awareness, through the investigation up until the finalisation of each subsequent fraud outcome.

Section C has a unique start. It commences with something that I am quite excited about sharing, as it has paid many dividends for my personal development and for the development of those that I have shared my learnings with in the past. Section C commences with the general rules that I have assimilated over my career and which have provided me with much guidance throughout my fraud risk management career. These are the proverbial pearls of wisdom that the retiring Silverback Fraud Risk Officer would have imparted to the young protégé at the retirement party, as mentioned in the introductory anecdote at the commencement of this book. These rules are referred to throughout the book to reinforce practical learning in the same manner that I conduct on-the-job training with my staff in real life.

After the rules, the detailed discussion of how to structure a fraud investigation is supplemented by key techniques (interviewing, lifestyle audits and something that I call 'the group approach').

SECTION D – SUBSEQUENT ACTIONS AND REPORTING

The completion of an investigation does not, however, mark the end of fraud risk management. Section D discusses the subsequent actions needed to take investigative output to finality, including the instituting of criminal cases, embarking on internal labour actions, pursuing civil suits, recovering losses and bolstering controls.

We end section D with a detailed discussion of fraud risk management reporting.

SECTION E – PRACTICAL EXAMPLES AND REFERENCES
Section E contains valuable examples of fraud. In continuation of the ideal of hands-on practical knowledge of fraud, section E purposefully steers away from traditional categorisation and fraud schemes. The fraud examples are, in this section, divided into actual functional and business process topics faced by all employees on a daily basis. The fraud examples have been divided broadly into general fraud topics, fraud related to typical balance sheet accounts, as well as income statement accounts. Fraud schemes are discussed within each of these sections under typical daily business processes such as 'accounts payable' and not under 'theft of assets', etc. Each fraud example contains a description of the specific fraud topic, as well as a list of practical methods through which to investigate the specific matter at hand. Section E is very complete and provides a lot of reference tools. It is intended to provide quick and focussed guidance on specific fraud matters. It will also be helpful in serving as an overall guide to the characteristics of many typical types of fraud schemes.
SECTION F – ADMINISTRATION PRACTICALITIES
Section F discusses how to practically motivate and set up a forensic function. The bulk of this section is dedicated to in-house forensic functions, but reference is made to external forensic consultancies as well. Section F covers such aspects as motivating the need for a function, resourcing and time management.
SECTION G – INDEX
A helpful index to facilitate the quick reference of key concepts, topics and words is included.

INTRODUCTION

Each of us comes into this world with an empty suitcase. This suitcase is attached to our arm and we cannot get rid of it. There is no limit to the size of the suitcase and it can enlarge or shrink as required. As we walk through life, we place various articles into this case. Some of these articles are memories, others are experiences and some are specific skills.

When we come to a situation we stop and look into our suitcase for things to help us. You can only draw things out of your own suitcase to help you in your situations. If you only have a few skills in your suitcase, you will not be in the best position to sort out your problems.

Some of the articles that we place into our suitcases can be unnecessary articles that just weigh us down. Guilt, blame, fear, resentment, anger, prejudice, etc are examples of things that weigh us down. These articles are much heavier and bulkier than skills and useful articles. We spend all our time dragging these articles around with little use. The good news is, however, that we can stop at any time to put articles in or to take articles out. We just have to want to do this.

The idea is to place as many useful articles in your suitcase that you can to assist you in life. We can acquire articles in 'good' and 'bad' situations. For example, if I am in a situation where I believe that I have an unpleasant boss, I can say: 'Well, I have an unpleasant boss and there is not much I can do about that. I plan to leave the organisation. I will however try to make the most of the time that I have here to gather as many skills as I can to benefit me when I am in my new situation.' It is bad enough to have to endure an unpleasant boss, but to endure the boss without any benefit is soul destroying. So, I am going to make the best of this bad situation and be as positive as possible.

I suppose it is all about having an internal locus of control, where you realise that you are in charge of your own situation and that you can decide on how well it ends. It also about having a positive attitude to recognise the good in all situations and to make the most of every situation.

I have seen too many examples of colleagues and contemporaries who do not have the skills and experience to deal appropriately with situations. They reach down into their suitcase and take out the same old tick-box mentality that did not work previously, and muddle through the problem regardless, without adding value and expressing unsubstantiated opinions. The worst thing is that people in the business recognise this, which frequently has a direct negative bearing on the team or on the field in general.

There is no pleasure in making mistakes, nor in running out of options. So, if you get to a situation where you just do not know, put up your hand and say: 'Whoops, sorry, but I just don't know.' Then make sure that you go out of your way to acquire the missing skills to avoid being in that situation again.

If you are a student, you might think that this is less applicable to you, as you are not in the workplace. Not true. Make the most of what you are studying. You will probably never get to go back to redo the specific aspects that you are studying. The learning experiences that you place into your suitcase while you are studying are the tools that you will take with you into the workplace. Everyone knows that a person lacks experience when entering the workplace directly from their studies. It goes without saying therefore that you would want to have as many tools as you can when stepping into the workplace.

To the reader: There are a multitude of practical skills and trade secrets in this book, which will, if you elect to make them your own, put you in a powerful position to be able to react correctly to many situations. What will you be putting in your suitcase today?

CONTENTS

CHAPTER 1

STRATEGIC FRAUD RISK MANAGEMENT

1.1. CHAPTER OVERVIEW AND INTRODUCTION

The management of fraud in any organisation deals with both the management of risks (being potential future events that could occur) and the management and of actual incidents after they have occurred. Complete fraud risk management deals with both these elements and does not favour one element over the other.

The dealing with fraud risks is by its nature, more strategic, while the dealing of actual incidents is largely tactical. We are, in this chapter, going to deal mostly with the strategic and procedural elements of fraud risk management. Subsequent chapters concentrate on how to deal with actual incidents of fraud.

This chapter is essentially split into three parts. We commence with a discussion of the four steps (the fraud charter, fraud policy, fraud strategy and fraud procedures) that are involved in fraud risk management. This is followed by a detailed discussion on the proactive and reactive fraud strategy processes (being one of the elements of fraud risk management). Lastly, we discuss the execution of the fraud risk strategy.

1.2. THE FRAUD RISK MANAGEMENT PROCESS

The management of fraud risks commences with the authority to manage fraud risks. The authority to manage fraud risks is contained in the fraud charter, while the organisation's stance on fraud is defined in a policy document on fraud.

How to manage future fraud risks (the proactive management of fraud risks) and actual fraud incidents (the reactive management of fraud risks) is described in the fraud strategy document. The fraud strategy is supported by various detailed fraud risk management procedure documents and other related activities.

The diagram below depicts the typical high-level steps required in the overall fraud management process in any organisation:

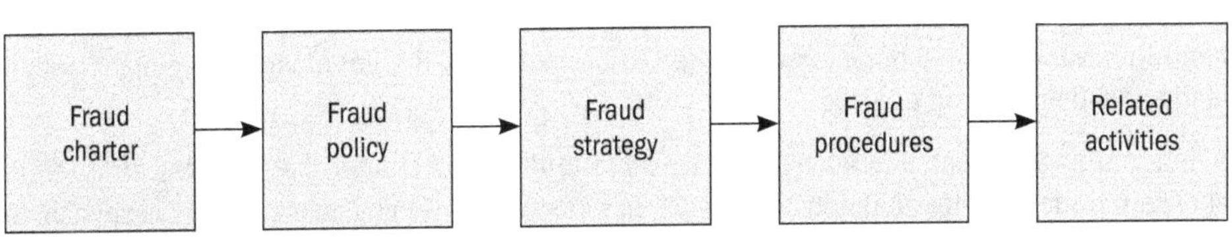

Diagram 1.1 *The fraud risk management process*

1.2.1. Fraud charter

A forensic function is established based either on a formal instruction to do so or in reaction to the need to investigate an actual fraud incident. In either event, the establishment of the function needs to be formally ratified and/or approved. A single investigation or ad hoc use of a forensic function may require less formal authorisation. In that case, a specific authorisation per event may suffice. An incident-specific letter of appointment, a contract or an investigation execution memorandum may be used to document the authorisation per event.

It is advised however to err on the side of conservatism and to rather formalise the authority of a forensic function in a formal fraud charter document, for the following reasons:

- The function may grow very quickly into something more than initially intended before the formal authority exists. In terms of this, the function may move from a once-off investigation to proactive activities with multiple investigations being conducted simultaneously. It may be restrictive for fraud risk officers to operate in the absence of formal authority.
- It may not be possible to predict when the legitimacy/authority of the function/specific right to investigate will be challenged. If the authority has been formalised, then you can refer to it and hopefully dismiss the challenge.

The formal approval of the forensic function is contained in the fraud charter. The fraud charter is normally approved by the most senior organisation leadership and/or the board of directors/the audit committee. The fraud charter defines the:

- Independence, objectivity and organisational status of the forensic function
- Scope of the forensic function
- Authority to investigate matters
- Authority to involve outside forensic practitioners and subject matter experts
- Authority to access premises, records, information and personnel
- Responsibilities (fraud investigators and management)
- Reporting requirements

The 'fraud' authority may be contained in a standalone fraud charter or it may form part of the organisation's internal audit charter, depending on the structure of the individual organisation.

The fraud charter is the starting point of fraud risk management and it legitimises the forensic function. Fraud investigators can refer people to the authority defined in the fraud charter if their authority or mandate to investigate matters is questioned.

The fraud charter should be subject to an annual review or at least to the consideration of the need for review. All amendments would need to be ratified by the board/approving organisation leadership before being enacted.

A 'letter of engagement' is a document equivalent to the fraud charter that provides an external service provider with the authority to conduct an investigation. An engagement letter is specific to an investigation, a group of investigations or a contractual period (for example three years). The letter of appointment is normally sufficient to commence the investigation. Further authorisations may be required within the specific assignments though. The engagement letter is normally preceded by the signing of a 'confidentiality agreement'. Organisations are reluctant to engage external service providers until the service provider has committed to treat the organisation's information confidentially.

The fraud charter typically authorises unrestricted access to all company records in line with investigations. Having the authority to access company records needs to be dealt with responsibly and it does not mean that investigators can access any records at any time that they wish. Confidentiality and privacy requirements remain despite this blanket authority. Records should only be accessed in line with and as reasonably required in an investigation or another activity (for example: predictive profiling, fraud vulnerability testing, etc) being conducted by the forensic function.

The authority to access records, premises and people is given to the forensic function as a whole and not to each member of the forensic team. As such, it does not mean that each member of the team will have unconditional access to all records, etc. No limitation of forensic activities is expected, as long as the 'forensic function' has the right to access records. Normal considerations of confidentiality, sensitivity and seniority apply. The head of forensics or the head of audit oversees and delegates this authority as required.

As an example: the head of the forensic function may be required to investigate a main board director suspected of being involved in misconduct and not a less senior fraud investigator.

The exclusion of junior staff members from 'important' investigations normally evokes emotional responses from the excluded parties. They need to understand however that it is normal (dare I say 'sensible' or 'responsible') business practice to do this. As long as the broader forensic function ensures that the matter is dealt with appropriately, there will be no limitation of scope. There is no requirement and there should be no expectation that they should be involved. It is a privilege if they are involved. Forensic function staff members should, despite any feelings about fairness, not have the expectation that they all need to be involved in all activities. It is the function as a whole that must be involved, not individuals.

Fraud prevention and detection activities should also not be used as an excuse to indiscriminately access people's e-mails and files to determine if they may be involved in something untoward. The access to files and records should only be given on the basis that 'grounds for reasonable suspicion' exist and that an investigation (which is subject to oversight) has been formally registered within a structured and approved proactive profiling programme.

1.2.2. Fraud policy

The fraud charter gives the authority to investigate fraud and to engage in the management of fraud risks. The fraud policy is the document that flows from the fraud charter. The purpose of the fraud policy and some of the topics typically covered in a fraud policy include the following:

a) Organisational position

The fraud policy tells people what the organisation's stance is on fraud. The fraud policy may be limited to a single paragraph document, but is typically not more than two pages long.

b) Purpose of the policy

The fraud policy normally contains a statement as to the purpose of the policy to inform the reader why there is a policy. While this may seem self-explanatory, there may be specific statements that an organisation wishes to emphasise to the reader of the policy. The attached fraud policy (see Annexure 1.1 attached hereto) refers as an example.

c) Definition

The fraud policy may also provide a definition of what the organisation sees as fraud. Again, this may seem like a strange thing to need to specify, as there may be a presumption that we all know what fraud is. This may however not always be the case.

Firstly, there are many different users of the fraud policy. The organisation has a responsibility to inform all readers, of all levels of sophistication, of the fraud policy as to what fraud entails. The fraud definition should also not contain a list of all examples of fraud, as this is not within the purpose of the definition and it may also be too easy to exclude a specific example. The fraud definition should be a concept discussion of the type of behaviours that the organisation considers as incorrect. The organisation may however have a need to specify certain items.

The definition used should be easy to understand and to relate to, and should avoid long, complicated and technical or academic definitions. The definition needs to be able to serve the audience for which it is intended. For example, are the readers of the fraud policy members of a financial institution, with a higher level of education, or are they unskilled labourers in a factory environment? Choose a definition of fraud that suits the reader of the policy.

There may be a tendency to want to make use of the international definition of fraud given by the Association of Certified Fraud Examiners (ACFE). While this may be a very good definition for fraud examiners, the question remains if it will speak to the user of the fraud policy. Furthermore, the organisation may want to specify certain aspects in its fraud definition. It may, for example, want to exclude 'external' matters, and this may have the effect of limiting frauds which need to be investigated to internal/own employee-related matters. The organisation may also want to include specific categories of employees (such as contractors) who might otherwise believe the organisation does not have the right to investigate them.

While not part of the fraud policy, but leading on from the aforementioned specifications, bear in mind that the organisation may want to include a clause in contracts to compel business partners, vendors, suppliers, clients and service providers to cooperate in investigations.

It is common practice for some employees to misinterpret HR issues or commercial matters as frauds. Notwithstanding this, it is advisable in terms of the fraud policy to be as broad as possible so as to prevent restricting people upfront. The fraud policy should not discourage people from reporting fraud. The fraud policy should:

- Give guidance to the readers of the policy
- Define broadly what is acceptable and what is not
- Define what the organisation's stance is on fraud matters
- Serve as a reference point against which to measure when misconduct is identified

- Define the roles and responsibilities of fraud investigators, general employees and management
- Describe possible actions to be taken by employees and management

It is advisable to encourage employees to report all matters. It is unimportant to ensure that only matters that fall within the definition of fraud are reported. It is relatively easy to direct incorrectly reported matters to the appropriate areas for attention after they have been reported. This approach increases the chances that all matters will be reported.

d) Responsibilities

The fraud policy also describes responsibilities with regards to all aspects of fraud and fraud-related activities, including the following:

(i) Reporting of fraud incidents

It is very important to make it clear to all organisation members that it is the responsibility of everyone in the organisation to report fraud. Both management and non-management members of an organisation are equally responsible to report fraud. Management may have access to additional reporting avenues, due to access to additional formal organisational reporting lines. Management may, on the other hand, have perceived additional pressures which lead them not to report fraud, including the following:

- They may feel pressure to be seen as a team player and not to 'make waves' for the organisation
- They may feel pressure to achieve key performance indicators (KPIs) and/or targets
- They may have more to lose personally if they lose their job
- They may have more to lose if they do not receive incentives
- They may have more to lose if they are implicated/complicit
- They may have more to lose if they were negligent or if they should have detected or prevented (through the establishment of a suitable control environment) the fraud

There may also be a moral requirement for people to report fraud:

- People need to assist their fellow man
- There is an imperative to 'do the right thing'
- In general, people should not complain about the moral decay of society if they are not prepared to report wrongdoing and/or be part of the solution

The employee's responsibility to report wrongdoing may also be defined in their contract of employment. Employment contracts frequently require employees to 'act in the best interest of their organisation' and/or may even provide a specific clause as to the need to report wrongdoing.

While there may not be any labour law requirement (other than contractual) in many jurisdictions to report wrongdoing to organisational leadership, there may very well be a statutory (relevant criminal Act of Parliament) requirement to report fraud to the authorities. These reporting requirements may be specific to a single country (for example the US and the UK's requirements are particularly onerous) or a union of countries (like the European Union).

Failure to report matters may hold consequences (imprisonment, fines and penalties) for the:

- Individual
- Organisation leadership
- Organisation

The statutory reporting requirement is based on the need to hold individuals or organisations criminally or economically liable for not reporting crimes. Failure to report a known criminal act falls within the criminal concept of 'wilful blindness'.

The aforementioned legislation may include a wide range of specific Acts of Parliament/ government, like those aimed at preventing and combating organised crime, anti-terrorism, corruption, anti-competitive behaviour, etc.

It may be sufficient to include a broad sentence in the fraud policy to cover the need of individuals and the organisation to abide by relevant laws and regulations.

From an organisational point of view, it is important to specify in the fraud policy that failure to report matters may lead to the need to invoke the organisation's disciplinary code.

At the end of the day we really just want people to report fraud. Part of this may necessitate showing that the organisation is serious about the employees' responsibility to report fraud. This may entail taking action against people that can be proven to have known about fraud and who failed (neglected) to act on/report fraudulent matters.

In an internal labour disciplinary tribunal, the organisation may wish to send a strong message that 'wilful blindness' is unacceptable. This message would need to be realistic and consider the pressures that employees are under, but still be firm.

It is advisable when disciplining people for not reporting known frauds that the organisation has an appreciation that people may be fearful to report matters, but that the organisation provides multiple avenues through which to report matters. The avenues available should be listed again to place this fact on record. It can be concluded in general that there is so much being said and done in the world against wrongdoing that, even if they do not want to be involved, people cannot plead ignorance about the need to report matters or the methods or means by which to report matters.

Society itself also generally provides various avenues through which to report matters, which include, but are not limited to:

- Police services
- Government authorities (tax, border control, etc)
- External auditors

- Professional societies (bar society, accountant institutes, etc)
- Religious leaders, political leaders and other trusted people

(ii) *Detecting and preventing fraud*

While every employee has an obligation to report fraud, they also have an obligation to act in a way that prevents and/or detects fraud.

The board of directors, as the custodians of the leadership of the organisation and the shareholders'/owners' interests, have the additional fiduciary responsibility to prevent and detect fraud. Board members' responsibilities would not be defined in the fraud policy, but would be specified in organisation governance documents, country-specific governance codes (for example: Commission of Sponsoring Organisations of the Treadway Commission (COSO - USA), Criteria of Control Framework (COCO - Canada), the King Code - South Africa, The UK Corporate Governance Code, etc) and applicable legislation (like the Companies Act).

The board of directors delegates its authority with regards to fraud to management. The senior executive organisational leadership therefore has a fraud management responsibility.

The fraud policy only specifies a broad sentence of what management's responsibilities towards fraud are and does not detail how they are to enact this responsibility. The details of how fraud is to be managed are contained in the fraud procedures and other organisational documents (see point 1.2.4).

(iii) *General decorum and professionalism when matters are detected*

The fraud policy may need to specify that people should:

- Be professional, courteous and respectful and treat all people with dignity
- Neither assume peoples' innocence or guilt in matters
- Ensure that all matters are reported to those charged with the responsibility to investigate them
- Not act in a different manner towards those implicated unless the unique situation requires it (for example to prevent further loss or if there is a specific instruction not to communicate with implicated people until the investigation can be completed)
- Duly assist those charged with conducting the investigation

(iv) *Investigating fraud*

The fraud policy may specify who is charged to investigate fraud matters. This is important because people should not shirk their responsibility to investigate matters. They should also prevent unauthorised people from being involved in matters or disrupting/jeopardising the investigation.

The responsibility to investigate fraud (for example by management) may not be the same as the responsibility to physically conduct fraud investigations (for example by fraud risk officers). Management can delegate this responsibility to fraud risk officers. The responsibility may differ from situation to situation. Less serious matters may be investigated by management and more serious or complex matters may be investigated by internal audit or the forensic team.

In conglomerate-type organisations, individual business units may have their own auditors/controllers/forensic resources and/or responsibility to investigate frauds. The holding company may only have an oversight role to play. Execution of the fraud strategy will be discussed later (see point 1.6).

All employees must, as part of the requirement to act in the best interest of the company, make themselves available to assist in the investigation, as required, to provide information, assistance and/or understanding of events, processes and people. Intentional withholding of support or assistance is tantamount to wilful blindness and may be seen as obstructive behaviour which may invoke the organisation's disciplinary code.

(v) *Funding investigations*

The funding of investigations is a common bone of contention. It is both a legitimate concern and a means by which to unduly control or prevent investigations. It is strongly recommended to specify in the fraud policy that management has the responsibility to pay for investigations and that internal audit or the forensic team must oversee all investigations.

Common complaints by management with regards to the funding of investigations include sentiments such as:

- 'Why must I throw good money after bad? I have already lost X. Now you want me to still pay Y?' Possible replies may include: It is important for the organisation to show that they have a zero tolerance for fraud. I agree that this will cost more money but look at it as an investment in sending a strong message to the organisation to reduce the likelihood of recurrence.
- 'Why must I investigate something, the answer to which I already know?' Possible replies may include: Because you may not know the full extent of the loss and all who are involved. It will also send a strong message to the organisation (which will act as a deterrent) that the organisation will investigate every matter completely.
- 'The investigation is not going to change anything. The fraud has already been perpetrated.' Possible replies may include: An investigation will send a strong message to the organisation. We will not be sure if we know the full extent of the fraud and who is involved unless we investigate the matter completely. An investigation will help us to understand the causes which will be necessary to bolster controls to prevent recurrence. The facts gained in the investigation will be used in civil claims to recover misappropriated funds and in the criminal case.

- 'The subject has already left the organisation, why must I carry on investigating it?' Possible replies may include: To send a strong message to the organisation. To determine the full extent of the fraud. To obtain information to be used in subsequent actions to bolster controls, in civil recovery claims and criminal matters.
- 'The group fraud function must pay for and conduct all investigations. That is why we have a fraud unit.' Possible replies may include: The incident occurred in this area and as such, we need to reflect the losses and investigation costs in this area. This may act as an incentive for managers to ensure that they have strong controls in place to prevent and detect fraud.
- 'If I pay for something, I have a say in it. Why must I pay for something that you (central forensic team) dictate to me how to do?' Possible replies may include: While we appreciate your assistance in this matter, there is a strong need for independence. You are, unfortunately, not independent of the matter. An investigation of this type takes a lot of time and you would not have the time available to conduct such a protracted investigation. Investigations of this nature require specialised skills. While your skills are valuable to the business they may not be directly suited to conducting complex fraud investigations. We will still definitely need your input and assistance. We will welcome your input as we see the need. There is unfortunately a need for confidentiality on this matter. If you investigate the matter, then you may be required to testify and you may not be comfortable with this.
- 'We do not have the budget for this.' Possible replies may include: It is not normal to budget for fraud. The incident unfortunately occurred in your area and as such the loss and costs need to be booked to your cost centre to ensure that it is correctly reflected in the responsible area.
- 'The investigation of fraud is a group rule. The group/holding company must therefore pay for this.' Possible replies may include: Group rules are applicable for all entities within the group. Costs need to be correctly reflected in the areas where they are incurred.
- 'If I pay for this, then I want to be able to go to market to see if I can get the same service for a smaller fee.' Possible replies may include: We already have framework agreements in place with service providers. We have already vetted service providers that we know operate at a particular standard, with whom we have already negotiated rates and who have already signed confidentiality clauses. While price is of concern, it is not the only determinant of service providers. We can only accept service providers who we know comply with best practice. There would not be sufficient time to vet a new service provider at this key time of the investigation. We require particular skills.
- 'I am already paying a monthly administration fee to the group; why must I also pay for the group to dictate investigations to me? The cost should be covered by the existing group monthly management fee.' Possible replies may include: The administrative fee is applied for other group costs. This is an extraordinary item and as such must be correctly reflected in the responsible area of occurrence and not in the holding company.

(vi) Remedial actions

Specifying the need to take remedial action in all applicable situations is important to ensure that action is taken and that it is taken by those responsible for doing so. You do not want management to ask you where it specifies that action is their responsibility.

Management may want the forensic team to take the remedial action and/or run disciplinary hearings. The forensic team should only be responsible for carrying the company's case in complicated matters or to serve as a witness in normal/non-complicated matters, as applicable. As a rule, management should conduct all their own disciplinary hearings. The forensic service may testify as an expert witness in normal/non-complicated matters, where they acted as such.

A lot of success is derived in complex matters by having a single, skilled person to lead the case from end-to-end. This ensures continuity of thought and prevents the 'broken telephone' scenario when presenting the case (criminal or labour matter).

(vii) Fraud strategy

The forensic function should only be responsible for the overall drafting and oversight of the fraud strategy. Different parties may, depending on the size of the organisation, have various roles to play with regards to the execution of the fraud strategy, including:

- The forensic function - which could be involved in the drafting, rolling out and providing of training and awareness, monitoring progress, reporting on fraud matters, providing support, etc.
- Management - which could, in single company structures/less complex type organisations, be responsible for some degree of implementation of the fraud strategy.
- Individual business units (in conglomerate/more complex type organisations) - which could have a high degree of responsibility for fraud strategy implementation.

The fraud strategy is a document that describes how anti-fraud measures will be carried out across the entire organisation. The fraud strategy is not limited to what the forensic function will do. Each organisation element involved in and/or contributing to anti-fraud efforts should be described in the fraud strategy.

(viii) Preventative controls and strategies

The board of directors (delegated to management) has the overall responsibility to ensure that sufficient controls exist and are being carried out to prevent and detect fraud.

Internal audit and the forensic team (third line of defence) may independently evaluate and report control deficiencies that were exploited to perpetrate the fraud, but management has the responsibility to ensure that:

- Fraud risks are identified
- The adequacy of anti-fraud controls is assessed

- Controls are bolstered to prevent fraud
- Sufficient resources (in the broader sense of the word) are provided to ensure a proper control environment

(ix) *Communicating and reporting*

The purpose of specifying who is responsible for reporting on fraudulent matters that have occurred includes:

- Ensuring that frauds and the outcome of investigations and remedial actions are reported to the organisational leadership
- Specifying who should physically conduct the reporting to prevent multiple uncoordinated reporting efforts

1.2.3. Fraud strategy

If the fraud policy defines the organisation's stance on fraud, then the fraud strategy defines what the organisation wants fraud risk management to achieve. The details of how the fraud strategy will be achieved are specified in the fraud procedure documents (see point 1.2.4). The fraud strategy is such an important element that we dedicate the entire second part of this chapter to it.

The fraud strategy is not a widely circulated document. It is a document that is circulated and presented to those members of the senior organisational leadership to whom the fraud risk management has been entrusted, including the audit committee and relevant senior divisional/ business unit-level management. A more sanitised/summarised version of the fraud strategy may be circulated to lower organisational levels from an informative, educational and deterrent point of view only. As an analogy, army generals do not widely circulate their battle plans, and neither should you.

The fraud strategy is what it says it is, namely 'strategic'. It is therefore a high-level document with less detail. It points out the strategic direction and the elements that will be followed. The fraud strategy normally defines the strategic direction within two elements, being:

- Proactive fraud detection and prevention work
- Reactive fraud investigation work

The fraud strategy also specifies more specific roles and responsibilities, especially applicable to conglomerate/multi-business-type organisations where the group fraud function defines the strategy and the individual business units carry a large part of the fraud strategy out. Each of these areas is discussed in detail below.

1.2.4. Fraud procedures

As per the above, the fraud procedures specify the detailed methods through which the fraud strategy will be achieved. The fraud procedures are normally a collection of detailed documents and not just one document. Trying to put everything into one document may result in the diluting of the individual areas or the creation of a very cumbersome document. Cumbersome documents are not easy to use and are resultantly used less than simpler documents. Multiple individual documents are also easier to maintain than one large, all-encompassing document. It is also easier to tailor individual documents to specific users. Furthermore, it may be easier to control the circulation of individual documents than it is with one large document, as not all elements of the single document may be applicable to all recipients.

The fraud procedure documents specify the mandatory requirements to be followed by the business in fraud-related matters and provide guidelines on how the business is to respond.

The documents that may be included in the fraud procedures are listed below and discussed in detail under the proactive and reactive fraud response sections. They include, but are not limited to, the following detailed fraud procedure documents:

a. **Fraud charter** – The forensic function's mandate with regards to fraud (may be part of the internal audit charter).

b. **Fraud policy** – Defining the organisation's stance on fraud.

c. **Fraud strategy** – How the organisation will carry out the fraud policy and manage fraud risks.

d. **Fraud risk assessment** – The fraud risk assessment is the starting point of fraud risk management (discussed later). A fraud risk assessment may be conducted at the following levels:

   - Enterprise (holding company)
   - Business/divisional unit
   - Geographic region
   - Product grouping
   - Individual company
   - Functional area
   - Key business process
   - Individual (key) employee
   - Specific incident

   The fraud risk assessment is more strategic in nature and is not confined to the detail of transactions. The purpose of the strategic fraud risk assessment is to identify the highest potential areas of fraud risk in one of the aforementioned levels. Detailed and/or specific fraud risk analyses are subsequently performed on the highest identified fraud areas through the conducting of 'fraud vulnerability assessments' as described below. The strategic-level fraud risk assessment can be conducted by:

   - The business itself
   - The forensic function
   - The internal audit function
   - External consultants
   - The business owners facilitated by the external consultants or the internal forensic function

e. **Fraud vulnerability assessment methodology** – While a fraud vulnerability assessment can be conducted at any of the same levels as the strategic fraud risk assessment, the value of a fraud vulnerability assessment lies in the detailed analysis of a specific area. A fraud vulnerability assessment is really a detailed and focused fraud risk assessment of a particular high-risk area (normally a specific business process). It is performed in much more detail than the strategic fraud risk assessment and identifies very specific fraud risks (even at a transactional level). The need to conduct a fraud vulnerability assessment can come from one of two sources. First of all, and most commonly, the need to conduct a fraud vulnerability assessment will stem from the overall enterprise-wide fraud risk assessment. The enterprise fraud risk assessment process identifies fraud risks. One method of mitigating these fraud risks is to conduct detailed fraud vulnerability assessments of the business process from which the fraud risks stem. The second need for a fraud vulnerability assessment will stem from specific fraud incidents. One of the subsequent actions to be taken upon the conclusion of a fraud investigation is to bolster the internal controls to prevent recurrence. The fraud investigation may point to a larger underlying structural control problem. Such structural control deficiencies are best analysed in detail in a fraud vulnerability assessment of the errant business process.

f. **Fraud awareness programme** – Fraud awareness refers to overall general fraud awareness. These are the programmes and steps through which the organisation will create awareness of fraud, the consequences of fraud and anti-fraud initiatives.

   Fraud awareness may be aimed at any number of levels or types of staff members within the organisation. It is best however to tailor separate programmes that appeal to specific categories of staff members. Fraud awareness programmes may consist of:

   - Presentations
   - Reading material
   - Evidence examples
   - Statistics of fraud incidents
   - Video clips
   - Posters
   - Illustrative examples and/or case studies
   - Online material

g. **Fraud training material** – Anti-fraud training is more specific than general fraud awareness. Fraud training is aimed at educating those individuals in the organisation charged with the management and combating of fraud. This material is in much more detail than the fraud awareness material and gives specific instructions on how to deal with fraud and how to respond to fraud situations.

h. **Fraud incident response plan** – The fraud incident response plan provides a guideline to the organisation detailing how to respond to known or suspected frauds. This is the kind of document that is available on the company intranet. The fraud investigator may also furnish this document to the people who are to investigate the misconduct. The fraud incident response plan specifies the detailed responses to be followed when a fraud becomes known and/or needs to be investigated. The fraud incident response plan details the initial response to the incident, but not the detailed investigation methodology.

i. **Fraud risk management programme** – The fraud risk management programme is in support of the fraud strategy and details how the organisation will manage anti-fraud efforts. The fraud strategy provides the overall anti-fraud strategic direction, while the fraud management programme specifies the practical steps on the ground required to execute the fraud strategy.

j. **Fraud investigative methodology** – The fraud investigative methodology is largely a document for the forensic function. It is not a document that is widely circulated, as it specifies tools and methodologies that should not be widely known, so as to prevent circumvention thereof. The fraud investigation methodology document is a 'reactive' document, as the document is only used when an act of misconduct is known or is strongly suspected. The document specifies a list of possible investigative tools and their application. The fraud investigator should determine the applicability of each of these methodologies at the commencement of an investigation (Chapter 3 on structuring fraud investigations refers in this regard). Seasoned investigators would not need to refer in too much detail to such a document to plan each investigation. After many years, fraud investigators tend to react intuitively rather than work from a programme. The document specifies the investigative methods favoured and also assists as a training guide. Excerpts of the document may be sent by the fraud risk officers to management to provide specific guidance on how to respond and/or to investigate frauds.

k. **Fraud reporting** – The fraud reporting document specifies:

- What needs to be reported
- To whom it needs to be reported
- By whom it needs to be reported
- When it needs to be reported

The fraud reporting document is not a detailed document and will specify a table of reporting types and how and when this reporting is to be conducted. This could be a standalone document or form part of another fraud procedure document, as applicable.

l. **Whistle-blower process/system/policy** – The whistle-blower policy is important, as it can add to the credibility of the whistle-blower system as well as document the protection required for whistle-blowers. The whistle-blower policy will also define the roles and responsibilities in terms of responding to incidents, including:

- Normal/general incidents
- Incidents in which senior members of staff are implicated or where an investigator's boss needs to be investigated
- Incidents when those charged with investigating the incidents or to whom incidents are normally reported are implicated
- Very serious incidents

The whistle-blower policy will define the generic steps to be followed per incident. The document will refer to detailed fraud procedure documents to prevent duplication.

1.2.5. Related documents/activities

There may be a need to link or read some of the following documents together with fraud procedure documents, and/or to take the following documents into account, when drafting fraud related documents or responding to fraud incidents:

- Shareholder agreements
- Joint venture contracts
- Anti-corruption legislation
- Anti-competitive behaviour legislation
- Foreign trade control legislation
- Conflict of interest policies
- Insurance policies and strategy
- Enterprise risk management documents
- Governance guidelines (internal and external requirements)
- Organisational culture and ethics documents
- Information security documents
- Procurement policies
- Supplier contracts
- Access to information legislation, privacy laws and policies, and information exchange policies
- The authority hierarchy
- Employment contracts
- Disciplinary procedures
- Commercial agreements
- Customer agreements
- Vendor/supplier agreements

The fraud policy and procedure documents may refer the reader to the aforementioned related documents and other organisational functions that need to be informed or consulted in fraud matters. Examples of functions to be consulted in fraud matters include:

- The legal department
- The human resources department
- The enterprise risk management function
- The ethics or corporate governance function
- Internal audit
- The IT security or forensics function

Examples of related documents are specified and discussed under point 1.2.4.

1.3. THE FRAUD STRATEGY PROCESS

The fraud strategy process is a little bit of a 'chicken-and-egg' conundrum. The purpose of the fraud strategy (the proverbial 'chicken') is to manage fraud risks (the 'egg'). But how do you know which risks to manage until you have conducted the fraud risk assessment? Which comes first – the strategy document or the fraud risk assessment?

Practically speaking, we have to start somewhere, and I suggest starting with the fraud strategy document. This is a very academic argument and adds little value to what we are trying to do, so I do not encourage it. It is rare that we have the opportunity to start a forensic function from scratch, so it is not often that you will be faced with this problem. After doing this for a few years in your organisation, it will not really matter which came first, as you will be renewing 'living' documents.

So, for all intents and purposes, the fraud strategy process commences with the drafting of the fraud strategy document of how the organisation plans to manage fraud risks.

The next step is to identify the fraud risks to be managed. The fraud risks are identified by performing a fraud risk assessment (discussed in detail in point 1.3.2 below). Mitigation strategies are then chosen and implemented to manage the risks (potential events) and incidents (materialised risks).

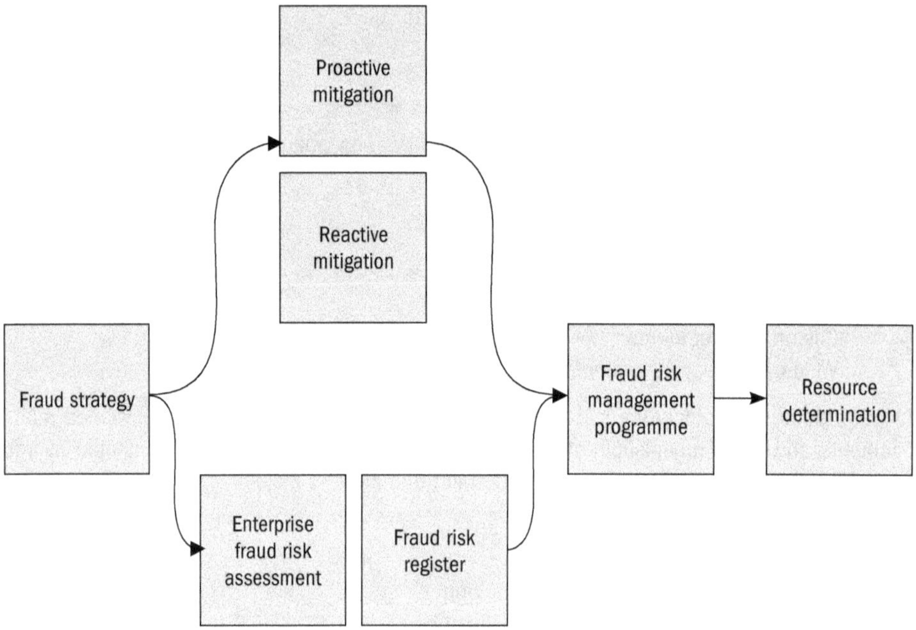

Diagram 1.2 *The fraud strategy process*

1.3.1. Fraud strategy document

The world has grown in knowledge over the last many years, much of which knowledge has been translated into sound theory, governance frameworks, risk models and legislation. Despite all of this, the media remains full of examples of corporate frauds. Most of the organisations in which these media attention-grabbing frauds occur had audit departments and forensic functions. Why therefore do significant frauds continue to occur? It is important for us to understand this so that our fraud risk strategies can be crafted to prevent these ongoing frauds.

To address the continuing fraud dilemma, it may be necessary to sweep in front of our own doors as fraud investigators, before passing the blame to anything or anyone else. There is a plethora of regulation and more regulation is certainly not the answer. The solution may be far simpler than expected. It is wise to commence by identifying where these significant frauds occur and who is perpetrating them. While the frauds occur in various industries and in many functional areas, the one common element is that the significant frauds are all perpetrated by more senior members of staff. It is certainly an interesting statement that it is the senior people perpetrating the big frauds. This is supported by the headlines.

Compare this revelation to our own behaviour, as fraud examiners. Where do fraud examiners typically pitch their anti-fraud campaigns? Fraud examiners spend an inordinate amount of time conducting fraud awareness presentations in the staff canteens, analysing systems of control for fraud weaknesses and conducting investigations of known lower-level frauds and thefts. This is all good and well, but there only needs to be one fraud to hit an organisation from the boardroom to bring the entire organisation down.

It is as if fraud examiners have the Pareto principle the wrong way around. Fraud examiners spend 80% of their time on 20% of the problem. Anti-fraud campaigns need to be moved out of the canteen and into the boardroom to resolve this.

There has also long been spoken about the 'risk-based approach to auditing', which involves concentrating audit efforts on the highest risks to the organisation. It may therefore be time to have a *real* 'risk-based approach' to fraud risk management, by prioritising fraud risk management efforts on the highest fraud risks (and in this case most senior positions and processes) in the organisation.

The fraud risk officers in the organisations where the significant frauds are perpetrated need to be respected. While there are many aspects that determine respect, we are going to discuss one: organisational status. In the animal kingdom, the most respected animals are at the top of the food chain and they tend to have the sharpest teeth. In the organisational world, the sharpest teeth tend to be found at the top as well. The first step to implementing a sound fraud strategy is therefore to lift the fraud risk function in stature in the organisation.

The fraud charter, as discussed previously, is what provides the organisational status to the fraud risk function. It gives fraud risk officers the authority to go where no fraud risk officer has gone before, as it is endorsed by the sharpest teeth in the organisation, being the board of directors.

The fraud charter not only provides the fraud risk function with the authority to investigate senior leadership, but also to ensure that robust fraud risk management is applied at the highest fraud risk organisational levels. Putting a strong fraud charter in place is a relatively easy step. Ensuring that it is applied as intended is however the more challenging task.

As the cliché goes, 'no man is an island' and the fraud risk function cannot solve the fraud scourge by itself. The fraud policy, as discussed previously, informs the organisation what the fraud risk management roles and responsibilities are and who is responsible for controls, fraud detection and prevention, as well as defines the duty to report fraud. Indicatively, management should, under the guidance of the fraud risk services function, investigate 85% of all frauds. External consultants should investigate 7.5% of all matters (where independence or special skills are required) under the direct supervision of the fraud risk services function. Fraud risk services should investigate the remaining 7.5% of all matters (which typically includes the more material and difficult-to-investigate matters). This will ensure that fraud risk services only concentrate on the most important aspects and provide the formal basis to ensure that adequate fraud risk management exists.

Therefore, the key elements needed to move the fraud risk strategy out of the canteen (lower-level frauds) and into the boardroom (higher-risk frauds), are:

- The organisational status of the fraud risk service function
- The ability to identify key fraud risks
- Management's involvement in the management of fraud

It is important to recognise that fraud risk officers themselves have an important role to play in ensuring that the most significant fraud risks are identified and mitigated. This starts with the fraud risk strategy. We should therefore ensure, when drafting the fraud strategy and when conducting the fraud risk assessment, that we concentrate on the highest risks.

1.3.2. Fraud risk assessments

As discussed above, fraud risk management commences with a determination of which fraud risks need to be managed. It is therefore important to determine what the fraud risks are for the entire organisation. This is performed in an attempt to 1) know where best to direct anti-fraud efforts and 2) to be able to provide the organisational leadership with an overview of 2a) the fraud risks as well as 2b) how well and/or to what extent the fraud risks are currently being managed.

Fraud risks can essentially be identified at one of three levels, namely:

- The enterprise-wide level
- The business process level
- The specific incident level

These are discussed below. The enterprise fraud risk assessment should concentrate on the most significant fraud risks. These will not be at a detailed transactional level.

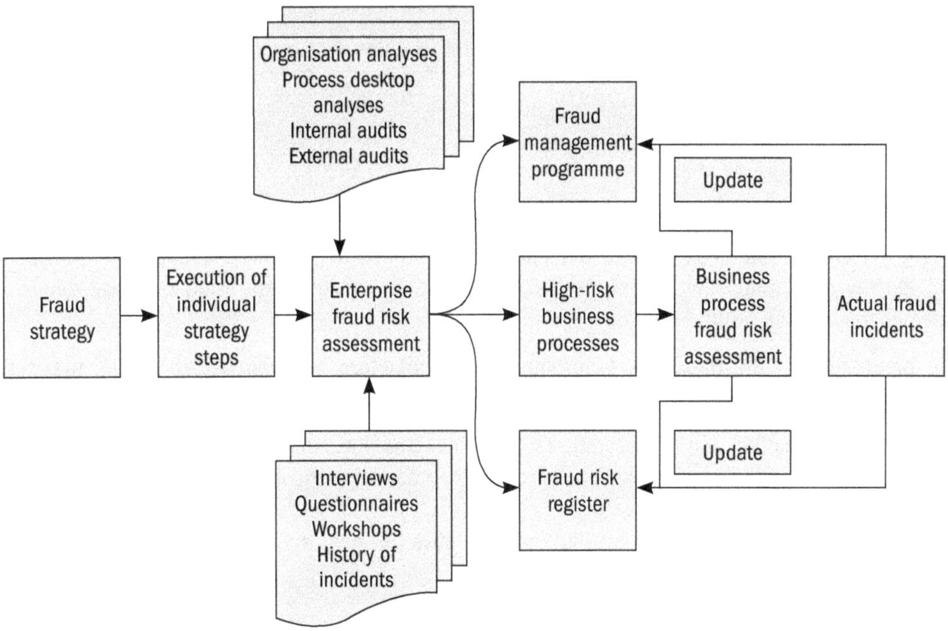

Diagram 1.3 *The fraud risk assessment process*

i) Fraud risk assessment philosophy

The purpose of the fraud risk assessment is to obtain a complete list of fraud risks across all business activities and processes and to prioritise these from the most significant to the least significant. The fraud risk assessment process does not screen fraud risks. All fraud risks are to be included. Not all fraud risks will however be selected for mitigation strategies.

When we talk about fraud risk assessments, we instinctively think about detailed transactional analyses of business process fraud risks. As discussed previously however, the most significant frauds are perpetrated by the more senior members of organisations. It is safe therefore to assume that the more senior members of staff represent greater fraud risks. How then do we ensure that we identify all fraud risks from detailed transactional fraud risks through to high-level senior management fraud risks? The solution lies in the ability to include and actively analyse all responsibilities performed by each organisational level and process.

The transactional business process fraud risk identification can be identified by inviting the business process owners to participate in fraud vulnerability workshops where transactional level fraud risks can be debated and identified.

As discussed previously, the more senior staff members have the ability to perpetrate financially significant frauds. The scoping and directing of fraud risk analysis needs therefore to include the activities performed by senior management/executives. Some examples of senior executive activities to be included in fraud risk analyses are:

- Business structuring
- Business deals (for example mergers, joint ventures, acquisitions, etc)
- Capital projects
- Authorisation of key business activities
- Governance, oversight and control
- Incentives

It is suggested that you sit with key senior executives and leadership to understand what their daily activities entail. Each of these activities will then need to be walked through and analysed to identify how fraud could be perpetrated within each activity. These fraud risks will then be documented in the fraud risk register for further action.

In preparation of the fraud risk assessment it will therefore be important to ensure that the following are considered:

- Identification and consideration of fraud risk enablers (discussed below)
- Identification and inclusion of the key fraud risk business areas, activities and responsibilities
- Inclusion and consultation with the respective business activity owners

ii) Fraud risk assessment identification methods

Fraud risk assessments, regardless of organisational level, can be carried out using any one of the following methods:

- *Interviewing key personnel and stakeholders*
  This approach is well suited for very senior company directors who do not have the time to participate in protracted workshops or to provide detailed business insights. Interviews should be structured and not just be conversations about what the interviewee feels are the risks. While there is room for understanding the interviewees' concerns, a structured interview that touches on numerous topics will prompt improved considerations of fraud risks. Failure to do so will result in interviewees limiting their reflections to their most recent experiences only. It is also recommended that this technique is used to supplement more detailed fraud risk assessments.

- *Questionnaires*
  Questionnaires can be written or online surveys could be used. Survey software is readily available to facilitate this process. Questionnaires ensure improved coverage of employees or business units, functions or geographic locations. The downside is that questionnaires do not lend themselves to a lot of detail. Questionnaires also tend to ask the questions for the answers that they seek, meaning that they have in-built bias and the questions were selected based on presupposed risks. They are therefore limited by the drafter's knowledge and experience. They also do not solicit debate nor invite additional areas not included. Questionnaires cannot be too long and may only be able to cover limited areas. Questionnaires are recommended to supplement detailed fraud risk assessments or to validate known fraud risks.

- *Workshops*

Facilitated workshops are the traditional method of identifying fraud risks. Key personnel (functional and line leaders) are selected to participate in a fraud risk assessment workshop. Workshops continue to be a valuable method by which to identify risks, as it is possible to go into a fair amount of detail per process/business unit and improve fraud risk understanding. It is however important to ensure that there is a wide representation of people at the workshop. The downside is that, if there is not a wide range of employee coverage, the output is limited to the views of a few dominant people. The more senior staff members may have a myopic view of the organisation and expect that everything is fine and working. Senior management may not want to admit that they have weaknesses in their areas. Workshop participants may also be reluctant to contribute in the presence of senior staff members.

The workshop facilitator does not need to have detailed knowledge of the processes and industry to be covered in the workshop. The facilitator will however have to conduct some research on the areas to be covered in the workshop. The facilitator's task is to encourage debate and to ensure participation and coverage of all relevant areas. The facilitator will need knowledge of generic fraud risks. Workshop delegates, unfortunately, do not think in terms of fraud risks. The facilitator's role is to prompt and guide to ensure that the maximum number of fraud risks are identified. The workshop should also follow a structured process to ensure that all high-risk areas are considered. Having a panel of experts to identify fraud risks is also highly recommended.

- *Desktop exercise*

Forensic investigators can perform their own analysis of where they feel the fraud risks are. They do this based on system walkthroughs and knowledge of the history of incidence. While fraud risk officers are control and fraud specialists, this analysis can be a very one-sided view and it does not consider other people's inputs. It is always good to supplement the fraud risks with the investigator's views as well.

- *History of incidence*

Fraud risks should be supplemented with categories of risks based on the actual occurrence of these events.

- *External audit and internal audit*

It is wise to request the auditor's input as to the areas that they see as fraud risk areas. These are traditionally not good sources of fraud risks though, as fraud risks do not represent the main driver of external and internal audit.

iii) Fraud risk assessment methodology

The fraud risk assessment process has the following generic stages:

Planning

The fraud risk assessment commences with planning, to determine:

- **The fraud enablers.** These are the organisational aspects that may promote fraud and are discussed in detail below.

- **The areas of emphasis**. Even though we may be performing an enterprise-wide fraud risk assessment, we may not wish to include all organisational areas for practical reasons. Document these reasons for completeness reasons and ensure that the required authorisations are obtained and/or agreement is reached. It may, for example, be wise to exclude obvious low-risk areas or areas that have known challenges or are undergoing significant changes. Specific business processes would also need to be selected for inclusion in the business process-level fraud risk assessment. Geographic location, legal entities and product types may also need to be assessed for inclusion.
- **The sequence of execution**. Consider if there is a logical sequence in which the planned areas of inclusion should be covered.
- **Information requirements**. What information will you require upfront to familiarise yourself with the areas included in the fraud risk assessment?
- **Participants**. Who will the participants be? Who is available and who is unavailable? What effect will this have on the assessment?
- **Timing**. When will it be best to conduct the fraud risk assessment (business pressures, vacation, etc)?
- **Audience**. Who will the eventual recipient of the information be and what will the information be used for?

Preparation

Request sufficient information (as planned above) to give an adequate understanding of the areas of inclusion and of high-risk areas, business processes, practices and personnel. Review the material received and determine if any further action is required. Suggested information sources include:

- *Flow diagrams and system descriptions*
  To provide an understanding of systems, processes, controls, deficiencies, degree of formality, etc.

- *IT infrastructure overview*
  To understand the degree of automation, vulnerabilities, stability of systems, reliability of information, etc.

- *Financial statements, operating volume information, product information, customer and supplier breakdowns and demographics, etc*
  This information should not be at a consolidated level as obvious trends may be lost when thrown together with a lot of other information. The information is used to understand how financially strong the organisation is, areas of pressure, how the organisation is funded (eg debt) and corresponding pressures, volume of business and transactions, risk of errors, etc.

- *Accounting policies and practices*
  Aggressive accounting policies may indicate risky/fraudulent practices, increased pressure on management to deliver, a degree of formalisation, a degree of compliance with internationally accepted standards, etc. Negligent or weak practices may provide fraud opportunities.

- *Tax philosophy and compliance history*
  May point to financial pressures or to an unethical culture. How aggressive is the organisation's pursuit to avoid tax? Is this tax evasion (illegal) or tax avoidance (normal business structuring to pay less tax)?
- *Organisational diagrams and key job descriptions*
  Will provide an understanding of the scale of the organisation, complexities, communication lines, roles and responsibilities, span of control, ability to control, key personnel dependencies, etc.
- *Authorisation hierarchies*
  Key personnel dependencies, roles and responsibilities, who has the official power to authorise transactions. Is this sufficient? How does actual practice compare to the theoretical authorisations required?
- *Governance and oversight*
  What is the extent of independent governance and oversight conducted? What is the ability of key individuals to ignore, override or circumvent these processes?
- *An understanding of revenue drivers, remuneration and incentive schemes*
  Will point out potential pressures, give an indication of management risk appetite, etc.
- *Recent relevant reports in the areas*
  Examples include repairs and maintenance, health and safety, internal audit, external audit, insurance claims, accident/injury/workplace incident reports, etc. This is used to determine whether, if there is financial pressure or excessive volume pressure, the organisation may not be able to invest in repairs. What are the types of findings being raised? What do these say about the general environment?
- *Personnel files*
  Consider applications for loans, garnishee orders, disciplinary issues, star performers, salaries, etc. This may point to personnel that are under financial pressure or those who are associated with known discipline issues. Some of this information may also be required for the public domain checks discussed below, for profiling and for lifestyle audits (discussed in Chapter 6 on lifestyle audits).
- *Public domain checks*
  of key personnel in the areas (properties owned, vehicles owned, company directorships, educational background, credit histories, etc). Certain information in the public domain can provide insights into personnel and companies that are under some form of pressure or that show unknown relationships. Consider including key personnel, suppliers and customers in these searches. The chapter on lifestyle audits refers in this regard.
- *A breakdown of know incidents*
  in the areas (fraud, HR, industrial relations, customer complaints, production issues, supplier complaints, etc). Known incidents are very useful to provide insights into:
  - the type of fraud committed

  - the types of people who commit these acts
  - the areas where these acts occur the most frequently
  - the organisation's response.

- *Prior period's fraud risk register*
  It is not encouraged to just take the previous year's fraud risk register and check if any additional fraud risks need to be added. The thoughts of the person preparing the fraud risk register will be prejudiced by the limitations of the previous fraud risks. It is recommended that the exercise is independently conducted from the start. The last risk register should be compared after the fact to the newly compiled fraud risk register to check if any significant matters have been missed in the revision. Internet searches of companies/divisions included (conglomerate type organisations), recent business deals, suppliers, clients and business partners may provide useful information of high-risk people and activities.

- *The enterprise risk management (ERM) risk register*
  While the ERM risk register may not contain too many fraud risks, it does provide useful insights into risk areas in which fraud may occur, as a result of the ERM risks.

- *An economic forecast*
  Obtain a high-level economic forecast of the market segments and countries in which the organisation operates. This will provide insights into the pressures (economic, political, legislation, etc) on the organisation.

- *The organisation's strategic initiatives*
  Obtain the organisation's strategic objectives. This will again provide insights into the direction that the organisation is moving and the corresponding pressures on the organisation and its personnel in these areas.

Risk gathering
Using one or more of the aforementioned fraud risk identification methods, gather the potential or actual fraud risks. List these in a fraud risk register as described below.

Analysis and reporting
The list of potential or actual fraud risks should be analysed to identify trends and their relative control maturity. Improvements should be identified and all results should be reported to the appropriate levels and responsible parties within the organisation.

Mitigation
Practical and cost-effective control strategies to mitigate fraud vulnerabilities should be identified, prioritised, resourced and implemented.

Monitoring and reporting
Continuous monitoring should be designed and implemented to monitor recurrence and to determine the effectiveness of implemented mitigating strategies.

Fraud risk identification

When identifying fraud risks, keep the ACFE's three categories of fraud in mind, being: misstatement, asset misappropriation and corruption. The following are examples of the general areas that should be included in fraud risk identification activities:

- High-risk personnel
- Undue pressures from the organisation's side
- Pressures that are on individuals
- High-risk practices
- Unethical climates/cultures/practices
- History of an incident of fraud
- Degree of structure control and formality
- Skills, qualifications and experience of staff members
- Degree of supervision and control
- More lucrative/high-risk products or services
- Degree of competitiveness
- Degree of laws, regulations and enforcement thereof.

iv) Enterprise-level fraud risk assessment

As discussed previously, a fraud risk assessment can be conducted at three levels, being at an enterprise level, at a business process level or at an incident level.

The purpose of an enterprise-wide fraud risk assessment is to gather the highest-level fraud risks to the group/organisation. Other than the obvious focus on fraud, there is no real process difference to that of an ERM risk assessment process, which is typically a well-established organisational process.

An enterprise-wide fraud risk assessment can be achieved through a single fraud risk assessment in an organisation with a simpler organisational structure. This will be a more encompassing and involved process in larger, more complex organisations. For example, in conglomerate-type organisations, the group level forensic function will need to define the fraud risk assessment process and ensure that the various business units understand and implement the process. The group level forensic function may also provide a template for the individual business units to guide their risk assessment process. Individual business units should submit their completed fraud risk assessments to the group forensic services function. The group forensic function should assess the adequacy of the fraud risk assessment and update the group fraud risk register.

There is no requirement to restrict fraud risk gathering to a single method. Multiple fraud risk gathering techniques can be used simultaneously to identify fraud risks in the same period of assessment. Not all inputs are however equal and it may be important to consider the need to weight different inputs to prevent skewing of the overall results.

v) Fraud risk enablers

When we think about fraud risk assessments, we tend to think about specific fraud risks. An example of a fraud risk is that procurement staff members may receive kickbacks for unfairly approving non-qualifying suppliers on the organisation's preferred supplier list. Like fire needs oxygen, fraud risks need certain enablers to 'burn' at a higher rate. The stronger the enabler or the more enablers there are, the greater the chances are of fraud/greater frauds. There will be a greater chance of procurement fraud in our previous example, if the environment is highly complex with very few people understanding it or performing any form of oversight.

Therefore, before we dive into identifying fraud risks, we need to know and understand the fraud risk enablers in the environment that we are assessing. It is therefore important, as part of the lead-up to the fraud risk assessment, to consider the influence (encouraging or deterrent) that each of the below aspects could have on fraud risks in the organisation. This may help us to focus our fraud risk identification efforts optimally.

The factors listed below are examples of prompts that can be used in discussions to identify enterprise-wide fraud risk enablers. The idea is to provide prompts to get the compiler of the fraud risk assessment to consider all areas of fraud risk. These factors should be supplemented to suit the specific industry on which it is being applied. Each of these aspects may increase fraud pressures. Try to understand how each aspect affects the organisation in general and what organisation-specific fraud risks may result. The factors include:

- *Macro economic*
  These are all the macro economic aspects that may cause pressure to commit fraud or that may weaken the control environment. Examples include: the downturn of the world economy, falling oil prices, shortage of commodities, commodity price fluctuations, etc.
- *Micro economic*
  These are all the micro-specific aspects that affect the specific industry within which the organisation operates. These may place pressures on third parties to perpetrate fraud against the organisation or on management to achieve targets or on employees. Micro economic pressure examples include: changing industries (such as the movement away from steam trains to diesel locomotives, the reduced dependency on post offices, changes to the telephone and communication industry changes, etc), commodity dependencies, etc.
- *Political*
  How stable is the political environment in which the organisation operates? How corrupt are the politicians? Do robust and fair political mechanisms exist within the country? What impact does the political situation have on the organisation and fraud? Is the organisation dependent on good political relations? Does the organisation deal directly with the government in the course of conducting its business? Is the organisation dependent on the government for survival?
- *Legislative*
  What is the impact of potential or current legislation? How easy or difficult is it to conduct business from a legislative point of view? How onerous are the laws? What industry-specific laws and regulations exist (for example in the mining industry, financial services, pharmaceutical industry, agriculture, etc)? What are the penalties for transgressing the laws? How strictly are these laws enforced? What impact can this have on the organisation?

- *Contractual*
  How easy is it to get contracts? What is the organisation's portfolio of contracts? Are there particularly onerous contracts? Which material contracts are coming to an end in the short-term? How will this affect the organisation?
- *Key personnel*
  What is the dependency on key personnel? Are there any tyrant-type leaders? How well-trained are staff members? How easy is it to obtain the skills required in the marketplace?
- *Competitors*
  How many competitors are there? How aggressive and ethical are competitors? Does the organisation operate in a free economy? How do the competitors compare in size?
- *Complexity*
  What is the degree of complexity in the industry/organisation?
- *Accessibility*
  How easily accessible is the industry/organisation to new joiner organisations?
- *Business process level*
  What is the degree of automation? How mature are the business processes? Are the business processes well documented and understood? Are the business process controls adequate and mature?
- *Organisational strategy*
  Is it too aggressive, unattainable or is it putting undue pressure on executives to achieve? Are the proposed strategy and the achievement mechanisms fraudulent or do they encourage fraudulent practices?
- *Organisational culture and ethics*
  What are the general organisational culture and ethics like and what are the ethics of the key leaders like? Do they participate in, encourage or turn a blind eye to fraud and unethical practices? How ethical is the organisation? What kind of industry does the organisation operate in? Is this an industry that is notorious for unethical dealings? What is the history of incidents?
- *Organisational structure*
  Is the organisational structure adequate (span of control, reporting lines, seniority, etc) to detect, prevent and report fraud?
- *Known enterprise risks*
  Do any of the risks identified as part of the enterprise risk management (ERM) process have a direct or an indirect bearing on fraud? Do any of these promote fraud or strengthen or weaken anti-fraud initiatives?
- *Organisational leadership*
  What are the skills, expertise and track record of leaders like, including their visible commitment to anti-fraud measures? What actual examples are there to evidence this?

- *Fraud schemes*
  What are particular fraud schemes that could occur, based on the:
  - Industry (different industries seem to have a predisposition to a particular type of fraud, for example the scrap industry is renowned for being less ethical)
  - Area where the organisation is situated (for example in drug and gang infested areas)
  - Degree of automation (the expectation is that the higher the degree of automation, the less opportunity there is for deviation)
  - Maturity of the control environment, etc
- *Parties*
  Who are the parties that could be involved in fraud and why?
- *Area/s of operation*
  In which area does the organisation operate in terms of industry (government, arms industry, mining, financial, pharmaceutical, retail, production, farming, shipping and logistics, medical, etc), markets, competitors, customers, suppliers, partners and countries. Do any of these raise the risk of fraud?
- *Product*
  What are the product offerings, product portfolio, unique strengths, dependencies and main revenue drivers of the organisation? How do these affect the risk of fraud?
- *Financial statements and other pertinent information*
  (for example the operating system, stock records, etc) - What are these saying in terms of fraud and related risks? Is the information credible or is it just too good to be true?
- *Assets*
  Is the organisation asset heavy? What are the asset types (movable, immovable, tangible, intangible)? Are there many costs associated with the assets? What is the age of the assets? Has adequate provision been made to replace or decommission assets? Which opportunities exist for fraud in each of these?
- *Product value*
  Does the organisation deal in lucrative products (precious stones, electronics, etc)?
- *Organisation type*
  What type of organisation is it? Is it sales driven, a service organisation, production-heavy?
- *Cash*
  What degree of cash is there in the organisation? High cash can represent a high risk of theft. Is there trapped cash in countries? How good is the organisation's cash flow? What is the management of cash like?
- *Funding*
  What type of funding does the organisation use? What is the debt-to-asset ratio? What pressure does this create? What are the types of equity and debt used (for example: shares, debentures, etc)? Does the organisation make use of complex financial

instruments, hedge funds, etc? Are all loans recorded completely and accurately on the balance sheet? Are any of the shares or assets used as security for finance obtained?

- *Security*
  What is the degree of physical security, ease of access to the organisation? Are there many public accesses, does the organisation make use of e-commerce, how strong is IT security, etc?
- *Accounting*
  Are there any accounting complexities, is there a high number of transactions, what is the degree of computerisation, what is the degree of data available and staff knowledge? Are the company's accounting policies in line with International Financial Reporting Standards (IFRS)? Are there any controversial accounting policies? Are the external auditors in full agreement with the policies? Did any significant accounting policies change recently and did this have a material effect on the profitability of the organisation?
- *Controls*
  Are there any control deficiencies that exist and controls that could be circumvented?
- *Incentives*
  Are there any unusual incentives, pressures, and opportunities to commit fraud? Are directors or sales staff highly incentivised? What checks and balances are there over this process? Are staff members incentivised to do their jobs (for example bonuses paid for deal closure)?
- *Impact and probability*
  In general, what could the potential impact of a fraud incident be and what is the probability of occurrence?
- *History*
  What is the history of incident – known issues that have occurred, the number of times they occurred, the value (and/or potential) of each occurrence, the parties involved?
- *Relationships*
  Do any unusual relationships exist (within the organisation, with suppliers, with clients, with government agencies, etc)?
- *Lifestyle indicators*
  Are there any people clearly living beyond their known financial means (in terms of lifestyle costs)? This may occur where the person is under financial pressure and where their legitimate income is being diverted to another area (for example: gambling, sex workers or drugs).
- *Ability*
  What is the organisation's ability to respond to fraud threats and incidents? The higher the ability, the less incentive there may be to perpetrate fraud.
- *Tolerance*
  What is the organisation's demonstrated tolerance to fraud?

vi) Business process-level fraud risk assessment

A business process-level fraud risk assessment is one form of preventative and detective fraud method. It will be discussed in detail in section 1.4.1 on preventative fraud methods. It is mentioned here as it completes the picture of the three levels (being level two) of fraud risk assessment and shows another source from which the fraud risk register is populated.

vii) Incident-specific fraud risk assessment

The final fraud risk assessment level is the incident-specific level. You will see that we commenced the fraud risk assessment at a high enterprise level and then toned down to a business process level and we are now at a detailed incident-specific level.

For every actual fraud incident, retrospectively determine why it occurred and how it could have occurred. Identify the failed and/or weak controls that resulted in the fraud or that would have (if they were present and functioning/were not circumvented) detected or prevented the fraudulent activity. Identify mitigating controls to bolster the deficient internal controls. The business unit level fraud risk register should be updated with all new and previously unrecorded fraud risks.

viii) Fraud risk register

The output of all three levels of fraud risk assessment should be captured in the fraud risk register. The purpose of the fraud risk register is to record all fraud risks in one central place so as to have one central place from which to manage fraud risks. The risks captured in the fraud risk register will include the high-level enterprise fraud risks, the medium-level business process fraud risks and the detailed incident-specific fraud risks. Not all fraud risks will be equally significant.

The fraud risk register is not a public domain document. The fraud risk register is a highly confidential document that highlights fraud vulnerabilities and the actual history of incidents of fraud. This information could be used fraudulently to the detriment of the organisation if in the wrong hands. Circulation of the fraud risk register should be restricted and not placed on a general file server.

A war story comes to mind of an audit report that I wrote of vulnerabilities in a large multifaceted distribution centre. This was at the time when the concept of 'participative management' was very much the fashion. The organisation misguidedly thought that it needed to share all information with all organisation levels in the distribution centre. My audit report was unceremoniously circulated to the entire distribution centre staff. The dishonest staff members amongst them could not believe their luck and used my report as a prompt list of vulnerabilities (many previously unknown to them) to exploit.

Managing fraud risks means having a mechanism by which to prioritise all fraud risks based on importance, imminence of threat, magnitude of consequential effect as well as the cost to mitigate. Managing fraud risk does not mean that each fraud risk will be able to be successfully mitigated by one direct control (for example a check and release of a transaction upon approval). Multiple indirect controls may collectively mitigate risks (for example: training, HR policies, fraud awareness, etc). Management of fraud risks could entail:

- The mitigation of the fraud risk by the introduction of sufficient controls
- The acceptance of the risk, with no or little risk mitigation
- The transference of the risk to another party, for example by insuring against the event occurring

The fraud risk register is the central place in which fraud risks and fraud management activities are documented. The following fields may be included in the fraud risk register:

- Fraud risk description
- Fraud risk category based on the type of fraud
- Potential direct impact (financial or other, such as reputational) in the event of occurrence
- Potential indirect/subsequent impacts
- Probability of occurrence/imminence of threat
- Business unit, department and/or people affected
- Date aware (if relevant)
- Existing mitigating control description
- Existing mitigating control effectiveness
- Mitigating owner
- Mitigation strategy
- Mitigation due date

The prioritising of fraud risks can be successfully achieved by rating risks according to the relative probability of occurrence and the impact on the organisation if the risk was to materialise. The scale against which the fraud risks are to be rated should be predefined and approved. Only one fraud risk rating scale should be used within the organisation to ensure continuity and comparability.

A five-by-five impact probability rating is fairly standard. Impact and probability are two dimensional. Prioritising which fraud risks to focus on typically requires focusing on the product of the scores, for example:

Fraud risk name	Impact	Probability	Net score
Fraud risk #3	5	5	25
Fraud risk #1	2	3	6
Fraud risk #4	1	4	4
Fraud risk #2	3	1	3

In this illustration, fraud risk #3 represents the highest risk and should be prioritised.

	Probability					
Impact						

The probability of occurrence and the potential impact of a fraud could be different in different situations. The scales used should therefore suggest multiple types of considerations for each scale to cater for multiple situations. The scales below can be used as an example to rate the impact and probability of specific frauds:

Probability scales

- *Certain*

The logical question is if there will ever be a situation in an organisation where there is 100% certainty that fraud will occur. If the answer is yes, then the natural next question is: 'Well then, why don't we just combat it before it happens?' That would unfortunately be an oversimplification. In certain industries like in the retail industry, there is just no getting around it, the chance of stock theft is certain. In such industries fraud risk officers concentrate their efforts on reducing the effect of fraud to the minimum, while never totally eradicating it.

- *Highly probable or a reasonable chance of occurrence*

There is a highly likely chance that this fraud will occur.

- *Probable*

In this case, we say that it is probable that the fraud being rated will occur.

- *Improbable*

remote, little or no chance of occurrence – In such cases there is a very low chance of occurrence of fraud.

- *No chance, extremely remote*

For this rating, the logical question to consider is if there could ever be absolutely no chance of occurrence of the fraud being rated. The short answer is no: even the Eiffel Tower has been 'stolen' more than once in its history. While that seems improbable, the Eiffel Tower was 'sold' to an unsuspecting scrap dealer. I suppose that what this tells us is that if we feel that there is absolutely no chance of fraud, then we probably have not applied our minds well enough. 'No chance', is more about the fact that, while there is an extremely low chance of occurrence, there is not (from a risk-based approach point of view) sufficient basis for considering it. A no chance rating will only be used in exceptional circumstances.

Probability scale considerations

When deciding on the probability scale to rate a particular fraud, consider the following aspects:

- *Complexity of the environment*
  Highly complex environments may only be understood by a few people. It may be easier to perpetrate and conceal fraud in such environments, as collusion may be easier or the chance of detection is reduced. Alternatively, highly complex environments may be less accessible to fraudsters, thereby reducing the chance of occurrence.

- *Number of people holding an understanding of the environment*
  As per the above point on the complexity of the environment.

- *Dependency on key personnel*
  How dependent is the organisation on key people in that area? How much power do these key people hold in terms of an ability to override controls, give unquestioned instructions, etc? As with the aforementioned discussion, do they hold all the knowledge of the area? Are these people in a position of trust and what is the chance that they will be questioned, their work checked, etc?

- *Lucrative nature of products*
  Does the organisation deal with cash, jewels, retail products or high-end electronic products? Alternatively, does the organisation deal in general services or mass-produced, low-value plastic widgets? The nature of the product or service may make theft or fraud of the product more desirable. Some products are more desirable to fraudsters themselves or may be more easily sold within their networks. Fraudsters are going to be more attracted to those products that they can sell for a higher price. They will look for the most money for the lowest effort. The lucrative nature of products may also differ from environment to environment. As an example: medical products may be more lucrative in Africa and less lucrative in a large developed city in Germany. *An example that I dealt with refers: South African-based fraudsters tried to fraudulently obtain delivery of a large consignment of maternity sanitary towels. These were destined to be taken over the border and sold on in poorer, under-resourced neighbouring African countries.*

- *Environment*
  What are the environments in which the organisation operates? Are these environments that are normally associated with unethical behaviour and shady deals? For example: scrap dealers, second-hand automotive part dealers and trucking services may be less ethical environments to deal in and there may be a greater occurrence of fraud in these industries. There is fraud in all environments; it is just more prevalent in some environments than others. *I recall being at lunch at a national ACFE annual seminar. I introduced myself to the people at my table and enquired in what capacities they worked and for which organisations. One gentleman worked for a large national church group. While I found the obvious contradiction humorous, he assured me that his organisation fell prey to fraud as well.*

- *Volume of transactions*

Volume and value of transactions go hand-in-hand and should to be read together. A greater volume of transactions may represent a greater opportunity to perpetrate frauds or less chance of detection due to the sheer number of transactions.

- *Value of transactions*

High-value transactions may be more desirable to fraudsters and therefore represent a higher fraud risk. Alternatively, there may be fewer high-value transactions with greater opportunity for detection of fraud and therefore a reduced chance of fraud.

- *Degree, maturity and visibility of controls*

Good companies have good controls. The stronger the control environment, the less chance there may be of fraud occurring due to the prevention or detection of the fraud.

- *Ability to measure compliance and visibility of measures and KPIs*

The general rule is that the more things are measured and monitored, the less expectation there is that fraud will occur or remain undetected. This is very true. On the other hand, too much emphasis on KPIs may drive the incorrect behaviour to misrepresent these measures or to conceal underperformance.

- *Extent of system documentation and formalisation*

The better systems of control and processes are documented, the better chance there is that the systems of control will be known and understood and therefore the less the chance there is for fraud. The reason for this is that there is a greater chance that more people will have an understanding of the systems. This in turn means that there are more people to identify if behaviour (fraudulent behaviour in this case) is occurring because it goes against their understanding of how the system should be functioning. There will therefore be a greater chance of detecting the fraud and this will in turn act as a deterrent because controls in the system will be more visible.

- *Degree, frequency and reliability of independent checks and audits*

The more effective controls there are, the greater the chance of detection or prevention of fraud there is. There will be correspondingly less chance that fraudsters are going to take a chance to perpetrate such frauds.

- *Degree of automation*

The general principle is that the more automated a process is, the less chance there will be of manipulation of that process. The alternative is also possible, that automated transactions may not enjoy any degree of scrutiny and may represent less chance of detection of fraud.

- *Amount of manual intervention*

The aforementioned discussion on automation refers. Chapter 9 on examples of frauds also refers, particularly with regards to manual journals, which represent a high fraud risk transaction.

- *Stability and frequency of changes in systems and environment*

Environments that are changing constantly may be less understood and represent a greater opportunity to perpetrate and conceal frauds than environments that are stable and well known to all. On the other hand, a system that has remained unchanged for years may not be as secure as a new purpose-built system. Older systems were less secure and built in the times when programmers did not have to consider such high degrees of control. Legacy systems are, in the main, less secure than enterprise resource planning (ERP) systems.

- *Length of time that systems have been in place*

The aforementioned discussion of degree and extent of change refers.

- *Staff competence, knowledge, length of service, training, attitude and discipline issues, etc*

The aforementioned discussion of degree and extent of change refers. The general principle is that the more competent and knowledgeable staff members are, the less opportunity for fraud there may be as everyone knows what is expected and a fraudulent transaction may be more easily identified. The length of service of staff members does not guarantee a reduced opportunity of fraud as, in reality, frauds are more frequently perpetrated by long-serving members of staff than new-hires.

- *Average span of control*

The span of control speaks to the degree and extent of internal controls. The expectation is that the fewer areas a manager has to control, the greater the degree of control will be. Organisations frequently retrench more expensive managerial staff members and increase the span of control of remaining managers in times of economic downturn. This widens the span of control of remaining managers and reduces the effectiveness of control thereby increasing the chance of fraud and reducing the opportunity of detection.

Impact scale discussions

The following potential effects of fraud may be considered to rate the impact of a specific fraud occurring:

- *Catastrophic*

Frauds with catastrophic consequences are few and far between. When they occur, they receive a lot of attention. Enron and Barings Bank refer as examples of catastrophic frauds. A catastrophic fraud would refer to the total disruption and/or demise of the organisation. The biggest travesty is that most people (management and fraud investigators) persist in believing that this sort of degree of fraud will not occur in their organisations.

- *Significant business disruption*

This level of fraud will result in a significant disruption to the business, but the organisation will still be able to continue thereafter, albeit worse off.

- *Medium impact*

The fraud will have some noticeable impact, but nothing that is insurmountable.

- *Little or low impact*

The organisation can absorb the effect of this type of fraud without any noticeable disruption or effect (financial or other).

- *No impact*

Again, the logical question to be considered here is if there will ever be a situation where there is no effect of fraud? There may be an assumption about the situations where fraud is successfully prevented. Even if there has not been a direct financial loss and/or if only one person is aware that there was a fraud, there will still be an indirect cost (investigative costs, productivity losses, effect on morale, hiring costs, training costs, reputational damage, etc). Also, even if there is no fraud, the cost of fraud to the organisation is the anti-fraud measures that are in place. The short answer is therefore 'no', as there will always be a cost to fraud in some form or another.

Impact scale considerations

Use the following aspects when considering how to rate the impact of a specific fraud occurring:

- *Size of direct financial losses*

What could the financial value of the fraud be? How does this compare to the organisation's revenue and reserves? Can the organisation absorb such a loss?

- *Total investigation costs*

What will an investigation into such a matter entail? Will it just be a few standard interviews, reviewing accessible documents and an internal HR process thereafter? Alternatively, will it be a protracted complex investigation requiring specialist skills?

- *Total legal costs*

What will the costs of litigation, prosecution or defending be?

- *Commercial losses, exclusion from business and lost contracts and business*

Which business does the organisation stand to lose and what is the value thereof?

- *Lack of access to finance or higher cost of finance due to increased risks*

What will the effect of such a fraud be on the organisation's ability to raise capital?

- *Penalties, fines and embargos*

Will there be any direct fines or penalties imposed by the authorities? The actions of a rogue employee may result in the non-compliance of the organisation to regulatory requirements. The authorities are frequently indifferent to the fact that the organisation may already have suffered a loss and that the organisation had little or no ability to control or prevent the occurrence. Authorities tend to push the responsibility of prevention of such occurrences back to organisations themselves.

- *More frequent and/or stringent enforcement of controls and checks by the authorities*

Knowledge of the occurrence by the authorities may attract attention by the authorities and result in them carrying out more frequent checks of the organisation. These checks may involve greater and more frequent scrutiny of documents, stop-and-searches being conducted, audits, inspections, etc. Such checks are generally time-consuming, disruptive to the business, require preparation, may have an effect on the organisation's ability to deliver value to its customers and cost the organisation money (directly or due to lost productivity).

- *Reputational damage*

The organisation may suffer reputational damage and lose the goodwill and/or trust of customers and suppliers as a result of the fraud. Management frequently wants to sweep fraud under the carpet to avoid reputational damage. Research has shown that the value of organisations that have a more transparent approach generally increases, while the value of organisations that conceal matters generally decreases.

- *Rehiring costs*
Dismissed staff will almost certainly have to be replaced. There are numerous costs associated with hiring new staff members, including advertising costs, employment agency staff placement commission costs, payment of notice periods, hiring temporary staff members, loss of productivity, etc.

- *Staff training costs*
New staff members will have to be trained to bring them up to the same level as dismissed staff members. This may involve direct staff training costs and productivity costs (of learners and internal trainers).

- *Loss of intellectual capital*
When people leave the organisation, knowledge leaves with them. Longstanding employees are frequently those that perpetrate fraud. It is safe to assume that longstanding employees have more knowledge than new-hires. This knowledge may be required to deliver on the organisation's objectives and it will have to be replaced. Additionally, the knowledge (scientific formulas, customer databases, special techniques, etc) that individuals have may be unique to that organisation and be the means through which the organisation derives its income or what sets it apart from its competitors.

- *Effect on/lowering of staff morale*
It is frequently difficult to share any degree of detailed information to the organisation in a fraud case. Remaining staff members may not always understand the true extent of fraud and or perceive unfairness to the perpetrators. The lack of sharing of information may be because the matter is sub judice or to respect privacy (of the organisation, victims or perpetrators). Remaining staff members may have been friends with the dismissed employees and may be struggling to come to terms with what has happened to their friend. Fraud is also simply an unpleasant matter with which to be associated.

- *Costs of additional controls*
New and additional controls may have to be introduced. This may result in more time to process transactions due to additional steps required, productivity costs due to retraining, implementation costs, system development and changes, testing timeframes, etc.

- *Lost productivity costs and system downtime*
The absence of people (involved in investigation, counselling sessions or trial, or suspended or dismissed due to involvement) may result in lost productivity. Systems affected by fraud may need to be brought down for investigation, repair and improvement.

Fraud risk management programme

Once all the fraud risks have been identified and prioritised, a programme needs to be designed on how to manage, mitigate and/or assume the risks. A fraud risk management programme formalises how the organisation will approach the management of identified fraud risks. Only the key fraud risks need to be addressed in this programme. All potential fraud risk management initiatives are discussed at length in the sections on proactive and reactive fraud risk strategy below.

The fraud risk management programme should be approved by the organisational or business unit leadership. In larger conglomerate-type organisations the individual business units should submit their fraud risk registers and fraud management programmes to the group fraud risk services. The group fraud risk services should evaluate the adequacy of the individual business unit fraud risk registers and fraud risk management programmes. The highest-group fraud risks and salient mitigation actions should be collated, summarised and reported to the group leadership.

A good fraud risk management programme contains:

- A summary of the fraud risks
- Proposed fraud risk management initiatives
- Fraud risk owners and anticipated completion dates
- Anticipated benefits

1.4. PROACTIVE SIDE OF FRAUD STRATEGY

As discussed above, there are two elements to a fraud strategy, being proactive and reactive activities.

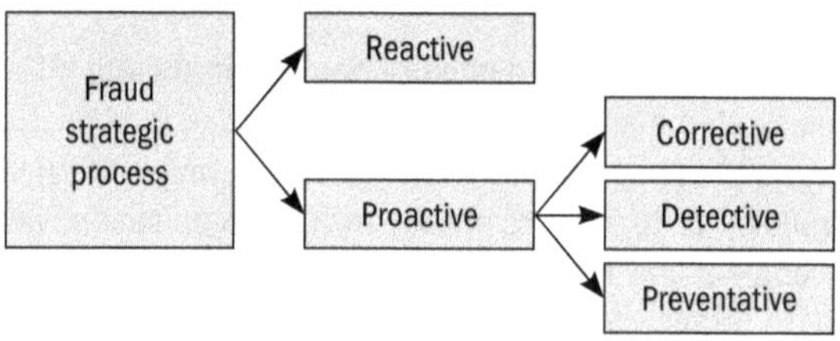

Diagram 1.4 *Proactive and reactive fraud strategy*

Proactive fraud risk management has preventative, detective and corrective anti-fraud strategic initiatives. The intention of this categorisation is to provide logical groupings to ensure that all elements are covered by the fraud strategy. The groupings are not intended to be an academically accurate split, as there is some natural overlap between the categories that occur. These are discussed in detail below.

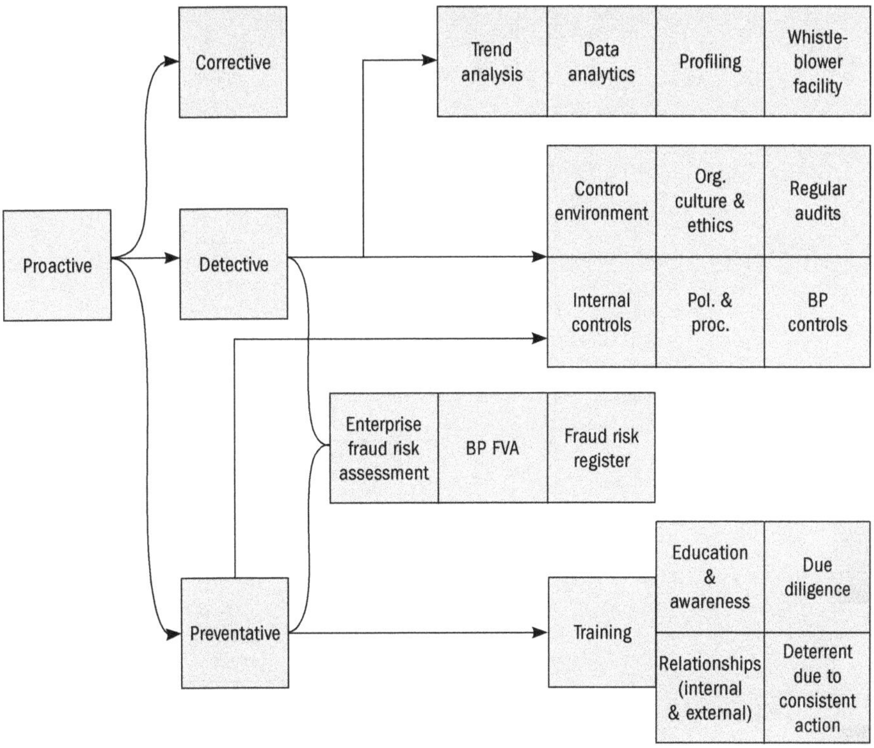

Diagram 1.5 *Proactive fraud mitigation*

1.4.1. Preventative fraud risk management

Preventative fraud measures are geared toward preventing fraud occurring in the first place. Many preventative fraud measures could however also be detective fraud measures. We will for practical reasons to avoid duplication, only discuss measures under either one of the 'preventative' (point 1.4.1) or 'detective' (point 1.4.2) sections. Some preventative fraud measures that are discussed in detail below include:

- Fraud risk assessments
- Internal controls (preventative, detective controls, discussed below)
- Policies and procedures
- Regular audits
- Organisational culture and ethics
- Control environment
- Education and awareness
- Training
- Due diligence
- Deterrents
- Relationships

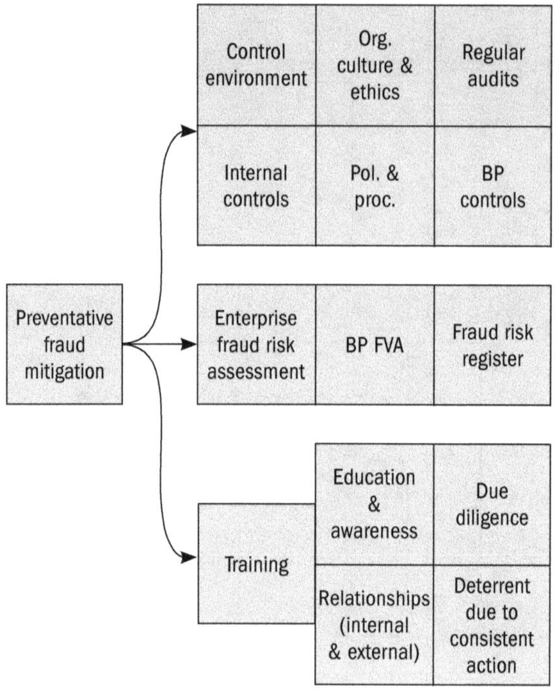

Diagram 1.6 *Preventative fraud mitigation*

a. Business process-level fraud risk assessment

The second level of fraud risk assessment is fraud risk assessments conducted at a business process level. A business process-level fraud risk assessment is a fraud risk assessment that is carried out on specific high-risk business processes, for example: the procurement process, the requisition to pay process, the order to cash process, the tendering process, the asset acquisition process, the recruitment process, business travel process, the payroll processes, etc.

The need for a business process fraud risk assessment can stem from two places, being the enterprise-wide fraud risk assessment (highlighting a specific business process as having a high risk of fraud) or a specific fraud incident that occurred, which highlights structural control deficiencies in the underlying business process as the cause for the fraud having occurred.

In most cases, the enterprise-wide fraud risk assessment process would have identified high-level fraud risks in specific business processes, product types, geographic locations, company, business unit, entity, and concerning practices.

If a high-risk company has been identified within a group of companies, then a further (more detailed) fraud risk assessment may be conducted to identify the highest fraud risk aspects within the identified area/company. This may be a simplified/more focused version of the enterprise-wide fraud risk assessment. This is done to understand why the company/area was regarded as a high fraud risk. The high-risk areas highlighted in the enterprise-wide fraud risk assessment will typically equate to business processes. For example: If the enterprise-wide fraud risk assessment identified company X in country Y where the organisation operates as a high fraud risk, then further analysis may identify that a specific vendor contract is behind the concern. Vendor contracts stem from the procurement process. The detailed business process fraud risk assessment can then be concentrated on the procurement process in company X in country Y.

The business process fraud risk assessment is one tool in the prevention of fraud. The detailed analysis of the high-risk business processes aims to identify fraud vulnerabilities in the business processes prior to actual fraud incidents occurring.

The key is for business process fraud risk assessments to be at a process level. It is therefore imperative to obtain an understanding of the business processes under review in advance, as part of the planning process. The business process fraud risk assessment involves the identification of fraud risks along the entire business process.

The business process fraud risk assessment is conducted separately for each business process under review. Different business processes should not be combined in a single risk assessment process and documentation.

A business process may not be limited to one department or to one IT system. The business process risk assessment spans functions, departments and systems for the business processes under review. The business process has an origin (for example, the placing of an order by a customer) and an end (for example, the application of the payment by the finance team). Concentrating on only one department would ignore potential fraud risks in other areas. Also, the mitigating control for a particular fraud risk in the procurement department may lie in the finance function. It is imperative therefore to look at the end-to-end business process. The business processes that are in the German ERP system known as 'SAP' ('Systeme, Anwendungen, Produkte in der Datenverarbeitung') are good examples of end-to-end business processes. Examples include the order to cash (OTC) cycle and the requisition to pay (RTP) cycle.

Commence the business process fraud risk analysis by documenting and understanding the end-to-end business process. Flow charts are useful to provide an overview of the process. Be sure to show the flow of information and documents through people, functions and across computer systems. These diagrams may be used by individuals in a desktop fraud risk assessment analysis or by a group of people in a workshop.

The first step in a business process fraud risk assessment is to identify the key objectives of the business process under review. Examples of generic high-level objectives include:

- Authorisation and validity of all transactions within the specific business process
- Completeness, accuracy and timely processing of all transactions
- That all transactions/actions are within organisational policies and procedures and abide by relevant laws and regulations
- Safeguarding of assets
- That all information (operating and financial) is complete and accurate (accounting period, general ledger account, amount, date, other details, etc)
- The economy and efficiency with which resources are employed

The purpose of defining business process objectives is to focus our fraud risk analysis on the purpose of the business process. These generic objectives should therefore be tailored to suit the specific business process under review. For example, when using our second objective, 'that all revenue is received, banked and recorded completely, accurately and in time.'

The identification of fraud vulnerabilities then involves walking each of the business process objectives through the business process to understand the points in the business process where the specific objective is determined. In other words, at which point in the business process are accuracy and completeness determined? For example, accuracy may be determined when the order is initially captured, when the sales system reads the price from the price master file and creates the warehouse 'picking slip' (the document that is used by warehouse staff, known as 'pickers' who 'pick' stock out of warehouse slots where stock is stored) and at the point when the pro-forma customer invoice is created and when the invoice is interfaced to the financial system.

The Business Process Fraud Risk Assessment Template (see Annexure 1.2 attached hereto) may be used to document the end-to-end business process fraud risk assessment.

Next, consider what, from a fraud point of view, could go wrong (risks) at each of these points. For example: stock could be dispatched without capturing an order. Not all orders could be captured, thereby unfairly prejudicing the organisation's orders. Orders could be captured against the incorrect customer while the stock is fraudulently issued to another customer. The incorrect customer is charged for the stock. Unauthorised credit notes can be processed after the stock is issued to fraudulently prevent the customer from being charged. The incorrect products, quantities or prices may be captured, etc.

The idea is to consider all risk possibilities, whether a control exists or not and/or no matter how unlikely it seems that the fraud risk could materialize. Do not screen any fraud risks in advance. Try to be as complete as possible. List all the potential risks in one document (Annexure 1.2 refers as an example). Fraud risk assessment workshop participants are frequently of the opinion that the suggested risks will not occur at all. While it may be unlikely that a particular fraud risk could materialise, as long as there is a risk, there is a chance that the risk could materialise, no matter how slim. Participants also frequently personalise the risks. They know what they do or they have worked with their colleagues for so long that they trust them and do not think that they could perpetrate fraud. We need to depersonalise the fraud risk assessment.

As a further example: The objective of a particular business process is the 'completeness and accuracy of revenue'. Completeness and accuracy of revenue may be achieved at multiple stages of the business process such as when:

- Customer orders are captured by a sales representative onto an online ordering system
- The sales program runs and processes all new orders to the warehouse
- The processed sales orders are interfaced to the financial system

Let us consider two fraud risks to illustrate our point:

- There is a risk that the sales representatives do not capture all orders on the system and make deals directly with the customers.
- There is a risk that the accounting staff members process manual journals to fraudulently increase revenue.

The non-functioning of a control is not the risk. The non-functioning of a control is non-compliance and the effect of the non-functioning of the control is the risk. For example, the risk is not that the bank reconciliation will not detect unauthorised/fraudulent payments. The objective is that all payments are valid and correctly authorised. The risk is that fraudulent payments may be made undetected. The control is that a bank reconciliation is performed.

Next, assign a potential impact and probability of occurrence for each of the risks. The impact and probability scales discussed below refer.

Lastly, we identify the controls that exist to mitigate the risks. The non-existence of a control points to a control deficiency. This will, depending on the purpose of our analysis, tell us why a fraud actually occurred (due to the deficiency of the control) or where a fraud could potentially occur (proactive analysis of fraud risks). Also, consider the adequacy of the design of these controls. So, while a control may exist, consider how strong the control actually is. Document all fraud risks and mitigating controls (Annexure 1.2 refers).

There may be more than one control that collectively contributes to objective attainment. Please note that there can be a one-to-many or a many-to-one relationship of risks to controls. So, one control could satisfy many risks or one risk may be mitigated by many controls. It is the strength of the portfolio of controls that we are interested in and not necessarily the strength of a single control.

The many-to-one concept frequently creates confusion. If, for example, a particular control is mitigating three different risks, then it will need to be ensured that the control is physically the same activity that is performed resulting in the mitigation of the different risks. The control should not just be the same sounding or purpose control (for example supervisory check) that is performed in different places in the business process. For example: A supervisor performs three accuracy and completeness checks at the start, middle and end of a particular business process, being at points A, B and C. In this example: there are multiple risks present in the middle of the business process that we suspect are all mitigated by control check B. It would be necessary to ensure that the control is physically the single performance of supervisory check B that mitigates all these risks. If it is not, then a separate control should be listed for control check A or C as applicable. This is important when concluding if there are sufficient controls in the business process to mitigate the fraud risks per objective.

Lastly, determine where there are control deficiencies or inadequately designed controls. Design mitigating controls to balance the fraud risks. The operative word here is 'balance'. We are looking for cost-effective controls that are not prohibitive. Communicate the reasons for not implementing controls to the stakeholders so that agreement for the associated risks can be attained.

Please also note that at this point we are merely considering the adequacy of the design of the controls and not the effective performance of the controls. The testing of the effective functioning of the control/s is not normally part of a fraud risk assessment. The known functioning of the control may have a bearing on our adequacy assessment though. The effectiveness of controls may be conducted as a separate activity. We may however, depending on the purpose of our analysis, want to test to see if the control is functioning as intended and/or if fraud exists. Testing may involve testing all controls, specific controls (in line with an investigation or specific risk) or only the key controls.

A key control is minimum control, without which the system of internal control will fail. The key control is normally the final control in a sequence of controls. For example: A clerk performs a check and a supervisor re-performs the check and authorises the transaction. If the clerk control fails to detect a discrepancy, then the supervisor control is the final control to detect discrepancies. So, the supervisor control is the most important control. You may elect (if following a risk-based approach) to only test the key control. If, in this example, the supervisor is not required to re-perform the check but only to authorise the payment, then the clerk's check would be the key control for completeness and accuracy and the supervisor's control would be the key control for authorisation.

Try to understand why the fraud risk participant regards the area as a fraud risk. Most fraud risks tend to be self-explanatory. Also, ask the participant:

- If the fraud risk has already materialised
- How the actual occurrence of such a fraud risk would be demonstrated/evidenced
- Where and when it has occurred
- Who is involved
- How prevalent it is/they think it is
- What needs to be done to mitigate the risk
- How material it is

If analytical reviews and trend analyses are being used, commence by establishing a benchmark/ baseline of what you anticipate seeing. Conduct the analytical review and compare actual trends to the benchmark. Obtain explanations for deviations.

One method to test deviations is to factor these into the original assumptions and to redo the analytical review to see if the trend has adjusted after the previously unknown factor was taken into account.

All business process fraud risks should be added to the business unit fraud risk register.

b. Internal controls (preventative)

(i) Introduction

Internal controls are the best defence against fraud. The chairman of the board of directors in one of the groups that I worked for used to tell me: 'Good companies have good controls.' He went on to explain that the companies on whose boards he sat, which had good controls, had noticeably fewer problems and did better than companies that did not have good controls.

Determining the adequacy (sufficiency/existence of) and effectiveness (correct functioning/ compliance to) of an organisation's internal controls can be vital not only to combat fraud but for the achievement of the organisation's objectives.

Internal controls can, from a fraud perspective, be either preventative, detective or corrective. In this section, we are going to discuss the preventative nature of internal controls. Our interest in internal controls is slanted towards how these controls can combat fraud.

An analysis of the adequacy and effectiveness of internal controls can be used at the following stages:

- In advance, when a new business process is being designed and before implementation to ensure that sufficient controls are included in the new process
- Once a business process is already implemented, to determine if there are sufficient controls in the existing business process
- After an actual fraud has occurred to determine why it occurred and/or which controls failed and/or were circumvented and/or do not exist
- After an actual fraud to know which controls to bolster to prevent recurrence.

Sound business process analysis skills are therefore a key skill required by fraud investigators to be able to evaluate the adequacy and effectiveness of fraud preventative and detective controls.

(ii) Methodology

There are two areas of control that we are going to discuss. The first is the general control environment and the second is the controls within business processes (known as control activities in the COSO governance framework). It is traditional to focus on the controls in business processes. These controls are more tangible and easier to relate to. The strength of the control environment is however probably more important. The strongest business process controls will not help prevent fraud in an organisation with a totally unethical culture, as controls can be circumvented or ignored.

International governance models like COSO, COCO, COBIT (Control Objectives for Information and Related Technologies framework) and King provide much guidance and input on the control environments of organisations. The COSO model includes some of the following topics under the control environment:

- *Integrity and ethical values*
  Existence and implementation of codes of conduct and other policies regarding acceptable business practice, conflicts of interest, or expected standards of ethical and moral behaviour may demonstrate an organisation's stance on integrity and ethics. These documents should cover dealings with employees, suppliers, customers, investors, creditors, insurers, competitors and auditors, etc (for example: whether management conducts business on a high ethical plane, and insists that others do so, or pays little attention to ethical issues). Also consider if there is pressure from organisational leadership to meet unrealistic performance targets, particularly for short-term results and the extent to which compensation is based on achieving those performance targets. This may encourage employees to take shortcuts and/or perpetrate fraud to derive or appear to achieve the expected results.

- *Commitment to competence*
  Formal or informal job descriptions or other means of defining tasks that comprise particular jobs contribute to strengthening the control environment, by ensuring that all role-players know what is expected in these jobs. Analyses of the knowledge and skills needed to perform jobs adequately may also be useful.

- *Boards of directors and audit committees*
  It is important that boards of directors and audit committees are independent of management to ensure, as required, that difficult and probing questions can be

raised. Organisations with strong control environments have effectively functioning boards and audit committees. Effectively functioning boards:

- Have frequent and timely meetings with the chief financial officer and/or with other accounting officers, internal auditors and external auditors
- Receive sufficient and timely information provided to them to allow monitoring of management's objectives and strategies, the entity's financial position and operating results, and terms of significant agreements
- Are appraised of sufficient and timely information, investigations and improper acts (eg travel expenses of senior officers, significant litigation, investigations of regulatory agencies, defalcations, embezzlement or misuse of corporate assets, violations of insider trading rules, political bribes or facilitation payments and other illegal payments)

- *Management philosophy and operating style*
  The nature of business risks accepted by management can affect the control environment. The control environment could be adversely affected if management often enters into high-risk ventures. The degree of oversight that organisational leadership has over operational management and geographically dispersed business activities may also adversely affect the control environment. What is organisational leadership's stance on financial reporting and accounting policies? Do they apply conservative policies consistently or do they aggressively pursue favourable financial reporting?

- *Organisational structure*
  Control environments will also be strengthened by suitable organisational structures that are sufficiently resourced and with the correct reporting lines. Managers should also understand their responsibilities and have the right skills and experience for their respective positions.

- *Assignment of authority and responsibility*
  Authority and responsibility need to be documented in an authorisation hierarchy and in job descriptions. Are decisions made outside of these responsibilities?

- *Human resource policies and practices*
  A good control environment has robust HR policies and procedures to ensure that the correct people are recruited, appropriately remunerated and that appropriate and consistent discipline is maintained.

The COSO governance framework lays out the detail on control environments. Organisations should choose and implement a suitable governance model to bolster their control environment. The possible fraud risk assessment questions that arise out of the aforementioned control environment issues can be invaluable in identifying strategic fraud risks. Focusing on the control environment will however ensure that emphasis is maintained on the most important fraud risks.

The adequacy and effectiveness of the control environment can be tested by using questionnaires, conducting interviews, performing system walk-throughs and conducting desktop evaluations of internal controls. It is important to obtain examples and evidence to substantiate management's assertions as to the adequacy and effectiveness of the control environment.

As discussed previously it is important, with regards to business process analysis, to understand what the purpose of the business process is. For example: the objective of a payment business process may be to ensure the timely payment of all liabilities. The purpose/objective of the business process is important in terms of:

- *Risks*
  If we know what the purpose is, then surely the highest-level risk is that the objectives of the business process will not be achieved. If we accept this argument, then we can start to identify more specific risks that could occur within the business process to prevent the objective/s from being achieved.
- *Controls*
  When we know the risks, then it is easier to know which controls there should be in place.
- *Tests*
  In the same way, if we know what the purpose is, then it is easier to know what to test. We need to test those aspects that ensure that the objectives are attained. In this manner, we will concentrate on testing the important aspects only.
- *Opinion*
  Lastly, once our testing is complete, the purpose helps us to know how to structure our opinion. What do the people, to whom we are reporting, want to know? They want to know if the business process will achieve its objectives or not. For example: the objective of a system is to ensure that we only pay for goods and services actually received. Our opinion would be, for example: 'We can or we cannot conclude with reasonable assurance that sufficient controls exist and are being complied with to ensure that the organisation only pays for goods and services actually received, as ... the following control deficiencies exist or ... as long as the controls continue to be complied with.'

Anti-fraud objectives are more or less the same as normal business process objectives, just with a fraud flavour. Business process objectives were discussed in detail in section 1.4.1 on the business process fraud risk assessment process.

c. Regular audits

Audits can be both preventative and detective in nature:

- Regular audits proactively assess the adequacy of internal controls. Fraud vulnerabilities can thus be identified and mitigated in a timely manner thereby preventing frauds from occurring.
- Regular audits also create a deterrent to potential fraudsters, as employees see controls being tested and thereby may be discouraged from perpetrating fraud for fear of detection. A strong deterrent is preventative in nature.

- The reality is however that fewer frauds are identified from standard audits. The reason for this may be because the purpose of regular audits is different and not primarily focused on fraud detection. For example: an audit may determine that transactions are incomplete ('... we cannot conclude that the XYZ transactions are complete ...'), but not why the transactions are incomplete (no time is spent to understand why the number sequence is incomplete). Audits may however, in their conduct, detect fraud that has already occurred. A further consideration may be that auditors' skills and experience may not include fraud. It may be unreasonable to expect first-year article clerks to detect frauds if they are not specifically trained to do this.

d. Organisational culture and ethics

As already mentioned under the discussion of the control environment under internal controls, the organisational culture and an ethical climate can promote or discourage unethical practices/ fraud.

While it is only criminal organisations that actively pursue unethical climates, not all organisations:

- Pursue ethical means in all areas of the business and/or do not practice what they preach (for example: they may say that theft is unacceptable, but then pay a bribe to obtain a government contract, which they justify by the fact that they are dealing with an unethical regime)
- Sufficiently discourage unethical behaviour (have robust policies and procedures to prevent, deter and consistently enforce ethics)
- Actively promote ethical behaviour (programmes, HR practices, etc)
- Have a means by which to measure the ethical climate
- Consistently enforce remedial action against perpetrators of unethical acts

e. Policies and procedures

As discussed above, numerous documents form a direct or indirect part of the anti-fraud documents. The documents that form a direct part of the anti-fraud documents tend to be owned by the forensic function, while the indirectly contributing documents tend to be owned by other business owners. The previously mentioned documents refer, including:

(i) Forensic function

- Fraud charter
- Fraud policy
- Fraud strategy
- Fraud risk assessment methodology
- Fraud vulnerability assessment methodology
- Fraud awareness programmes
- Fraud training programmes
- Fraud response plan
- Fraud investigation methodology
- Fraud reporting policy
- Whistle-blower policy and procedures

(ii) Related and supporting documents

- Shareholder agreements
- Joint venture contracts
- Anti-corruption legislation
- Anti-competitive behaviour legislation
- Foreign trade control legislation
- Conflict of interest documentation
- Insurance policies and strategy
- Enterprise risk management documents
- Governance guidelines (internal and external requirements)
- Organisational culture and ethics
- Information security
- Procurement policies
- Supplier contracts
- Access to information legislation, privacy policies, information exchange legislation
- Authority hierarchy
- Employment contracts
- Disciplinary procedure
- Commercial agreements
- Customer agreements
- Vendor/supplier agreements

(iii) Business process-specific documents

Most indirectly contributing anti-fraud documents are not classified as anti-fraud documents at all. They have another main purpose, which also contributes to anti-fraud interventions in some or other manner. Some of the strongest anti-fraud documents are in fact the normal standard operating procedures (SOPs) that the organisation has by which staff members are instructed and guided. This is because in many cases in a fraud investigation, the fraud investigator will compare the subject's behaviour to the standard approach/anticipated behaviour. See Chapter 7 on subsequent actions for more detail – in a labour matter you may need to prove that there was a rule and the subject had knowledge of the rule. The SOP can evidence the existence of the transgressed rule. Strong general business process and specific SOPs are therefore vital in the fight against fraud.

Strong SOPs also have strong internal controls built into them for the prevention and detection of fraud. Anti-fraud professionals all acknowledge that sound internal controls represent the best tool to combat fraud.

There are many policies and procedures within organisations. A few examples include:

- Asset usage policy
- Accounts payable procedures
- Payment approval policy or authorisation hierarchy
- Procurement policy

- Bank reconciliation procedures
- Accounting policies and procedures
- Travel policy

The degree of documentation/formalisation strengthens the control environment.

(iv) Authorisation hierarchy/limits

Authorisation limits define the organisation's risk tolerance level in so far as they define the risk that the organisation is prepared to take before requiring a more senior approval for transactions/events.

The automation of authorisation limits makes the control stronger, as it ensures that the control will always be executed as required as long as predefined criteria are met.

As discussed under SOPs, the authorisation hierarchy also provides a base (rule) against which to compare actual behaviour.

(v) HR policies, procedure, practices and records

Robust checks at the time of recruitment may be a sound preventative fraud control. These include the following:

- A candidate's ability to practically conduct tasks should be assessed – can they do what their CV purports they can?
- Background checks should be conducted.
- Reference checks should be conducted. References should be vetted in advance and independently contacted. Do not just assume that you are speaking to the person they purport to be. Say to the referee that you would just like to ask them a few validating questions. They will not mind if they are legitimate. Make use of multiple references and cross-reference what they are saying. Be mindful to understand what the referee is not saying, as much as what they are saying. People feel compelled to say good things about a person, not say bad things, give people a second chance or may even have a desire to get rid of their problems. One final test question that I like to ask is if they would rehire the person. A long pause is your answer.

Two examples refer to when candidates used friends as references. In the first case, the candidate's ex-prison cell mates served as her reference. The referees gave a glowing reference and the candidate was duly employed. Needless to say, it was not long before she was up to her old tricks that landed her in prison in the first instance. She was eventually dismissed for theft. An expensive lesson. In the second example, I was conducting a reference check myself and I realised halfway into the conversation that the referee was in fact a friend of the candidate. They had started as colleagues but later became close friends. The reference was consequently considered as insufficiently objective.

Also, ensure that the organisation conducts exit interviews. People leaving may be disgruntled and/or have nothing to lose and/or want to get even and/or have a need to unbundle all their frustrations. There have been numerous examples where departing staff members unbundle their frustrations. I frequently say jokingly that I get some of my best information from disgruntled housewives and dismissed employees. It is however important to substantiate assertions made by exiting employees before reacting. *One bad example comes to mind where management and HR unjustifiably castigated the supervisor based on the sour grapes that his departing employee had alleged in the exit interview. The supervisor was not asked to provide his side of the story and the assertions were immediately held against him. It later transpired that the employee had lied.*

Performance appraisals and remuneration policies are owned by management. These show a history of performance and are a good source of reference.

The existence of sound records also ensures that information is available when required.

(vi) Roll-out evidence

As discussed above, part of proving a labour case may require proving that there was a rule and that the employee had knowledge of the rule. The rule may be a policy or a procedure. Knowledge of fraud or having attended anti-fraud training in which certain concepts (for example conflicts of interest) are discussed may qualify as the employee having knowledge of the rule. Employees cannot plead that they were unaware of the rule if they attended fraud awareness training when this precise concept was discussed.

Proving that they have knowledge of the rule may be achieved through:

- Witnesses (less reliable)
- Policy roll-out attendance registers
- Mailing lists (the recipients of which the policies were e-mailed to)
- System logs (showing who accessed the policies and procedures and/or electronic training)
- Certificates of attendance (of policy roll-outs)
- Examples of situations in which they were present when the policy was upheld

Managers are furthermore encouraged to keep a record of when they gave instructions to employees concerning fraud-related matters so that they can refer to it in the event the employees engage in misconduct. For example: A manager should keep minutes of all management meetings at which policies and procedures were discussed. Management may also e-mail all participants to confirm points discussed. These e-mails should be retained in a special folder, as these may serve as evidence that specific employees had knowledge of the 'rules' under dispute.

f. Education and awareness

A significant portion of fraud prevention lies in education about:

- What fraud is
- Roles and responsibilities with regards to fraud
- The correct response to fraud
- The consequences of perpetrating fraud

Fraud awareness is not aimed at providing a detailed understanding of fraud. The discussion on fraud training below refers concerning a more detailed understanding of fraud. Fraud education can be carried out in numerous direct or indirect manners, including:

(i) Internal training workshops

Probably the most commonly practised form of fraud awareness training would be in-house fraud training workshops. These are normally easy to compile and execute. A workshop would normally involve some sort of presentation supported by examples and may include role-play and allow for discussions. It would typically be an hour or slightly longer.

(ii) Internal online courses

Some organisations additionally have training courses on their intranets for their staff members to complete. Some of these courses are prescribed and others will be discretionary. These courses are designed to be simple and to appeal to a wide range of employees.

(iii) External training

Employees may enlist in external training courses themselves or may, as part of their agreed-upon development plans, be required to conduct external training. This training may be specific to fraud or could include fraud learning as well. External training would range from high-level awareness training to more detailed and specialised training. Some examples of external training include:

- Pre- and post-graduate courses
- Short courses
- Specific anti-fraud training
- Conferences

(iv) Reading

Employees could also learn about fraud by reading about it. Reading could be self-initiated or it could be prescribed by the organisation. Examples of fraud reading sources include:

- Internal fraud newsletters
- Industry-specific journals (for example the ACFE's *Fraud* magazine)
- General print news and internet sites
- Websites
- Textbooks

(v) Fraud awareness campaigns

A fraud awareness campaign is a short, non-detailed presentation, with the purpose of educating delegates about fraud. Fraud awareness campaigns are normally targeted initiatives to refresh or inform employees about fraud.

(vi) Fraud assessment workshops

Employees could also learn about fraud while participating in workshops constituted to analyse business processes for fraud vulnerabilities. The discussions on fraud vulnerability assessments to follow.

(vii) Fraud risk assessments

Employees may learn about fraud when they provide inputs into enterprise-level fraud risk assessments.

(viii) Questionnaires

Employees could be requested to complete questionnaires about fraud and in so doing learn about fraud.

(ix) Audits

Employees can learn about fraud while participating in and assisting in various audits, reviews and investigations, including:

- Internal audits
- External audits
- Tax audits
- Customs and excise audits
- Security audits
- Fraud investigations

(x) On the job

Employees may be taught about fraud while being trained to perform their jobs.

(xi) Secondments

Employees may be seconded to work for a defined period with the internal audit or fraud functions, before being cycled back into the business to apply their broadened skills.

(xii) System implementations

Employees may learn about fraud while being part of IT system implementation teams. Controls and risks may be discussed as part of the implementation.

(xiii) Management communications

Management may communicate directly with employees about fraud. Management communications include:

- E-mails
- Talks
- Announcements
- Memos
- Meetings

(xiv) HR counselling

Employees may receive counselling as a result of their involvement in misconduct or as a result of their colleagues being involved.

(xv) Sanction

Employees learn about fraud through the sanctions (punishments) that are handed down to them in internal labour hearings for any misconduct that they are found guilty of. Sanctions are discussed in Chapter 7, covering subsequent actions of fraud matters.

(xvi) Investigations

Employees may learn about fraud through their participation in fraud investigations.

(xvii) Testifying

Employees may learn about fraud from their participation in internal disciplinary hearings or by testifying at external labour tribunals or criminal courts. The chapter on subsequent actions refers.

(xviii) Fraud reporting

Employees may learn about fraud when they report fraud and interact with the person to whom they report the fraud. The chapter on reporting refers.

(xix) Networking

The advent of social media has widened the concept of networking. Networking may include traditional rubbing shoulders with anti-fraud professionals. It may also include subscribing to various specialised chat forums and groups.

(xx) Posters, screensavers, in-house TV screens, etc

Fraud awareness can be as simple as employees seeing posters in a canteen or banners on screensavers.

g. Training

Fraud training is conducted in more detail than general fraud awareness. Fraud training is normally aimed at those individuals in the organisation charged with fraud investigation and other anti-fraud activities. Fraud training can be conducted internally by the organisation or externally. Education is however not forever and completion of a training course cannot guarantee that an employee has processed all training material delivered or that they will retain all training material in future. 'Good' training includes the following characteristics:

(i) Simplicity

The training material must be geared to the audience to which it is delivered. For the greater part, it should not be too technical. Normal English-language terms and phrases should be used. Avoid the use of jargon.

(ii) Quantity

The quantity of the material should be manageable. It should be sufficient to convey the message, but not too much to overwhelm the participant. The length of the training course (hours or days) should also be manageable and not be too long or too short.

(iiii) Delivery

The training should be delivered in a professional manner. An experienced and professional trainer should be used if possible. The trainer's voice pitch should also be easy on the participants. The voice should not be:

- Low/deep or excessively high-pitched
- Monotone (boring)
- Unclear

Trainers should maintain eye contact across the venue. They should have minimal/concise notes that are easy to navigate. They should practise their delivery of the material and ensure that all faults are ironed out and that they can navigate the material even if side-tracked. A trainer should have a strong but polite and professional personality and be able to keep the participants on track.

(iv) Materials

The training materials should be:

- Correct and complete
- Available
- Easy to navigate
- Manageable

(v) Recall

The training materials should encourage a high recall factor. In order to do this, materials should:

- Not just be reams of endless text without natural visual breaks
- Include many pictures, diagrams or videos
- Contain minimal Microsoft PowerPoint bullets
- Have practical exercises and calculation examples
- Have small rewards for correct answers

(vi) Practical

The highest recall will be derived from training material that has a high practical content and less theory. The measure of the degree of practicality of the training material is if the material can be directly applied in the workplace after the training. Use actual case studies or examples that participants can relate to in their industry or field of work.

(vii) Interactive

While training implies a one-way classroom-type set-up, good training makes use of alternatives to ensure that participants are actively engaged throughout the training. This increases the amount of material retained and recalled later. Some examples of interactive training include:

- Participants interacting with online training material
- Completing exercises in workbooks
- Working in workgroups
- Completing assignments for presentation after the completion of the initial classroom training

- Making presentations of their understanding or workgroup outputs
- Exams (oral or written)
- Building models to demonstrate issues
- Role-play
- A panel of experts' discussion setting
- Trainers engaging participants and asking for their input

(viii) Repetition

Frequent refreshing of principles is required to keep concepts fresh in the minds of employees. The fresher the concepts are in the minds of employees the greater chance that fraud learnings will be used.

(ix) Timing

Most employees have heavy workloads and having to step out of the work environment is rarely ever at a good time. The danger is that participants are not engaged, or may be resentful or distracted. The timing of the training course should be when it is suitable to most participants.

(x) Hygiene factors

The venue and refreshments provided over the period of the training should be of a reasonable standard.

- The venue should be:
  - Neat and tidy
  - Free from distraction
  - At an ambient temperature
  - Accessible
  - Not excessively costly
- The food should:
  - Cater for special dietary needs
  - Be healthy
  - Be able to sustain participants but not be too heavy
  - Be timed to coincide with natural breaks
- Technology should:
  - Be tested in advance
  - Be easy to use
  - Be useful and not included just for the sake of having it
  - Have technical assistance available on site to sort out any problems
- Establish basic etiquette to all training delegates at the commencement of the course in terms of:
  - Use of technology/electronic devices
  - Taking calls
  - Visitors and other disruptions
  - Breaks
  - Starting and ending times and returning after breaks

(xi) *Needs-based*

All training should be conducted to satisfy a particular need. Sending people on training just because they have reached a particular organisational level or because the list dictates certain training to them at a particular point does not ensure that participants will be engaged and find value in the training.

Other than general fraud awareness training, the need for specific training could arise out of personnel development discussions. For example: a business unit-based employee may be requested to assist holding company fraud investigators going forward. The employee may require fraud training to assist with the new responsibilities.

Personnel should be debriefed upon completion of the training course and before their normal workload resumes. Implementation objectives should be defined and milestones agreed as to when development success can be measured.

Participants should be selected on an equitable basis. Employee morale may be negatively affected if they do not perceive course selection and attendance criteria to be fair.

h. Deterrents

There should be strong deterrents in place to employees to discourage them from wanting to participate in misconduct. Having the best designed controls without any visible enforcement of the controls is really no more than an academic exercise. Employees will be reluctant to engage in misconduct if they perceive that there is a good chance that they will be caught and that there are severe consequences to their misconduct.

Deterrents commence with the 'tone from the top'. While the concept of tone from the top can be over utilised, it is important that those in senior organisational leadership roles:

- ❑ Show their support of anti-fraud initiatives
- ❑ Voice their zero-tolerance stance on fraud and misconduct
- ❑ Consistently act against misconduct

- Those in leadership roles should lead by example, by:
  - ❑ Not engaging in misconduct themselves
  - ❑ Not valuing performance/KPIs above honesty and controls
  - ❑ Not turning a blind eye to misconduct
  - ❑ Actively participating in anti-fraud training and interventions
  - ❑ Allowing their staff members the time to participate in anti-fraud training and interventions
  - ❑ Ensuring well-designed controls
  - ❑ Enforcing controls consistently
  - ❑ Consistently subjecting themselves and their staff to all rules
- Organisational leadership needs to act in a consistent, fair and transparent manner to apply the company's disciplinary procedures.

Examples of additional deterrents include:

- Robust policies and procedures that are communicated. Employees should be aware that defined methods exist to define how they are to work. The policies and procedures should also define the actions to be taken in the event of a transgression.
- Publicised positive effects of controls and the negative effects of not following the guidelines.
- Sound enforced controls. If there are no or only a few control deficiencies and if employees know that there are no loopholes to exploit, then they are less likely to engage in misconduct if the controls are going to catch them out/prevent them from proceeding. Employees will also be reluctant to engage in misconduct if they can see that controls are consistently complied with and that there is a high probability that they will be caught out.

Part of the assessment of how effective deterrents are is to ask management if they can give any recent examples (within the last year) of where:

- The organisation's disciplinary code has been enacted
- Management has communicated its stance on fraud
- Management has communicated the results of misconduct identified

i. Due diligence

It is common practice to vet candidates before employing them. Why therefore do we less frequently vet the people that we conduct business with?

It is recommended that the following parties are also vetted in advance:

- Suppliers
- Customers
- Business partners
- Business funders

Formal vetting criteria will need to be:

- Drafted in advance
- Formally included in business processes and/or contracts
- Based on industry standards
- Communicated and agreed
- Measured and enforced

j. Relationships

Our rule discussed in the next section of this book refers: 'Forensics revolves around contacts.' This is perhaps a broad statement, but strong relationships can:

- Help to get things done internally or externally
- Help obtain internal buy-in to ensure that anti-fraud measures are implemented completely and consistently
- Help to report actual frauds and misconduct or potential fraud vulnerabilities
- Provide learning on how to proceed

All relationships should be managed within the ambit of the law. Information should never be obtained in an illegal manner and no undue influence should be exercised over or requested from parties.

The purpose of these relationships is to:

- Create a mutual understanding of each other's priorities, challenges and constraints
- Network and exchange ideas
- Pool common challenges facing multiple parties so as to facilitate the more coordinated and concentrated request for action of the issue/s from the responsible parties
- Determine how each party can help the others (voluntary)
- Understand the communication channels required and to set up working relationships in advance to facilitate communication when it is actually required
- Understand (in advance) the information requesting requirements/protocols - this will help in understanding how long in advance to make the request (for example a subpoena typically takes X days) and from whom to request the information.

The fostering of strong relationships with the following parties can be beneficial:

A. Internal relationships

(i) Audit committee and the board of directors

The audit committee is a working committee of the board of directors. The audit committee performs and oversees tasks on behalf of and reports back to the main board. The board is charged with the governance and oversight of the organisation. While the board may delegate the responsibility for control and fraud to management, it remains accountable. The audit committee will therefore directly or indirectly be the ultimate client of the forensic function. It is unlikely that the forensic function will have too much contact with the other board members. The forensic function will tend to have its relationship with the board via the audit committee.

The audit committee provides the forensic function with its mandate through the endorsement of the fraud charter and/or the audit charter (if part of the internal audit function).

Obtaining the audit committee's authority is imperative to ensure the true objective and independent functioning of the forensic function. Independence can be demonstrated by the audit committee:

- Appointing the head of forensics/internal audit
- Requiring reporting on all aspects of fraud to them - practically this will involve detailed reporting of key frauds and statistical reporting of less significant matters
- Measuring and holding management accountable for fraud prevention and detection
- Requesting the forensic function to perform special tasks/assignments
- Providing/mandating/approving required resources

If the audit committee is the forensic function's client, then it will be important to understand what the audit committee's/client's needs are in terms of fraud. Time should therefore be set aside periodically to discuss the audit committee's requirements and to obtain its insights as to the performance and success of the forensic function.

Please also bear in mind that you may have to deal with multiple audit committees in your organisation:

- A single audit committee in the organisation is the most typical.
- Conglomerate organisations may have a holding company audit committee (most important) and individual audit committees per business unit/sub-company/entity.
- Organisations may have one 'normal' audit committee and then they may, despite the lack of regulatory requirement, also have their own 'pseudo' audit committees per brand, geographic region, company, etc. Organisations do this to try to put the responsibility for governance and control at the right level/with those who have direct influence over it. These may not be legally required, but may strengthen the control environment. The downside is that it tends to layer in levels of onerous reporting.
- Medical aid/insurance companies may have an audit committee per medical aid or investment fund that they administer. Each medical aid is a separate legal entity with reporting and governance requirements. The medical aid company will, in addition, most likely also have its own audit committee.
- Likewise, life insurance organisations may have multiple audit committees for each pension fund that they administer. Each pension fund is a separate legal entity with reporting and governance requirements.
- Finally, you may work for a consulting firm serving multiple unrelated client organisations each with their own audit committee.

(ii) Chairman of the audit committee

It is highly recommended to establish a strong relationship with the chairman of the audit committee. The person meeting with the chairman of the audit committee would be the chief audit executive (when the fraud function resides under the internal audit function) or the head of the forensic function (where it is an independent/standalone function). Meet periodically off-site and independently with the chairman of the audit committee to discuss challenges, progress, key risks and to obtain input and direction.

This is also a manner in which you can build trust and support for what you/your function is doing. This type of meeting also helps to prepare the chairman for the formal audit committee meetings. Reports often have to be drafted in a particular, carefully worded manner that does not always carry the true picture. A one-on-one meeting offers you the opportunity to say things that cannot always be said in a report. It is advisable to use this sort of meeting to give the chairman prompts to know which questions to ask when findings are reported. It may also be beneficial to role-play what will be said in the actual audit committee, what responses could be expected and how to respond to adverse responses.

The chairman of the audit committee is responsible for the audit committee and therefore the chairman is really the person for whom the forensic function is working. It is important to be able to warn the most senior members of the organisation of very serious matters as you become aware of them. You should not be alarmist or inundate them with detail, as this will not instil confidence. Be selective and balanced. If a serious fraud comes to your attention, then request a meeting. Be open and honest about the amount of information that you have and/or the stage of the investigation. Inform them that you are just keeping them abreast of what you have heard before you have had an opportunity to investigate, as relevant.

Also, be sure to say who you have and who you intend to inform of the serious matter. This is also part of the trust relationship and they will in turn know who they can communicate with about the matter. They may also advise you who to communicate with and who not to communicate within the event that they are aware of things that you are not aware of.

The audit committee should also have its own budget to conduct its business. In the event of a very serious fraud involving the most senior staff members (for example the FD and/or the MD), the audit committee may be able to authorise and/or fund these types of investigations.

Meeting with the chairman of the audit committee is normally most suited for holding company type/single audit committees. It may not be required for all of the aforementioned types of audit committee.

(iii) Chairman of the board

As with the chairman of the audit committee, it is beneficial to build a relationship with the chairman of the board, as similar benefits apply.

The more people trust you, the more they will entrust you with. They will also allow you more freedom to do the things that you need to do and be less restrictive/imposing.

(iv) Key senior organisational leadership

There are also numerous business leaders with whom it may be beneficial to build relationships. This is again to explain the value added by the forensic function, to obtain support and to build a trust relationship. Assuming that none of the leaders are implicated in a fraudulent matter, it is always wise to keep key leaders informed of what is happening. In this regard, it would generally be wise to always keep the CEO, MD and FD informed of important matters and/or obtain their permission to proceed, as required. It may also, depending on individual reporting lines and the unique situations of certain organisations, be beneficial to build a relationship with other key business leaders and/or keep them informed of fraud occurring in areas under their responsibility. Other organisational leaders to consider include: the chief commercial officer (CCO), chief operating officer (COO), chief information officer (CIO), Company Secretary, and enterprise risk manager. Tailor this list to suit your unique organisation or individual circumstance.

(v) HR

The forensic function normally has a narrow working relationship with the HR department. The HR function can:

- Provide information (for example employment data, salary information, disciplinary conduct, performance history, demographics, etc)
- Provide support for the fact that investigations should occur
- Assist with anti-fraud campaigns and fraud awareness training
- Conduct internal labour hearings
- Ensure that employee records are appropriately updated

- Ensure that HR policies and procedures and other organisational policies and procedures support anti-fraud efforts and/or are updated in response to incidents that have occurred

(vi) Internal audit

The forensic function may very well fall under/report to the internal audit function. In that case, keeping the chief audit executive (CAE) informed will be part of the normal department reporting lines.

In other cases, the internal audit or forensic function may provide support (in meetings and forums) and/or skills (for example, data analytics, business process analysis, computer forensics, resources, etc) to the forensic function. Building a relationship with the internal audit function will therefore facilitate and perpetuate the providing of this support.

The internal audit function and the forensic function also share many similarities. They:

- Have a similar interests in controls
- Have similar governance objectives
- Report to the same people
- Operate in the same domains
- Access the same organisational people
- Have similar information needs
- Have similar skills and techniques

It would therefore be of mutual benefit to the internal audit function and the forensic function to share:

- Identified risks, frauds and concerns to ensure that learnings are shared
- Areas of emphasis to avoid duplication of effort
- Areas of emphasis to avoid auditees becoming suspicious of confidential investigations and reviews

The internal audit function and/or forensic function may be in-house or outsourced functions. The relationship that you form may therefore be internal or external to the organisation.

(vii) Business fraud champions/chief fraud risk officers (CFROs)

There may, in larger/conglomerate-type organisations, be multiple people responsible for fraud in different entities within the larger organisation. These will be the people on the ground in the different entities that will be investigating fraud and implementing anti-fraud campaigns. Developing a relationship with them will ensure that:

- Matters are investigated correctly
- Risks and learnings are shared
- Anti-fraud efforts are implemented and coordinated

(viii) Key functional leaders or staff members

As with key business leaders, organisational function heads may also be able to provide support to the forensic function to assist with investigations or provide support with anti-fraud efforts. Examples of organisational functions with which to build relationships include:

- IT
- Operations
- Legal function
- Public relations
- Security

B. External relationships

(i) Authorities

Strong relationships with the authorities are some of the most important relationships to develop and maintain. A lot of success can be derived in matters because of the relationships built with the police and prosecutors. This helps to know what is required to process a criminal charge, as well as to be able to follow up on a regular basis and in so doing encourage the actioning of the matters.

Company lawyers do not always agree with the idea of working with the authorities. But experience has taught us that working with the authorities is better than not working with them at all, even when the organisation is guilty of transgressing the law (albeit knowingly or unknowingly due to a rogue employee). This may however differ widely for particular countries and/or authorities. Take the matter of relationships with authorities under advisement before embarking on them.

Examples of authorities with which a relationship can be extremely beneficial include:

- The police – to expedite investigations
- Interpol – where cross-border investigations/actions are required
- Tax authorities – for both individuals and businesses
- Customs and excise authorities – concerning the movement of cross-border goods/ trade
- Border police – to help with the movement of individuals across borders
- Harbour and port authorities – for the movement of aircrafts, vessels and people
- The courts, more specifically the:
    - Chief prosecutor (who decides if your matter will be prosecuted or not and who appoints the prosecutor to ensure that a good prosecutor is assigned to your case)
    - Clerk of the court (who assigns and administers court dates and/or the court role)
    - Prosecutor (who will prosecute on behalf of the state in your matter)

(ii) Industry bodies

Certain industries have bodies that have oversight of the specific industry. Industry bodies may be useful as they:

- Can provide information required in your matter
- Can provide the expertise required in your investigation
- Can provide resources
- Have knowledge of industry risks
- Have access to other industry experts or members
- Can ensure that collective efforts are made to fight common industry issues

There are too many industry bodies to name them all. Some examples of industries with oversight bodies include:

- The Chamber of Commerce
- Mining sector bodies
- Shipping industry bodies
- The Estate Agency Affairs Board
- Various agriculture boards
- Various medical bodies
- Horse-racing fraternities

(iii) Competitors

Working with competitors needs to be done very carefully to prevent actual or perceived anti-competitive relationships.

As an example: I personally formed a retail internal audit special interest group when I worked in the retail sector. We only exchanged auditing ideas and benched auditing data at this forum and it was very beneficial.

It is quite common for telecommunication organisations and financial institutions to cooperate with each other and with authorities on anti-fraud efforts.

Competitors may be subject to the same industry-specific fraud risks. Coordination of efforts and sharing learnings may be beneficial.

(iv) Professional bodies

Professional bodies are the bodies that oversee particular professions. Some examples include:

- Institute of Chartered Accountants
- Association of Certified Fraud Examiners (ACFE)
- Information Security and Audit Control Association (ISACA)
- Institute of Internal Auditors (IIA)
- The Law Society/the Bar
- Various engineers' guilds
- Actuarial Society of South Africa
- South African Institute of Architects (SAIA)

Professional bodies can be helpful to your investigation as they can provide:

- Expertise
- Resources
- Field-specific risks
- Field-specific knowledge and standards
- Member information
- Assistance to sanction members guilty of misconduct

(v) Embassies

Working in specific countries can be challenging. Embassies may be able to assist in your investigation by providing:

- Citizen-specific information
- Country-related information and support
- Assistance to obtain local government support
- Diplomatic immunity

(vi) Contemporaries, peers and colleagues

Depending on the nature of the matters that you are dealing with, it may be beneficial to have another person/people who can:

- Serve as a sounding board for ideas
- Mentor you to help you improve your skills in a particular area or in general
- Enable professional networking

(vii) Trade unions

Depending on the nature of the industry and the appetite of the respective trade union, it may be beneficial to build a relationship with the trade union leadership and/or local shop stewards. Trade unions can be tricky though, and they may be driven by different motives than you and/or the organisation. There may also be better or worse times to hold discussions with trade unions. For example, it would not be advisable to open discussions with trade unions at wage negotiation time. You would not want an innocent request for assistance in a fraud investigation, or the need to give union members anti-fraud training, to be used against the organisation in other negotiations. Such a relationship should be coordinated and approved by the senior organisation leadership in advance.

There can be pros and cons to working with trade unions. They can ensure the cooperation of their members, provide information, and represent transgressing employees in tribunals, but they can also be disruptive if they do not perceive that their members have been treated fairly.

(viii) Service providers/suppliers

A service provider could be any individual or organisation providing any service to the organisation, including forensic services. Many benefits can be derived from coordinated anti-fraud efforts and investigations with suppliers.

As an example, when I was working in retail we formed working groups with manufacturers and distributors of high-risk products. We strove to improve the controls throughout the supply chain from the manufacturer to the retail outlets.

Suppliers may be able to provide information, evidence and/or testimony in support of investigations. A supplier may also be the victim of the matter under investigation. For example, they may be forced into paying kickbacks or they may have lost business due to the corrupt relationship between an organisation employee and another supplier.

Supplier relations can also be strengthened through close cooperation in common areas.

(ix) Key business partners
As with suppliers and service providers, key business partners may be able to provide valuable information. These are external business partners, for example joint venture partners. Business partners are not the same as suppliers or financers of the organisation. These are parties that have a close common relationship with the organisation.

(x) Banks
Banks may be able to give you information and/or benefit from working closely together with you on matters to prevent their own losses. Banks also sometimes offer anti-fraud training to big clients or host interesting educational talks.

Banks are bound by strict regulations, however. Banks will therefore be cautious not to transgress regulations. Banks are also in business and they may be cautious not to say anything that could be construed as an admission of guilt or that could bind them contractually or cost them unnecessary money.

I recall an example where the bank was, based on the strong relationship that the organisation had with the bank, prepared to freeze bank accounts and reverse misappropriated funds without signing onerous paperwork and/or obtaining court orders.

In other cases, I reported matters of interest to them (where it came to my attention via contacts that they were potential victims of fraudulent acts) and they were able to take action by themselves.

(xi) Educational institutions
Tertiary training institutions can provide valuable pre- and post-graduate education. Such education can be in the form of full-term graduate programmes or short courses. Educational institutions may be a source of valuable research as well. Educational institutions can also be used as a source of graduate-level candidates to be recruited.

1.4.2. Detective control measures

Detective control measures are the second of the two areas of proactive anti-fraud efforts. Detective fraud measures are designed to detect fraud after it has occurred. The following are measures by which to detect fraud that has occurred/is occurring (discussed in detail below):

- Internal controls (detective)
- Application controls (part of internal control, but specified for clarity)
- Whistle-blower facility
- Fraud vulnerability assessments
- Trend analysis and data analytics
- Profiling

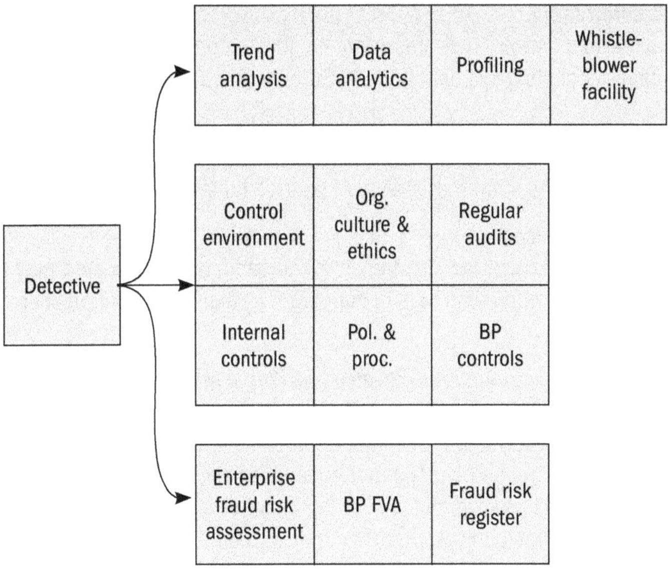

Diagram 1.7 *Detective fraud mitigation*

a. Internal controls (detective)

(i) Introduction

As mentioned in the discussion on the preventative nature of internal controls (point 1.4.1.b), we know that internal controls are the best safeguard against fraud. They are then by default, as long as they are complied with, also the best method by which to detect fraud.

So, the first requirement is that the controls must exist and they must be adequately designed. Next, the controls must consistently be complied with/effectively performed.

There are very few 'silver bullets' (single controls) that adequately prevent or detect fraud. It would also not be wise to pin our hopes on a single control. Portfolios of controls are the best defence against fraud. Different controls may achieve different things and the correct alignment of controls may be a stronger anti-fraud measure than a single control. It is also important for us to take a broad view on control and to include the previously discussed control environment aspects with traditional business process controls.

(ii) Control environment

We discussed the control environment under the preventative side of internal controls (point 1.4.1.b). The control environment can be preventative and detective. We are not going to re-discuss the control environments here. It should be noted that control environments can detect fraud as well. Some examples of control environment activities include:

- HR policies and procedures
- Organisational culture
- Consistent application of the rules

(iii) Other controls

When it comes to controls, it is important to think more widely than governance models and traditional accounting system controls. Examples of other activities that increase control include:

- *Lighting*
  Sometimes the simple existence of good lighting can prevent fraud/theft.
- *Open-plan offices*
  In a similar manner having staff sit in the same open-plan area may prevent corrupt relationships with customers or suppliers, as their conversations can be heard by all.
- *Competition*
  A bit of healthy competition can also go a long way. When staff members need to openly list their work in meetings and it is compared to all colleagues' work, then employees may feel too exposed. They may be reluctant to enter into corrupt relationships, as there is an increased chance that colleagues will ask difficult questions and expose them. This will however not work if the benefit that the employee is deriving from the corrupt relationship is greater than that of their legitimate job.

Please note that none of these controls is a strong control in its own right. They will each however serve to strengthen the general control environment. At the end of the day, we seek to promote a robust portfolio of controls.

(iv) Business process controls

We know from COSO that internal controls can assist organisations to achieve their objectives. There are no special anti-fraud internal controls. Any of the traditional internal controls can serve as anti-fraud controls. For example, the internal controls that ensure the transactional completeness and accuracy of billing in the order-to-cash cycle are the same controls that ensure that billing is not fraudulently incomplete or inaccurate. The only difference is how we look at the same control. Are we specifically trying to prevent or detect fraud or are we just trying to ensure the transactional accuracy of the transactions?

There are numerous business processes in organisations. Many of these will be similar across organisations (for example: accounts payable, accounts receivable, fixed assets, etc). The control principles will also tend to be similar across organisations for these activities. It will not be possible to discuss every control in all traditional business processes. There is however benefit in discussing traditional categories of controls and some specific controls that are well known as strong anti-fraud controls. There may be some academic overlap between the controls. Try to understand the spirit of what the controls are trying to achieve and then apply these to the business process under review.

Examples of anti-fraud traditional internal controls include:

- *Accountability*
  Ensuring that people can be held accountable for what they have done is a good control. People (guilty or innocent) generally do not want to be associated with wrongdoing. If they know that they can be linked to a transaction or event, then they

are going to be less likely to do something incorrectly. Accountability results in my identity being associated with the transaction that I have performed (it could be with a system log-on or the physical writing down of my name).

- *Authorisation*
  Authorisation is one step higher than accountability. Authorisation is a mix of holding someone accountable for having given them the go-ahead for a transaction and also about having a degree of independence from the person who performed the transaction. Authorisation is also normally defined according to the organisation's risk appetite. The organisation's authorisation risk appetite will be listed in an authorisation hierarchy of who may approve what. Generally, the higher the financial value of the transaction or the greater influence the transaction can have on the business, the more senior the person needs to be to approve the transaction.

- *Supervisory checks*
  Authorisation is a go/no-go stage-gate control. A supervisory check is just a check for validity, accuracy, completeness or that performance occurred. Having a senior person who is independent of the task checking the task is a sound control. Supervisory checks are normally more detailed than management checks and are therefore good controls. Of course, the downfall is if the supervisor is colluding with the person performing the task being checked.

- *Management checks*
  These follow the same logic, as supervisory checks apply to managerial checks. Managerial checks are however not always in sufficient detail. Management checks may also only be spot/sample/trend/reasonability/principle checks.

- *Trend analysis, analytical reviews*
  Trend checks include comparing actual trends/behaviour to expected or historical trends/benchmarks.

- *Re-performance*
  Frequently the full re-performance of a task may be the only foolproof manner to ensure that the transaction is correct/valid. This may be performed by a colleague ('buddy checking'), a supervisor, a manager, an internal audit or an external party.

- *Existence*
  Consider what the transaction was purported to have been for. For example, if the transaction was for the purchase of an item, establish if the item actually exists. Also ensure that the existence resembles what it is expected to be (the standard)?

- *Reconciliation*
  Reconciliation is unfortunately a term that is loosely used in organisations. The term may, in the process, have lost some of its impact as a result. The effect is that people may place too much reliance on controls that are not as strong as true reconciliations. Let us understand this a little more: a reconciliation is what it implies. It is the reconciling of two things or the bringing together of two things. In terms of business records, we have two independent records that are supposed to be equal

to each other, but which may not be due to timing differences or because one record may have been updated and another not. In an organisational context, the one record will almost always be a general ledger account and the other will be another record like a bank statement, a register of sorts, a stock ledger, a creditors' ledger, a creditor's statement, etc. The reason why we perform a reconciliation is that we want to ensure that our financial records are accurate. The organisation's financial records are based on the general ledger. We are generally comfortable with our records and we have control over them. For this reason, we always want to use our records as the base. As an example: if we are reconciling the bank account, we find the difference between the cash book and the bank statement received from the bank. We then list all the differences in the one record which are not on the other and vice-versa. In our bank reconciliation example: we list all payments we have processed in the cash book, but which were not reflected in the bank's records at the time that the statement was drawn up. Likewise, we list transactions (like bank charges or deposits) processed by the bank which we have not yet processed in our books of account. In this way, we understand and explain the difference between the two records and we validate the accuracy of our accounting records. We may even process transactions that are missing in our books thereafter or refer in the reconciliation to where/when the correction was posted. I often hear about people having 'performed a balance sheet reconciliation'. What they really mean is that they have performed a reasonability review of the balance sheet accounts and not a full reconciliation of them. Many of the balance sheet accounts do not have an independent record against which to compare them. When we look at what people have done, then we see that they have merely created a listing of the transactions making up the balance. They then scan this listing and try to understand if these items should still be carried in the balance sheet or if they should have been processed in some or other way. People typically concentrate on the 'aged' items that have been carried for a long time in the balance. Part of this check may entail ensuring that the transactions are adequately supported (like accruals) with documents/explanations/history of follow-up/calculations/opinions. Bank reconciliations are, from a fraud point of view, one of the most important controls in an organisation.

- *Limit checks*
  Limit checks could mean that a transaction above or below a particular value will require special approval before being processed or will be automatically rejected and not processed.
- *Sequence checks*
  Sequence checks ensure that the full spectrum of transactions is present. A missing sequence number would imply that a transaction record is missing.
- *Dependency checks*
  Some transactions are dependent on another transaction and it may not be normal to see them as standalone transactions. A control may be performed to see that the necessary supporting or dependent transactions exist. As an actual example: in the medical insurance industry, there may be two surgical procedures for the draining

of an abscess on a patient's hand. The cheaper one may be less complicated and can be safely performed in the doctor's consulting rooms. The more complicated and expensive procedure may have to be performed in theatre. Theatre procedures would also require the services of an anaesthetist and a hospital. Analysis of a sample of claims submitted by doctors would identify examples of the second more expensive procedure, which does not have anaesthetists and hospital bed charges. In such cases it is highly probable that the doctor/service provider is overcharging for services not actually rendered.

- *Physical access controls*
  Physical access controls ensure that access to an area, documents or assets is restricted to authorised personnel.
- *Virtual access controls*
  These are discussed in application controls below.

b. Application controls

Many systems of internal control that fraud risk officers deal with will contain some form of computerised control. It is important therefore for fraud risk officers to understand the different types of computerised controls that exist. Application controls are normal internal controls. There is however less understanding of application controls than non-automated internal controls. Application controls are discussed separately here as a result, but please bear in mind that they are just a category of internal control.

1.4.2.1. IT control overview

There are essentially two categories of IT controls, being general IT controls and application controls. All other IT controls fall somewhere within these two categories.

General controls are those controls that are specific to the IT environment (that is to say not the business environment, such as finance, operations, procurement, etc). The list of these controls is extensive, but finite. The COBIT governance framework provides a good overview of the general control environment. Some examples of general IT controls include:

- Change control procedures
- Software library controls
- System development life cycle controls
- Management of third-party suppliers
- Disaster recovery
- IT Infrastructure controls

It is unlikely that we will be interested in IT general controls from a fraud point of view. For the greater part fraud will touch on the applications within business processes. Fraud with, for example, third-party IT service providers (while strictly speaking an IT general control) will be dealt with as part of a normal corrupt relationship type of fraud and not specifically as an IT general control issue. It is good to note that this category of IT control exists though. Our discussion is going to concentrate on application controls in the context of our previous conversation on internal controls.

1.4.2.2. Introduction

An 'application' is a computer program. Application controls are those controls within the computer programs that the organisation runs.

While there are generic categories of application controls (for example 'input controls', 'processing controls', etc), we can say that application controls are specific to a particular application. For example: the 'input controls' in a particular finance application are not the same as the 'input controls' in a procurement application in the same organisation. In this example, they both ensure the completeness and accuracy of data that is inputted into the respective systems, but uniquely for each application.

Application controls differ from general controls in this manner, as one general control (eg systems development methodology) may be the same control process that governs the development of all applications.

The following are the categories of application controls that we are going to discuss:

- Access controls (specific to the application or operating system access control in the case of a 'single sign-on' type of IT environment)
- Input controls
- Processing controls
- Output controls
- Data transfer
- Log controls

Other interesting controls that we will discuss below include:

- Data conversion controls
- Technical environment and configuration (can be specific to the application or a general control)

Database controls can fall within IT general controls or application controls. It will be important to understand the logic of the database and which controls would best serve the applicable objectives.

1.4.2.3. Importance

Application controls are at the end of the day part of a normal system of internal control. Our interest in application controls from a fraud point of view includes:

- *Adequacy testing*
  We are concerned about application controls when assessing the adequacy of the design of the controls in business processes. As a general rule, it is considered to be inadequate to express an opinion as to the adequacy of the controls in an entire business process without due consideration for the application controls within the respective business applications. Care should therefore be taken to include the application controls when the manual controls within a business process are documented. Some of the application controls (as with manual controls) may serve as anti-fraud controls. The adequacy of the controls may be determined as part of a scheduled audit, a fraud vulnerability assessment or as part of a new system development initiative.

- *Post-mortem*
  Once a fraud has occurred it is important to understand all controls in the business process (in which the fraud occurred) so as to determine which controls failed/did not exist to allow the fraud to have occurred. Application controls should be included to ensure that the full spectrum of controls is evaluated. Recommendations to bolster controls to prevent and/or detect future occurrences should then be made.
- *Evidence-gathering*
  An understanding of application controls may be required to know where to gather evidence, which controls failed/were circumvented or which control deficiencies were exploited. Insights may also be gained as to who was involved (via transaction logs). Lastly, knowledge of application controls will assist to know where to obtain evidence of fraudulent transactions (transactional data) and acts of misconduct (for example transaction logs).
- *Preventative tools*
  An understanding of application controls may also assist when designing computer-assisted audit techniques (CAATs) and anti-fraud preventative measures.

1.4.2.4. Adequacy testing

The assessment of the adequacy of application controls is no different to the assessment of the adequacy of manual controls in the wider business process. The same objective/risk/control process described earlier should be followed through the end-to-end (manual and automated controls) business process. Application control assessments should not be conducted separately. They should be conducted as part of the business process control evaluation (described earlier).

With regards to the application controls, non-IT investigators frequently are at a loss to know which controls exist. The discussion below lists examples of application controls within the aforementioned categories. You can use this list as a prompt sheet to know which questions to ask.

1.4.2.5. Compliance testing methods

Once satisfied that the controls are adequately designed, it may be important to test the effective functioning of the controls. Compliance and/or effectiveness tests of application controls may be conducted in combination with or in isolation of any of the methods listed below:

- *Manual checks*
  Identify inputs. Independently calculate (outside the application/s) what the answer should be and compare it to the automated output. The downfall of this test is that only a limited number of transactions and permutations can be tested in this manner.
- *CAATs*
  Application controls can be tested in some instances through the use of computer-assisted audit techniques (CAATs). CAATs are purpose-made programs and automated routines to conduct audit tests. Chapter 5 on data analytics to follow.

- *Audit software*
  Specialised audit software can be used to run CAATs. Chapter 6 on data analytics refers. The packages are generally not limited by volume or type of transaction. Examples of software packages include: ACL, Idea and SAS.
- *Embedded programs*
  Programs can be specifically written and embedded into systems to test application controls on an ongoing/perpetual basis.
- *Queries (SQL)*
  Specific queries can be written in, for example using standard query language (SQL) to run and test application controls.
- *Excel*
  Excel can also be used to test application controls. This can be achieved for example through recalculation and comparison of audit-calculated outputs to application-generated outputs. Excel is understood by many people worldwide and is more accessible than specialised data analytic software.

1.4.2.6. Test environment

A separate test environment in which to conduct tests is frequently used. Test environments are separate environments from the production environment into which data is taken for testing. This is to ensure the integrity of production data, confidentiality/restricted access or not to impact on system performance (large tests may take significant system resources). Examples of data used in a test environment include:

- *Same data*
  Investigators may use actual system data to conduct a test in a test environment.
- *Calculated data*
  Investigators may 'manufacture' their own data to be used in tests. This will ensure that specific elements are tested.
- *Incorrect data*
  Investigators may purposefully utilise incorrect data in tests to determine if the application controls function correctly.

1.4.2.7. Application control discussion

The following discussion of application controls may serve as examples when fraud risk officers conduct system evaluations. The *Handbook on IT Auditing* (J Donald Warren; Lynn W Edelson; Xenia Ley Parker; Michael A Murphy, 1994, continually updated resource) presents more detail on application controls. The categories of application controls to be discussed here include:

- Access controls
- Input controls
- Processing controls
- Output controls

- Data transfer
- Log controls

A detailed list of application controls can be found in Annexure 1.4.

c. Whistle-blower facility

1.4.3.1. Introduction

Most frauds reported on the whistle-blower system will already have been perpetrated and/or are currently being perpetrated. It is rare that someone will report that a fraud is still going to happen. The use of the whistle-blower line is therefore, strictly speaking, more reactive in terms of finding the fraud than preventing the fraud from occurring in the first place.

The distinction is however (and the motivation for including the whistle-blower line in the proactive detective anti-fraud area) that we wish to proactivity identify frauds occurring in the organisation. The whistle-blower facility is very successful in doing this.

1.4.3.2. Required elements

As per the ACFE, most frauds are reported via a whistle-blower facility. The importance of an effective whistle-blower facility can therefore not be underestimated. An effective whistle-blower facility has the following elements:

Anonymity
Whistle-blower facilities should provide the option for reporters to remain anonymous, including:

- Full anonymity - where the identity of the whistle-blower remains protected (the whistle-blower system normally enforces such restrictions)
- Full anonymity in communication to the whistle-blowers (discussed later), but facilitated by the whistle-blower system
- Partial anonymity - limited people, such as the investigators, knowing who the whistle-blower is
- Full transparency - when the whistle-blower openly communicates about the matter or expressly states that their identity can be revealed.

Independence
The whistle-blower facility should be administered by an independent party. A third-party external service provider would be preferable. Whistle-blowers, despite the heinous nature or seriousness of the misconduct, want to feel safe to report matters. They do not want to be victimised. Whistle-blowers may be risking a lot to report matters and organisations need to be sensitive to this. So, even though an organisation may feel that it can administer an internal whistle-blower facility independently, it is the perception of independence to the reporters that is important. The perception of independence of the whistle-blower facility is one of the greatest contributors to the success of the whistle-blower facility. Independence also has to do with the perception of being able to be traced (the discussion of communication with whistle-blowers later refers).

Multiple methods

The whistle-blower facility should provide multiple methods by which to report matters. Examples of reporting channels include:

- E-mail
- Telephone
- Website
- Post
- Direct contact with those in the organisation charged with investigating such matters is an alternative channel (where whistle-blower facility contact details are posted or given in awareness sessions). It is recommended that the forensic or internal audit team's work contact details be published. Some people (who already have a relationship with the team or who have a fair number of details or if the matter is complicated) may elect to report directly to the investigation team. This is all about trust and a reporter's desire to report wrongdoing

Language

A good whistle-blower facility should offer reporters a variety of languages to report in. This is also a strong motive to use an external third-party service provider. The organisation could most likely not justify having multi-linguistic operators. Establish the languages used in the areas that the organisation operates in and ensure that these languages are represented by the whistle-blower facility.

Availability

Reporters may wish to or may only have the ability to report matters outside of normal working hours. The whistle-blower facility should therefore always be available.

Trained operators

The benefit of a whistle-blower facility lies in the reporter providing sufficient information for investigators to be in a position to investigate matters adequately. Frequently the only contact that the organisation will have with a whistle-blower is when the whistle-blower reports the matter. There is therefore a very narrow window of opportunity in which to obtain sufficient quality information. Whistle-blowers also frequently underestimate the amount of information required to direct an investigation. It always seems as if whistle-blowers feel that they can make a passing comment and the matter will miraculously be investigated. Operators should therefore be adequately trained in the art of communication and in drawing out the essence of the matter. Operators should also be trained in and/or have a prompt sheet of the questions to ask to solicit all the necessary information.

Clarification and feedback

Investigators frequently need to clarify the allegations and/or the facts in a matter. Investigators may have the need to seek clarification from whistle-blowers as the investigation progresses. Very few whistle-blowers are however prepared to provide their details. Good whistle-blower facilities offer whistle-blowers the ability to:

- Anonymously receive queries and clarifications from the investigators – the whistle-blower then has the ability to provide further details to the investigator
- Log on and determine the status of the matter they reported
- Receive outcomes of the investigation from the investigator

Awareness

Awareness of the whistle-blower facility is probably the most important aspect contributing to the success of the facility. Fraud reporting generally increases just after a fraud awareness campaign or as a result of investigations being conducted in a particular area. These all serve as methods to keep the whistle-blower facility fresh in people's minds.

The aim is for people to immediately think of the whistle-blower facility when they see wrongdoing. Awareness campaigns go hand-in-hand with whistle-blower facilities.

Reporting

A good whistle-blower facility also provides the means by which to generate reports on matters raised on the whistle-blowing system. Reporting includes reporting to:

- The organisational leadership – fraud statistics, case status, etc
- The whistle-blowers themselves on the status of matters
- Fraud investigators and fraud risk officers to be able to guide anti-fraud activities.

The positive aspect of reporting on reported matters is that people want to know that the matters that they report are being taken seriously by the organisation. Failure to demonstrate this could negatively impact the likelihood of matters being reported in the future. Information shared in reports may need to be sanitised first.

The success of a whistle-blower facility may be determined by factors wider than the facility itself. Some examples of additional factors that may affect the number of matters reported on the whistle-blower facility include:

- Management's support – If managers do not actively support the facility, then there is a good chance that their subordinates will not have faith in the facility and refrain from reporting matters.
- Span of control – Whistle-blowers are less likely to identify fraud and discrepancies if the span of their control is too wide. This is because they will not be able to delve into the required degree of detail and therefore not identify the discrepancies. As an example, if an organisation were to increase regional managers' responsibilities on the back of 'cost-cutting initiatives', this may result in the regional managers having to oversee more entities/branches/areas. A span of control that is too wide has two outcomes, being: a) fewer matters being identified and reported by those with the oversight responsibilities, and b) more misconduct being perpetrated, as there is a perception of non-detection/lack of an adequate deterrent for perpetrating the misconduct.
- Whistle-blower responsibilities – The actual job title that a whistle-blower holds may not be indicative of their actual responsibilities. For example, the duties of one financial manager may be very different from those of a financial manager in

another organisation. The effect of this on the ability to raise whistle-blower cases will mean that the actual tasks performed by the whistle-blower (and not their actual job title) will have the greatest influence on their ability to identify and report discrepancies. As an example, if an organisation centralises many of a country-level financial manager's duties in central global transactional service centres, then the branch-level financial manager's duties will be greatly reduced due to the offshoring of common duties. The branch-level financial manager will therefore no longer deal with all transactional matters in the same degree of detail as before the offshoring and there will therefore be less opportunity for them to identify transactional discrepancies. The service-centre staff members on the other hand are normally measured on transactional turnaround and not on control. Their focus will not be on identifying discrepancies, but on increasing transactional throughput. The number of identified and reported matters will therefore diminish.

- Whistle-blower's workload – If whistle-blowers are inundated with projects and work, they simply may not have the time to analyse discrepancies, conduct controls or take the time to report matters.
- Organisational changes – Frequent or significant organisational changes (structure, reporting lines, incumbents, etc) may result in matters dropping between the cracks and not being identified. This is partly due to people being focused on delivering the changes, fear of job security resulting from the changes or lack of knowledge caused by the changes.
- Fear of reprisal – Whistle-blowers may be less likely to report matters if they feel that they may be identified and/or victimised for reporting discrepancies. If for example there are only two staff members in a small retail branch, then the perpetrator will know by default that their colleague blew the whistle on them.

Completeness

After working in an organisation for a while, people get to know you as a fraud investigator and/or you develop a bit of a (hopefully positive) reputation. Whistle-blowers will develop the confidence (based on your positive reputation) to report matters of concern directly to you. In those cases, it is recommended to request whistle-blowers to in addition report the matter themselves directly on the whistle-blower system. If the whistle-blower declines/refuses to do so, then phone the report from the whistle-blower through yourself. Report the matter verbatim to the whistle-blower line in terms of what was relayed to you. Do not embellish or omit any details.

The reasons for reporting all matters on the whistle-blower system include:

- To have one central place where all matters can be coordinated from and thereby reduce the chance of something dropping through the cracks
- To facilitate efficient fraud reporting (statistics)
- To create 'grounds for reasonable suspicion' which may assist when reporting matters to the police and to obtain subpoenas, etc

Campaigns
Ensure that regular whistle-blower awareness campaigns are scheduled. Low-value items branded with the whistle-blower contact details can be presented to staff members attending awareness campaigns to take away with them to ensure that they recall the whistle-blower facility. Examples of take-home items include:

- Lanyards
- Keyrings
- Stickers
- Desk flags
- Caps
- T-shirts

Anti-fraud and whistle-blower promotional posters should be displayed at central points (for example recreational areas, areas where shared network printers are kept, etc) in the workplace to ensure awareness and access to the call centre details. Some organisations also include the whistle-blower contact details on:

- Organisation invoices and other organisational documents
- Screensavers
- Call waiting voice messages
- Organisation websites
- Organisation vehicles

Third-party whistle-blower service providers have a wealth of marketing and awareness material that can be tailored to suit your individual organisation's needs. Agree and coordinate campaigns with management. Budget would also have to be allowed for such campaigns.

d. Fraud vulnerability assessments

Fraud vulnerability assessments are proactive exercises that are conducted on high-risk fraud business processes, to identify fraud vulnerabilities. This process was described in detail under the proactive preventative anti-fraud methods, as the business process fraud risk assessments.

Once a fraud vulnerability has been identified, detailed tests can be conducted on the transactions and control compliance evidence to identify actual fraud.

e. Trend analysis and data analytics

Trend analysis and data analytics are discussed in detail in Chapter 5 on data analytics. These techniques can be proactively harnessed to detect actual fraud based on:

- Data that does not follow an expected trend
- An analysis of data against established rules

f. Profiling

Chapter 6 on lifestyle audits refers to a detailed explanation of profiling. Profiling can be both a proactive and a reactive fraud strategy.

- Proactive preventative profiling - proactively profiling key employees in high-risk jobs who have the potential to commit fraud due to financial pressures.
- Reactive detective subject profiling - once fraud has been identified to identify the most likely subjects of the investigation.
- Subject profiling (reactive) - the detailed profiling of the subject (once they have been identified) to prove that they are living beyond their declared financial means.

1.4.3. Corrective

Corrective controls are designed to automatically detect and correct transactions that do not fall within predefined criteria. Corrective controls are not common and can be found in some specialised computer programs.

The automatic correction of transactions may have implications if legitimate transactions are being reversed. Auto-corrected transactions should generally be 'parked' in a file for review and/or possible further action.

1.5. REACTIVE SIDE OF FRAUD RISK MANAGEMENT

In this section, we are going to discuss the strategic elements of how to respond to actual fraud incidents. These are the preparatory measures that can be set in place to ensure that the best response is given to actual incidents. See Chapter 3 on conducting investigations for guidance on how these strategic elements are carried out.

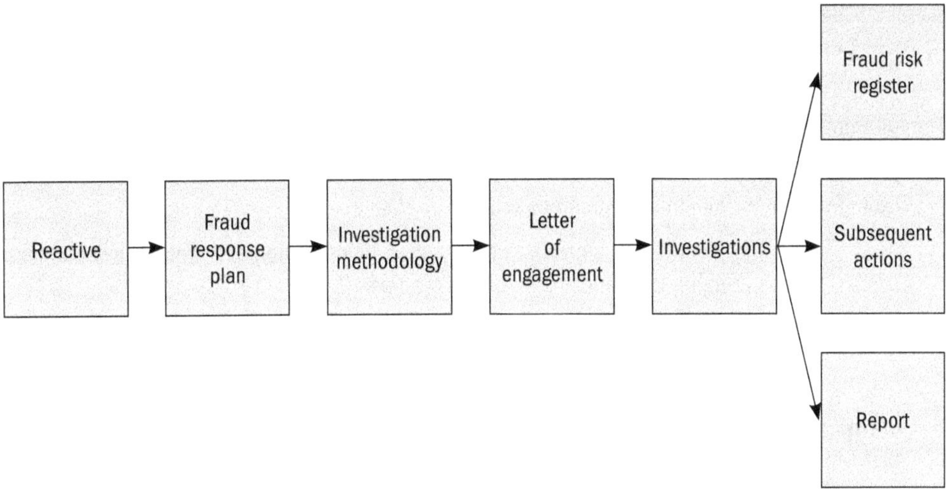

Diagram 1.8 *Reactive fraud mitigation*

1.5.1. Fraud response plan

When a fraud case or suspected fraud is brought to the attention of the fraud risk services function, the fraud risk officer will need to know how to respond to the initial notification. The primary objective of the first notification is to:

- Become aware of the matter
- Determine if there are any immediate steps to be taken
- Obtain sufficient initial information
- Obtain initial clarifications
- Develop an initial hypothesis
- Commence more detailed investigative planning

A fraud response plan is a document that helps the organisation determine how best to respond to a fraud incident. The purpose of a fraud response plan is to ensure that:

- There is a structured, consistent and complete response to all incidents
- Roles and responsibilities are defined
- Required parties are informed in a timely manner
- Decisive steps can be taken in a timely fashion to prevent prolonging the problem/continuation of the loss
- Important steps are not missed
- Responses are legally, ethically and procedurally correct
- We ask the right clarifying questions up front
- We request/obtain the correct documentation and/or evidence early on
- The investigation is not prejudiced
- No one suffers undue damage, slander or loss
- Unnecessary concern is not caused

- Communication is restricted to those who need to be involved
- Evidence is not lost or inadmissible
- No or minimal reputation damage is done

The following are steps that should be included in a formal fraud response plan:

a. **Immediate steps**
   Examples of possible immediate steps include:
   - Possible removal/suspension of the offending individual/s from the workplace (depending on the seriousness of the matter)
   - Securing evidence (documents, electronic, physical items, footage, people's recollections, etc)
   - Ensuring the safety of individuals and securing property/assets

b. **Clarification**
   Clarifying the allegation and/or nature of what has occurred. This may involve holding discussions with the whistle-blower and/or specialists in the area.

c. **Registration**
   Registering the matter on a central fraud case management tracking system.

d. **Drafting an initial hypothesis**
   Formulating an initial hypothesis of what occurred based on the information at hand.

e. **Informing key stakeholders**
   Based on the seriousness of the situation there may be a need to inform key stakeholders of the matter before proceeding.

f. **Drafting an investigation plan**
   Defining initial investigative steps to be covered.

g. **Responsibilities**
   Assigning initial responsibilities for the individual elements of the investigation.

Each of these steps is discussed in detail in Chapter 3 on conducting investigations.

Investigations are dependent on good information. Annexure 1.3 provides a summary of considerations that may assist the person to whom the fraud incident is being reported to ensure that they obtain the most complete information to assist the investigation team.

1.5.2. Investigation methodology

It is important to give people guidance as to how to respond to an incident and how to conduct an investigation. Investigations may be conducted by different people. More complicated investigations may be conducted by the fraud risk services team or by an external service provider. Other matters may be investigated by management itself.

Draft therefore a complete formal investigation methodology that can be tailored at the commencement of an investigation. Chapter 3 on conducting investigations refers.

The typical investigation steps listed below will need to be expanded into a detailed investigation guide, including:

a. **Awareness:**
- Receive notification
- Register the matter
- Immediate steps
- Commence investigation journal

b. **Planning:**
- Clarification
- Develop an initial hypothesis

c. **Investigate:**
- Craft an investigation plan
- Conduct the investigation
- Detailed information gathering
- Physical information gathering
- Subject information gathering
- Analysis of information
- Information interviews
- Finalise hypothesis
- Additional investigation

d. **Complete and conclude:**
- Further planning
- Subsequent interviews
- Volunteered evidence
- Corroborating checks
- Final subject interviews
- Conclude on hypothesis

e. **Subsequent actions:**
- Compile subsequent actions
- Register criminal matter
- Initiate civil claim
- Initiate labour case
- Voluntary recovery
- Inform senior management
- Inform the audit committee
- Inform relevant industry bodies

The possible outputs of an investigation include:
- Knowledge and closure of what occurred
- Statements and affidavits
- Evidence (all forms)

- Resignations/dismissals/internal labour sanctions
- Recoveries
- Initiated actions
- Outcome/progress reports
- Control improvements

1.5.3. Letter of engagement

A letter of engagement may be required to initiate an investigation depending on the size of the organisation. Larger organisations tend to be more formal in their approach.

External third-party forensic service providers would normally require a letter of engagement to define the scope and to authorise access to records, business areas and people. The use of an engagement letter has advantages and disadvantages, including:

a. The letter provides an early opportunity to formally manage expectations of:
   - Roles and responsibilities
   - The timing of the investigation
   - The scope of the investigation
   - Costs and/or the responsibility for costs

   An incomplete letter may however provide management with the opportunity to limit the scope of the investigation.

b. The authority to investigate matters may be expressly stated in the letter. For example: 'Group Forensic Services will, in line with their responsibility, as defined in the fraud charter, investigate ...'

   The letter may however give management the expectation that it has the right to influence and/or limit the investigation. Management may also use the letter to restrict the investigation scope if the authority is too limited or too broad in definition.

c. The letter could inform management that an external service provider will be providing assistance in the matter and who the internal contact people are.

   Management may try to influence who may be involved in the investigation. Management typically tries to use all kinds of seemingly legitimate concerns to prevent the use of external service providers. A common method used is to say that 'big four'-type organisations cannot assist as there are confidentiality concerns. The counter-argument is to have the external party sign a confidentiality agreement.

d. The letter may force specific action to be taken, for example:
   - Reporting to the authorities
   - Initiation of recoveries
   - Internal disciplinary action (subjects and those that did not perform the required controls

Management may be reluctant (for various reasons) to take action and may use its supposed concern about bad press or attracting attention from the authorities, prompting an audit, to:

- Limit or prevent subsequent action
- Restrict the investigation

e. The letter can show (to authorities or to other key stakeholders) that the organisation is taking the matter very seriously. This can count in the organisation's favour when the organisation stands to be penalised for not complying with the prescripts of the law, as a result of the corrupt actions of a rogue employee.

   The letter is however 'discoverable' and can be used as evidence in a dawn-raid against the organisation by the authorities to prove that the organisation has known about an illegal activity for a while and not acted appropriately/timeously.

f. The letter could define responsibility for the costs upfront. Management may however also try to control the investigation by pulling the purse-strings. Management will typically ask who is going to cover the investigation costs and say that they do not have the budget and therefore the investigation cannot continue.

g. The letter can name the investigation sponsor. The investigation sponsor is important, as this is the person who will unblock investigation bottlenecks and resolve problems. The sponsor is typically a senior person with the required degree of organisational status/clout.

1.5.4. Reporting and communication

A reporting and communication strategy or policy is helpful to define who needs to be informed on which matters, when and by whom. Chapter 7 on subsequent actions presents details in this regard.

a. Communication and coordination

A big part of the success of the fraud risk strategy will depend on the degree of communication and coordination. The formalising of a defined communication and coordination strategy will assist to ensure that the communication and coordination actually occur as desired. Communication and coordination sessions that may need to be held include:

(i) Daily coordination
between fraud risk services (FRS) and management conducting the investigation or the FRS investigator. This is for specific individual high-risk or complicated or important investigations.

(ii) Weekly coordination
between FRS and management conducting the investigation or the FRS investigator. To ensure coordination of the status of cases and practical problems.

(iii) Monthly communication
between the FRS panel (senior FRS leadership) and the specific FRS coordinators. To discuss which cases are to be closed, any additional work and any special actions required.

(iv) *Quarterly communication*
between FRS and the business unit senior management. To advise on:

- Specific outcomes
- Trends
- Issues
- Additional actions

(v) *Annual communication*
between FRS and the group senior leadership or FRS and the audit committee to advise on:

- Specific high-risk/important outcomes and on trends and issues
- Progress of the FRS strategy
- Resource requirements

b. Reporting

Chapters 7 and 8 present a detailed discussion on reporting. At a summary level, the reporting policy should cover all types of reporting, including:

- Criminal matters (police)
- Authorities (other than police)
- Audit committee
- Board and senior management
- Management
- Specific entities and business units within the group
- The general organisation
- Specific colleagues affected by the matter
- Shareholders, owners, holding companies and subsidiaries lower down
- Key clients, business parties, key suppliers and other parties
- The stock exchange
- Financing institutions
- Insurance houses
- External parties and/or the press
- Industry and professional bodies
- Internal audit
- External audit
- Third parties, suppliers, clients, etc

Some of these reporting types can be grouped in the policy. The reporting strategy should consider the purpose of the reporting and define the type and frequency of reports accordingly.

1.5.5. Subsequent actions

Chapter 7 on the subsequent actions sets forth more detail. Define a possible list of subsequent actions to be taken upon conclusion of an investigation. Include whose responsibility it is to conduct each of these. Possible subsequent actions include:

- Registering criminal cases
- Initiating civil cases
- Registering labour disputes with external labour tribunals/courts
- Conducting internal disciplinary hearings and formal counselling
- Obtaining recoveries
- Bolstering internal controls to prevent recurrence/detect future cases
- Reporting to:
    - Management
    - The audit committee
    - External parties

1.6. STRATEGY EXECUTION

1.6.1. Introduction

Having all the required documents and methods defined is only one part of the fraud strategy. The other important part of the strategy is how these individual steps will all be implemented. The execution of the fraud strategy will differ from organisation to organisation.

Generally, the number of specialised fraud investigators will be limited and insufficient in any organisation to ensure the complete execution of the fraud strategy. So too will the number of people in the business to carry out the strategy.

The principles remain the same for big and smaller organisations. In a smaller organisation the forensic team/person will carry more direct involvement and responsibility. This is just not practical for larger organisations. Most in-house forensic teams will be in larger organisations.

1.6.2. Fraud function motivation

Chapter 10 on setting up a forensic function refers. It is best to get the business itself involved in the fraud strategy. This is so for multiple reasons, including:

- Increasing the number of people working on anti-fraud efforts
- Putting the responsibility for anti-fraud on the source where it belongs
- Helping the source of the fraud problems to appreciate and see the effect of fraud
- Raising the general anti-fraud awareness and skill level in the organisation

In a larger group or conglomerate-type organisations with multiple businesses/business units it may be necessary to do the following:

- Ensure that the group fraud risk strategy encompasses a multifaceted organisational structure.
- Obtain the audit committee/main board's buy-in and authorisation to such an approach. Start at the top. The board members are the decision-makers and these are the people charged with the governance of the organisation. If they agree with the fraud strategy, then things will be a lot easier. Without their endorsement, the forensic strategy will just be a side issue that someone is trying to implement.

- 'Sell' the concept to the leaders of the individual business units. While they may not be able to decline the concept if the main board has already approved/required/endorsed the concept, they can certainly be a good or a bad proponent of the concept. Strategy execution will be a lot smoother if there is support for it.
- Have fraud risk officers appointed and/or have these responsibilities assigned in the individual business units. Smaller businesses may not have the budget or need to justify a full-time fraud risk officer in their employ. This does not mean that the business does not need someone to perform these responsibilities. The duties may form part of the responsibilities of an individual.

1.6.3. Fraud strategy execution summary

The group-level forensic function should define the fraud risk strategy and provide sufficient guidelines (discussed below) on how to carry it out.

Group fraud risk services should commence by setting up formal interactions with the business unit leadership and the business unit fraud risk officers. These forums will assist to:

- Discuss group anti-fraud effort direction
- Communicate fraud risk trends
- Understand business unit-specific challenges
- Provide guidance

The fraud risk strategy should require individual business units to commence by conducting their own business unit-wide fraud risk assessment. Group fraud risk services should define the minimum requirements and method by which the business units should conduct their fraud risk assessments (the previous discussions on fraud risk assessments refer).

The business units should then forward their prioritised fraud risk registers (previous discussions on the same refer) to the group fraud risk services. Group fraud risk services may perform some degree of oversight control to ensure that the business unit-level fraud risk assessments are performed correctly. Oversight should not be left to an annual assessment, as this will severely limit the opportunities to redirect misguided efforts in a timely manner.

The business units should also compile a programme on how they plan to mitigate and manage fraud risks (the previous discussion on fraud management programmes refers).

Group fraud risk services should provide templates of how to compile a fraud management programme and which anti-fraud proactive and reactive initiatives could be considered for inclusion in the programme.

Group fraud risk services should then collate a group fraud risk register based on the top fraud risks from the respective business units. Group fraud risk services should also compile an overview of the anti-fraud efforts for the group. These should both be reported to the main board of directors. The potential benefit of this to the main board members is that they will:

- Obtain a view of the highest fraud risks to the group
- Be aware of what the most important anti-fraud strategies are to the group
- Be able to direct efforts, as required

Group fraud risk services should also define the standards and provide guidance and coordinate investigations. Group fraud risk services would be best suited to negotiate and set framework agreements with external service providers in place. Group fraud risk services should also build and maintain external relationships with the relevant authorities.

Business units should be required to ensure that all fraud matters are reported centrally to group fraud risk services as they become known (but are not necessarily proven). Group fraud risk services should:

- Ensure that the business units deal with matters in a timely manner
- Provide guidance to the business units on how to approach the specific investigations
- Follow up on and monitor progress periodically
- Determine which matters will be centrally investigated by group forensic services
- Report on actual fraud cases to the main board

1.6.4. Effectiveness assessment

At the end of the day, we want the organisation to have strong anti-fraud efforts. Human nature is such that people tend to do the things that they are measured on. The trick is therefore to measure people and hold people accountable for the drivers that we want (the discussion on metrics in Chapter 10 refers). This will largely be achieved by requiring the business units to:

- Conform to group fraud risk standards
- Report to group fraud risk services
- Seek group fraud risk services' approval oversight
- Be reported on to the main board (retain positional power)

Holding the business units accountable for the turnaround time on fraud investigations and the conducting of fraud risk assessments is only part of what will drive an effective fraud risk strategy. There must also be some degree of assessment of the effectiveness of the fraud strategy and of the fraud management interventions. This is important to ensure that they are doing the right things and to know where to direct efforts in a practical and timely manner. The measurement of success should be communicated on a regular basis to the board of directors.

Some factors by which the effectiveness of the fraud risk strategy can be measured include:

- Recurrence of incidents (fraud/conflict of interest/complaints)
- Value of losses/disruption to business
- Degree to which fraud procedures assisted in fraud detection
- Degree to which fraud procedures were followed in an actual incident
- Degree of compliance to controls
- Degree to which non-compliance was identified by controls
- Degree of completion of anti-fraud training and awareness campaigns
- Assessment of visibility of anti-fraud material/posters
- Degree of use of the fraud whistle-blower line
- Results of fraud risk assessments
- Results of fraud surveys

- To a lesser degree, analytical trends
- Internal/external audit fraud assessments
- Success in closing cases
- Period of time taken to resolve matters
- Number of recoveries/insurance claims/convictions/disciplinary action taken/civil action taken/bolstering of controls
- Degree to which budget constraints restricted investigations/closure/success of matters
- Degree to which confidentiality was maintained as required during the investigation of matters
- Degree to which sufficient evidence was obtained.

Annexure 1.1
Fraud policy example

The following is an example of a fraud policy. Not all aspects discussed above are demonstrated by this document and it is for illustration purposes only.

The ABC company fraud policy

Purpose

The purpose of this policy is to provide guidance on fraud within the ABC company in terms of the organisation's stance on fraud and the responsibilities surrounding the reporting of incidents, the investigation thereof and of fraud risk management within the organisation.

Organisation's position

The ABC company was established to achieve its objectives, as determined from time to time by the board of directors. The organisation has, in pursuit of these objectives, the right to protect its interests so as to deliver value to its owners, employees and business partners. Fraud is against the values of the ABC company and erodes value.

As such, the organisation has zero tolerance for all acts of fraud and misconduct. The organisation will investigate all suspected or actual incidents of fraud and initiate the required internal and external remedial actions, as required.

Definition

Fraud includes any known misrepresentation of the truth or concealment of a material fact to induce the ABC company, its employees or business partners to act to their detriment.

Fraudulent acts include any acts of bribery and corruption, the inappropriate or unlawful use of assets and any misstatements.

Responsibilities

- *Incident reporting*
  The reporting of suspected or known fraud is the responsibility of each and every employee of the ABC company. Suspected or actual incidents of fraud must be reported to the Group Forensic function within one day of awareness thereof. Failure to report all suspected or actual fraud incidents may be seen as 'wilful blindness' and invoke the company's disciplinary code. Actual or suspected acts of fraud can be reported at AntiFraud@ABCforensics.co.za (e-mail), www.ABCCompany.co.za/fraudreporting (website) or on +27 (0)21 555 666 7899 (24-hour telephonic fraud hotline).
- *Fraud investigation*
  The investigation of fraud is the responsibility of management in concurrence with the Group Forensic Function who will coordinate and provide guidance on all fraud investigations. Management must ensure that investigations are adequately resourced. All employees must make themselves available to provide assistance in investigations, as required.

- *Fraud prevention*
  The Board of Directors, as the custodians of internal control, have delegated the operational responsibility of fraud risk management to management. Management has the responsibility to ensure that:
  - All fraud risks are identified
  - Anti-fraud controls are adequate
  - Anti-fraud controls are effectively performed
  - Sufficient resources are provided to ensure a proper control environment

While management has the overall responsibility for anti-fraud interventions, all employees have an obligation to act in a way that prevents and/or detects fraud.

- *Remedial actions*
  Management must, as an outcome of fraud investigations, ensure that all fraud incidents are adequately remediated, including the opening of criminal matters, the initiation of internal disciplinary actions, the recovery of losses and the adequacy of the control environment, as relevant.
- *Communication and reporting*
  Management is responsible to ensure the timely and relevant reporting of all fraud-related reporting to the senior organisation leadership.

General decorum

All fraud risk management and investigative activities should:

- Be conducted in a manner that is professional, courteous and respectful and should treat all people with dignity
- Assume neither innocence nor guilt in matters
- Ensure that all matters are reported to those charged with the responsibility to investigate them
- Not act in a different manner towards those implicated unless the unique situation requires it (for example: to prevent further loss or if there is a specific instruction not to communicate with implicated people until the investigation can be completed)
- Duly assist those charged with conducting the investigation

Annexure 1.2
Business Process Fraud Risk Assessment Template example

The following is an example of a business process fraud risk assessment template that can be used:

Objective: 2
To determine that only goods and services actually received were paid for.

No	Risk	Impact	Probability	Existing or proposed control	Report Ref	Test Ref

Annexure 1.3 Fraud Incident Information Question Template example				
No	**Consideration**	**Prompt**	**Action**	**Responsible and due date**
1.	What: ▪ Did they do/are they doing? ▪ Was/is the nature of the behaviour in question?	For example: misuse of assets, theft, kickbacks, etc.		
2.	How are they doing this?	What was/is their modus operandi: was/is it a particular type of transaction, a particular supplier, a particular time or day, below a floor limit.		
3.	What benefit(s) was given to the supplier/customer/third party/the subject/s of the investigation.	For example: cash, holidays, gifts, free use of assets, discounts, etc.		
4.	How did/does the money flow?	Is it paid in cash? Is it paid to the supplier who pays a cash kickback to the employee?		
5.	Who was/is involved?			
6.	Which are the organisations involved?	Please list all legal entities involved.		
7.	What relationship do the parties have to each other?	Supplier and company, supervisor and employee, etc. Do they have shares in conflicting entities, do they hold directorships, do they own specific assets like trucks, etc? Are there any other unique facts/information that we should know, eg they both play the horses or they have a family member in common, they own a boat together, they go to the same Mosque/temple/church, they used to work together, went to school together, studied together, etc?		
8.	Who has benefited?			
9.	Who is the victim and are they aware that they are the victim?	Name the specific legal entity.		

No	Consideration	Prompt	Action	Responsible and due date
10.	Who needs to be informed?	Senior organisational leadership? Special government agencies or serious crime units? Suppliers, customers, etc if they too are the victims?		
11.	Dates: ▪ Chronological history of what happened and frequency. ▪ What should the trends be showing and what are they actually showing?	Use a timeline and identify conflicts.		
12.	What records exist (very important as this speaks to how we prove the matter)?	Examples of documents would include: ▪ Letters ▪ E-mails ▪ Cheques that have been honoured by the bank and returned to the business for record-keeping – please provide a copy of front and back ▪ Cheque counterfoils listing the payee and/or purpose ▪ Printouts of the cash book or other general ledger accounting records ▪ Invoices, receipts, statements, cheque vouchers, etc ▪ Petty cash slips/records with the name or purpose of the payment written on them ▪ Documents with the accuseds' signatures on them ▪ Contracts that formalise the corrupt relationship ▪ Registration documents (of vehicles or companies) showing the names of the people concerned ▪ Company minutes (if applicable) describing any of the relationships ▪ Bank statements ▪ Photos or video footage, eg of parties or any of the above.		

No	Consideration	Prompt	Action	Responsible and due date
13.	What other evidence is there?	Electronic files on computers and devices, telephone records, access records, etc. Physical evidence, fingerprints, forced entry, etc.		
14.	Other details	Please provide: ▪ Account numbers ▪ Supplier codes ▪ Seal numbers ▪ Product codes ▪ Container numbers ▪ Batch numbers ▪ Etc.		
15.	Asset names, description, amounts and quantities?	What assets were involved in this matter? Abuse of assets, theft of assets, etc.		
16.	Who paid the money to the accused?	Was it the accused himself, a finance person in the company, an external person, supplier, etc?		
17.	When and where was the money paid?	Openly in the office, at the accused's house, at a pub, etc.		
18.	What did they do with the money?	Did they squander it or did they buy assets? Knowledge of what they did with the funds may be useful in directing lifestyle audits or for recovery or for evidence purposes.		
19.	How much of the fraudulently obtained funds/assets remain?	Kept in cash, in specific bank accounts, etc.		
20.	Where is this money?	In whose name is the money kept?		
21.	Who authorised the payments/transactions?	Please evaluate the signature on the document and/or who performed the transaction/signed the company documentation.		
22.	Who received the money?	Is there evidence of this: a witness, an electronic record, did they sign for it?		
23.	Who should have known?	Maybe they were aware and they kept quiet or maybe they are complicit? Were they negligent? Do they need to be counselled for dereliction of duty? Do we need to bolster controls?		

No	Consideration	Prompt	Action	Responsible and due date
24.	Who knows about/witnessed the corrupt relationship/ fraudulent activity?	Who have they told? What have they done about it? Are they complicit?		
25.	Who can supply more information?			
26.	Who must we protect and why?	For example: whistle-blowers.		
27.	Who can be trusted and why?			
28.	Who cannot be trusted and why?			
29.	Who processed the transactions in the company's books?	For example: a finance clerk, a routine computer program. Were they aware of what they were doing?		
30.	What were the payments processed in the books as?	For example: commission, finder's fee, etc.		
31.	Are there any other people involved and if so, how are they involved?			
32.	How long has this been going on?	Quantum, extent and scope.		
33.	How and by whom was this discovered?			
34.	Why has it only been reported now?	Previously unknown, only recently looked at these aspects, subject went on leave, etc.		
35.	What happened to allow this to occur/continue for so long/ be undetected?	Circumvention of controls, collusion, lack of controls, non-compliance with controls, etc.		
36.	Please list all applicable dates and/or times.	When the money was paid/benefits received, periods in which the transactions occurred.		
37.	Give a detailed listing of the amounts received.			
38.	What is the normal procedure/ rule/standard?	List the SOPs, etc. We need to prove that there was a rule and they had knowledge of the rule.		
39.	How does what they did differ to the normal procedure?	Compare the fraudulent behaviour to the rules.		

Annexure 1.4
Application control examples

The following is a summary of application controls. *The Handbook on IT Auditing* (J Donald Warren; Lynn W Edelson; Xenia Ley Parker; Michael A Murphy, 1994; continually updated) refers.

1. Access controls

Access controls have a lot to do with determining the 'validity' and/or 'authorisation' of the person or system accessing the program or data.

Background

There are essentially three areas of 'system' access, being:

- Operating system and/or infrastructure access – The operating system program is the interface for the user between the infrastructure and the hardware and the applications that run on the hardware. An operating system is therefore the overall 'infrastructure access' that a user has to go through to access a system. Operating systems normally have basic file management type functionality (file copy, create directories, etc). A lot of PCs make use of Microsoft Windows as their operating system. Servers also have operating systems. These operating systems are not specific to one application (and fall within general controls) and are therefore excluded from our discussion on application controls. System access control is mentioned here to complete the picture for the fraud risk officer. Some systems make use of 'single sign-on'. In these environments, the operating system controls the access to the applications as well. The operating system will be considered an application control in these cases and will be relevant for our discussion. The same controls described below may be assessed in such cases.
- Application system access – This is the access to specific programs or applications. This is discussed below.
- Database access controls – As mentioned previously access to a database could fall either within the general control environment or the application controls.

Application system access controls include:

- *Physical access controls*
  Physical access controls restrict unauthorised access to buildings, computer rooms, facilities, hardware and software.
- *Unique passwords*
  Unique passwords are necessary to ensure that access authorisation cannot be compromised through the use of another individual's authorised data access. Individual passwords also provide accountability for data changes.
- *Password complexity*
  Password complexity is a control that is set to define the length of passwords, the requirement for alphanumeric characters or special characters, etc. The general rule is that the more complex a password is, the less likely it is that it can be guessed or 'cracked' and therefore complexity represents sound control.
- *Password renewal*
  Passwords should be renewed within a fixed period (normally 30 to 40 days). Failure to renew passwords will result in a user being locked out of the system. This restricts the long-term use of passwords by multiple users when they become generally known.

- *System timeouts*
  It is good control practice to deactivate access to a system if an open session has not been used for longer than a fixed period (normally a few minutes).
- *Lockouts*
  Access is restricted at an application/system level if:
  - An incorrect password is attempted more than a specified number of times
  - A system is not accessed within a predetermined timeframe
- *Segregation of duties*
  Clear roles and duties need to be defined and care must be exercised to ensure that staff members do not have conflicting duties and profiles to allow them to conceal invalid transactions or for errors to be undetected. Consider which staff members have 'read', 'write', and 'approve' profiles within the application under review. Staff members who have access to 'write' (perform) transactions should not have the access to 'approve' the same or other conflicting transactions.
- *Online access controls*
  These controls ensure that only authorised individuals may access data or perform sensitive functions/transactions. Access may be restricted via special programs or physical firewall devices.

2. Input controls

Inputs can be manually inputted or originate from another system interface or program. Input controls are concerned with the validity, completeness and accuracy of the inputs. There are three types of input controls that are discussed below, being the following:

a) *Input validations*
   This is the validation of input to one of the following:

   i) Historical data
   Comparing inputs to historical data within the same system.

   ii) Manager's specifications
   Checking to see if inputs fall within parameters/conditions as specified by a manager.

   iii) Other data
   Comparing inputs to other systems.

   iv) Expert systems
   The use of a program written and embedded in an application to make decisions. The decisions are based on profiles calculated from the inputs (eg credit rating profiles). The expert systems often use weightings of good and bad to make their decisions.

   v) Authorisations
   consider the sequence of authorisation, the timing of authorisation and programmed authorization. At what point must authorisation occur? Must processing occur first or is other data required? Requiring authorisation of inputs at the time of input or at a later stage (processing, output). Authorisation will occur if inputs comply with predefined parameters.

b) *Completeness of input*

These are the controls that consider the completeness of data inputs and include:

i) Sequence checks

Is the sequence of transactions/documents complete, for example for pre-assigned, serially numbered documents or transactions? This may be a pure sequence check or a comparison to a file of issued numbers. Sequential numbers entered are flagged to indicate that they have been entered for processing. Reports of missing numbers are generated and followed up on.

ii) Duplicate checks –

All duplicate transactions should be rejected and written to a file for investigation.

iii) Batch totals

This involves the comparing of computer-calculated totals to corresponding inputted totals. Batch totals include document counts, financial value totals (eg USD), item/line counts and hash totals. Batch and hash controls involve adding a particular column of data before input and comparing the total of the column of data after it was inputted into the system. If the totals are equal, then the presumption is that all the data was inputted correctly for that column. A hash total is the sum of figures to form a 'nonsensical' total. For example: the adding up of product codes would result in a nonsensical total. The adding of the total value of a particular transaction would on the other hand provide a 'sensible' total. The basis of batch and hash totals is however not the sensibility of the total calculated. The basis of the total is to determine the completeness of input by the comparison of totals prior and post input.

iv) Matching

Matching/comparing of data to master or suspense files.

c) *Input accuracy*

i) Edit checks

- *Reasonableness checks*
  Inputs are tested to determine if they are within predetermined limits.
- *Existence checks*
  Checking that a particular field actually exists (eg department or supplier codes).
- *Mathematical accuracy*
  Extending and checking the manually calculated and inputted totals to the computer-calculated totals.
- *Document reconciliation*
  Reconciliation of a document hash total to a calculated one.
- *Dependency checks*
  Check to ensure that inputs bear the correct logical relationships to existing data.
- *Format checks*
  Check that only certain formats of inputs are allowed (eg alpha-numeric checks).

- *Check-digits*
  Check the computed calculated check-digit (a predetermined algorithm of the numbers captured in a field) against the check-digit that was captured, thereby determining that the individual numbers were captured correctly.
- *Prior data matching*
  Checking inputs to existing data before changes can occur. For example, requiring that the old price of a product code be input and verified before the update of the product master file can occur.
- *Pre-recorded input*
  Matching inputs to previous inputs or system-generated data.
- *Key verification*
  Certain fields of machine-readable documents that have been entered are keyed in manually to ensure that the machine read them correctly.
- *Automatic completion of fields*
  The machine predicts and completes fields being entered.

3. Processing controls

Data can either be 'updated' data or 'standing' data that is being stored.

a) *Standing data*
   This is data that has been processed or captured previously and is being stored. The integrity of this data must be ensured until the file is amended, deleted or appended to, etc. This data may be referenced by applications, eg price master files. Examples of processing controls on standing data include:
   - *Currency checks*
     Checking a date mark or matching data from a prior period to ensure that no changes have occurred.
   - *Reconciliation of file totals*
     Comparison of an accumulation of records to an independent control total.
   - *Access control*
     Restricting the ability to change master file data.
   - *Exception reports*
     Identifying records that have not been changed in a long period or which do not have a logical relationship to other records (eg cost greater than selling) or which do not fall within predetermined parameters.

b) *Updates*
   Examples of processing control on updated data include:
   - *Sequence checks*
     To identify missing or duplicate processed numbers. Alternatively, transactions are assigned a sequence number on being processed. The completeness of these assigned numbers is checked.
   - *Batch totals*
     Agreement of batch totals (discussed previously).

- *Reconciliations*
  Computer agreement of an accumulation of records.
- *Exception reports*
  Identifying processing that does not fall within predetermined parameters.
- *Matching*
  Matching processed data to a master file or to a suspense file.
- *Duplicate processing*
  Checking for duplicate processing.
- *Rejections*
  Rejected transactions should be stored and actioned.
- *Transaction logs*
  Logs all changes made to master files, when they were made and who made them.

4. Output controls

Output controls are frequently an area of application controls that are forgotten about or ignored.

a) Consider the intent, timing and authorisation of the output required. The answers to the questions below will assist in determining which controls need to be in place:
   - *Sensitive forms*
     How sensitive is the content of the output?
   - *Access*
     Who should have access to the output?
   - *Actions*
     What action needs to be taken on the output? Is it used as input to another system for decision-making or is it a file of rejected transactions that needs to be investigated?
   - *Job scheduling*
     Who has access to change the prioritising of jobs or termination thereof?
   - *Distribution*
     How and when should the distribution of output occur? Paper output, electronic reports, etc.
   - *Retention*
     For how long should the output be retained and how accessible should it be during the retention period?

b) System-generated output
   Output is generated by the system once certain criteria have been met (eg just-in-time replenishment systems ordering stock once the minimum re-order level has been reached).

5. Data transfer controls

Data is frequently moved from one system to another. Controls need to be in place to ensure that this data transfer is valid, complete, accurate and timely.

a) Consider the purpose of the data after the transfer. Establish if there is a control in place (for example batch totals) for each element of the data that is used after the transfer. Many data transfer controls only consider total value transferred and number of lines of data transferred. There is a risk that the data within the line transferred becomes corrupt. For example, the product code or the transaction date in a line of data becomes corrupt. Hash totals on each field used after the transfer (in this example product code and date) will determine the accuracy of specific fields used later.

b) Controls include:
   i) Encryption - encrypting data in a non-readable format prior to transmission and decrypting the data upon receipt.
   ii) Completeness, accuracy and validity of data - to ensure that all data that was sent was received completely, accurately and is valid. As discussed above, controls should ensure at least that all data used subsequent to the transfer has controls to ensure the complete and accurate transfer. It is also important to ensure that the data was received by all applications (there may be more than one) scheduled to receive it. Finally consider if the table mappings and conversion from source to destination are correct. Frequently data being sent may not be in the correct format of the destination file into which it is being uploaded. In these cases, a conversion or translation needs to occur. The conversion may entail the consolidation of some data. The consolidation of data may diminish the chance to use batch and hash totals.

6. Log controls

Log controls are concerned with creating an audit trail of data creation. Consider the following concepts when reviewing log controls:

- *Accountability*
  This ensures that users who access data, changed data or used transactions can be identified. Transaction logs should not be able to be changed and should record all users, including the systems administrator's movement within the application or database.
- *Recreation*
  Transaction logs may help to understand the events that transpired and gave rise to problems. They may also assist with the recreation of data, etc.

7. Data conversion controls

Legacy system master files or transactional files may not be in the required format before they are uploaded into a new system. This data will need to be converted into the new system formats prior to uploading.

Input, processing and transfer controls may be used as inspiration for the controls that are applicable.

8. Technical environment

Where the technical configuration of the system is unique to the specific application (for example, a dedicated machine on which an application runs) it can impact on the completeness, accuracy and timeliness of the data.

It is also possible that unauthorised changes to the technical environment may expose these applications or access to other IT resources. Technical controls fall under the general IT control environment and do not form part of application controls.

CHAPTER 2

THE RULES

2.1. CHAPTER LAYOUT AND INTRODUCTION

As in so many aspects of life, there are 'rules' applicable to fraud investigation, which can, if known and understood by you, help you to achieve your goals.

The rules that are discussed here are not really rules by the pure definition of the word. They are, as is the theme of this book, practical learnings that have been observed, picked up or handed down by fellow fraud investigators. Some are totally original and based on my own experience, while others stem directly from what I have been taught. Others, still, are good old-fashioned clichés that remain relevant. What they do is to summarise my general philosophy of fraud investigations.

When I am on the job with one of my less experienced colleagues, I continually repeat these rules at applicable stages. This slowly conditions their thinking and helps them to understand the importance of the principle of what the rule is trying to tell them. My goal is to provide them with a guiding voice which can sit in the back of their minds and provide guidance to them when they are alone and faced with an unfamiliar situation. This will provide them with a basis against which to reflect when they are stuck in a situation, to know how to proceed.

It always brings a smile to my face when, after a while, the people that I interact with start to apply the rules themselves when in a particular situation. It is at this stage that they are successfully interpreting the rule in the context of their particular situation and I can see the proverbial penny dropping and them becoming very confident in how to proceed.

The philosophy of this book is to provide practical learnings which you would not usually find in a book. These are possibly the gems of experience that the retiring fraud specialist would have imparted to the young protégé in the anecdote at the commencement of this book. So, while this chapter of rules is not a conventional manner to start a book, I believe that the rules will provide the needed background before going into the detail. My rules are not what you will expect in a conventional textbook. Do not judge them. Give them a chance. Wait until you read the detailed chapters before deciding whether to adopt them or not. There is no requirement to use them, but I can tell you that these rules have proved invaluable to me in my work and to the staff members who I have trained.

Read the rules and take note of them. You do not need to memorise them. I will be quoting some of these rules at various stages in the book when I want to anchor the principle of the rule. You can then refer back to the detailed rule discussion for a deeper understanding, as required.

The rules are listed in order of relative 'importance'. The rules are totally independent of each other and any perceived link is purely coincidental and unintended. The relative importance of the rules becomes blurred as the list lengthens. The first ones are more important, while the latter ones are just 'good to know'. Before long you may even develop a few 'rules' of your own.

The rules that are discussed below include the following:

- Secure the evidence.
- The best time to do something is immediately.
- The three things you should always do are: number 1, plan; number 2, plan; and number 3, plan.
- Follow the money.
- Get yourself a yardstick.
- It is simpler than you think.
- It is always the people who are the closest.
- The people who tell you they are good are the ones that you should worry about.
- If it is too good to be true, then it probably is.
- The devil is in the detail.
- He with the most paperwork, wins.
- Take whatever was found when the fraud was discovered or whatever they (the fraudster) admit to and multiply it by three. This is what has been lost in the fraud.
- Forensics is less about fact and more about psychology.
- People always do and say things for a reason.
- Be aware of the 'fear factor'.
- When all else fails, interview.
- Keep the end-game in mind.
- They always make a mistake.
- The thing that drives people will make them fall.
- An old Japanese saying goes something along the lines of: 'If you stand at the bank of the river long enough, you will see the body of your enemy come floating past.' I think the English equivalent is: 'All good things come to those who wait.'
- Robin Hood was a fairy-tale.
- It always involves sex, drugs or gambling ... or some form of addiction/vice.
- Forensics revolves around contacts.
- Be careful who you share information with.
- Management is your biggest challenge.
- How long is a piece of string?
- Maintain an attitude of professional scepticism.
- Play the ball, not the man.
- We have a duty towards the truth.
- Queensbury rules apply.
- Principles are for rich people.
- In this game, we take any score we can get on the board.
- There is life after the subject leaves.
- Every criminal/crime is known to/by someone.
- 'You will get more right with honey than with chilli.'
- Accountability is a team sport.

2.2. DETAILED DISCUSSION

These are the 'rules' that will be discussed in greater detail and referred to in various parts of the book. My 'rules' of forensics include:

2.2.1. Secure the evidence

There is no other rule more important in a fraud investigation. This single rule can make or break your investigation. The times that I have disobeyed this rule, or allowed others (in the area affected by the fraud and/or when acting under their direct instruction/advice) to divert me from it, have invariably ended up in evidence being intentionally or unintentionally lost or unusable. The integrity of evidence may also be vital in a criminal matter (Chapter 3 on conducting an investigation and Chapter 7 on subsequent actions guides more detail in this regard). There are essentially two elements to this rule, namely: 1) obtaining the evidence and 2) the integrity of the evidence. These both talk to the ultimate use of the evidence. Evidence can be physical evidence (documents, items, etc), electronic evidence (information, computers, telephones, etc), video (CCTV footage) and people's recollections.

2.2.2. The best time to do something is immediately

I suppose that this rule is a natural progression from the first rule of securing the evidence. As per the above I have learnt hard lessons by taking too long to secure physical evidence and to obtain affidavits.

A few clichés come to mind:

- A stitch in time saves nine.
- Don't put off to tomorrow what you can do today.
- Regret always comes too late.

There is a big 'BUT' attached to this rule though, in so far as it is subject to the next rule of planning.

This rule is also in line with the general police guidance (typically see in murder and missing person's investigation dramas) that the first 48 hours are the most important. This has to do with the diminishing chance of success as time progresses due to the low probability of finding a person alive after 48 hours and due to testimony/evidence being less available/reliable as time progresses.

We do not always have the luxury of the first 48 hours in a fraud investigation, as fraud cases normally come to light after they have been progressing for some time. I have been involved in numerous cases where I have had to try to obtain evidence that backdates years. This is very challenging.

The spirit of this rule is not about the Hollywood movie with the same name (*48 Hrs*). The spirit of this rule is that investigation efforts should not be delayed, but rather conducted as soon as possible.

2.2.3. The three things you should always do are: number 1, plan; number 2, plan; and number 3, plan

So, in short, 'planning is everything'. As the old clichés say:

- Only fools rush in.
- Look before you leap.

To illustrate the point of planning further, let us use the game of chess as an example. To me the best moves in chess are those moves where you force your opponent to respond to your attack without allowing them the opportunity to move in any other manner (for example: the use of 'discovered check').

Similarly, in forensics you want to be in control of the pace and the manner in which the subjects respond to your moves. Planning will allow you to do this. We discuss the merits of this at length in Chapter 4 on interviews.

2.2.4. Follow the money

If you are at the beginning stages of an investigation and do not know how to progress, it is advisable to 'stop and follow the money'. At the end of the day, the most common motive for committing acts of fraud is to get money and/or influence the effect of money. What fraudsters do with the money and why they want the money may differ, but in the vast majority of cases, perpetrators are motivated by money. So, if you want to find out what they did or how they did it, then follow the flow of money in or out of the organisation being investigated and/or for the transactions under review. This will give you very good insights with which to progress your investigation.

2.2.5. Get yourself a yardstick

This is something one of my old bosses taught me. When reviewing something you need a baseline or standard against which to measure the activity being tested. Without a baseline, you are using your own judgement to determine if the activity is acceptable or not. While you may be highly experienced, your opinion remains your opinion. The rule below of 'how long is a piece of string' also refers in this regard. The standard or baseline may be a policy, a procedure, a law, an industry standard, etc. As far as possible, try to get yourself an independent and defendable baseline. The more independent your baseline is, the less convincing others of its credibility you will need to do.

2.2.6. It is simpler than you think

Somewhere we seem to have acquired the impression that fraudulent schemes are all terribly complicated. I am not sure if it is the fault of the media or our education. Perhaps it is our own inherent inferiority complexes that make us believe that the perpetrators of frauds are that much more intelligent and ingenious than ourselves? We tend, as a result, to spend our time looking for elaborate schemes and/or methods. In reality, fraudsters are not that sophisticated. In fact, they frequently 'go for the easy money (perhaps a sub-rule of this is the simplicity rule). Unless the perpetrator is a highly skilled criminal (and you certainly get them), the perpetrators tend to utilise the methods that are the closest and/or available to them. The methods available to them tend to be those performed as part of their daily duties, most of which are regular daily transactions (eg payroll transactions, creditor payments, procurement, etc).

2.2.7. It is always the people that are the closest

Fraudsters do not wake up one day and decide to cross town and go into a business that they are not sure exists and gain access to funds which may very well not be there. Too many Hollywood movies have taught us that even bank robbers meticulously plan where and when they are going to strike. Fraudsters, while often opportunistic (see discussion later on the personality traits of fraudsters), use a particular modus operandi because they see (albeit in their mind's eye) that it can be done on a regular basis (in their daily routine) and/or because they have regular access to the opportunity (due to their responsibilities).

So, a fraud in the accounts payable area was most likely perpetrated by one of the accounts payable staff members and even more likely by the accounts payable clerk who works with the afflicted suppliers. Our judgement, as investigators, could be clouded by the fact that the person who is the closest to the fraud is often a long-serving employee or a well-liked person. As a result, we tend to be less suspicious of them or disbelieve that they could have been party to the crime.

In one example that I dealt with, the perpetrator was an extremely helpful lady (and I do not mean helping herself, as she was doing), with six years of experience in her job (accounts payable in this example) and who outwardly seemed to be a devout Christian. Her manager found it difficult to accept, even long after she had been dismissed, that she had defrauded the company of so much money and over such a protracted period.

2.2.8. The people that tell you they are 'good' are the ones you should worry about

This is one of my pet hates. I am sure that many people can relay a story about someone who pretends to be devoutly religious and then does exactly the opposite to what their faith decrees. Bear in mind that we are looking for red flags/early warnings that can lead an investigator to the most likely suspects. In isolation, such behaviour may, while irritatingly hypocritical, be quite normal and not a sign that fraud has been perpetrated. At the end of the day, though, people who are really good or who do good deeds do not need to tell others about it. They are perceived to be good by their actions. Truly good people rarely have the need for recognition of their good deeds (Gandhi, Mother Teresa, Princess Diana and Nelson Mandela refer as iconic examples). People who continually tell you that they are good are concerned that they will not be perceived as such. We will discuss detecting deceit in Chapter 4 on interviewing. We will also discuss the deterrent to fraud that is created by the likelihood of detection (Chapter 10 on setting up a forensic function refers). It is my supposition that people who continually tell you that they are good are in fact acutely aware of their shortcomings and misdeeds. They nevertheless have a need to be perceived to be good so that they can continue to engage in their misconduct, undiscovered.

2.2.9. If it is too good to be true, then it probably is

If something just seems too good to be true then it is most probably untrue. The tools of the fraud investigator's trade are evidence, facts, logic and sound reasoning. Go back to the basics and follow a logical approach to testing what has been asserted. As with most of the rules being discussed in this chapter, this rule has multiple facets, including the following:

- Victims need to be realistic and not fall for unbelievable schemes. Fraudsters offer compelling reasons for how their victim is going to make 'easy money' if they follow the scheme. Victims should not be naive.
- Suspects may offer excuses in interviews. Actual examples of excuses offered to me before include: 'I have very rich in-laws who pay for a lot of things for my wife and I and that is how we can afford to have such a good life' and 'I frequently win at the casino and that is how I can afford these luxury items.'

2.2.10. The devil is in the detail

The television has successfully romanticised the greater realm of investigation with Gucci-clad models in exotic sports cars arriving at the scene of the crime with great theatrics, miraculously solving the crime, returning the misappropriated items and 'getting the girl' all within a record-breaking 30 minutes (including advertisements). Perhaps I am just slow, but this easy and glamorous picture has certainly not been my experience of investigations.

For those fraud investigators who come from an auditing background, it may also be a bit of a shock to learn that they can no longer draw a sample, check a few isolated documents and express an extrapolated opinion of the entire population. Fraud investigation does not work that way. If there is a box of invoices suspected of being tainted with fraud, then you have to go through every single invoice to see if it matches your fraud criteria!

There is just no getting around it: fraud investigation is very detailed work. Detailed work also typically takes a long time and requires a methodical, pragmatic approach (See Chapter 3 on conducting an investigation). Fraud investigation may therefore not be suitable for everyone. It takes a rare animal to be able to keep focused on the end-game while wading through masses of detail over a protracted investigation. This is not a criticism against those people who are not suited for this. This is merely a statement that different people have different aptitudes and lines of work that they are suited to.

2.2.11. He with the most paperwork, wins

This is something that I learnt from the quantity surveyors in the construction industry who need to get clients to pay for variations and special requests over and above the original scope of work. Their clients try to argue that the work performed formed part of the original scope of work and is therefore covered by the standard contract price.

The same is true for fraud investigations in a couple of regards, including the following:

- Evidence – Simply put, the more documentary evidence that you have, the stronger your case is going to be.
- 'Chain of custody' – We will discuss this in detail later, but it entails documenting the chain of evidence to ensure the integrity thereof so that it will be submittable in court.
- Your investigation and methods – You will need to document what your investigation entailed, why you did it as well as what your findings and conclusions are, as you may be required to testify to this.

2.2.12. Take whatever was found when the fraud was discovered or whatever they (the fraudster/s) admit to and multiply it by three. This is actually what has been lost in the fraud

One of my contemporaries taught this to me at the early stages of my fraud investigation career. This rule has held true for me over the years.

I could add to the rule and say that in my experience, the 'three times rule' is most likely a good estimate of the minimum amount of the fraudulent loss. I have had many instances where this multiple has been exceeded.

In one particular example, I was able to prove that the actual loss was in excess of 11 times greater than the original discovered amount.

2.2.13. Forensics is less about fact and more about psychology

This is not necessarily the most important rule, but certainly one of my favourites. We use the 'psychology' to get to the facts. The facets of this rule include:

- Using psychology to get perpetrators to confess to their involvement
- Getting people to divulge information
- Identifying the modus operandi (the psychology of what the fraudster was thinking) that enables the fraud investigator to identify the full scale of the fraud; for example, the subject used a particular supplier or only transactions below the authority limit.

Forensics is all about identifying those psychological levers which, when pulled, will open the facts of the case to you.

In terms of interviewing, forensics is also less about what you actually know and more about what the guilty party thinks you know. The more they think you know, the more fearful they will be and/or the less resistance they will offer. The more fearful they are, the more likely it is that they will make a mistake and/or confess. See Chapter 4 on interviewing for a detailed discussion on this.

2.2.14. People always do and say things for a reason

This is the rule that I quote the most frequently. This was taught to me by my brother (who is a medical doctor) many years ago. This rule has helped me to look beyond what is said or not said. It helps me to look, as per the previous rule, for the psychology behind what is being done or said. Whether talking to a person giving information or looking at evidence, what has been done or said tells a story. Once you understand the psychology behind what the person was doing, you will then be able to apply this to the situation to identify the facts and use these to prove the case.

2.2.15. Be aware of the 'fear factor'

This rule is really a subsection of the 'people do and say things for a reason' rule. In this case we are discussing the fact that fear is frequently the reason that people do things which may not be commensurate with your expectation of rational behaviour. Trying to detect deceit and/or solicit a confession is discussed at length in Chapter 4 on interviewing.

As an example: Subjects may be part of a syndicate and they may fear what their syndicate bosses can do to them (bodily harm) more than what you can do to them (dismissal).

Other than trying to put people at ease, there is not a lot that you can do about this. You should be aware of the fact that people in extreme situations are frequently motivated by fear. Some examples of fear include:

- Fear of not having (and hence electing to steal to obtain)
- Fear for their lives/of retribution from their co-conspirators
- Fear of their bosses
- Fear of shame by their family, friends or peers upon their misdeeds being publicised
- Fear of dismissal

Management may also be fearful of the results of an investigation (due to their failure to implement adequate controls, loss of incentives, brand damage, etc).

2.2.16. When all else fails, interview

It is common to reach a situation where you have very little to go on. This could be at the commencement of an investigation or even after some time performing the investigation. There may only be a very 'thin' allegation from a whistle-blower or there may even have been a physical loss of sorts (funds or assets) that has occurred, but very few facts to proceed on. Too many times I have seen investigations closed/never commenced in the face of a perceived lack of evidence or insufficient detail to go on.

Fraudsters do not make things easy for us. The evidence is rarely out in the open. In most cases you will need to find the evidence yourself. So, if you have very little to go on initially and you are at the point of closing the case, then you have 'nothing to lose' from a last concerted effort. Interview a wide cross-section of people related to the matter. You will be surprised by what people tell you. You will then be able to direct your investigation efforts based on the information supplied by the interviewees and hopefully obtain the evidence required.

2.2.17. Always keep the end-game in mind

In all things that you do, keep the 'end-game' in mind. The ultimate end-game in forensics is the criminal case and/or any other subsequent actions.

A criminal case is the most important end-state to strive for and the end-state that supersedes any other action. It is also the most onerous to be successful with. Act, therefore, right from the time that an actual or potential matter is brought to your attention, in a manner that will enable you to be able to 'go criminal' with the matter in the end. It is better to get to the end of a matter and decide not to go criminal, than to get to the end of a matter and to want to go criminal, but not to be able to due to the lack of integrity of the evidence. If you therefore do not ensure the integrity of information and/or gather the required evidence in advance, it may be too late once you realise that you will be going criminal with the matter. Proceed therefore in all aspects and immediately from the point of awareness of the matter, as if you are going criminal and ensure that you follow all the required protocols, gather all possible evidence and consider all aspects that may need to be proven in a criminal matter.

Another dimension to this rule is to keep your initial investigation brief in mind throughout. Keep reminding yourself what your initial objective was or what you have been asked to determine. When you find something, ask yourself what it means in terms of your initial objective. Adjust your approach to ensure that you stay on track.

2.2.18. They always make a mistake

Do not become despondent when you cannot see how or by whom the crime was perpetrated or if you initially feel that you have inadequate evidence. There is no such thing as a perfect crime. They have either already made a mistake or they will still make a mistake, which once discovered will assist you in prising open the case. All you must do is find it.

Of course, I am over-simplifying things and it may not be that easy. What I can say in consolation is that in my experience, perpetrators actually make many 'mistakes' in any one single crime. The question then is how do you identify what you cannot see? I have to say that the longer I am in this field, the easier it becomes for me to spot their mistakes. Mainly because I have formed a body of knowledge from which I can draw to assist me. Training and experience are therefore key.

As an example, if you walk through a forest, you will probably come out on the other end not having noticed many of the things that were there. Walk through the same forest however with a trained game ranger at your side and he will point out all types of plant and animal life to you that you did not see previously. The ranger may even point out signs of the type of animals that were there recently and where they have gone based purely on the signs (which we call evidence) that they have left behind them.

In the words of Gary Player (world-renowned golfer): 'The more I practise, the luckier I get.'

This book will teach you some of the general aspects to look for. For the rest, it will be up to you to practise them until they become second nature.

2.2.19. The thing that drives people will make them fall

Perhaps another take on this is that 'you are your own worst enemy'. People who are driven by power and greed will pursue these to such a degree that they will eventually succumb to them.

It seems to me that at a certain stage fraudsters become overconfident or so consumed by what they are pursuing that they lose touch with other normal aspects of life. History is full of examples of powerful empires and individuals that have fallen as a result of decadence and pursuing the wrong things.

What this means to us, in terms of fraud cases, is that the very fraudulent ways that drive people will cause them to be caught out and fall. We can therefore identify the potential involvement of people by identifying people who demonstrate unethical values/pursuits. We can also investigate these pursuits to obtain evidence in terms of a lifestyle audit or an actual trail of what they have done incorrectly.

2.2.20. An old Japanese saying goes something along the lines of: 'If you stand at the bank of the river long enough, you will see the body of your enemy come floating past.'

I think the English equivalent is: 'All good things come to those who wait.'

Part of this is about being patient and part of this is about being resilient. One interpretation of this rule is that if you do not get them the first time, then be patient. They will always re-offend and you will get them the next time. I have had experience of this.

Another interpretation is that you should be patient in your process of gathering evidence. If you are patient you will get the desired outcome. Patience in this regard does not mean waiting for the evidence to come to you. It means persisting and not giving up.

The spirit of this rule is not that you should sit back and wait for a conviction to fall into your lap. It rather means that being vigilant, observing and lying in wait will put you in a good position to strike when the opportunity presents itself.

2.2.21. Robin Hood was a fairy-tale

I can remember reading a very old version of *Robin Hood* that my father had on his bookshelf when I was a child. I recall that the preface of this book maintained that Robin Hood had really existed and that he was buried in the grounds of a chapel in Sherwood Forest in 1145 AD. The author went on to explain that much of the legend of the Robin Hood character was handed down over time. The author implied that in reality, Robin Hood was no more than a common criminal, but that his stature had grown each time the story of his crimes had been retold and embellished on. Whether or not this is true I would not be able to say. I do however recall deriving much pleasure from the story and being in awe of this charismatic fellow who stole from the evil rich people (never the nice rich people) and who gave generously back to the poor people that the evil rich people had deprived in the first instance.

In reality though, there is no such phenomenon as Robin Hood. People steal for greed. Even if they start off needing food, they quickly move into greed. In fact, I would go so far as to say that if they have already elected to steal, then they have already taken the easy/quick way out. This should be read together with the next rule.

I am sure that we could enter into many academic debates about how a person would respond if their children were starving and/or in need of medication. I am merely saying that in my experience, I have never found a fraudster whose motives come close to the selfless motives of Robin Hood.

Sure, fraudsters will justify to themselves why they are entitled to steal (discussed in greater detail below), but this does not mean that their motives are pure.

Furthermore, I am not going to downplay the realities of people's situations or what has made them what they are or brought them to that point. I just maintain that I have never met a Robin Hood and I predict that you are not likely to meet him either.

2.2.22. It always involves sex, drugs or gambling ...

... or some form of addiction/vice. This rule was taught to me by my contemporaries in the early stages of my fraud investigation career.

Part of identifying who perpetrated the crime may entail looking for indicators (red flags) to identify people living beyond their known financial means. This will indicate to you that they may have utilised funds that they would ordinarily not have had access to (see detailed discussion later). When looking for the areas where the fraudster may have spent the illicitly obtained money, you can safely look for one of these three common addictions. These addictions are all 'expensive hobbies' and they need to be 'fed'. The idea is that these people have a higher need for money as they indulge in expensive hobbies. Their legitimate income will therefore be applied to these pastimes and they will need to fund their hobbies and their normal lifestyle from somewhere else. These people have a higher than normal probability of having perpetrated a fraud to obtain the funds that they use to fund their addictions.

Perhaps the use of the word 'always' is a bit strong. I would say that this has certainly been a common theme. In my career, I have mostly dealt with fraudsters who have fallen prey to the vices of sex or gambling. This may however not be your experience. Again, this is a generalisation, but as a blunt instrument, it is a good place to start. Remember if you are looking for the most likely suspect in a group, then the known gambler must enjoy a higher probability of being a perpetrator.

Maybe it is the kind of person who has a higher disposition towards stealing who is also attracted to these avenues. Alternatively, maybe it is the habit that causes them to go into a life of crime as it were? As mentioned above these are expensive pastimes that need to be funded. Chapter 6 on lifestyle audits sets forth a more detailed discussion.

Somehow, the old cliché of 'easy come, easy go' also comes to mind. The fraudsters I have encountered were often wasteful with their ill-gotten gains. There is definitely an irony to that. They rationalise to themselves why they are entitled to the fraudulently acquired funds, but then go about wasting the funds once in hand. It does not make sense, but then fraud rarely does.

In my experience, many of the fraudsters I have encountered often had relatively few of the misappropriated funds left by the time their crimes had been identified. Numerous business owners and senior members of management have said to me that they cannot understand why the perpetrator squandered all of the money. They then continue to say that they would have used the money to acquire assets. Well, fraudsters do not think like us (see discussion later on the personality of a fraudster).

A particular war story comes to mind – in this case a young man who worked for retailer 'A'. He fronted a renovation contracting company that specialised in the refurbishment of retail stores. His uncle was one of the directors of a large international retail chain ('B'). His uncle was responsible for approving the contractors that performed the store refurbishments. In this way, his uncle was able to award the work to his nephew. The subpoenaed bank account of the nephew revealed that almost all of the funds (ZAR 2M/USD 200K in this case) had been withdrawn at an automatic teller machine at a local casino.

2.2.23. Forensics revolves around contacts

Over time you will need to build up a network of contacts, simply because it is not possible/practical from a skills point of view to be able to do everything (well) or have access to everything (information) yourself. It is also unlikely that it will be cost effective to pay for all required services.

What I am talking about is an unspoken code of professional courtesy that exists amongst trusted forensic practitioners. This is not about doing something illegal, but rather about doing favours for favours. It is not something that can be rushed either. It is about building professional relationships over time, and knowing who to call when you hit a problem – someone to point you in the right direction or to give you advice on how to proceed.

For example, you have a subject's identity document that you suspect is fraudulent. You phone a friend who is a forensic document expert at a local bank. He is able to give you tips on how to identify if the document is fraudulent.

It is vital that fraud investigators never stoop to the levels of the very fraudsters they are trying to catch and engage in unethical or illegal means to gain information and/or evidence. It does not matter how frustrating this game can be; never do something illegal or against your professional code of ethics.

Remember it is give and take. So, for example, if someone helps you with data mining, then you might help them with legal advice if this is your field of expertise.

2.2.24. Be careful who you share information with

I have unfortunately had very bad experiences around this rule on too many occasions. This cautionary part covers numerous aspects:

Firstly, you very often do not know (certainly in the early stages of an investigation) who is involved and who is not. When talking to witnesses and people involved in the business unit/functional area under investigation, remember that you may very well be talking to someone who is involved in the crime themselves. Even when you have the main culprit, there may be other parties involved that you have not contemplated yet.

Secondly, even if you are not talking to an accomplice, you may not be aware of all of the alliances and loyalties that are in play. Fraudsters also have an ability to convince people to keep them up to date or to convince colleagues that they are innocent and that the company is treating them unfairly.

An example comes to mind where an outside individual managed to convince the group FD to appoint his son (despite being an insolvent as well as being technically incompetent) as one of the organisation's regional financial directors. The group FD was later angered and tried to hold me accountable for highlighting how his friend's son's incompetence had aided a material fraud. I suspect that the loyalties of the FD and the father were stronger than the need for good control within the organisation.

Thirdly, I have also had bad experiences in two companies in which I worked where senior executives tried to cover up an identified fraud because they were friends with the implicated party or because they did not want to look bad in front of the main board of directors.

Fourthly (and most importantly), once you tell someone something in confidence, you have no control over what they do with that information. They may innocently pass it on out of sheer excitement or naivety. Different people also react differently to information given to them. They will react in a particular way depending on what they want. For example, a director or owner may want decisive action and react prematurely. I have been in situations where senior management calls people in to discuss what has occurred without all the facts. I have also been in situations where you mention that person A or B could have been involved. The director decides that the person must have been involved and the relationship of trust is ruined regardless of the outcome of the investigation.

This also applies to your eventual report. Audit reports and forensic investigation reports typically detail control weaknesses and how a person could or did misuse control deficiencies to defraud the company. An example comes to mind of a company which was obsessed with the concept of 'participative management'. All reports were circulated to everyone in the area reviewed. In this case the criminals utilised my report (with detailed descriptions of the control deficiencies) to misappropriate physical stock.

Of course, the reverse is also applicable. If you know who you are talking to or if you know which alliances there are, then you may be able to get information indirectly back to the subject or to engineer a nervous response by selectively releasing information that you know will run back to the alliance partners. This may cause the fraudsters to make a mistake.

2.2.25. Management will be your biggest challenge

When we are students we are taught that it is all about doing a good job. The subjects are the 'bad guys' and the fraud investigators are the 'good guys'. Unfortunately, that is not the only determinant of success. Organisations can be full of politics. The bigger the organisation, the rifer the politics. The smaller the organisation, the fewer people you will have to assist you.

Some of the biggest challenges that I have had in fraud investigations have not been the subjects at all. They have been trying to convince management to pursue the matter or that the matter is in fact a fraud. Maybe it is about expectations. We expect subjects to be evasive and non-cooperative. On the other hand, we expect management to be 'on our side' and we do not expect them to be 'against' us. Remember one of our previous rules: 'People do and say things for a reason'. Well, this applies very much to management. Management may:

- Be avoiding blame due to not having identified the fraud or not ensuring that the required controls are in place
- Be covering for a friend/a crony
- Not want to highlight weaknesses in the systems and processes
- Keep general attention away from their division or area of responsibility
- Not want to have additional work or controls
- Want to save costs

It is suggested that you prove value as much as you can, always be professional and develop allies, and report to be transparent about the process.

2.2.26. How long is a piece of string

This point is about the dangers of presumption and the fact that you should not expect others to have a similar understanding to you. The old analogy of not knowing how long a piece of string should be when someone requests one from you, refers.

Do not to presume that management or another party knows:

- What an investigation entails (steps and tools)
- How to structure an interview
- How to analyse information (conducting a detailed investigation)
- What subsequent actions should be taken or how they are to be conducted

Our previous rule of obtaining management's assistance may also be easier if they have a greater understanding of what needs to happen/is happening.

In an example where we were assisting management to investigate fraudulent expenses, we requested them to analyse the data at hand. We even went so far as to list the analyses that they could conduct (specific examples of trend analysis, exception identification, etc). Standard stuff, or so we thought, until shortly before the subject interview was to take place. We then realised that all they had done was to list some of the expense details contained on the invoices in a column in a spreadsheet of the questioned expenses. We eventually performed the analytics ourselves (using pivot tables, 'if statements', graphs, etc) and spent time understanding the exceptions with management (analyses and interpretation). It is doubtful that we would have been able to have a meaningful or credible interview with the subject without this information.

So, the message is not to presume that people have understood what you require, but rather to give explicit guidelines and to check their understanding/progress at regular intervals to allow sufficient time to intervene and/or provide additional guidance.

The same is true for subjects. If they make a general statement, do not presume that you understand what they mean. Ensure that you obtain explicit clarification of what they have said. Part of their generalisation of answers may be an attempt to be deceitful and/or avoid detection.

2.2.27. Maintain an attitude of professional scepticism

This rule comes from the Institute of Internal Auditors (IIA-USA). In terms of fraud we can apply this rule to mean that we neither trust nor distrust anyone. We consider all possibilities and that all parties may be involved. We then set about obtaining facts and evidence to substantiate our suspicions and findings either way.

Even if someone tells you that a particular party is involved, you must not presume the role of judge and jury. This stance may cloud your judgement and lead you in the wrong direction or cause you to overlook vital facts.

2.2.28. Play the ball not the man

As with the previous rule, ensure that you separate the subject from the emotion of their misdeeds. This can be very difficult, but we need to be professional. We, as fraud investigators, have a job to perform and we need to investigate the fraud or misconduct and obtain the fairest and optimal result.

2.2.29. We have a duty towards the truth

I think I picked this rule up in a Hollywood drama. This should be read together with the previous rule on professional scepticism. This rule requires telling the truth and ensuring that you get to the truth by gathering all possible evidence.

This rule can be onerous, as we need to stand by this duty regardless of the outcome: being the innocence or guilt of the subject or whether we win the case or not. The truth is more important. This rule also entails standing up to management and ensuring that the truth comes out when they want to squash matters.

2.2.30. Queensbury rules apply

I am giving away my age by including this rule. This is something that is typically said when we want to emphasise that the rules of fair play/good sportsmanship should apply.

The actual 'Queensbury rules' relate to the rules on which the sport of boxing is based today. John Graham Chambers (a sportsman) drafted a code of generally accepted boxing rules in London in 1865. The code became known as the 'Marquess of Queensberry rules', as the 9th Marquess of Queensberry publicly endorsed the code.

Fighting fair in a boxing match is no different to investigating fraud cases (fighting crime). Even though we may dislike the subject of the investigation and/or what the subject has done, we always ensure that we 'fight' fair and stick to the rules. We want to win, but we want to win right!

I frequently quote this rule to inexperienced fraud investigators who are frustrated by investigations that are not proceeding as they would wish and/or who suggest unethical methods.

2.2.31. Principles are for rich people

When we are students and when we grow up we are taught to 'do the right thing'. After all, does not good always triumph over evil? So, it is a matter of principle then: when we find someone doing something wrong, we have to ensure that justice is served and must do what is necessary, correct?

Well, not always. I am certain that the readers of this are frowning at this notion and wondering what this can mean. We all agree that each person that we catch perpetrating fraud should go through an internal disciplinary procedure and that a criminal case should be opened, the relevant industry regulatory bodies informed of their member's transgressions and the necessary civil claims put in place. Well here comes the shock: not actually.

In reality, we need to do what is right for us or the business that we work for. All the actions that we can take, take time and cost money. The problem is that different people have different opinions of how far we should go on each case. Let me explain before you start to doubt my personal integrity:

I agree that we should always open a criminal case if a crime has been perpetrated. How much time and effort we spend on it may differ from case to case though. In most cases, you (as the fraud examiner) will be chomping at the bit wanting to go the whole hog. It will be those who control the purse strings who will be saying: Wow cowboy.' There is no point in throwing good money after bad.

I can think of numerous cases where the organisation that I worked for was right, but where it would have cost too much money to prove this. In an actual example, the company dismissed an employee in an internal disciplinary process. The employee then took the decision to external labour arbitration and 'won' by having the company's ruling overturned. In this case the ruling was overturned because the external arbitration commissioner did not apply their mind correctly. The problem was that we needed to appeal the matter in the High Court where the cost of advocates would have been exorbitant. We estimated that the appeal would have cost a minimum of ZAR 200K, while the incorrectly awarded damages payable by the organisation were ZAR 20K without the requirement to re-employ the subject. So, the company put its principles in its pocket and paid the compensation. It was not 'right' in terms of the fraud that was committed, but we did it because it was the cheaper option and therefore 'right' for the organisation.

If the company had unlimited resources and/or time, it could have thrown all sorts of expensive resources at the case and ensured that it won. This sort of thing hurts us 'principle-driven' people. So how do we console ourselves then? We ensure that the decision-makers know why we chose to walk away from the issue. We could make use of a fraud newsletter to circulate to the staff members in which we make a high-level statement that a person was dismissed for fraud.

This does not, however, always have to be the case. In some matters the organisation may spend the additional money just to send a strong message. The short-term additional expenses may pay deterring dividends over the medium-term.

This point should not be used as an excuse not to investigate a matter or to do a poor job and blame it on costs or lack of resources. Remember we have a duty towards the truth and to be professional. We therefore always try our best.

2.2.32. In this game, we take any score we can get on the board

This point builds on the previous point. As a rule, when building a case (an internal labour case or an external criminal matter), try to 'paint the picture as black as possible' by getting as much evidence as is available to build the strongest case possible, and to cover all possible outcomes.

The reality is, however, that we cannot guarantee that all our arguments and facts will be accepted. I am always happy if I get two-thirds of my arguments to stick in a case. This does not mean that we are cheating or manufacturing evidence. What this does mean is that we 'hedge our bets', by arguing as many points as we can, as we do not always know what the judge/commissioner will accept. Place a bet on as many horses in the race as you can to avoid losing because your one argument was rejected.

A second positive spin on this rule is that the subject sometimes chooses to resign in the face of the mountain of evidence presented, and declines to proceed. My advice is to always accept the resignation and move on. Take the path of least resistance and accept the resignation. The first objective is to get the perpetrator out of the organisation. The point is not to be able to have them dismissed by proving all elements of the case, but for them to leave in the easiest manner.

Criminal cases, labour cases and civil claims are independent of each other. You may still be able to open a criminal case, if you have sufficient evidence for a criminal matter, despite the resignation. Alternatively, you walk away knowing that you never quite got to the bottom of the matter and console yourself that at least you stopped the bleeding and that the person chose to leave without you having to defend a complicated internal labour matter.

2.2.33. There is life after the subject leaves

There are two elements to this rule. Firstly, picture this: I am standing at the coffee machine when the financial manager of a large concern comes past and starts making small talk with me. I comment on the fact that I have just returned from seeing the prosecutor on the Mr X matter. He says in a quizzing manner: 'Mr. X? Didn't he leave us a long time ago?' Almost as if to say: Why are you still busy with this? This is out of your hands now and you should be doing other things.

This scenario encapsulates managements' general attitude after the subject of an investigation has resigned and/or left the employ of the organisation. This is partly due to the fact that they do not have an understanding of what the wider process entails and partly because they just want the matter to 'go away' after the subject has left.

Your duty, as a fraud risk officer, is to educate them as to the end-to-end process. Their confidence will only be built after dealing with numerous such matters with them. Success breeds success.

There is a lot to be done after the subject leaves the organisation's employ. Chapter 7 on subsequent actions discusses this. Some examples of subsequent actions after the employee leaves the organisation are to:

- Report the matter to various parties, bodies and authorities, etc
- Open a criminal case
- Initiate civil recovery claims
- Embark on an external labour case
- Counsel victims
- Bolster internal controls
- Determine the full extent of the irregularities if not determined in the original investigation
- Bring the losses into the books of account
- Manage public image

The second element of this rule entails how people feel when the subject leaves the premises. Subjects seem to have a degree of control over other employees (Chapter 4 on conducting interviews refers in terms of the fraudster's personality and in terms of interviewing witnesses) despite being suspended. People seem to be much freer to talk once the subject is physically off the premises.

2.2.34. Every criminal/crime is known to/by someone

This rule has a direct and an indirect side. On the direct side, it is about identifying who knows what the criminal did. On the indirect side, it is about what people know, but do not realise that they know. People see things. Fraud investigators have a privileged view of all the information on a matter. Something that seems irrelevant to a witness can be highly relevant to the fraud investigator once seen in the context of the investigation. Some examples refer to demonstrate this point:

- *Sally was always irritable when she was doing the bank reconciliation. You later find out that she was manipulating the bank reconciliation to cover the cheques embezzled by her. Her aggressiveness was an attempt to keep people from looking at the manipulated bank reconciliations.*
- *A young bank clerk was driving an expensive high-performance vehicle. He told his colleagues that his mother had financed the vehicle for him. It later transpired that he was embezzling funds.*
- *An investigation was progressing steadily. I, out of pure chance, happened to ask one of the ladies who sat opposite the subject if she had noticed anything out of the ordinary. This lady turned out to be a keen observer who furnished me with many details of the subject's lifestyle and doings. These proved to be very helpful in resolving the matter.*

Try therefore to identify the things that did not make sense to the witnesses or that seemed out of place. Do not dismiss or reject anything that is said. Put these to one side, as their relevance may become clearer later.

2.2.35. 'You will get more right with honey than with chilli'

This phrase was first introduced to me by one of my friends and is his version of the phrase: 'You will catch more flies with honey than with vinegar.' I loved it so much that I said I was going to use it myself.

What this rule really means is that you will achieve far more by being nice to people than by being tough with people. This rule does not mean that you need to be passive or submissive. It simply means that you are respectful, persistent and pleasant. The rule definitely does not mean that you bribe people.

It is very difficult to refuse people or to be nasty to people who are being nice to you. I can think of numerous examples when I went to 'complain' about an issue, but decided in advance to be extra nice to the service staff. The service staff initially tried to respond in an aggressive manner, but were met with pleasantness. They then tried again and eventually gave up and were equally pleasant back to me.

Friends and family frequently tell me that I have 'the luck of the devil' and that it is unfair that I always just seem to get helped. I do not think luck has anything to do with it; I think it is about attitude. If you are pleasant and positive then people will respond in a similar manner to you. Everyone has enough pressure and unpleasantness in their lives, they do not need your bad attitude as well. Being angry is a decision you take to respond in a particular manner. When I am being angry it is about me wanting to show the other person that I am cross and not about me trying to resolve the issue. It is a choice that you can make. Refer to Chapter 4 on interviewing for further discussion on this.

As a side issue, always ensure that you are nice to PAs and receptionists, as these are the people who can open or close doors for you depending on your attitude.

2.2.36. Accountability is a team sport

I am looking at a newspaper cartoon picture of another corrupt government official found guilty of accepting bribes and I am thinking to myself: 'He could not have achieved this by himself.' We tend to focus on the subject/s of an investigation when dishing out accountability and taking action, when in truth there are typically many people who contributed (directly or indirectly) to the continuation and/or concealment of the fraud. We must ensure that all people are held accountable for the part they played in the fraud. Sanction handed down should be proportionate to their role and the severity of their actions, as dictated by individual circumstance.

For example, in a procurement-related fraud case:

- Did the senior procurement officer act in the organisation's best interests when he failed to conduct any due diligence and accepted the word of the operations manager when he said that he regarded the supplier as 'good'?
- Did the colleague who sat opposite the operations manager and who kept quiet when they became aware that the operations manager was running his own business, make themselves guilty of 'wilful blindness'?

- Is the finance manager, who blindly authorised the substantial payments for 'consulting services' in the absence of a contract or proof of delivery, guilty of dereliction of duties?
- Is the supplier who paid a bribe guilty of bribery and corruption and should the organisation continue to conduct business with them?
- Was the HR manager (known to have gone on many expensive weekends away with the subject) acting independently and objectively when he dismissed numerous whistle-blowing reports on the subject as slanderous, because the subject was a highly regarded senior leader within the organisation?

The fraud risk officer should ensure that all people who played a part are investigated and places where controls failed are evaluated to understand how best to intercede to prevent recurrence and/or to punish errant behaviour.

The fraud risk officer should also report on all people involved to ensure that their involvement is formally documented. The fraud risk officer should also recommend subsequent actions to be taken on these individuals (See Chapter 7 on subsequent actions in this regard). This would also be in line with the rule of 'Queensbury rules apply' in terms of the fairness of holding all people (not just one) accountable and that subsequent actions should be in line with their involvement.

Subsequent actions may involve:

- Opening criminal cases
- Embarking on civil cases
- Conducting internal disciplinary labour tribunals
- Holding counselling sessions
- Bolstering controls
- Reporting

CHAPTER 3

CONDUCTING THE INVESTIGATION

3.1. CHAPTER OVERVIEW AND INTRODUCTION

Each new investigation will differ from the previous investigation in terms of the type of misconduct committed, the modus operandi of the perpetrators and the methods you will need to employ to investigate the issues. There are however common 'categories' of investigation steps that can be considered. Each of these may be used to a greater or lesser degree, as the individual circumstances dictate.

The chances of 'success' (used widely in this context) are increased significantly if a structured approach is followed to investigate and address the matter. The purpose of this chapter is to give guidance on different investigation steps, which you may wish to consider employing in your investigation.

We commence with an overview of what investigations could entail. Then we discuss each of the five interrelated areas of the investigation. Some of the individual investigation building blocks (interviewing, data analytics, lifestyle audits and the 'group approach') are discussed in greater detail in their own chapters, as these are important aspects and require more in-depth discussion. All other investigation aspects are discussed in this chapter.

Finally, we refer to possible subsequent actions to investigations, including: reporting, and criminal, civil and labour cases, as well as bolstering of internal controls. These are also discussed in detail in subsequent chapters.

The primary goal of this chapter is to give you a mental picture of a typical investigation process to enable you to be able to walk through this process at any stage of an investigation for guidance.

3.1.1. Investigation overview

The 'divergent/convergent' diagram below is an interesting way of looking at investigations. The ribbon on the top of the 'kite' diagram below is a graphical representation of the high-level investigation phases in a typical investigation over time. These are discussed in more detail hereafter.

The kite section depicts the type of thinking that prevails over the investigation steps. The kite diagram is a widely used divergent/convergent thinking model. The model essentially demonstrates that your thinking will be 'divergent' at the onset of the investigation, in that you have to consider multiple options. The investigation thinking becomes refined as the investigation progresses and eventually becomes 'convergent' and focused on specific known aspects.

The kite part of the diagram has a delayed start in the awareness phase. This demonstrates that the awareness of the fraud may be known for some time before the matter is seen as something that needs to be addressed in a structured manner.

Once the fraud or the possibility of fraud is recognised, an approach can be planned. The investigation is then conducted in line with the plan, after which a conclusion is reached. Subsequent steps are embarked on as required.

The kite part of the diagram ends before the subsequent actions finish. This depicts that the subsequent actions may continue long after the organisation's investigation is complete and/or after any significant involvement by the organisation.

3.1.2. Detailed investigation steps

The subsequent diagram (spread over two pages) is a view of the most common detailed steps in an investigation. The purpose of the diagram is to represent the possible steps to give guidance to allow you to select the steps that are suited to your investigation. It will be helpful to keep this picture in mind when embarking on an investigation and to walk through it on a regular basis to check where you are in the process. Each of these possible steps is discussed in detail below.

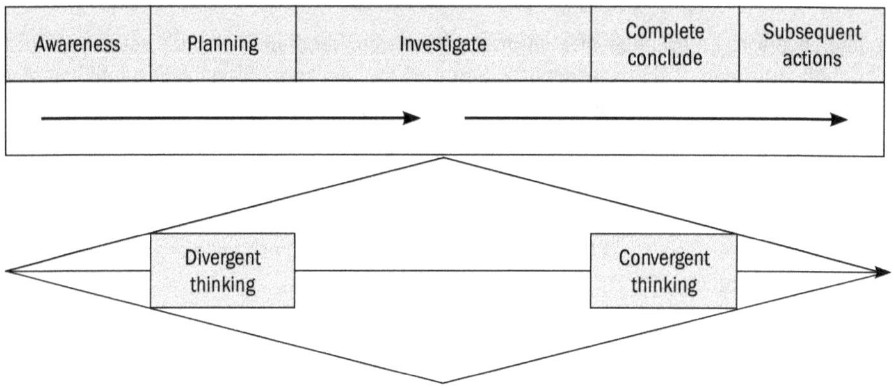

Figure 3.1 *Overview of the investigation process*

The following is a diagrammatic representation of the high-level stages in an investigation, as well as the degree of clarity that prevails over the course of a typical investigation.

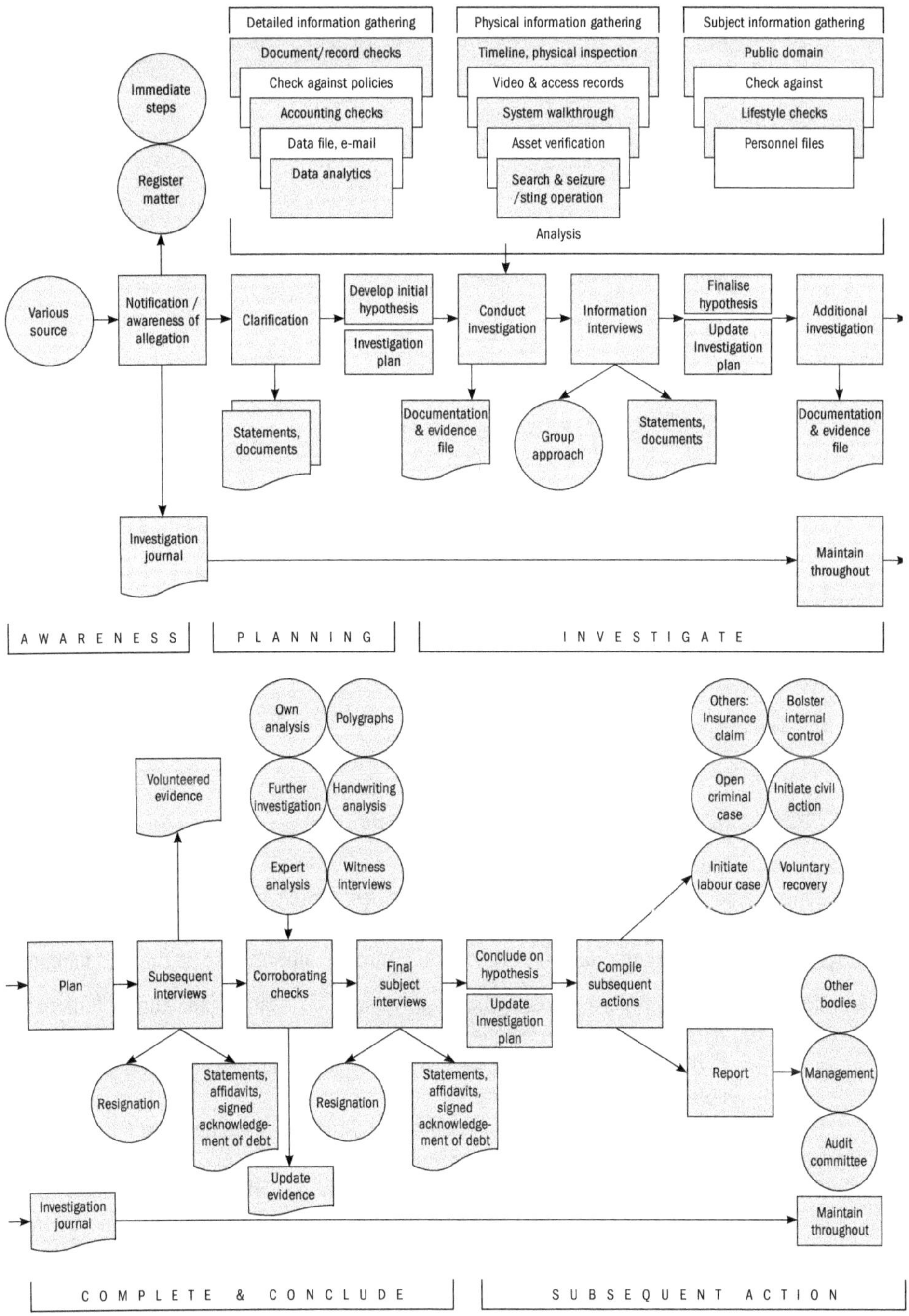

Figure 3.2 *Detailed investigation steps*

3.2. AWARENESS PHASE

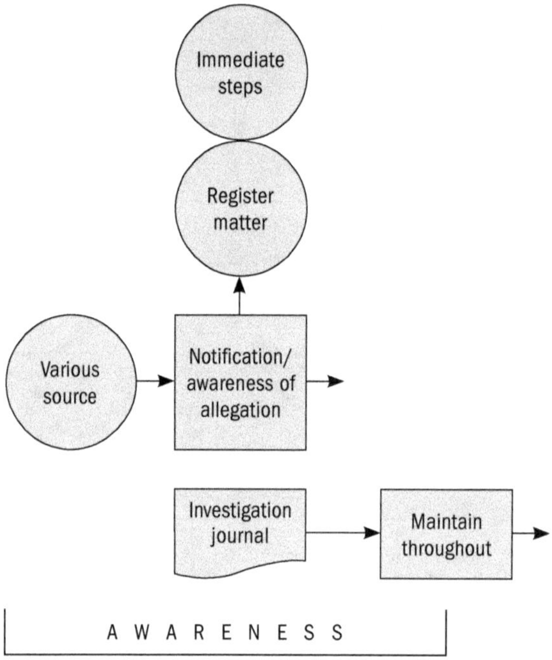

Figure 3.3 *Awareness phase*

3.2.1. Reporting and awareness of fraud cases

In general, there is a poor rate of identifying and reporting fraud matters. All fraud matters (suspicion of or proven) should be reported to the fraud risk services (FRS) function of an organisation. Chapter 1 on strategic fraud risk management sets forth the methods to increase fraud incident reporting. Figure 3.4 depicts the degree to which fraud matters are reported to the FRS function:

- If we consider the ACFE's statistics that on average 6% of an organisation's turnover is lost to fraud, then we have to presume that most fraud cases/acts of misconduct remain unknown, as this degree of financial loss (6%) is typically not visible, and 6% is high, so if it was visible, people would react to it.
- Some matters only become known to management and may even have been investigated to some degree by them, but are never reported to their organisation's FRS function.
- Other matters are reported late to the FRS function. This normally occurs after management has conducted their own investigation. Some of these matters are screened or only reported to the FRS function if they were able to prove them. Matters that they are unable to substantiate are dropped off the list.

- Even fewer matters are reported to the FRS function on time. These matters have the best opportunity for support and structure provided by the FRS's specialised skills.
- Very few matters by comparison are proactively identified by the FRS function and reported back to the senior organisational leadership.

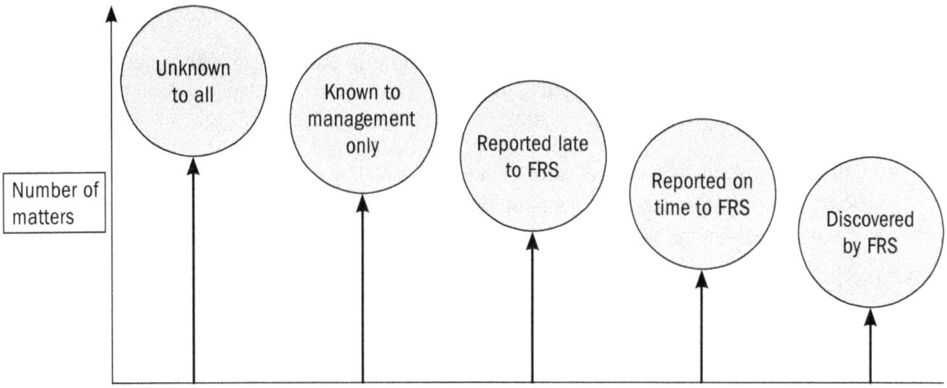

Figure 3.4 *Extent of fraud incident reporting*

3.2.2. Registration of fraud matters

All investigations commence in reaction to some initial information and/or suspicion. All fraud matters (suspected or proven) should be recorded in a central register under the control of the FRS function.

It is important to register the matter in a fraud database as soon as it becomes known. Do not wait for the matter to become clearer or to determine if there is a case to investigate. Reasons for early registration include:

- To ensure that all matters are dealt with and that none drop between the cracks
- To be in a position to give guidance as to how to conduct the investigation and/or on the treatment of subjects and which evidence is required – late registration of a matter may deny the opportunity for such advice to be given, which may negatively impact the investigation's successful outcome
- To ensure a more complete reporting picture of fraud matters within the organisation – part of fraud reporting is to report the number of matters reported per category and the outcome and/or status of current investigations
- To identify trends as soon as possible so as to be in a position to respond as quickly as possible.

3.2.3. Immediate steps

Different matters may, depending on the nature of the matter and/or the seriousness of the matter, require some immediate steps. These initial steps may include:

- The securing of evidence (our first rule refers)
- Ensuring the safety of individuals
- Removal (suspension) of offending individuals (depending on the seriousness and nature of the misconduct and the information available)
- Preparing of a formal response in the event that the media gets wind of the matter
- Some form of reporting (to the organisation's leadership or authorities)

The initial steps are normally conducted as soon as there is awareness of the matter and even before the matter has been investigated. It is also normal to make the following clear to the parties to whom the matter is being reported:

- An investigation has not yet commenced or that the investigation is in the very early stages and that no conclusions should be drawn yet.
- No pronunciation of innocence or guilt should be made at this stage.
- No action (unless agreed with FRS) should be taken by them until more facts are known.
- The purpose of your reporting is to ensure that they are aware of important matters in a timely manner.

The following factors may influence the need to immediately report matters:

- *Financial materiality*

  The financial value of the anticipated or actual loss will most definitely determine how quickly a matter is escalated and to whom. More material matters will need to be brought to senior management and the board's attention early on.

- *Strategic nature of the matter*

  More strategic matters could have a greater impact on the organisation and would therefore require bringing to the senior leadership's attention earlier. Perhaps the organisation is in the process of a strategic deal. The matter may need to be taken into account in terms of the financial value of the transaction or need to be highlighted to specific parties involved. The matter may also mean that the deal needs to be put on hold until an investigation can be completed. Examples of strategic deals include mergers and acquisitions and strategic contracts.

- *Reputational damage*

  Some matters could tarnish the organisation's name. On the other hand, the decisive and correct dealing with matters can also improve an organisation's standing/reputation. *One organisation in which I worked was renowned in the marketplace for being upright. Companies liked dealing with this organisation, as they knew that 'everything' would always be above board.*

- *Legal reporting requirements*

  There may, depending on the local laws, be a need to report matters of a particular nature or value to the authorities. Examples of criteria that may require reporting include:

  - Financial materiality of the fraud
  - Involvement of syndicates
  - Stock exchange requirements
  - US, British and EU regulations also require certain matters to be reported to their respective authorities, as soon as they are known or suspected

- *Heinous nature of the matter*

The nature of the crime may be such that it needs to be reported. As an example, the theft of petty cash by an old lady will not require early reporting. On the other hand, crimes involving drugs, extreme violence, sophisticated crime syndicates, human trafficking, minors, sexual offences, etc will require immediate reporting. Failure to report some of these matters to the authorities may result in fines to the organisation and/or imprisonment of the directors of the company.

- *Seniority of the subject or position of trust held by subject*

If the subject of the investigation is a very senior person and/or in a particular position of trust, then the board or senior management would want to know in a timely manner that they may no longer be able to trust this person. Failure to do so may continue to expose the organisation to the risk of losses and other damages.

- *Interested and affected parties*

The people (senior leadership, etc) and/or parties (suppliers, customers, authorities, etc) who are affected by the matter may dictate when and to whom the matter needs to be informed. In a similar fashion, those who have an interest in the organisation (financing institutions, shareholders, stock exchanges, etc) may dictate keeping these parties informed as soon as the matter is highlighted.

- *Timing of the event*

There may be a particular event that may require the early reporting of fraud. The events that we are talking about here have an external driver. Some examples include:

  - Financial reporting
  - Stock exchange submissions
  - When material contracts are being concluded
  - At the time of a merger, an acquisition, a joint venture, a sale of a legal entity, etc.

- *Expert requirement*

Certain matters may also require the use of an expert or a particular authority (for example Interpol) to proceed. The timing of when this person/body is involved may be key. Early notification and inclusion are advisable.

- *Claims*

Certain contractual and insurance claims require early reporting in order to qualify to be claimed. Non-reporting may result in disqualification of the claim.

- *Risks to others*

The likelihood of others being negatively affected may also dictate early reporting of the matter. Risks to others include:

  - Personal safety
  - Likelihood of the same event occurring to them/continuing to occur
  - The organisation may be held liable if they were aware of the matter and failed to inform others.

- *Nature of the goods*

Dangerous goods may necessitate special and decisive handling to prevent others being exposed to associated risks. The US has a list of goods that will require reporting to them if an entity/individual is found dealing in them. These goods all tend to be armament/explosive/military-type goods. A lot of the goods on this list will not be obvious to a normal person. Do not guess therefore and rather consult the list/an expert.

- *Recoveries*

The likelihood of recovery of misappropriated assets, funds and property may diminish as time progresses (our rule of: 'the best time to do something is immediately' refers). The timely seizure of assets and the recovery of illicit funds in bank accounts may be required. Many financial institutions will require a court order to freeze accounts or to release funds back to an organisation. Banks typically only freeze funds on the strength of a court order. Some may also, depending on their relationship with the organisation and the obvious nature of the matter, return funds regardless of the judicial process. The organisation may be required to sign a document protecting the bank for the early release of the funds. Banks may also be prepared to freeze illicit funds and retain them (not releasing them to anyone, but preventing them from being moved/used) until a court order can be obtained.

- *Evidence*

The integrity of evidence may be unable to be guaranteed after the matter becomes more widely known. Our first rule of forensics is: 'secure the evidence'. Early securing of evidence in line with all evidence protocols may, therefore, be imperative. Timely commencement of the gathering of evidence is always wise. For example: subpoenaing evidence can be a time-consuming process. Timely subpoenaing may prevent unnecessary investigation delays. It may, therefore, be wise to commence this process as soon as possible.

Various parties may also need to be informed early on in the process. There may not be a direct requirement for the fraud risk officer to report to the parties discussed below. The fraud risk officer should at least bring the reporting requirement to the senior organisation leadership's or external auditor's attention. It is recommended that this is done in writing to protect yourself. The parties who may require early notification of new fraud incidents include:

- *Police*

This should be done for all criminal cases. As mentioned before, local legislation may require early reporting of serious crimes, organised crime and/or syndicate crime. Early reporting of criminal matters and the developing of a cooperative relationship with the investigating officer, as soon as possible, is recommended.

- *Specialised government services and authorities*

Some examples of specialised units include the narcotics unit, customs, tax authorities, human trafficking unit or even a specialised commercial crime unit for material and sophisticated fraud matters. Other examples of specialised authorities include border control, customs, maritime authorities, coast guards, Interpol, EU, US, British authorities, anti-bribery and anti-competition authorities, maritime authorities and even the military.

- *Directors/senior management*

The confidentiality of investigations may be key and the likelihood of disrupting an investigation and losing the element of surprise always needs to be considered. Organisations however typically employ professional people at their senior levels who know how to ensure the integrity and confidentiality of investigations. It is always a good idea, if not a requirement, to keep the senior decision-makers aware of key events as they unfold. You can expect very bad reactions from senior executives whom were not updated on matters but feel that they should have been. It is not necessary to inform too many people of matters and you may also need to manage the expectation of leaders who feel that they should also be informed. A tactful explanation of the reporting that was already conducted with more senior people is advisable in such instances. You may be able to say that the senior members to whom you reported the matter felt that it was not necessary to communicate the matter any wider. It is recommended that you report to the most senior leadership first. Discuss and agree with them who else should be informed. The decision will be theirs in this way and you can always refer to their decision when confronted by those who were not informed.

- *Shareholders, owners, holding companies and subsidiaries lower down*

Similar to senior management, these are the parties that have the highest interest in the company. Consider when and if making these parties aware of a serious matter is required.

- *Clients, business parties, suppliers and other parties*

These are the parties that have significant business dealings with the organisation. There may be contractual obligations to report significant issues to them. Be selective in making these parties aware of matters. Also, ensure that awareness to parties outside of the organisation has senior leadership's sanction in advance.

- *Stock exchanges*

If the company is listed on a stock exchange, there may be a requirement to report serious matters to the respective stock exchange/investing public at a very early stage. Refer to local laws, as some countries have very onerous stock exchange reporting requirements.

- *Financing institutions*

Those parties providing the finance to the organisation may require notification. Again, there may be a contractual obligation to inform financial institutions of matters putting them at risk.

- *Insurance houses*

Reporting to an insurance house may be required to ensure that you have a future claim with the insurance house.

- *External auditors*

The external auditors may require notification of fraud matters to ensure that they design and conduct the required audit steps, and/or ensure that their opinion is representative of the true picture. External audit normally only requires notification around the time of their audit though.

- *Professional societies*

Professional societies include those for medical, legal, accounting, etc. Members can be disciplined within their own institutes as well. Members found guilty of misconduct may lose their professional qualifications. It is doubtful if reporting to professional societies would be an urgent requirement and may be required only at the conclusion of the matter.

3.2.4. Consequences

The failure to report matters on time and to the correct parties may result in any of the following consequences to individuals or the organisation:

- *Fines, penalties, imprisonment, etc*

  These can carry financial impacts to the organisation, which can be material. In extreme cases, company directors may be imprisoned for non-reporting of material matters. The local laws refer.

- *Reputational damage*

  Failure to report may result in unnecessary money and time being spent on press releases, conducting damage control and rebuilding the organisation's name.

- *Undue time spent defending actions*

  Unnecessary expenditure of cost, time and application of resources may be required to defend why the matter was not reported in a timely manner.

- *Trade disqualifications or exclusions*

  The organisation may be disallowed from entering or continuing to trade in a particular area. The organisation may no longer qualify for future contracts, with direct financial bearing on the organisation.

- *Professional body repercussions*

  Stock exchanges, accounting professional societies, etc may impose their own sanctions. Sanctions may be on their members holding professional designations. Sanctions may also be on professional firms who have failed to practise in line with the particular institute's regulations.

- *Dismissal or disciplinary procedures*

  You, as the fraud risk officer, may be subject to disciplinary procedures from the organisation for not conducting your work or for not acting in the organisation's best interests and for not informing the required parties.

- *The halting or restriction of the investigation*

  The investigation may be terminated or be significantly slowed down while those to whom notification was not given, or given late, decide how to proceed.

- *Future restrictions*

  The decision-maker's trust in you may be damaged resulting in a lack of confidence in future investigations or the restriction of future budgets.

- *Credit rating*

  The organisation may be downgraded on their credit rating which would impact their ability to obtain future funding.

- *The awarding of the investigation to another party*

  You, as the fraud risk officer, may be removed from the investigation and it may be given to another person or external party to conduct. We all take our investigations very seriously and we want to deal with 'our own' matters. We do not therefore want 'our' matters to be given to someone else to investigate because we made an error.

- *Cancelling of contracts*

Your firm (in this case a professional consulting firm) may lose the contract to investigate or other contracts already held with the organisation.

- *Misstatements*

Material events need to be declared in financial statements. Failure to do so could result in financial statement misstatements, business feasibility misstatements, or misstatements by the organisation to the public or press due to the lack of inclusion of the matter at hand.

3.2.5. Fraud reporting policy

It is recommended that a policy is drafted (may be part of the general fraud policy) to provide guidance on the requirements to report fraud. It would be best if an organisation-wide policy of reporting all suspected and actual matters within 24 hours of becoming aware of the matter, is established. Emphasis should be placed on the fact that there is no need to prove the matter, just becoming aware of the matter is sufficient to warrant reporting the matter.

Explaining the concept of 'willful blindness' to people may encourage them to report matters. This will introduce the notion to them that they may be held accountable/complicit due to the non-reporting of a matter. This may be sufficient to encourage them to report all matters.

Employment contracts and conditions of employment normally require employees to act in the best interests of the organisations that they represent. Employees may not be doing this if they fail to report misconduct that they are aware of. In extreme cases, where an employee purposefully did not report a matter, their contract of employment and/or the requirement to act in the best interests of the organisation may be used against them in an internal disciplinary hearing.

Reporting trends improve with education and visible investigation and/or action. Most people will report matters when they are aware of the requirements. People are more likely to report matters if they see other matters being investigated and if they see action being taken against perpetrators.

General fraud reporting trends will increase in the geographic areas, branches and companies where investigations are being conducted in unrelated matters, as people are aware of action being taken. By the same logic fraud reporting trends will typically dwindle and reduce in the areas where there is little investigation. Maintaining uniform organisation-wide awareness is an art.

3.2.6. Trend analysis

A lot of unsubstantiated misconduct claims may be an indicator of the need for fraud awareness training. It may also be an indicator of other organisational culture problems and/or dissatisfaction issues. Alternatively, it may be an indication of bigger problems.

As an example, in one company, we would send a team of people into a branch to investigate if we received three to four seemingly unimportant whistle-blower reports. Our interviews and control reviews always identified more serious aspects. The discussion on the group approach below refers.

3.2.7. Software

It is good practice to make use of some form of software to assist with the management cases. Your fraud registration system may be purpose-built case management software with whistle-blower reporting functionality. Alternatively, it may be an Excel spreadsheet or a manual register. The case register is not the place where detailed information concerning your investigation and/or proving your case is stored. The register is a single central repository where all matters can be registered, tracked, monitored and analysed for trends.

There are distinct advantages to using purpose-built software. Be cautious however when choosing software. Software salespeople will always promise that their software can do everything (including providing world peace). The problem is that you do not really know what software features you need until you have the wrong product. It is important to bring yourself up to speed in terms of what you are going to want in the future. Part of this will involve:

- Thinking about what your vision is for your work/the fraud function
- Speaking to your colleagues about their vision and needs
- Speaking to the organisation leadership about where the organisation is heading and how you will support this strategy
- Speaking to fellow fraud investigators and professional bodies (for example the ACFE) to understand in which direction the field is going
- Speaking to multiple software providers about features and traps)
- Speaking to fellow software users (for references and their needs and frustrations)

When selecting software, keep the following in mind:

- Avoid the trap of going with the one 'known' name or the most spoken-about name. It does not mean that this is the best product. Marketing is not everything.
- Avoid gimmicks. At the end of the day, the software needs to be used on a daily basis. Be practical! Ensure you involve the people who are going to use the software on a daily basis.
- Software is not a status symbol. It is a practical tool to make our lives more efficient.

Use a few demo versions of the software before acquiring a package, as the software does not always pan out to be as useful as promised by the salespeople. Play the one software provider off against the other. While they may not badmouth another product, they will be quick to tell you what their product can do. There are a number of criteria you should consider.

- Try to list how you work and how you wish to work in the future.
- Who needs to have access?
- Locations to be accessed from (travelling, regional offices, business, etc).
- Which features does the software have? Which are real usable features and which are gimmicks that will never really be used? Which problems does it solve and which does it not?
- Reporting requirements.
- Scalability.
- What is the largest and smallest number of users currently using the software?
- Number of users concurrently and individually.

- Licence fees and annual fees.
- Performance (desktop level, over the internet and conventional network) and performance capacity requirements.
- Database used, programming language, communication basis, interface protocols, etc.
- Ability to interface with other packages.
- Ease of installation.
- Ability to import legacy data.
- Data storage requirements (capacity, archiving, accessibility, data privacy, etc).
- List the current specialised packages that you have and determine if the new software will replace these (and if so how well), supplement these or slow these down.
- Ease of use.
- Ability to customise.
- Training available.
- Used by which other (similar) clients.
- What is the history of the product? Who developed it and for what purpose? How has it been changed over the years? How much support is there and what is the availability of support (international time perhaps)?
- Provide a history of version upgrades (what, when and why).
- What is planned for their next upgrade?
- Who owns the software?

Arrange a test of your data. Get the software service providers to work for their money. Have them set up and demonstrate exactly how your work will function on their software. Lastly, contact as many references that you can.

There is good and bad software out there. It is tough enough to investigate matters. Working with bad software aggravates frustrations. The person who will be using the software should have significant input into its selection. Department heads or IT professionals may not be the best people to make an isolated decision, as they are not the people who are going to work with the software on a daily basis.

3.2.8. Criminal cases

A printout of a reported matter from the organisation's whistle-blower system can be successfully used as the basis to register a criminal case. The police generally need at least 'grounds for reasonable suspicion' before they will register a case. The police investigation can then commence and necessary subpoenas, etc may be served and information and documents obtained.

3.2.9. Responsibility

As far as possible, encourage the reporter to register the matter themselves. Alternatively, register the matter yourself on behalf of the reporter to ensure that it gets registered.

In most organisations, the whistle-blower facility is operated by an independent service provider. This is good, as it creates credibility through independence. Only isolated organisational employees (fraud risk officers) should have access to the system to input matters over and above the whistle-blower service provider. The whistle-blower system should be used to report all matters on. As discussed previously, call the whistle-blower line yourself and recited the reporter's assertions verbatim if the whistle-blower reports a matter directly to you, but does not want to register it themselves. Do not amend their words, but ensure that it is registered completely on the whistle-blower system and as stated by the whistle-blower.

In other organisations, the fraud risk services personnel will have the ability to capture allegations onto the system themselves in addition to direct reporting functionality via the whistle-blower operator company. In this case, it would be possible to capture whistle-blower reports verbatim too.

3.2.10. Fields

The following are some of the information fields that may be included in a fraud database:

- *Date registered*

This is the date that the matter was reported to the investigation team/forensics team/group internal audit/etc. It may also be the date that the whistle-blower registered the matter on the online whistle-blower system. Alternatively, it will be the date that the fraud investigation team lists the matter on the whistle-blower system.

- *Date of event/s*

This may be the:

  - Actual date of the fraud event/s
  - Suspected date of the fraud event/s
  - First date of occurrence of the fraud event/s.

- *Name of reporter*

Try to get all names of the persons reporting the matter.

- *Position of the reporter*

This will be the position of the reporter of the matter in the organisation or in which capacity they are making the report.

- *Company/organisation of reporter*

The organisation which employs the reporter of the matter or who they represent.

- *Does the reporter want to remain anonymous?*

This is a key field. Whistle-blowers are protected by law (individual countries' laws refer). Remaining anonymous may be vital to the reporter's safety. Anonymity may also influence the success of the investigation by helping to ensure the integrity of information and evidence (not being tampered with due to the element of surprise). Guilty parties should not know who to try to influence and/or exercise pressure on. Investigations are generally not for public consumption and confidentiality may be key to protect innocent parties. There is also a chance that the subject of the investigation may turn out to be innocent and/or the allegation may be less serious than initially anticipated. It will then be important not to have unduly tainted the subject's reputation.

- *Contact details of the reporter*

This is important when further clarification and/or an affidavit and/or additional evidence is required. The need for further information will not necessarily be immediately apparent.

- *Preferred method of communication*

Sometimes the reporter would like to receive ongoing feedback on the status of the matter reported. Reporters may request the investigator to only e-mail them or to contact them on their mobile phone or between specific hours, etc. It is ideal if the whistle-blower system makes allowance to note report-back preferences. In other cases, the investigator may wish to clarify information with the reporter and need to contact them. The investigator would need to know what the reporter's communication preference is in advance.

- *Category of the event*

It is frequently useful, for reporting statistic reasons, to categorise matters reported into broad categories. As with the status of the matter, do not choose too many categories. Too many categories result in a merely academic exercise of working out into which category the matter falls, which does not add value. It is recommended that some (not all) of the ACFE's categories of fraud are used. Some examples include:

  - Bribery and corruption
  - Theft or misuse of assets
  - Misreporting

Having fewer categories also reduces unnecessary debates around the 'correct' category into which the matter should fall. This is not productive and does not add anything to the outcome of the matter. A lot of time can be wasted on the categorisation of frauds. It is advisable to get the audit committee's approval of the list of categories to ensure that you satisfy those to whom fraud statistics are being reported.

- *Summary of the event/s*

A short summary of what transpired and/or what the broad allegation is.

- *Attachments and other documents*

Reporters may wish to provide scanned or other electronic documents in support of the allegations.

- *Subject(s) of the investigation*

List the people who are alleged to be/have been involved in the matter. Be sure to list all relevant details of the subjects:

  - Names
  - Job titles
  - Organisations they work for
  - How they are involved
  - Contact details

- *Amount of loss*

The amount recorded may be an estimate of the loss, the suspected amount, or the known or proven amount.

- *The applicable currency*

Try, as far as possible, to record the local currency as well as the dollar/Euro/major currency used by your organisation, where relevant.

- *Status of the investigation*

As mentioned under fraud categories, it is better to have fewer status indicators than too many. Some examples include:

- Open:
  - Registered
  - Under investigation
- Closed:
  - Proven/substantiated
  - Unsubstantiated/suspicion unproven
  - Dismissed as untrue
  - Further action required
- Criminal case
  - Registered
  - Trial ongoing
  - Conviction (specify)
  - Acquittal
- Labour matter:
  - Registered
  - Awarded in employer's favour
  - Awarded in employee's favour
  - Taken under appeal
- Civil case:
  - Opened
  - Recovery obtained (specify claimed and obtained)
  - Claim dismissed (specify if with costs)

- *Investigator to whom the case has been assigned*

This will be a fraud investigator or the person in the business who you request to conduct the investigation.

- *Other parties who have ready access to case material*

In larger organisations, there may be more than one person who requires access to the case database.

3.3. PLANNING

Sound and flexible planning is imperative for successful investigations. Remember our rule: 'The three things you should always do are: number 1, plan; number 2, plan and number 3, plan.'

Sound planning of an investigation has a direct bearing on the degree of success of the investigation and includes consideration of:

- The sequencing and executing of logistical and administrative aspects
- Technical investigation aspects (interviewing skills, criminal psychology, IT forensics, etc)
- Stakeholder management
- Subsequent actions (civil cases, criminal cases, internal labour tribunals, bolstering of controls and building the ethics and morale of the organisation)

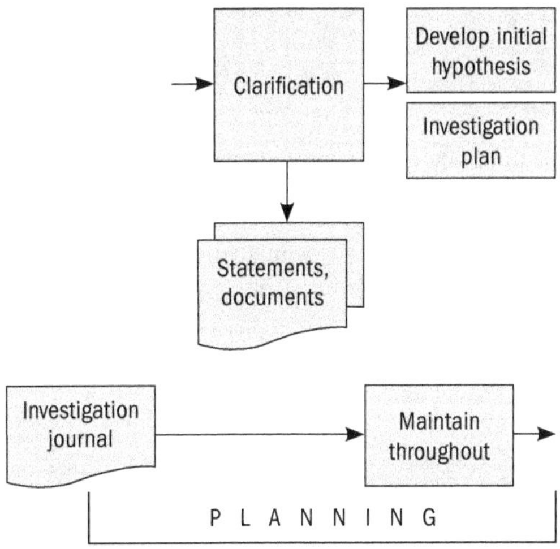

Figure 3.5 *Planning phase*

3.3.1 Stakeholder management

Stakeholders can make or break an investigation. It is wise to anticipate and manage stakeholders in a manner that ensures an optimal investigation outcome for the organisation.

Commence by listing the most important stakeholders that may have an interest and/or influence in the investigation. Formally anticipate and record their support of you, the investigation, the FRS function and/or the organisation. Design suitable interventions to manage stakeholder interests to prevent derailment of the investigation.

Stakeholders may include:

- The audit committee or the board of directors
- Senior management
- Direct line management
- The fraud risk function (internal politics)
- Internal audit
- External audit
- The organisation, colleagues and friends of the subject or victim
- External parties (suppliers and clients)
- Investors and financiers
- Whistle-blowers

- Government agencies and authorities
- The public.

Stakeholder management is largely to do with the optimal management of the interests of specific people and less about groups of people unless the group has a common goal and/or viewpoint. Potential stakeholder management interventions are discussed in Chapter 1 on strategic fraud risk management.

3.3.2. Classification

The next phase is to start to clarify, classify and structure the information that you have. This will determine the next steps in terms of:

- Investigating or not investigating ('stay or go' decision)
- Conducting an initial investigation
- How to structure your investigation
- Gaining early insights into the nature and extent of what has happened.

3.3.3. Obtaining evidence

Remember our discussion on 'the rules'? The most important rule was to secure the evidence. The integrity of evidence may also be vital in a criminal matter (discussed later). There are essentially two elements to this rule; namely, 1) obtaining the evidence and 2) the integrity of the evidence. Both of these elements talk to the ultimate usability of the evidence.

a. Element of surprise

The element of surprise may be imperative when obtaining evidence. The evidence (physical and/or electronic) must be secured as soon as the fraud/possibility of fraud becomes apparent to you. This will prevent it from being destroyed by the perpetrator in an attempt to prevent being detected or implicated. Evidence may also be inadvertently destroyed through the normal course of business. For example: older camera footage may be overwritten by newer footage. If the misconduct was captured on the older retained footage, this may be overwritten and lost unless copied in advance.

b. Integrity of evidence

The integrity of evidence has many facets. All of these facets include the usability of the evidence, either in your internal investigation or in subsequent external proceedings. Most of the facets are concerned with securing the evidence in a usable form from the perpetrators or from the scene of the fraud. Others are concerned with keeping the evidence away from inadvertent destruction or corruption.

c. Use of evidence

The ultimate goal of assimilating evidence is to use it. Evidence can be used:

- To prove your case (in the investigation phase still)
- In internal labour or external labour tribunals
- In criminal cases
- In civil cases
- In internal enquiries to bolster controls

The eventual use of the evidence will dictate how the evidence is to be collected. Another important aspect to be introduced here is how your investigative methodology supports 'the chain of evidence'. If the evidence is to be used in a criminal court (and you will rarely be aware of this at the onset of your investigation) you may, as the investigator, need to testify as to:

- What your investigation entailed and why you did it
- How you obtained the evidence and how you ensured the integrity of the evidence from the time that you gathered it up until the trial.

Documenting of these aspects and how best to secure evidence as well as which evidence is of value to an investigator is discussed in greater detail under point 3.3.6. Some examples include:

- Setting down witnesses' recollections into an affidavit
- Obtaining physical documents (may require a court order – discussed under points 3.2.3 and 3.4.2.e)
- The use of specialised electronic tools and methods
- Documenting the 'chain of evidence'
- Documenting investigators' testimonies.

d. Chain of evidence

The chain of evidence (also called the 'chain of custody') is a simple but important concept to be borne in mind during investigations. This is because defence teams frequently try to discredit evidence by arguing the following:

- Their client is innocent, as the evidence could have been tampered with.
- The evidence was not retrieved by a suitably qualified person and/or using an 'acceptable' method.
- The evidence is incomplete and/or inaccurate.
- The evidence does not prove what is being testified to.
- It cannot be guaranteed that their client was the author of the evidence.
- The evidence was intentionally manipulated or manufactured to some degree.

Investigators may be required to testify in criminal matters as to their investigation steps and more importantly, to the 'chain of evidence'. The 'chain of evidence' is the chain of events that transpire from prior to the time that the evidence is first identified up until it is presented in court. I say 'prior to the time' as we need to consider any events or people who could have affected the integrity of the evidence even prior to the evidence being identified. Try to determine, therefore, once you become aware of the evidence if there were any events or people that could have affected the integrity of the evidence.

The chain of evidence is a legal concept and not something that must be left to trial and error or guesswork. If you get it wrong, your evidence may be inadmissible and this may cost you your case.

It is imperative therefore that you understand and abide by the laws of the country in which you are conducting your investigation.

3.3.4. Types of evidence

The following includes some of the different types of evidence that you may be required to attest to the chain of evidence for:

- *Source documents*
  Source documents are the source of transactions. Examples of documentary evidence include: invoices, receipts, delivery notes, purchase orders, requisitions, reconciliations, creditor statements, etc. These are diverse and would include all documents associated with a transaction and/or the matter that you are dealing with. These documents normally show amounts, sources of funds, destinations of funds, companies used, accounts used, etc.
- *Accountability setting documents*
  While these documents form part of the larger aforementioned group of documents, this requires emphasising as a subcategory, as some documents create a unique accountability and/or demonstrate knowledge of and/or involvement in a matter. Examples of such documents include signed contracts, meeting minutes, disciplinary proceedings, e-mails sent to or from people, written requests for something, etc. Fuel bills, restaurant bills, credit card slips, vehicle tracking information (standard security devices fitted to vehicles) are all examples of documents and information that could 'place' a person at a particular point in time. For example: if a person signed a contract, they must have had knowledge of its contents or if a person signed a restaurant credit card slip then they must have been in the restaurant.
- *Transactional information*
  Transactional information includes all operating information, accounting information, payroll transactional information, etc. Most information these days will be electronic in nature (be in electronic media or have its source in electronic media and be printed out). So, while a lot of information will fall under the 'electronic' information category, it is important to see transactional information separate from e-mail and other general electronic information, as it deals directly with the transactional side of the matter that you are dealing with. An example could be a transaction listing of all transactions including the disputed transactions.
- *General information*
  - General information includes:
  - Contracts
  - Correspondence (letters)
  - Meeting minutes
  - Training courses (to prove that a person had knowledge of a policy or a procedure).
- *Electronic evidence*
  This would include any electronic file found on any electronic device (actual or virtual device):
  - Computers and servers
  - Firewalls, routers and network devices

- Internet service provider (ISP) records (these are the records from the company that provides internet connection to the organisation)
- Cell phones, tablets, etc
- Digital cameras
- Electronic storage devices (flash drives, external hard drives, cloud-based servers, 'drop boxes', 'NAS' databases, etc).

Examples of electronic evidence on these devices include:

- Access records
- Transaction logs
- 'Mac' (machine) numbers (a computer device's unique number)
- IP addresses (internet protocol address)
- Photos and videos
- E-mails
- Metadata (data about data).

- *Video footage and still photos*

These may originate from the organisation's own camera systems. Alternatively, examine nearby organisations and buildings to determine if they have camera systems that could assist you by showing what actually occurred in the period you are investigating. Be sure to obtain a copy of the footage to prevent it being overwritten in the normal camera storage cycle.

An example of where company cheques were being fraudulently cashed: The bank had camera footage of the cheques being cashed. The footage was imperative to place the one subject at the scene and to prove their involvement. The bank was successfully convinced to secure the video footage on a separate device for possible later use in court and to prevent overwriting. The bank did not give a copy of the footage to the investigator, but they did, however, view the footage and they could advise who had chased the cheques. The police were directed accordingly.

The advent of mobile devices has seen an increase in the number of privately recorded video footage and photos. This footage may be volunteered directly to you and/or may be circulated on social media. It is also good practice to take photographs of the scene when you arrive and before people carry on with their normal day. Try to get photographs under normal circumstances and at the time that the crime was committed (for example at night). Smartphones typically save the location where and the time that the photo was taken, which may be useful.

- *Office plans and layouts*

In some cases, the layout of the premises may be required:

- For evidence
- To solve aspects of the investigation
- To give context and to illustrate aspects to the members of a tribunal

It is also recommended that you physically walk through the area where the misconduct occurred. Try to understand what happened and compare this to what you know and what people are alleging. Determine if this seems plausible.

Sit at the subject's desk/workspace and try to visualise the area as the subject saw things on a daily basis. Time the duration to do things. Determine if they could have seen or done what they are purporting to have seen or done.

- *Audio recordings*

As with video footage, audio recordings may be those made by yourself or alternatively by a third party. Ensure that you establish what the local country's privacy legislation dictates are in terms of the recording of conversations:

  - In some countries, you require the person's permission to record them.
  - The recording of a third-party conversation of which you are not a part will most likely be prohibited unless submitted by a person who was.

The discussion on the recording of interviews in Chapter 4 on interviewing also refers. Other examples of audio recordings include voice recordings (for example, from telephone operators/call centres) and telephone history records.

- *Registers*

Registers can form part of electronic information or hardcopy documents. Registers are singled out here to focus you on their usefulness:

  - Physical access records (electronic or manual registers) – these can prove who had access, when and for how long.
  - Asset registers – to prove who had access to which assets.
  - Vehicle tracking records – organisations frequently subscribe to the technology ('in-vehicle' monitoring devices) that gives them information on the location of their vehicles and driving speeds an styles (for example acceleration and braking). This can place a person or vehicle at a particular place at a particular time and date (for example: in a scrap yard, where scrap metal was illegally sold). Please note however that in some countries (US and Europe) unions may regard the use of such records as an invasion of the driver's privacy and do not allow the use of such records without the driver's express consent or at all,
  - Document or record registers – to prove who had access to which files and records. In some organisations, original files need to be signed out to an individual.
  - Logical access records (who logged onto the computer systems and when).
  - Social media. What do the person's public domain social media accounts say that they were doing at the time? Compare this to the other facts. For example: a subject's Facebook account shows a picture of him walking hand-in-hand on the date in question with his girlfriend on a beach with brown sand (typical of the east coast of Africa) and not white sand, which is typical of the west coast where he is purporting to have been.

- *Physical evidence*

Physical evidence includes what you see and/or find when you look at the subject's physical workspace or the area in which the matter transpired (for example the place where the theft took place):

  - Workspace environments
  - Fingerprints, footprints, tyre prints, DNA, blood, dirty marks against a wall, dust and dirt, hair samples, skin, etc

- Physical items (doors, windows, items left behind like gloves, items interfered with by the perpetrators)
- Any articles left on a scene of a crime by the perpetrators, including items of clothing, items that they used to obtain access (eg crowbar, bolt cutters, cutting torch, etc), containers that they used to carry items (eg bags, trolley, crates, etc), items they used to cover their tracks (eg gloves, balaclava, etc)
- Measurements and timing (how long does it take to walk from one point to another, etc).

It is very useful to photograph the physical environment and to walk through the area where the incident took place. Try to place yourself in the position of what the subject and/or witnesses saw. Think in terms of practicalities and compare this to what is alleged to have occurred. Some of the information about the physical location may only have been known to a person who works for the organisation. What does this tell you about who the subject could be?

- *Assets*

These may include assets that were taken and/or recovered, which may also be a form of evidence. Some examples include:

- Stock of finished goods
- Raw materials
- Computers
- Vehicles
- Livestock on farms.

- *Policies and procedures*

These will be documents and files detailing how the organisation has decided to work.

- *Recollections*

One of the most important forms of evidence is a person's recollection of what transpired. Lock down the investigator's and all other people's recollections. This can be achieved by putting this evidence into an affidavit. These affidavits may include reference to the chain of evidence as well. Affidavits are discussed at length in Chapter 8 on reporting.

3.3.5. Testimony

It is imperative that you are able to recollect and recount in your testimony:

- From whom you received the evidence
- When you received it
- Where the evidence was stored before and after you obtained it
- Who had access to the evidence before and after you obtained it
- For which period/s they had access
- The purpose of them having the evidence
- When you handed it to the authorities
- To whom you handed it.

Use an investigation journal in which to record details of the evidence. Your investigation journal could even be submitted as part of your evidence to support your testimony.

Do not try to hide the fact that the source of your evidence may not have been perfect. It may discredit your evidence if it comes out later and that you were trying to conceal it. You do not have to advertise the fact, but the 'Queensbury rules' should always apply and you need to be ethically correct even if you are unable to prove something.

If you have a significant amount of evidence that multiple parties are accessing during the investigation, then it is recommended that you maintain an evidence register. Sign evidence in and out, clearly stating:

- Date taken
- Date returned
- Taken by whom
- Returned by whom
- Reason taken.

As far as possible, do not work on originals – rather make a working copy.

3.3.6. Integrity of evidence

Before taking the evidence into your control, determine what may affect the integrity of the evidence and/or if a subpoena is required to legally obtain the evidence. Take advice from local legal counsel, as required.

As far as possible, only give copies of the evidence to those who need it. It is also wise for you to only work on copies of the evidence and not to work on the original documents. This is because it is easy to write on the documents while you are working, which may affect the integrity of the evidence. The following aspects may affect the integrity of evidence:

- *Legal aspects*

  If a subpoena is needed then try to ensure that the investigating officer obtains one at their earliest convenience. Expect that obtaining a subpoena could delay the investigation. Do not obtain evidence without a subpoena if required. Illegally obtained evidence may be dismissed and you may be subject to sanction for your actions. Financial institution records and telecommunication records normally require a subpoena. If you can encourage the subject to volunteer evidence, then you will not need a subpoena. Ensure that you have a witness to this or in exceptional cases that they sign that they are volunteering the evidence to you. The person volunteering the evidence may specify restrictions of its use, however. You may need to consider these restrictions before accepting the evidence. If they volunteer evidence, it is suggested to obtain it as quickly as possible to prevent them from changing their minds. Negotiate the usage thereof afterwards. Our rules refer: 'The best time to do something is immediately' and 'The most important rule is to secure the evidence.'

- *Method of evidence retrieval*

  For example: did you request a general finance department clerk to sort through boxes and to obtain the invoices in question on your behalf or did you identify and retrieve the documents yourself? Is the evidence made up of manual documents or electronic evidence? In each case, how was this obtained and by whom? In terms of electronic files, did you switch on the computer yourself when it was seized? Did you copy the files yourself onto a storage device? Alternatively, did you make use of an expert to access the machine and to retrieve the information? Did the expert follow the required protocols and was the electronic evidence encrypted?

Consider that more than one person may need to attest to the chain of some evidence, as you can only attest to what you did. For example, a computer forensic specialist may have retrieved the information and you may have analysed it.

- *Person who retrieved the evidence*

Who retrieved the evidence? Are they sufficiently independent? Do they need to be qualified or authorised to retrieve the information (like an IT forensics specialist)?

- *Method of storage*

How has the evidence been stored? For example: was it stored in a plastic evidence bag? Were electronic devices stored in non-static containers, etc? Were documents stored in a fireproof safe with restricted access?

- *Medium*

Is the evidence in an electronic format or is it hardcopy paper? Each may require a different treatment. Are the hardcopy documents originals or copies?

- *Purpose of the evidence*

In line with our rule, 'Keep the end-game in mind', understand the purpose that the evidence will serve. This will dictate the method of treatment of the evidence. For example, will fingerprints be required or is the document to be used for illustrative purposes only? It is recommended to be conservative with your treatment of evidence, as the purpose of the evidence may change over the progression of the investigation. Certain evidence might not be contested and special treatment may therefore not be required.

- *Status of the evidence*

Is the evidence an original or a copy? The 'best evidence' rule requires:

  - An original document
  - Alternatively, a copy of a document with a person's testimony as to the authenticity of the document
  - Lastly, a copy.

Why is the original not available? How do you know the copy is complete and accurate?

- *Place of storage*

Where was the evidence stored prior to you obtaining it and where have you, as the investigator, stored it subsequently? You may need to be able to answer to the restricted access to the evidence. Consider exposure to the elements or other aspects that may affect the evidence (such as strong electronic or magnetic fields).

3.3.7. Investigation journal

It is recommended that you maintain an investigation journal from the time that it is decided to investigate a matter. While we all work on numerous matters at the same time, it is recommended to maintain a journal per case or at least a separate journal per significant matter that you investigate. This is a habit or a discipline that needs to be formed.

A handwritten journal tends to be the most practical. A hardcover bound journal will also:

- Demonstrate that no pages have been removed
- Show that the chronological sequence has been maintained
- Prevent you from losing individual pages/notes.

It may not always be practical to have your journal handy every time that you take a call or perform some small aspect of the investigation. In that case, it is recommended that you make notes in some other place (handwritten or electronic) and that you later transcribe these into your journal when you get the opportunity.

Similarly, if you forget something, then just record it in your journal with the date that you recorded it, but refer to the original date to which the event is applicable to. Furthermore, if you only start using the journal sometime after the commencement of the case, then write the date from when you commence the journal and then give a recount of the events that transpired prior to commencing the journal. Ensure that you carry a reference over to a new journal from a completed journal so that there is a clear link between the journals.

The investigation journal is a valuable source from which to compile affidavits. Some of my colleagues record all their related interviews in the journal as well. You can record the following in the journal:

- Your investigation plans
- Your thoughts
- Outstanding steps
- People to include in the scope of your investigation
- People spoken to
- What was discussed
- Pieces of evidence collected.

If you are asked, in an attempt to discredit your testimony, how you managed to recall all the events and how the court can be sure that these are correct, you can simply present your investigation journal and they can cross-reference it to your affidavit and/or to the evidence that you are presenting and/or your testimony.

3.3.8. Clarification and structuring

As per the introduction, in this stage of the investigation we wish to structure, clarify and classify the information and/or evidence that we have as early as possible to determine:

- What information and evidence we have
- What evidence is still required?

- Which investigation steps will need to be conducted to obtain evidence
- What the potential charges could be (this will define the evidence required, for example, if you need to prove a movement of funds from the organisation to the subject, a bank statement may be the best evidence to show the transaction out of the one and into the other)
- Who the subject/s of the investigation could be.

'Mind maps' are very useful to draw high-level views of the information at hand and what is still required to be done. Lists are less user-friendly for this purpose. Lists are good for summarising what is already known, but not for showing gaps of what is missing. Chapter 10 on structuring the forensic function also refers here with regards to the fraud response plan.

3.3.9. Notification source

Commence by understanding how and from where the fraud or potential fraud has come to your attention. This is important as it may have a bearing on the integrity of the information/evidence. Some examples of the source of the notification include:

- *Whistle-blowers*

As per the ACFE's annual report to the nations, the most common source of fraud identification is whistle-blowers. There is a fundamental difference between a whistle-blower and any of the other parties mentioned below. A whistle-blower's notification has a strong voluntary element to it. Fraud identification may be considered an organisational duty (albeit partial) of all of the other sources discussed below. Whistle-blowers have a reason for bringing to matter to your attention. Some reasons for reporting matters include:

  - Strong personal moral continence
  - Personal vendetta
  - Ignorance of the full matter/consequences.

The reason why the person is reporting it is less important, but try to understand it nevertheless. Concentrate on trying to understand who the whistle-blower is and then on what their motive could be. The more important aspect, however, is that the matter has been brought to your attention. All information will need to be corroborated (whether from a disgruntled dismissed employee or from a credible, highly ethical employee) and the corroboration of the evidence is what determines its integrity. Do not dismiss any allegations just because they come from a disgruntled person. As said previously, take all the information that you can get and corroborate it later.

In a particular example, a corruption matter was repeatedly reported to the organisation but never finalised. When it was reported to me again after I joined the organisation, I researched the previous investigators' work. I saw that they had asked the whistle-blower to provide direct evidence of the alleged corruption. Corruption cases are the most difficult to prove, but there are established methods by which to investigate these (see Chapter 9 on examples of fraud). Not surprisingly, the whistle-blower was unable to provide direct evidence. Shockingly enough the inept investigators dismissed the very serious allegations as unsupported mutterings from a disgruntled supplier. However, using standard techniques,

I was able to prove the case without too much trouble. This was not because I was such a competent investigator, but rather because the previous investigators were so incompetent and unwilling.

Another difference between whistle-blowers and other sources, discussed below, is that there may be a material risk of reprisal for whistle-blowers reporting matters. This risk is greatly diminished when fraud identification is part of the source's functional duties, as it is for internal auditors (ie not a whistle-blower). This is because it may be perceived that they were just doing their job and did not go out of their way to report the subjects. Exceptions apply, for example, when crime syndicates want to silence any witnesses and/or investigators. It is however impossible to know precisely if a person may be in any type of danger or not. It is therefore advisable to treat each situation as if you are trying to avoid the worst possible outcome.

I have had one occurrence when a whistle-blower was beaten up and had to flee his job to another town 200 km away. Whether or not it was my fault and/or if I could have been more careful still haunts me.

- *Management*

Management may detect irregularities as a result of the performance of their normal management duties. The irregularities found may be fraud. Discuss with them what they found and why they regard it as suspicious.

An example follows of when a regional financial manager phoned me up and started to ask me control-related questions, based on irregular account postings that he had identified. He was reluctant to tell me why, but I persisted and he gave me some background. I told him that he had a fraud on his hands and that the lady who was responsible for posting the questionable transactions was the subject. He rejected my notion. I nevertheless jumped on a plane and went to investigate. Sure enough, my suspicions were correct and I proved that the lady had embezzled large sums of money by circumventing the controls due to a lack of adequate segregation of duties in the area of her responsibility.

- *External party*

I suppose that anyone reporting an unknown fraud matter to management can be regarded as a whistle-blower. In this case, we are not referring to a whistle-blower as such, but more to an external institution who (in the course of their daily activities) identifies irregularities or who provides information. Examples of external parties that have brought frauds to my attention in the past include:

  - Banks
  - Suppliers.

- *Internal audit*

Internal audit may detect fraudulent activity as a result of their audit tests. A lot of internal auditors do not, however, have a 'fraud' mindset. The purpose of their tests is also frequently only to prove if controls are functioning as intended. The purpose of their tests is mostly not to detect fraud. Auditors also make use of sample testing and it cannot be guaranteed that their sample will include a true cross-section of the population and/or fraudulent transactions. My experience of a low rate of fraud identification by internal auditors is supported by the ACFE's annual 'Report to the Nation'. *On several occasions, I do however recall how surprise petty cash counts by my internal audit colleagues identified misappropriation of funds.*

- *External audit*

As with internal auditors, external auditors' procedures may detect fraudulent activity. External auditors are generally concerned with the reliability and integrity of the financial numbers that are being reported. Fraud outside of this scope is unlikely to be detected by them. External auditors' materiality cut-offs are also normally very high (sometimes in the millions) and frauds/fraudulent transactions may fall outside of their sample parameters. External auditors furthermore do not always concern themselves with why the numbers are not accurately stated. So, on a positive note, they will say that yes, the financial statements are materially correct and/or a true representation of the financial position of the organisation. In other words, there is not large-scale financial misstatement fraud present. So, if the balance sheet says that there are one million in debtors, then this is reasonably accurate.

What they do not do is say that there were no other occurrences of fraud unrelated to the financial statements. Also, if they are unable to substantiate the numbers, they do not dig through each number to understand if there was fraud. They just say that they are unable to conclude on the completeness and correctness of the numbers. It is up to management to do this. The reader of the financial statements will be informed that they cannot rely on the numbers.

As an example, let us say that the external auditors were unable to satisfy themselves as to the completeness and correctness of the accounts receivable (AR). Management may tell the board that yes, they are aware that they have an AR problem and they are in the process of implementing a new AR system. What management might not tell the board is that the reason why AR is in a mess is that they have been misappropriating the receivables. Fraud will not be identified in this case.

The board could contract the external auditors over and above their annual audit, to investigate the AR system and/or AR balances in detail. This would result in a greater chance that fraud could be identified, but is not part of the external auditor's normal duties. The aforementioned discussion is not a criticism; it is merely stating that auditors (internal and external) generally have different focuses and purposes.

- *Forensic auditors/fraud examiners*

Formal fraud investigation of a matter may identify wider previously unknown areas or extents of fraud.

I have experienced numerous situations where the fraud examiners of one organisation detect potentially fraudulent activity in another organisation and then alert that organisation as a professional courtesy. I am also in the habit of preparing management by saying that it is normal that the investigation will identify more fraud or the true scope of the fraud. They should therefore not think that the initial questionable transaction is the full extent of the fraud.

- *Authorities*

Police and/or other officials (customs officials, border control, tax officials, immigration authorities, etc) may approach the organisation and inform them that they have identified fraud and/or are investigating irregularities.

- *Accidental discovery*

Accidental discovery is also a common source of fraud identification. As an example, the fraudster goes on leave and/or resigns from the organisation and they are no longer able to continue their scam/hide the irregularities. Someone else takes over their responsibilities and detects the fraud.

Numerous cases that were brought to my attention come to mind after a person had resigned or had absconded. While there is very little that you can do to change accidental discovery, you may want to:

  - *Increase detective controls*
  - *Encourage disclosures and highlight reporting in fraud awareness training sessions*
  - *Enforce minimum leave policies*
  - *Ensure job rotation, where applicable.*

- *Effective functioning of internal controls*

The best antidotes to fraud are sound internal controls. Sound internal controls may prevent, detect and even correct irregularities. Common examples of good controls identifying fraud include:

  - A bank reconciliation that detects a fraudulent payment that was honoured by the bank without being processed in the organisation's books first
  - Pre-payment authorisation detecting an unauthorised payment prior to processing/ honouring the payment
  - The approval of a payroll master file change by a person independent of the change, detecting a fraudulent change.

- *Computer-assisted audit techniques (CAATs) and/or embedded parameter testing*

Highly mature organisations may have designed and implemented special computer programs to detect and prevent fraud. These are different from standard internal controls as they are purpose-built routines.

- *Professional insight and experience*

As an experienced anti-fraud practitioner, you may gain insights into aspects over and above a formal investigation that may indicate fraud. I pride myself on continually sharpening my professional instinct to improve my insights to detect irregularities. Furthermore, I find that I am able to apply more industry-specific knowledge to identify common frauds the longer I am in a particular industry.

- *Fraud vulnerability analysis*

A formal analysis of fraud vulnerabilities within a business process may detect fraud. These types of assessments may be conducted by:

  - Auditors
  - Fraud investigators
  - Risk managers

- Management themselves
- Loss control specialists
- External consultants.

Fraud vulnerability assessments may be performed as part of a formal management consulting exercise on wider business processes. Alternatively, they may be targeted on known high-risk transactions/activities.

- *Lifestyle profiling*

The proactive profiling of high-risk employees may indicate out-of-kilter lifestyles. The investigation of the activities that the employee deals with may detect fraud. This can be likened to scanning a searchlight over a broad group of people. Chapter 6 on lifestyle audits refers.

- *General lifestyle indicators*

As with targeted lifestyle audits, general lifestyle indicators may identify employees who are living beyond their known financial means.

For example: in the past, many fraudsters that I have dealt with have been identified by the fact that they drive expensive vehicles.

- *Detailed lifestyle analysis*

The detailed analysis of a person's incomes and expenditures, as part of an investigation, may identify that the person has been funding their lifestyle from irregular activities. This can, in turn, be likened to looking at specific people under a microscope.

- *Publication/mass media*

The organisation may only become aware of the fraud after an article on it has been published or a television show aired.

- *Social media*

Social media chatter may highlight the irregularities. Some organisations have their own social media accounts on which issues may be raised. Alternatively, issues may be discussed on an individual's private social media accounts or on social media accounts designed specifically for such discussions (the Hello Peter website refers as an example).

3.3.10. Contact

Establish if you can engage with the person at the source of the information to gain more details/provide clarification.

Whistle-blowers (and for that matter anyone who requests an investigation to be conducted, like management) typically do not have a realistic idea of what is involved in an investigation and of possible further action. They do not understand the degree of and the type of information that is required to conduct the investigation. It always seems as if they think that they can make a comment in passing and that this will be sufficient to commence an investigation. They are probably not to blame, as it is unlikely that investigations are their skill-set. Their only frame of reference would typically be Hollywood, where everything miraculously always seems to fall into place within a relatively short period of time.

An important part of the fraud investigator's job is therefore to establish a relationship with the information-giver and to help them to understand what is involved. As the fraud investigator, you will then need to 'work' the relationship to get the information that you need. This process requires patience and persistence.

You will also find that the longer you work with people and the more matters that you deal with during your tenure, the easier obtaining information will become. This is because people get used to the type of questions that you ask and they become comfortable with the typical investigation process. After a while, you will find that people start to pre-empt your questions and volunteer information to you without you even needing to request it. You will know that your relationship with them is maturing when they start to quote your own catch-phrases back to you. In my case, I have my 'rules' that were discussed in Chapter 2. When people tell me one of my own rules, as if they are telling me for the first time and/or teaching me something, then I just smile and agree with them. That is when I know that I have made a difference.

3.3.11. Information

When asking for information, keep our rule in mind: 'Remember the end-game.' In terms of this, picture a criminal trial throughout your investigation. Try to picture what will need to be proven it and who will need to testify to this. Request the information that you need therefore to support the 'end-game'.

Furthermore, keep our most important forensic rule in mind, namely: 'Secure the evidence.' Obtain all physical evidence possible and 'lock' witnesses' testimonies down in affidavits. The use of affidavits is discussed in detail in Chapter 8 on reporting. Chapter 4 on interviewing may also provide valuable inspiration on how to structure your information-seeking interviews.

Annexure 3.1 provides an example of a template that can be used to gather information from the source of the fraud information. This will primarily be used during your initial contact with the reporter.

Analyse the information received and decide:

- If any further clarification is required from the reporter
- On the usefulness of the information
- On the subsequent actions.

Record the decisions and the basis for the decisions.

3.3.12. Security and protection

Fraudsters are unfortunately rarely the nicest people on Earth. Fraudsters may stand to lose a lot through the uncovering of their misconduct. This could be in the form of dismissal, lost money and property, loss of their basic freedom due to imprisonment or even reputational damage. It is not always clear what lengths they might go to in an attempt to save themselves or their family, friends and co-conspirators from potential consequences. Examples of extreme lengths that they could go to include:

- *Destruction of evidence*

Two examples refer of matters that I dealt with in which the main culprits set a fire to destroy evidence. In the first example, the culprit set fire to an entire floor of an eight-storey building. Other floors also suffered residual damage. In the second example, the matter had commenced many years previously. There was only one large private document archiving and storage firm in the region, which was widely used. The offending supplier company, their bank and the tax revenue authorities' documents were all archived at this single regional private archiving facility. The supplier was known to be an ethically challenged individual whom people also feared physically. He was further alleged to be linked to other dubious people. The independent archive was burnt to the ground by an unknown arsonist and with it all historical paper evidence. Luckily the bank retained scanned electronic copies of documents. The matter was therefore still able to be handed to the prosecution for the original criminal case (excluding arson).

- *Interfering with witnesses*

Offending parties may try to unduly influence witnesses not to testify at all or to omit or amend details. This may be done by threatening them, bribing them, emotional blackmail, appealing to their good nature or by exploiting their friendship.

- *Physical harm to investigators or their families*

Investigators are murdered in extreme cases. In one example, in one of the companies in which I worked a local country branch manager had acid thrown in her face when she threatened to expose wrongdoing.

- *Getting authorities to act against the investigators or the company*

Three examples of where this happened come to mind:

  - *In one instance, we were working on a large fraud case. One of my colleagues who was the key investigator was wrongfully arrested by the police late at night from his hotel room, denied of all his rights, detained for almost 24 hours and treated horrifically. This was all based on false complaints that were laid with the police and/or possibly because the police were paid to do this. The irony is that this occurred in the Netherlands, a developed country where the International War Tribunal is held. He subsequently took action through the European Union, the outcome of which is not known at the time of writing. It just goes to show that no country is totally immune from police blunders and/or corruption and also underpins the fact that you can never be too careful.*
  - *We also had, in the same organisation, numerous examples of where the border police would miraculously show up to check visiting officials or expatriate visas. The visiting officials or resident expatriates were frequently deported or incarcerated and traumatised for days.*
  - *In other cases, the tax revenue authorities turned up at the organisation to conduct a detailed audit. While the organisations were not knowingly party to tax evasion, the untimely audits were disruptive.*

- *Slanderous campaigns against the investigators or their employers*

This may be as simple as slanderous social media campaigns or leaked and/or influenced media reports. It could go as far as the fabricating of evidence. Campaigns may also be levied against the organisation's clients or suppliers to tarnish relations.

- *Holding of the organisation or investigators to ransom*

This may entail threatening to expose an individual's previous indiscretions or misconduct previously practised by the organisation. Fraudsters may threaten to disrupt key projects, destroy or deny the organisation of key information, take or make public intellectual property or sensitive information (frequently leaked sensitive e-mails refer) or take clients away.

- *Bribery of officials*

Officials may be bribed to make matters or evidence go away. Alternatively, they may be bribed to act unfairly against the organisation or individuals as per our previous examples.

- *Absconding*

The guilty person may simply abscond and/or move to another area or country to avoid having to face the consequences.

- *Suicide*

The guilty people may take their own lives rather than go through an investigation or trial.

The key point is to always protect yourself. Some of this may seem over the top, but when it happens it is too late. The trick is to be prepared and conservative. Fraud investigators are defined by the work they deliver and not by the exposure they enjoy while doing it. The ideal is to go in, conduct the job and depart without too much ceremony and without attracting too much attention.

The aforementioned experience of my colleague being falsely arrested and detained was a very surreal experience. It was like being in the movies. It was one which traumatised him for a long time thereafter.

My original mentor, who is responsible for many high-profile cases, once told me: 'When you land at your home airport and you get into your car to go home, you don't have to think before you start the car! I do, every time!' The investigating police officer in one of the matters that he dealt with was gunned down while driving on the highway! This is the harsh reality of the society that we live in. The trick is to be defensively prepared.

Practical suggestions by which to protect yourself and your investigation include:

- Do not tell subjects that you will be coming to interview them and/or the exact dates and times that you will be travelling. However, it may not be possible to keep your travel itinerary secret, especially where you need an invitation letter from a local organisation representative for visa purposes or when airport collections and transfers need to be arranged.
- As far as possible, do not tell people in which hotel you will be staying. But again, this may not be practical.
- Be observant of apparent 'coincidences' and things that seem out of place (people watching you, spotting known people in places where they are not expected, vehicles tailing you, etc). Record and report these incidences to your trusted colleagues.

- Only bring the necessary documents and files with you. Ensure that you always lock documents, files and electronic mediums away, even in your hotel room. Carry everything with you and do not leave documents and devices unsupervised.
- Only bring copies, no originals.
- Back up all electronic information. Try to upload electronic information to the cloud during field visits to allow for recovery.
- Make use of secure passwords and encryption.
- Avoid connecting to the internet on public networks.
- Be careful about what you discuss in public places (airports, restaurants, while being transported, etc). There can legally be no expectation of privacy of anything discussed in public. Everything discussed in public is deemed to be in the public domain.
- Lock and bolt/chain your hotel room door. Do not open the door unless your lawyer is present if someone who you do not trust comes. Do not open the door unless you look through the peephole to identify who is there.
- Talk to people through the door or with the chain on. Do not open the door fully. Only open the door for the police if:
    - You can see that it is real police (uniform and photo ID)
    - They slide a search warrant under your door
    - You have your lawyer present
- Immediately phone or ask for your local embassy representative to be informed/present.
- Resist subjecting yourself to blood tests. These may be a health risk (HIV/Aids and other infections) and you have no control over how the results will be scientifically determined or used.
- Ensure that your vaccinations are up to date and keep a copy of your vaccination card in a safe place. In one instance, my boss forgot to have one of his vaccine boosters and the local country wanted to give it to him upon his departure. A facilitation payment was unavoidable to prevent him from having to go through this. Facilitation payments (not bribes) are allowed in this circumstance.
- When you go out, leave the TV on (so that it seems like someone is inside) and put the 'do not disturb' sign on the door to keep the housekeeping staff out.
- Upon return to your hotel room, look for things that are out of place (I once returned to my room door being ajar).
- Keep the curtains of your room drawn.
- Walk through your room/the location you wish to establish as being secure with an old-fashioned small transistor radio turned on. The radio will experience signal disturbance when brought close to certain types of wireless transmitting listening devices (bugs). Professional firms can also be used to conduct such tests.
- Be observant of the subtle details in the manner in which you left your things before leaving the room. Place items in a very specific fashion that will need to be disturbed if someone opened or went through your things.
- Do not trust hotel safes. They have a generic master key (in the event that guests forget their codes) that is available to the hotel staff. One of my colleagues had items and cash stolen out of his hotel safe in two different countries (one of these countries is rated the lowest for crime and corruption).

- Develop the habit of taking all important items with you from the hotel when you go to the office.
- Do not dispose of organisation documents in hotels. One European hotel (known to be frequented by staff from the organisation for which I worked) told us that they collect all the disposed of documents and that there are individuals who bought these from them in order to obtain organisation information. Remember if you throw a confidential document away in a public place, it is deemed to be in the public domain.
- Resist giving hotels memory sticks from which to print. This can transfer viruses and the staff may electronically copy documents. Similarly, avoid using internet cafes.
- Do not leave documents or items in meeting rooms unsupervised. Have one colleague remain in the meeting room while the others take a break or collect lunch. Alternatively, order lunch in.
- Only eat from trusted sources. Avoid street food. Drink from sealed containers.
- Eating cooked food reduces the chances of upset stomachs. The cleanliness of water used in the growing or washing of green or uncooked items cannot be guaranteed. Similarly, do not use ice in drinks, as you do not know the source of the water/how clean it is. Local stomachs may be accustomed to the local water sources, but you may not be.
- Arrange to have a local lawyer on speed dial for all hours (not just office hours).
- Have a list of all important numbers on your phone and on paper (police, senior company officials, medical personnel, the driver, the embassy, etc).
- Have a copy of your itinerary and all addresses to be visited. Keep copies of all important documents (permits, visas, invitation letters, a local representative's passport, etc) in the event that you are stopped by officials.
- Determine if an independent (big four-type) firm of investigators should rather conduct the interviews. This is a way of screening organisation staff members from harm.
- Do not drive yourself if you are in a foreign and/or a difficult country. If you are involved in an accident the locals may extort money out of you or be less than friendly/want to exact vengeance.
- Determine if you need a security escort. We typically have drivers and sometimes armed guards to escort us in difficult geographies. In very difficult countries we have two vehicles in the escort.
- Determine if you need a security member to accompany you (such as a bodyguard). We sometimes make use of a professional independent outside security firm to provide us with personal protection staff to accompany us in challenging countries when we are dealing with serious matters.
- Research the place that you are going to. Keep abreast of local news (for example conflict areas). Find out and respect local customs. Find out where hospitals, police stations and airports are in relation to where you are staying and working. Understand traffic patterns. Identify alternative routes to be used in emergencies to and from destinations. Inform trusted people when departing and arriving at destinations.
- Do not argue with or be impatient with officials (police, border control, airport staff, etc). Our rule refers: 'You will get more right with honey than with chilli.'
- Do not go to risky places (neighbourhoods that are dangerous, nightclubs, etc). You are there to do a job and not to be entertained. Do these things on your own time thereafter if you must.

3.3.13. Develop an initial hypothesis

Once you have gathered the initial information, summarise everything that you have. The purpose of this is to determine:

- If there is a basis for the allegation/suspicion
- What information you have
- What additional information you still require
- Which investigative steps you need to undertake.

Update and redraft the mind maps that you drafted initially to more accurately depict what you have and to visualise what you do not have. Then start to develop an initial predication or hypothesis of what has been done, by whom, when, where, how and the quantum. This will help you to define an investigative direction. From this initial hypothesis, develop an initial investigation plan. It may be prudent to test your hypothesis and investigation plan with your colleagues (trusted colleagues only).

Your initial hypothesis and investigation plan will also identify questions and inconsistencies that need to be tested. The hypothesis is important, as it provides the initial direction and you will refer back to it on numerous occasions throughout the investigation to ensure that you are on track.

In exceptional cases, you may be in a position at this early stage to know that no further investigation needs to take place. If that is the case, ensure that you document the reasons why you have decided not to proceed with an investigation. The reason for the formal documentation is to act as reference material in the event that the decision not to proceed is questioned in the future. You may or may not agree with the reasons not to proceed, like an instruction from a senior member of staff. Ensure that you document the reasons for not proceeding, who was aware of the decisions or who took the decisions. Retain all required correspondence, minutes and documentation to support this decision. Communicate the decision not to proceed with an investigation to the required parties.

3.3.14. Investigation plan and objectives

Develop a high-level investigation plan according to the standard investigation steps. Annexure 3.2 provides a useful investigation plan template with all standard investigation steps.

3.3.15. Outputs

You will, at this early stage of the investigation, already have some outputs. Examples of outputs resulting from the planning stage of the investigation include:

- Working papers
- Interview notes
- Evidence (some)
- Information
- Analyses (albeit limited)
- Conclusions

- Admissions
- Resignations
- Recoveries
- Signed acknowledgement of debt
- Affidavits
- Statements
- Expert opinions:
    - Subject matter expert opinions (engineers, lawyers, etc)
    - Polygraph results
    - Handwriting analysis
- A next step high-level plan of action
- An updated investigation journal.

3.4. INVESTIGATION

3.4.1. Conducting the investigation

A full investigation is, from start to finish, about gathering information and evidence, analysing this information and evidence, drawing conclusions, reporting on the facts and conclusions and initiating some form of subsequent action/s.

While the specifics will differ from one matter to another, there are well-established generic methods which can be followed and general places from where information and evidence can be obtained. An investigation is also an iterative process of obtaining evidence, analysing it, drawing conclusions and reverting and refining information gathering, until a suitable conclusion can be reached, which is adequately supported by evidence and/or testimony.

It is wise to ensure that management is aware that more matters than are initially known will be identified once the investigation commences. Continue to tell them that this is not a reason not to proceed with the investigation, but rather an opportunity to mentally prepare themselves for further matters that they were unaware of.

Emphasise that it is unlikely that the investigation will identify the full extent of the fraud, but that it should get to the bottom of most of the aspects. It is also common practice that some aspects only come to light after the subject has left the organisation (dismissed or suspended) or a long time after the investigation is concluded. So, they should not expect to find out about everything and/or be able to prove everything. This is about managing stakeholders' expectations.

Annexure 3.2 lists the broad steps that can be used in an investigation. Select those that are the most appropriate to your investigation. These are discussed in detail below.

The planning and the conducting of the investigation tend to blur into one and there is not a clear line between the two. It is important to understand, as stated previously, that investigations are an iterative process, which require flexibility of planning and regression and rework.

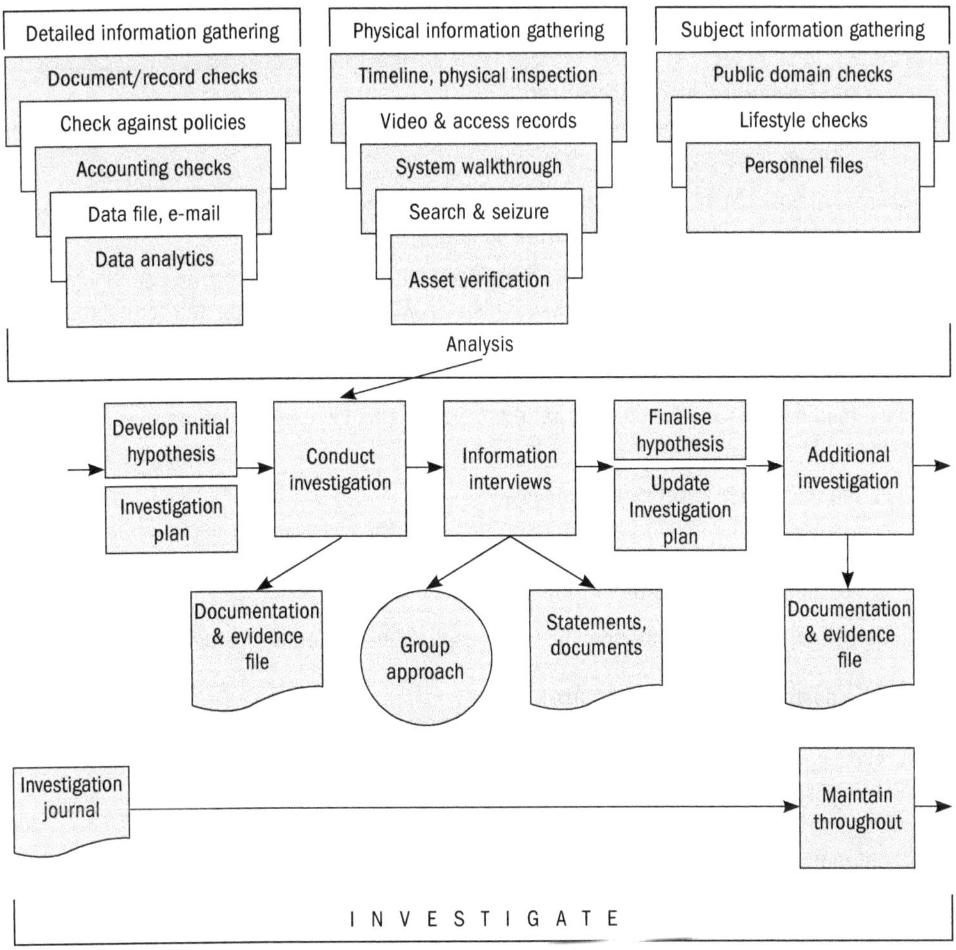

Figure 3.6 *Investigation phase*

3.4.2. Subject information gathering

a. Introduction

Upon completion of your contact with the source, you will have as much information as you can obtain from the source concerning the misconduct. This will most likely highlight the following or part thereof:

- An actual/known subject
- An actual/known group of subjects
- A potential target group of subjects

The next logical step would, therefore, be to commence gathering general information about your subject/s, so as to:

- Know who you are dealing with, or
- Narrow down their most likely degree of involvement so as to direct you to subsequent investigation steps.

The sources of possible information and the methods used to obtain and analyse information are discussed in detail in Chapter 6 on lifestyle audits.

If you have not identified any potential subjects, stand this step over until you have conducted your detailed information gathering and analysis. This step will need to be repeated for each subject identified.

As a general rule start 'wide' with your search of potential subjects and include as many people as possible, then narrow your search as a pattern starts to emerge. Use this information to develop a profile of:

- The most likely investigation subjects
- Additional information that you need to gather (because of who has been included as a subject)
- Additional subjects to be included.

The flowing general sources of information can be used for the gathering of information on subjects:

b. Public domain checks (open source)

- News sites/forums
- Social media
- Professional and/or recreational associations.

c. Semi-public domain checks (official databases)

Numerous official (but restricted) databases exist, which may be accessed by approved professionals for, amongst other reasons, fraud investigations. Possible data sources include:

- Credit checks and applications
- Company directorships
- Property deeds office
- Qualification verifications
- Employment history
- Bank account ownership detail confirmations (not transactional history).

d. Restricted records (company records)

The following information may be useful from the company's personnel records:

- Personnel files for general information (address, number of dependents, contact details, education, etc)
- Superiors
- Position, career progression
- Salary analysis

- Loan applications
- Internal disciplinary history.

e. Subpoenaed records (restricted records via a court order)

Certain information needs to be obtained by the investigating officer assigned to the case with the permission of the courts. You may, depending on the stage of your investigation, be in a good position to offer guidance to the investigating officer as to the records to be subpoenaed and for what reason:

- Bank accounts (specific or banking trawl)
- Cell phone records
- Other financial institution records (life cover insurance policies, investment schemes, etc).

f. Volunteered information and records (subjects and sources with or without specified use)

Subjects and/or sources may volunteer information and records to you in the course of your investigation, as requested by you in interviews with them. This may be used in detailed lifestyle audits later:

- Bank account details
- Other sources of income (inheritance, prizes, etc).

g. Informed information (subjects and sources with specified use)

Various parties may provide you with information concerning subjects. This information will need to be corroborated. Some of the parties that may inform you are:

- Whistle-blowers
- Senior management
- External parties
- Colleagues
- The subjects themselves
- Family or friends of the subject.

h. Conduct history (official databases)

The investigating officer can check if the subject has a criminal record. Alternatively, the subject may give you permission to conduct a criminal record check on them. Please be mindful that recent updates to criminal records may take time to reflect. Criminal matters underway would also not reflect yet on the system:

- Criminal convictions
- Criminal profile.

Over and above actual criminal convictions, the police maintain a 'profile' of each individual of all matters that they have been implicated into some or other degree. This could include the fact that a subject has been arrested and released, but not convicted. Request the investigating officer to pull the subject's profile as well.

The subject's criminal history may even be listed in their personnel file, in which case you could use it without their permission.

3.4.3. Detailed information gathering and analysis

a. Introduction

Detailed information gathering can occur at various stages of your investigation. The bulk of detailed information gathering will, however, take place just after the subject has been identified and the broad allegation is known. The need to gather this information may be highlighted from any of the sources of the fraud allegation. The source of your detailed information may or may not be the same person as the one who highlighted the initial allegation/suspicion of fraud. The source of your detailed information may commence with the source of the allegation, but will generally be wider than the source. The sources of information were discussed previously.

b. Request for information

Each piece of information will need to be requested from those people who are responsible for it. Your request for information (RFI) will in most cases be an informal request directly from the responsible person.

On certain occasions, it may be better to formally request the information that you require. Formal RFIs are almost always in writing and may be directed via a senior staff member or an officially appointed organisation person. A formal RFI is almost always about 'putting something in writing' and/or putting the request on record. This is done to protect yourself and/or to 'control' those from whom you are requesting the information. Annexure 3.3 is an example of an RFI document that can be used.

The following are some examples of occasions where you may want to utilise a formal RFI:

- *If you are working in a hostile environment*
  Hostile environments are environments where the organisational culture is generally hostile. The culture may be driven by a few key individuals (normally key leaders) or just be an organisation-wide phenomenon. Doing anything in such environments may be construed as difficult. Fraud investigations and anything that could attract negative attention may be even more difficult. Examples of hostile environments include:
  - Some government organisations
  - Organisations which do not like the control of a head office or their holding company.
- *When you are working for a client and/or organisation leadership with whom you do not yet have a well-established relationship*
  The client or business leadership may be completely cooperative, but it is better for you to be more formal until you establish a freer and more open relationship with them. As the client or area of the business grows in confidence in your methods and results, you will find that they will ease up. You will then be in a position to adopt a more relaxed approach to requesting information.
- *When people are trying to restrict your access to information*
  In this section, we are referring to individuals, as opposed to the organisation-wide culture. It is commonplace to have people within the organisation who try to limit access to the information required in an investigation. You will almost always find that the person restricting

the access is not the person who commissioned the investigation. Alternatively, the person requesting the investigation may be trying to use you to investigate certain elements only. They may do this for a number of reasons:

- The investigation of the specific elements suits their personal political agenda.
- They do not understand the full extent of an investigation or the scope of your current investigation.
- They do not want certain elements to be highlighted.
- Even though they may not be directly involved in the fraud, they may be concerned that a full investigation may somehow reflect poorly on them or the organisation.

Numerous occasions come to mind of when senior company officials said: 'This is easy; all you have to do is to investigate [xxx]. There is no need for you to do all of this ....' In one organisation, we had to get a particular manager to sign for receipt of information, as he would deny having received the information so as to try to evade any consequences related to the information.

- *People may be trying to discredit you or the function that you represent or the person who appointed you*

You may have 'history 'with the individual and they might use this opportunity to 'get back at you'.

The political motives for trying to derail the investigation may reach further than you as an individual. The players may be using your investigation to fuel their agendas and/or to get back at their opponents.

One of my clients requested me to investigate the other partners in the business that they shared. Two of the partners later ensured that I was denied access just when I was getting to the most important elements of the investigation. This is very frustrating, but there is very little that you can do if the requesting party does not or is unable to back you. You just have to walk away.

- *There is something else happening that the organisation wants to concentrate on or that they do not want to adversely influence if the fraud investigation comes to light*

Examples of activities that organisational leadership may be concerned will be adversely affected by a fraud investigation include:

- Acquisitions, mergers and sales of businesses
- The raising of capital, attracting of new investors and the obtaining of new business
- Existing trade impact.

In one organisation, the executives were trying to sell one of the companies in the group to a competitor. My team and I were expressly instructed to refrain from investigating a fraud in another unrelated part of the group. I did not receive any support from the audit committee, as they were betting on the executive turning around the organisation. I eventually left this organisation some months later and half of my team followed voluntarily soon afterwards, as the organisation became unbearable to work in.

In another organisation, I was frequently told that the organisation may be subject to fines and penalties or experience trade restrictions by customers and authorities in the event that the misconduct was highlighted. I always managed to convince the management that the organisation should rather work together with the authorities and comply with the laws despite the isolated actions of rogue employees.

It is recommended in these occasions that you draft an official 'request for information' (RFI) type document. Determine if someone needs to:

- Acknowledge receipt of the RFI
- Sign that they have given you the information requested
- Show evidence that you have returned the information upon completion.

c. Counter-measures

The RFI is only one measure to help you obtain information. The broader need to ensure that the investigation is conducted within reasonable timelines is the bigger issue.

The following aspects may assist you to ensure that your investigation stays on track:

- *A formal charter*

A charter is a formal document that is normally endorsed by the main board members or the audit committee. The charter defines the powers, organisational status and independence of your function. Your function (forensic team) may be part of a larger function like the internal audit function and may consequently fall under their charter. It may be useful to quote the fraud function's authority as outlined in the charter if organisational individuals do not want to cooperate/assist.

- *Letter of authorisation/appointment/contract*

Your letter of appointment should define the scope of your investigation, your right to access people and information and your deliverables. An example of a letter of appointment is given in Annexure 3.4. Engagement letters are used by internal fraud investigation functions in larger conglomerate-type organisations and by external consultants providing fraud services to an organisation.

- *Authorisation hierarchy*

Your decision powers may be defined by the organisation's authorisation hierarchy document. In this case, people will either know that you have the authorisation, as they know the authorisation hierarchy, or you can refer them to the authorisation hierarchy to convince them that you have the authority.

- *Direct access to the person who appointed you*

You may decide to revert back to the person who has appointed you to conduct the investigation. This person may be in a position to intervene (especially if they are senior enough) to instruct the parties to give you the requested information/assistance. Request the person to do this in a non-prescriptive manner. Rather try to explain to people why they should assist and win their favour than instruct them to do something they do not want to do.

- *Direct access to senior organisation members*

In a similar fashion to the discussion on the person who appointed you, access to any of these people may be of great assistance to you for direct or indirect support:

- Chairman of the board
- Chairman of the audit committee
- Managing director/chief executive officer/chief financial officer/chief information officer/chief operating officer
- Head of audit.

These people may:

- Openly display their support for the investigation
- Take an interest in and ask pertinent questions to key individuals if they have knowledge of the incident
- Intervene and speak directly to the uncooperative parties
- Table the matter in a formal meeting.

It is wise to develop the habit of having regular meetings with these people to ensure that they are always up to speed and that they have confidence in what you are doing. Request special meetings when an important issue crops up if you are unable to wait for the standard scheduled meetings.

- *Solicit the help of outside organisations*

Examples of outside bodies that may be approached to give you support in your investigation include:

- External auditors
- Authorities (revenue authorities, police, customs officials, etc)
- Industry regulatory bodies
- Independent bodies that have the ability to pressurise people/organisations to assist
- Professional bodies (IIA, ACFE, Institute of Chartered Accountants, etc)
- Legal counsel.

- *Budget*

Having a pre-approved budget may entitle you to certain freedoms to perform work without having to request funding. If you stay within the budget, there may not be a requirement to seek anyone's approval and in so doing you may avoid scrutiny or the opportunity for them to unduly influence your investigation.

- *Convincing discussions*

Attacking people with documents and forcing them to cooperate is the last option. Our rule refers: 'You will get more right with honey than with chilli.' First, approach the people who are creating the bottleneck and try to win them over to your side through discussion before using a forceful approach.

- *Communicating*

If you communicate with people on a regular basis, they are more likely to gain confidence in what you are doing. If they do not know what you are doing, they may presume the worst.

- *Sticking to your word*

As far as possible, ensure that you stick to what you have committed to do. If there is a change, then call the people you are dealing with and inform them about the change, why it has arisen and what they can expect.

- *Including a wide range of people*

It is difficult to suppress something if it is out in the open or if more people are aware of it. People who are trying to hide the issue may not want to be seen by a wider audience to be doing something underhand. People mostly want to be seen to be part of the solution.

The number of people with whom you can communicate about the matter will depend on the nature of the issue though. Our rule of being careful who you share what information with refers, as you have little or no control of information once it has been given to another party.

- *Education campaigns*

Hold education campaigns to inform people what you do or what your function does. This may assist in improving people's understanding of the importance of your investigations and methods.

- *Success stories*

Success breeds success. Publishing success stories is a form of education and deterrent. This may be done in meetings or with a periodic fraud newsletter.

- *Put your opinion in writing*

A lot of people (especially people who occupy senior positions in the organisation) will try to influence your investigation, but without going on record. They seem to change their mind as soon as the issue has been committed to paper. This is because your document is 'discoverable' and there is suddenly evidence that they had knowledge of the issue and potentially did not act on it.

Ensure that the investigation or the need for assistance is formally tabled at an audit committee level. Alternatively, and if time allows, send the decision-makers a tactfully worded e-mail to motivate why you feel that the matter should be investigated. You will almost always obtain the required assistance once the matter is in writing. The reason for this is that if the organisation was the subject of a 'dawn raid' by the authorities or if there was an investigation after the fact, there is a chance that the correspondence may be found and indicate that they were aware of the matter and failed to act appropriately. People are reluctant to formally associate themselves with potential future blame.

In one organisation I worked in, I used to say to the board: 'You are the custodians of the control and you have to sign the corporate governance statement in the financial statements. Please tell me how you would like to proceed?' They would invariably say: 'No, no... please go ahead and conduct the work.' Be sure to thank them profusely for their 'generosity' and do not look smug.

d. Records

You will need to access many different types of documents in investigations. The following detailed records may be useful in your investigations:

- *Records such as:*
    - Accounting records
    - Other records (operating information, assets registers, organisational charts, etc)
    - Access records
    - Video footage.

- *Documents such as:*
    - Invoices
    - Statements
    - Receipts
    - Contracts
    - Bank statements
    - Delivery notes.
- *Electronic files such as:*
    - Data files
    - E-mails
    - Metadata
    - Program code
    - Browsing history.

e. Standards

Company policies and procedures can also be very helpful in an investigation. The following include some reasons for this:

- *Familiarisation*

To familiarise yourself about the process and to establish how things are supposed to work. You may be looking at an area of business that you have no or little background in. Policies and procedures can give you a good starting understanding.

- *Interviewing*

Policies and procedures also provide you with a measure against which to compare actual behaviour to. This can be successfully used during the comparison and contradiction phase of an interview. Chapter 4 on interviewing refers.

- *Subsequent actions*

Policies may be used in hearings and/or in criminal cases as the standard against which to measure the subject's performance. In a labour matter, you may have to demonstrate that there was a rule and that the subject had knowledge of the rule. The existence of a policy helps with the first. Chapter 10 on structuring the forensic function refers for more detail.

Examination of policies and procedures may also be of assistance if internal controls need to be bolstered and/or business processes amended in response to the fraud case to prevent or detect recurrence.

- *Reporting*

Findings may also be reported against the backdrop of existing standards and policies and procedures.

The following standards may be useful to obtain, as part of the detailed information gathered:

- *Company policies and procedures*

These may be general policies and procedures (for example general decorum) or they may be specific to the function that you are testing (for example the procurement policy).

- *Training manuals*

Training manuals are particularly useful as they normally contain a lot of detail (pictures, examples, screenshots, etc).

Determine if the subjects of your investigation attended these training sessions. This will help to prove if they have knowledge of the rules/procedures.

Furthermore, if the subject uses a particular system on a daily basis, it may be common cause that they are au fait with the functioning of the system. It may be difficult for them to purport that they have no or little knowledge of an area if you walk them through the detailed steps of the training manual and say: 'But you perform each of these steps on a daily basis, please help me to understand how you could not know?'

- *Job descriptions or job profiles*

Job descriptions typically describe the roles and responsibilities of staff members. Job profiles are less specific than job descriptions.

These may both be useful to show what the subject was supposed to do. Compare their behaviour or assertions to this. Their actual behaviour may also be compared to their job description/profile in an internal disciplinary hearing, for example on a charge of dereliction of duties.

- *Authorisation hierarchies*

Authorisation hierarchies list the people who may approve specific areas, to what value they may approve and any special circumstances that may apply. They also list who should have done something in the absence thereof.

These are commonly used documents. It may be difficult for a subject to explain why they approved a transaction outside of their responsibility when faced with the authorisation hierarchy.

- *Industry standards*

Industry standards are not so much 'hard and fast' rules as they are guidelines. These may be best practices and can become common knowledge, as to how things should work in certain industries. It also helps to create credibility to compare behaviour to independent sources or when recommending what is considered to be best/good/common practice. This will counter the standard response that 'we are different here'.

- *Professional standards, codes, guidelines, etc*

Professional standards relate to standards such as accounting standards (IFRS). They could also relate to codes of ethics. For example, a registered accountant knows that they need to subscribe to certain ethical standards. Compare actual behaviour to these standards.

- *Laws and regulations*

Laws and regulations may be specifically applicable to the type of business that you are dealing with or just general laws. Determine if there are any special laws and regulations that you should be aware of, including:

- Customs and excise laws
- Border control laws
- Tax laws
- Hazardous goods
- Foreign trade laws
- Competition laws
- Stock exchange laws
- Laws of contract
- Labour laws
- Privacy laws
- Criminal laws
- Electronic communication laws.

- *Letters of employment or contracts of employment*

Contracts and letters of employment may specify 'do's and don'ts', as well as rights and obligations.

Contracts of employment also frequently contain a standard clause to say that employees are to dedicate their time to their employer and that they need to act in the employer's best interest.

- *Meeting minutes, memos, instructions, notifications, etc*

Businesses issue various instructions to staff members advising them how to proceed in certain circumstances, as part of the normal course of business.

Try to determine if any such special notifications were issued relating to the area that you are investigating. These could be in the form of e-mails with a distribution list, memos, intranet, etc.

- *Established practice/precedent*

In some cases, there are both formally documented policies and also 'practice'. It is often the practice that is more important than the letter of the law. The revenue authorities are an example of where policy and practice may differ. The Receiver of Revenue frequently interprets their laws in a manner that is more lenient than the letter of the law suggests. Practice advisories may even be issued to assist people.

Practice is mostly set through repetitive precedent. Practice may be commonly known. We talk about the practice being 'repeatable and undocumented' from a 'maturity modelling' point of view.

f. Search and seizure

- *Introduction*

There may be occasions when a search will be required. Examples of searches may include a search of:

- An employee, a contractor or a supplier's person (body or clothes) and/or bags
- An employee, a contractor or a supplier's vehicle

- An employee's workspace
- An individual's private residence or other property
- A supplier's premises.

Searches need to comply with strict conditions and are not an automatic right.

- *Principles*

A person can either agree to a search or be required to subject themselves or their property to a search. If they agree, then there should not be any complications, as they are giving you permission. You nevertheless still need to be respectful in the conduct of the search and you are limited to the nature of what you are looking for (for example weapons, stolen goods, etc). You cannot break people's things or touch them inappropriately. If you are searching their person you should perform the search or offer to perform the search in a private area (like a cubical). As a rule, the same gender should conduct a search of the person. You can never force them to comply with a search request.

When searching someone's bag, their vehicle or their place of work, the basic guiding principle that applies is that of the 'expectation of privacy'. You need to establish if there is an expectation of privacy before conducting the search. If there is, then you will need their permission; if there is not, then you will not need their permission.

If a person refuses to be subject to a search, there are a few options that you can exercise. Remember that a search can be of the person, their bag, a vehicle, or property or place. Options include:

- Respect their refusal and walk away.
- Respect their refusal and subject them to disciplinary procedures. This may be an option if it is company policy, or part of their employment contract, to subject oneself to searches. Company policy would need to be clearly displayed, consistently practised and regularly repeated.
- Respect their refusal and deny them any further privileges, subject to the outcome of further proceedings. Privileges include:
    - Access to the organisation
    - Right to work (suspension from work pending disciplinary action)
    - The right of their vehicle to leave the premises
- Respect their refusal, but request that a police officer or security official conduct the search.

When you are searching someone's person, their bags or their private vehicle, they need to be present. You cannot just look into their bag or take their keys and open their vehicle without them being present. If they have a company vehicle, you may be able to search it without them being present if the vehicle is a general organisation vehicle that they make use of as well. If the vehicle is part of their remuneration package and only they have use of the vehicle, there may be a high expectation of privacy. In that case, they would need to be present when a search is conducted.

If there is a legitimate reason why the person cannot be present (for example, they are in the hospital) then obtain documented approval from senior leadership to proceed without the person. Photograph the items to be searched before, during and after the search. Have a senior independent person present to witness the search. Limit your search to the scope of what you are investigating.

When conducting a search, it is important to be open and transparent. As a rule, do not conduct searches alone.

When you are searching a person's workspace there are some differences to searching their person. For example: the expectation of privacy of my person and my clothes are generally high. The expectation of privacy in the cupboards in my office where I store the company files is low. The expectation of privacy in the one drawer (out of a bank of drawers on my desk), where everyone knows I keep my private things, is high. The protocol for searching a person's workspace is discussed below.

- *Data privacy*

Ensure that you understand and abide by local and other regional (EU, UK and US) data privacy requirements. Two important questions to consider include:

(i) *Are you, as an employer, allowed to access data on an employee's machine?*

For clarity's sake, we are talking about a machine given by the employer to the employee to perform their duties. This machine's primary use is the employer's work. It would also access the employer's network and computer resources and be subject to the employer's security conventions (active directory, etc). The basic rule (to be confirmed in line with local requirements) is that yes, you can. Data privacy laws normally allow for the provision to access data for specified and legitimate reasons. Legitimate reasons must be in the line of conducting your business. Conducting investigations is a legitimate business activity.

If you are conducting an investigation, you may only access data in line with the purpose of your investigation. You cannot make use of the opportunity to access other data not required for your investigation. It is highly recommended that the purpose, authority, methods employed and subsequent analysis and use of the data are documented. Only access data via legal means.

It is also strongly suggested that a senior person's approval is required before data can be accessed. This will reduce the likelihood of unnecessary accessing of data. Fraud investigators can, on occasion, be too focused on their investigation objectives. Part of this focused approach can involve firing off the typical investigation techniques without sufficient consideration of their necessity. Some of this focus might also involve being overly careful and embarking on unnecessary investigation steps. Requiring authorisation will provide an opportunity for a person independent of the investigation to question the need to access electronic data. The senior person should not misuse the need to approve data access to screen or limit investigations. An escalation process should exist to provide the opportunity to reconsider denied reasonable data access requests.

Data can also only be used for the purpose collected. It can never be used for another purpose, sold or distributed to other people uninvolved with the investigation/not required in terms of the investigation.

Data should be suitably stored in a restricted area. It should also be password protected and/or encrypted. Data should only be retained for the period required and/or in line with local data retention requirements.

(ii) *Is there a requirement to inform the person that you are accessing 'their' data?*
The general answer is no. You do not need to inform them, as long as the data is being accessed for the reasons and in the manner discussed above.

It might very well come out later in the course of the investigation when people are confronted by evidence that data was accessed. Prepare your response to possible pushback in advance.

It is also advisable to be aware that despite the legitimacy of the investigation and methods used, the accessing of people's data has a negative effect on morale. This needs to be managed correctly.

- *Private property*

You cannot search a person's private residence without their permission. The searching of a person's private residence by people other than the police will almost never be acceptable. Try to get the police involved as far as possible. The police may however not react within the period that suits you.

An example refers of a tip-off that was obtained that the assets of an organisation (for whom I worked) were being misappropriated and being stored in the subject's house. A police raid was arranged and the company's assets were recovered. The company was required to attend the raid to identify its assets, but were not actively involved in the police procedures. This example proceeded well as the whistle-blower was a resident on the larger property and gave an affidavit to the police. The subject did not suspect anything and there was no danger of the goods being taken somewhere else in the short-term.

- *Anton Piller order*

What recourse do organisations have if the police do not wish to get involved? Is there any method to still have a search conducted? The answer is yes. An individual or organisation can apply to the High Court to request that an order is issued for another person or organisation's premises to be searched and so that evidence can be seized without warning. This action is reserved for very serious matters and there needs to be a very strong case with good evidence to convince the court to proceed.

Such a court order has its origins in the English legal system and is known as an 'Anton Piller order'. This option is available in England, Wales, India, New Zealand, Australia, Hong Kong and South Africa. Anton Piller orders are available in most other countries in some form and/or under copyright matters.

This can be a very expensive option. It is also a complicated exercise involving the police and legal counsel on the day. Strict protocol also needs to be followed during the search.

You need to be very certain before going down this route. It is normally only used in complex matters, where there is a reliable basis to believe that a search will identify valuable information, and with the complete alignment of senior leaders in the organisation.

- *Work place*

It is wise to always, as a general investigation step, to conduct a search of the work place of the subject/s. This almost always highlights valuable previously unknown information.

The following are examples:

- *A subject had just been suspended pending an investigation. He asked if he could take a few personal effects from his drawer. He took a few brochures/supplier catalogues and he placed a scrunched-up blue plastic carrier bag on top of the books. I recall wondering to myself why he would want to take some business-related brochures with him. Surely if you have just been suspended then the last thing that you are thinking about is to ensure that you have some work-related material to browse through at home. I also recall thinking: 'I wonder what is in the bag'? The atmosphere was already very tense and I decided that it would be better if I did not ask him what he had in the bag and I let him leave. I was told afterwards by one of the interviewees that he had ZAR 80,000 (about USD 8,000 at the time) in hard cash in the bag, as the proceeds of a corrupt scheme that he had together with the subcontractors on site. The moral of the story is that we are not paid for comfortable situations and you should always go with your gut feeling.*
- *A signed copy of a vital policy was found in the subject's desk. This provided the evidence that the subject had knowledge of the company policy on the misconduct that he stood accused of.*
- *The subject's work diary with interesting notations concerning the embezzlement that he was busy with was found in his work desk.*

- *Protocol*

Be mindful of local privacy laws when conducting searches. Always conduct the search together with a colleague. Commence by photographing the environment and any specific more detailed aspects to be recorded as you progress.

Record any items taken in a register and sign the register together with your colleague as a witness. Maintain the investigative/evidence journal throughout. Place the seized items in suitable storage containers. Seal the containers and restrict access to them.

- Computers should be placed in non-static boxes.
- Original documents should be placed in plastic sleeves.
- Other items should be placed in plastic sealable evidence bags or boxes.

Some of the typical areas and items that you may want to concentrate on during the search and seizure processes include:

(i) *Work place*
offices, desks, cupboards and filing cabinets.

(ii) *Electronic items*
desktop computers, laptops, phones, cameras, data storage devices (memory sticks, external drives, SD-cards, etc), iPads, etc.

(iii) *Contacts*

Be sure to look in the subject's Microsoft Outlook, on their cell phones or in paper address books for contacts. This may be useful to understand who they called on their telephone logs or to prove that they had knowledge of a particular person. Obtain the subject's call history from the organisation's desktop phone system.

(iv) *Photos and videos*

Look on computers, on desks, on phones, on Facebook, iPads, etc. People like to display or show off what drives them. Look for photos, as these may give you insights into who they are friends with and their lifestyle. Knowing who the subject's friends are will give you valuable insights into loyalties and who you should trust or distrust or at least regard with suspicion.

Photo and video searches have also frequently revealed who the subject's mistress is. Mistresses (apparently) do not come cheaply and may need to be funded from sources other than the subject's declared income.

An example refers where our live e-mail monitoring showed pictures of the subject walking with his secretary in a holiday destination while chatting with his wife back home. There was no business reason for him to be in that destination.

Photos may, therefore, provide insights into:

- The subject's general morals
- Financial pressures and the need to fund their lifestyle with their mistress
- Loyalties if this person is an organisation employee
- Any additional conspirators
- How the subject could have used an employee under the guise of a relationship to give them information or to do things for them.

Remember our rule: 'It normally involves sex, drugs or gambling.' A subject's 'defective' morals are not normally limited to the scheme that they are engaged in. Subjects normally suffer from general moral decline. Photo and video searches frequently also unearth pornography on devices. This may:

- Provide insights into addictions or lifestyle choices
- Explain what the misappropriated funds were used for
- Explain what the subject spent their work time on
- Explain what the subject used organisation resources for – this may serve as a 'charge' in terms of misuse of organisation resources or abuse of authority
- Be contrary to organisational policies
- Provide useful negotiation tools in interviews with them.

An example refers of a person who portrayed himself to be an upstanding Christian. Our search of his laptop identified extensive pornography. The subject's main counter-argument in the internal hearing that he could not have stolen from the organisation, as he is a good person, was consequently successfully negated.

(v) *Files*

These may be electronic or hardcopy files. Concentrate on active as well as deleted files. It is amazing how many files get deleted on computers around the time that an investigation becomes known.

In a particular investigation, electronic statistics identified that the subject had deleted masses of files around the time that the investigation became known. This was clearly out of kilter with the subject's normal deleting trends.

Also ask around to see if there was any disproportionate or noticeable shredding of hardcopy documents.

Subjects frequently keep track of their schemes in files saved on their machines. The trail of their schemes may also be seen in normal documents and on computer systems. Subjects sometimes try to hide these files in obscure folders on the computer. A file type (Excel spreadsheet, Word document, pdf, pictures, etc) search will identify files saved anywhere on the machine.

(vi) *E-mails*

E-mail searches are consistently an excellent source of information during investigations. There are normally thousands of e-mails, so try, as far as possible, to make use of specialised software to simplify your task. Start wide and then use an iterative process to refine searches. Make use of keywords, date periods, communication between key people or organisations, etc to narrow your search.

Also, ensure that you comply with local privacy laws and company policy. The integrity of electronic evidence also needs to be maintained. Follow acceptable electronic evidence gathering protocols.

(vii) *Browsing history*

Flip through the person's browsing history and Google searches. This may provide valuable insights, for example:

- Pornography (vices)
- Residential estate agents (places where misappropriated funds were applied)
- Holiday sites (lifestyle indicators).

In an example where the accountant of a small company stole a laptop, his internet log files showed that he had advertised the computer on a general internet selling site shortly before he took it. Funnily enough, his Google search also included 'how to pass a polygraph'. He 'failed' his polygraph despite his research.

(viii) *Archives*

These may be electronic archives or hardcopy document filing areas. Out of sight is out of mind. Subjects may neglect to destroy evidence retained in such archives. While periods may differ, organisations will typically have three levels of storage, being:

- The current year's documents and information retained within the department
- Three years' information and documents retained in on-site archives
- Five years' information and documents retained off-site

(ix) *Desk phones*

The degree of information obtained from a desk phone will depend on the sophistication of the PABX system through which it operates. IP (internet protocol) phones will have the most information. Voicemail messages may also be automatically available electronically on the subject's laptop. Try to obtain the telephone exchange's call history and analyse it to establish interaction between subjects.

In an example: the subject's telephone records showed a high call history between him and the corrupt supplier. This successfully disproved the subject's assertion that he did not know the corrupt supplier and had no contact with him.

(x) *General search warrants*

On some occasions, you may work together with the authorities to get them to obtain search warrants. You may also be able to accompany the police while they conduct the search, as they may require assistance identifying items or people. The previous 'search and seizure' discussion refers.

(xi) *General 'stop and searches'*

Stop and searches may be conducted by authorities or by security staff members. The security staff members may be general building security or people employed/contracted by the company for the specific purpose. Stop and searches are typically routinely conducted when people enter or leave certain premises. They may also be targeted searches.

In one successful matter, a subject had just returned on an aircraft from meeting with a corrupt supplier. The subject was a buying-executive and he and the supplier were loading the unit price of retail stock by a few cents. The amount did not seem significant per unit but made for a sizable amount given the volumes. The subject and the supplier would share the proceeds from the increased price.

His rental vehicle (paid for by the company) had a tracking device so his movements were known to us. The funds were however exchanged in a private residence to which we did not have access. A 'stop and search' was arranged to be conducted on him when he entered his home airport. The subject was found to be carrying a significant amount of cash. The subject initially said that he had won the money at the casino. He eventually admitted to the scheme when he was showed the vehicle tracking records, which were nowhere near a casino.

Some organisations have a system of searching all people and vehicles (high-risk areas) leaving the premises or of conducting random searches (lower risk areas). This is a sound control when enforced. Others have a random search protocol. Others still make use of a system where employees are asked to draw a ball out of a bag and must be subjected to a search if they choose a particular colour ball.

A buddy system should be adopted for the people entrusted with the security themselves to ensure that they are also included in the search. Frequent supervision of the searches is important to continually reinforce the discipline.

Local laws and organisational policies need to be taken into account. It is good practice to have:

- A policy stating that the company will conduct searches
- Notices at entry points stating: 'By entering these premises you agree to be searched.'
- Staff members periodically sign their acceptance of this possibility.

(xii) *Routine verifications*

Organisations may conduct routine periodic verifications of stock, assets and/or cash. These may identify discrepancies that need to be investigated.

(xiii) *Anton Piller order dawn raids*

Authorities may conduct 'dawn raids' from time to time depending on whistle-blower information and their own investigations. Anton Piller orders were discussed under point 3.4.3.f. above.

3.4.4. Sting operations

A sting operation is used to try to catch a person committing a crime. Sting operations are the frequent subject of much Hollywood embellishment and resultantly carry an air of excitement about them. The practicality of sting operations may be less than portrayed in Hollywood pantomimes.

Sting operations are also not permitted in all countries. They can be construed as entrapment. *The John Zachary DeLorean story is an early example of the entrapment defence. John DeLorean started his own car manufacturing company (the 'DeLorean' vehicle enjoyed much airtime in the now very old* Back to the Future *movies), but experienced a delayed launch of his vehicle and incurred significant debt. The authorities caught DeLorean in a cocaine sting operation and he argued that the authorities had approached him (not the other way around) and that they knew that he was in financial difficulty (and therefore more likely to be swayed to take the bait) and that he would not have done this if they had not approached him.*

Other considerations include the following:

- It is important to understand what you are trying to prove. What is the objective of the sting operation? If a person agrees to commit crime B when approached by an investigator, does it mean that they committed crime A previously? The short answer is no. While it may point to their general ethics and morals, each crime needs to stand on its own evidence. Catching a person red-handed is no guarantee that they will confess to their wider scheme.
- A sting operation generally needs to be closely linked to the original crime that you are trying to prove. A sting operation is most useful when you are aware that a crime is going to take place and you want to catch a person red-handed to make the evidence irrefutable. As an example, if you know (by way of a whistle-blower) that an asset has been misappropriated and that it will be sold by the subject on a particular day, a sting operation may be useful to directly link the subject to the misappropriated asset.

- The question is, though, whether the sting operation can be successful to link all parties involved with the crime. Criminals also have hierarchies. Frequently the more hierarchically 'important' criminals do not perpetrate the crimes themselves. They issue instructions and they make use of less important foot soldiers to carry out the dirty deeds.
- A correctly executed sting operation can be useful to obtain access to information about methods employed, people involved and the extent of the fraud. Sting operations can also provide investigators with access to premises not normally available.
- Understand who and what is being put at risk through the sting operation. What reprisal is possible and/or likely?
- Obtain legal opinion as to the usability of the sting operation.

3.4.5. Analysis

The real value of information and documents lies in the analysis thereof and the conclusions drawn therefrom. Some examples of analyses include:

- *Analytical reviews*

This is discussed in detail in Chapter 5 on data analytics. Analytical reviews are the analysis of mostly financial information and sometimes of operating information over time and in relation to specific aspects with the purpose of identifying out of trend figures. The out of trend figures are examined to identify discrepancies.

- *Data analytics*

This is also discussed in detail in Chapter 5. Data analytics is the independent analysis of electronic information contained in databases to identify errors, exceptions, deviations or to substantiate amounts.

- *Computer forensics*

This involves understanding and proving how data was generated, moved, accessed, stored, amended and used.

- *Profiling*

This is discussed in detail in Chapter 6 on lifestyle audits and entails the profiling of potential subjects based on public domain data.

- *Detailed lifestyle checks*

This is discussed in detail in Chapter 6 and entails the detailed analysis of the funding of a person's lifestyle against their declared/known income and from other public domain information to either:

  - Identify people who occupy high-risk positions, who are under financial pressure and who may be tempted to succumb to the temptation to perpetrate fraud
  - Identify the most likely people to have perpetrated an actual fraud - remember our rule: 'It is always those who are the closest'
  - Prove that a particular subject funded their lifestyle from undeclared sources

- *E-mail analysis and searches*

An e-mail search can be a very laborious, detailed and iterative process. E-mail searches are however a vital tool in fraud investigation, so prepare yourself for a long haul. Commence your search for all e-mails within a wide range and try to identify e-mails that provide key information. Once you find the key e-mails, understand what it is about these e-mails that help you. Some examples include specific authors, recipients, amounts, contracts or deals, company names, dates, etc. Apply this newly identified key information to the database to extract all e-mails with these keywords, etc. Analyse the reduced population to see if it helps. If it does not help, then revert back to a logical point (for example your initial extraction) and try again to identify keywords/aspects to narrow your search. Continue until you find a meaningfully reduced population.

If on the other hand, it helps, then analyse the newly reduced population to find key works or aspects to search further on. Continue to do this and narrow your search each time a trend or keyword becomes evident.

For example, in a typical procurement type fraud, begin by obtaining all e-mails of the subject (Population 1 = P1a). Extract all e-mails between the subject and the supplier in question (P2a). You may even do this for a period (P3a) when your analytical review highlighted that the procurement expenditure spiked. Look at a few e-mails to see if you can identify anything obvious. Perhaps you identify correspondence that suggests that a particular product seems to have been manipulated. Extract all e-mails with this product word in (P4a). Analyse these e-mails that have this product as a keyword. Perhaps later you identify that another person may have been involved. Regress back to your initial cross-section (say P3a) and then include this person and re-perform your searches to obtain a meaningful population to search (P4b).

It is best if a person with knowledge of the area analyses the mails. This will help to identify the key search words easier. This is however not always possible. If it is not possible, try at least to discuss the matter with someone to identify key aspects to use as possible search criteria.

The search function in Microsoft Outlook is cumbersome to employ. Much specialised software exists to assist investigators with this type of e-mail search. It is wise to invest in such software.

- *Timelines*

The drafting of a timeline of the chronological events is extremely helpful in identifying otherwise invisible information.

Plot basic events along a timeline, as alleged to you/identified in your investigation. Then sit back and logically try to understand if this makes sense and if it supports the subject's assertions. You may find that it is physically impossible for events to have occurred as alleged as:

- Events do not occur in the alleged sequence
- There would have been insufficient time
- Etc.

- *System walkthroughs and site visits*

In a similar manner, walk theoretically, in a desktop exercise, through a computer system or business process. This will typically identify information and anomalies when compared to actual behaviour.

Also, physically walk through business premises where matters transpired. Sitting in the subject's chair and looking at what they saw normally also gives a unique perspective. Try to put yourself in their shoes and try to retrace their purported steps to identify facts or to try to understand what they were thinking.

If required, time the physical walking through the premises to prove that it would not have been possible for the purported event to have occurred, as there was insufficient time available. When presenting this evidence, ask the subjects how long it typically takes to perform the tasks in question. Once they agree on the normal time/process, then compare this to the walk-through and ask them for their explanation of the difference to what they are alleging and what you found.

Also, stand where witnesses purport to have stood and determine if they could have seen everything that they are alleging. Sometimes we are consumed with catching the subject out and we forget about the witnesses. The credibility of your witnesses is also important.

- *Computer forensics*

Most information is in an electronic form or dependent to some degree or other on an electronic device. This is a good thing because computers are machines and machines are predictable, as they work according to a predefined set of rules. The set of rules is far narrower than human behaviour and it is fixed.

It is highly likely that you will require some degree of computer forensics in an investigation. Skill yourself with a working knowledge of computer forensics and set up access to various experts to assist as required. You do not have to know how to perform every aspect of computer forensics, but you need to understand the principles and what is possible and when to call an expert.

The term 'computer forensics' is very broad. It can involve the highly technical experts that dig into program code and metadata or it can involve the analysis of data as described in Chapter 5 on data analytics. There are as many sub-fields and nuances in computer forensics as there are IT job profiles.

At the highest level, computer forensics is concerned with the following:

- Understanding how data was generated
- Where data, applications and infrastructure are stored
- How data and systems are changed and/or updated (interfaces, program logic changes, program run updates, etc)
- System and data dependencies (authorisations, timing, program runs, interfaces from other programs and databases, etc
- Database and file structures
- What the system or program rules are and what the exceptions are
- Data available, file headings, file names, formats (including metadata)

- How data, systems and resources can be accessed
- Backup protocols
- The security of data, applications and infrastructure
- The formats in which data is stored
- If encryption is used or not and the degree of encryption security
- The size of data
- Who the author of a file/data was
- Who amended the file and when
- Who accessed (read, copied, e-mailed, amended or approved) the file
- Comparison of files (to identify changes to know if, for example, it is the same file in terms of intellectual property rights)
- Was the file moved, copied or mailed (when, by whom and what was the difference to the file before and afterwards)
- Who has access (system rights and privileges) to different transaction types, data, infrastructure, systems and resources
- Segregation of duty conflicts and mitigating controls
- Transactional trends and history
- Who performed which transactions, when and the effect of the transaction
- How IT infrastructure is set up (networks, servers, cloud computing, security, access, performance, etc)
- Who the (real) author of an e-mail was
- The machine and/or location from which the e-mail was sent or from which a transaction was performed (the actual perpetrator may have taken remote control of the suspected subject's machine to perform the transaction, for example a bank transfer)
- To whom the e-mail was sent and when
- Files and attachments sent/information exchanged
- Common correspondents (users, machines, locations, times, organisations, communication methods), correspondence themes, correspondence volumes and keyword correspondence
- Detecting identity theft
- Browsing history
- Error handling and logs
- Securing and extraction of evidence
- Monitoring and checking network traffic
- Monitoring and checking internet traffic.

This is by no means a complete list. How do you know which computer forensic steps to perform in an investigation? At the end of the day, as fraud investigators, we want evidence. Approach the need for computer forensics from the investigation side and not from what could be performed, as the list is endless and may not support your investigation objectives. Approach the need for computer forensics from your test objective point of view. 'Keep the end-game in mind' and determine which evidence you require to prove your case and what protocols must be followed to ensure the integrity of evidence.

At the end of the day, do not fret: computer forensics is just logic, not black magic. Get yourself a yardstick and determine what are the rules are. Computers support business processes, so a sound knowledge of the specific business area will be vital to know what should have occurred and what actually occurred. If you understand the business process then you will have a good idea of what the computer systems that support it are required to do.

Remember, when developing your investigation hypotheses, that 'people do and say things for a reason'. See this against the backdrop of the examples of fraud (see Chapter 9) and build your hypotheses. Conduct initial planning and investigative work and refine your hypotheses, as required. Identify the touch points that the business process or the fraud modus operandi had on the computer applications, files, networks, or electronic communication methods. Then determine at each of these points if a computer forensic test is required and which test will be best suited in your investigation. Use an iterative process. Walk your logic through with an IT forensic expert in the identification and design of tests.

The methods by which computer forensics is conducted are less extensive. An understanding of the detailed technical methods, while interesting, is less important, as a computer forensic expert will be required to testify to these, as required.

Our rule concerning the securing of evidence refers. As discussed previously, it is not ideal to work on actual data/machines. For this reason, we make 'copies' (this term is used loosely). The difference between a 'copy' and a 'mirror' needs to be understood. The English terms are actually quite descriptive as they relate to computer forensics:

- A copy is just a copy of all active files. A copy may also just be a copy of specific files or directories. The advantage of a copy is that it is quick and does not require a computer expert to conduct. Copies do however not enjoy protection against loss of integrity and are not admissible in a court of law if brought into question.
- A mirror is a total 'copy' of the entire contents of the hard drive of the device being copied; it is a 'mirror image' captured just as it is. It includes a copy of all files, active and deleted. What a lot of people do not realise is that a deleted file is not removed from the drive. It is merely not visible via conventional software (such as Microsoft File Explorer). Specialised software can retrieve deleted files, depending on whether they have been overwritten by new files or not. Even formatted drives can be partially recovered. Some recovery restrictions apply though. The downfall is that mirroring takes a long time to perform (about four hours per laptop) and must be done according to strict protocols and by a suitably qualified person. You may not always have the luxury of this time. Mirror images are however admissible in court. Mirrored drives are the advised route, as they cannot be amended. It is normal practice to have two mirrors of the same machine. One kept by the person who performed the mirror and one given to the fraud investigator to work with. Mirrors can be made of mobile devices, servers, laptop and desktop hard drives, storage devices, cameras or any electronic media.

- *Evidence files*

Keep the end-game in mind throughout your detailed information gathering phase. Maintain an evidence file (hardcopy and/or electronic files). Develop a good structure (electronic folders and physical dividers) right from the start. Do not wait until the end; you can always rearrange as you progress if your initial file structure turns out not to be fit-for-purpose. Do it as you go to prevent it from becoming too much in the end or losing important elements or forgetting facts. It is always amusing to me just how disorganised many fraud investigators are. Organisational skill is a disciplined habit that can be learnt and practised. The physical file may serve as your evidence file. Topics are not always discussed in the logical sequence in which you structure your evidence files. You should, therefore, in an internal hearing or the like, be able to navigate and jump around your files quickly to get to all the necessary evidence, as topics are discussed.

You may later need to set up or assist in the setting up of the actual criminal case evidence files for court purposes. Evidence files are structured per charge mostly. Charge 1, and all its evidence, charge 2 and all its evidence, etc.

Witness schedules (of who will be testifying to each charge) will map across these as well. Evidence files are discussed later in Chapter 7 on subsequent actions as part of criminal cases.

3.4.6. Interviewing

Alternatively, and/or additionally, information may be gathered through conducting interviews. Refer to Chapter 4 on interviewing for a detailed discussion on interviewing. Interviewing is possibly the most important skill that an investigator needs to have. Conduct interviews with:

- Subjects
- Friends and family of subjects
- Colleagues
- Experts
- Senior members of staff.

You may also want to request subjects to undergo polygraph tests to establish the credibility of their statements. Use the results of the polygraphs in your interviews.

The 'group approach' (discussed in point 3.4.7 below) also refers as a technique where investigators descend on a functional area, branch or business unit and start to interview all staff members and review documents and procedures as part of a wider investigation to identify/prove fraud.

3.4.7. Group approach

a. Background

A group investigation is conducted when a multifaceted team of investigators descends on a corporate function, a business unit or a branch and executes a coordinated investigation to uncover previously unknown facts concerning misconduct. Group investigations are held in situations where:

- There are actual/known or suspected occurrences of gross irregularities.
- These irregularities are however of such a nature that they affect or involve more than one person, usually a larger group of people.

- The extent of the irregularities and/or the degree of individual involvement is however unknown.
- A focused investigation of an individual or on a single area of the business will not suffice at this stage of the process.

These investigations may be done in the presence of one or more of the following:

- A suspicion only and/or little or no initial facts and evidence
- Amidst adverse trends (financial information, operating information, abnormal staff turnover trends, a high number of complaints or a high degree of dissatisfaction, etc)
- In response to a tip-off of irregularities. A single tip-off or a trend (three or four) of seemingly less important tip-offs may be seen as an indication that there are many/ serious problems in the area.
- On the basis of partial information of irregularities
- Against the backdrop of complete information about the irregularities.

Group investigations are conducted by a coordinated team of investigators. They are:

- Led by one designated investigator
- Supported by others representing multi-functional disciplines (forensic team, audit, finance, operations, estimating, corporate functions, etc)
- From internal and/or external resources.

b. Process

The group investigation has, at the highest level, three phases, being:

- Planning and initial information gathering
- Conducting the group investigation
- Subsequent investigation, follow-up and intervention actions.

c. Outcomes

The expected outcomes of a group investigation may be summarised as follows:

- Greater clarity of existing suspicions of irregularities
- New information of previously unknown irregularities (invariably other matters will be identified as part of this investigation)
- Information of other irregularities (not necessarily directly related) and pertinent information
- A plan of action and required responses
- Reduction or eradication of current irregularities
- A deterrent to future potential or current perpetrators of irregularities
- Improved staff morale of remaining staff members.

d. Success

The success of the investigation is dependent on:

- The degree of support from senior leadership within the business
- The involvement of senior leadership in the investigation
- The investigation team's skills and coordination.

A group investigation is unlike other investigations as it requires:

- A well-coordinated effort
- Active senior management involvement and presence.

Remember our rule: 'Forensic investigations are less about fact and more about psychology.' The successful use of psychology in an investigation involves identifying the right psychological levers and determining how to use them to identify the truth/facts. The presence of members of the organisational senior leadership shows commitment and that the group is serious about eradicating such occurrences. Honest people may be reluctant to talk in front of senior people, but most often their desire to expose the truth will supersede their fear of senior management.

e. Planning and information gathering

- *Planning*

Commence by appointing a single person to coordinate the investigation. This should be a senior person with investigation experience. Constitute a multifaceted team of individuals to conduct the investigation.

Discuss and evaluate the information at hand with the team or at least the most senior members of the team. Decide on a desired objective and plan the investigation accordingly, as per the below.

- *Parties involved*

Identify those parties that need to be involved as well as those parties that need to be informed of the process. Bear in mind that this type of investigation must be 'surprise' in nature.

The group investigation works well if there are multiple, simultaneous and coordinated investigations. Suitable people should be chosen to ensure that the best people are conducting those individual investigation activities.

Please also ensure that you pay equal attention to identify those parties that should not be aware of and/or involved in the investigation. These may be parties that are perceived not to be independent due to:

  - Their own potential or actual involvement
  - Actual or perceived loyalties to those involved (colleagues, family or friends)
  - The fact that they may have been responsible for the area and may wish to evade blame for not identifying or preventing the irregularities
  - The fact that they are just too close resulting from their direct involvement in the processes or knowledge of/relationship with people and their consequent inability to see the proverbial 'wood from the trees'
  - Their ability to leak information, adversely affect the investigation and/or destroy evidence.

- *Evidence*

As per our number one forensics rule, all physical evidence should be secured as soon as its relevance to the investigation is apparent, to prevent it from being destroyed or altered. This becomes increasingly important in a group approach as there may be many people involved and it is more difficult to control a lot of people/prevent a wide range of people adversely affecting an investigation.

It is best to draft checklists for each member or sub-team involved.

- *Information*

Investigators should obtain as much information in advance as they can, concerning:

- The allegation/s (date made, time made, made by, persons involved, what happened, other facts, etc)
- The site (history, layout, nature of the work, stage of completion, profitability, etc)
- Personnel (own employees and sub-contractors)
- Clients and suppliers
- Suspects/subjects (previous history of incidents, garnishee orders, default judgments, dependencies, habits and hobbies, marital status, service record, etc).
- Computer systems and documentary evidence that is expected to be on site
- History of incidence
- Reporting lines.

Chapter 6 on lifestyle audits provides a comprehensive guide to gathering information on suspects. Possible sources of information include:

- Personnel files
- Lifestyle audits (Chapter 6)
- Management
- Colleagues
- Public domain searches.

f. Group Investigation

- *Sequence*

The investigation team should arrive unannounced at the site/business area concerned normally at the time that the site is opened and before work commences, but when the whole business unit's team is on site.

The site/area should be closed and no work commenced, unless of a critical nature, while the initial address is given. The initial address should only last ten minutes. It is a good idea to prepare 'closed for technical reasons' – type notifications in advance that can be displayed outside the premises where public trade is applicable.

All staff members should be called together in a central area. The investigation coordinator should read the script, as per the example (see Annexure 3.5 attached hereto) and the day should progress thereafter as per the process outlined below. The wording may be amended to suit the audience and/or the individual circumstances.

- *Questionnaire*

In some instances (typically used for more sophisticated employees than average general labourers), staff members may all be requested to complete a predefined questionnaire straight after the initial address. The merits of the use of this tool must be debated before use. It may not be applicable in all circumstances.

This tool may be used:

- To cover a wider group of staff members and to gain inputs from people who will otherwise not be included in the interview process
- To determine who is to be interviewed
- As inputs to the interviews (discussed later)
- As evidence against people (identified to be involved during the investigation) in hearings where they have denied knowledge and/or involvement and/or failed to provide information/make declarations.

g. Interview process

A cross-section of people should be interviewed to obtain information. Chapter 4 on interviewing refers, but interviewing is typically about:

- What you know (to a lesser degree)
- What you are perceived to know by the interviewee (most important)
- The interviewee's perception of:
    - How much trouble they can be in if they do not cooperate
    - Their need to 'get in first' and in so doing not to be implicated too deeply by co-conspirators
    - The favour that they may win from management if they cooperate
    - Their need for revenge/retribution (disgruntled)
    - The strength of their loyalty to or fear of the perpetrators.

The interviews should be planned as far as possible, irrespective of whether you are on a 'fishing expedition' to identify unknown facts or whether a specific point needs to be proven. About eight to nine normal-length interviews can be conducted comfortably on average in a day. The key people may need to be interviewed on day one if the process is going to span more than a day. The critical momentum and the greatest impact of this approach will be achieved early on day one.

One person should lead the interview process. The investigating team should be careful not to interrupt the lead interviewer, as they may be trying to lead to interviewee down a specific path. The interview team should identify signals and/or set a protocol in advance of when the other members of the interview team may ask their questions. For the greater part, they should write down their questions as they come up and ask them once the lead interviewer is finished.

Interviewers should be mindful not to ask:

- Leading questions
- Questions that require a 'yes' or 'no' answer.

Interviewers should ask interviewees:

- What they think is going wrong in the area and why
- Who else they think should be included in the interview process and why
- Who they think is involved and to what degree
- Where we will find the evidence/who will be able to assist the investigation team.

Interviewers should decide what outcome they want from the interviewee in advance. They should not come straight out and ask the interviewee if they perpetrated the irregularity, as it may be difficult to progress with the interview if the person just answers 'no'.

Questions should be structured, as discussed in the interviewing chapter. The sequence of questions should be in such a way that interviewers commence by asking questions that block possible untrue answers later before asking the questions that will get to the crux of what is required.

The sequence of the interviews of the various people and the structure of each interview should be planned to ensure that:

- The identities of the informants are not revealed
- There is a cross-section of people interviewed (senior to lower-level staff members, those perceived to have knowledge and some unknown).

The sequence in which people are interviewed may also be important because there is a high probability that as soon as one person has been interviewed, they will relay the gist of the discussion held. It is also anticipated that the interviewee will be questioned by their colleagues and/or co-conspirators on what the interview covered. Suspects could plan/practise their responses in advance.

The venue where the interviews are to be conducted is also important. It should be in a place free of interruptions and where the confidentiality of the interview can be guaranteed.

h. Concurrent investigations

The person coordinating the investigation should monitor the outcomes of the other investigation activities and evaluations that are being conducted simultaneously with the interviews.

The team leader should utilise new and/or additional information from the investigators in the interviews. Likewise, the team leader should also pass information back to the investigators to guide their detailed efforts.

i. Business processes

The other investigation team members should begin with their focused investigations concurrently while the interviews are taking place. Areas of focus include:

- Determining the degree of compliance with business processes and controls
- Evaluating documents and computer systems
- Assessing staff members' level of understanding of activities and processes
- Physical verification of assets, stock, etc
- Identifying physical aspects that may be important, for example disabled security systems, physical damage, etc
- Feeding any information provided and/or identified back to the investigation team.

j. Subsequent follow-up

(i) General

A debriefing should be held by the investigation team on the completion of the site investigation each day. Lessons learnt, information identified and subsequent actions required should be discussed at a sanitised level, agreed and scheduled.

(ii) Policy and procedural changes

Specific and immediate actions may be required. All required policy and procedural changes to be made should be discussed in principle, drafted and implemented to prevent and/or identify recurrence. Such enhancements should be made with a special bearing on bolstering internal control, but not to disadvantage any ongoing investigation.

(iii) Communication and feedback

Communication of what has transpired and the outcomes of the investigation are very important to the success of future investigations. Positive feedback will assist to instil the culture of zero tolerance and to act as a deterrent.

Only a salient and sanitised overview of the process followed and outcomes obtained should be communicated to the general staff members.

The morale of the remaining staff members once such an investigation has been completed is very important. These staff members are often left as victims and need to be made to feel that:

- Their contribution was important
- They are valued despite the difficult situation
- The group does not tolerate irregularities
- Their colleagues and friends who have been implicated in the irregularities will be given a fair procedure, that they are not being targeted and that the outcome of the hearing, etc has not been predetermined.

Clients and suppliers may also need to be informed of the decisive action taken by management in an attempt to repair goodwill.

It is also important that the business owners and management are kept abreast of developments. Chapter 8 on reporting refers. This is required both in terms of their duty to manage risk and from the confidence that they need to develop around the security of their investment.

(iv) Disciplinary action

Any required disciplinary actions should be held within the normal process of the organisation's disciplinary code. Refer to Chapter 7 on subsequent actions.

3.4.8. Outputs

Again, as you progress, 'keep the end-game in mind'. As far as possible and unless patently obvious, presume that every matter is going to go as far as a criminal case. Build your evidence in support of this. This means that you should secure every possible piece of evidence, as you find it. Obtain statements and affidavits as you progress. You can always add supplementary affidavits, but get the ones that you can, while you can. Chapters 4 and 8 on, respectively, interviewing and reporting, refer for detailed discussions on this.

The same is true for documentary and informational evidence. Do not wait to see if you might need to mirror a subject's hard drive. Spend the money (to get an expert to mirror the drive) and ensure that you lock down the integrity of the electronic evidence in the event that you need it later. It is unfortunately not possible to predict what you will need in advance. Our rules of: 'the most important thing to do is to secure the evidence' and 'the best time to do something is immediately' refer.

The potential outputs of the detailed information gathering and analysis stage include:

- Working papers
- Interview notes
- Evidence
- Information
- Analyses
- Conclusions
- Admissions
- Resignations
- Recoveries
- Signed acknowledgements of debt
- Affidavits
- Statements
- Expert opinions:
    - Subject matter expert opinions (engineers, lawyers, etc)
    - Polygraph results
    - Handwriting analysis
- A next step high-level plan of action
- An updated investigation journal.

3.4.9. Finalise hypothesis

As your detailed analysis of information progresses, what really happened with the fraud will become clearer. This is a good time to revert back to your initial hypothesis and refine it, adding in the required detail. This will be used for:

- Deciding on additional work
- Reporting
- Drafting charges.

3.4.10. Update investigation plan

Update the investigation plan to reflect insights obtained to date.

3.5. COMPLETE AND CONCLUDE

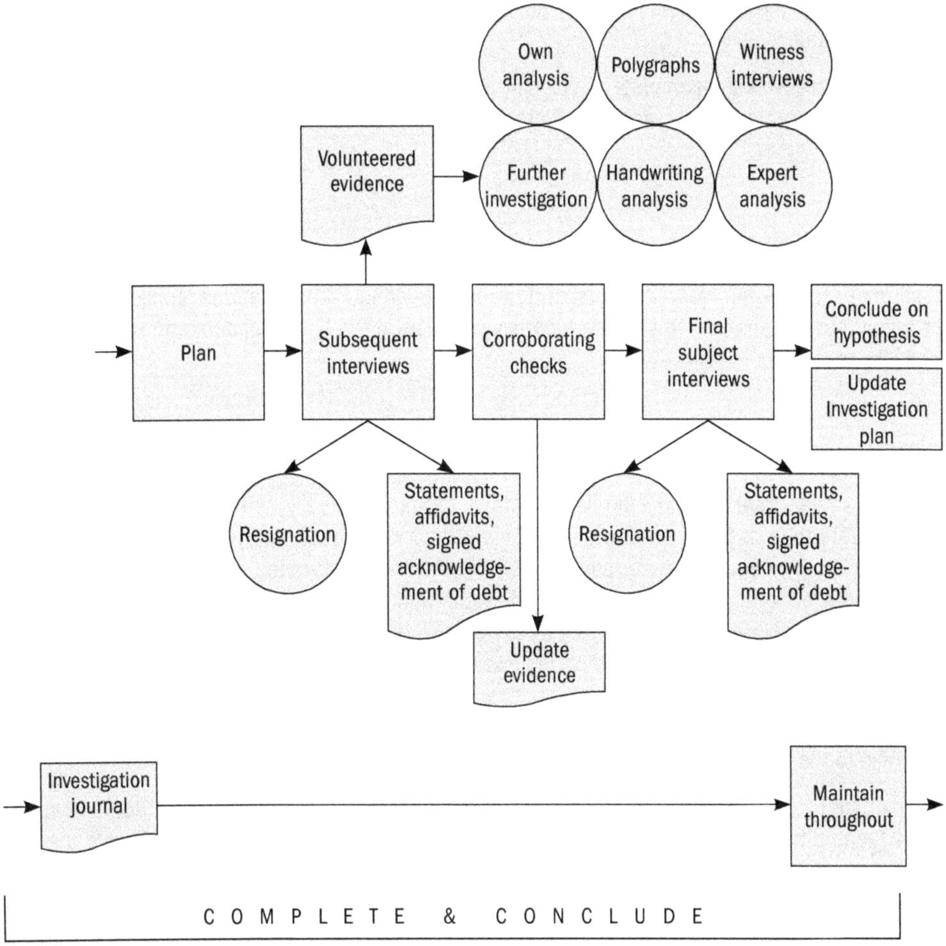

Figure 3.7 *Complete and conclude phase*

3.5.1. Additional investigation

Decide, by comparing the information and evidence that you have to your refined hypothesis, if any additional work needs to be conducted. Repeat those steps of the detailed information gathering and analysis phase that you need to until you are comfortable that you have sufficient evidence and understanding of what has transpired. 'Sufficient' means that someone else, 'looking cold' at the evidence that you have, will come to the same conclusions that you have reached.

It is likely that you will only feel completely comfortable that you have everything once you have drafted your affidavit, which summarises your investigation or when you have finalised how you plan to present your internal labour case. This is because this is the stage when all aspects are pulled together in your mind. Drafting of an affidavit and the structuring of a labour case come later, but keep the end-game in mind, as you will need to decide if you need to conduct any additional work.

In addition to covering incomplete areas, new aspects will be identified as you progress. Plan how you are going to cover these aspects. Redo the relevant investigation steps that were discussed previously.

3.5.2. Investigation journal

Remember to maintain your investigation journal throughout. Your notations should be at a level of detail that will enable you six months or six years down the line to understand what was done and why you did it.

3.5.3. Volunteered evidence

Subjects make assertions in interviews. Refrain (certainly initially) from telling them just how unbelievable their assertions are. Attempt to win their confidence and obtain their cooperation. Try to get them to commit to certain answers (the concept of layering refers, as discussed later in Chapter 4 on interviewing). Once committed, thank them for their assertions and ask them to help you substantiate this by supplying documents to prove this. Copies of bank statements are one of the most common categories of documents that you will want them to volunteer. If they do not volunteer their private bank statements to you, you will be required to go through a protracted process of subpoenaing them. There is no guarantee that you will obtain the subpoena and it may just take too long.

If they agree to give you documents, do not wait for them to bring them to you. Remember our rules: 'secure the evidence' and 'the best time to do something is immediately'. Bundle them in a car and take them to get the evidence wherever it is (their house, the bank, etc). Offer to pay the bank costs if there is a fee for obtaining their bank statements. For example, tell them: 'No problem, you are doing the organisation a favour and it is only fair that the organisation covers the costs of the investigation.'

In one case, we were convinced that the person procuring IT services was involved in a corrupt relationship with IT service providers. He volunteered his bank accounts and we rushed off to get them. As it turned out he was innocent and we needed to rethink who the subject was. We saved valuable time in determining this immediately.

3.5.4. Plan

Plan your next steps and refer back to your plan frequently to ensure that you remain on track. Being able to communicate that you have a plan and your progress against this plan also inspires confidence in the people that you report to.

It is suggested that you document your progress updates to people in one of two ways, being:

- By adding a date column with a progress update on a spreadsheet register of all cases. This also assists when you need to give regular progress updates on cases. Imagine the cases' names and numbers running in column A from top to bottom (row: 2, 3, 4, etc). Columns with follow-up dates run from left to right (column: B, C, onwards). It is very easy to be able to refresh yourself on what has transpired to date by reading each of the follow-up notes for a particular case.
- Alternatively, and/or additionally, forward previous e-mails to these people in which the planned steps were originally laid out and add the additional correspondence/steps to the new e-mails each time. This will create a chronological e-mail thread of updates. It is also advisable to give a status of previously planned steps in subsequent e-mails. This option is more applicable when giving management and/or outside service providers ongoing guidance on how to progress. In this manner, all correspondence is in one place (e-mail) and they cannot dispute knowing what to do, as there is a complete e-mail thread.

3.5.5. Subsequent interviews

It may be necessary to interview additional people after the detailed information and analysis stage. There may also very likely be additional facts that you would like to question the subjects on. Plan and conduct these at this stage.

3.5.6. Outputs

This marks the end of the information gathering and analysis stage. Outputs are added to the previous options and include:

- Updated and additional working papers
- Updated and additional interview notes
- Updated and additional evidence
- Updated and additional information
- Updated and additional analysis
- Updated and additional conclusions
- Admissions
- Resignations
- Recoveries
- Signed acknowledgements of debt
- Affidavits
- Statements
- A next step plan of action
- An updated investigation journal.

3.5.7. Corroborating checks

Statements and assertions made by interviewees cannot just be accepted and they will need to be corroborated. Corroboration can occur via any of the previous methods used in the investigation. Some of the methods by which to corroborate assertions include:

- Own analysis (analytical reviews, data analytics, etc)
- Further investigation
- Testimonies of others that confirm or deny assertions
- Comparison to previous witness/interviewee interviews
- Comparison to existing documentary evidence (accounting records, invoices, statements, etc)
- Making use of expert opinions to corroborate assertions:
    - Subject matter experts (engineers, doctors, lawyers, etc)
    - Polygraphs
    - Handwriting analysis
- Corroborating may also include broadening the investigation to additional:
    - People
    - Processes
    - Types of transactions
    - Transactions
- Assertions may also be corroborated against volunteered evidence.

3.5.8. Final subject interviews

Based on the information, analysis and inputs received in all the preceding steps, you may wish to conduct final interviews with the subjects, as:

- The concept of 'layering' of interviews discussed in the chapter on interviewing is of particular relevance at this stage of the investigation. The subject may have committed to answers in previous interviews. These answers may now be seen by you in a different light based on the investigation work completed. Additional layers of interviews will allow you the opportunity to contradict the subject's previous assertions.
- Alternatively, it is reasonable to expect that you will not have contemplated all the questions to ask the subjects at the time of the initial interviews.
- New and additional facts that you have not had an opportunity to discuss with the subject will most likely have surfaced during the investigation.

This stage of the investigation process will, therefore, represent an ideal opportunity to hold any final interviews that you require. Conduct your interviews along the same lines as per all other interviews. The chapter on interviewing refers.

The final interviews will primarily be admission-seeking interviews and they are less likely to be information-seeking interviews at this late stage of the investigation.

Ensure that you document your interviews and conclude on the outcome. Update your investigation journal. Bear in mind that minor additional work may be required.

3.5.9. Conclude on hypothesis

Now that all work has been completed you are at the stage to conclude on what you set out to prove. Reflect on your updated hypothesis based on all information, analysis and evidence. Refine your hypothesis as required.

Congratulations, your investigation is now complete! You now need to bring the whole process to some form of fruition. Decide therefore on the subsequent steps, as discussed below.

3.5.10. Update investigation plan

Update the investigation plan to reflect the insights obtained and steps performed to date.

3.5.11. Outputs

This marks the end of the 'complete and conclude' stage. Additional outputs that could be added to the previous outputs include:

- Finalised working papers
- Additional and final interview notes
- Updated and the most complete evidence available
- Updated and the most complete information available
- Finalised and complete analysis
- Final conclusions
- Admissions
- Resignations
- Recoveries
- Signed acknowledgements of debt
- Affidavits
- Statements
- A plan of subsequent actions to be undertaken
- An updated investigation journal.

3.6. SUBSEQUENT ACTIONS

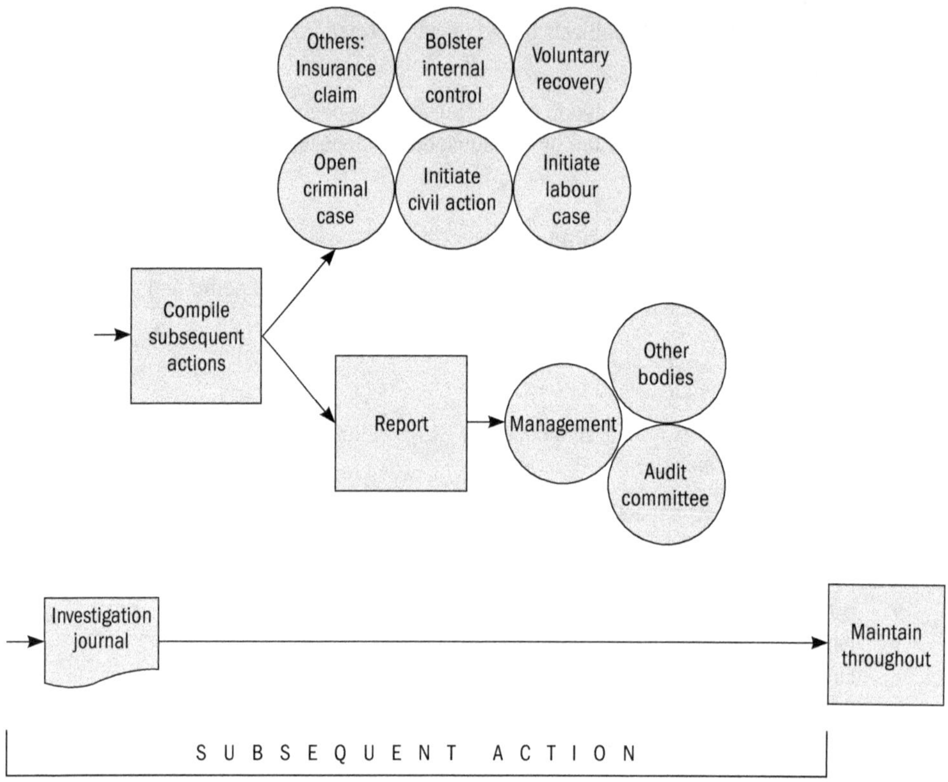

Figure 3.8 *Subsequent actions phase*

3.6.1. Introduction

The investigative portion of the process is now complete. We now move to the stage of making use of what we concluded based on our investigation. There are essentially three areas that we concentrate on after the investigative stage, being:

- Reporting
- Direct actions
- Indirect actions.

3.6.2. Plan

Commence by compiling a list of subsequent actions to be undertaken once your investigation is complete. Draft a plan for each action to be undertaken.

3.6.3. Investigation journal

Review your investigation journal and ensure that it is complete. Compare it to the working papers and the notes of any colleagues that assisted during the investigation. Ensure that you update any incomplete sections of your investigation journal.

3.6.4. Reporting

Each of the reporting areas listed below will be discussed in detail under the reporting chapter. They are mentioned here to complete the end-to-end process in your mind. Please refer to the chapter on reporting for a detailed understanding of each of these. Local privacy laws are vital to understanding when reporting matters. It is not important that you as the fraud investigator inform all these parties. It is only important that someone within the organisation complies with reporting requirements. The possible parties to whom you may report include:

a. Criminal matters

This involves the opening of a criminal case with the police. This is a very important action and should be the aim of all investigations. The chapter on subsequent actions supplies a detailed discussion.

b. Other authorities

There may be a legal, a moral or a professional obligation to report matters to other authorities. Examples of other authorities and specialised police units include:

- Narcotics units
- Tax and revenue authorities
- Border and custom police
- Environmental bodies
- The military
- EU union, USA and British anti-bribery and anti-corruption units
- Interpol
- Etc.

Establish which authorities are relevant to your investigation and what the reporting requirements are. Take the reporting to these authorities under the advisement of legal counsel if required to ensure that you do not make any incorrect statements. Incorrect admissions could inadvertently incriminate the organisation.

c. Audit committee

The audit committee is normally an important client, especially if you are working for an in-house forensic function. There are normally formally structured reporting protocols in place for reporting to the audit committee. See the chapter on reporting for a detailed discussion.

d. Board and senior management

While the audit committee is a working committee of the board, you may be required to report separately or in greater detail to the board. The organisation's internal reporting conventions would need to be established. The seriousness of the matter may also dictate specific reporting requirements. See the chapter on reporting for a detailed discussion.

e. **Management**
Management is responsible for the day-to-day running of the organisation and may need to have greater detail on the matter, as they will need to take action. The chapter on reporting discusses this in detail.

f. **The general organisation**
People in the organisation may need to be informed of the outcome of serious matters. This may entail a specific communication from management or it may be done via a periodic fraud newsletter. Facts will need to be sanitised. Failure to communicate important matters to the wider organisation can have a negative impact on morale.

g. **Specific colleagues affected by the matter**
There may have been specific colleagues who worked closely with the subject/s. They will also have a need to understand what has transpired. Conduct any such discussions with the support of HR or a suitably qualified counsellor. They should be given slightly more information than the general organisation, but it should still be highly sanitised. These are the people who remain behind and who are going to run the business. They sit with all kinds of emotions including:

- Pity for the subject
- Support for either the subject or the organisation
- Guilt and remorse because they were somehow involved
- Anger at either the subject or the organisation.

Such reporting, despite what the subject did, needs to be factual, free of emotion and respectful. It is advisable to err on the side of giving less detail rather than giving too much. Please also bear in mind that legal processes may still be ongoing (the matter is sub-judice) and you do not want to be guilty of adversely affecting proceedings or, in the worst case, defeating the ends of justice. Sensitive facts will need to be sanitised.

h. **Shareholders, owners, holding companies and subsidiaries lower down**
Shareholders and holding companies may need to be informed of the outcome of serious matters. This may be done via the organisation's own reporting channels or you may be requested to do it.

i. **Key clients, business parties, key suppliers and other parties**
As with shareholders and owners, the key parties that the organisation deals with may need to be updated on the outcome of matters. Facts will need to be sanitised.

j. **The stock exchange and/or the investing public**
Determine any specific stock exchange's reporting requirements. Ensure that you take the reporting under the advisement of suitable people such as legal counsel and professional accountants.

k. Financing institutions

The institution that is providing funding may require reporting to as well. Even if there is not a formal reporting requirement, it may be good practice to inform them of the occurrences and what the organisation has done about it. This will contribute to building a relationship of trust.

l. Insurance houses

Insurance houses will need to be informed of all matters for which the organisation intends lodging a claim. In some cases, the organisation may have an obligation to report all matters of a particular type to the insurance company even if the organisation is not intending to claim and is self-insuring the specific incident. Determine the relevant insurance policy's requirements.

m. External parties and/or the press

Informing of internal matters to external parties should be well planned and handled by those people in the organisation authorised to communicate to the public. As far as possible a statement should be prepared and approved in advance. Alternatively, the message to be communicated should be role-played and practised. Facts will need to be sanitised. Examples of external parties include:

- The general public
- Specific private individuals affected by the matter
- Landlords or properties that the organisation is renting
- Private security companies.

In a particular incident that I dealt with, a painter had climbed up scaffolding during lunchtime and tried to gain access to an apartment in the block that the company was painting. Feedback was given to the apartment owner after the matter had been handed over to the police to say that they were dealing with the culprit. The owner was understandably disturbed and emotional. The owner was significantly calmer after being listened to empathetically and having the facts at hand explained calmly. The company received a compliment from the apartment owner, the neighbourhood association and the police station commander for the manner in which the incident was handled. This was important, as the company did a lot of work in the area and one of the company owners lived in the area.

n. Industry and professional bodies

There is an element of trust associated with professionals. Failure to uphold the ethics of the industry is a poor reflection of the whole industry and brings everyone down. It is therefore important to report the misconduct of members to the responsible professional body to allow them the take any actions they deem necessary. Please also bear in mind that you cannot make any declarations if the subject has not been found guilty yet. The punishment also needs to suit the crime. Barring a person for life from their professional status may not be the fairest option. Examples of industry bodies to be contacted include:

- SAICA
- IIA SA
- Bar/law society
- Estate agents' board.

o. Internal audit

Internal audit should be aware of all fraud matters, as they evaluate the adequacy and effectiveness of internal controls. Auditors try, through various analyses, to identify high-risk areas. The area in which the matter occurred may represent a higher risk area for inclusion in a future audit cycle. You may also wish to direct internal audit to conduct an immediate evaluation of the internal controls in the business processes around the matter. Internal audit would be able to make recommendations to bolster controls to prevent and/or detect future occurrences.

p. External audit

External audit will need to be aware of all material matters that may affect their audit procedures and opinion. Provide the external auditors at year-end with a list of all matters dealt with. It is then up to them to decide what further work procedures to apply.

q. Third-parties, suppliers, clients, etc

While organisations do not like airing their dirty laundry, it may be required to meet with suppliers to define a way forward if they were affected by the matter as well. These parties may have been the employer of the offending party. Alternatively, your organisation may have employed the subject that affected them. Facts will need to be sanitised.

3.6.5. Direct actions

Other than reporting, you will most likely need to consider taking one or more of the actions discussed below. Based on the outcome of the chosen actions, there may be some further reporting required. This could be reported separately or the aforementioned reporting may be delayed to ensure more complete reporting at one time. Ongoing status updates and reporting to the relevant parties, as listed previously, is however recommended. The chapter on reporting refers in this regard. Some of these subsequent actions are discussed in greater detail elsewhere in the book. Possible further actions to be considered may include:

a. Internal labour case

The first priority in most organisational matters is to 'stop the bleeding'. While we cannot presuppose the outcome of a labour matter, we will most times need to conduct some form of internal labour case to address the errant behaviour. This may entail simple counselling or a full disciplinary hearing. How to structure a labour case is discussed in detail under the chapter on subsequent actions. An independent chairperson will give a sanction based on a balance of probability.

Unless the subjects have resigned, internal labour cases will always involve the subjects of the investigation. If the subjects have resigned, you will need to ensure that HR records are suitably updated to record the events. This is important to prevent reemployment and for when references on the subjects are requested.

There may also be a requirement to address the actions of people other than the subjects. Organisations frequently focus on the subjects and forget about those people whose actions assisted or perpetuated the misconduct. The most important rule of labour law is that of consistency. It is therefore important to ensure that each person is given the opportunity to amend their behaviour and to improve. Determine who was responsible for the controls or who should have detected or prevented the fraud. These people may require counselling.

b. External labour case

In some cases, an employee may take the organisation to an external labour tribunal or court based on their perception of an unfair labour practice related to their internal labour case. Again, these employees could include the subjects of the investigation or other general employees. You may have to represent the organisation in such matters or you may just have to testify.

c. Civil matters

Civil matters are private lawsuits raised by the organisation against one or more individuals. The importance of raising these within the prescription period and the benefits to criminal matters are discussed in the chapter on subsequent actions.

d. Voluntary recoveries

The 'first prize' is if subjects voluntarily repay misappropriated funds. As discussed previously ensure that you have an acknowledgement of debt form handy at the time of the subject's interview. In this manner, you will have a longer period in which to lay claim to the funds.

Inform subjects that it is important to them that they show any potential court that they:

- Cooperate
- Show remorse
- Show restitution.

In this way, you encourage them to volunteer to repay the money. Subjects may have spent their ill-gotten gains and may not be in a position to repay the funds. You will, therefore, need to suggest different ways in which they can repay the money.

Some suggestions of manners in which they can repay funds include:

- Repaying the misappropriated funds they are still holding
- Repaying out of their own funds
- Signing an acknowledgement of debt and repaying the funds in instalments
- Selling assets to cover the losses
- Signing over their rights to fixed investments
- Volunteering the proceeds of their pension to the organisation
- Getting a spouse, family member or friend to repay the funds or acknowledge the debt on behalf of the subject.

It is not suggested to accept assets in lieu of losses as:

- The actual proceeds may not cover the organisation's loss.
- If the proceeds exceed the loss, you will have a legal obligation to pay the excess to the subject.

- The selling of assets will most likely not be the organisation's business.
- The selling of the assets may be more complicated than envisaged.
- The subject may claim duress.
- It may not be possible to verify the actual ownership/source of the assets (may also be misappropriated).

It is better that they do the selling themselves and give the proceeds required to the organisation.

In some organisations that I worked with we even went so far as to write letters in mitigation of subjects to the prosecution when sentence is handed down to say that they cooperated. Similarly, we have also written letters in aggravation when they refuse to cooperate.

e. Asset forfeiture

Some countries have legislation which will allow the assets of a subject to be frozen if it can be sufficiently proven that the assets were funded from illegal activities. In this manner, you are able to prevent the subject from making the money 'disappear'.

The court will then instruct the assets to be sold if the matter is proven. Determine if this legislation is applicable to the matter and the country that you are dealing with.

f. Bolstering of internal controls

The old cliché 'fool me once, shame on you; fool me twice, shame on me' comes to mind. Organisations need to learn from mistakes. An analysis of the internal controls should be conducted to ensure that any control deficiencies are bolstered to ensure that future occurrences are:

- Prevented
- Detected in a timely manner
- Corrected.

The controls, on the other hand, may exist and may have been adequately designed. Perpetrators may just have not complied with controls or may have successfully circumvented (normally through collusion) existing controls. The reinforcing of existing controls may, therefore, be all that is required.

Be sure to document the attendance of training and reinforcing sessions, to prevent people later saying that they were unaware.

g. Therapy of those remaining

Organisations always seem to forget about the people that remain behind. The subjects (the people that we do not like) have gone. We now need to concentrate on the people who remain behind and who are going to run the business going forward. Senior management typically are too angry about the losses that the organisation has suffered or are too uncompassionate to consider such suggestions.

Employees may not want to be counselled, but it is suggested to at least make the offer to them. Senior management normally likes to make a quick suggestion that the organisation will pay for anyone that wishes to undergo therapy and that they should come and see them if they want to exercise this option in the hope that they never do.

There have been many positive reports from people who have exercised this option. The victim (mostly an organisation in our type of work) represented by the experiences of the people left behind will be more important in traumatic (for example in the case of armed robbery or assault) or heinous crimes.

3.6.6. Indirect actions

Some aspect, less related to the matter will also need to be conducted upon conclusion of the matter, including:

a. Updating of HR records

The updating of HR records to record the events is important to:

- Ensure that recommended actions are recorded and completed
- A record of performance is maintained for use in possible future matters
- Ensure that matters are recorded for inclusion in future periodic performance discussions
- Prevent reemployment where relevant
- Ensure accurate references are given.

b. Investigation post-mortem

I strongly suggest conducting a documented post-mortem of all investigations to ensure that lessons learnt are not lost.

c. Customer satisfaction questionnaires

The use of formal or informal assessment of the satisfaction of clients is always a good idea. Results will, however, need to be seen in the light of the case and who is giving the feedback. Difficult matters sometimes result in sour grapes in feedback. On the other hand, some people are just too reluctant or scared to give negative feedback to the investigators, which is also not helpful.

d. Investigator performance appraisals

It is recommended to conduct a job-related performance appraisal of each staff member after each large audit or investigation. This ensures that they have an opportunity to correct development areas soonest. Collate all performance appraisals for use in their annual performance reviews.

e. Overall investigation wrapping up

Some examples of general forensic department administration that may need to be conducted include:

- Submitting of expense claims
- Filing and storage of documents.

3.7. DOCUMENTATION EXAMPLES

The following are examples of documentation and records that may be used in an investigation:

a. **Investigation journal**
A chronological summary of investigation events.

b. **Interview notes**
A close to verbatim record of what was asked by the interviewers and what the interviewee said and/or did in response. These can be typed or handwritten.

c. **Meeting minutes**
These are summaries of the actions of previous points undertaken and of new undertakings, discussion points and decisions.

d. **Transcripts**
These are verbatim summaries of meetings/interviews/proceedings that were held.

e. **Planning notes**
All planning documents drafted in the course of the investigation.

f. **Calculations and analyses**
All calculations and analyses conducted over the course of the investigation.

g. **Lifestyle reviews**
The reviews of the subjects' lifestyles and the conclusions and results of how these are funded.

h. **Public domain documents**
All records obtained during public domain searches.

i. **Correspondence**
All correspondence undertaken over the course of the investigation.

j. **Reports**
All reports written, as per above.

k. **Hardcopy financial documents and records**
Documents used during the investigation.

l. **Computer records and files**
All electronic records, including; financial records, cash books, price databases, transactional history, supplier data bases, customer databases, stock lists, debtors or creditors' history, etc.

m. **Photos, video footage, voice recordings, CDs and DVDs**
Any multimedia files used during the investigation.

n. **Registers**
Examples of registers include: asset registers, access registers, etc.

o. **Working papers**
Any working papers completed during the investigation.

p. **Test plans/audit programmes**
Any documented specific tests performed during the investigation.

q. **Business process risk assessments**
Any risk assessments of control deficiencies conducted.

r. **Evidence files**
All evidence (including aforementioned) gathered in the course of the investigation in one group of files.

s. **Labour, criminal or civil case material**
All material used in any of these matters.

3.8. NEED FOR INDEPENDENCE

It is important for investigators to be independent of the matters that they investigate. The following reasons support the need to make use of a person independent of the subject and/or business area under review:

- Interviewees may make disclosures more freely to a stranger.
- Senior people may not want to talk to an investigator whom they perceive to be junior to their organisational status.
- Your investigatory skills may not hold sufficient credibility with people you have worked with for a long time. They may perceive you as their friend or contemporary and not as a skilled investigator. As the old cliché goes: 'A prophet is never accepted in his hometown.'
- A non-independent investigator may not want to believe that a person they have known for years could have done something like that (the description of the fraudster's personality in Chapter 4 refers). It is easier for an independent person to distance themselves from the emotions of the person/people being investigated and look objectively at the facts.
- A non-independent investigator may be reluctant to 'punish' a person with whom they have had a long friendship or about whose difficult personal situation they are aware or whose family are friends, children go to school together, etc.
- It may not be in a person's (who is responsible for a business area) best interest to expose the full extent of a fraud for fear of making themselves look bad for allowing the fraud to take place and/or not detecting it.
- A non-independent investigator may be angry with the perpetrator and they may want to exact revenge. This could impair their independence and make them jump into situations without due consideration to the detriment of the investigation.
- The actual or perceived lack of independence may be used against you in subsequent actions in an attempt to discredit your investigation/the subsequent action taken (internal disciplinary hearing).

Raise any independence concerns with your senior if you think that you are in a situation where you not independent. Ensure that you recuse yourself from the matter. Ensure that you put your reasons in writing.

In some situations, it may be unavoidable that you investigate a matter in which your independence may be questioned. In such cases:

- Ensure you always have a witness to all your actions and dealings with subjects.
- Document everything, even verbal conversations.
- Obtain multiple people's opinions on your decisions.
- Make use of external/independent advisors.
- Stick to professional, ethical and defendable actions.

Annexure 3.1
Example of an initial incident notification information template

No	Information required	Discussion/reasons for information	Information declared	Next steps/ further action
	What is being done/ are they doing?	This is a high-level explanation of the irregularity.		
	What is their modus operandi?	This provides a more detailed explanation than above and includes a description of the steps that they are following.		
	Who is doing this and/or is involved?	This will tell you: ▪ Who to interview ▪ When to interview them (the chapter on interviewing refers) ▪ Whose work to include in the scope of the investigation ▪ The possible scope/extent; for example, a clerk may only have access to 'X', while a manager may have access to 'Y' ▪ Who is the most likely to have been involved, when they were involved and how they were involved.		
	What amounts are involved?	This could be an estimate of the quantum of the fraud or indicate the modus operandi of the fraud, for example, amounts: ▪ Below a specific authorisation limit ▪ That pertain to a particular supplier ▪ That fall within a particular date range, etc.		
	When did this come to your attention?	How long have they known? This will have a bearing on the chance of you obtaining evidence if the matter is being reported long after the fact. What does the length of time taken to report tell you about the reporter's motives (potential involvement, revenge, etc) if it has been known to them for a long time?		

No	Information required	Discussion/reasons for information	Information declared	Next steps/ further action
	How did this come to your attention?	If we know what they did to discover the irregularities, then perhaps this will help us to: ▪ Corroborate what they are alleging ▪ Identify the modus operandi of the perpetrator/s ▪ Emulate what they have done to identify the full scope of the irregularities.		
	Why are you reporting this now?	As a word of caution, I would tend not to ask this. Your primary motive is to get as much information as you can, as soon as possible and to set up further discussions if required. At this early point, your purpose is not to put the information that you are receiving on trial. If you are seen to be too attacking, the reporter may become defensive and clam up/decline to assist you further. As strange as it may sound, let it flow. We will worry about the integrity of the information later. Only ask them if the opportunity presents itself. Maybe this is something that you can try to understand yourself without asking them directly. Many of our informants are not the most upstanding people. It is important for us to understand their motives. This may have a bearing on the truth and/or additional facts required. For example: Is there something they are trying to hide? Are they reporting the matter now to appear to be assisting and to prevent being associated with the perpetrators? Try to determine when they should have reported this matter.		

No	Information required	Discussion/reasons for information	Information declared	Next steps/ further action
	At which dates and times did/does this occur?	Remember our rule: 'Forensics is about psychology, not fact.' It will be easier to find and/or prove irregularities if we know what the perpetrator 'was thinking'. We can then apply this to the entire transaction population to identify the full scope of irregularities. For example, consider if the irregularities occurred: ▪ Early in the morning ▪ Late in the afternoon ▪ When the supervisor was in a hurry to go home ▪ As an 'emergency'/'urgent' transaction ▪ When a supervisor or the normal responsible person was on leave/absent. *In one example, the perpetrator used to come to the financial manager just as he was about to go home and ask him to approve the payments. The financial manager was notorious for going home early and was typically irritated if anything delayed his 16h00 departure. The financial manager signed the fraudulent expenses without checking.* *In another matter, the perpetrator used to convince the cheque signatories that he required a 'stock' of approved blank cheques for the period that they were away on business. He used these 'approved' blank cheques to misappropriate company funds.*		
	Who else knows about this and for how long have they known about this?	This will tell you: ▪ How long it has been known ▪ How long has it been going on ▪ Who else to talk to ▪ If the organisation's fraud reporting requirements have been complied with.		

No	Information required	Discussion/reasons for information	Information declared	Next steps/ further action
	Who will have information to assist with the investigation? Please specify which information they will have and why.	As per above.		
	Who should I trust and why?	This is very important, as you may wish to limit knowledge of the investigation to prevent the destruction of evidence, influencing witnesses, ruining the element of surprise and providing the subject with the opportunity to rehearse, etc.		
	Who should I distrust and why?	The element of surprise is most important in the early stages of the investigation. It is also difficult to understand the loyalties at play when the investigation commences. Remember there is honour amongst thieves and they may be feeding information about the investigation to their complicit friends.		
	Where does this occur?	This will assist you in knowing: ▪ Where to look ▪ What will be involved in the investigation ▪ What the chance of a favourable outcome will be, for example, if it occurs in a 'difficult' country where the chance of a fair trial is unlikely.		
	When last did these irregular activities occur?	This will give you an idea of the possible extent of fraud. The integrity of evidence may diminish over time and/or be increasingly more difficult to obtain the longer after the event that it is required.		
	When will these irregularities occur next?	This will help you to know: ▪ If further loss can be prevented ▪ If it is still ongoing ▪ If you can set up a sting-type operation ▪ If you can more easily obtain evidence ▪ What the likelihood of recovery is (more likely if more recent).		

No	Information required	Discussion/reasons for information	Information declared	Next steps/ further action
	What evidence (documents, video footage, etc) is available?	Remember our most important rule of forensics: 'Secure the evidence.' This is partly about securing the evidence to support your investigation and/or further actions. It is also about guiding your investigation steps.		
	Is there any threat of loss of money, property or is someone's safety at risk?	Your first responsibility would be the safety of others. The investigation/ principles of right and wrong all come second.		
	What else should you know before starting?	This will direct your initial steps to the investigation.		

Annexure 3.2
Example of an investigation plan template

Investigation phase	Possible investigation process	Investigation objectives and steps
Awareness	Case registering	
	Immediate steps	
	Immediate reporting	
Planning	Clarification	
	Develop an initial hypothesis	
	Develop an investigation plan	
Conducting the investigation	Detailed information gathering	
	▪ Document/record checks	
	▪ Check against policies and procedures	
	▪ Accounting checks	
	▪ Data file and e-mail checks	
	▪ Data analytics	
	Physical information gathering	
	▪ Timeline and physical inspection	
	▪ Video and access record analysis	
	▪ System walkthroughs	
	▪ Search and seizure	
	▪ Asset verification	
	Subject information gathering	
	▪ Public domain checks	
	▪ Lifestyle checks	
	▪ Personnel files	
	Information interviews	
	Finalise hypothesis	
	Update investigation plan	
	Additional investigation	

Investigation phase	Possible investigation process	Investigation objectives and steps
Complete and conclude	Subsequent interviews	
	Corroborating checks	
	▪ Own analysis	
	▪ Further investigation	
	▪ Expert analysis	
	▪ Polygraphs	
	▪ Handwriting analysis	
	Final witness interviews	
	Final subject interviews	
	Conclude on hypothesis	
	Update investigation plan	
Subsequent actions	Compile subsequent actions	
	▪ Initiate labour case	
	▪ Bolster internal controls	
	▪ Voluntary recovery	
	▪ Other	
	Report	
	▪ Audit committee	
	▪ Management	
	▪ Other bodies	

Annexure 3.3 Example of a Request for Information (RFI) document	
Request for information number	DD/MM/20X1/001
Date request presented	
Person request presented to	Mr A Client
Request from	Mr S Sleuth, Fraud Services Company
Date request closed	
Person received from	

Please furnish us with the following information to assist us with our review:

No	Description	Date received
1.		
2.		
3.		
4.		
5.		

Thank you in anticipation.

Regards

____

S Sleuth
Telephone No
email@FraudServices.co.za

Annexure 3.4
Example of a Letter of Appointment

Date
Consultancy Address
Zip code

Mr A Client
Client address
Zip code

Dear Mr A

1. INTRODUCTION AND PURPOSE

Thank you for the opportunity to work together again. The letter sets forth the objectives, nature and scope of the proposed engagement with the primary intention to prevent possible misunderstanding.

2. PARTIES TO THIS AGREEMENT

The parties to this agreement are the ABC company and the Super Sleuth Forensic Service Company.

3. ENGAGEMENT OBJECTIVES

As per our initial scoping meeting that was held on the day [xxx] of month [xxx] [year], the engagement will seek to understand

- >>>
- >>>

4. SCOPE OF THE ENGAGEMENT

The review will cover >>>:

- >>>
- >>>

The review will be limited to >>> and >>> will not be included.

5. TIMING

The engagement will commence on the date that this letter is signed whilst considering all preceding planning and scoping discussions.

6. REQUIREMENTS

We will require free and unencumbered access to premises, people, records and information of the aforementioned entities in line with our review at the ABC company. This may necessitate your express instruction to persons and entities concerned to authorise such access.

We will also require full disclosure on all related matters from you and all parties concerned to ensure that we have the information that we require to conclude the engagement.

7. RESPONSIBILITIES

We undertake to provide you with a full and detailed report of our methods, findings and opinions at the conclusion of this review.

The frequency and detail of interim feedback on the review can be mutually agreed from time to time.

Your responsibility will be to engage with the senior and executive management of the ABC company and/or any other related parties to ensure that this assignment progresses as described in this letter.

Your responsibility will also include the payment of the fees and disbursements described below.

8. LIMITATION OF LIABILITY

The matters reported during this review will be those deemed to be necessary to be brought to your attention. They will not necessarily be a comprehensive record of all matters that may exist. In particular, we cannot be held liable for reporting all fraud matters related to the aforementioned entities or related records and issues.

The findings, conclusions and opinions of this review are intended for the sole use of the senior executives of the ABC company. As such they should not be quoted in whole or in part nor should they be relied upon by any third party for any reason. No responsibility to any third party is accepted as this review is not being conducted for or intended for any other purpose.

While this review will be conducted in terms of international standards for the professional practice of fraud investigations, it should be understood that the opinions and conclusions thereof cannot be used to determine the:

- Fair value any of the underlying legal entities
- Guilt or innocence of any person or entity

It is also understood that we cannot be held liable for any negative outcome to or adverse reaction to this review.

9. FEES

Professional fees will be charged on an actual time spent basis and at a rate of ZAR >>>.00 per hour for the 20X1 calendar year. Monthly billings of professional fees supported by timesheets will be presented.

Disbursements will be charged on an actual cost incurred basis, as supported by invoices. Disbursements may also be paid directly by the ABC company should the need arise.

10. ACCEPTANCE

We would appreciate it if you would sign this letter to indicate your acceptance of the terms and conditions of this engagement. Please return one original signed copy to us for our records.

	CLIENT	**WITNESS**
DATE		
PLACE		
SIGNED		

Regards

____

S Sleuth
Telephone No
email@FraudServices.co.za

Annexure 3.5
Example of: a Group Approach script

The following is an example of a generic script that may be considered, as the basis for the opening address to the staff members:

Good morning everyone. My name is >>> and I am the >>> of ABC COMPANY.

We have called you all together here this morning to inform you of a process that will be taking place here over the next day/>>> number of days on this site.

With me I have:

- *>>> the >>> of ABC COMPANY*
- *>>> the >>> of ABC COMPANY*
- *>>> the >>> of ABC COMPANY*
- *>>> the >>> of ABC COMPANY*
- *>>> the >>> of ABC COMPANY*

The reason that we are here is because certain irregularities have come to our attention.

These irregularities have been happening on this site and have been perpetrated by the people working on this site. We have therefore commenced an investigation into these irregularities and we are at the point now when we need to look at certain aspects on this site.

ABC COMPANY sees these and all such irregularities in a very serious light. ABC COMPANY has a policy of zero tolerance for misconduct, irregularities and fraud. We will investigate all such matters and hold the perpetrators of such irregularities liable. ABC COMPANY will also press criminal charges as relevant.

As you can see we have assembled a very senior team of ABC COMPANY management. ABC COMPANY is determined to get to the bottom of these irregularities. Over the next >>> day/s we will be examining various aspects and documents in detail on this site. You are to continue with your work as normal, but be advised that you should not try to destroy any evidence or to intimidate anyone into not talking to us. This will be seen in an extremely serious light and any such actions may invoke the company's disciplinary code.

We will be interviewing people who we believe may be able to assist us in the investigation. The fact that we have chosen to interview specific people does not mean that they are guilty of anything. Please inform us if you have not been selected for an interview, but feel that you could make a meaningful contribution.

There are >>> people on this site. We will not be able to interview everyone and we will be putting our contact details up on the outside of the >>> office and >>>> in case you would like to inform us of any irregularities that you are aware of.

Should you be aware of any irregularities, it is imperative that you make us aware thereof prior to it coming to our attention that you were aware of the irregularity, but chose not to inform us. You now have an opportunity to inform us of anything that you have done wrong or anything else wrong that you are aware of that has happened. Just because you admit to something will however not guarantee that we will not prosecute you. It will, however, be seen in mitigation when we decide how to proceed against you. Failure to bring irregularities to our attention will be seen in a very serious light.

We must also inform you of the legal concept of 'willful blindness'. In terms of this concept, you can be held criminally liable if you are aware of something wrong that has happened and you do not report it. Your contract of employment also requires you to act in the best interests of the company and we look forward to your cooperation in this regard.

You may either speak to one of the investigation team or you may speak to one of your superiors. Alternatively, you may call us on the numbers provided at >>> as mentioned previously. You may also call the tip-offs/whistle-blower number and give the information to the telephone operator on the number as per the tip-offs posters to be found >>> and >>>.

We will also be requesting you to complete a questionnaire. This should not take more than five minutes to complete. This questionnaire provides you with an opportunity to provide information and make declarations. Please complete the questionnaire on your own now and hand it to >>>.

Are there any questions at this stage?

[Short Q & A]

Thank you. Please go to your workstations now and commence your normal work.

CHAPTER 4

INTERVIEWING

4.1. CHAPTER OUTLINE AND INTRODUCTION

Interviewing is arguably the most important skill required by a fraud investigator. It touches almost every element of the identification, investigation and resolution of a fraud case. You may be involved in every aspect of a case from start to finish or you may have a specialised role to play according to your personal strengths and experience (for example: data analytics, computer forensics, accounting, etc). Regardless of your degree of involvement in the case, it is almost certain that you will need to interview someone at some or other stage of the process. Your ability to obtain information, whilst still maintaining the integrity and momentum of the investigation, is paramount to the success of the investigation.

In this chapter, we discuss who could be interviewed as well as the types and purposes of interviews. We also discuss many practical and logistical elements to interviews. Lastly, we will discuss two aspects of the pre-interview phase, the seven typical phases of an interview, as well as six possible post-interview aspects.

The purpose of this chapter is to give you a mental picture of the typical interview process as well as a firm understanding of the many practical aspects that need to be borne in mind throughout. The goal is for you to be able to navigate the phases naturally and flexibly to optimise the interview.

4.1.1. Interviewees

When we talk about interviewing our attention naturally first goes to the interviewing of suspects and accused parties. After all, that is what we do as forensic practitioners. We catch crooks!

Many different types of interviewees exist, however. When we commence interviewing people, we are not always aware of who is involved and/or to what extent. Suffice to say, a large portion of the people that we interview will not be the guilty parties. Depending on the individual situation, it is safe to assume that at least 50% of the information that we require in our investigations will come from parties other than the accused/suspects. Such information will be a valuable stepping stone to assist us when interviewing the suspected parties and/or proving our case.

4.1.2. Setting

The second place that our attention naturally goes to when we talk about interviewing is to assume that we are talking about a formal interview situation. That is to say, one that is predefined fully planned and in a traditional 'Hollywood' setting. 'Traditional' is used loosely here but is one that refers to the paradigm of the lone chair (designated for the interviewee) in the middle of a room facing a 'firing squad' of interviewers' chairs. That is Hollywood and we definitely do not work in draconian interview settings like that.

You would probably only get an opportunity to set up an interview room in the way that you want in less than 30% of the interviews that you are going to conduct. In the majority of interviews, you will most likely have to play the cards that are dealt to you in terms of the setting. In fact, most times you will just be happy to have been granted an interview. The setting (while important) is the least of our worries. A quick shuffle of some chairs may be all that you are able to do.

4.1.3. Conversations

It is therefore important that we widen the definition of an 'interview' to include any information-seeking conversations that we hold in the course of our investigation. Maybe just pause to think about what is being suggested. That will mean all conversations held over the course of the investigation. This would naturally also, therefore, include a wider range of interviewees. It goes without saying that this also includes a wide range of forums and settings. Therefore, we need to keep the following in mind:

- We need to plan all our conversations.
- Even if we did not have the opportunity to plan, we need to think quickly (as per the commencing goal of this chapter) and put some form of structure to the conversation (naturally and without the interviewee knowing that we are directing the conversation, as we require) so that we derive maximum benefit from the conversation.
- We need to document all our conversations.
- We use the guise of an informal conversation to interview someone without them knowing that they are being interviewed.

These points are discussed at length below.

4.1.4. Types

The type of interview that you conduct will also differ depending on the type of person being interviewed and the purpose of the interview. The differences between the types of interviews stem from:

- *The type of interviewees (as per the list of interviewees below)*

  You will interview an accused person differently to an informant or to a person who is going to give you general information on a business process under review. The type and intensity (discussed later) of the interview will differ.

- *The type of person the interviewee is*

  Some people are more nervous than others, while some have the gift of the gab. You will more than likely need to adapt your style and tempo to obtain the best result.

- *How the interviewee personally relates to the investigation*

  A guilty person may be a reluctant interviewee. Similarly, a member of senior management who feels that the highlighting of the fraud will be a poor reflection on them (despite them not being personally involved) may also be reluctant to cooperate in an interview and/or investigation.

- *Their degree of involvement in the actual fraud*
A victim may still be psychologically damaged, a general worker with no involvement may be indifferent and find the investigation a distraction and a waste of their valuable time, a disgruntled spouse may desire revenge, etc.

Try to anticipate these different aspects and plan your questions accordingly.

4.2 INTERVIEWEES

The types of people who may need to be interviewed in a fraud investigation are discussed below. The different types of interviewees listed have been separated so that attention can be drawn to different interviewees and not because of an academically accurate classification. They include:

- *The accused/subject of the investigation*
This is the main person who is or parties who are, suspected of being or known to be involved in the irregularities. These interviewees could include any internal or external party to an organisation or to the victim/s of the irregularity.

- *Co-accused/conspirators*
The people or the parties who are suspected of or are known to have been involved (not the main driver of the fraud) in, assisted in, benefited from or had knowledge of the irregularities. As per the above, this could include any person working with the transgressor of the irregularity. The accused and co-conspirators may be internal or external to the victim organisation or split across multiple organisations.

- *Witnesses*
Those people or parties who have direct or indirect knowledge of the activities that gave rise to the irregularities or that occurred during or subsequent to the irregular activities. Types of witnesses include:
    - An eyewitness who had direct first-hand knowledge of the occurrence/s.
    - A general witness who had second-hand or third-hand knowledge of the occurrence/s. While their information may assist in your case, they can rarely testify, as their testimony is deemed to be 'hearsay'. Exceptions apply though. Their evidence can provide valuable insights into your investigation.
    - A specialist witness – see below.
    - An expert witness – see below.

Knowledge of the irregularity includes being an eyewitness to the irregularity and/or knowing what should have occurred, as opposed to what did. In the latter case, the witness testifies to what the norm is. The witness typically does not say that what the subject did was incorrect. He merely testifies as to what the standard practice/ procedure is. Inference is thereby created for the court or labour tribunal as to what is conspicuous in the subject's behaviour, by its departure from the standard practice; that is, what is different between what did happen and what should have occurred. For example, in a case of the theft and sale of intellectual property (IP): As background, witness #1 wrote part of the original document (the IP of which was stolen) while in the employ of Company A. Witness #1 testifies to the fact that:

- They wrote the original document attached as an annexure (W1) to their affidavit.
- They have, at the request of the fraud investigator, compared their original document to the document under dispute of Company B, attached as Annexure W2.
- The documents are, for all intents and purposes, identical.
- They do not understand why a document written by them will have Company B's logo on it.
- They do not understand why a document from Company B will have identical wording to a document they wrote in Company A.

Witnesses are more than likely going to be the people who are going to testify in criminal and/or internal labour tribunal proceedings. In other cases, they will just give you valuable information/insights into the irregularities and not be required or be unable to testify. Witnesses may however typically:

- Want to remain anonymous
- Be scared of being identified
- Not want to be blamed for blowing the whistle or any other wrongdoing
- Not want to make the effort to be involved (plain indifference)
- Not want to have to testify.

The dilemma that the fraud investigator faces is that they will want to obtain the required information from the witnesses, but cannot provide any guarantees that the witness will not be required to assist or will not have to be involved to any degree in the future investigation or subsequent proceedings. The concept of confidentiality and how to motivate witnesses is discussed in detail below.

- *Victims*

Those people who suffered an actual loss or who had the potential to have suffered a loss or who have been prejudiced in some manner by the actions of the accused and/or co-accused. This could include the company and/or its representatives, managers, owners, shareholders, investors, financing institutions, suppliers, etc. These people or representatives may be required to testify in criminal proceedings.

- *Informants*

Those people or parties who are going to give you information about the subjects and actual fraud activities that will assist in the investigation. The informants we are referring to here are not general witnesses nor whistle-blowers per se. They are the people that have made a tip-off to you and/or passed you a piece of information that is helpful in the investigation. The whistle-blower is the person who blows the whistle and highlights the fraud. The informant is the person who is feeding you valuable pieces of information over the course of the investigation. Whistle-blowers could do this as well. Whistle-blowers are the ones who initiate the highlighting of the case. Informants are typically approached to assist. The distinguishing factor between a normal general witness and an informant will probably come down to:

- The requirement of confidentiality and the requirement of the informant to remain anonymous
- The value of the information to the investigation and/or if the irregularity would have been discovered without the informant. Could any office worker describe the business process to you (if so they are a general witness) or could only the informant

have told you that specific piece of confidential information about the misconduct that no one else knows (then they are an informant). Some of the best information is obtained from co-workers, disgruntled spouses, family members, friends, business partners, co-conspirators who have been prejudiced, etc.

The Association of Certified Fraud Examiners' *International Fraud Handbook* advises never to write down the names of an informant or a whistle-blower. It may be difficult not to write down some identifiable particulars in your working papers/interview notes. The problem is that the information from every witness needs to be treated with confidence to some degree or other. Your interview notes, working papers and case diary are not public domain documents. As soon as you write down the particulars of your confidential source/s, you run the risk of someone getting their hands on what you have written. Please also ensure that you understand the data confidentiality/privacy laws of the country in which you are working.

Care needs to be exercised when discussing informants and whistle-blowers in documents that are to be circulated. I agree that whistle-blowers' and informants' names should never be mentioned in a report on the irregularity or in your affidavit where the informant has requested confidentiality. The Association of Fraud Examiners advises talking about 'source 1' (S1) and 'source 2' (S2), etc when referring to confidential sources in written documents.

I like to think of informants as a special 'class' of witnesses. Confidentiality of information is discussed below. Resist using their initials as this might make it too easy to identify them.

- *Whistle-blowers*

Whistle-blowers are a more specific category of informant. Whistle-blowers often (as demonstrated in many high-profile international fraud cases) need to eventually reveal their identity. Legislation provides for special protection of whistle-blowers. Ensure that you understand the whistle-blower protection laws of the country in which you are working. Whistle-blowers normally have highly privileged and incriminating information. They are also the ones who do the initial highlighting of the irregularity. Whistle-blowers are discussed in greater detail later.

- *General witnesses*

These are people who will be providing general information, background information or who will help you to understand how a particular process works. General witnesses could include the subject's friends, family, spouse, partner, co-workers, advisors, suppliers, subcontractors, service providers, business partners, etc.

- *Trade union representatives*

Trade unions are there to protect their members. This does not mean that they work against you; they just ensure that their member's right to a fair proceeding is maintained. Trade unions may very well want to represent their members in internal hearings. Representation at internal hearings is discussed in Chapter 7 on subsequent actions. The protection of members should not be used to conceal a crime or to interfere. If you develop a good relationship with your union they will generally work closely together with you to protect the innocent and to bring the guilty to justice. Some (normally those with political aspirations) may just be difficult and try to 'protect' their members at all costs and despite their guilt.

Your employer - The category of employers includes the organisation's owners, shareholders, the board of directors, audit committees and subcommittees of the board, executive and non-executive directors, senior managers, managers, the chief audit executive, the head of forensics, etc. If you are employed internally by a company, the senior management of the company may have information that may assist you or they may just require periodic feedback on your progress. There may be some challenges dealing with these people including the fact that they may:

- Cover up to some degree so as to evade blame or to avoid publicity.
- Have a lack of understanding of the fraud investigation process. They may therefore intentionally or unintentionally be uncooperative.
- Not be committed to/convinced of the fraud investigation and resolution process and/or reluctant to provide the funds required.
- Be angry and be seeking vengeance. They may try to use the investigation or yourself to assist with the achievement of their personal agenda. Some rush off with an emotional response stemming from something that you have told them. This can cause damage to the investigation based on their reaction.

- *The client*

Your client may be any one of the preceding 'internal' parties or their representative. If you are employed by an external client, you may need to gather information from them about the fraud or so that you can understand their motives. There are strong similarities between a client employer and a permanent employer. The aforementioned points refer.

- *Government agencies*

Some examples include revenue services/tax officials, border officials, etc. Evidence from government agencies will more than likely be independent and defendable. Such evidence (testimonies and documents) may (in certain circumstances) only be obtained via a court order/subpoena. Original, official documents (for example tax returns) already in the possession of the company/client can be used to great advantage in proceedings.

- *Private investigators*

The company or client may already have hired an investigator to look into the irregularities. A private investigator is not a fraud examiner. These are people who investigate infidelity claims, etc. Private investigators are high risk. There will inevitably be exceptions on both sides, but private investigators do not always have the required fraud investigation skills or follow acceptable or even legal methods. Numerous experiences come to mind where private investigators come across a relatively insignificant detail and then approach a company requesting the company to hire them on a retainer so that they can investigate the matter on the company's behalf. Other examples include where they offer money to staff members (tantamount to entrapment) to sell them stolen items. The private investigator then goes to the company and purports to have information of widespread theft in the company (showing footage of the one theft or evidence of company property). Private investigators are also notorious for milking companies when billing. Never pay private investigators on a daily/time spent and disbursements incurred basis. Unscrupulous private investigators milk companies by never actually solving the case and/or delivering outcomes. In such cases, they continue to create a 'need' in the company's mind by promising to solve the irregularity whilst billing for time spent pursuing an intangible irregularity. Alternatively, they deliver minor perpetrators and make promises of greater findings. Further high-risk activities concern the illegal attainment of evidence. *As an example: In one matter, we had to spend a lot of time to negotiate with the police not to act against the organisation on illegally obtained bank statements by a private investigation type organisation. The police refused to return the illegally obtained bank statements and left them in the docket. Luckily for the organisation, the prosecutor did not identify the statements and the illegally obtained statements went no further. It was touch and go for a while.* If you must use private investigators, then agree on a fixed fee for a defined positive outcome. Only pay them once they have delivered on what they have contractually agreed to.

- *The police services*

People to be 'interviewed' include the investigating officer, station commanders, fingerprint experts, etc. The police may see you as an amateur, a stumbling block, ignorant of the law and/or their field. Alternatively, they see you as a soft target to conduct all of their work. If the fraud investigator performs all the work and the investigating officer does very little, then there is a risk that the case can be seen as a 'complaint driven' case. Work hard to show cooperation with the police. It is important that they see that you are there to assist them and not to hinder them and that you will work together. In most instances, you will be able to perform tasks that they are unable to due to your specialised skills and experience or due to your access to specialised tools (eg computer software). You can also give them insights into the general business processes that they will not be privy to as an outsider. You may have access to budget to pay for legal counsel, expert witnesses, etc.

- *The prosecution*

The chief prosecutor, the prosecutor, the clerk of the court, etc. The chief prosecutor is the person who is going to assign the prosecutor to your case. Good relations with the prosecution are imperative to positive criminal outcomes. This is discussed in detail in Chapter 7 on subsequent actions.

- *The defence*

It is unlikely that you will ever have to interview a defence attorney. You may very well have discussions with them or even need to negotiate settlements or information. The purpose of a defence attorney is to protect their client's rights. They are not going to volunteer anything to the contrary. They want to know what you know and what you want. Obtaining anything from them is like pulling teeth.

- *Legal experts*

These are people who may be giving advice in the process or they may be the people that you employ in a 'watching brief' capacity. Again, discussions with these parties are less likely to be in the form of a traditional interview. The discussion should nevertheless still be structured to optimise the outcome. This is discussed in the chapter on subsequent activities.

- *Specialist witnesses and experts*

These are professionals who may give you advice (that is unique to an area of specialisation or an industry) or who you may need to use as specialist witnesses. Some examples of specialist witnesses include: medical doctors, pathologists, psychologists, engineers, accountants, tax specialists, software specialists, chemists, graphologists, polygraph administrators, computer specialists, audio/visual specialists.

- *Third parties*

These are the people or parties who have other dealings with the victim and/or accused. Some examples include: banks, creditors, employees, investors, shareholders, liquidators, etc.

- *Industry bodies*

These are the bodies that control the field in which you may require insights for your investigation. They set the professional industry standards and they have codes of ethics, disciplinary guides, etc. Examples include: chartered accountant institutes, legal societies, engineers' guilds, etc.

- *The press*

These may be general reporters or they may be investigative journalists or tabloid journalists. Dealing with the press is handled in Chapter 8 on reporting.

4.3 PLANNING THE INTERVIEW

4.3.1. Interview purpose

There are some subtle and some obvious differences that need to be sketched in the interviewing processes of these aforementioned different parties. These are discussed below, but before we go into the specifics of interviewing different parties, it is important to always bear in mind that the purpose of an interview is to obtain information, albeit different information. The broad types of interviews include:

- *Information seeking*

Information seeking interviews can be held with general witnesses and with accused parties. The purpose of an information seeking interview is to:

  - Gather information for the first time
  - Corroborate existing information.

- *Admission seeking*

Admission seeking interviews are those interviews where we are able to turn the accused party to cooperate and admit to their indiscretions. In such interviews, it is important to be able to:

  - Prevent deception
  - Detect deception
  - Make it easy for the subject to confess to their misconduct.

Interviews do not have to have one or the other purpose. They can have both purposes or just evolve from the one to the other. Choose the purpose of each interview and document it in your interview notes or working papers.

4.3.2. Interview intensity levels

The intensity of an interview has to do with the pace of the conversation and the assertiveness used. When conducting an interview, you will inevitably vary the intensity of your interview in response to the:

- Purpose of the interview
- Type of interviewee
- Interviewee's response to the review/interview
- Degree of dishonesty demonstrated during the interview
- Duration of the investigation
- Time and resources available for the review
- Scope of the review

There are three levels of interview intensity, including:

- *Interview intensity 'level 1'*
  This is a normal level of conversation. There is nothing antagonistic or threatening about the approach. It is merely a structured and focused conversation with a specific goal in mind. You have done well if the interviewee contributes to the conversation without feeling like they are being led down a specific path. This level of interviewing will be used predominantly.
- *Interview intensity 'level 2'*
  While we would typically commence all interviews at intensity level 1, it may be necessary to step up the pace slightly, especially when deception is detected. I would say that the interviewee will in most cases not detect that you have stepped up the pace. They will merely start to make mistakes and run out of excuses/explanations. The interview is still courteous, but firmer. This approach must be planned. In this approach, we start to trip the interviewee up and highlight their deception through contradiction and comparison to previous things that they have said. This is discussed later under 4.13.1. below, in the 'comparison and contradiction' phase of interviews.
- *Interview intensity 'level 3'*
  While frequently portrayed in Hollywood, this level of intensity is seldom to be used. When it is used it must be carefully planned and well executed. While the interview intensity is heightened, the interviewer is never rude. The pace is fast and the questions are very precise so as not to give the interviewee a chance to think of an excuse. The interviewee typically catches themselves out by committing to answers before thinking of the consequences of their answers. It is then up to the interviewer to compare their answers to the norm or standard and show up their errors and deceit. This level of interview intensity is only suited to a limited number of interviewees. *An example of a case where the accused was very arrogant and uncooperative follows. A level 3 interview was planned and agreed with management. The accused party was told, upon my unannounced entry into his office, that I just wanted to ask a quick clarifying question. Once in and once progressing the pace of the interview was increased. The Interviewee was unaware that this was planned and probably believed that the interview naturally evolved into the heightened pace. Questions were posed to the subject and no sooner had he replied than the next question was fired off. The result was that he was unable to plan his responses and he got himself into an awful tangle and his lies started*

to contradict themselves. He did not admit to his indiscretions, despite his obvious lies. An admission was not the plan of the interview, as we anticipated that he was not the type to confess. What it did do was to prepare us well for the internal labour tribunal (as he had used many excuses that we were able to counter in advance), at which we were able to show his dishonesty and the inconsistencies in his story.

These different interview intensity levels may be used during the different phases of an interview. The interview phases are discussed later in section 4.11 and also in section 4.13 on the structuring of interviews. Choose the desired intensity level when planning the interview.

4.3.3. Interviewees

Plan and decide on who you are going to interview during the review. Remember that the different interviewees will give you different information. For example, a manager may tell you the way things should have worked while the subordinate is more likely to tell you the way in which they actually performed the work.

Try to get a cross-section of all the people. When in doubt, interview the person. The problem is that 'you don't know what you don't know until you know it'. As confusing as that little riddle is, it is very true. It means that you basically will only know if an interviewee has good information once you have interviewed them and they have told you what they know. Only at that stage can you make an informed decision whether to include or discard the information. Do not, as a rule, discard any information. Instead, 'place' information (the value of which is unknown) where you can refer to it in the event that its importance and/or relevance to the review becomes elevated.

The sequence in which interviews are conducted has a huge bearing on the amount and the integrity of information obtained and/or if admissions are obtained. Some reasons for this include:

- *Timing of Information*
  The sequence in which you interview people can also be very important. The importance is concerned with:
  - When, over the period of the review, people are to be interviewed, and
  - In which sequence people in a particular group are to be interviewed.

  Different people will have different motives and demonstrate differing degrees of cooperation over the various stages of the review. You will also inevitably gain more information over the period of the review, which will assist you in your overall interview process. The incorrect sequence of interviews may, however, result in you only finding important information out after key interviews have already been conducted, or not at all. It may not always be possible for you to re-interview the key people. Alternatively, you may have lost an ideal opportunity to use the information at all or to use it in a certain context in the initial interview.

- *Layering*
  Layering is an important technique that I have developed over the years. Layering applies to the build-up of questions across multiple interviews with the same person or persons. In terms of this technique, you may choose to conduct an initial interview with a subject, so as to get them to commit to their excuses or their version of the story before conducting a follow-up

interview once you have all or more of the facts. In this way, you will be able to highlight their dishonesty when you compare their responses in the first interview to their responses in the second interview.

Determine in advance, as far as possible, if you want to hold single or multiple interviews with a person. It may only become evident to you later that you need to have multiple conversations with a person. Start to plan the layers of your questions as soon as the need becomes apparent. Think about how the topics you spoke about previously impact on your overall conversation and/or the ability to obtain information.

It is often necessary to conduct multiple interviews before obtaining the desired result. This really involves stretching the aforementioned phases over multiple interviews. Once again, this may be done intentionally or it may just occur naturally as you find out more information during the progression of your review.

People will often just shut down if you come at them with too much at one time. You basically frighten them away. In other instances, you may need to get the interviewee used to you or even used to the idea of the review.

The sequence of questions within a single interview is not the same as the layering of multiple interviews. The sequencing of questions within a single interview is concerned with the concept of placing blocks in advance, which is discussed under point 4.7.5.

- *Fishing expedition*

On many occasions, you may be completely unaware of who the perpetrators are or even what has gone wrong or to what extent. In such a case try to cast the net as widely as possible in terms of who to interview in an attempt to see what you draw in. Follow this process on multiple occasions each time, narrowing the span of the investigation and questions, until what occurred or who is responsible is identified.

An alternative to this (when you know what went wrong, but not who perpetrated the irregularity) is to start with a small group (remember the rule, 'it is always the people that were/are the closest') and then to widen the net to include more people and possibilities, as required.

- *Groups*

The interviewing of a group of people does not mean that all the people in the group are interviewed at the same time. It merely means that there is a known group of subjects who need to be interviewed over the course of the investigation. The people in the group may all be subjects of the investigation or some may be, while others are not. Avoid, as far as possible, including more than one interviewee in an interview, as this may restrict the information disclosed during the interview.

Remember, when interviewing groups of people, that people talk. As soon as the first person has completed their interview, the other people are going to ask what was discussed in the interview. Deceptive people will immediately (if not before) start to align their stories and/or plan their responses. While this is impossible to stop, the correct sequence of interviewees and interview questions may identify 'story-building' or ensure that the most important information is obtained before it has been adversely influenced.

Try to predict who will give you what information when planning the sequence of your interviews. Be flexible as you progress through the interviews and adjust the sequence in response to information gained, as required.

- *Confidentiality concerns*

Interviewee disclosures will almost always need to be treated confidentially and not discussed with other interviewees in a manner that identifies who made the disclosure/s. For example, if you said to a subject of an investigation: 'Jane has just said that you always stayed late to work on the office computers.' This may put Jane, as the source, in a very difficult position.

That example is quite an obvious one, but there is another element to be aware of: people may be able to deduce who has said what, based on the sequence of interviewees. If you are talking about a particular piece of information in an interview with a subject, they may deduce that it could only have been one of the previous interviewees that told you that. Depending on the esoteric nature of the piece of information it may be possible to conceal who made specific disclosures, by one of the following methods:

- In the manner that questions are posed to subsequent interviewees
- By conducting key interviews at the end once a lot of interviews have already been held, making it less likely to identify the source of the disclosures
- By conducting interviews with a cross-section of people.

When interviewing a group of people, tell the people that there is no specific sequence to the interviews, even if there is. Alternatively, tell them that:

- 'I am starting with the most senior persons first and then working my way down.'
- 'I need to interview person "A" first as they need to leave first' etc.

- *Summary of interview sequencing*

In summary, the sequence of interviewees would be determined by:

- How much you know about the matter under investigation prior to conducting the interviews
- What you are trying to achieve in your interview process.

As a rule, try to start with those interviewees you think will give the most general information first, and then move to people who will give more specific information. Save the 'guilty' person for last if the subject is known. In the event that you are layering many interviews, ensure that you keep the 'comparison and contradiction' type questions (discussed under 4.11, phases of an interview) to the final subject interview towards the end of the investigation. These are the questions in which we compare the subject's assertions of what happened to other evidence.

Sometimes you only find out during the interview process who the 'guilty' person is. The layering of interviews then comes into play and subsequent interviews may be required.

Layering is most successful when you have knowledge of who the main subjects are in advance, and a conscious decision is taken to get the subjects to commit to certain answers in the first interviews, and then to have a follow-up interview in which you catch them out once you know more.

a. How many?

You will, on average, be able to conduct nine normal interviews in one day. You will not be able to do the interviews justice if you try to cram too many into one day. The objective of an interview is to obtain information and not to cover as many interviews as possible in a day. You (as the interviewer) may also 'shut down' and reach a saturation point, and stop listening properly or taking in all of the vital information if you try to get through too many interviews in a day. Do not, therefore, be too ambitious in your scheduling/planning of interviews.

b. Questions

In the planning phase of interviews, we want to be cognisant of which questions are going to be asked and when they are going to be asked. Part of the answer to this lies in the answer of 'why' we want to ask the question. The 'why' has to do with our expectation of what outcome, answer/response or effect will be created if we ask specific questions at certain times. The questions to be asked in interviews are discussed in detail under points 4.2 (interview questions) and 4.11 (phases of the interview).

4.4. PARTIES TO THE INTERVIEW

Interviews should not be overcomplicated or crowded. The inclusion of unnecessary parties may have an adverse effect on the interview and prevent the required information being identified and disclosed. As far as possible there should only be three parties present in the interview, being:

- The person conducting the interview (interviewer)
- The person assisting the interviewer
- The person being interviewed (the interviewee).

Notwithstanding this, circumstances may dictate that any number of the following people are present at the interview:

- *Interviewer*
  To guide and direct the interview. This person plays the dominant role and leads the interview. How to conduct an interview is discussed at length under point 4.11 (the phases of an interview).
- *Interviewer's assistant*
  The interviewer's assistant may fulfil any number of multiple roles, including:
  - To play a specific 'role' (for example: 'good-cop, bad-cop')
  - To document the conversation
  - To raise questions unthought of by the interviewer
  - To give interpretations after the fact of what was said/not said and on the behaviours that were manifested
  - To fetch items/people/documents, etc
  - To be a witness of what was said

- To protect the interviewer in the event that they are accused of doing or saying something incorrectly
- To close the interview if the situation gets out of hand and the interviewer is too emotional or caught up in the interview.

The interviewer's assistant is a very important role to be played. While the party may be quiet for most of the interview, do not underestimate their role. The word 'assistant' does not mean that the person is subordinate to or junior to the interviewer. While this may be the case in reality, in the interview they are team members. Having two experienced and equally senior fraud investigators who work together in a team in an interview situation is ideal to maximise results.

- *Minute taker*

To take minutes of the conversation. This is a passive role. While the minute taker may also very well be a witness (as with the interviewer's assistant) they need not necessarily have any knowledge or experience of fraud investigation/interviewing. They also do not contribute in any manner to the interview. The useful part of having a minute taker present is that the minutes may be immediately available. A copy can be made of the minutes and signed by all parties at the end of the conversation to evidence that the minutes are a true reflection of what was discussed.

- *Interviewee*

The person being interviewed. See the aforementioned list of interviewees.

- *Interviewee's representative*

Someone who the interviewee requests to sit in on the interview to protect their interests. Interviewee representatives are discouraged, as far as possible. If the interviewee suggests it then try to discourage them from having a representative in the room. Invariably they are scared of the interview and want a support structure in the room with them. If you are able to put their fears at bay, then they will no longer require the representative.

I normally say to them that it is not a hearing, that no charges have been laid and we are just trying to gather information/obtain clarity on some issues at this point, and that there is no need for representation. This is just a normal employer/employee conversation.

The problem with the representative is that they may:

- Prevent the interviewee from talking freely, as they may be reluctant to look bad in front of their colleague.
- Interrupt the interview with their questions and comments.
- Try to answer on behalf of the interviewee. In these cases, it is advisable to thank them for their assistance but to emphasise that this is the interviewee's interview and that it is important that they give their own answers.

In other situations, the presence of an interviewee's representative works well because the representative provides a balance to the interview. In such cases, the representative recognises the fact that the person has done something incorrectly and encourages them to cooperate. At the end of the day, we want to be able to interview the person. If it comes down to a choice between having the representative in or no interview at all, then opt for the interview with a representative. If they insist on having a representative, then say: 'Well this is your interview and you may have anyone present that you feel comfortable with.' Then request to set some ground rules. In the worst case if things get out of hand or the interview is not going in the way that you would like because of the representative, then you can always say that this is not working out and that you are calling the interview to an end.

- *Human resources/industrial relations-type person*

This is a person who fulfils this type of role in the organisation. This can work very well. The inclusion of HR/IR people will depend on the skill level and the maturity of HR/IR in the company. The HR/IR person is normally on the company's side and it is in their best interest that the truth is revealed. They can be a damper to the conversation though if the interviewee does not want to be perceived as 'bad' in front of them. They can also play a valuable role to 'represent' the interviewee. They can tell them what their rights are (in terms of company policy and procedure). The HR person can also provide valuable insights if they have expertise in psychology. The HR person can also be your ally when reporting back to management. The building of your subsequent internal labour case may also be easier with them already being on your side.

- *Employer/client representative*

To represent the employer/client's interests. There are occasions where an employer/client (especially when they have not had a chance to build a relationship of trust with you as the fraud investigator) will want 'their' representative to sit in on the interview. They do this to ensure that they know what was said in the interview or to ensure that the questions that they want to have asked are asked. Again, the success of this will vary from company to company. As far as possible, avoid it. In many situations, you may not have a choice in the matter.

- *Legal counsel*

This may be the company's internal or external legal representative. This may also be the interviewee's legal representative. Now, the lawyers amongst us are not going to like the statements that follow, but experience has taught that as soon as you get a lawyer involved, things are not going to go your way as a fraud investigator. Lawyers like to do the things that lawyers do. They want to:

  - Control the conversation themselves
  - Write letters
  - Represent their clients
  - Impose injunctions
  - Go to court
  - Write complex agreements.

They discourage their clients from speaking to you even in simple conversations. The process will become protracted and you will become frustrated. Some unscrupulous lawyers just want to draw the process out so that they can milk their client for professional fees. Many lawyers like to dominate and be in charge. They do not like anyone else, least of all a fraud investigator, to tell them what to do. With regards to the organisation's legal representative, it is wise to surround yourself with experts/have access to them. In this regard, it is wise to obtain legal opinion as soon as possible in the cases that you are dealing with. Try however to keep the legal support in the background. As soon as a lawyer is visible, it then prompts the other party to respond by producing their own lawyer and slowing down the process.

- *Police services*

This will invariably be the investigating officer (IO). Over time you may work with many of the local IOs in the police stations where your organisation is situated. You may also develop a trust relationship with them during a specific investigation. The IOs are normally less motivated than you are. They also quickly realise that you have the business insights, specific experience/skills and resources to assist them. A good relationship with the IO is to be encouraged.

- *External auditors*

These may be the external auditors of the company, an affected supplier company, etc. In any case, they will be the accounting experts. They may even have identified the irregularity. Their presence may be required to give technical insights into certain complex accounting transactions and/or principles.

- *Other specialists such as actuaries, engineers, quantity surveyors, computer specialists, etc*

The purpose of the participation of these types of people would be to assist the interviewer with factual content. These people may provide valuable insights into otherwise complex or esoteric topics. They provide balance and ensure that the facts are not twisted by the interviewee. They give you support on topics that you may know very little about. These individuals are normally very professional. They typically have no direct interest in the fraud investigation. They are normally only interested in the facts of their field.

4.5. GENERAL INTERVIEW CONSIDERATIONS

General interview considerations are concerned with the influence that certain aspects (listed below) have on the 'psychology' of the interview. While it cannot be guaranteed that these factors will always influence an interview, in the same manner, it is helpful to be aware of the possible influence of these factors on an interview so as to allow you to adopt an approach that avoids potential adverse effects.

The points discussed here have a lot to do with our rule: 'Forensics is less about fact and more about psychology.'

4.5.1. The setting

When conducting an interview, it is best to get the person out of their own office environment and into a neutral interview room or your own interview room. The reasons for this include:

- They are less likely to be interrupted.
- People feel more confident when they are in familiar surroundings. In sporting terms, we like to talk about a 'home ground advantage' when a team plays at their own stadium and/or town/country. In interviewing terms, this is true for both the person being interviewed and for the person conducting the interview. If, therefore, you are able to get the subject of the interview out of their environment, then there is a higher probability that they will be less confident and/or more likely to manifest nervous behaviours. Nervous behaviour may be an indication of deceit (discussed later) and may force the subject to make mistakes.

a. General

As far as possible, try to visit the interview location in advance. Make alternative arrangements if the meeting room is unsatisfactory. It is advisable to consider phoning ahead to enquire if a suitable venue is available to conduct the interviews in if you are unfamiliar with the interview facilities.

The setting should be free from distraction, free from interruption and it should be non-threatening.

The interview room may be able to assist you in your interview process in terms of making the person more comfortable and therefore more relaxed. The idea is that the more comfortable people are, the more willing they will be to cooperate. Other than that, the interview environment is not a 'tool' to assist you in your interview. Only medieval-like torture chambers with bright lights, shackles and other cruel devices are used to extract information from people. We live in modern times, where the interviewer's skills and information at hand are what is going to assist in obtaining the desired result. The room is not a highly important factor in interviews, so do not put a disproportionate amount of emphasis on it. You are aiming for a generally relaxed atmosphere, that is all.

b. Freedom

Under no circumstances should a person be (or perceive that they are being) held against their will. The door should never be locked. They should never think that they cannot get up and leave at any time or that they would be stopped if they tried to leave. For this reason, avoid sitting between them and the door. Even if you are not going to stop them physically, they may feel caged in and less relaxed.

c. Glass

Many meetings rooms have glass doors and/or windows. The view through glass doors and/or windows can be a distraction (to the interviewee and interviewer) in terms of people walking past and disrupting a thought pattern. For example, you may be building towards and/or leading an interviewee in a specific direction. A disruption of any sort (person entering the room, walking past, a phone call, etc) may break the mood or their thought pattern and make it too easy for them not to cooperate and/or to make declarations.

There may also be a psychological disadvantage in so far as the interviewee may feel that they are being watched. This may impact on their willingness to declare information.

It is proposed that you paste paper or work-related posters over the glass in meeting rooms and/or doors to minimise the potential negative effects. When designing and/or setting up meeting rooms within departments, try to ensure that frosting is applied to the glass. In the absence of any of the above, try to seat the person with their back to the door/window to prevent them from becoming distracted/feeling like they are being watched.

d. Lighting

The room should be well lit, and it should be neither too bright nor too dim. You should be able to see the entire person. If there is a window in the room, make sure that you are seated with your back to the window/strongest light source. This will prevent the interviewee looking like a silhouette.

Remember that you are more than likely going to be spending whole days in the meeting room completing all the interviews. It can also be a strain on your eyes to look into/concentrate on a strong light source for protracted periods.

The reason for wanting to be able to see the subject of the interview is that you want to be able to observe any involuntary, tell-tale signs of deceit. These are discussed below.

e. Seating

Try not to have a desk or a table between you and the person you are interviewing. Physical barriers are also mental barriers. You want the subject to open up as much as possible.

If the interviewee comes into your space/office, stand up and come around from behind your desk and sit at a round table, next to them on the same side of the desk or at a boardroom table. In the event of a boardroom table, do not sit at the head of the table. You want to avoid a 'boss/subordinate' or a dictatorial atmosphere. Sitting next to someone also reduces barriers. They may feel less likely to hide things.

If you go into their office, request that you rather sit at a table if they have one in their office. Alternatively, book a meeting room and invite them to the meeting room. This will get them out of their environment. Their own environment is an area where there is a higher probability that they can be distracted and interrupted easily. Their environment is a point of strength for them and a place of comfort. It is a place in which they may be less likely to concede.

Try to sit close enough to the person (about 1.2 to 1.8 metres/four to six feet), but not so close that they can read what you are writing or any other important or confidential notes (the figure below refers as an example).

In general, you should sit close enough to the person without getting into their personal space. They should not have the desire to back away. You should be able to see the entire person. It should also be easy for you to hear them. Too much distance between you is also not conducive for stimulating conversation.

Have the person sit facing you, not too much to the side. You want to be in a position to observe all the involuntary signs of deceit should they demonstrate them. Turn yourself to look directly at the person. You will see that people tend to orientate themselves in response and will frequently turn toward you. The feeling that you want to create is that only you and the subject are having a conversation. Anyone else in the room should sit slightly away and even behind their line of sight. After some time, the subject of the interview may become less aware of others in the room and focus more clearly on what you are talking about.

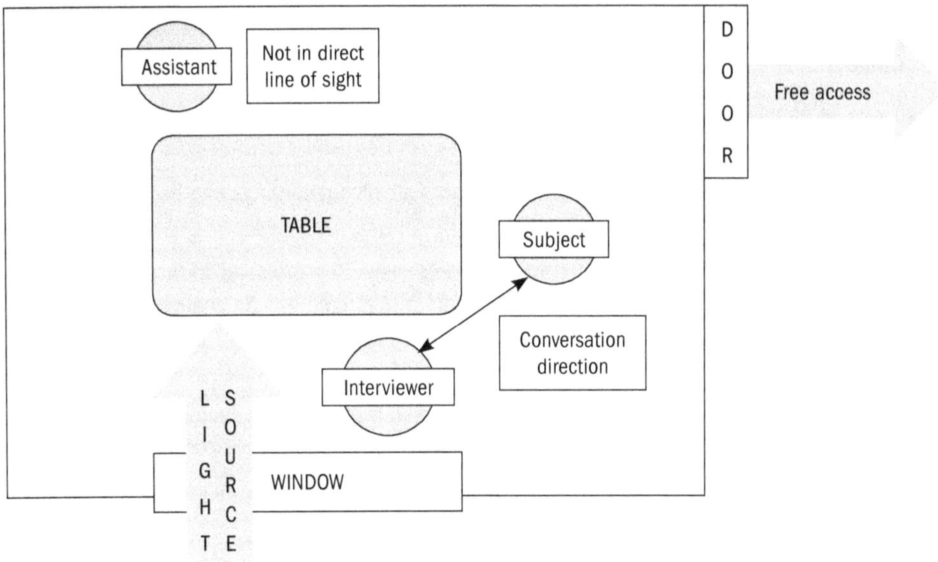

Figure 4.1 *Typical interview seating plan*

f. Waiting area

When interviewing multiple people, you may not always want one interviewee to see another when they walk out of the interview location or while awaiting their turn.

It is highly unlikely that you will have a waiting area or an alternative exit to the entrance. Scheduling of interviews may therefore become important to resolve this practical problem. Consider if it is necessary to have delays between interviews to prevent people from bumping into each other. The time between interviews can also be used practically to reflect on the completed interview and to plan for the coming interviews or subsequent steps.

g. Other setting considerations

Some other practical considerations include access to:

- Power sources for laptops, recording equipment, specialised equipment, external hard drives, etc.
- Place to write. It is difficult to write on your lap and to maintain the desired degree of eye contact with the interviewee.
- Access to amenities like toilets, tea and coffee and/or something to eat if you are going to spend a protracted period of time interviewing multiple people.
- Place to make copies of documents, identity documents, etc. Printing facilities. A network connection for the subject to access the system to explain matters.
- Although less of a concern these days with the advent of cellular technology, the ability to telephone and/or access the internet.

4.5.2. Recordings

a. General

When we talk about recordings, we are actually talking about:

- *Audio*
The recording of voice during an interview. Quality of voice recordings can be an issue.

- *Video*
The recording of voice and image during an interview. This is useful as it also shows the reactions of the person being interviewed. Amateur recording has its challenges and quality may be an issue depending on the equipment used and the setting.

- *Transcripts*
Transcripts are a more detailed/mostly verbatim record of what was said in an interview.

- *Interviewer minutes*
Minutes maintained by the interview team are discussed later, but also serve to preserve/record the conversation.

Video proceedings may be less practical than audio proceedings because of set up and the equipment required. Video proceedings do however give greater detail, as a person can see and hear what occurred. Many of the negative psychological aspects that we mention in this section will be more pronounced with video proceedings than with audio proceedings.

For the larger part, investigators make use of audio recordings. The bulk of our discussion below is therefore aimed at audio proceedings. You will, however, be able to apply what is discussed to video recordings as well.

b. Reasons

There are three main reasons (and some secondary reasons) why we would want to make recordings of interviews. These include:

- *Reference*
It is often difficult to ensure that all salient points of an interview are denoted in written notes (*completeness*). Even when there is more than one person taking notes, each person is exposed to the probability that they will miss something and each person has their own interpretation of what is important or not. Furthermore, you cannot always remember why you wrote something down during an interview. Alternatively, you may have taken a point out of context or begin to doubt that you wrote down all the *correct* facts. Recordings are therefore highly suitable for record purposes. The limitation of interviews will be discussed under the comments on the psychology of recordings.

  Recordings should not be relied on totally, as there are often technical/practical issues (for example: batteries dying, excessive background noise, limited recording space, etc) and not all recordings physically work. The environment in which the recording is made may not be conducive to recordings and the end result may not be audible (eg due to background noise). There may also not be power to perform the recording.

- *Evidence*

A recording may serve as evidence of what a person has said. This may be useful for admissions of guilt to prove what was said in the event of disputes or changes of heart. Recordings are also useful when there are many detailed facts/information provided.

The limitations include the fact that the recording may be inadmissible in proceedings if the correct protocol was not followed. Furthermore, if the recording is of an admission, the admission may be inadmissible if the correct protocol to confessions/admissions was not followed. Lastly, a recording of a witness testimony may be inadmissible in proceedings if the witness is unavailable for cross-questioning. Establish what local country laws are applicable with regards to recording interviews.

- *Protection*

A recording can protect you as the interviewer. If an interviewee falsely accuses you of duress or improper behaviour, the recording may provide evidence of your innocence and the interviewee's dishonesty. We need to consider that desperate people may do desperate things. *As an example: I was dropping off a lady (late Friday afternoon) close to her home after I had just interviewed her alone in the office. She looked at me with big puppy dog eyes and said: 'I will do anything to make this go away.' Needless to say I just kept on staring at the road ahead and pretended to be unaware of her proposal.*

If, in another example, a lady tears her blouse and runs screaming out of the meeting room in front of the general office, you are going to have a tough time trying to clear your name. In fact, most people are going to see the subject as the victim. There goes your investigation and your reputation and maybe even your career with it! Again, the admissibility of the recordings may be a problem.

- *Other*

Voice stress tests may be applied during interviews in an attempt to detect deception. Voice stress tests are similar to polygraph tests.

These are more likely to be used for your own reference, as a blunt instrument to indicate honesty of the interviewee. The problem is that these are not widely used and less widely accepted, as their accuracy is doubtful. It is doubtful if a person would volunteer to undergo such a test. A covertly conducted test would most likely not be admissible in proceedings. The admissibility of voice stress tests is doubtful from a scientific point of view and even less likely to be accepted in proceedings than a polygraph, the validity of which is also frequently denied.

c. Psychology of recordings on interviewees

People are very reluctant to talk if they know that they are being recorded. When you reach forward and ask if you should switch off the equipment, then they agree. Once the equipment is switched off they proceed to talk a lot more freely. This is often despite the fact that there may be more than one person in the room. It is almost as if they think that they can deny having said something if it is not recorded. Perhaps they are also concerned about what happens to the recording once they walk out of the interview.

What is said in an interview may be confidential, said in privilege or of a whistle-blowing/tip-off nature. The interviewee may be prepared to trust you as the interviewer with the information, but not anyone else that they have not agreed to. They will have no control over a recording of themselves and may therefore be reluctant to be recorded when giving information that could incriminate others.

d. Admissibility of recordings

If you want a recording to be admissible in proceedings there are a few factors that must have transpired, including:

- The person must have given their permission as per the protocol below and/or
- In the absence of the person's permission, the person must be party to the conversation (you cannot record third-party conversations that you are not part of) and/or
- The person must not dispute the recording in the proceeding (whether or not the protocol was followed and/or if it is a true copy of all that was said and/or was not manipulated). Basically, the recording will be admissible if they agree to allow it as evidence despite them not knowing that the interview was being recorded. In the absence of their agreement, the chairman or judge will have to decide as to its admissibility.
- There must be no tampering (actual or perceived) with the recording itself. There should be no loud clicks (when equipment could have been put on and off or edited) on the recording or unaccounted for pauses or unexplained/suspicious changes in pitch or speed of the recording.

e. Recording protocol

If you are an officer of the court, evidence may be inadmissible if you did not read the person from whom you obtained the evidence their Miranda rights (discussed later in this chapter).

The recommended procedure below is very cumbersome and will more than likely have a negative impact on the interviewee's willingness to divulge all pertinent information.

The correct procedure would be as follows:

- Before switching on the recording equipment, tell the person that you would like to record the session.
- Then ask them if they will agree to the recording of the session.
- If they agree then follow the formal recorded protocol.
- Switch on the equipment and state the following:
  - 'My name is Mr A. Smith.'
  - 'I am the Group Audit Manager (your official title) of the XYZ company.'
  - 'This is a recording of an interview held (today's date and time).'
  - 'In the room with me are: Mr A.N. Other, my assistant and Ms D Jones, XYZ company human resource consultant.'
  - 'This interview is being held with Mr A. Crook.'
  - 'The purpose of this interview is to seek clarity into the serious allegations of misconduct around the fraudulent use of... or the misappropriation of....'
  - 'Please state your name and position for the record.'

- 'Please state that you agree that this session may be recorded.'
- 'I would like to read you your rights (read their Miranda rights - not required if you are not an officer of the court/a police officer).'
- 'Please state if you understand these rights.'
- Then proceed with the interview.
- Going off record, taking a break or any pause in the recording, should be 'marked'. The person leading the interview should state on the recording: 'We will be taking a tea break or we will be going off record', etc.
- When the recording break is complete, the equipment should be switched back on and the person leading the interview should state: 'This is the recommencement of Mr DEF's (subject's name) interview. We are going back on record/we have completed our break and are recommencing the interview/the document previously requested has been delivered and we are going to recommence the interview.' Anything said off record will be inadmissible if the interviewee does not agree with its authenticity. If you want to bring something on record that was said while off record, then say: 'While we were off record, it was agreed that.... Please indicate that you agree with this statement.'
- The recording must also be ended correctly. The person leading the interview says: 'This is the end of the interview. There is agreement that nothing further needs to be discussed. The next step is that .... Thank you to all who participated in the interview.'
- Switch off the equipment.

The best manner to obtain the interviewee's acceptance of the recording it to have it transcribed and then to have them read and sign the transcription for authenticity/accuracy. Alternatively, you can give them an electronic copy of the recording and ask them to sign for receipt of the electronic copy and/or for its authenticity. Software compatibility may be an issue if the recording only plays on propriety software/equipment.

The suggested protocol is a costly and time-consuming process. It will rarely be necessary to follow this process. It is suggested that you just record the interview for your own protection and do not inform the person, as you do not intend submitting it as evidence. Some subjects pick up that they are being recorded. If they make a scene and want it put off, then rather continue the interview unrecorded than have no interview at all.

f. Physical recording

Many different methods exist by which to record interviews. These include:

- Dictaphone-type recorders – out of date technology.
- Traditional tape recorders – out of date technology.
- Modern MP3-type recorders – small, discrete and added functionality. Some size and compatibility issues.
- Recording software on laptops, cell phones, iPads, etc – cheap, freely available, flexible.

The need to be discrete, the length of storage available on the equipment and the cost and availability of the recording equipment may dictate the type of equipment used. Recording software on laptops is the most accessible and easiest to use. Various 'freeware' packages are available on the internet. Laptops may however not be subtle enough and it may not always be possible to cart them around and/or you may not have the chance to set them up or not have them handy.

In such cases an MP3-type recorder is small and can be kept on a key ring ready for use most of the time. Battery power and being charged when you require it may be an issue. MP3 recorders have limited capacity and the recording has to be transferred to other electronic media and/or edited and/or the storage/recording/file format changed. Backing up and loss of device and/or data may be a higher risk with smaller MP3 recorders.

g. Practical considerations

As far as possible, always have a back-up recording device. Situations may arise where the interview is about to commence and your recording device fails. You will need to have a plan B ready and waiting.

Always test your device with sufficient time before the interview commences. As an example: the microphone of the laptop may need to be switched on manually in the control panel of the laptop to allow recording to commence. This takes time and you do not want to be fumbling about during the interview.

Never rely only on your recording. Always continue making manual notes as if you do not have a device. This is good from a psychological point of view in so far as the interviewee forgets about the device. It is also good in so far as you cannot check if your device is working during the interview. You will not be in a position to make comprehensive written notes once the interview has been completed and you realise that your device has failed. You will need to have made notes already.

h. Transcripts

Some organisations have an HR representative present to record verbatim minutes of the interview. This enables you to give the interviewee an opportunity to read the minutes through at the conclusion of the interview and sign the original to evidence that they were a true reflection of the interview. The interviewee would be given a copy of the minutes and the original would be retained on file. This is particularly useful when admissions are made, as long as the person does not dispute the admissions or cry duress later. The use of transcripts is advisable in highly unionised environments.

The interviewee tends to go back and study the minutes, and tries to dispute specific aspects of the interview or to say that they actually meant 'this' and not 'that'. In most cases, the very detail of what was said is less important and they become unnecessarily distracted in the detail.

4.5.3. Confidentiality of interviews

a. General

Witnesses often request to remain anonymous and that their identity is not divulged as the person who disclosed the information.

b. Who

In most cases, it is the witnesses who want to remain anonymous. On some rare occasions, it is the guilty person who wants elements of the transgression to remain confidential. They sometimes also want to declare information about other people's involvement or other unrelated irregularities in a bid to gain favour with you, misdirect you or to cut a deal with you.

As a general rule, try to skirt around the issue of confidentiality and/or avoid it. Never introduce the concept yourself, as it creates expectations that you will most likely be unable to commit to. It may however not be possible to avoid it when the person is very concerned about it. Discuss it directly with them in those events.

c. Why

It is important to try to understand why the person wants the interview to be confidential. Remember our rule: 'People do and say things for a reason.' In this case, they are not saying that they do not want to talk to you; they are just saying that they do not want other people to know where the information came from. This is actually a positive place to be in and one that a person can work with.

In that case, ask them why they want to remain in confidence. We need to try to understand if it is just because they:

- Do not want people to think badly of them
- Are scared of being victimised
- May carry some form of blame in the irregularity (directly or indirectly).

If it is purely a confidence issue, then say to them that you will try your best to keep the matter confidential, but if it is serious then you may have to take it further. Most times it is not a serious issue and it is just the fact that they do not want to be labelled as a person who is going behind people's backs.

A suggested response is to say that you have been doing this for a very long time and that there are many ways to conceal their identity and/or to arrange that the information is stumbled upon by chance. In almost all of the cases when the information needs to come out without identifying them, run through a role-play of how you plan to highlight the issue. Then ask them if they would be comfortable with this. Build their confidence in this manner.

d. Serious matters

If they have had some part in the irregularity then tell them that they should rather disclose it to you, as it may be far worse if it comes out later and that things always eventually come out. Say that it is better to deal with these things up front. Request them to make the disclosure to you so that you can decide how best to present their disclosure.

The important point is always to be totally honest with the witness. In certain instances, you could tell them that you cannot guarantee their absolute anonymity. In such instances, tell them that you are aware that it is very difficult for them. Tell them that they are making a significant contribution to the investigation so as to appeal to their ego or to their good nature or desire to see justice served.

If you realise during the course of the disclosure that this is a serious matter and that it will have to be brought out into the open, then tell them this. Try, in most cases, to get them to make the declaration themselves. In other cases, agree to assist them to highlight the declared information in a manner that reflects positively on them for coming forward and making the disclosure.

In one example: a reluctant witness eventually admitted having received stolen company equipment (a power drill and some electric cord for his home renovations) from the main subject. He did not want to be a witness as he was concerned that the main subject would use this against him. I told him that I could see that he had accepted this in good faith and that it was a long time ago. I told him to make this disclosure to his superior to break the power of the main subject if he tried to use it against him (yes, I did, but I have declared this to ABC). I said that I did not see it being an issue, but suggested that he act with greater caution in future events. He did this and was relieved.

e. Testifying

In some cases, the witness does not mind making disclosure in the interview, but they say that they do not want to have to testify in any proceedings. In such cases, say that you can or you cannot (depending on the situation) determine if they will be required to testify at this early stage of the investigation or say: 'I will first need to know what they know before determining if it will be required as evidence. At this stage I am merely gathering evidence and we are a long way from knowing who was involved and from formulating charges. I cannot say what will be required at this early point. I am deeply grateful for your assistance and please be assured that I will come to you should I require further assistance.'

Once you have heard what they have declared, say that the information has certainly helped you to understand the background. Then summarise to say, for example, that this is not something that you will be able to use in a hearing or court of law, as it is hearsay. Alternatively, say that this is a material piece of information and this is the reason why. Then tell them how this piece of information will be used in any potential proceedings.

Also tell them that they need not fear any proceedings, as you will help them through every step of the way in such proceedings and explain how you will assist them. I usually draft an affidavit on their behalf which they read into evidence. Chapters 7 and 8 on subsequent actions and reporting refer.

f. Client confidentiality

Fraud investigators are not in a client confidentiality relationship, as a professional lawyer may be with their client. You nevertheless do not want to act unethically by:

- Making promises that you cannot keep
- Concealing otherwise vital information to 'save' a witness
- Unnecessarily exposing a witness to risk of reprisal.

As soon as you see that the information is going to require that they are involved in proceedings (for example that they will be required to testify) or that the information is going to need to be divulged to a wider group, you will need to inform the interviewee of the change, especially if the expectation of complete confidence was created. Then set about trying to get them to agree to assist in further proceedings.

g. Willful blindness

The concept of willful blindness should not be confused with the requirement for confidence. The concept of willful blindness is a criminal concept by which a person can be held liable for having knowledge about a criminal matter but choosing to remain silent about it to protect themselves or others or because of apathy.

People who want to remain anonymous want to declare what they know; they just do not want others to know where the information came from. People who choose to remain silent do not want to make any declarations at all. The reasons why they want to remain silent and/or confidential may be the same (possibly out of fear). The difference between requesting confidentiality and willful blindness lies therefore in the desire to make disclosures.

On these occasions, tell the person that there is a criminal concept called 'wilful blindness' through which they can be held criminally liable if they know about an irregularity and choose to remain silent. Then say that you are sure they would not want to be held liable for something that someone else perpetrated and which they just happen to know about. Willful blindness is actually applicable at any stage that a person becomes aware of a crime. The difference is that we are now telling the interviewees about it in an attempt to:

- Encourage them to make full disclosures
- Provide them with a forum in which to make the disclosures.

Telling people about willful blindness is often perceived as threatening, and it is therefore a less desirable method. How you tell them about the concept is important. It is advisable to convince them that they are doing the right thing. Only tell them about the concept of willful blindness when you can see that they are not declaring all that they know. As in the case of informing a person of their Miranda rights, you also have a duty to tell people (in a professional manner) of the possible consequences of their actions (our rule on 'Queensbury Rules' refers).

4.5.4. Challenges

a. General

Numerous cultural and other differences may pose challenges to an interview situation. These challenges range from simple cultural customs to complex social injustices. The truth is that forewarned is forearmed. If we are aware of the challenges, then we can understand how they could potentially impact on our interview/s and plan around them.

It is likely that the statements below may attract criticism. If, however, you are offended because of a list of potential challenges, then you have missed the point of listing them. Issues of race, religion, gender and age are all very emotive and widely debated issues. The reality is that these issues exist and we have to deal with them as best we can to ensure that we deliver a professional service at the end of the day. The purpose of mentioning them here is to ensure that you are sensitive to potential negative reactions in your interviews and to provide you with an opportunity to prepare suitably in advance.

b. Specific challenges

The following specific challenges need to be considered in an interview situation:

- *Pregnancy*

  As far as possible do not interview pregnant women. If anything happens to the mother or the unborn baby, the interview may be seen as the cause of the problem and the organisation may be blamed. While we may think that an adverse effect on the mother or the baby is unlikely, we are not doctors and cannot make such a call. The loss to the pregnant subject, the mental trauma endured by you and the possible litigation to the organisation are just not worth the chance. One solution is to have the lady agree to be interviewed amidst warnings of the dangers and to have her sign a limitation of liability-type document. This route is however not recommended, as regardless of the probability of occurrence, the cost of a negative effect on the mother and child is just too high. It is suggested to either postpone the interview for a reasonable period after the birth or to close the matter altogether.

- *Gender*

  Women interviewing men and vice versa may have an impact on the ability of the interviewer to hold a professional interview. This is not from the interviewer's side, but from the interviewee's perspective. *Examples of interviews come to mind where the male interviewee did not like being interviewed by a female interviewer because in his culture women are seen to be inferior to men.* Interviewees like that are less than cooperative and it is unlikely that the interviewer will obtain the required information. While we all frown heavily on these archaic paradigms, the reality is that they exist. Our interviews are not there to shine a torch on social injustices, as painful as they are. We need to put our principles in our pocket, put our game-face on and hold a professional interview and get the truth, whether in favour of our case or not. The best way in which we can do this is to be aware of the potential challenges and to plan and work around them in such a way to ensure that we optimise every interview situation. Try to find out in advance what your interviewee is like. If he is a 'Ku Klux Klan-type' then it does not help to send a highly qualified and professional African woman to conduct the interview. Remember our rule: 'Keep the end game in mind.'

  It could, of course, be used to your advantage to send someone (forewarned) obviously wrong to conduct the interview. It would be a dangerous game to play, but there may be a situation where the interviewee would be so agitated or caught off guard that it could unsettle them sufficiently to cause them to make mistakes. This approach is not recommended though. You are advised to err on the side of conservatism and to go with a better fitting interviewer. It may be a case of losing the battle and winning the war. It is better to gloat over a successful conviction and mumble under your breath in terms of what a racist or a sexist the interviewee was than have no conviction and proving an unrelated social injustice point. And there with the controversy of this point.

This is all well and good in a situation where you have a selection of resources to choose from, but what happens when you are in a situation and you have to get the job done? Well, then you:

- Plan your interview questions well.
- Record the interview (covertly if required) to protect yourself/staff members.
- Take a (credible) witness with you.
- Ensure you follow all the basic steps, such as getting the interviewee to sign that they were Mirandized (discussed later).

- *Religion*

In a similar fashion, religious differences may impact on your ability to hold a successful interview. The most common challenge I have had to deal with is the differences that need to be respected with regards to the Islamic religion. This may be combined with the gender issue as well. For example: depending on how orthodox the interviewee is, it may be unacceptable for you to walk straight up to an Islamic woman and shake her hand. *An example of such a situation refers, which left me feeling foolish when the lady concerned declined my hand. It was my fault of course for not being sensitive to the difference and assuming that she would be the same as the other Islamic ladies in the same office.*

Some interviewing literature suggests that you touch the interviewee (shaking hands, touching on the shoulder, etc) as often as possible to develop a rapport with them. You are however not encouraged not to touch interviewees, as there is a greater chance of getting it wrong than there is of getting it right. The associated risks to your interview success are too large and not worth the chance. Only go as far as shaking hands if local custom allows for it.

The lesson is: When in Rome, do as the Romans do. Try to understand the local customs in advance. Talk to other expatriates and buy a book on the relevant culture or religion. Try to learn as much as you can in advance. Do not talk about food when people are fasting. If you will excuse the pun, it is in 'poor taste'. Do not talk about alcohol to Islamic people. That is disrespectful to their convictions. The same goes for jokes. You might want to use humour to lighten the situation, especially when you know the person. Choose your jokes very carefully. Do not make Catholic and Protestant jokes in Ireland. In fact, rather do not make jokes at all. Often you cannot read all aspects of a person. Smile and be friendly. That should suffice.

The bottom line is that you are advised to be professional and courteous in every situation. If you have someone on your team who is of the same cultural or religious background as the subject, then rather send them to conduct the interview or at least to assist if they are too junior.

- *Race*

Two examples refer, firstly, of an interview where the interviewee would not even look at me. He looked at my colleague (who was of the same ethnicity as him) and answered towards him, even though I was asking the questions.

Secondly, all my requests for interviews were declined (for weeks) until I asked a person internal to the organisation and of the same ethnicity to broker the interviews. Take it on the chin, walk away and get the job done.

Another example includes the simple matter of shaking hands. Some cultures are brought up to respect someone who has a strong handshake, as it is supposed to be a reflection of their character. They believe that if the person breaks your hand, then they must be a person to be respected. Alternatively, if they have a 'wet fish' handshake, then they must be of weak character. Of course, that is a complete generalisation and any similarity is more likely ascribed to coincidence or culture. In contrast to that, in some African cultures a person who crushes your hand is seen as aggressive. For example, picture this: a white interviewer crushes the hand of an African interviewee. The interviewee thinks, wow he is aggressive and obviously out to get me. The interviewer thinks he is weak and obviously guilty due to their weak character. We will laugh at how ridiculous some of our paradigms are, but they exist. Let us be sensitive. In some African cultures, it is preferred to shake with both hands. This apparently comes from old days when it was a concern that you might shake with one hand and have a weapon in the other. The Asian culture is also not to shake with a strong grip. I have made the mistake many times of crushing someone's hand. It is very difficult to recover from that sort of a start.

- *Country*

While far less of an issue than some, there may be some differences that result from people that hail from different countries. These differences may be due to:

  - Accent (difficult to understand or the frequent butt of Hollywood humour)
  - Mannerisms
  - Particular terms or ways of saying things
  - Dress style or hair styles
  - Personal hygiene.

Again, try to find out as much as possible about local custom. Prepare yourself to avoid being surprised.

- *Age/senior citizens*

Senior citizens have expectations of how they should be addressed and/or treated. It is not to say that you will be disrespectful on purpose, it is just that they come from a different era and they are not always used to the 'modern' (used loosely here) ways. Young people often talk very colloquially and older people may not like this and/or do not relate to this. They like you to speak in the 'Queen's English'. Young people again do not want to be perceived to be 'stuck up'.

Older people may not like having a younger person interviewing them, seeing them as beneath their status, inexperienced or just too young. They may well even go ahead with the interview, but not relate to the interviewer. *As an example: in an interviewing of a person some 30 years my senior, I was so fixed on the matter at hand that I 'charged off' headlong into the conversation. The subject was quite taken back by my fast pace and I had to stop abruptly and apologise for being too energetic.* Again, know your interviewee. If they want to sit and have a cup of tea and first get to know you, then that is what you do.

- *Minors*

You cannot just interview a minor. You need to first get the permission of their parent or guardian and they need to be represented in the interview by a parent, guardian or legal counsel. The opportunity for you to make a mistake is great. Ensure that you do everything in line with local laws if you need to interview a minor.

- *Sexual orientation*

We live in a more enlightened society today. Things are far more open than they were many years ago. In the past, we pretended that some differences did not exist. Now they are paraded around. Not everyone has embraced the changes with the same degree of acceptance. 'Don't play the ball, play the man.' Put your personal beliefs to the side and conduct a professional interview. Do not make insensitive jokes, do not volunteer or give your opinion on controversial issues of race, gender, abortion, religion, etc. If it comes up, say to the interviewee that you would not want to get into a debate about those issues and say that you would appreciate it if you discuss the matter at hand (being the purpose of the interview). Do not be drawn in. If the shoe is on the other foot and you (as the interviewer) are the one who has to bear the brunt of their prejudice, then be professional (and the better person) and keep to the issues at hand.

- *Seniority*

Seniority here refers to a person's actual or perceived position in a company and not their age. This is more applicable to company directors and senior organisational leaders. Some may just be 'a big fish in a small pond'. The more senior the appointment or the larger the salary or the larger the company and the more power they wield, the worse the ego could be. Some examples of responses that I have received from so-called senior people include: 'When you have been here as long as I have...' and 'But I am entitled to it because I am a director'. This is especially true when you came through the ranks in a company and now you have to interview the person who mentored you or who was (or still is) senior to you.

So, what do you do when you have to interview managing directors and very senior people in charge of millions of dollars of assets or turnover and/or in charge of thousands of staff members; people with many more years of experience than you? At the end of the day, it is about the facts. Stick to the matter at hand and the facts. Always be courteous. The old saying, 'a prophet is never accepted in his hometown' comes to mind.

If the budget allows, it is advisable to use an outside fraud examiner to conduct the interview/s. They may have their own credibility (for example: partner of a firm) and they can get away with saying things or asking questions that you may be less than successful saying or asking. They are also not subject to the same pressures/threats that you are. If you are employed by one company, then you have one job and you can be fired or worked out. The independent fraud examiner can walk away to their other clients.

- *Heinous crimes*

What if you have to interview someone who has been part of something particularly bad, such as a scam that caused people to lose all their money and commit suicide as a result of, or a ring that was exploiting children? Pretend, in such interviews, as if you hear those kinds of things every day. Do not act surprised or shocked, as you want the informant to continue talking. If you act shocked, then the interviewee may not want to divulge more (some of which they may have been directly involved in themselves) due to your disapproval. So, sit and take notes while being unemotional.

At the end of the day, do not be judgemental. We do not know what has brought these people (right or wrong) to this place and what about their lives made them do the things they have done. Even if we know about their childhoods and backgrounds, we do not know what their emotions have been. Not even greed is a simple assumption. We do not know why these people feel they need to have excess. Modern science has taught us that these things are complicated. Our job is to solve the crime and/or get the conviction and/or to recover what we can. Again: 'Play the ball, not the man.' As difficult as it can be, stick to the issue at hand and leave the person out of it. Get the facts that prove how the crime was committed and by whom. Do not talk about the people who have suffered and why the subject is such a bad person for having perpetrated the fraud.

When we get personally involved or if our emotions overtake our logic, then we move more from a point of emotion and less from a point of fact. We may even start to purposefully sway the facts in the direction that suits our emotions. This would be a complete no-no. If you are a sensitive person or if you are less independent (due to personal or work relationship or previous negative experiences) then rather recuse yourself from the investigation and have someone else conduct it. It also helps to have a trusted person that you can talk to about these types of difficult situations.

- *Family or friend*

We typically work many years for organisations. Friendships will develop; we cannot avoid it. While we can keep relationships professional and to a minimum, there may come a time when you have to interview a friend. Worse still, you may have a family member in the same organisation as you. The subject may also have studied with you or know some of your acquaintances or attend the same outside events as you.

The subject of the interview may want to play on these facts and try to get you to be lenient. They can use all kinds of emotional blackmail to try to get you to compromise the situation. Alternatively, you may be insufficiently independent to interview the person. You may be too harsh (out of anger or the need to prove your independence) or too lenient.

As an example: I have been in situations where I was required to discipline colleagues that had become friends. I was told that the power had gone to my head and that I was a disloyal friend, etc. It is strange that the subjects never brought up the fact that they had done something wrong.

Possible courses of action in these sorts of situations include the following:

- The first and best option is to declare the potential conflict and to recuse yourself and withdraw from the matter.
- Declare the potential conflict. Consider putting the potential conflict in a subsequent report or affidavit.
- Explain the conflict to your management and the potential dangers. Get management to agree on the chosen course of action.
- Explain the potential conflict to the subject and the potential danger. Inform them of the chosen course of action.
- Have a colleague support you in the process.
- Have an independent person review what you have done after the fact.
- Pre-empt potential criticisms and problems. Plan how to counter them.
- Record your logic and/or conversations in your working papers.

4.6. MIRANDA RIGHTS

a. General

While a lot of people will not come from a police background, we have all watched movies where the police officer reads the subject their rights. These rights are called the 'Miranda rights'.

Miranda rights are about being fair. They are about the duty that an investigator has to inform a suspect that things are serious and that there could be consequences to what they say or do.

The rights were put in place to ensure that the police and investigators do not use trickery to obtain information or that suspects do not say something without realising the consequences of what they are saying. It is not permissible for investigators to misrepresent matters or to mislead interviewees.

b. United States

The following is an excerpt from 'The Miranda Warning', which provides a history of the Miranda Rights in the United States (available at http://www.usconstitution.net/miranda.html):

> 'This was the crux of the issue in *Miranda v Arizona*. In 1963, Ernesto Miranda was accused of kidnapping and raping an 18-year-old, mildly retarded woman. He was brought in for questioning and confessed to the crime. He was not told that he did not have to speak or that he could have a lawyer present. At trial, Miranda's lawyer tried to get the confession thrown out, but the motion was denied. In 1966, the case came in front of the Supreme Court. The Court ruled that the statements made to the police could not be used as evidence, since Miranda had not been advised of his rights.
>
> Since then, before any pertinent questioning of a suspect is done, the police have been required to recite the Miranda warning. The statement, reproduced below, exists in several forms, but all have the key elements: the right to remain silent and the right to an attorney. These are also often referred to as the "Miranda rights". When you have been read your rights, you are said to have been "Mirandized".
>
> Note that one need not be Mirandized to be arrested. There is a difference between being arrested and being questioned. Also, basic questions, such as name, address, and Social Security number do not need to be covered by a Miranda warning. The police also need not Mirandize someone who is not a suspect in a crime.
>
> As for Ernesto Miranda, his conviction was thrown out, though he did not become a free man. The police had other evidence that was independent of the confession, and when Miranda was tried a second time, he was convicted again. After release from prison, Miranda was killed in a barroom brawl in 1976.
>
> *The following is a minimal Miranda warning, as outlined in the* Miranda v Arizona *case:*
>
> You have the right to remain silent. Anything you say can and will be used against you in a court of law. You have the right to speak to an attorney, and to have an attorney present during any questioning. If you cannot afford a lawyer, one will be provided for you at government expense.'

c. South Africa

Section 35 of the Constitution of the Republic of South Africa, 1996 states:

> Everyone who is arrested for allegedly committing an offence has the right:
> - to remain silent;
> - to be informed promptly
>   - of the right to remain silent; and
>   - of the consequences of not remaining silent;
> - not to be compelled to make any confession or admission that could be used in evidence against that person;
>
> ... and later in the section:
> - Every accused person has a right to a fair trial, which includes the right
>   - ....
>   - not to be compelled to give self-incriminating evidence[.]

d. Admissibility

As per above, testimonies may in certain circumstances be inadmissible in a court of law if the person who made the declaration/admission was not Mirandized.

The trick is to know when to Mirandize and when not to. Surely the safest would be to Mirandize everyone all of the time? This is however not practical. Mirandizing is not required by all people. It is only required by officers of the court. Most people reading this book will not be police officers or officers of the court. Mirandizing people too soon (by people not required to do it) may also have a negative impact on their willingness to disclose matters.

e. When

- *General*

When do you read them? The rule is, as soon as you know that the matter has become serious.

- *Prior to the interview*

You need to anticipate if the suspect is guilty or not. If they are guilty and it is a very serious offence/crime, then you must Mirandize them.

- *During the interview*

If at a certain stage during the interview it becomes apparent to the interviewer that the person is guilty of a very serious offence, then there would be a duty on the interviewer to inform the interviewee that the matter is serious and that they have rights and what these rights are.

- *The rights:*
  - The right to remain silent.
  - Anything said may be used in evidence against him/her.
  - He/she has the right to consult an attorney of their own choice before answering any questions.
  - The right to have an attorney present during the questioning.

- The right not to incriminate themselves.
- The right to discontinue answering any questions put to them at any stage during the interview.
- The right to end the interview at any stage.
- The right to leave the interview at any stage.
- The right to exercise any of the above rights at any time before or during any questioning and the making of a statement.

- *Miranda rights template*

The Miranda rights template (attached as Annexure 4.1 hereto) may be used when conducting an interview in which a person needs to be informed of their Miranda rights.

4.7. INTERVIEW QUESTIONS

Questions are the 'meat' of the interview. This is what we have been leading up to in this chapter. In this section, we are only going to be discussing the background to interview questions. Specific examples of questions are discussed later under the different sections of the physical interview.

4.7.1. Types of questions

There are essentially three types of interview questions, being:

- Leading
- Closed
- Open.

While open questions are generally the most suitable type of questions, we must recognise that there are times that the other questions may be applicable, albeit to a lesser degree. Part of the planning of which interview questions to ask should include a decision as to which types of questions to ask.

- *Leading*

Leading questions lead a person to a particular answer. As a general rule, leading questions should not be used in criminal proceedings or in internal labour matters, as they suppose a particular answer and can be unfair in so far as they may cause a respondent to inadvertently answer to their detriment. For example: 'Mr Smith, please answer me yes or no. Do you still beat your wife?' Well, that supposes that he already beats his wife. If he says yes, then he is admitting to beating his wife. If he says no, then he is admitting to having beaten her in the past. Leading questions can, however, be used wisely to get an interviewee to inadvertently admit to something. As an example: 'What were the reasons that you needed the money?'

- *Closed*

Closed questions do not elicit any additional discussion. We should rarely use closed questions. There may be times when these are warranted. At the end of the day, the purpose of our interview is to obtain information. An example of a closed question is: 'Did you take the money?" – answer: 'No'. You cannot progress any further with this line of questioning, as the interviewee is just going to refer you back to their answer and say: 'But I already told you that I did not do it.' Closed questions may be required in circumstances when a subject is being highly evasive and avoiding your questions. You may want a subject to give you a direct answer of 'yes' or 'no'. Once they have committed to an answer, you will then request reasons for their choice and/or further clarity.

- *Open*

Open questions are those questions that prompt an interviewee to volunteer information and divulge what they have done or know. Open questions should be used in most circumstances. For example, do not ask: 'Do you fully understand the procedure?' This will be leading or may be a matter of the subject's opinion. Rather ask: 'Can you please help me understand how the procedure works?' In this way, the respondent has to tell you what they know about the procedure. You will, therefore, be able to deduce if they know about the workings of the procedure, based on the completeness of their reply.

4.7.2. Planning of questions

The most important element of interview questions is planning. Start with what the purpose of your interview is or what the desired outcome is. This may be as simple as information-seeking or admission-seeking or it could be more specific (for example to get the interviewee to demonstrate knowledge of a policy, admit knowing the corrupt supplier, etc). Then work backwards by asking yourself which questions are going to get you the desired result.

4.7.3. Testing of questions

We then play different scenarios off against the questions to understand what impact different respondent replies may have on our ability to achieve the desired outcome. We then adjust our questions and retest the scenarios. Sometimes we need to develop alternative approaches. For example, if they answer 'A', then we will ask 'X' and then 'Y' to bring them back on track before asking 'Z' which is the actual question we want to ask. Alternatively, if they answer 'B', then we go straight to asking 'Z'.

4.7.4. Decision trees

Decision tree-type diagrams combined with 'If this, then this, otherwise that' types of questions may be a useful tool to plan the structure of an interview. A decision tree is dangerous as it is inflexible. It is supposed to help inexperienced interviewers, but it can be counterproductive if the interview does not pan out as planned. If you want to use them, ensure that you build in sufficient variations. They are more suitable for more formal/hearing-type situations when you control the questions.

4.7.5. Blocking techniques

Blocking techniques are a vital tool in the interviewer's toolbox. Blocking techniques stem from planning. As discussed above, the interviewer predicts during the planning phase what the interviewee's response could be and, more importantly, which excuses they could offer and how they could evade the truth. The interviewer then skilfully crafts the questions (planning backwards, as always) in such a manner that when delivered, they place certain 'blocks' in place to prevent the interviewee lying or not divulging the truth later when the 'actual' question that needs to be asked is delivered.

As an example: In a previous interview (interview A), the girlfriend of the gentleman being interviewed in interview B had said that she had been legitimately given goods by her boyfriend. The girlfriend was the actual guilty party who had stolen the items and she was just using the boyfriend as an excuse. She did not think that we were going to call him. She quickly primed the boyfriend how to respond when we told her that we were going to check her story with her boyfriend. The catch, in this case, was the fact that the recovered stolen goods were marked as having been purchased from various widely dispersed national outlets. The goods were also date stamped as being purchased within a wide range of days within normal working hours. The interviewer adopted a very 'friendly' approach at the commencement of interview B with the boyfriend. This was a clever guise to put the required blocks in place. The interviewer began seeming to be very interested in the boyfriend's work. The boyfriend was only too keen to tell us what he did (answering non-threatening questions). The interviewer continued to play the boyfriend's ego by saying: 'Oh, I suppose you cover a wide area?' This was something that we had previously confirmed with his employer. The boyfriend took the bait and responded by saying: 'Yes, the area that I cover begins at the highway on the left and extends all the way down to the railway lines on the right.'

So, the blocks were in place. Then the interviewer said: 'Wow, that is fantastic, but let's get down to the real reason why we are here. We just want to confirm if you gave these goods to your girlfriend.' The boyfriend then confirmed that he had given them to her and that he had purchased them. The interviewer then said: 'But I don't understand, how could you have purchased these goods from all these different places around the country?' The boyfriend began to get a sinking look on his face as he realised that he had set his own 'work' boundaries to us. He made a quick comeback to say: 'I have a friend who owns a taxi and I sometimes accompany him on trips around the country when I am off.' The interviewer then came in for the kill. He said: 'But these goods are all stamped with different dates. Normally when a person takes leave, it will be for a fixed period and to a single destination. Did you take off all of these different times?' The last question was a cleverly placed leading question which at this point the interviewer was confident that the boyfriend would grab. The boyfriend made one last desperate attempt to save the situation and said: 'Yes, I like to help my friend out when he needs me.' To which the interviewer sat forward in his chair and looked directly at the boyfriend and said very seriously: 'Sir, you are not in trouble here at this point. We did not come here for you.' He then explained the criminal concept of willful blindness to the boyfriend. He continued to say: 'We know you are a good person and you are just trying to help your girlfriend out here, but she is busy making trouble for you. We can easily ask your employer to show us your leave records. What are those records going to say? How is this going to look to your employer? Why don't you rather tell us the truth?' At this stage, the boyfriend gave up the fight and started to cooperate resulting in the conviction of his girlfriend.

4.8. COMMUNICATION INHIBITORS AND PROMOTERS

4.8.1. General

In this section, we are going to discuss what causes people to talk and what motivates them not to talk. More importantly, what causes people to be deceitful or truthful. Not talking can be a form of deceit.

4.8.2. Safety

In general, people talk when they feel safe to talk. That may sound contradictory when we are talking about a guilty person. It is true that a guilty person may not feel safe talking to an investigator (for fear of being discovered). They may not feel safe to make admissions. Well, not entirely. There are circumstances in which all people will feel more comfortable to make admissions. Our job as investigators is to create an environment in which all interviewees will feel safe to talk.

4.8.3. Inhibitors

The inhibitors that we need to consider are more than those concerning the fear of being caught out. We also need to consider how to get people (innocent and guilty) to make disclosures (all information about the matter), not just admissions (that they perpetrated the wrongdoing). The inhibitors that we are concerned about are those inhibitors that prevent us from obtaining the vital information that we require for our investigation. The discussion below provides examples of possible approaches to some typical situations of communication inhibitors:

- *Innocent parties*

  In some situations you can clearly see that the person is not telling you everything. Alternatively, it may, based on the facts at hand, seem highly unlikely that they could not know more. One technique that is used is to tell innocent people about the criminal concept of 'willful blindness'. Willful blindness is not applicable to guilty people. It is only applicable to people who are not directly involved in the crime. The idea of the concept is to motivate innocent people, through their fear of being held criminally liable, to disclose all the information they have about a crime.

  Here you are trying to motivate people by fear, using scare tactics. This approach is often less effective, as there may be stronger fears at play than the prospect of being held accountable for not making disclosures. They may, for example, still elect to remain silent if the fear of reprisal from their peers or the guilty person is greater than the fear of the trouble they may get into for not making the required disclosures. They will weigh up the possibility of being caught out for making disclosures against the possibility of being held accountable for not making the disclosures. Our rule, to 'be aware of the fear factor', refers. Remember the people with the information are those people who are living with the fear of reprisal every day. This is not a small matter in their lives. This is their reality that they are living with. They have spent a long time convincing themselves not to say anything because of the potential negative effect. It may be difficult (but not impossible) for you to change that perception in just one interview.

So, the strongest communication promoter is trust. They need to trust you before they will make disclosures. They will contemplate what you are going to do with the information once you have it and/or how this will impact them and/or how likely it is that their disclosure will become known to others. It is useful to tell people (in order to build this trust) that you have been doing this for a long time and that you never divulge your sources. Say, where applicable, that you can arrange something to seem as if the information was stumbled upon by accident or that it came from another unrelated source. In other instances, where it is unavoidable, I think that honesty is the most important policy. You need to tell them that you are obliged to take the matter further, but that this is how you are going to communicate the matter. Check if they are comfortable with this approach.

- *Witnesses*

The fear of being labelled as the whistle-blower may be far worse when there is another person in the interview room. This is worse in some cultures than in others. Seniors and colleagues may be a serious damper on the conversation. The possibility of anyone knowing what the interviewee has said now becomes a reality with all the colleagues in the room. As discussed previously, the same is true for interview recordings. The mere notion that an interviewee is being recorded frequently prevents the free flow of information.

To a lesser degree, written notes may be perceived in the same light. Some interviewees say: 'Don't write this down, but...' and then they make their disclosure/s. This is of course a futile exercise, as you will more than likely remember most of what they have said to you and you can just write it down once they have left the room. Alternatively, you and your colleague can each provide affidavits of what was discussed at the meeting. The trick is, therefore, to put people in a position where they are comfortable to talk.

- *Non-judgemental*

Part of trust is not to pronounce judgement. Once the disclosure is made, do not jump up and say: 'Aha, I knew you were hiding something.' Thank them for the disclosure and tell them what the next steps are. One of the fears that people have is the fear of being judged. If you are seen to be empathetic and non-judgemental, then they will trust you more. People also typically dip their toe into the water before jumping in. So, the initial disclosure may only be the tip of the iceberg. If they feel safe they may make further disclosures.

When you build a rapport with people, they trust you more. If they trust you more, they are more likely to make disclosures. You should therefore try to form more than the normal rapport with the interviewee. One manner to do this is by letting them know that you see their side of the story or by siding with them or sympathising with them. Remember people rarely get thanked for what they do. People often feel mistreated and unappreciated by the employer/seniors. So, if you are seen to be on their side, this will help build rapport.

When trying to convince people to implement controls that they deem to be unnecessary or too much additional work, it is advisable to tell them that they really need to protect themselves in the event that something goes wrong to prevent them from getting blamed unnecessarily for something that they have not done wrong. They are normally much keener to consider and actually implement the recommended controls to avoid being associated with wrongdoing or to avoid getting blamed for something that they did not do.

To this end, people (even guilty people) do not want to be associated with wrongdoing. Ask them therefore what they could be blamed for. People do not want to be blamed for something they did not do. They will be quick therefore to shift the attention away from themselves and tell you about the problem at hand. The blame that is being referred to here is a general blame for the situation.

Another type of blame is a result of false accusations. Tell the reluctant witness that there is a chance that the guilty person may try to pass some/all of the blame on them. Then encourage them to rather tell you what happened so that you can decide how best to protect them.

Another approach is to understand if the interviewee is satisfied or not. If they tell you that they are unhappy with certain aspects then you can play the empathy card. Alternatively, some interviewees complain the whole way through the interview. They keep turning the interview to how they have been affected and how they are doing so much for the company. Try to be an ally to such people. This involves empathising with them. Some of the empathising only involve listening to them and agreeing that they are working very hard, etc. In other cases, you may actually be able to assist the interviewee by offering advice or making recommendations in your report. As auditors, investigators or consultants we often talk directly to more senior people. Our reports are also treated with greater consideration than the ideas of a lowly employee. In such cases tell interviewees that you will definitely be taking the actual or perceived unfairness further and ensure that you do. The rapport is cemented if you actually give the interviewee feedback once you have taken the matter further.

Coalface employees generally know what the issues are and also what the solutions are. They may not be able to put it as eloquently as a trained consultant can, but they see what is going on around them on a daily basis. They may also not have the benefit of a bird's eye-view or of your specialised training to draw the bits of information together, but they will more than likely have a good idea of what has gone wrong. These people are mostly just looking for a willing ear to listen to their problems or frustrations; this is a type of therapy for them.

As stated previously, the bulk of the interviews that we conduct as fraud investigators will be with innocent people. When it comes to guilty people or people with some degree of involvement, they too need to be comfortable to make disclosures.

As discussed throughout, people do not want to be seen in a bad light. Even if the person has done something wrong, they still do not want to be perceived in a bad light. The trick then is to create a situation where the person does not feel that they are being perceived in a bad light.

How is this possible if what they have done is obviously wrong? Surely they are by default going to be perceived in a bad light?

You achieve this by 'distancing them from the wrongdoing'. Say things like:

- 'I understand that it must have been hard for you.'
- 'I can see that you have been unfairly treated.'
- 'I can only imagine how difficult it must be for a single parent in your situation.'

A common fear of guilty subjects is the fear that their family, friends or colleagues will find out what they have been doing and that they may be seen in a negative light and/or lose favour and/or be ostracised.

Examples come to mind, where the perpetrators used part of their ill-gotten gains to 'buy favour' with their colleagues, friends or family. They spoil or indulge the people whom they want to see them in a good light. It is as if they feel that these people like and accept them by doing this.

Again, try to distance the subject from the wrongdoing by identifying something that will somehow rationalise to them what they have done and/or make it easier for them to explain why they did what they did. For example, you could say:

- 'I understand that you have been through a tough time.'
- 'It is easy to see how you felt forced to do what you did.'
- 'Yes, it is not really your fault. Circumstance has pushed you to it.'
- 'I can see that you are a good person. Let's work together to see how we can solve this in the best manner for all.'

Try to encourage people (innocent and guilty) to make disclosures as soon as possible. Tell them that things always come out eventually and that it is better to get things out in the open sooner rather than later. Then say that you can then try to see how best to deal with the matter.

Another tactic, where applicable, is to empathise with them and to highlight how the main guilty person has mistreated them and used them. Using people is part of the criminal's personality, discussed under point 4.9.2 below.

In terms of very serious matters, when the subject will have to be charged, say that you are willing to make a statement in mitigation or not to oppose a lenient sentence if they cooperate. Also tell them that it is important in these matters for them to:

- Cooperate
- Show remorse
- Show restitution (eg repay the stolen funds).

Emphasise that such actions are seen In a favourable light by the court. Sometimes people are reluctant to talk at all because they have had some minor part in the misconduct. If the person's actions (while morally reprehensible) are not such that criminal charges will be levied, say:

- 'I cannot think why you should be charged for what you did.'
- 'I encourage you to disclose what you have told me to your senior (as relevant).'
- 'Thank you for making this disclosure, but this particular disclosure or known fact is not under review. We will handle it as a separate issue.'

Alternatively, say that you are glad that they have given you the background, but that you are really interested in information about the following areas.... In this manner, they will trust you and hopefully be more open about the areas that you are interested in.

Some of the best information that one gets comes from scorned wives, disgruntled employees and cheated friends. *An example refers of one case where the informant had frequented brothels with the guilty party and where the informant, his wife and the guilty person and his wife had participated in regular orgies. In this particular case, the informant was very close to the guilty party and his disclosures of his indiscretions were played down so that he would disclose information of direct relevance to the case.*

If you pick up that the informant is angry with the guilty person, then play on that fact. Empathise with them. In the aforementioned case, the indulgences had eventually cost the informant his marriage. He was only too keen to provide me with information on the guilty party.

There also comes a stage when people want to unburden themselves. It seems that sometimes, when the weight of what they have done gets too much for them, they reach a stage where they almost want to get caught. This may be so that they can finally get some relief.

In such a case, when you can see the worry in their eyes, then start to make it easy for them to disclose to you what they have done. Say something like: 'I can see that it must have been very difficult for you' or 'You were clearly in a very difficult position' or 'I am not sure how I would have reacted in such a case, but rather tell me what happened and we can see how best to handle it.'

4.9. INTERVIEW OBSERVATIONS

4.9.1. Introduction

During the entire interview, observe the interviewee's reactions. Remember the rules:

- 'Forensics is more about psychology and less about fact.'
- 'People always do and say things for a reason.'

So why are they saying certain things? Why are they behaving in that manner (perhaps with aggressive responses)? Are they sitting still, are they covering their mouth when they talk, etc? These things can be strong indicators that the person is not telling the truth. This will help us know who the guilty person/s is/are and which questions to ask.

4.9.2. Fraudster's personality

I have noted that colleagues and friends of a subject frequently struggle to understand why the subject perpetrated the crime. Fraudsters walked among them and worked with them for a period and seemed quite 'normal'. Why the would they do something so bad and perpetrate a crime? The reasons why a person did something could be very complex. The easiest manner that I have found to this question, is to look at the personality of a fraudster.

I attended an Institute of Internal Auditors (IIA) conference many years ago at which doctor Micki Pistorius was a speaker. Dr Pistorius is famous for profiling serial killers in South Africa. She is an accomplished author and continues to have an illustrious career. She taught the delegates that a fraudster is basically a psychopath, which demonstrate some typical behaviours.

One of the other statements that she made which stands out, was that you will know one to two psychopaths in your personal life. While this may be a scary thought, I think it speaks to how common psychopaths may be.

Criminal psychology is a very interesting science and you are encouraged to learn more about it. Over the years I have seen many different classifications, but have found Dr Pistorius' 12 traits to be the most useful. I have seen these traits in every fraudster that I have interviewed. The different fraudsters do not necessarily demonstrate each trait to the same degree, but they all demonstrate the same traits.

What I have also noticed is that you can work with a person for years and not see the traits. Many times, you feel there is just something strange about them that you can just put your finger on. Perhaps the more accurate description is that you do not see the traits in the correct context.

When you interview them in a fraud investigation however, it is as if they change in front of your eyes and all of a sudden you see the traits come to light. *I recall interviewing a lady with whom I worked for three years. When I interviewed her in respect of misappropriated expense claims, she changed in front of my eyes and I recall thinking while watching this metamorphosis that I could be wrong about her being a fraudster, but there is a greater chance that I am right in terms of what I am seeing.*

Getting back to the explanation of why they did what they did, I find it easier for people to understand and accept why if they understand these traits. Some of a fraudster's typical personality traits include:

- *Use*
  Probably one of the most disturbing traits of a psychopath is the fact that they do not care who they sacrifice to get what they want. They will use friends, family and colleagues in any manner to get what they want. I think they are able to do this due to the next point, concerning their sense of conscience. *I recall an example of a lady who eve got colleagues of her to take out loans in their personal capacity on her behalf. She did not care that they eventually had to foot the bill for these loans when she was unable to repay them.* Victims will often say, but they were my friend. Why did they do this to me?

- *Conscience*
  Psychopaths do not have the same sense of conscience that a normal individual has. When you interview them, they just stare back at you with a complete blank face. It is quite uncanny. There is no sense of shame, guilt or remorse. Just blank. A sociopath still has an (albeit numb) sense of conscience, but a psychopath has no sense of conscience.

- *Fault*
  In the mind of the psychopath, it is never their fault. They always blame someone else for their behaviour. One example relayed by Dr Pistorius was of a serial killer that said that it wasn't their fault that they had bludgeoned a particular individual to death. They said that they didn't tell the individual to be there!

- *Opportunistic*
  Psychopaths are opportunistic. They will take what they can (property/victim) at the time it is/they are available to them with total disregard for the future. They don't think about the future or the repercussions. They only think about satisfying themselves now. Another example relayed by Dr Pistorius was of a fraudster walking in the yacht-basin in Cape Town, South Africa. On seeing an elderly couple looking at a yacht, he asked them if they wanted to by

"his" yacht. They said that they did and they then proceeded to close a deal in the harbour café, despite the fact that the fraudster did not own the yacht and was merely walking in the yacht basin.

- *Rationalise*

Psychopaths tend to rationalise their behaviour to themselves, as to why they are/were justified in doing what they did. This is also something that the ACFE's fraud triangle also teaches us. For example: I am entitled to it, as I work so hard here and I never get any gratitude. Or, Jonny does X so it is fine if I do this. Alternatively, I am only going to do it once, etc.

- *Religion*

Psychopaths typically "use" religion when it suits them. This is one of the most common traits I have seen. In a previous company I worked at, it became a standing joke as most of the people that were caught for fraud were 'highly religious'. This speaks to our rule on people doing and saying things for a reason. I believe that they are acutely aware of their misdeeds and try to find religious excuses to avoid being detected.

- *Charismatic*

Psychopaths are typically very charismatic. They can be highly convincing and get people to do things or overlook things based on their ability to convince people. This is another reason why they are able to perpetrate fraud and remain undetected so long. People often say once the misconduct is detected that they can't believe it because X was such a nice person. Examples in the media of religious ministers who committed crimes serve as an example.

- *Intelligent*

Psychopaths are typically very intelligent. Intelligence combined with no sense of conscience is a lethal combination.

- *Educated*

Psychopaths are typically well educated. This may have a direct correlation to the fact that they are typically intelligent people.

- *Liars*

Psychopaths are typically compulsive liars. You will see that psychopaths lie all the time in interviews without even flinching. When a psychopath argues, they tend to jump around in their argument. If you talk about one point they move to the next. The manner to argue with a psychopath is to remain calm, stick to your one argument and to keep bringing them back to the original point: no, we are not talking about Y now, we are talking about X. Please tell me about X.

- *Reoffend*

Psychopaths will most likely reoffend. This is also something that I have commonly seen. I have phoned previous and subsequent employers of fraudsters and they almost always reoffend. I think this also speaks to their lack of conscience and an overall inability to change who they are.

4.9.3. Identifying deceit

a. General

Deceit is the best example of our rule that 'people always do and say things for a reason'. For example: people generally have no reason to be deceitful if they are having a casual chat about their weekends on a Monday morning around the coffee machine. So, they are typically honest. What if, on the other hand, you approach a person on the Monday morning and ask them where the bank reconciliation is that you asked them for on Friday past? They may respond in a deceitful manner if they know that the bank reconciliation was not done and/or lists unreconciled fraudulent payments that cleared the bank without legitimate entries having been processed in the company's books. They may choose to respond deceitfully to avoid their wrongdoing being detected.

A subject's deceit may be in response to direct questions, as per the example above, or it may be planned by the subject in anticipation of subsequent questions. In the latter case, the subject may spend time fabricating a story long in advance so that:

- People will not think that their behaviour is out of trend/question their behaviour at all.
- The subject can later refer enquiring parties back to their story in the event that they are questioned on how, for example, they manage to fund their extravagant lifestyle. In this way the subject can say, 'yes but remember I told you that I received this money as a prize' or 'everyone knows that I have a rich family'.

Examples of fabricated stories include:

- *The subject comes to work making casual mention of the luck that they had betting on the horses and how much money they won. They do this frequently so that people will always believe when they see them with nice things that they got the money from their winnings. This also speaks to our rule that fraud is linked to some form of vice like gambling. The subject, in this case, elaborates on something real in the hope that it will be perceived as more plausible to people.*

  In another matter, it came to our attention while we were profiling the possible perpetrator/s that a lady in the office had previously alleged that she had won a sizable prize from the bank in a lucky draw competition. At that stage of the investigation, while we knew who one of the perpetrators was, we did not know if there was someone else involved. We therefore regarded this as highly suspicious and decided to confirm it with the bank without upsetting/accusing the lady. Our enquiries with the bank confirmed that she was, in fact, telling the truth and she had won the prize.

- *The subject talks about how successful their spouse is and what a high-powered and high-earning job they have. This explanation is frequently used.*

- *The subject tells people how successful their family is and how much money they have, and how generous they are to the subject. In one matter, the subject said it was his in-laws who were rich and generous. He probably felt that they were distant enough for people not to detect that this was not the case. He may have felt that there was a greater chance that his own family situation may be better known to people or more easily detected.*

- *The subject tells people that they have inherited money. The subject may make use of an actual death in a family to create more credibility or refer to some long-lost distant family member that co-workers could not authenticate.*
- *The subject tells you that the cars, jewellery or other luxuries belong to a friend or were paid for by a rich friend. Of course, no one ever meets this friend.*

To compound these aspects, people generally are competitive, and they want to believe that everyone else is earning more than them and having an easier and more comfortable life than them and that they just have rotten luck. It is therefore easy for fraudsters to justify their expensive lifestyles to people. There are generally two aspects to identifying honesty or dishonesty in an interview. These are the things people say and the way in which people act (physiological indicators).

b. What they say

To be more accurate it is:

- What people say
- What people do not say
- How people say it
- What people are doing whilst in your company or otherwise
- What they are not doing.

In my experience people use the following general lines of defence in interviews to avoid their dishonesty being detected:

- *Avoidance*

  The first line of defence by subjects to prevent their deceit from being detected is to avoid being asked in the first place. Avoidance can take many forms, including:
  - Avoid having the investigation. More senior people will try to prevent the investigation from being conducted at all.
  - If they are unable to avoid the entire investigation they try to limit the scope of the investigation.
  - Avoid agreeing to an interview. Subjects will typically say that they are too busy, refer you to someone else who they say is more appropriate, say that they had no or limited involvement, say that they have no knowledge of the topic, etc. In this way, they avoid answering any questions. This is typically short-lived, as most fraud investigators are very persistent.

- *Control*

  Some people will say that they want your questions in advance. In this manner, they are trying to control your process, restrict you and limit the number of questions and types of questions to be asked. This is a method for them to ensure that their deceit is not identified because they have a sufficiently well-prepared reply and will not be caught off guard and make mistakes. You are not recommended to allow this. It is inevitable that new things come up in any conversation that you will want to explore. A big part of our interview psychology is centred around surprise and the possibility of catching deceit out in the manner in which questions are asked. This is discussed in great detail below in section 4.11 on the various interview phases. Even giving the discussion topics in advance can be restrictive. Later in the conversation they may restrict you and say: 'You did not tell me in advance that this is what you want to discuss so I am not answering the question.' You will be bound by the process that you have agreed to. This is not a process that needs to be perceived as fair from the interviewee's point of view. It needs to be respectful, but it does not have to be evenly weighted in either the interviewer or the interviewee's favour. Not even in hearings or criminal cases do the questions get circulated in advance. An interview is a normal employee/employer (albeit employer representative) conversation. They are not charged with anything and there is nothing that they need to prepare for. If they are unable to answer a question then they should say so, and maybe also provide a reason why not. They should also be free not to answer questions if they do not want to. Again, it would be nice if they provide a reason why they are not answering the question. If on the other hand a matter requires referencing files and records or is one that happened a long time ago, it may be helpful to your process to tell the interviewee in advance that you wish to broadly discuss certain matters. Be sure to emphasise that the conversation may not be restricted to these topics only and other areas may also be explored as required.

- *Aggressive defensive response*

In general, subjects (not only senior people) may respond in an aggressive defensive manner to an interviewer's questions. This is an avoidance tactic, as the people to whom this is directed are typically put off by this sort of behaviour and may withdraw from the situation in response or cease asking questions for fear of the response. The correct response is to remain calm and not to respond aggressively. Say to people like this that it is not within your value system to shout at people, so they should please not shout at you. You may have to calm them down more than once. They tend to look a bit sheepish at having been cautioned and normally comply thereafter. Alternatively, once they see that you are not going to give up, they may concede and agree to the interview.

Very senior people like to use this tactic. They try to intimidate you as the investigator. This is a bullying tactic, to keep you from prying into what they are trying to conceal. They are tacitly saying: 'I am bigger and more powerful than you, so back off or I will have to unleash my power onto you.' It could be that they are trying to conceal their deceit or that their ego does not like the fact that someone that they perceive to be of a lower rank than them is questioning them. You are advised to always be firm and professional. Refer to your mandate (as an external consultant) or to your instruction from the audit committee (request to investigate) or to the department's charter that authorises you access to records and requires you to investigate.

One of my colleagues handled this bullying tactic extremely well by responding to the aggressive questions that were being fired back at him with 'Good point' and then carrying on with the interview topics that he wanted to talk about: 'In terms of aspect A...'. In this manner, the wind was completely taken out of the aggressor's sails as he got no response. He tried once or twice more, but eventually gave up and answered the questions.

- *Say they do not know or cannot remember.*

This is again an avoidance tactic, as they avoid answering the question and they avoid lying. It is a very convenient response. It is therefore important to place blocks in place earlier on in the interview to prevent them from saying that they do not know. The discussion above on blocks refers in this regard.

- *'I do not have access to those records anymore.'*

This may or may not be true, but what is reasonable to expect a person to remember? Remember our rule: 'Queensbury rules apply'. We need to be fair. This may also be a question that you pose to the subject. For example: 'But Mr X, you were the project manager of this project for two years. How could you not have knowledge of the ABC document?' Another example includes: 'But you have just said that you were the financial manager for year X1 and that you were never ill. Why then would you not be able to recall who signed the payment, as this was part of your normal daily responsibilities?' Also, are you expecting them to precisely recall or describe or recite a particular document or do you wish to explore their knowledge around an issue with the document? It is recommended that you put into context what you are requesting.

- *Avoid answering a specific question.*

Again, this is an avoidance tactic. It is frequently done by talking around the issue, without addressing the issue. Alternatively, it involves leading the conversation in another direction. In terms of this, they will typically mention a few topics in their reply and then go off and explain an unasked area in great detail. In this manner, they appear to be very cooperative, honest and complete without addressing the question and sometimes without the interviewer being aware.

- *Answer as little as possible.*

They typically do not volunteer any information or answer anything above exactly what was asked. Open (as opposed to closed) questions are suggested to solicit an improved response.

- *Ask for specific clarification.*

Interviewees like this do not ask for all clarifications at one time, they will continue to ask clarifications and become very pedantic about knowing exactly what it is that you want to know. This behaviour is an attempt to demonstrate that:

  - The reason why they are not answering is that you are unclear and not because they are being deceitful.
  - They are only willing to answer the minimum.
  - They appear to be cooperating very well.
  - They appear to be a very precise sort of person and therefore by default not someone who would do something untoward.
  - To try to shake you and discredit you as the interviewer by making it appear as if you do not know what you are talking about.

For example:

Interviewer: Thanks Joe for agreeing to provide us greater understanding of the service contracts that we are looking into. Could you please give us a high-level understanding of how these contracts work?
Interviewee: What do mean?
Interviewer: We would appreciate it if you could give us an understanding of how these contractors are selected.

Interviewee: Well there were many contracts in that period.
Interviewer: Yes, but we would really like to understand the service contracts and not the raw material type contracts?
Interviewee: Well we had many of those in the period, which one are you concerned about? (and so on).

This is essentially an avoidance tactic. They ensure that they only need to answer you on one specific highly academic point and argue with you if you try to steer them back to the actual question. They may say: 'But you asked this ... and I answered you, why are you now changing?'

- *'Remove' themselves from what is being said, so that they cannot be blamed*

These are essentially also avoidance tactics. These include:

  - Blaming other people
  - Talking in the third person
  - The work which is being discussed was (always) performed by someone else.

- *Put themselves in a more credible light, so that they will not attract attention.*

Some examples of how subjects do this include saying things like:

  - 'But I am a Christian, I would never do that.'
  - 'Yes, I have worked here for X number of years.'
  - 'I do not need the money; why would I do that?'

- *Distraction*

Another tactic to avoid being in the focus of an investigation is to try to make someone else or something seem more 'attractive' as a subject/area of investigation. In the animal kingdom, a predator will focus attention on the prey that is moving the most. So, in this analogy, you as the investigator are the predator and the subjects are the prey. The person is therefore hoping that you will turn your attention to the new subject introduced by them and not on them and their deceit. The counter to this is to say: 'Thank you for that piece of information, but as per our introduction we would like to know more about X. We will make a note of Y, but for now, it will be most helpful if you could tell us about X.'

- *Cooperate too much*

Some people also try to appear as if they are more cooperative than they really are. This is really to put themselves in a credible light. Secondly, they may elect to give unnecessary information. This may result in your attention being swayed onto the new information that is irrelevant to the investigation or that is 'away' from their deceit when information is relevant.

- *Use emotional blackmail*

Subjects, especially employees with long service, will frequently ask in response to your questions if you as the investigator or the organisation do not trust them. This is trying to force you to answer either yes or no. So yes, they would go off on a tangent to explain that they had been working for so many years and that they cannot believe that the organisation does not trust them anymore. A suitable response may be to say that this is not about trust, but rather about the organisation's right to look after its interests.

If they say: 'Well then, the organisation must come and ask me if they think that I was involved in the misconduct.' You could respond by saying that you are representing the organisation in this matter.

If you answer 'No', then they will ask you why you are questioning them (if you trust them in this case).

- *Lie*

Misconstrue all or part of the truth. This can entail telling a direct lie or it can entail lying by omission. Lying by omission is when a person does not tell a direct lie, but purposefully omits a pertinent piece of information, without which the truth does not come out.

- *Discredit the outcome/results*

Once the results of the investigation have been published, a last-ditch attempt may be made to try to discredit the results to prevent them from being blamed totally or in part. Deceitful people do not necessarily use all of these lines of defence every time or even in sequence. The trick is to get them past all of these to a position where they have no option but to tell you the truth. Knowledge of how these various lines of defence are acted out is therefore imperative to a successful interview.

Persistence and possibly the support of a more senior person to ensure their cooperation may suffice where subjects use avoidance. Detecting deception in an interview requires a more artful approach. There is, however, science to give us assistance in this regard.

c. Linguistic analysis

Behavioural scientists have observed that people will subconsciously amend what they say and/or write in a certain manner depending on whether they are being honest or deceitful. This science is called 'linguistic analysis'. It is being discussed here as it is both interesting and important. This technique requires a lot of time to apply properly. Time is a luxury that you will most times not have leading up to, during or after an interview. In most cases, you will have to decide on the spur of the moment (frequently in the interview) if a person is being deceitful or not and more importantly why they are being deceitful. It is not a great help to be too academic about the subject. Linguistic analysis typically requires a lot of time to perform correctly and may be of less help to you as a tool.

It is also only possible to concentrate on a few indicators of deceit at any one time during an interview. The trick is to concentrate on a few that you are comfortable with and also to give yourself tools to help you structure your approach to identifying deceit. Examples of tools are covered in the section on documentation of interviews. Linguistic analysis is very useful when you are analysing a person's written statement. In this circumstance, you will most likely have the time and you will be able to use a checklist-type approach to identify indicators of deceit.

Paul M Clikeman (*PhD, CFE, Associate Professor in the Robins School of Business at the University of Richmond*) lists ten signs of deception in his January/February 2012 ACFE *Fraud Magazine* article. These are discussed below:

- *Lack of self-reference*

Clikeman says that truthful people make frequent use of the pronoun 'I' to describe what they have done, while deceptive people use one of two ways to adapt their language to move attention away from themselves.

The first manner is to describe events in the 'passive voice'. Clikeman gives the following examples:

  - 'The safe was left unlocked' rather than 'I left the safe unlocked'.
  - 'The shipment was authorised' rather than 'I authorised the shipment'.

The second manner to reduce self-references is to substitute the pronoun 'you' for 'I'. Clikeman's examples include:

Question: 'Can you tell me about reconciling the bank statement?'

Answer: 'You know, you try to identify all the outstanding checks and deposits in transit, but sometimes when you're really busy you just post the differences to the suspense account.'

Guilty people may also direct the conversation to other people and/or to the wrongdoing of others. They do this despite the lack of relevance of the misdirection. It is as if the misdirection takes the attention away from them and as if it puts them in a favourable light with the interviewer for being helpful.

Interviewee: 'You know, at the time that the upgraded cell phone handsets were taken there were major problems in the department. Mary was on maternity leave and the contract lady did not know what she was doing with the payments. The petty cash was also a problem.' I believe that this information was given to me to send me rushing off solving all kinds of other irrelevant issues. I said: 'Thanks for that information, as said earlier, I am here to try to understand the missing cell phone handsets. I will make a note of your concerns and I will take them up with John later. Getting back to the handsets then ...'.

It is advisable to let them talk freely initially, as you never know what they might tell you out of nervousness and you do not want them to clam up. If you see that they are really going off on a tangent, then bring them back to the issue at hand. Alternatively, during the clarification phase of the interview, try to pin them down: *'So just to help me understand then, who is responsible for locking the safe?' or 'Thank you for telling me how the reconciliation works, but who was the person who performed the January reconciliation?' or 'So what is your role in the reconciliation process?'*

The deceitful person may persist with the avoidance, in which case you will have to persist on a specific answer.

In the aforementioned interview concerning the disappearance of cell phone handsets, the interviewee would not tell me who had requested the upgraded handsets from the cell phone company at contract renewal time.

Question: Who requested the upgraded handsets for company A? Answer: *Mary is responsible for the administration of cell phones.*

Question: Mary was on maternity leave for two months prior to the disappearance and for four months afterwards. Who took over those responsibilities from her? Answer: there were numerous people in the office.

Question: There were only two people other than yourself in the office at the time. Jackie, a contract worker, whose only role was to give temporary relief doing subcontractor payments, and Joe, who is only the bookkeeper for company B. They had no reason to request the upgrades from the cell phone company. It could only have been you. Did you do the upgrade? Answer: I cannot recall; it may have been me.

Question: I am sure that the cell phone company will have retained proof of who requested the upgrades. They would need this to protect themselves. Answer: I may have done it, but you know that our manager never told me directly when Mary left that I had to do it.

Question: But Peter said that he spoke to you when his contract came up for renewal. Did you not contact the cell phone company and request his upgrade? Answer: I may have done, I don't recall. You know when Mary was gone, things were mad here. We don't have any job descriptions of what we must do.

Question: I will have to call the cell phone company then. Answer: I may have sent the e-mail request to them, but anyone in the office at the time could have received the delivery of new handsets.

In this case, the lady concerned would not admit that she had requested the upgraded handsets. In such cases, you have to rely on the testimonies of other people and evidence (e-mail correspondence and proof of deliveries).

- *Verb tense*

Clikeman says truthful people usually describe historical events in the past tense. Deceptive people on the other hand sometimes refer to past events as if the events were occurring in the present. Paul says that deceitful people do this as describing past events using the present tense suggests that they are rehearsing the events in their mind.

He illustrates this point with a statement made by an employee purporting that a pouch containing $6 000 in cash was stolen before she could deposit it at the bank.

'After closing the store, I put the cash pouch in my car and **drove** [past tense] to the Olympia Bank building on Elm Street. It was **raining** [past tense] hard so I had to drive slowly. I **entered** [past tense] the parking lot and **drove** [past tense] around back to the night depository slot. When I stopped the car and **rolled** [past tense] down my window, a guy ***jumps*** [present tense - not jumped] out of the bushes and ***yells*** [present tense - not yelled] at me. I can ***see*** [present tense - not saw] he ***has*** [present tense - had] a gun. He ***grabs*** [present tense - not grabbed] the cash pouch and ***runs*** [present tense - not ran] away. The last I **saw** [back to past tense] him he was headed south on Elm Street. After he was gone, I **called** [back to past tense] the police on my cell phone and reported the theft.'

You will note that the change of tense only occurs at the critical part of the description whereafter it reverts back to past tense.

- *Answering questions with questions*

This is something that you will experience frequently. Interviewees may say:

- Don't you trust me?
- Are you accusing me of stealing?
- I have a good job, why would I do something to jeopardise that?

This is primarily an avoidance tactic and you may reply:

- *This is not about* trust. *I am just trying to understand what happened at the time. Can you help me?*

You must be very careful how you answer these questions. If you answer them incorrectly, you will be pulled into a long irrelevant debate that the interviewee controls. You need to ward off the question without being drawn in and by directing the conversation back to the matter at hand, whilst still keeping control of the conversation.

- *Equivocation*

The interviewee makes frequent use of statements with expressions of uncertainty, weak modifiers and vague expressions.

Noncommittal verbs are: think, believe, guess, suppose, figure, assume. Equivocating adjectives and adverbs are: sort of, almost, mainly, perhaps, maybe, about.

Vague qualifiers are: you might say, more or less.

Again, this is an avoidance tactic. They are giving themselves plenty of leeway to manoeuvre themselves out of a tight spot later if you corner them later by modifying previous statements without directly contradicting the original statement.

- *Oaths*

We can go back to the rules here: 'The people who tell you they are good, are the ones you should be worried about.'

Deceptive people are aware of their deceit and nervous about being detected, so they try to make their story more believable. Clikeman says that they use statements like: 'I swear,' 'on my honour,' 'as God is my witness,' and 'cross my heart.'

In the same vein, people often say: 'To be completely honest with you...'. That really makes a person concerned. Why do they need to tell you that they are being honest at this specific point in time? Is it because they are being honest at this time only and they have been dishonest about the other things that they have said or is it because they are being dishonest at the time?

Some similar examples of what people say to create credibility are to state strongly: *'I am a very ... kind of person.'* The kind of person that they may or may not be is not under scrutiny. Why do they feel it is necessary to emphasise it?

'You know me, I am very ... kind of person.' The chances are that you do not know the person. Or even if you do, you could not say 'no, actually you are a poor worker'. In their mind, by keeping quiet or by agreeing, you have established them as credible.

'You can ask anyone here.' Of course, there is not anyone else to ask at the time in the interview room. Even if there were someone else it would not be relevant or correct to ask for a reference at the time.

'I am here early in the mornings. I work very hard.' Or 'I have been here for X number of years.' Again, their work ethic or length of service is not under review. It is, for example, the disappearance of the funds that are being reviewed. Hard work is irrelevant. They are hoping that the investigator will move their attention to a less 'credible' person – someone who is less hardworking. But it is not less hardworking people and people with short service who always perpetrate crimes.

'I am a senior person' or 'I have a responsible job' or 'This place wouldn't survive without me.' In other words, they are saying they are senior, so you should not question them. They are above reproach or senior people who do not have to be subjected to petty accusations.

For example, I dealt with a person who thought he was senior and beyond questioning, that not being questioned was his right after so many years of service. He thought that senior people have certain privileges in the organisation, as the management trusts them. However, it is not that they are trusted, it is just that there were no controls in place – so trust was the only thing to rely on.

Alternatively, *'Don't question me as I am too important to lose and the company will have to overlook this indiscretion.'*

'I am a very direct person.' Being 'direct' in this example is an excuse for not being tactful and to be blunt and/or rude.

- *Euphemisms*

The deceitful person, in this case, is choosing to describe their action using softer or less harsh words so that they or their actions are seen in a more favourable light.

Some examples include:

- 'missing' instead of 'stolen'
- 'borrowed' instead of 'took'
- 'bumped' instead of 'hit'
- 'warned' instead of 'threatened'
- 'looked at' instead of 'checked'
- 'thought' instead of 'knew'.

- *Alluding to actions*

This is also an avoidance tactic. The deceitful person does not say directly that they did something. They mention actions at a high level. For example: *'I normally glance over the reconciliation after it was performed.'* So did they review it this time and what did their review entail?

The trick is not to assume anything. The deceitful person wants to gloss over the questionable actions without attracting too much attention. They will try to be as casual and general about their description as possible so as to sneak it in under the radar. Ask the interviewee directly. For example: 'So did you lock the door or not?'

- *Lack of detail*

This one is fairly obvious. The deceitful person is again coming in under the radar with what they are saying and leaving sufficient room to manoeuvre if they are caught out later.

With a lack of detail, we also refer to an apparent 'failure of memory'. It is funny how deceitful people seem to have detailed recollections of irrelevant details, but only selective recounts of incriminating aspects.

In one example, it was the incumbent's selective memory that caught him out. The incumbent was a friendly, well-liked, long-serving driver who had colluded with an accounts person to cash fraudulent cheques. He had an established relationship with the bank and she had access to the cheques. It was established from the interviews held with him that he could not recall any details whatsoever when it came to the cashing of the fraudulent cheques. It was anticipated that he was going to use character references in his internal labour hearing, so this was used against him. Witnesses were called during the presentation of the company's case (prior to his defence), who told the chairman (amongst other things) what a great and honest person he was. The character witnesses recounted numerous instances where he was able to recall details from many years in the past. He was established and a person with an exceptional memory. He smiled from ear to ear. During the organisation's questioning of him, the examples of his good memory were emphasised. Questions were then asked about the activities around the cashing of the fraudulent cheques (with a lot of documentary support). Of course, he was unable to recall the details and his deceit was obvious.

- *Narrative balance*

At the end of the day, this point is really a technical grammatical explanation of a lack of detail at a critical time. It is unlikely that you will remember or have the time to break the interviewee's statement down to this degree while the interview is occurring. This would be more suitable to apply during the analysis of a written statement or an analysis of a transcript or recording.

Clikeman explains in his article that a narrative consists of three parts, being: a prologue, a critical event and an aftermath. Clikeman explains that the prologue 'contains background information and describes events that took place before the critical event. The critical event is the most important occurrence in the narrative. The aftermath describes what happened after the critical event. In a complete and truthful narrative, the balance will be approximately 20% to 25% prologue, 40% to 60% critical event and 25% to 35% aftermath.' The logic is that detail could have been trimmed if one of the three parts of the narrative is significantly shorter than expected. Alternatively, false information could have been added if one part of the narrative is significantly longer than expected.

- *Mean letter of utterance*

This is again a fairly technical manner of saying that deceitful people's sentence structure is not always balanced. It comes down to too much or too little detail.

Clikeman explains that the average number of words per sentence is called the 'mean length of utterance'. He goes on to say that most people's sentences are between 10 and 15 words long. He says that anxiety causes people to use sentences that are either significantly longer or significantly shorter than the norm.

As an example, one particularly nervous individual used to speak in such long (monotone) sentences, that it made the listener want to take breaths on his behalf. It was later discovered that he was busy with service delivery fraud.

In this case he felt that he needed to create credibility around what he was supposed to be delivering when in truth he knew that he was just charging the company for doing very little.

d. Physiological indicators

There are certain involuntary physiological indicators that tell us that a person is being dishonest. Remember people are dishonest for different reasons, not only because they were the ones who perpetrated the crime and wish to avoid detection. They may be covering for a friend or not want to be blamed for their own negligence or for not identifying the fraudulent activity, etc. So, there are degrees of honesty that we are concerned with.

We must differentiate between nerves and dishonesty. Honest people start off nervously, but they settle down as the interview progresses. Deceptive people will either maintain a constant level of nervousness or become increasingly more nervous as the interview (and therefore the pressure) progresses.

Some people are too calm throughout the interview. This is also a concern, as it is unnatural. What therefore are they trying to hide by pretending not to be fazed at all? Alternatively, are they possibly psychopathic and consequently have no sense of conscience and therefore show no fear and emotion?

Everybody is nervous in an interview, both innocent people and guilty people. Their own personal experience, their degree of guilt and the type of person they are will determine how nervous they are and to what degree they demonstrate their nervousness externally. Deceptive people are nervous because they fear being detected. Innocent people fear being blamed for something they did not do or for being blamed for an indirect effect of the fraud. An example of this would be if a company lost money because of a procurement fraud and the financial manager is in trouble for not putting sufficient controls in place.

There is, in my experience, only one clear physiological indicator that will conclusively tell you if a person is being dishonest. This is a pulsating vein. If the subject demonstrates this factor, then they are definitely being dishonest. If on the other hand, they do not demonstrate the factor, it does not mean that they are innocent.

As for the other physiological indicators, these are just indicators. At the end of the interview, you will conclude, based on your subjective experience of all of the physiological aspects demonstrated, whether or not the person was honest.

If you see one of the indicators listed below you cannot jump up in the middle of the interview and point at the interviewee and scream that they are the guilty party. With the exception of the pulsating vein, described below, these indicators cannot conclusively determine dishonesty. These are merely indicators to show you who is most likely being honest and who is being dishonest. The cumulative picture of all indicators will sway the balance of probability of who is being honest and who is not.

Commonly considered deceit indicators include:

- *Pulsating vein*

This is an all-time favourite physiological indicator and the one indicator that will never let you down. When you see it (and you do not always see it), you will know without a shadow of a doubt that the person is being deceitful. It will not tell you why they are being deceitful, however.

When some people lie, one of the veins on the side of their neck just under the jawline pulsates furiously. The pulsating vein may also be seen on the temple or on the forehead.

Try as far as possible and without being too obvious, to physically position yourself in the interview so that you can see the subject's neck.

An example comes to mind of a person who came into the interview room with his collar turned up and a cap on. He sat low in the chair so that his shoulders were up and his neck was well under his collar. He also wore a scarf around his neck. The scarf was the type that is associated with certain 'gang colours'. He also later tried to manipulate his polygraph test with his breathing. It is rare that you will encounter people like this in a corporate environment. Knowledge of physiological countermeasures by a subject is an indictment in itself. The fact that he tried so hard to disguise his involuntary physiological deception indicators was sufficient to tell me that he was deceitful.

In another example, a young forensic protégé's face lit up when his glance was caught by the interviewer who was casually tapping the side of his own neck to draw the protégé's attention to the pulsating vein on the interviewee's neck. He had been told about it before, but this was the first time that he had seen it in reality. There is no better learning experience than seeing something like this first-hand.

- *Blushing and/or a flushed complexion*

Some people blush when they are feeling guilty. Others develop big red patches or red flushes on their neck and chest. Again, this could just be innocent nerves. An example refers of a particularly self-conscious young lady, whose complexion would erupt in a sea of red whenever anyone spoke to her. She was not dishonest, jut extremely self-conscious. Look therefore for supporting indicators with regards to this physiological indicator.

- *Perspiration*

People tend to perspire more when they are under pressure/nervous. Some people just perspire more than others, but if accompanied by other signs the excessive perspiration may be a sign of deception.

- *Sitting position*

What position is the person sitting in? The sitting position may either indicate nervousness or over-confidence. Unnatural nervousness may be a sign of deceit. So too, may overconfidence be a sign of wrongdoing. Is their body slumped forward in a huddle, shoulders bent forward, and head down? This may indicate submission, an acute awareness of their wrongdoing. Are they sitting too far back, very casually, when you would expect them to be nervous? People are inclined to sit slightly forward when listening.

- *Hands*

Fidgeting with hands may indicate nervousness. It is up to you to decide if the nervousness is 'normal' nervousness experienced by someone in an interview situation or if it is nervousness about having their misdeeds discovered? Hands may also be sweaty when a person is nervous. Some people perspire more than others. You will need to decide why they are nervous. No single factor should be seen in isolation. Rather develop a picture from multiple factors.

- *Folded arms*

Folded arms are an indicator that a person is 'closed' and/or protecting themselves. If you are suggesting new ideas and the person sits back and folds their arms, they may be mentally closing down to your ideas, and not wanting to consider them.
Annoyance – A person may be irritated with having to be interviewed. Again, it may be quite normal to be irritated by the interview. So, you will need to determine if the irritation is normal or not. Is it accompanied by a lot of 'huffing and puffing'? Normal irritation should settle down as the interview progresses unless a deadline is looming and they need to go to their next appointment. People may use subsequent appointments as an excuse to evade interviews. It is suggested that you tell people that this is a very important aspect and one that the organisation sees in a serious light, so it would be best to cancel the next appointment and to dedicate their time to the matter at hand.

- *Fidgeting or doodling*

People fidget when they are nervous. Please consider why they are nervous in the situation. Look for other indicators to sway your opinion either way.

Doodling is the practice of writing or drawing playfully while listening. The specific doodle does not necessarily mean anything. It is normally an indication of boredom. The doodle could be the embellishment of an existing word or letter and just the colouring in of a punched hole in a pad of paper.

- *Covering mouth*

A lot of people cover their mouth when they are talking. This may be an indication that they want to hide what they are saying. Why are they hiding what they are saying? Do they not want other people to know that they are telling you so much, or are they fabricating all or part of a story?

- *Hand on the chin*

When people put their hand on their chin while they are talking, they are being contemplative. It just means that they are thinking. It does not mean that they are being dishonest. What you should try to establish is what they are thinking about. Are they fabricating a story or are they just trying to recall foggy details? In this case look for other indicators to sway your opinion either way.

- *Touching the nose*

Touching the nose is said to be an involuntary indicator of dishonesty. There is no scientific basis to substantiate this.

- *Shifty eyes*

Nervous people do not like to look another person in the eye. Cultural differences (of how we relate to or communicate with women, older people or senior people) may also come into play here. Generally, there is a difference between not wanting to look someone in the eye, and a courteous glance away. In a similar light, an aggressive stare-down should be regarded with caution.

- *General aggression*

Aggression is a type of defence. Some people attack others when they want to ward them off. This is called aggressive/defensive behaviour. You will need to decide why they are being aggressive. Are they irritated by the interview or are they trying to keep you away? The logic is that if you attack someone then they would tend to get a fright and back off. A firm but professional response is advised. They become sheepish once they realise that their tactic has not worked.

e. What they do and what they do not do

We have discussed what the interview subject does (knowingly or unknowingly). Next, we look at the general situation and more specifically at what they have not done. This is to get a feel for the way that they should have reacted or things that they should have said, but just did not. This may be indicative of a planned response that is being acted out. Innocent people are typically angry when they are (or feel as if they are) accused of a wrongdoing. They will typically voice their dissatisfaction and reluctantly cooperate. If a person is too cooperative and does not show any anger, this could be indicative of deceit.

In the same light, consider topics that they should have raised, but did not. Honest people would be concerned about certain aspects. Failure to raise certain issues may be an indication of them not wanting to attract too much attention.

f. Clothing

There is not too much that you can do about what your interviewee is wearing. A dishonest person demonstrates numerous involuntary signs. A seasoned criminal may be aware of some of these signs and may try to hide them. Clothing covering the neck (to hide a pulsating vein), a big, broad-brimmed hat or sunglasses may be used to hide these signs.

In an aforementioned example, a subject was taken to have a polygraph test. He started to cough on the way there and he continued to cough the entire time until we left. The cough was so insistent, it was as if there was a medical reason for it. Then, on the way back in the car, his coughing miraculously stopped. The coughing was a ploy to interfere with the polygraph results. He also slouched in his chair and he had his collar turned up to hide his neck. He wore a scarf, a peaked cap and sunglasses. As mentioned before, the scarf was the same as the type of scarf that is worn by gang members and his mannerisms reflected someone who had been in/was in a gang. It was put to him in the interview that he was an 'old gangster'. He smiled, but neither agreed nor denied the accusation.

It would not be unreasonable for you to request a person to take off their hat and to remove their sunglasses. If the item covering them is a religious item (eg a headscarf worn by a Muslim woman), then you should not ask them to remove their religious attire. Be respectful of local and personal customs and beliefs.

There is not a single rule to assist you to determine what the interview subject's dress code is telling you. Try to understand what their dress code is telling you within the context of the situation. In most instances, people come dressed for work and then are called into an interview. Subjects will have less opportunity to come dressed specifically for an interview. Therefore, few psychological indicators can be read into dress code. There are some prompts that you may consider, however, such as the following:

- *Too conservative*
  Is the person purposely 'dressing down'? Are they trying to appear to be conservative and less likely to be a person involved with the misconduct? *The example below of the lady dressed all in black refers.*
- *Too revealing*
  Are they trying to use their sex appeal to distract you or woo you into overlooking their indiscretions?
- *Too flashy/ expensive*
  This is the opposite of too conservative. Are they trying to tell you that they are too sophisticated to have done this? Alternatively, does their dress code suggest an extravagant/ expensive lifestyle that may need to be externally funded?
- *Overt display of religious symbols not normally worn by them*
  The person would be trying to build credibility by associating themselves with symbols of good in the hope that you would think they could not have been involved and/or that they are a good person.
- *Covering*
  As mentioned previously, are they trying to cover up physiological indicators of deceit?

It is normal for a person to dress in anticipation of an event. Whether you are going to the theatre, to court, for a job interview, or to meet your mates at a sports bar, you are going to dress in a way in which you believe will suit the situation and make you more 'acceptable' to the audience that you will be appearing in front of.

The interview subject may not have had an opportunity to dress in advance for the interview. Do not attach too much value to dress code unless it is something obvious. The absence of a dress code indicator does therefore not mean anything. The presence of an indicator may be showing you something. You will have to decide what it is telling you and how to use it.

g. Other indicators

Remember the rules: 'People always do and say things for a reason' (even if involuntarily). In this situation, we are concerned about behaviours that indicate dishonesty.

In one case, a colleague and I went to a lady's house to interview her. She had previously admitted to me that she had misappropriated petty cash and minor expense reimbursements. She was at home on suspension and we were going to interview her for a second time.

When we walked in we were introduced to a male. She said that he was her local church representative. We sat down in the lounge. She was dressed completely in black, as if she were going to a funeral. There was an open Bible displayed prominently on a small table near me. There was also a very large television set (about 55 inches) that was on with the sound muted. The programme (satellite) being aired was that of an American charismatic-style preacher who was pacing up and down delivering a fiery sermon. The lounge was a smallish room and the television (that would have been the envy of many a sports fan) was clearly overpowering in the small space.

I recall thinking about what my mother would have said in such a situation. She would have said that you put the television off when guests arrive to show them that you are giving them all your attention. My mother regarded watching television while guests were in the house as disrespectful to your guests (even if the TV is on for background noise and the set is muted). I may be showing my age, but I believe that my mother is correct in this regard.

I will refer to this interview again in this book. When we left I asked my younger colleague to tell me about what he had observed. He spoke about a few unimportant aspects. I asked him to tell me what he thought about the television. He said: 'Yes, what was that about? I found it really irritating.'

I then gave him my synopsis based on the 'psychology' I believed that she was trying (knowingly or unknowingly) to project. I believe that she was wearing black to project a sombre mood, almost like she was in mourning or outwardly trying to project remorse. I did not feel that she was sincere, however. I had previously (during her initial admission interview) observed strong similarities in her behaviour to that of a psychopath, behaviour which is common to white-collar criminals. I believe that this was just another one of her eye-blinds. The television, the church representative and the Bible were all there to say: See, I really am a good person (hence the Christian association). I have made a mistake, but I am sorry (sombre/black clothing) and I am trying to turn my life around (Christian association).

I never did understand why the church representative approached from the bedroom side of the house when we entered and not the lounge side. Perhaps he was returning from the bathroom?

h. Polygraphs

Polygraphs can also be used to identify deceit. The use of polygraphs can, however, be a controversial topic. There is both good and bad use of them. The proper use of polygraphs is an important weapon in the fraud investigator's arsenal. Polygraphs can be used successfully to determine a person's honesty. They are merely an indicator and they cannot be used in isolation. They can be used in corroboration of other evidence only.

What many people do not know is that polygraphs are not 'lie detectors'; they are in fact 'fear detectors'. They show the questions that the subject fears the most. You then have to understand why they fear the question.

It is very important to choose the right time to suggest to the interviewee that they avail themselves for a voluntary polygraph. We will discuss this in more detail below when we discuss the physical interview.

Polygraphs can be used successfully in the following two situations:

- To identify who, out of a group of subjects, to concentrate the investigation on.
- Once you know who the subject is, to try to obtain an admission in a subsequent interview, based on the evidence and the 'failed' polygraph results.

Never use polygraph results in isolation, as evidence. Polygraph results are rarely advisable as evidence in labour hearings. Polygraphs are not always accepted as evidence. Also, bear in mind that the subject has the right to cross-examine all witnesses. The person who administered the polygraph would then need to be at the hearing to testify if the subject so wished.

There will also be occasions when you will knowingly send innocent people for polygraphs. In those cases, you will already have told them that you do not think they are being dishonest, but that from a consistency point of view and to treat everyone the same, you need to send them. Ask them then to assist you despite the unpleasant nature of having to subject themselves to the test. You will have many different reactions to the request to polygraph-test an individual. *One youngster I requested got excited at the prospect, as he could not wait to go back to his mates to tell them that he had done a polygraph, as in the movies. He was far too keen and passed with flying colours.*

Some aspects to keep in mind when drafting polygraph questions include:

- Do not have more than five to six questions.
- The questions cannot go back further than one year.
- The questions need to be specific and cannot be general. For example: 'Did you steal that item from that box on that day?' Not: 'Did you steal something?'

You cannot force a person to undergo a polygraph. Agreeing to undergo polygraphs may be part of their employment contract, but it still cannot be forced.

i. Interviews

There are numerous other techniques (discussed below) to determine, by virtue of your questioning, if a person is being truthful or not. Placing 'blocks' early in the interview and planning the sequence of your questions are crucial.

j. Handwriting analysis

Handwriting analysis may be used to determine if a person is telling the truth or not. *In an example: An employee was adamant that the local MD had signed a document to authorise him to make a disputed payment. The local MD said that he had not, but was starting to doubt himself, as the event had occurred some time ago. The help of a qualified handwriting specialist was enlisted. The handwriting specialist concluded that it was 'highly unlikely' that the signature on the document in question was that of the local MD. The handwriting specialist testified to such effect at the employee's hearing.*

k. Corroboration

Another way to verify the authenticity of the assertions made by someone is to corroborate it by verifying what they said against:

- Someone else's testimony
- Documentary evidence
- Video, timekeeping records, computer logs, etc.

It remains good practice to try to corroborate all key evidence and testimonies.

l. Multiple parties

Remember our rule: 'Take whatever you find or whatever they admit to and multiply it by three and that is your real loss.' You will find when interviewing a person that they typically only admit to what they think you know or to what they think they need to declare. They rarely voluntarily admit to everything/make full disclosures up front. It is as if they, despite being caught out, still want to be perceived as being 'good', by not letting the full extent of their deception be known.

You can expect to experience something very similar when interviewing multiple complicit subjects. The difference is that each one is only serving their own interests and responding to their individual fears of being detected. As with individual subjects, neither of the parties will declare the full story. Each will tell you the part that they want to declare to you. You should, therefore, anticipate this behaviour and wait until you have interviewed all subjects before responding in any manner to the information of an individual. You may even need to interview the subjects on multiple occasions before obtaining a more complete picture. Compare and collaborate all information received.

m. Conclusion

Ultimately it is what you do with the knowledge of possible deceit that is important to your investigation. It may not always be advisable to directly accuse a person of being deceitful, but if done in the right way and at the right time this may work for you. Alternatively, you may want to corroborate your suspicions.

You may be happy to know who was involved or who is loyal to whom. You may also be happy that you know the person is lying and use this in a hearing (where you present the contradiction) or in a criminal testimony.

4.10. INTERVIEW PROTOCOL

4.10.1. Introduction

As with all other aspects of our investigation, interviews need to be planned and structured. In this section, we are not referring so much to the questions and interviewees as we are referring to how the interviewer structures their delivery, and who does what in the interview.

4.10.2. Roles

For the greater part and as practical, never conduct interviews alone. This is for many reasons, including:

- *For the protection of the interviewer.*

  There needs to be protection if the interviewee alleges that they were mistreated, that their rights were violated, or that they were not informed about something. It is also less likely that an interviewee will attempt to falsely accuse two people. There is a greater chance that they will attempt this with one person where it is their opinion against the interviewer's. The discussion above on interview recordings refers. While interview recordings may be inadmissible as evidence, they may serve to protect you against slanderous accusations.

- *To act as a witness.*

  In the event that the interviewee changes their statement or denies having said something or if they refuse to give a written statement later, the interviewers can each submit an affidavit of what was said in the interview.

- *To create redundancy.*

  Things are not always straightforward and investigations may be interrupted for any number of legitimate reasons. An interviewer can fall ill, be unavailable due to personal commitments, etc. All interviewers should be equally au fait with the topics to be covered in the interviews. This will enable any of the interviewers to be able to lead and/or conduct the interviews in the event that the scheduled interview lead is unavailable.

- *As a check and a balance.*

  It is possible that the lead interviewer becomes distracted and does not cover all aspects or misses a subtlety in the interviewee's reply. A second person may pick up on this and be able to ask for additional clarifications.

It is also important that all of the interviewer's representatives understand the structure and the protocols for them to follow. Failure to do so may result in an adverse effect on the interview process and therefore your ability to obtain the information you are seeking.

It is important that one person leads. One person must lead even if you are playing distinct roles (for example: 'good-cop/bad-cop'). It will typically be the most senior/experienced investigator (unless you are training a protégé) who will lead. In the latter case, you will need to let the less experienced person lead so that they can gain experience.

Some complications include the fact that you may not want to or be able to, brief your counterpart on how you plan to lead the interview. Alternatively, you may think of a particular line or tactic whilst conducting the interview. If the person leading the interview is interrupted it may end a line of questioning. For example, if you were putting blocks in place first with your initial questions (and delaying asking the 'real' questions until later) an interruption may derail the process. Alternatively, you may be trying to maintain a particular atmosphere (for example, one in which the interviewee is feeling remorseful) and a disruption may put you right back at the start (where they do not want to make any admissions).

Less experienced staff investigators may be keen to ask the obvious questions first. You, on the other hand, may purposely be leaving these questions to the end.

There may also be sound reasons why your counterpart needs to interrupt. Perhaps you are in training or they see something (in the interpretation of an answer or a behaviour) that you missed.

Agree therefore on a protocol (raising a hand, displaying a pen in a particular fashion) for interruptions in advance. The more you work with people, the less you will need to instruct them upfront. They will get used to the protocol based on prior experiences. A prearranged hand signal (which will not distract the interviewee if you do not want to give your counterpart the opportunity at that moment to ask their question/s) is the most appropriate.

4.10.3. Distractions

Younger generations have an unhealthy preoccupation with mobile phones, which far outweighs any possible benefit afforded by them (phones, not the younger generation). The other problem with mobile phones is that you are always reachable when you have one.

Preferably conduct the interview in an area free of phones or an area where the interviewee will not feel compelled to answer the phone each time it rings. It may be a good idea to request the interviewee if they could please turn all mobile devices off. Do not, as a rule, take any calls yourself. This may be unavoidable, however, for example to receive evidence. If you are expecting to receive a call, it would be wise to tell the interviewee upfront that you unfortunately need to take an important call. Once you have received the call, thank them and then put the phone off or on silent.

In general, avoid iPads/tablets, reading e-mails while you speak, landlines, cell phones or any other interruptions.

4.11. INTERVIEW PHASES

Interviews have phases to them, like so many other things in life. The phases may play out over a single interview or over multiple interviews (the concept of layering refers) with the same person.

It is very important to note that the interview phases commence prior to you speaking to the interviewee and endure after the physical interview ceases. Interviews typically include the following phases:

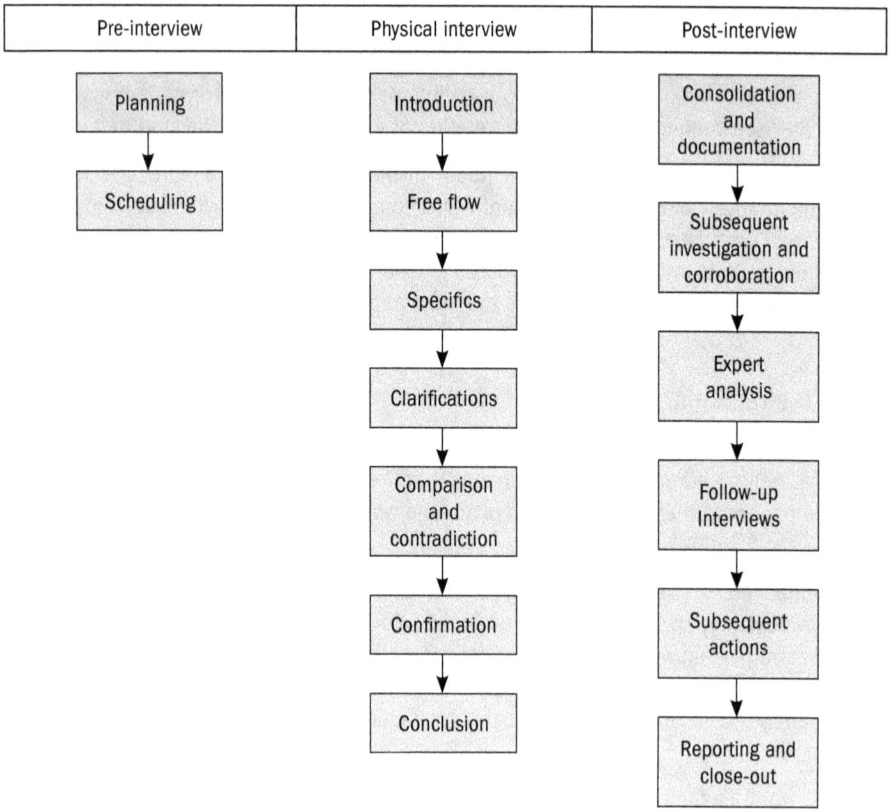

Figure 4.2 *Interview phases*

4.12. INTERVIEW PLANNING

4.12.1. Introduction

Bridging the gap between the investigation and structuring interviews is frequently a challenge for fraud investigators. We talk a lot about the planning of interviews. Planning an interview includes knowing:

- Who to interview
- When to interview each person (sequence)
- The number of times to interview different people (layering)
- Which questions to ask in each interview
- The sequence of questions.

4.12.2. Interviewee information requirement summary

One method to bridge the gap between the investigation outputs and the interviews is to summarise what you have per interviewee and what you still require. Then build questions and design the interview structure to best obtain the outstanding information, commitments (to assist, provide documents, etc) and admissions that are required.

The purpose of this summary is not to have reams of documents or to have documents for the sake of having documents. This is one possible practical method to see at a glance what you have and what you still need. The usefulness of this may increase as the number of interviewees increases and the amount of information you have and require increases. The idea is also not to rewrite your interview summaries. This is a very high-level planning document. Annexure 4.2 attached hereto is an example of an interview information requirement summary. Amend the column headings to suit your individual requirements.

Mind maps are particularly useful for this purpose. The one (a list) is not better than the other (mind maps); it is rather a case of the method that best suits you. The tabular summary is a little more formal though, and can form a valuable working paper.

It is also important to see the interview in the context of the investigation stage that you are in. Figure 4.3 is an excerpt from the fraud investigation process (that we discussed in Chapter 3 on structuring the investigation). Interviews conducted earlier in the investigation process tend to be information-seeking interviews. The final subject interview may be an admission-seeking interview.

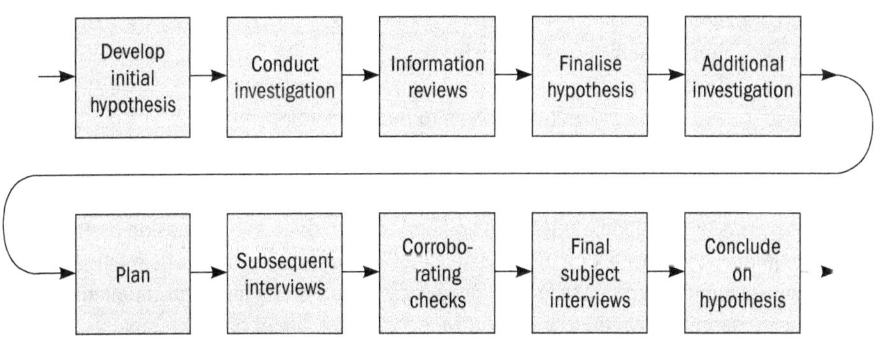

Figure 4.3 *Excerpt of the investigation process*

4.12.3. Question per interview phase

The objectives of interviews, discussed under point 4.3.1 on the purpose of an interview, include information-seeking and admission-seeking. While an interview takes on a similar structure regardless of the purpose of the interview, we can say that we place different emphasis on each of the phases depending on the interview purpose. The interview phases applicable to each of the possible purposes of an interview are listed below:

a. Information-seeking interview

- Gain information
    - Planning
    - Free flow
    - Specifics
    - Clarification
    - Comparison
    - Conclusion.
- Corroborate information
    - Planning
    - Free flow
    - Specifics
    - Clarification
    - Comparison
    - Conclusion.

b. Admission-seeking interview

- Prevent deception
    - Free flow
    - Specifics
    - Clarification.
- Detect deception
    - Comparison
    - Contradiction.
- Make it easy for the subject to confess to their deception
    - Conclusion.

Annexures 4.3 and 4.6 attached hereto have sample questions that may be considered when planning interviews. It is recommended that you first work through the discussion on the different stages of an interview, before trying to make sense of the question prompts below. It is important to understand the context/purpose of the questions before diving into the detailed questions. This list is just a sample. Over time, you will develop your own list of questions that work for you.

4.13. STRUCTURING THE INTERVIEW

- *Planning*

In addition to the planning of the questions to be asked during the physical interview, the interviewer needs to consider the following and put appropriate steps in place around:
    - What the purpose/goal of the interview is
    - Where the interview will take place
    - When the interview will take place
    - Who will attend the interview
    - Are there any special considerations?

As per Chapter 2 on the rules, the three most important rules of interviewing are, firstly: planning; secondly: planning and lastly, planning. In this context try to predict the effect that various people who may attend an interview will have on the outcome and where the interview should be held, so as to optimise the interviewer's ability to obtain the required information. Some special considerations may include:

- Will the interview be recorded?
- Will it be necessary to read the interviewee their Miranda rights at the commencement of the interview?
- Do you need to have any form of documents/information/exhibits present during the interview?
- Do you need to arrange for a translator?
- Is it necessary to have any people on standby in response to the conclusion of the interview (eg polygraph specialists, someone that can check the responses of the interviewee, someone that can have case relevant information available in the event it comes up and the interviewer does not want to break the momentum of the interview, etc)?

- *Scheduling*

Some contact/conversation with the interviewee may be required prior to the physical interview. The scheduling process is the process where you physically set up an interview with the interviewee. The scheduling of an interview may:

- Be a natural progression from the broader investigation
- Be an instruction from their employer to avail themselves for an interview
- Not even seem like an interview to the subject and may just be perceived as a general conversation
- Require you to telephone the interviewee and request an interview
- Require you to walk into their office unannounced and inform them that they are going to be interviewed at that point
- Require more skilful manoeuvring, support and intervention by others.

You may, for conversational-type interviews, not want to approach the interviewee directly and rather want it to seem like a 'perchance' meeting or let it seem that the suggestion of the discussion came from their side. Such cloak-and-dagger will rarely be required though.

Annexure 4.5 attached hereto provides a basic template by which to plan interviews with interviewees.

- *Interview background*

Some of what is discussed with the interviewee during the scheduling process may overlap with what is mentioned to them at the introduction that occurs at the commencement of the physical interview. This will occur when you are compelled (by request of the interviewee) to give more information about the purpose of the interview before they will consent to the interview. In that event, the interviewer will give a summary of the purpose of the interview. If they pressure you for more, then it is recommended that you say that those sorts of details will be discussed at the 'meeting'. At the introduction phase of the physical interview, the interviewer will only need to remind the interviewee (for example: '...you will recall that...') of the purpose. Do not duplicate unnecessary details already discussed with the interviewee, as you may irritate the interviewee.

- *Attendees*

When scheduling your interviews, remember never to interview more than one person at a time. Also, avoid having a senior in the room with a junior staff member. The one may be reluctant to speak in front of the other. The senior may not want to divulge too much confidential information in front of the junior and the junior may not want the senior to see them giving the information about the bad things that are going on, which may make the senior or the company look bad.

As far as possible, do not allow any representatives. You want the interviewee to talk. You do not want the representative to speak on behalf of the interviewee; you want to hear it in the interviewee's words. You also do not want the representative to suggest to the interviewee that they should not say anything for fear of incriminating themselves. People are also less likely to speak in front of someone else, even if they have asked them to sit in and represent them.

An interview is not a disciplinary hearing and therefore does not have the same onerous requirements as a hearing. Tell interviewees (that are concerned) that this is not a hearing and they are not being charged with anything. Tell them that this is just a normal employee/employer discussion. So, while they do not have an express right to a representative, at the end of the day you cannot refuse them the right to have a representative if they wish to have one. You should encourage them as far as possible not to have a representative. You may say: 'You are free to have whomever you wish with you, but really it will not be necessary to have someone with you. This is not a hearing and you are not accused of anything. I would just like you to help me understand aspects that I am working on...' or 'I would like you to be able to speak freely. You may leave at any time that you feel uncomfortable with the interview.'

- *Salesman tactics*

This is the phase in which you need to be firm, charming and convincing. A lot of people will initially decline your request for an interview. You have a very brief chance to gain their cooperation without making them fearful of you or the process or without giving them a direct instruction. They will say: 'I don't want to get involved' or 'I don't know anything, I don't work with that part or I didn't see a thing.' You may reply in response: 'Yes, I understand that, but I was wondering if I could come and chat to you about the 'ABC' part of the work...' or 'I am currently looking at [X] and I was wondering if you could help me understand how it works.'

You should never get angry or irritated with them, but you also do not want to take no for an answer. To get the interview, I say things like: 'Just chat to me, it won't take long...' or 'I realise that this is difficult for you, but it would really help me if we could have a quick chat.'

In reply to the 'I don't want to get involved' gem, it is advisable to say this person that you understand their reluctance, but that it would be a big help to you. Appealing to their good nature and assistance is also a positive way to gain their buy-in. If they are concerned about confidentiality (our previous discussion refers), say that you have been doing this for a long time and that there are many ways in which to make it appear as if you have stumbled upon the information, without identifying them as the source. Once in the interview, if you realise that you will be unable to keep the declaration quiet, then say: 'I did not realise that the matter was that serious. We are unfortunately going to have to take this further.' Then discuss and agree on a way forward.

Alternatively, you could say: 'Well, unfortunately you are involved due to ..., but let's talk about this and see how best to handle it...' or 'You are the only one who can assist me with this.' The trick at this stage of the interview process is to get the interview and hope that they turn up for the interview.

4.13.1. Physical interview

- *Introduction (Pace: level I)*

The introduction starts from the time that you first see or speak to the person. Maybe it is more correct to say that it starts from the time they first see you or become aware of you/your reputation/what you do. A poor introduction may set the incorrect tone and/or fail to create rapport. As far as possible, meet the person at the door. Be friendly, without being false. Greet them with a handshake if local custom and religious beliefs permit this.

Two scenarios exist for the first contact:

- *The person comes into the office that you are in*
  If you are sitting, then get up and go to them. Never greet them sitting down. It is arrogant and disrespectful. Even if you look up and they have already come in, then stand up and apologise. Walk towards them if you can. Preferably meet the person at the door, as they come in. This will have a welcoming feel to it. If local custom permits, give them your hand and greet them. Walk them to a chair (the arrangement of which should be predetermined) and offer it to them to sit on. Thank them for coming and say that this will not take too long.
- *You go to their office*
  Knock and say hello in a friendly manner. Ask them if you could just ask them something quickly. The idea is that you need to get your foot in the door. Be careful not to give them too much information upfront otherwise they will have an excuse to delay/decline. At this point you could again have two responses:
  - If they are extremely agitated or if they have a real excuse (difficult to determine) apologise and then ask them when it will be more appropriate to come back. Again, when they enquire why you want to see them, do not give them too much information. Just say that you need some help with some work that you are doing. In a case where you urgently need to talk to them, retain the element of surprise or if the matter is of such importance that it cannot wait, then explain to them that you realise that they are extremely busy and that this is an inopportune time, but you really need to speak to them briefly.
  - They reluctantly agree to talk to you.

If the interview was prescheduled or if you walked into their office or workspace, then always make sure that you thank them for their time once you have entered the interview location. Reach over and shake their hand if local custom permits. Introduce yourself without your official and 'scary' title. Sit down and tell them that this will not take long.

In either instance (pre-arranged or walk-in interview) it is advisable to go with the approach that you need their 'help'. This makes people feel good that they can help you. It also piques their curiosity as to how they could help you. Lastly, the idea of helping someone is generally non-threatening.

Start off with a general introduction. Give the purpose of the interview without going into too much detail and without being formal. Do not formally say that the 'purpose of this interview is...'. It should seem like an unrehearsed conversation, for example: 'I have been asked to look at the invoicing process and I was wondering if you could help me to understand how it works.' They may try to shrug you off. Perhaps they will suggest that you speak to someone more important than them. If so, reply:

- 'Your manager? Yes, I have already spoken to them.'
- 'Yes, they advised me to speak to you.'
- 'Yes, I will try to speak to everyone. I am beginning with you.'
- 'I have been advised that you are the most suitable/knowledgeable person to speak to in this regard.'
- 'I just need to know at a high level.'
- 'I think you will be the best person to assist me, as you work with this on a daily basis.'

This stage of the interview is very important as it sets the tone for the rest of the interview. Exercise caution, as it may be impossible to undo 'damage' sustained at the commencement of the interview. If you irritate them or if they fear you, they may never talk to you. It is therefore important that you put the person at ease. You must gain their assistance and willingness to participate in the interview. The interviewee may perceive the interview to be a waste of time or an irritation, as they may have other pressing deadlines. Alternatively, they may not understand the extent of the investigation. They will, therefore, fail to understand how their input could be of assistance.

As you progress with information-seeking interviews, encourage interviewees to tell you anything that they can think of about the aspect, no matter how trivial they may think it is. Say to them that the piece of information may seem insignificant to them, but that you have an overall view of what happened and something that seems insignificant to them may be enlightening to you. Also, say that everything helps to colour in the picture for you. This way they are less likely to edit what they say.

If they perceive themselves to be more senior or more important than you, they may not want to assist you. In such a case, you may have to stroke their ego initially, until you get the questions going.

At the end of the introduction ask them if they have any questions and then ask them if they will be willing to help you. This is a general commitment to assistance. The more times you get them to acknowledge this, the more likely they are to cooperate.

If relevant, introduce the people in the interview room and explain their roles (eg to take minutes, to represent the company, a translator, or from an HR perspective, etc). State what the high-level purpose of the interview is and ask them if they will be willing to assist. Guilty people typically say things like: 'Well, that depends on what you want me to assist with.' Innocent people say things like: 'Well sure, I will try to help as far as possible' or ' I doubt if I will be able to help you as I had very little to do with it, but let's see how I can help.'

Avoid using auditing or forensic jargon. The people we interview are lay people. These people do not attach the same meaning to technical terms, as you/other auditors/ investigators do. Also, do not use 'scary' police language (for example: numbers of forms - J50, section-105 subpoena, etc). Do not use words like arrest, charges, court, guilty, accused, interrogation, criminal charges, etc). It is also not advisable to describe what you are doing as an 'investigation' or as an 'audit'. This may put people unnecessarily on their guard and make them less likely to cooperate/talk freely.

Request help. Say that you require clarity or ask for assistance. Do not tell or demand. Do not use positional power (due to rank or experience). Use words like:

- 'Review'
- 'Assignment'
- 'I am working on a matter.'
- 'As you are aware, there have been some problems and I was wondering if ...'
- 'There are some matters that need clarity.'
- 'Some differences have been identified and I require some help understanding them.'

Always ensure that you as the interviewer are respectful, as:

- The people we, as fraud investigators, are interviewing are our fellow human beings. We cannot, despite what they may or may not have done, play judge and jury.
- We may not have all of the facts yet. Skilful interviewing will help us to determine more facts, while insensitive interviewing may cause the interviewee to clam up.
- We may be incorrect about our suspicions or facts and we do not want to end up with egg on our faces, so go carefully.

Disrespectful interviewing may damage your rapport with the interviewee or affect subsequent matters that you deal with in the organisation. It may also place you, your employers, your clients, witnesses and other third parties at risk of:

- Lawsuits
- Reputational damage
- Retribution or acts of vengeance
- Demotivation of existing employees.

Being respectful does not mean that you have to lie down and admit defeat. Skilful interviewing can turn the balance of power in your favour and result in a favourable outcome.

Be mindful to observe behaviours during the introduction. These tell-tale signs may be vital in assessing honesty or dishonesty at an early stage. It would however be premature to conclude on their honesty at this point. It is suggested that you put to one side what you see in terms of their behaviour. Never disregard behavioural indicators, as its relevance may only become apparent later. If they provide information that is not directly relevant, thank them and say that you will return to it later.

- *Free flow (Pace: level I)*

At this point, things are starting to get exciting. Up until now, your main goal has been to secure the interview. This was a tactical manoeuvre. Now that the interview has commenced, your game becomes very strategic. This is the point where you set them up for your 'end-game'. The chess players amongst us will recognise the importance of the opening, the middle-game and the end-game. Getting the interview and the introduction are comparable to a chess opening. Once the interview commences, you shift into the chess equivalent of the middle-game. How well you do during the end-game will depend on how you set yourself up during the middle-game.

The interview starts with a stage that is called 'free flow'. This is mostly just a free flow of information in a casual manner. This may differ depending on:

- How well you know the suspect
- What the purpose of your interview is (information-gathering, admission-seeking)
- How many interviews you have already had with them and how many you are still planning to have with them (layering).

The basic idea is to let the person settle (a certain amount of nervousness is normal) and try to build rapport with them. You may even use this time to put blocks in place to prevent them from lying in the next phases of the interview.

Subjects will typically try to establish what you know. If they ask you what you know, it is advisable to 'play dumb' and to say: 'Well I actually don't know. I was hoping that you could shed light on the matter' or 'That is why I am so grateful that you are able to speak to me, as I am hoping that you will be able to shed some light on the matter for me.'

Subjects tend to talk about the things that they are the most nervous about early on in the interview. This is the 'free flow' section of the interview. It is as if they cannot contain themselves and they need to set the tone to convince you that they are innocent even without you asking directly about the matter. Do not stop them or guide them; let them speak while you make notes. Try to identify the topics they are concerned about for later use in the interview.

Do not read off your questions to them. This part of the interview must be like a normal, free-flowing conversation. A skilled interviewer has their interview plan in their head and can react to changing points of discussion and jump around to ensure that all points are covered so that the interview seems unstructured and free-flowing.

If they do not begin to talk spontaneously, then you may need to prompt them to talk. Have a few prompts planned to get the conversation going. Some sample prompt questions include:

- 'What do you do for the company?'
- 'How long have you been with the company?'
- 'What did you do before you joined the company?'
- 'Who do you work with?'
- 'What have you heard about the incident?'

Once they are talking generally, it is easier to lead them with other questions to where you want them to go.

I also find that subjects practice their 'excuses' with me very early on in the interview process. These excuses are valuable bits of information, as they will tell you first what they are scared of and secondly they will give you early insights into their defence. Note these for now. You will use them later in the process.

Continuing from the aforementioned example, let us presume that you are investigating a new organisation cell phone that was stolen out of an office cupboard. Subjects may say early on in the interview something like: 'Well I don't know how that could have happened, as I was not there and Jane always locks the office door when she goes out at lunchtime.' In this case, they are removing themselves from the situation and blaming someone else for not doing the right thing (the discussion later on the fraudster's personality refers).

Now let us presume that you have seen camera footage or you have building access log information to prove that the subject was in fact there on that day. It would not be advisable for you to jump up and say: 'Aha, you are lying. I have proof you were there!' They will calmly just say: 'Oh dear, I have made a mistake. It was some time ago and I have forgotten.' That will leave you high and dry. At this point in time, we are just setting them up and then we reel them in later. The idea at this point is only to get them talking freely. The more nervous they are, the more they will say in the beginning. You want them to commit to what they have said about what they actually do/did, as opposed to what they should have done. Remember at this stage they do not know what you know, so they are at a disadvantage.

Do not say too much. Make notes, acknowledge that you are listening ('Uh-huh, yes, and then?'). Do not interrupt. You can come back later to the missed point or points that require further explanation. One technique that can be used is to circle or underline the things they say that you want to refer back to later. When they have finished talking, page back and say: 'Thanks very much for that background, but there are just one or two things that I want to clarify based on what you have just said.'

- *Specifics (Pace: level I)*

Free flow is not necessarily as free as it implies. It is purposeful, but without the subject knowing. The difference is that the subject is doing most of the talking and you are listening with very few conversational prompts from the interviewer's side.

The free flow conversation will come to a natural end. At that stage, you need to assess if you have heard all the things that you wanted to hear at the initial stage or if they responded well enough to your prompts. If not, you may need to ask them some direct questions. This is the 'specifics' part of the interview. The purpose of this is to move the interviewee to say the things you want them to say and in so doing set the blocks in place to prevent/detect their deceit later in the interview. The interviewee is still doing most of the talking and you are still gathering information.

Blocks are important. If, for example, you present them with a piece of evidence upfront and/or ask them the actual question that you want to ask them, it may be too easy for them to offer an excuse to explain the abnormality. So, when planning, we start from the ending questions that we actually want to ask and then work backwards to the starting questions.

The whole interview must seem like a general conversation and not like an interview. They must not know that you are leading them to a point. The idea is to ask them non-threatening questions that no normal (not even guilty) person would mind answering. They will answer these questions without realising that their future answers are being blocked.

In the example below, we ask the interviewee 'what position they are in' and 'what their duties include'. It is unlikely that this will be perceived as a threat. In fact, people often like to tell you what they do. It is important when asking questions never to ask without knowing:

- What the answer could be
- Why you are asking the question
- What your reply/subsequent questions will be to guide them back to the point that you want to ask them about.

As a general rule, the fifth or the sixth question that you ask (that is specific to the topic) is the actual question that you want to ask. As an example:

- 'So Jane, what position are you in?' '*FD.*'
- 'Tell me about your duties.' '*I am responsible for the entire finance function.*'
- 'Fantastic. What are some of the specific things that you do?' '*I am responsible for approving payments, monthly reporting, drafting budgets and reporting to the board, etc.*'
- 'Payments, wow, okay. As a start, please tell me how many different types of payments you get.' '*Well, trade suppliers, expense creditors, etc.*'
- 'And what are the payment methods?' '*Bank cheque, manual cheque or electronic funds transfer.*'
- 'I am relatively new here; please take me through the payment process.' '*Well firstly the invoice arrives at ... it is sent to ... for approval and then it comes back to the finance departments where ....*'

In this way, we place a block in place for later, as the subject has now demonstrated knowledge of the process and cannot lie later and say that they were unaware of the process. As discussed before, common excuses used by fraudsters include that they did not know or that it was someone else's responsibility. In a labour case, you frequently have to prove that, firstly, there was a rule, and secondly, that they were aware of it. Try therefore to get the interviewee fairly early on in the interview to admit (without knowing what they are doing) that they knew what the rule was. Ask them to tell you about what they do in their job. Ensure that you seem to be interested and ask further clarifying questions. In this way, drill slowly down to the detail and get to the point that you want them to say unbeknown to them that they are admitting to being aware that there was a rule. For example: '*I work in the finance office, I do bank reconciliations and I capture information onto the accounting system.*' 'Bank reconciliations, that must be a lot of work.' '*No, not really. It was previously, but then the FD put the ABC process in place.*' They have just described what their responsibilities are (so they cannot use the 'not my responsibility' excuse).

At this point (specifics) we are just putting the blocks in place for later. It is not advisable to ask them at that point if they understand or if they were aware of the rule. If they answer in the negative, you will have run out of opportunities to ask. It is preferable to seem to be interested in what they do and ask them to tell you as a form of an introduction.

Some interviewees are very keen to impress you with irrelevant information, perhaps to make themselves look competent. Not all of these matters will be relevant to the matter at hand. Let them talk, but also keep them focused on the topics you are interested in. Keep them happy to chat in general, without realising that blocks are being set in place around them.

Do not assume anything. Try as far as possible to get them to say things in their own words. If they did not say something directly, then ask for clarity: 'Just to test my understanding, if I understand you correctly ...' or 'Sorry I don't understand, you mentioned just now that ...' or 'So do your duties include that or not?' Alternatively, if they say: 'You know ...' then say 'No, sorry I don't know. I am new here. Can you please elaborate?'

This is also important for your recordings and in the third part of the interview when you start to compare what they have said to what has actually happened. This can be used in your interview summary afterwards. When making your summary afterwards, review your interview notes and those of your colleagues as well. Refer back to recordings and fill in the gaps to ensure that you have one complete transcript of the interview.

Review the transcript to identify further questions that need to be asked in subsequent interviews (layering). Try also to identify the times that deceit took place. Remember, deceit is always in response to the possibility of being detected. Try to understand what was being discussed at that point and what they feared detection of at that point.

By the end of the specifics phase, we want people to have committed themselves to what they have said. As discussed previously, subjects also give away their excuses in advance. It is as if they are practising their excuses to see if you will fall for them. They do this regardless of your ability to disprove what they have said. It is therefore strange that they stick to the same excuses in subsequent hearings, despite the fact that you have overturned their untruths in the interview. This is probably because this is the best excuse they can give and they simply use it again.

- *Clarification (Pace: level I)*

This is the stage of the interview when you double check what was said. The difference between this section and the previous sections is that in this section you are more involved in the discussion. It is more of a 50:50 conversation. It is here that you gather your last bits of information before homing in on the real purpose of the interview that you have been building towards the entire time. The mood is still very friendly and informal and very much an information-seeking one. If you are just conducting a general information-seeking interview with a non-guilty/non-deceitful person, you will most likely stop after this section of the interview.

If you started off conducting an admission-seeking interview and then realised that you have the incorrect party or that you have insufficient information to pursue the individual at that precise point, it may be necessary for you to back-pedal and stop the interview here, to prevent an unfavourable outcome or to allow you to have a follow-up interview later without having to regain rapport.

Let them see you writing down the things they say. This is important for the next contradiction phase when you refer to your notes in terms of what they have said when you are checking a subsequent statement made by them. When you refer to it you will page back to your notes and read their statement/s to them and they will recall what they said, and realise that they are in a corner due to what they have said (actually due to the blocks that you have put in place). For example: After hearing a lie about something for which you had already put a block in place, page back in your notes and say: 'But earlier you said .... Now you are saying ... I really don't understand; can you please clarify?'

This is the last point of the interview where you ask direct questions about what they do or what has happened. You need to be confident at this point that you have sufficient information to proceed to the next phase and that they have committed sufficiently for you to proceed with the next section of the interview. There is a possibility that the interviewee will just not know the answer or that they are being deceitful. We test this in the next section of the interview.

- *Comparison and contradiction (Pace: level I or II)*

This is the 'fireworks' section of the interview. This is the section that all the movies you have seen and the novels you read have prepared you for. We have done the groundwork in the preceding phases and now we get to the fun section. The difference is that we do it respectfully and not in the 'Hollywood style'.

The pace of the interview may very well increase at this point. You must however always be professional and polite. This is where things get tricky for the interviewee if they have been dishonest up to now. This is also the most appropriate section to discuss the 'elephant in the room'. The elephant in the room is the obvious and often uncomfortable topic of why you are interviewing the person and the reason for the investigation. Frequently everyone in the room knows about what happened, but interviewees do not want to ask about it and interviewers do not want to give too much away until now. Something has happened (for example, money is missing) and that is why you are here. As plain and simple as it is.

As far as possible, delay the discussion on the elephant in the room until you reach this section of the interview, when the groundwork has been done and the blocks are in place. If the interviewee approaches the subject before you wish to or if it is unavoidable, then mention it in as little detail as you can.

You could say, for example, after the subject has explained the bank reconciliation process to you: 'Joe, as you are aware some discrepancies have been identified with the bank reconciliations. I was hoping you could help me understand what has happened.' If on the other hand, they do not know that there is a problem, then do not volunteer the information just yet.

Let us get back to the exciting bit. In this part of the interview, you compare what they have said to what has occurred and you seek clarity on any differences. You have, for the greater part, been fairly strategic in your approach so far, thereby ensuring that the interviewee has committed themselves to what they have said. It should, therefore, be easy to compare what they have said to what has occurred.

For example: 'Sorry Joe, I don't understand: at the start of our conversation you said that the bank reconciliations were part of your responsibilities, but now you are saying that you did not perform the bank reconciliations in question? Is my understanding correct?'

Answer: 'Yes.' 'So, if you didn't perform them, then who did?' *Answer: 'I don't know.'* 'Let's look at this logically: there are three staff members in the finance function. Esther does the debtors, Mary does the creditors and you do the cash books ...' And so on. In this example, Joe is starting to catch himself out by painting himself into the proverbial corner.

If, on the other hand, it was not possible to put blocks in place, then just run through each item and check that the process is correct or that they agree with the amounts, dates, etc and compare them to what seems logical.

For example: 'But Mary, I don't understand. Why is this invoice for USD 25 000.00 made out to a company that your husband is the sole owner of? Does your husband supply goods or services to the company?' Answer: *'My husband has lots of contacts and sometimes he helps me get goods at special prices for the company.'*

I think that Mary has done something wrong. She does not want to admit to having done something wrong, so she is trying to let it seem like she is (through her misconduct) doing something good for the company. She is distancing herself from the wrongdoing. She has, however, just given you the opening that you require to explore what she has done in greater detail.

As far as possible, try to consider the logic and probability of the situation without ever accusing the person of having done something. Never accuse the person, even when the situation is blatantly obvious. Do not say, for example: 'But I can clearly see you stealing the boxes and loading them into the back of your car.' Rather try something like: 'But who is that on the camera carrying out the boxes? Isn't that you?' Answer: *'Yes.'* 'Why were you carrying the boxes out and putting them in your car?' *Answer: 'Sometimes I purchase goods on my staff account.'* 'Okay, so that is you taking the boxes out. If I go to your staff debtor's account for the day listed on the camera, am I going to find an invoice for the five boxes charged to your account?'

Another effective technique is one which can be used if the person is not cooperating. This entails looking at them (normally, not aggressively) and remaining silent. Use this if you have tried many things and you are just not breaking through. Maintain this silence for as long as practical. This silence is very uncomfortable and the subject will feel a very strong urge to want to fill the silence with something. They will often start to talk to fill the uncomfortable silence. The silence will be uncomfortable for you as well. Try to persist and resist the temptation to talk, as this will break the effect. Once they start to talk, return to the stage of the interview that will help you progress, for example: 'free flow', 'specifics' or 'clarification'.

- *Confirmation (Pace: Level I or II)*

Up until now, we have been concerned with getting an interview, obtaining information, and determining the person's honesty. The second-last step is to try to get the interviewee to admit guilt if they have been dishonest.

Catching the interviewee out on their deceit is relatively easy. Getting them to admit to it is much more difficult. People are strange. Even in the face of compelling evidence they frequently will not admit their guilt. So how do you help them to make that admission? You have to soften the blow for them. You have to distance them from the wrongdoing.

At the precise point that it is obvious that they are guilty, lean slightly forward in your chair towards them, look kindly at them, lower your tone and say caringly:

- 'I know you are a single mom of two kids; tell me what happened.'
- 'It must have been very tough for you. Were you in financial difficulty?'
- 'I can see that you are a good person. It must have been difficult for you. Tell me when it started to happen.'
- 'How much did you take the first time?'
- 'Did you mean to put it back later?'
- 'Was it just going to be the once?'
- 'You probably just needed a little bit of help and then things became more difficult.'

Asking them when it first happened seems to get the best results. The next thing you know, they are telling you what happened. You then need to maintain your empathy and look with concern at them and listen attentively without disrupting, nodding your head as they talk. Alternatively, you could ask: 'Why don't you start from the beginning?' You may also play the cooperative interviewer, for example: 'Rather tell me what happened and I can see how I can help you out.'

Always thank them for telling you. Listen attentively so that you seem to be sympathising with them. Never appear to be judging them. Once they have told you, empathise with them: 'Yes, I realise that it must have been very difficult for you, but thank you for telling me.'

If you can see that the person is guilty or if they have made a partial admission and you are sure that there is more, tell them that it is important that they do three things, namely:

- *Cooperate*
  They must cooperate and help with the investigation. They must not conceal details, as these details will always come out and then they are going to look bad. Tell them that if they cooperate that you are prepared to put in a good word for them with the prosecutor.
  In one case where a retail store manager had been making fictitious refunds on his personal credit cards, we recovered the money and he cooperated fully. He was convicted and received a criminal record. When it came to sentencing, we kept quiet (as prearranged with the prosecutor) and we did not give any aggravating arguments. The young man received a suspended sentence. We were happy and he was relatively happy, as he got off lightly.

- *Show remorse*
  They need to show that they are sorry for what they have done. A judge is not going to be lenient if they do not show remorse.

- *Show restitution*
  They must try to put the complainant (the person against whom they perpetrated the crime) back in the same position that they were before the fraud. In most cases, this involves repaying misappropriated funds. This is discussed in Chapter 7 on subsequent actions.

When more than one party is involved and if you get the impression that the parties are holding back, play the one person off against the other in their separate interviews. As discussed above, people frequently want to shift attention from themselves onto someone else. They are normally quicker to sacrifice someone else than give themselves up. Perhaps it is survival instinct. Regardless of the reason, it is a good opportunity for you to obtain information on the other party. Try therefore to get the person to give you as much 'dirt' on the other party as they are willing to. As long as they are feeding you information about the other person, they feel that the attention is off themselves. They may also feel that they are seen to be pleasing in your eyes by cooperating (kind of like the teacher's pet). Try to let them think that they are going to get all the blame unless they give the other person up. Ask questions such as:

- 'Did he approach you?'
- 'Was it his idea?'
- 'What can he use against you?'
- 'Tell me what his involvement was so we can see if he is trying to pin the blame on you.'
- 'Has he called you yet since this incident came to light? No? I didn't think so. This is not how a friend should be.'
- 'Has the supplier offered you a job yet? It seems like he has used you and now he is leaving you out in the cold. I think you are the victim here.'

You then do the same with the other party in their separate interview. In some instances, a follow-up clarifying interview to catch the other person out may be required, now that you are armed with more information about what they did. With multiple investigation subjects, the question is if there is honour amongst thieves. We are concerned about this, as ultimately we want people (especially subjects) to disclose information and/or to make admissions. As discussed above, one way of obtaining information is to get one subject to make declarations about another subject.

- *Conclusion (Pace: Level I or II)*

This is the phase where we pull everything in the interview together. This could just be a conclusion of the interview or it may involve setting up a subsequent interview, a request to undergo a polygraph, a request to review specific documents or conduct the next action, etc.

There are a couple of possible outcomes of an interview, including the following:

- There is no need for any further action.
- There is a need to have subsequent interviews with the same subject.
- There is a need to interview others as a result of information provided in the interview.
- The subject has made a full or a partial confession. The need may, therefore, exist to formalise the confession and to use this in subsequent actions.
- The subject has indicated that they will cooperate and provide some form of recovery. Alternatively, the subject communicates (directly or indirectly) that some form of involuntary recovery could be made.
- The information provided by the subject will be required as evidence in subsequent actions. The subject's testimony will need to be locked down in an affidavit. Chapter 8 on reporting refers.
- The subject indicates their desire to resign.

- There is a need to confirm certain facts and assertions.
- There is a need to obtain documents and evidence.
- The subject has volunteered documents or evidence to be obtained.
- There is a need for subsequent actions (discussed below) such as a polygraph test.
- There is a need to initiate a criminal, civil or internal labour case.
- If the subject has volunteered evidence, as discussed earlier, ensure that this is obtained immediately before they change their mind.

If the subject has made admissions, get them to provide a confession written and signed by them. In serious matters, you may wish to take the subject directly to the police station to have them make a statement there.

If the matter is complicated, you may have to assist them to prepare an affidavit afterwards. Try to do this immediately, but this may not be possible. Try to get them to do one of the following:

- Write a statement in their own words.
- Give a written confession.
- Sign a transcript of the interview or minutes to confirm that this is what was discussed.

If they are reluctant to sign it, write on the bottom of the minutes that by signing this they:

- Acknowledge that this is what was discussed.
- Do not necessarily agree with what was said.
- Are not making any admissions of guilt.

Remember our rules:

- Go with the path of least resistance.
- In this game, we take what score we can get.
- Principles are for rich people.

The first and most immediate requirement of a fraud risk officer is to 'stop the bleeding'. The bleeding in the organisation's case is the loss of money to the organisation due to the fraudulent activity. In this case ensure that all future dealings with implicated suppliers, etc are suspended pending the outcome of an investigation. Any activity related to the fraud should be suspended, funds frozen, etc. This will freeze everything in time pending the outcome of the full investigation or subsequent actions if the investigation is already far progressed.

If the subject is guilty of fraud, then it is unlikely that the organisation would want to continue to have an employer/employee relationship with them. They would need to leave the organisation. They could leave voluntarily by resigning or they could leave as a result of being dismissed, as the outcome of an internal disciplinary hearing. The second most important aspect then is to have the fraudulent subject leave the organisation.

Take the path of least resistance. If they want to go, then let them go. Do not resist it to prove a point. Do not give yourself a lot of additional work for an outcome that cannot be guaranteed. Hearings are chaired by independent chairpersons and it cannot be guaranteed that the hearing will proceed as you expect it to proceed and that the chairperson will make a ruling that you expect.

If they resign, do not question it or try to stop them and force them to undergo a disciplinary hearing. Accept it. Your primary goal is not to make a point, but to stop the bleeding. Our two rules refer in this regard: 'take the path of least resistance' and 'principles are for rich people'. Prepare letters of resignation in advance in anticipation of the outcome of the interview. The trick is not to threaten people. We do not do that. Rather we talk calmly and factually. We give them sound advice and/or tell them what the options are so that they can make an informed decision themselves. If they decide against what we are hoping for, then we accept it and say that it is their choice; we walk away and carry on with the standard next steps (hearing, criminal, etc).

Never say you will do something that you are not prepared to do. So, if you say you are going to hold a hearing, then you had better be prepared to do it. They may call your bluff, so you need to be in control and be seen to be doing what you said you would do, or you will lose credibility with them.

There is always the chance that they will choose to resign later. Sometimes they go through the hearing and then they resign when the outcome is to be given or if it is not in their favour.

Tell the subject:

- You cannot tell them what to do.
- You will be pursuing this matter to the end and you will be opening a criminal case and initiating an internal disciplinary hearing.
- You will be opening a criminal case regardless of what they chose to do, as it is company policy to do this. You will however not be following up on the matter with the police if they chose to cooperate and it is unlikely (depending on the country that you are in) that the police will take the matter further if you do not push it. You cannot speak on behalf of the police, however; you are just relaying your experience to date on such matters.
- You cannot presuppose what the outcome of the hearing will be. You can tell them that you will be aiming for dismissal.
- The organisation sees these matters in a very serious light.
- The organisation has zero tolerance for fraud and related matters.
- The organisation needs to be seen to be consistent and/or send a strong message that it does not tolerate such matters.
- The organisation has deep pockets and is prepared to see this matter out despite the costs (litigation) involved. This implies that they need to be prepared to foot similar bills.
- You will be representing the organisation and based on what you are seeing you are confident that you have a strong case.
- They are still young/in the early stage of their career/still have a long time to work. A dismissal would be a black mark against their record and will follow them for the rest of their lives. They then normally ask what their options are. Invite HR (prepared) in, who can tell them what they could do. Invariably they choose to resign. If they choose to resign, have them write a letter immediately.

Have others on standby to assist you with the following steps:

- Revoke system access.
- Amend banking signatory instructions.
- Obtain access cards, keys, mobile devices, computers, vehicles, records, files, etc.
- Prepare a notice to all staff members to advise them what has happened (sanitised) and what the way forward will be.
- Prepare a notice to customers, suppliers and business partners as to what has happened and what the way forward will be.
- Have a 'plan-B' or a deputy standing by and ready to take over.
- Instruct building security not to allow the subject access.

Escort the subject from the premises. You may first escort them to their workplace and supervise them to allow them to take a few personal effects.

Agree with management in advance (when you know who the guilty person is, but where the chance of successful outcome is unlikely or not worth the effort or will put the organisation in a bad light) that you are going to try to bluff the person into resigning. This approach can be very successful and can save the organisation a lot of time and effort.

You may decide, based on the information provided in the interview, that the employee needs to be suspended. Suspension is not a sanction in this case. It can be a punishment if recommended by the chairperson after an internal labour hearing. In an interview case, the purpose of suspension is to:

- 'Stop the bleeding' and remove the subject from the workplace.
- Remove the person from the scene to allow a full investigation to occur.
- Prevent disruption of or interference with the investigation.
- Think of the subject's morale and not to require them to sit in the work environment knowing that everyone is looking at them/talking about the matter at hand. Despite what people may have done, we treat them with dignity.
- Prevent revenge attacks by the subject.

Ask the subject if there are any reasons that they should not be suspended. They will probably say because they are innocent. Explain that the suspension does not mean that they are guilty. It is just to allow the organisation the time to conduct a complete investigation and that it is better for their morale not to have to sit through that. Listen to what they say. You do not need to accept their reasons. Then go ahead and suspend them assuming that nothing changes based on what they have said.

Prepare a letter of suspension in advance which you can take out if the situation demands it. Have them sign the organisation's copy and follow the same exit steps, as described for resignation.

If the subject indicates that they are prepared to assist with recovery, have an acknowledgement of debt form ready for them to sign. Denote any special terms on the acknowledgement of debt.

If what the subject has said will be required as evidence later, agree to have the subject provide you with an affidavit of their testimony. This may take some salesman tactics.

Chapter 8 on reporting presents more detail on drafting affidavits. Do this immediately or as soon as possible to ensure that you secure the evidence (our most important rule of forensics).

It is a good idea to run over key elements of what was discussed in the interview. The mood of the interview and/or the type of interview just held may however not be right to run through a summary of what was discussed. Only summarise as appropriate. The summary also does not have to seem like a summary. It can seem like an unplanned conversation. Look at your notes and say: 'Let me just check if there was anything else. We discussed your duties, the payment process, we looked at some examples and you committed to providing us with the ABC documents. No, that seems like everything, for now, thank you.'

It is important at the conclusion phase of the interview to give yourself options. Even if you do not think that there will be another interview, always keep the door open for the subject to contact you and tell you something. Let us assume that there is no further follow-up required as per below. Then tell them before you leave that there may be a need for you to clarify further matters with them and that you may call them for an additional interview. Give them your business card and tell them that this was a lot to absorb at one time and that they may very well think of additional matters once they have had an opportunity to reflect on the interview. In that case, they should feel free to contact you with the additional information.

Thank them for their assistance, their willingness to assist, or for making the time to talk to you. Tell them that the organisation takes these matters seriously and their assistance is greatly appreciated. There will frequently be a need for further action.

Let us presume in our previous example of Mary, who did business with her husband's firm, that you were not in a position to know if the prices were market-related or not, what the company policy was in terms of doing business with family, or what the quality of the products purchased was. In that case, thank Mary kindly for her assistance and say that you will contact her again if you require any further help. Then interview the production manager and the cost accountant to determine if the quality and the production costs were acceptable. You could then have a follow-up interview with Mary to ask her why she felt it necessary for her husband to help her out twice a week for the last three months when the production foreman had told her that the usual supplier's products were of a much higher quality.

In many instances, the purpose of your interview could be to get the subject to agree to the next step. Examples of next steps may include:

- Agreeing to undergo a voluntary polygraph test
- Giving you copies of their bank accounts
- Showing you their accounting and/or records
- Allowing you access to property or personnel
- Making a full confession (in writing, to a witness, at a police station or before a judge)
- Having a subsequent interview (the concept of layering refers).

You will want to act as quickly as possible when they agree to the next step. Again, you do not want to appear to be too keen (and frighten them off), but you want to maintain the momentum and get them to the next step before they can change their mind/be influenced.

As soon as they return to their comfort zone and once they have had time to think about the interview, they may become fearful. The psychology of the moment is also broken and they are on their own. If they promise you bank statements, then ask them to log onto the internet or jump in your car with them and take them home to get the copies or take them to the bank to print them. Do not wait if it is possible not to.

Determine the availability of the person conducting the polygraph in advance and time your interviews accordingly. If they agree, say 'Thank you, let's go, this shouldn't take too long' or 'Let's just get this done and then we can put it behind us.'

4.13.2. Post-interview

- *Consolidation, documentation and conclusion*

As discussed previously, interview notes should be made during the interview. Recordings (audio and video) of the interview should also be regarded as part of the interview documentation. All handwritten notes (no matter how rough) should be retained.

After the interview has been concluded, it is important to draft formal interview documentation from your rough interview notes, as soon as possible subsequent to the interview. Annexure 4.6 attached hereto provides a generic template that could be used for this purpose. Collect the notes from all the people who participated in the interview and compare and compile the formal interview summary form the notes. It is advisable to use a verbatim style. This way it is less likely that there will be interpretation errors later. When you are documenting the conversation, reflect very carefully on what was said. After the interview, go through your notes to ensure that you did not miss something, or to clarify something which you did not denote in sufficient detail or that may be misinterpreted later. Reflection often brings new insights into what was said or which behaviours were manifested.

If you have someone (a colleague) you can trust with the details of the investigation, then you can discuss the interview with them to obtain other inputs as to the background of what was said. The person giving you advice should preferably be someone more experienced than you or at a similar level to you.

The discussion of an interview may be with a fellow fraud practitioner or with an auditee to verify what was told to you. If it is with an auditee, you will need to be selective in terms of how much information you share. The possibility of discussing interviews in any detail with another party is remote, however. Let us say the person interviewed was a junior person and you are working with a senior person on the matter. You will only be able to test certain elements of what was said during the interview. They may be able to give your insights on matters that you would otherwise not have been privy to. This has to be done very carefully, though. Information is mostly confidential. Even if what was discussed was not confidential and the interviewee finds out that you discussed some of what was said, then this may impact on your credibility and their future trust in you. There are however often ingenious and indirect manners to test what was divulged in an interview without giving away too much detail or the names of those who made the disclosures.

- *Subsequent investigation and corroboration*

One method of testing what was told to you in an interview may be to test it (discreetly) in another interview. This may be in another interview with the same person (called layering of interviews) or with another person. Testimonies/assertions can be tested against people and documents, camera footage, calculations, analyses, etc. Do not trust anything that you are told. Test and independently corroborate, as much as possible. Even if people are not being intentionally dishonest, different people have different vantage points and perceive things differently.

What the interviewee is saying must also be seen in the context of a psychopath's personality (discussed under point 4.9.2) and in terms of our rules in so far as:

- A person always does and says things for a reason.
- Forensics is more about psychology than fact.

In short, try to understand why the subject said what they said, and then you can use that understanding to get to the facts. Further investigation may be required based on information obtained from the interviews.

- *Expert analysis: polygraphs, handwriting analysis, doctors, psychologists, computer specialists, engineers, accountants, lawyers, etc*

The use of an expert to verify and/or investigate subsequent information may be required. Ensure that you use credible/certified professionals. Obtain a written report of their analysis and conclusions. Verify if they are available to testify to what they have done. This is important as a report cannot be cross-examined and an accused person has the right to cross-examine all witnesses presented by the organisation in an internal disciplinary hearing.

- *Follow-up interviews*

After confirming the details in your subsequent investigation and/or corroborating additional information, you may want to hold additional interviews with the subject/s. The interview process described above is repeated in full or in part, as required.

- *Subsequent actions*

Subsequent actions are mentioned here from a completeness point of view. They really form part of the structure of the investigation process and are not really part of the interview process. These are discussed in greater detail under Chapters 3 and 7 on conducting the investigation and subsequent actions.

- *Recovery/civil cases*

Recovery (part of subsequent actions) can take many forms, but will largely be a voluntary action (eg where the person agrees to put the aggrieved party back in the same position as they were before the fraud) or an involuntary action (eg obtaining a civil court order). This is discussed in detail under Chapter 7 on subsequent actions.

- *Criminal cases*

Criminal cases (part of subsequent actions) may need to be opened.

- *Internal labour cases*

Initiate an internal labour case (part of subsequent actions) and/or counselling sessions with the subject/s and with anyone else who needs to be held responsible for actions.

- *Bolster internal controls*

Internal controls (part of subsequent actions) may need to be strengthened and/or reinforced in response to exploited weaknesses.

- *Reporting*

This is the final stage when we report (part of subsequent actions) on the matter in hand and close out on the investigation. See Chapter 8 on reporting.

4.14. DOCUMENTING

4.14.1. Introduction

Documenting your interviews is vital. You need to lock down what was said for future reference purposes. There are many aspects and considerations when it comes to interview documenting, including:

- Type or mode of documenting (eg recorded, video, handwritten or typed). Invariably you will make use of multiple aspects to document the investigation.
- By whom (yourself, your assistant, a minute-taker, an HR representative, etc).
- How to highlight key aspects and not to lose track in the interview.
- What is the most efficient method to take interview notes?
- The subsequent chain of evidence and your testimony as to what you did, when you did it and why you did it.
- Your interview plan and questions are also a form of documentation.

4.14.2. Planning documentation

This would include the retention of all the interview planning that you have done, including:

- People to be interviewed
- Sequence of interviews
- Possible questions and answers
- Dates, time venues
- Special requirements
- Attendees.

4.14.3. The interview itself

It is difficult to lead an interview and to make full notes at the same time. You will normally start off well, but the quality of your interview notes will tend to diminish as the interview progresses and you become more engrossed in the interview.

As per the protocol, agree upfront on which person will lead the interview. All the people in the interview should record minutes. At the end of the interview, the person who led the interview must take all notes and type up one master record of the interview. You will find when comparing the different interview notes that each person missed something that the others did not and/or which was interpreted differently and/or heard incorrectly. Unclear aspects could be verified in subsequent interviews if relevant.

You may have elected to have an HR person sit in and record minutes of the conversation and have the subject sign the minutes at the end to confirm that the minutes are a true reflection of the conversation held. This works well in terms of our rules of 'secure the evidence' and 'the best time to do something is immediately'.

As per the previously discussed interview protocol, do not interrupt the subject being interviewed when they are talking. Make notes as they talk. It is important that you do not forget your line of questioning and/or a new point that you want to ask them once they have finished. While they are talking, you can mark (eg circle, underline, asterisk, etc) your notes to remind you of what you want to clarify with them. When they have finished, go back during the clarification phase to seek clarity on the sections that you marked. If you jump in and seek clarity while they are speaking, they may clam up and it may be difficult/impossible to get them talking/to make disclosures on the specific point.

4.14.4. Documenting of deceit indicators

As discussed previously, a big part of an interview is deciding if the person was being honest or not. Consider keeping next to you a checklist of key linguistic and/or physiological indicators for you to note as you observe reactions of deceit, and in relation to which questions you observe them. Annexure 4.7 provides a template that can be used for this purpose.

4.14.5. Post-interview

This is the stage where you:

- Document the interview
- Check for completeness of your work and whether it satisfies your needs
- Decide on further action to be taken (further checks, other interviews, signing affidavits, etc)
- Conclude on the interview.

4.14.6. Templates

The annexures that follow provide examples of general interview templates that you may consider for use/adaptation.

Annexure 4.1
Miranda Rights template

1. YOUR RIGHTS

Please be advised that you have the following rights in the interview that is to be conducted with you:

1	You have the right to remain silent.
2	Anything said may be used in evidence against you.
3	You have the right to consult an attorney of your own choice before answering any questions.
4	You have the right to have an attorney present during the questioning.
5	You have the right not to incriminate yourself.
6	You have the right to discontinue answering any questions put to you at any stage during the interview.
7	You have the right to end the interview at any stage.
8	You have the right to leave the interview at any stage.
9	You have the right to exercise any of the above rights at any time before or during any questioning and the making of a statement.

2. CONFIRMATION

Please confirm that:	**Please tick one option**	
	Yes	**No**
These rights have been read to you.		
You understand these rights.		
You agree to continue with the interview of your own free will.		

3. SIGNED

	INTERVIEWEE	**INTERVIEWER**	**WITNESS**
Signed	______________	______________	______________
Full names	______________	______________	______________
Date	______________	______________	______________
Place	______________	______________	______________

Annexure 4.2
Interview information requirement summary

Interviewee	What we have	What we require/ objective	Type of interview	Interview intensity	Number of interview and sequence	Case relevance and importance	Date, time, place and method of interview	Investigation stage	Possible or key questions
Name and position	Documents, other testimonies, commitments, affidavits, footage, recordings, electronic information, physical evidence, correspondence, information, admissions, etc.		Information or admission seeking	Level I, II or III	For example: Interview 2 of 3	Ancillary, key witness, subject 1, subject 2, whistle-blower 1, etc.	Telephonic, face-to-face or video conference	Information interviews, subsequent interviews, final subject interviews	

Annexure 4.3
Generic interview questions per interview objective

No	Information required	Information seeking	Admission seeking
	General - All		
	What is your name?	Y	Y
	What is your position in the organisation?	Y	Y
	How many years have you been with the organisation?	Y	Y
	What do your responsibilities entail?	Y	Y
	Whistle-blowers		
	What is being done/are they doing/what is the problem?	Y	
	What is their modus operandi?	Y	
	Who is doing this and/or is involved?	Y	
	What amounts are involved?	Y	
	When did this come to your attention?	Y	
	How did this come to your attention?	Y	
	Why are you reporting this now?	Y	
	At which dates and times did/does this occur?	Y	
	Who else knows about this and for how long have they known about this?	Y	
	Who will have information to assist with the investigation? Please specify which information they will have and why?	Y	
	Who should I trust and why?	Y	
	Who should I distrust and why?	Y	
	Where does this occur?	Y	
	When last did these irregular activities occur?	Y	
	When will these irregularities occur next?	Y	
	What evidence (documents, video footage, etc) is available?	Y	
	Is there any threat of loss of money, property or is someone's safety at risk?	Y	
	What else should I know before starting?	Y	
	General information seeking		
	Please describe the 'X' business process.	Y	
	What do you think is the problem?	Y	
	If you were to direct me, where should I look and why?	Y	

No	Information required	Information seeking	Admission seeking
	General information seeking		
	Where do you see the risks?	Y	
	Why do you think this happened?	Y	
	What do you think can be done to resolve/prevent/detect this?	Y	
	Who is for this and who is against this and why?	Y	
	If you were in charge what would you do?	Y	
	Who will be able to give me more information and why?	Y	
	Who is involved in the misconduct?	Y	
	Who should I not trust and why?	Y	
	What could they blame you for and why?	Y	
	Would you hire them and why?	Y	
	Do you trust them and why?	Y	
	Do they receive any strange visitors? Aggressive conversations, people asking for money, dangerous looking people, etc?	Y	
	Is there anything in their lifestyle that indicates a lavish lifestyle?	Y	
	What are their hobbies, pastimes, interests, etc?	Y	
	Admission seeking		
	Please describe the 'X' business process/policy.		Y
	Are there any exceptions to this? Please describe these in full.		Y
	Can you please take me through an example of how you have done this?		Y
	I have identified the following examples. Can you please explain them to me/help me to understand what you have said?		Y
	Who else will be able to give me information and why?		Y
	Who gave you instruction?		Y
	Who else is involved and how? ▪ Did he approach you? ▪ Was it his idea? ▪ What can he use against you? ▪ Tell me what his involvement was. In that way, I will be able to see if he is trying to pin the blame on you. ▪ Has he called you yet since this incident came to light? Has the supplier offered you a job yet? It seems like he has used you and now he is leaving you out in the cold. I think you are the victim here.		Y

No	Information required	Information seeking	Admission seeking
	▪ When did it first happen? ▪ I know you are a single mom of two kids, tell me what happened? ▪ It must have been very tough for you. Were you in financial difficulty? ▪ I can see that you are a good person. It must have been difficult for you. Tell me, when did it start to happen? ▪ How much did you take the first time? ▪ Did you mean to put it back later? ▪ Was it just going to be the once? ▪ You probably just needed a little bit of help and then things became more difficult? ▪ What did you need the money for?		Y
	Why don't you start from the beginning and I can see how best to help you?		Y

Annexure 4.4
Generic forensic interview planning sheet

1. Generic forensic interview sheet

The following is a generic template that may be used wholly or in part during the interview of witnesses and suspects in a forensic review.

2. Background

The following is a summary of the incident/s that has given rise to the review:

3. Investigative methodology

The following is an overview of the investigative methodology:

4. Investigation team

The following are the team members who will be involved in the review:

No	Name	Title	Involvement

5. Interviewees

The following is a list of interviewees:

No	Name	Title	Relevance

6. This interview

The following are the details of this specific interview:

Interviewee	
Interviewer	
Minute taker	
Others present	
Date	
Place	
Time	

Annexure 4.5
Generic forensic interview questions

7. Generic questions

The following is a list of generic questions that may be used as prompts/suggested questions when interviewing witnesses and/or accused/co-accused:

No	Category	Question/s	Replies/Application of results
	Introduction	State name	
		Will this interview be recorded? If so, please state express permission.	
		State your job title.	
		Give the number years of service with the company.	
		Description of duties Link to: ▪ Those involved ▪ Knowledge of transactions/corrupt activities/indicators ▪ Authorisation of assets/movement of funds.	▪ Are they implicated? ▪ Is some other remedial action required (negligence/ disciplinary hearing/ criminal/etc)?
	Process	Give a description of the process under scrutiny.	
		Who is involved in this process?	
		What does each person do?	
		What are your: ▪ Functions? ▪ Area/region of responsibility?	
		What is the official policy/process: ▪ Verbal instruction ▪ Written instruction ▪ Evidence of knowledge of process by virtue of previous actions/practices/ communication.	

No	Category	Question/s	Replies/Application of results
	Physical evidence	What is the nature of evidence: ■ Affidavits ■ Bank statements ■ Electronic information ■ Surveillance footage.	
	Relationships	Internal:	
		■ Colleagues	
		■ Subordinates	
		■ Superiors	
		■ Performance history.	
		External:	
		■ Suppliers	
		■ Subcontractors	
		■ Clients	
		■ Professional teams/consultants.	
		Other:	
		■ Friends	
		■ Family.	
	Modus operandi	Who could it have been?	
		What could they have done?	
		How could they have done it?	
		Why would they have done it?	
	Assets	Physical assets:	
		■ Existence of	
		■ Control over	
		■ Issue/use of	
		■ Purchase of	
		■ Sale of	
		■ Financing of.	

No	Category	Question/s	Replies/Application of results
		Payments (process and approval):	
		▪ Trade creditors	
		▪ Expense creditors	
		▪ Cashbook payments	
		▪ Petty cash payments	
		▪ Staff reimbursements	
		▪ Suspense accounts	
		▪ Discounts, rebates, etc (control of, issuing of, authorisation of)	
		▪ Nett payments (debtors and creditors).	
		Debtors:	
		▪ Ageing	
		▪ Bad debts	
		▪ Discounts	
		▪ Cash.	
		Buying:	
		▪ Kickbacks, etc.	
	Lifestyle indicators	See lifestyle indicator generic template.	

Annexure 4.6
Generic forensic interview template

1. INTERVIEW DETAILS

CATEGORY		DETAILS
INTERVIEW WITH	:	
RELEVANCE TO INVESTIGATION	:	
INTERVIEWED BY (Name, company & position)	:	
OTHERS IN ATTENDANCE	:	None
DATE & TIME	:	Dd Mm 20yy 10h00
METHOD OF INTERVIEW	:	Face to face
PLACE OF INTERVIEW	:	
SUBJECT OF INTERVIEW	:	
CONTACT DETAILS	:	
ADDRESS	:	

2. CORRESPONDENCE RECORD

DATE & TIME	CORRESPONDENCE NOTES	REF
dd Mmmm 20yy During day	Phoned – booked interview	
dd Mmmm 20yy 10h00	Interview	

3. DETAILED INTERVIEW TRANSCRIPTION

No.	QUESTIONS	REPLY	ADDITIONAL ACTION	REF
1				
2				
3				
4				
5				
6				
7				
8				
9				
10				

4. PHYSIOLOGICAL INDICATORS

No.	INDICATOR & WHEN DEMONSTRATED	OPINION	REF
1	Pulsating vein		
2	Blushing and/or a flushed complexion		
3	Sweating		
4	Sitting position		
5	Hands		
6	Folded arms		
7	Fidgeting or doodling		
8	Covering mouth		
9	Hand on the chin		
10	Touching the nose		
11	Shifty eyes		
12	General aggression		
13	Other		

5. LINGUISTIC INDICATORS

No.	INDICATOR	OPINION	REF
1	Lack of self-reference		
2	Verb tense		
3	Answering questions with questions		
4	Equivocation		
5	Oaths		
6	Euphemisms		
7	Alluding to actions		
8	Lack of detail		
9	Narrative balance		
10	Mean letter of utterance		
11	Other		

6. OTHER INDICATORS

No.	INDICATOR & WHEN DEMONSTRATED	OPINION	REF
1	Too conservative		
2	Too revealing		
3	Too flashy/expensive		
4	Covering up		
5	Absence of expected behaviours		
6	Failure to say certain things		

7. OVERALL INTERVIEW OPINION AND SUMMARY

No	AREA	OPINION	REF
1	Credibility of witness		
2	Value of witness		
3			
4			

8. REVIEW

Prepared by:		Date prepared:		
Checked by:		Date checked:		

Annexure 4.7
Generic post-interview deceit indicator summary template

Interview deceit indicatory summary table

No	Area	Observation	In relation to	Interpretation
	Linguistic indicator			
	Lack of self-reference			
	Verb tense			
	Answering questions with questions			
	Equivocation			
	Oaths			
	Euphemisms			
	Alluding to actions			
	Lack of detail			
	Narrative balance			
	Mean letter of utterance			
	Physiological indicator			
	Pulsating vein			
	Blushing and/or a flushed complexion			
	Sweating			
	Sitting position			
	Hands			
	Folded arms			
	Fidgeting or doodling			
	Covering mouth			
	Hand on the chin			
	Touching the nose			
	Shifty eyes			
	General aggression			

No	Area	Observation	In relation to	Interpretation
	General indicator			
	What they do, what they do not do			
	Other, eg surroundings			
	Clothes			
	Too conservative			
	Too revealing			
	Too flashy/expensive			
	Overly displaying religious symbols not normally worn by them			
	Covering			

CHAPTER 5

DATA ANALYTICS

5.1. CHAPTER OVERVIEW AND INTRODUCTION

Data analytics can be used from a proactive or a reactive point of view with regards to fraud investigations and fraud risk management. Data analytics is merely the analysis of any data with the use of an automated tool. Data analytics could be the complex analysis of millions of lines of financial data or the analysis of large numbers of e-mails or a simple spreadsheet plotting a financial trend. Data analytics can be conducted with the aid of specialised, purpose-made software tools or a simple spreadsheet. The volume of data, type of tool used or complexity of algorithms used is not the determinant of what is defined as data analytics. At the most simplistic level, data analytics is just logic.

One difference between data analytics and other established analytics (for example financial ratio analysis) is that other analytics have more accessible examples. Other analytics are also entrenched much better in people's minds, as they are taught as part of specialist fields such as accountancy. This makes their knowledge applied, which is much more powerful than only theoretical knowledge. There is also the added technology barrier, which so many people battle with, which separates the data from the analysis in data analytics. The largest limitation to data analytics is, however, our imaginations. Our imaginations may be empowered through experience and education.

Data analytics is a topic that is frequently discussed by auditors, management and fraud investigators. It is however seldom used well, or at all. This may be because many people (the people saying that they want to use data analytics or those saying that they are using data analytics) want to be associated with the latest methods and want to be seen to be doing the right things. They tend however to inflate any electronic analysis to sound better than it really is. Their discussions are typically at a very theoretical level and without substance. When you question what it is that they really do and when you break it down, you find that it is rudimentary at best and limited in its application. This is not something negative; it is just the reality of the stage of maturity of data analytics in general. However, this gives us a fantastic opportunity to add value.

In this chapter, we will discuss the different types of data analytics and their applications. We will also discuss what is required to perform data analytics and some practical tips and tricks. Numerous examples are mentioned to demonstrate its practical application.

The purpose of this chapter is to improve your understanding of data analytics and to provide actual examples of data analytics in fraud investigations, supplemented by practical hands-on learnings.

5.2. MISCONCEPTIONS

People also seem to believe that there is a magical list of possible data analytic tests from which to choose. This is simply not true. While there are some more commonly used data analytic examples quoted, this is only the tip of the iceberg. There are in fact principles that can be successfully applied to most data to produce desired results. These are discussed below in terms of using dedicated, specialised data analytic software or using a simple spreadsheet.

5.2.1. Examples

Some examples of typically used data analysis tests include:

- *Missing documents test:*

To check if the entire sequence of numbers in a range is present and to isolate the numbers which are not.

Dedicated data analysis software
Missing and/or duplicate document tests are probably the most common data analyses exercises performed. Dedicated data analysis software typically has standard routines to test for document completeness.

Spreadsheet
Obtain a spreadsheet listing all documents in the sequence to be tested. Sort on the column to be tested. Then use an 'if formula' in the entire column to test if the one cell less the previous cell (for example: B3-B2) is greater than 1. If so, then denote a 'missing' text indicator in your test column, otherwise leave it blank. Thereafter copy your formula and past the values to replace the formula in the entire column in which the test was performed. This will eliminate the formula, but leave the test results, being blank or 'missing'. Sort on the column to float the 'missing' indicated rows to the top. Investigate the discrepancies.

- *Duplicate documents/numbers test:*

To identify duplicate numbers in a range.

Dedicated data analysis software
As per above, dedicated data analysis software typically has standard routines to identify duplicate documents.

Spreadsheet
Obtain a spreadsheet of the document numbers to be tested. Sort the column in the spreadsheet on the document number that you wish to test. Then use an 'if formula' to check if the one cell is equal to the previous (for example: B3=B2?). If so, then mark the column in which your formula is as 'duplicate'. Then copy the formula and paste the values to remove the formula. Sort on the column to float the 'duplicate' rows to the top. Investigate and explain the apparent duplicates.

- *Supplier/staff bank account check*

To identify if any staff bank accounts are listed as supplier bank accounts.

Dedicated data analysis software
Comparing staff members' bank account numbers listed on the payroll system to the suppliers' bank account numbers listed on the creditors' master file. This test is frequently mentioned as a data analytic example, but it is used less often, as it is a little more complicated in practice.

You may have to spend some time to get the data into the same (and clean) format before you can conduct this test. Also ensure that you include all payrolls in the organisation (executive, management, blue collar, contractors, etc), as these may be separate.

Spreadsheet
Obtain the following two extracts into your spreadsheet (two separate tabs):

- All payroll bank accounts for all staff members in all payrolls.
- All suppliers' bank accounts in all supplier master files within the organisation.

Ensure that you bring in sufficient reference information to allow subsequent investigation of anomalies. Define the staff members' bank accounts as a name range. Using a v-lookup formula, look up the supplier bank accounts in the defined staff range and return the account number if found. Alternatively, use a nested 'if statement' to denote a text indicator ('test') to identify that the account should be checked, as a possible duplicate.

It is most practical to conduct these tests both ways from the payroll to the supplier bank accounts and from the supplier bank accounts to the payroll.

- *Recalculation:*

To recalculate amounts calculated by a computer program and to identify differences between the recalculated amount and the computer calculated amount.

Dedicated data analysis software
Define an expression that can recalculate the value to be tested based on the raw data in the file. Compare the recalculated value to the value calculated by the program. Extract to a new file all occurrences where the two are not equal. Investigate and explain variances. Adjust the original expression with newly understood restrictions. Re-perform the test until a satisfactory result is attained.

Spreadsheet
Write a formula to recalculate the value based on the raw data. Pull all data into a spreadsheet required to recalculate the value being tested. Design formula to recalculate the values (for example discounts given). Use multiple formulae in separate columns to break up the recalculation of complex amounts. In this way, it is easier to identify errors in your logic and to regress to the last correct column before the error in logic (if any) occurred. Next, pull in the amount to be tested, as calculated by the actual program. Define an 'if formula' to test if the recalculated value is equal to the program-calculated value and mark those that are not as 'to be checked'. Use the copy-paste-special-values feature to replace the formulae. Sort on the 'to be tested' value to float the values to be investigated to the top. Investigate the anomalies and adjust formula with new information which needs to be taken into account. Re-perform the test until a satisfactory result is attained.

- *Identifying all values above or below or within a defined range test:*

Dedicated data analysis software
This will be an extract of all data to a new file where the value is greater than/below or equal to the value or range of values defined by you. Investigate a sample of values extracted. Identify additional limits to be applied. Refine your extract with the newly refined criteria. Re-perform the test until satisfied. Investigate and explain the differences.

Spreadsheet
Commence by copying the raw data to a working file. Then sort on the column to be tested and delete unrequired data that is obviously not within the range to be tested. In this manner, you are sure you are only dealing with the required dataset. Be sure not to delete required data. Filters may also be valuable in this instance. If you are performing multiple tests, create copies of the dataset for each test. Do not amend the previous test, as you will lose the evidence of amended tests. There is also a risk that errors may be perpetuated undetected in subsequent tests. A fresh test reduces the chance of carrying over errors.

- *Identify if a value complies or does not comply with a rule test:*

Dedicated data analysis software
Define an expression that re-performs the rule. Extract to a new file all occurrences where the rule has been satisfied or not satisfied. Investigate the anomalies and refine the expression as required.

Spreadsheet
Define an 'if formula' to mark all values (as an example with: 'exception') that do (as required) or do not equal the rule. Copy and paste the values of the test to remove the formula and sort on the column to float the exceptions to the top. You could also make use of a v-lookup formula to match the value to be tested to a file of rules. Use an if-formula thereafter to identify exceptions or sort on 'N/A' values not found by the v-lookup.

- *Identifying the user who performed the transaction test:*

Dedicated data analysis software
This will be an extract of data to a new file where the 'user' equals the valued defined by you. Investigate these user-performed transactions against the pre-established criteria under investigation.

Spreadsheet
Commence by copying the raw data to a working file. Create a working copy of the data extract. Then sort on the column to be tested ('user') and delete unrequired data or use a filter. Investigate the user performed transactions for the predefined criteria under investigation.

5.2.2. Case study

An employee (employed as an IT technician) was suspected of having a corrupt relationship with an external IT service provider. A visual analysis of costs highlighted that 45 printer cartridges were procured from September X1 to April X2. The local office had a total of 30 staff members. In one instance three cartridges were procured on one day and another two cartridges the very next day. This was highly suspicious and the following steps were embarked on:

- We Googled the cartridge yield and determined that each cartridge can print 6500 pages. We calculated the total number of pages purportedly printed. There were no cartridges in stock at the time of our review.
- The particular printers were dedicated to the customer service desk area. We knew that five copies of every customer transaction were printed. We had a system total of

customer transactions and we were able to calculate the actual number of copies printed for customer transactions.

- We also remotely (we were located in another country) looked at the printer tally totals of prints performed and extrapolated them for the period.
- We identified invoices of paper procured for the same period and calculated the theoretical number of pages used in the period.
- We compared the theoretical print totals and there was a significant variance (up to 50%).
- The incumbent was confronted with the discrepancies and other evidence that was gathered.

5.2.3. Conclusion

There are as many possible data analytical tests available as there are of permutations of computer systems, program combinations and industries. The most value-adding data analyses that you will perform will be those that you design to satisfy a particular need. The aim of this chapter is not to give you a list of X number of data analytic exercises that you can perform to identify fraud. The aim is to provide you with an approach and to highlight some of the pitfalls of performing data analytics.

The light at the end of this tunnel is that the software providers of generic systems (ERP systems and many more) tend, based on their experience with one package, to write standard analyses that can be applied generically. These may not suit every situation, but they will offer a better than average start to some typical analysis.

5.3. REQUIREMENTS

Data analytics is in itself not very complicated. There is, however, a notion, probably due to the need to access data and to perform computerised routines, that data analytics can only be performed by technical people. Data analytics has, however, been successfully performed for some years by many non-technical people as well as by highly technical people. The assumption is then that anyone should, therefore, be able to perform them regardless of how technically skilled they are. Data analytics is in fact not a technical IT skill at all; it is an 'analytical mindset' skill. If you are unable to utilise data analytic software yourself, ensure that you sit with someone who knows how to use the particular package to perform the desired tests designed by you. There are three things you need to do in order to perform data analytics. These include:

- *Learn how to use the specific data analytic software*

  There are many reasons for wanting to make use of data analytics. There are also many different methods by which to accomplish this and there are equally as many software packages to assist you. You will most likely end up using a combination of packages to suit the specific needs during your career. You will have to go through the normal four stages of learning to learn any new package, being:
  - Unconscious incompetence
  - Conscious incompetence
  - Conscious competence
  - Unconscious competence.

You will have to motivate yourself past the 'conscious incompetence' stage and the 'unconscious incompetence' clumsy stage. You will, however, start to build on your knowledge and things will become easier and easier as you progress. Learning the package is, for the greater part, the far easier of the requirements. In fact, while some people learn how to use a package (albeit an introductory course only) or make use of someone who can, they never really have great success with data analytics, as they never acquire the insights associated with the second requirement.

- *Acquire a 'data analytic mindset'*

Acquiring the data analytic mindset is the far greater challenge. Knowing what to compare to what and which tests to perform is really challenging. It is not just something that you can think up. It takes time to learn how to think with that type of mindset. It does get easier the more analysis you perform and/or are involved in. This is the single most important reason why the best intentions to use data analytics never result in tangible results. It has to be needs-based. Most of this mindset is generic thinking and has nothing to do with the package used and/or is not a technical IT skill-set. Some skills required may, however, be organisational or industry specific as well.

- *Knowing what data is about and what data is available*

A far less important requirement, and one which invariably comes with time as experience grows is to understand the basics about data (fields, formats, storage thereof, etc), as well as what data is available. 'Any-start' is better than 'no-start' at all. Sometimes the simplest comparison using the least sophisticated spreadsheet is the most eloquent solution. So, get going and grow your skills from there.

5.4. UTILISATION

Data analytics can be used by:

- Internal auditors
- External auditors
- Management
- Fraud investigators.

Data analytics can be used to:

- Monitor for events and exceptions
- Audit (substantive values or tests for control functioning) or general testing of data (integrity tests)
- Gather information, evidence or provide proof
- Show the effect of events.

More specifically, data analytics can be used:

- To identify data above or below a limit
- To identify data within or not within a specific data range
- To identify data equal to predefined criteria (figures, keywords, etc)
- To list specific occurrences of an event

- To show data transfer between points or communication between parties
- To identify machines or users used to perform transactions or events
- To prove that an event has not occurred
- To compare:
  - Data to each other (one file to another – transactional files and/or master data files)
  - A recalculated dataset to previously calculated data
  - Data to a predefined set of rules
- To determine completeness (for example: missing sequence numbers)
- To look for duplicates
- To recalculate data
- To build new datasets (merge, join, concatenate)
- For predictive modelling and forecasting
- For decision-making
- For 'what-if' scenarios
- To identify and analyse trends
- To compare unlinked datasets
- To stratify data
- To choose samples
- To provide totals and statistics of datasets.

5.5. FREQUENCY OF USAGE

Data analytics can be used with the following frequency:

- *Once-off (non-repetitive)*

This will be a test or analysis that is intended for a specific reason and/or will most likely not be repeated.

- *Periodic (repetitive)*

For example: to conduct monthly checks that run over datasets.

- *Continuous (repetitive)*

With real-time data updates, some data analytics can run in real time. Batch-processed data can also use continual analytics, as and when the data is processed.

5.6. MONITORING

Data analytics can be used:

- *For specific requests (can be used in fraud investigations)*

This will be dependent on the specific request. *For example: Please tell me what the organisation's exposure is in terms of the number of temporary staff members who have worked more than their allowed time in a month. These staff members will be deemed to be permanent and the organisation may have to pay additional benefits. Please give me this data per employee, per branch, per month.*

- *For system implementations (application reviews) (cannot be used in fraud investigations)*

To test to see if programs (particularly controls and routines within programs) are functioning as intended, to:
  - Validate the completeness and accuracy of data transferred
  - Clean data.

- *For fraud detection (can be used in fraud investigations)*

Using data analytics to identify activities that match known fraud indicators or that are not within expected trends and warrant inspection to determine their validity.

- *For information and/or evidence gathering (can be used in fraud investigations)*

To gather event history of known frauds.

- *To trigger events (can be used in fraud investigations)*

To notify the recipients of the data that a specified event has occurred.

- *For dashboards (can be used in fraud investigations)*

Dashboards are trend and event monitoring tools used to monitor repetitive datasets.

5.7. ANALYTICAL REVIEWS

5.7.1. Usage

Within these areas, data analytics can be used:

- *For substantive tests*

To prove a balance, total or transaction.

- *For compliance tests*

To prove that a control is or is not working as designed.

- *To draw samples/test sets*

To draw a sample of events from the full population to be tested in detail.

- *For identification of risk areas/areas of audit emphasis/investigation scope*

To identify areas of high risk through trend analysis to highlight areas of high risk or where to direct investigation emphasis.

- *For trend analysis (analytical review)*

To identify data patterns and to analyse these patterns.

5.7.2. Types

Analytical reviews are one form of data analytics. They are possibly also the simplest and most accessible form of data analytics. Most people are comfortable with performing an analytical review and have probably already performed an analytical review of some sort. There are essentially three types of analytical reviews:

- *One-dimensional*

This entails the identification and analysis of the trend of one set of data (mostly over time).

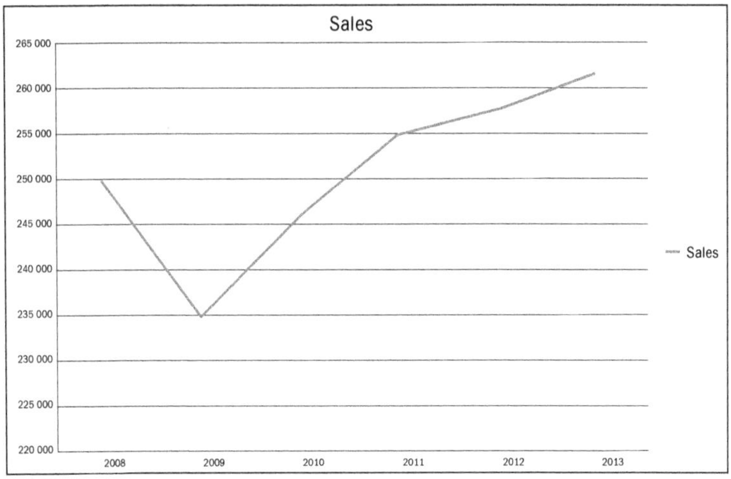

Figure 5.1 *One-dimensional analytical review*

- *Two-dimensional*

This entails the identification and analysis of the trend of two or more sets of data (mostly over time).

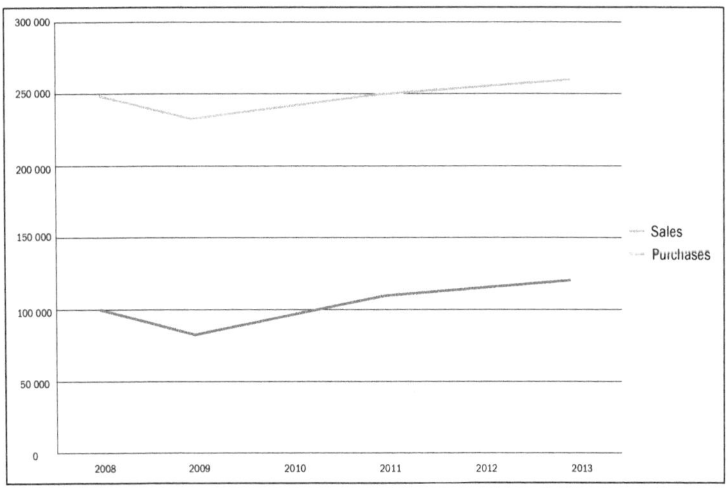

Figure 5.2 *Two-dimensional analytical review*

- *Three-dimensional*

This entails the identification and analysis of the trend that exists between financial and non-financial data.

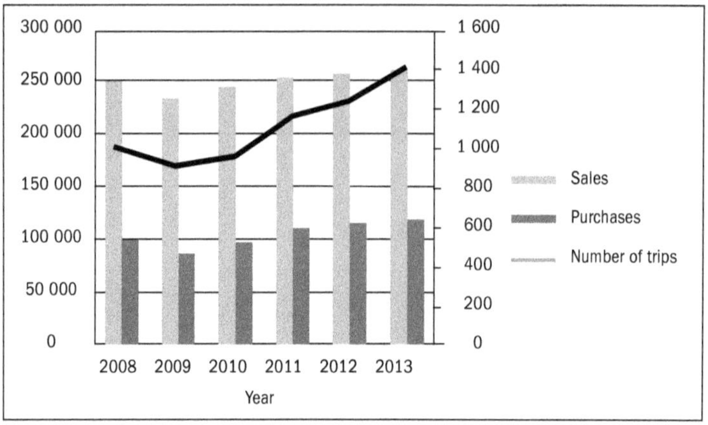

Figure 5.3 *Three-dimensional analytical review*

An interesting fraud analytical review lies in the ability to identify data outliers in datasets. This particular test can be applied to any data that has changed from one period to another to identify data to be investigated. In this example: we have plotted the annual salaries of staff members for the years 20X1 and 20X2. The presumption is that all staff members received close to the same annual inflationary increase and that they should all lie within the same increase trend. The test has identified three outliers: two being above the average and one being significantly below the average trend. Let us presume that our investigation of these three exceptions identified that the lower-outlier was for a staff member who voluntarily started to work half-days in 20X2 and that her salary was proportionately reduced. Let us also presume that one of the two high-outliers was a staff member who was promoted in 20X2 and that her salary had increased to be higher than the annual trend, as a result. Let us also presume that the second high-outlier is a payroll staff member and that no plausible reason could be obtained in our initial enquiries for the above average increase. Further detailed evidence would be required to determine if this was a valid increase or if it is fraudulent.

Annual Salaries	
20X1	**20X2**
1000	650
1000	1070
1060	1135
1500	1605
1450	1550
1670	1800
1075	1150
1200	1750
1150	1800
1375	1470
1250	1335

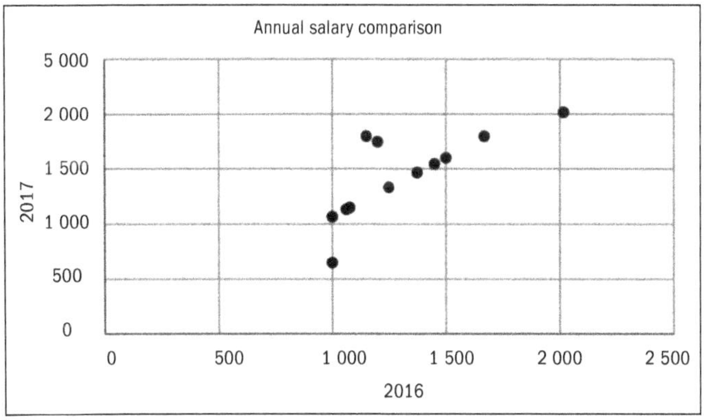

Figure 5.4 *Illustrative graph comparing annual salary increases*

5.8. DATASETS

The following are some examples of datasets that you may want to access in a fraud investigation:

- Financial data – Traditional financial transactional data, financial balances, master files, rates, prices.
- Operational data – Operational movements, master data, production run times and quantities, yields, etc.
- Operator/user information – Operators/users signed on, times signed on, duration signed on, last used, frequency used, machine signed on, place signed on, transactions performed, etc.
- Passwords – Signed on attempts, complexity, last amended, etc.

- E-mail history – Sent to/by, number sent/received, duration of time spent, attachments, subjects, keywords, etc.
- Call/breakout history, IP addresses, durations, other information stored on device, etc.
- To identify sites visited, duration, frequency, data uploaded or downloaded, etc.
- Applications listed, user access per application, versions, frequency of access, compliance to licence requirements, etc.
- History of dates and times, and people who have accessed a physical or virtual record area of a file, record changes (before/after), etc.
- Banking transactional history, medical records, external tables (tax tables, industry-specific tables), etc.
- Metadata is data about data. All machines retain data about the internal working of the machine and the movement of data. Data of this nature can be very useful to an investigator. This data can, however, be large.
- To identify and/or analyse files stored, author, subjects, file types, content, date last amended, nature of amendment, etc.
- Video or audio records, the history of retention, etc.
- Vehicle mileage, duration, access to vehicle, access to high-risk areas driven in, speeds, braking history, service history, consumption, etc.
- Lists of access to records, duration of access, who accessed, when accessed, etc.
- Active directory records, personnel files, customer databases, product files, pricing files, fixed asset registers, etc.
- Company registration data, properties owned, credit application history, etc.

5.9. TOOLS

5.9.1. Introduction

There are numerous good software tools that can be used. The tool used will depend on:

- *Test need*

What is it that you want to test?

- *Test result application*

How will the test result be used eventually? Does the electronically obtained evidence need to stand up in court?

- *Future use*

Do you want to repeat this test in future?

- *Resources available*

What are the technical skills required to perform the test/s?

- *Integrity of the data being tested*

How reliable is the data being tested? How much data is available? Is the data clean or will it require scrubbing?

- *Access to data*

Where is the data stored? What format is the data in? How easy is it to access it? Are there any special interfaces or programs required, etc?

5.9.2. Software categories

The software that is used to conduct data analytics can be divided into the following categories:

- *Specialised/dedicated software*

This is specialised software that has been specifically designed to perform some form of data analysis. This software can generally not be used for any other purpose. The software is generally designed for a purpose (eg analysis of metadata or the analysis of e-mails or general analysis of operating and financial data, etc). Examples of commercially available software include: ACL (Audit Command Language), Idea, SAS, Intella viewer, Analyst Notebook, etc.

- *Reporting tools*

Various standard utilities and/or languages can be used to extract and/or report data. For example: SQL, Click view, etc.

- *Custom programs*

You may wish to write a purpose-built program for a specific test. This would function as a standalone piece of software.

- *Existing programs*

You may want to include logic in an existing program to conduct your analyses. These days the top of the range ERP packages already include some form of analytical ability and or the ability to use exception reporting.

- *Database tools*

Many databases have standard reporting and query functionality built into them that can be harnessed to conduct a form of analyses. Examples of database packages include: Access, Oracle, DB4, etc.

- *Spreadsheets*

Write your own functionality in a spreadsheet to conduct your analysis. For example: Microsoft Excel, etc. Advantages include: the program is easily accessible, commonly known, and user-friendly. Disadvantages include: prone to errors, version control complications, may be used beyond its intended application/for less suited application, record size limitations, standard functionality limitations, can require a lot of manual manipulation, etc.

Spreadsheet functionality is commonly known and a natural first choice for many people commencing with data analytics. This is fine, but there are numerous other limitations which will severely hamper larger datasets and more complex analytics. The functionality of dedicate data analytic software, is on the other hand, relatively unknown and demands considerable effort to become proficient. This can be daunting for non-IT people.

Spreadsheets have built-in intelligence that tries to understand data and put it into a useful form for you. This is great for spreadsheet use but can be problematic when importing data, which you do not want to change the format of. Examples include the fact that when MS Excel tries to recognise numbers it cuts off zeros in the front of a data field. MS Excel also recognises dates and can inadvertently corrupt dates because of regional date formats (US: mm/dd/yyyy, EU: dd/mm/yyyy).

MS Excel, despite having greatly increased the number of lines/rows that it can accommodate, is nevertheless limited by the size of data that it can load. Performance can be severely hampered with too many lines of data. The reason for this is that MS Excel loads the entire dataset into memory and tries to apply its automatic intelligence to the entire dataset all the time. This results in significant delays between steps as MS Excel needs to run its intelligence for each step. This can be extremely frustrating and limiting from a time constraint point of view. A program like ACL on the other hand only creates a view of the dataset. Data is normally loaded in a text format, which is significantly smaller. ACL only loads the first 100 rows or so of data being viewed and loads more data as required. ACL can run directly on Sequel databases dedicated to data analytics. ACL can handle millions of lines of data relatively easily and without significant performance degradation.

5.10. HOW TO USE IT

Before embarking on a specific exercise, gain an understanding of the following:

- *Elements*
  - Get to know the package that you are using - the purpose of the specific software, what it can do, what it cannot do and how to do it.
  - Understand the general elements of data, formats, types, storage medium, how to access it, etc.
  - Acquire the data-mining mindset.
- *Define the need*
  - Define the need for your test.
  - Resist trying to do too much in one batch of tests.
  - Resist test-scope creep.
- *Understand the data flow*

Understand the source/s of the data, the controls at the source, the integrity of the source data, what happens when the program processes the data, where the outputs are sent to, etc. Dataflow diagrams are ideal for visualising dataflows. This will help you to know where to find data and highlight specific data integrity concerns (completeness, accuracy, timeliness of data, etc).

- *Understand the storage of the data*

Understand the number of tables and files in which the data is stored, the database format used, fields available within the tables, physical devices, access conventions/requirements, etc.

- *Plan*

Sketch a broad approach to which data you are going to access, the logic that you are going to apply and how the output will be used. Refer back to this plan throughout the tests to ensure that you remain on track of your goal.

- *Risks*

Define the risks and constraints to your tests. Plan around these.

- *Rules*

Define the rules of the data and the exceptions that you are looking for.

- *Initial download*

Pull the data that is required.

- *Test*

Sample the initial data that was pulled and test to see if it is what is required.

- *Rethink and rerun*

If it is too much, define filters in your extraction script to limit the amount of data pulled (for example limit the date range included).

- *Test*

Again retest the new dataset to see if it fulfils the refined criteria.

- *Analyses*

Define and run analyses to be conducted.

- *Test*

Test the outcome of a sample of analysed data to see if it is complete and accurate and in line with what was required.

- *Rethink, redesign and rerun*

Refer back to the test or original dataset just prior to the analysis which did not produce the required data. Redesign the tests to allow for the exceptions identified and rerun your scripts. Remember data analytics is an iterative process to refine tests until the desired results are achieved.

- *Repeat*

Repeat the rerunning and retesting for every step to ensure the completeness, accuracy and relevance of analyses.

- *Results*

Upon conclusion of your analyses, summarise results of your tests and apply these to the purpose of your test.

- *Record-keeping*

Understand up front what the record-keeping requirements of your test/s will be. Be conservative and document all tests well to ensure that you can:

  - Regress and redress errors and refine tests easily
  - Re-perform tests effortlessly in the future
  - Testify to what you have done
  - Prove your findings easily.

- *Reporting*

Understand how the results of your tests will be reported and used. Ensure that you gather pertinent information, screenshots, etc to assist you in this regard.

The largest portion of your time performing data analytic tests will be spent:

- Finding out what data is available
- Getting the data that you want and in a format that you require
- Understanding the exceptions that you find
- Refining your tests to cater for the exceptions.

Performing the actual tests will occupy the least of your time.

5.11. WHO

Choosing who should perform the test will again depend on a few considerations. Is this something that you must do yourself, can you make use of a colleague in your team, can you use an in-house IT specialist, do you need an external consultant, are there budget constraints, etc? Some considerations to be borne in mind when determining who should perform the tests include:

- *The need for independence*

Do the people giving you the initial data extract have a vested interest in the data? Is there a chance that they may restrict the data given to you or corrupt, taint or clean the data given to you?

- *The need for confidentiality*

What is the need for confidentiality of:

- The data that you are working with?
- Knowledge of the analysis that is being conducted? Is there a surprise element to the analysis? Will people destroy evidence or interfere if they are aware of the investigation?
- Knowledge of the test result: does the test give away your planned case logic before you can present it? Does the test highlight guilty people or people to be investigated, which information may be damaging if known to others?

- *The urgency of the request*

How urgent is the request to conduct the analysis? Can you take the additional time to learn how to perform it yourself?

- *Technical knowledge required/available*

What is the degree of technical or specialised knowledge that is required? That is knowledge of:

- The data analytical package/program to be used
- The field in which the analysis is being performed (engineering, actuarial, banking, etc)
- IT in general (file access, databases, download methods, query language, etc).

- *Recurrence of the test*

If you are going to be performing the test on more than one occasion, determine if there is merit in gaining knowledge of the underlying data analysed and of the software package. This will also ensure that the knowledge is retained within your team and not going to service providers outside your organisation.

- *Subsequent use of the test*

What is the requirement for the subsequent use of the results of the analysis? What is the need to testify as to the chain of evidence and/or the need to testify? Will the analysis serve as evidence and must it be able to stand up in court or in a labour tribunal? Will expert testimony be required? If so, who will be the best suited to do this? This is the person who should conduct the tests.

- *Access to software tools*

Do you have ready access to the tools that are required to conduct the tests or must they still be purchased? Can you justify owning the software in-house? How frequently will the software be used in the future and does the use justify purchasing the package?

- *Resources*

Do you have the budget to cover any costs (consulting fees, licence fees, training, outsourced costs, etc)? Do you have the skills to:
  - Obtain the data
  - Use the software/write the report
  - Analyse it?

5.12. GENERAL

Investing in your own development is important. The question then is whether your deadline and other requirements will allow for this. Many (larger) organisations make use of a separate team of data analysts to conduct their test. Smaller organisations may outsource, co-opt or perform the tests themselves. While the degree of integration will depend on the aforementioned factors, in an ideal situation, a combination of both (own conducted test and use of consultants) is ideal.

The best results are achieved when the person who requires the test results performs the test themselves. The analysis process is an iterative and learning process. The investigator holds the test purpose better in their mind. If you tell a dedicated resource to compare A to B, then that is what they will do and then stop. An investigator may see the applicability of an expanded analysis or of additional data to their broader investigation. The investigator will be able to adapt their thinking more quickly. The investigator is normally limited by the understanding of the data analytic package, though. Getting your investigators involved also reduces the long-term dependency on future specialised resources. I have successfully taught and/or influenced many of my (non-technical) staff members to conduct their own data analytics. There has never been someone to whom I was unable to teach this. I therefore strongly encourage this route.

5.13. PRACTICAL DO'S AND DON'TS

The following are some practical data analytic hints that may assist you when performing data analytics:

- *Ensure the integrity of source data*

Before you start, ensure that you test (normally a sample of) the source data extracted, to ensure the integrity thereof. Not all data mined is received electronically. Some may be manually captured or calculated. Even if it is obtained from an electronic database, there is no guarantee of its integrity. Record the totals (value, record counts, etc) before downloading and test to ensure that they match the final downloaded raw data.

- *Always obtain all the data that you can get*

The problem with data is that you invariably do not know what you want until you need it. Data analytics is an iterative process that involves learning, regression, adjusting and rerunning of tests. If you limit your initial dataset and you subsequently find out halfway through performing your tests that you should have extracted more data, then it may be too late. You will have to restart from the beginning. This wastes time, may result in abandoning the test, etc. The major limitation to this ideal is that most data is very large these days. Some degree of filtering will inevitably be required to ensure that a meaningful amount of data is extracted.

- *Maintain a diary/working papers*

Remember the rules: 'Keep the end-game in mind' and 'He with the most paperwork wins'.

  - If you encounter a problem with one of your tests, how easily will you be able to regress to a point and know what you have done? Good working papers will assist you in this.
  - Will you need to repeat the test now or in the future? Good working papers will prevent too much rework.
  - Do you need to maintain proof of your work done for a supervisor, external audit verification, the police, testimony, etc?
  - Who is going to rely on your work and how will they evidence what you have done?
  - Will you have to testify to the chain of evidence or what you investigated and how?
  - Will you have to report on what you have done or list this later in an affidavit? Good working papers make this an easier exercise after the fact.

As a rule, maintain a diary of what you do while you do it. This does not have to be complicated. It can be a few handwritten chronological telegraphic-style sentences.

- *Never touch the original data*

Never touch your original data that was extracted. Make a copy and work with the copy. This will help you when you have to regress. It can also serve as a start baseline for comparison.

- *File versions*

Save versions (tabs or files) per test step performed. Limit each step to a single test/event. Do not try to conduct multiple tests in one file or perform multiple steps in a single file instance. Perform one test step at a time and save it as a next version before moving on. This might seem like overkill, but it is an important and very practical step. For example:

  - Test/version 1 - Join file A and B based on employee number.
  - Test/version 2 - Sort on employee number.
  - Test/version 3 - Extract all employees with a category 'Y' number.

- *File-naming convention*

Do not make use of 'file 1, file 2' or 'version 1, version 2' type file names. It is very difficult to know after the fact what element of the data analysis is contained in a file called 'version 3.2', for example. There are almost no file-naming limitations with modern software. Use therefore a predefined naming convention and ensure that you use English-type names that describe the nature of the test element saved. For example:

- 1.1_Master_Data_Extract
- 1.2_Sort_Master_Data_Extract_on_employee
- 1.3_Join_Pay_rate_File_on_empl_No_to_Master_Data_sort

In this manner, it is very easy to know exactly what was done in file 1.3 by just looking at the file name.

- *Confirm the completeness and accuracy of data as you go*

Reconcile record totals of your source data and the extracted data to ensure that you have downloaded all records. When you save subsequent versions and/or when you do extracts and merges, ensure that all data is transferred. After you have performed a step, go back and draw a sample of your test results and confirm manually that they are correct. Record your checks in your data analytics diary/working papers.

- *Do not presume anything*

Do not presume that people understand what you know or what you require. Our rule, 'How long is a piece of string?' refers. In many cases, you will instruct others to conduct analyses on your behalf or in line with their investigation. These people may be your own staff members or from management. Your skills and experience, as a fraud investigator, will help you to know what to do fairly quickly. Fraud investigation is however not a common skillset and other organisational members will not always be able to know what to do. After all, that is why the organisation hires specialists like you. Ensure, when asking someone to obtain data or to conduct analyses that you:

  - Explicitly explain what you require.
  - Give examples and/or demonstrate what is required.
  - Define the objectives and goals, list the end product and specify success criteria.
  - Get them to explain your requirements back to you in their own words.
  - Put your requirements in writing.
  - Check their understanding and progress at regular intervals.
  - Clarify and/or intervene as required.
  - Are available for them to clarify as required.

5.14. A BACKGROUND TO DATA

You are going to have to learn a little about the more technical aspects of data in order to do well with data analytics. The following are some areas you will need to become familiar with:

- *Types*

Try to learn what the difference is between views and tables. This is discussed below. Understand what the following are:

  - Fields
  - Records
  - Tables
  - Views
  - Files
  - Objects
  - Databases.

- *Data formats*

Some examples include:
  - Numeric - numerous formats available
  - Date or time
  - Character or text
  - Logical
  - ASCII.

- *Access*

How do you get to the data? Do you make use of:
  - An open database connectivity (ODBC) connection (this is a universal connection/interface convention)
  - External drives
  - Standard utility
  - File format (text)?

- *Need for independence*

The need for independence of data may be defined by numerous aspects, including:

- *Integrity of data*

If, for example, you want to test the integrity of a supplier database, it will not serve the purpose if you request the creditors' database administrator to give you an Excel format extract of the supplier database. This is because she will be able to delete all fictitious suppliers on the database and give you a clean file without you being the wiser. Management may also not want you to identify errors and place them in a potentially bad light. It will be ideal if you can use, for example, an IT person who is remote and who does not have a vested interest in the transactions. This will provide the best chance of obtaining the full/true records requested. What is the need for confidentiality and/or the requirement for the element of surprise? Can the confidentiality requirements be satisfied based on the person you are requesting to extract the data? What is the anticipated future use of the test and/or data? If you need to re-perform the test frequently, then it may be best to learn how to extract the data yourself.

- *Data privacy constraints*

Most countries have strict data privacy requirements. Determine what the data privacy requirements are in the geography that you are working. Adapt your tests to ensure that you comply with local and international (UK, EU or US) requirements.

5.14.1. Views and tables

Understanding the source from which you are extracting the data is vital. As far as possible extract your data from the original source files. Do not extract the data from a data warehouse or a report file.

Databases are made up of numerous tables of data. A view is a file that has been created to give a combined view of the underlying data in a defined format that was required when the view was created. The very reason for creating a view of data tables is that not all data was required in the final view. The program logic used to create this view will therefore already exclude certain data not required by the programmer in their initial view. If you perform an extract from their view, then you are limiting the available fields and records from which to extract. You are essentially getting an extract of an extract. It is frequently difficult to identify a person who can reliably tell you what the logic was that was used to create to view originally.

As a rule, therefore, do not extract from data warehouses, even if people tell you that it is fine. Data warehouses may only retain specific elements of data that were deemed necessary at the time of creation of the data warehouse. The excluded data may be required by you.

You will frequently be told when requesting more specific data that the data does not exist or it cannot be done. This is because the people to whom you are making the request are used to using a particular report or they only have knowledge of a few views of data that they use in their daily tasks. They are unaware of the concept of views. If the data field does not exist in the view that they are used to looking at, then they conclude that your request is impossible. It may however very well be available from the source data. You will need to learn to be persistent with it comes to obtaining the right data.

The diagram below shows a view of three data source tables with only the data required in the view that was created.

Staff No.	Name	Date Eng	Date Term
10023	E Clapton		
10024	J Brown		
10030	A Young		
10033	B Tyler		
10035	C Norris		
10059	W Smith		
10060	R Waters		

Staff No.	Rate Date	Pay Rate
10023		
10024		
10030		
10033		
10035		
10059		
10060		

Staff No.	Date Eng	Pay Rate	Medical
10023			
10024			
10030			
10033			
10035			
10059			
10060			

Staff No.	Dependents	Pension	Medical	Tax
10023				
10024				
10030				
10033				
10035				
10059				
10060				

Figure 5.5 *An illustration of a view of multiple data tables*

5.15. PER ASSIGNMENT

Per assignment ensure that you understand:

- *Fields available*

Which fields are available? How can these assist you with your analysis?

- *Field character length*

How many characters make up the field?

- *Field separators*

How are the various fields separated in the table, for example: spaces, commas, etc?

- *Primary and secondary keys*

A primary key is the major field (eg employee number) that is the link between files/tables. For example, let us presume that we have three payroll tables, namely: A. demographics, B. pay rates and C. pay history. The first record in each of the files in this example is the employee number that corresponds to the record. The employee number will be the primary record to link all three files together. When joining, merging or using look-up logic in the analysis, you will create the logic that goes to look up the pay rate in file B based on the employee number, being the primary key between the files.

- *Which tables exist*

Which tables exist and what is the difference between them? What was the logic of creating different tables?

- *Electronic rules*

What are the normal electronic rules applied by the program? This will point to the logic of the program and the requirements of the business process. These are the types of data exceptions that are normally stumbled upon as you progress through the iterative refinement of your data analytic tests. An example is given below of such exceptions.

- *Exceptions*

What are the exceptions in the general program logic or data? Try to anticipate these in advance. These exceptions are not errors. They are the different types of data that you will find in the table. It is normal to commence your data analysis with a limited knowledge of the exceptions. As per above, you will identify anomalies when analysing the results of the test. You will then need to regress your tests back to the point where these exceptions can be taken into account. For example: let us assume that we are testing the automated calculation of an amount. Let's presume we find additional amounts that do not match our recalculated results. Inspection identifies that all these unmatched amounts have a "J" indicator. Discussion with the programmer tells you that the accountants process manual journals (indicated with a "J") at month-end. In this case, your test is focussed on testing the automated calculation. You then regress back to your initial extract and exclude all records with the "J" indicator. You then rerun your recalculation and comparison. If you had known this up front, then you could have saved a lot of time.

- *Key field indicators*

As per our previous example: a "J" in a particular column may mean that the transaction was processed by virtue of a manual journal, etc... Sit with the programmer and work through a few examples of actual data in tables to identify different indicators upfront.

- *Understand the convention of fields*

For example: the first three characters are the country abbreviation, the next three characters represent the town name, etc... ABDUK001 = Aberdeen, UK, company 001.

5.16. OTHER

Furthermore, it will also assist you greatly to understand the following:

- *Query language*

Most extracts from systems (into your data analytic software) will require some form of instruction written in an extract program/language, for example using SQL (Standard Query Language) to extract data. This is not very difficult and a commonly used functionality. It takes a bit of getting used to and I suggest that you begin to understand the conventions of the language/utility to be used. Even when you are in a data analytics program (like ACL) SQL knowledge will assist you to write expressions (these are like formulae in Microsoft Excel).

- *General logic*

There are some general data analytic concepts that you will need to understand as well, including:

  - *Concatenate*

    To concatenate means to add two separate fields (eg ABC and 123) together to form one new field (eg ABC123). The benefit of this is that the combination of the two fields in the one field may give you the unique indicator that you require to identify the records you want.

  - *Merge*

    To merge means to mix. For example, let us presume that we are going to merge file 1 and 2. What typically happens is that the data analytic program (for example ACL) looks to see which records match (based on the primary key) between two files (1 & 2). A new file (3) is then created with the records in file 1 that match to those in file 2. The records from file 2 are brought into file 3, for example:

File 1

Employee No	Sex	Age
12443	M	45
26899	F	36
37796	M	33

File 2

Employee No	Pay rate
12443	10/hr
37796	12/hr
77832	10/hr

File 3

Employee No	Sex	Age	Pay rate
12443	M	45	10/hr
37796	M	33	12/hr

It is possible to list the files that match, the files that do not match or a combination thereof. The nature of your test will determine which records you include or exclude.

- *Join*

A join requires the records in the respective files to be the same (same headings) in the two files. The join simply appends the records of file A to the bottom of the records in file B to create file C. The file structures need to be the same, though.

- *Expressions*

An expression in data analytic software is like a formula used in a spreadsheet. There are too many different expressions to mention here. Purpose-built data analytic software (like ACL) has many standard expressions. You are also able to build your own expressions. Get to know the most common expressions in the package that you are using. These packages are very sophisticated and it is unlikely that they will not have standard functionality to perform most basic tests.

- *A string*

A string is a data record made up of different fields. For example: '12443,M,45,10'. The different fields will be separated according to a predefined convention (a comma in this case).

- *Spreadsheets*

In spreadsheets it will greatly assist you if you can master the following concepts:

- *Sort functionality*

For example, sorting records in a file from largest to smallest or vice versa, etc.

- *V-lookups*

This is the functionality that looks up the first record in a table (in the most left-hand column of, say, spreadsheet 1 – S#1) in another specified table (say in spreadsheet 2 – S#2). If the record can be found in S#2 then the record in a specified column in the table in which it was looked up is brought back into the initial table (S#1).

- *'If statements'*

Use 'if statements' for more than the obvious. As an example, data is sometimes in a report format when you bring it into a spreadsheet from a database. The report breaks headings and totals up, which does not allow for sorting and extraction of data once in a spreadsheet. To eliminate this, insert a column and make use of an 'if statement' to extract the data that you want into the new column. Your 'if statement' will test to see if criteria specified by you are satisfied before placing the data in your inserted column by adding a text note (eg 'include'). Then make use of the 'copy-paste-special-values' functionality to remove formulae and sort the spreadsheet to float the 'include' fields to the top and delete unwanted data.

- *Text to columns*

This is used when you bring test files from other applications into a spreadsheet. This functionality helps you to put strings of data into columns in the spreadsheet. If you do not use this functionality all data in the string will appear in a single column. The text to columns allows you to break the string up into columns based on the string separation criterion or based on your own selection.

- *Left, mid and right*

These formulae look at the records in a specific place within a field. Either:

  - X-number of records from the left
  - X-number of records in the middle from a defined start to a defined end
  - X-number of records from the right.

You may want to use these in combination with an 'If formula'. As an example: see the formula: =If(mid2,3>C3,'test',' '). In this case, you are checking if the middle 3 records starting from record 2 are greater than the value in C3. If this is true then mark the records to be tested, otherwise leave the cell blank.

- *Pivot tables*

A pivot table is like a big pre-defined formula. It combines and summarises records as specified by you. This is a very powerful tool and one that you will use frequently in data analysis.

- *Concatenate*

As discussed previously, this entails the joining of the information in two separate cells into one new cell. For example: 'ABC' in cell A1 is joined to '123' in cell B1 to be 'ABC123' in cell C1.

- *Conditional formatting*

This is a type of a filter or manner to mark specific records that comply with specified conditions. Conditions could include values equal to a predefined value, greater than/ less than a range, which comply with the results of a formula, etc. The conditions are set per column in the spreadsheet.

- *Filters*

This is a standard functionality which can be switched on per column in a spreadsheet. You will then be able to select or deselect specific data in the spreadsheet based on the filter of one column. For example: click on the year column and select '20X2'. Only the records with 20X2 will then be visible to you in the filtered spreadsheet. You can use more than one filter. The spreadsheet will filter based on the sequence of filters enabled. Filters can include ranges of numbers greater than, less than or based on the result of a formula. The underlying data is still available; it is just not visible. The view of all data is restored as soon as you remove all filters or specific filters. Filters are good for quick tests, but they are not retained if tests are adjusted. It is better to save separate tests for test evidence reasons.

- *Graphs*

Graphs give us a picture of the progression of figures over time or in relation to themselves. A graph is very helpful to demonstrate a trend. A single graph can also make use of multiple scales (say value and volume) within the same graph to show the relationship of two or more aspects that cannot be compared based on their respective scales only.

You are encouraged, most importantly, to learn from others. Each person has their own style and they are used to doing different things in Excel or in their respective data analytic programs. If you are looking over someone's shoulder, do not let them progress to the next phase unless you have understood what they have done, how they did it and why they did it in that way. In this way, you will be able to add tools to your skillset.

In one company, we tried to challenge each other to see if we could give the other an impossible task to perform in Excel. We never encountered a challenge that we could not perform in Excel. That is where my two 'rules of Excel' were coined. These can be applied to any data analytic software/ situation:

- *If you can think of it, Microsoft Excel can do it*
  You are only limited by your own imagination.
- *Just because you cannot think how to do it, does not mean that Excel cannot do it*
  A bad workman blames his tools. Do not blame the program or the IT infrastructure.

- *Repeatable*

Consider if the test is to be repeated. For example: will this be a monthly or annual test that you are going to perform or is it a once-off test? Even if this is a once-off test, you are strongly recommended to type your data analytics in 'scripts'. Scripts are similar to 'Macros' in Excel. Scripts are essentially programs (short programmed instruction/logic) that can be rerun at a later stage. Scripts also help when you need to regress and adapt your initial analysis/tests in response to refinements that you invariably need to make. In this case, the script will allow you to go back into the script itself and amend the script. You will then be able to rerun the script, hopefully with improved results. It is rare that your logic will be correct the first time. You may, therefore, have to regress to a specific point to recommence to correct errors/add additional criteria in the initial attempt.

- *Time*

If you are writing fraud or risk identification queries, then do not try to do too much the first time. Do one or two tests well and then add to your arsenal of tests in subsequent periods. If you are doing a forensic investigation, prioritise the most important tests first, as far as possible. Do not perform all the tests possible. Focus on your main goal first. Performing data analytics takes a lot of time to conduct; time to:

- Identify, design and devise the tests
- Identify, understand and obtain access to the data that you require
- Obtain all the data that you require in the format that you require
- Run the analysis test/scripts
- Analyse outcomes
- Document what you have done and what your outcome was.

Choose wisely. Also ensure that you manage expectations of how much you can do, what your current analysis does and what it does not. Manage any expectations of your tests with others.

- *Regress and rework*

  Do not think that you are going to get your first analysis right the first time. In fact, do not think that you will ever get any data analysis that you perform right the first time. That only happens in Hollywood crime detection movies. Data analytics is an iterative process of trying, learning, adjusting and retrying.

- *IT dependency*

  A final piece of advice: keep your IT helpdesk on speed dial. But as far as possible, break the dependency on IT. If you can build your IT knowledge this will save you time long-term and save you a lot of rework. You will, however, be quite dependent on their input until you build your own knowledge.

5.17. ELECTRONIC COMMUNICATION SEARCHES

5.17.1. Introduction

Much communication is conducted via e-mail and text on computers and other mobile devices. Fraudsters also make use of these communication methods and as such, they are of interest to fraud investigators.

Fraud investigators typically spend a lot of time analysing e-mails. E-mail searches can be very useful to identify previously unknown information and to gather facts and evidence. Communication on other mobile devices may be less accessible to the fraud investigator than organisation-controlled e-mail servers. This as the devices may be privately owned (privacy laws may prevail), run over networks to which the organisation does not have access or be organisation owned but not accessible to fraud investigators (may require the physical device).

The analysis of any electronic communication, while deploying different methods and tools, follows the same principles. We are going to talk primarily here about e-mail communication, but the principles apply to all electronic communication.

5.17.2. E-mail searches

The analysing of the content of e-mails forms part of detailed investigations and is discussed in Chapter 3 on conducting an investigation. E-mail searches are mentioned here from a completeness point of view, as there can be a data analytic purpose to the searching of e-mails. A data analytic analysis of e-mails would concentrate less on the content of specific e-mails and be more focused on the pattern of communication.

The data analytic search of e-mails would analyse greater volumes of e-mails to identify trends and exceptions. The data analytic searches of e-mails would, if required, precede the analysis of the content of specific e-mails and/or be used to identify those e-mails to be searched in greater detail. The subjects may or may not be aware of the analysis at the time.

An example of the data analysis of emails is the analysis of the e-mail communication traffic between all the members of a tender committee, all the organisational procurement officers and all parties external to the organisation. Let us presume that our analysis showed that there was an increased level of e-mail traffic just prior to bid submission between one of the tender committee members and the organisation's procurement officers and also between the same procurement officer and one of the bidders. This would raise the concern that the bidder may be receiving competitor bid information from the tender committee member via the procurement officer. A more detailed content e-mail search would determine the nature of the correspondence and if anything untoward had occurred.

5.17.3. Need

Electronic communication can be analysed to:

- Proactively identify fraud that has occurred/is occurring
- Profile fraudsters
- Obtain information about fraudsters and their dealings
- Obtain evidence as to the perpetration of wrongdoing
- Identify communication patterns.

5.17.4. Confidentiality

Not all countries have the same legislation with regards to electronic communication searches. As a general rule, companies may access work-related e-mails under the following conditions:

- A company must have a legitimate reason for reviewing electronic communication. This is in terms of who the subjects of an investigation are, as well as the specific communication to be searched. The search cannot be a general 'fishing expedition'.
- There should also not be another less invasive method to conduct the investigation.
- The employee must give their permission that the company may search their electronic communication. This may be express permission per incident or it may be demonstrated in the signing of their employment contract with a clause to the effect that their electronic communication can be searched. Alternatively, they may sign the organisation's IT policy.
- Organisations should avoid reviewing or accessing private communications.
- The organisation should maintain an audit trail of the decision and approval of the access as well as of the searches conducted.

5.18. PROCESS

Select a tool most suited to the communication method to be searched. External forensic service providers will be able to advise you of the latest tools, costs and ease of use. E-mail analyses are a regular and fruitful tool in the forensic suite of tools. It makes sense, therefore, to try to have a tool in place (at least for e-mail searches) and trained resources prior to using such a tool. This will provide an opportunity to take care of authorisation and policy issues in advance. It will also be an ideal opportunity to resolve budget and become proficient.

5.19. SOCIAL MEDIA SEARCHES

5.19.1. Introduction

The modern generation is obsessed with airing all aspects of their lives on social media platforms. This is both scary (that people are willing to do this and from the point of view of how vulnerable they make themselves) and represents a good opportunity for us, as fraud investigators, to obtain information otherwise unattainable in a non-social media society.

The good thing about social media is that much of the information placed on these platforms is in the public domain or is accessible through known public exploits. Data privacy and access to information rules are vital. Only embark on such searches under the guidance of a professional/reputable firm (like big four accounting firms) and/or legal counsel.

5.19.2. Need

The purpose of conducting social media searches may be to:

- Track subjects' movements
- Locate subjects
- Profile subjects based on their social media behaviour
- Obtain lifestyle information about subjects (where funds were spent, holidays, hunting trips, vehicles owned, properties owned, hobbies, habits and vices, etc)
- Obtain evidence of statements made, groups associated with, knowledge of an event, etc.
- Identify known associates and possible collaborators or co-conspirators
- Show geographic preferences (countries frequently visited where funds may be stored, places where similar crimes may have been perpetrated, where associates may be, under which countries' rules the subject may fall, etc).

5.19.3. Process

As with any data analyses, commence by defining the purpose of your tests. Next, define the tool/s required to perform such a test and method to be followed. Determine how these tools can be obtained (purchased) or the use of them can be acquired (by contracting a specialist forensic service provider to perform the tests).

Conduct the searches according to the search plan and reflect on the results in terms of your search objective and investigation hypothesis. Amend and refine searches as required. Utilise results in interviews and to build evidence in the investigation or to initiate subsequent actions, as required.

CHAPTER 6

LIFESTYLE AUDITS

6.1. CHAPTER OVERVIEW AND INTRODUCTION

The logic of a lifestyle audit is that there are indicators reflected in a person's lifestyle that could highlight that a person/group of people is/are:

- More likely to be tempted to engage in misconduct/fraudulent acts. This can be used from a fraud risk management point of view to identify fraudulent acts that have already happened, that are still happening or that could potentially occur.
- Most likely, out of a wider group of people, to be involved in misconduct/fraud that has been identified. This can be used for fraudulent acts that have already been identified as having occurred/occurring.
- Already engaged in fraudulent acts unbeknown to the victim organisation. This can be used for fraudulent acts that are occurring unidentified. These are potentially the most concerning type.

Lifestyle audits can be very valuable in an investigation in identifying fraud or proving that a fraudulent act has occurred.

In this chapter, we discuss the different type of lifestyle audits as well as the requirements for performing these. We then have an in-depth discussion, supported by practical examples, on how to perform high-level and detailed lifestyle audits.

The purpose of this chapter is to provide you with an overview of the possible application of lifestyle audits as well as to equip you with the necessary tools and awareness of information sources to be able to conduct meaningful lifestyle audits.

6.2. TYPES

The subsequent use of the information from the lifestyle audit will define the type and/or extent of lifestyle audit carried out.

Remember the rule: 'People always do and say things for a reason.' In line with this rule, we note that there are general behaviours that may indicate deception and/or involvement in misconduct/fraud. These are covered in a fair degree of detail in Chapter 4 on interviews. These will not be discussed again here, except to say that you may want to note suspicious (and potentially deceitful) behaviours to supplement the lifestyle profile that you will build whilst conducting a lifestyle audit.

There are indicators that have a link (directly or indirectly) to some form of financial or other aspect that will indicate a person's probability of or actual involvement in misconduct and/or fraud. These are the indicators that we will discuss in this chapter under the following three categories of lifestyle audits:

- *Proactive*

This is the type of lifestyle audit that you will conduct to proactively identify:

  - Fraud that is otherwise unknown
  - The people who are most likely to perpetrate fraud - these are people who should be observed more closely and/or represent areas of control which require bolstering
  - The people who are actually already perpetrating fraudulent acts.

- *Profile (Reactive)*

Once a matter has come to light, the people involved may be unknown. Lifestyle audits can be used to identify who in a wider group is under financial pressure and who is the most likely to need to fund their lifestyle from unknown or illegitimate sources. As is discussed in detail later, this in itself is not evidence. It is merely a rough guide to help you decide on whom to concentrate on first to determine if there is any corroborating evidence of their untoward behaviour.

- *Proof (Reactive)*

This is the type of lifestyle audit that you will conduct once a fraud has been detected and once there is a strong indication of who the perpetrator/s is/are. This sort of lifestyle audit is a detailed review of the lifestyles of specific people who are suspected of being involved in the fraud. The objective is to prove that their lifestyle was funded from sources other than their known/declared income. There have been numerous high-profile cases where this has been used successfully. I have also used this sort of lifestyle audit to great effect.

6.3. GETTING STARTED

As a rule, always build some form of profile of the people whom you are investigating. Do this regardless of the fact that you may be certain of who is involved (possibly by way of an admission or highly compelling evidence). Elect to conduct the lifestyle audit in more or less detail and with more or less formality. The logic is that you may rely more or less on this profile later in the investigation depending on how conclusive the other evidence you obtain is. The aforementioned three lifestyle audit categories are discussed below:

6.3.1. Prediction

In Chapter 1 on strategic fraud risk management, we covered the proactive and reactive aspects of a forensic function. As mentioned above, lifestyle audits can be used in a proactive, predictive manner as well as in a reactive manner.

In one organisation in which I worked, we identified key positions and/or people in the organisation who were deemed to be 'high fraud risks'. 'High fraud risk' was defined as those jobs/people that were:

- Most likely to be approached to engage in misconduct/fraud. For example: public- or client-facing, with influence over business.
- Traditional areas associated with fraud and corruption. For example: procurement officers.
- Those areas in the organisation in which if fraud occurred, the organisation would sustain the highest losses. For example: treasury function.

The idea was that we performed a public domain lifestyle audit of all the people in these positions every six months. We told the organisation what we were going to do and we agreed on the list of people and jobs to be included in the exercise. We then asked the main board of directors, as a show of transparency and commitment, to subject themselves to the lifestyle audit first. The board did this and other than a few uncomfortable, reluctant moments, it worked extremely well.

We also ensured that we had an up-to-date conflict of interest policy in place and we communicated to everyone in the organisation what they are permitted to do and that they should make declarations to the contrary in line with this policy. This ensured that there was a known rule in place thereby strengthening any subsequent cases in so far as staff members identified as being in contravention to this policy could be referred to the opportunity to make declarations that they chose not to exercise.

The benefits derived from this exercise included the following aspects:

- It created awareness of what the rules were.
- It created deterrence for people contemplating engaging in misconduct of this kind.
- It highlighted those people actually in direct contravention (for example: with known directorships in rival companies).
- It identified people under financial pressure that should be watched to see if there were any corroborating indicators to suggest that they were engaged in misconduct.

The one that (almost) got away: *Some time later (in the same group) it was brought to our attention that a buying executive (who was part of one of the smaller companies in the group that were not included in this exercise) was running his own property investment company. While this was a retail concern and property investment was not in competition to the core business, we found out that he was playing two of the company's major suppliers off against each other in his private investment company. This put the retail company at high risk that these suppliers (on whom the company was dependent) may withdraw if the suppliers are associated with the retail company with the unethical conduct. The buying executive was confronted with the conflict of interest and dismissed after due process. The company managed to restore the relationship with the suppliers without disruption to its activities.*

The point of mentioning this example is that we could have highlighted the conflict in advance and addressed it sooner if we had extended the lifestyle audit to include this company as well. Proactive lifestyle audits can, therefore, be used to manage fraud risks in advance.

6.4. PROFILING

Profiling is the process of drafting a 'picture' of a person or group of people in relation to predefined criteria. The initial information that we utilise in the profile is quite wide and not necessarily 'lifestyle' in nature.

Profiling can have three purposes, namely:

6.4.1. Profiling of individual/s

For the purpose of identifying the most likely person/people to be involved in misconduct/fraud. When fraud is detected, the full extent of the fraud and all those involved may not be known. Even if some of the perpetrators are known, it would be prudent to consider possible involvement by others. As an example: A fraudulent payment has been identified in an office with ten staff members. Who of the ten staff members were involved? Lifestyle audits assist in the task of understanding who was involved in the fraud and to what degree.

Commence by obtaining background information on each of the staff members in the office from an independent, reliable source that is in the circle of trust about the incident. For example, if the local MD is aware of the fraud investigation, ask them for a short background on each of the ten finance staff members mentioned in our example. There are also wider sources of the background information which can be sourced. These are discussed in detail in the list of examples below. Further insights may be gained subsequently through:

- Information-seeking interviews
- Conducting polygraphs and interpreting and applying the results
- Analysis of:
    - job descriptions, organisational diagrams - to show who has the responsibility for the areas under review
    - documents and transactions – to show who the author, performer or approver of documents was and therefore who had knowledge of the fraudulent transaction/s
    - electronic information analysis - to show the transactional history of who the system has recorded as the author of a transaction
    - access logs, video footage and telephone records - to show who was available to have perpetrated it.

Use this information to build a profile of:

- Who the most likely people are to be involved in the misconduct/fraud (remember our rule, 'it is always the people who are the closest')
- Who might be a friend and who might be an enemy (and therefore who is more likely to provide credible evidence)
- Early indications of loyalties (to the organisation or between perpetrators)
- Who is the most and who is the least likely to provide you with information
- Who should be trusted and who should not
- The most likely sequence of interviews
- Any other evidence that you should obtain.

Chapter 3 on conducting an investigation refers for greater detail on investigative steps. Continue to build on these profiles as you progress; this is described below. Use this process if you are trying to identify the possible perpetrators as well as if you know who is involved. If nothing else, and even if the perpetrator has been identified, the information gives you a better understanding of the individual/s with whom you are dealing.

6.4.2. Profiling of specific subject/s

Once the subject/s has/have been identified to some degree of certainty and in order to understand the make-up of the subject/s and/or their lifestyles, it may be necessary to understand the subject's lifestyle in greater detail and how this is financed. This information may be useful:

- For general interest
- To understand the subject's motives
- To identify places where funds may have been sourced
- To identify friends and people who could have information on the subject/subject's activities
- To identify places where funds could have been applied, for example property held in other people's names, relationships with companies owned, etc
- For input into a detailed lifestyle audit - discussed in detail below.

6.4.3. Profiling of groups of people/subjects

For the purpose of understanding the relationship between subjects, general people and companies. The first use of profiling discussed was to identify potential subjects. The second use was to analyse specific subjects. The third use, discussed here, is to understand the relationships between:

- Subjects (may be multiple)
- Subjects and other people or organisations
- Organisations.

Understanding the relationships between subjects will, again, help you to understand:

- Potential sources of incomes
- Motives
- Methods/avenues used (for example payments made via a particular organisation)
- Potential places where incomes have been applied or where assets may be hidden
- The loyalties that may be at play
- Other perpetrators previously unknown
- Places where information can be obtained. Suppliers and outside companies and people may be totally unaware of the subject's schemes. These people, once informed, will be more than willing to cooperate and provide valuable information.

Relationships between people could be family, friendship or business-related. They could also be legalistic relationships (director of a company) or asset owners (registered owners).

The best method to depict this is to first obtain the information and documents that show potential relationships exist. These may also be required in support of the hypotheses that you will build later (Chapter 3 on structuring the investigation refers). Then summarise these in a relationship-type diagram (such as a mind-map). Specialist software may also be used to depict relationships. Examples of such software are Analyst Notebook and Netmap. You generally do not need expensive software if you are only dealing with one or two subjects with minimal information.

These software programs are generally expensive and it may be difficult to justify purchasing a licence if you are going to have limited use from the software. Consulting firms typically hold licences to such software and it may be cheaper for you to pay a usage fee once in a while, as opposed to buying the software outright.

The software is the most useful when there is a lot of data, such as thousands of telephone records. The software's algorithms can detect patterns in thousands of rows of transactions/data that the naked eye could not detect.

It is recommended that you always draw a mind-map or spider-type relationship diagram of all the pieces of information that you have, even if you do not think that there is a relationship. You will be surprised when, after having summarised the information, the trends that you previously overlooked just seem to appear on the page. A so-called 'aha' or 'light-bulb' moment.

6.5. PROOF

The final use of the information from a lifestyle audit is to be used as evidence and/or proof of fraud. This is only achieved by the subsequent detailed analysis of legally obtained transactional information. This process is also discussed below.

The detailed lifestyle analysis may detect illicitly obtained benefits. It most times proves that the person's lifestyle could not have been funded from their known normal and/or declared legal income.

6.6. LEGAL REQUIREMENTS

6.6.1. Introduction

Conducting lifestyle audits can be tricky from a legal point of view. Lifestyle audits also have a stigma attached to them, related to 'spying' on individuals. The professional, ethical and legal conduct of these must be managed. Even if information is in the public domain, no one likes someone looking at their information. The real reason is that no one likes being investigated and/or be suspected of being involved in misconduct even if they are totally innocent. It can be very demoralising to know that someone is watching you. This is a perfectly normal reaction.

With regards to the obtaining of information, we all know a friend who knows a friend who has access to information. While this might be a great manner to get information quickly, do not obtain information illegally and never use illegally obtained information. There may be many dire consequences for you, your organisation and your investigation if you do this. Even if you do not get caught, it is unethical. Fraud investigators are the custodians of ethical investigations. Our rule, 'Queensbury rules apply' refers in this regard.

6.6.2. Policy

Other than the predictive approach described above, it is unlikely that a company will have a policy on conducting lifestyle audits. The country in which you operate will have laws that regulate access to information and cover the right to privacy. Always ensure that you operate within the ambit of the law of the geography in which you are operating, and within the bounds of company policy, regardless of whether you agree with these or not. Rather comply and try to amend policy/ attitudes through other means (education, discussion and approval).

Some companies include an addendum to their employment contracts saying that they have a right to investigate employees, or a similar paragraph in their conflict of interest policy or disciplinary code. This can be helpful to remind subjects of when they become difficult and uncooperative.

You may have trouble convincing management that the organisation should conduct lifestyle audits (proactive or reactive). Any such request is normally met with understandable caution, given the stigma and many publicised examples of the illegal use of information. Most agree to the strictly legal and ethical conduct after hearing your explanation.

Do not preclude the fact that there may be hidden motives lurking behind the reasons offered by some management for not wanting to perform lifestyle audits. Perhaps this job has just made me too suspicious over the years, but a person cannot help to wonder if they were concerned that this may be used against them at a later stage and perhaps they feel the need to head it off before it becomes institutionalised. Management may just be acting within the strict privacy laws of their respective countries.

Suspicions aside, you will need to identify allies (who are open to the suggestion of conducting lifestyle audits) to support you in your quest. It can be quite frustrating knowing that you have a tool that is out of your reach because of people's fear or lack of understanding.

Management may be more open to the idea of conducting a lifestyle audit if they are still hurting from a 'fresh' fraud and want swift and decisive action/retribution. Also, success breeds success. If you are able to convince them to allow one lifestyle audit that delivers results and demonstrates ethical conduct, then they will be more open to considering future use thereof.

Lifestyle audits typically evoke an emotive reaction, so you are advised to inform your seniors that you intend to conduct a lifestyle audit or that it is a tool that you use regularly. Try to get principle approval so that you do not need to get approval for each investigation. Get the permission in writing or confirm your thanks for the permission via an e-mail to your senior. This may be required to protect you later if there are adverse reactions from others who were uninvolved in the process. You also cannot always trust that those who gave you the authorisation will stand up and defend you and/or admit that they were the ones who authorised the audit.

6.6.3. Permission

In most countries, if you have grounds from reasonable suspicion, you have the right (in accordance with the laws) to investigate people without their knowledge. Even if you suspend a person, pending the outcome of an investigation, there is no need to give them the full details of what is known to you at that point and your anticipated methods. This may not be the case in all countries in which you conduct investigations and you are advised to understand local requirements.

Invariably, public domain information is insufficient to give you the full insights into a subject's lifestyle that you may wish to have. Corruption cases are often reliant on this sort of analysis. In that case, get the subject to agree in an interview to a give you permission to:

- Conduct specialised searches that may require their permission (for example criminal records, vehicle ownership, etc)
- Access bank statement details.

The unfortunate thing is that people change their minds, so ask them to sign at the time they give their permission. If they promise you copies of their bank statements, then drive with them to their house or to their bank immediately and obtain the copies, give them a computer and ask them to download them. Pay the bank administrative fees if you need to. Remember the most important rule of forensics: 'Secure the evidence.' This will avoid disappointment. Also remember the rule: 'The best time to do something is immediately.'

Annexure 6.1 attached hereto is an example of a form that can be used to obtain written permission from prospective candidates for pre-employment screening. This form can be adapted to obtain written permission from subjects to be included in investigations if required. Alternatively, it can be adapted for inclusion in contracts of employment at the time of employment or as an addendum later.

6.6.4. Subjects

If you are transparent and honest about lifestyle audits, then people will accept them. They may not like them, but they will accept them. These are a little like security checks at the airport. We do not like being searched, but we are happy that the authorities are looking for dangerous and illegal items.

The following are examples of justifications and motivations that could be provided to the subjects of lifestyle reviews to gain their cooperation and to put them at ease:

- I understand that this is a difficult situation for you and I very much appreciate your assistance in this regard.
- We are not only focusing on you. We need to treat all people fairly and consistently. This is why you are included in this part of our review of the discrepancies.
- We cannot discriminate against certain people and you must therefore also be included in the search.
- We only consider information in the public domain and/or information that you volunteer.
- This information is restricted to those involved in the investigation.
- The information will not be publicised.
- We will request clarity from you, as required and you will have an opportunity to explain should it be necessary.
- But you have explained that you have not done anything wrong so this will be a pure formality and you have nothing to fear.
- If you have any conflicts to declare, you have an opportunity now to make such disclosures.
- If we find conflicts that you did not declare this will be seen in a serious light and may invoke the company's disciplinary code.
- I have to, despite declarations made by you, corroborate any declarations that you make to me. This process will allow me an opportunity to do this.
- The lifestyle audit cannot in itself indicate wrongdoing.

- In the face of any persistent objection: It is within the organisation's rights to conduct this sort of analysis and I do not require your consent (where relevant).
- But you have signed for permission at X point in time (contract of employment or other).

Chapter 4 on conducting interviews also refers with regards to when and how to introduce the notion of lifestyle audits.

6.7. BEHAVIOURAL INDICATORS

As per the above, please refer to Chapter 4 on interviewing for a discussion on detecting deceit. It is wise to note any behavioural indicators made by subjects at the time of discussing or performing the lifestyle audit. Remember our rule: 'People do and say things for a reason.' People may be providing you with involuntary indicators that they are uncomfortable with the lifestyle audit and that they are fearful that you may detect their deceit or misconduct.

6.8. HIGH-LEVEL LIFESTYLE AUDIT

6.8.1. Introduction

The following discussion adds to the manner to conduct a high-level lifestyle audit that was described in the previous paragraphs on proactive lifestyle audits and on profiling lifestyle audits.

6.8.2. Information sources

The following represent examples of possible sources of information to be used to obtain information used in lifestyle audits:

a. Public domain databases

Continuing from the profiling paragraph, supplement the profiles that you have started to build on the subjects with information that you obtain from conducting searches of public domain information sources, including:

- Properties owned (deeds office)
- Directorships held (Registrar of companies)
- Addresses and phone numbers held
- Employment history
- Credit applications
- Default credit judgments against them.

There are numerous such databases available. The local chapter of the Association of Certified Fraud Examiners or one of the big accounting firms will be able to direct you to the right databases to use. Sources of information include:

b. Interview with the subject

This is fairly self-explanatory. It is, however, important to check and/or substantiate the information provided by the subject with regards to their lifestyle and funding thereof.

c. Interviews with others

Interview those colleagues who socialised with the subject or who sit in close proximity to the subject. *An example refers of when I interviewed a lady who sat opposite the subject in an open-plan office. The ladies were clearly competitive and the colleague interviewed was very eager to give me all the details of the subject's lifestyle. I was consequently able to prove that the subject's lifestyle was beyond her salary.*

d. Personnel files

Lastly, obtain access to the personnel files of selected employees so that you can understand their:

- Performance history
- Disciplinary history
- Salary and package details
- Family problems
- Any applications for loans
- If they have or have had any garnishee orders against themselves
- Information that may be required later and which could be on file, including:
    - Bank account/s numbers and details
    - Identity numbers
    - Passport numbers
    - Nationality
    - Beneficiaries
    - Marital status
    - Dependants
    - Address/es
    - Phone numbers on file
    - Tax number
    - A copy of their CV
    - List of experience and qualifications.

e. Subpoenaed records

In a criminal case, the investigating officer (IO) or the prosecutor may subpoena records to be used in the investigation and/or trial. Subjects may refuse to volunteer these records. A court can 'force'/instruct a party (for example the subject's bank) to surrender records to it/its officials. The IO or prosecutor may also need to ensure that certain records are obtained independently to ensure the integrity of the evidence. The types of records that are normally subpoenaed are normally subject to some form of protection (eg banking records, mobile phone records, medical records, etc) or privacy legislation and/or which are not in the public domain. The subpoena process formalises the obtaining of the documents and prevents these types of records falling too easily into the wrong hands.

f. Volunteered records

These are any records which another party voluntarily provides to you. Always try to obtain the original documents. Alternatively, obtain copies with an explanation of why you cannot obtain the originals. These documents can come from various sources, including: the subject, the subject's employer, the party that suffered the loss, friends and family of the subject, suppliers, customers, etc.

g. Electronic device searches

This would be any form of device that records audio or video or data in an electronic form. Examples include: personal computers, memory sticks, external hard drives, cameras, mobile phones, tablets/iPads, etc. Chapters 3 and 4 on structuring investigations and conducting interviews refer with regards to electronic device searches. The concept of the 'expectation of privacy' (discussed in Chapter 3) is particularly important in this regard. The information may show relationships, assets, hobbies and other lifestyle indicators.

h. Photos

Photographs on the desks of subjects and on electronic devices and those obtained in interviews with colleagues are a good source of information to know what assets a subject has or what hobbies they have and places where they may spend 'their' money and what needs to be funded. *As an example: A subject's colleagues told me that the main subject (S#1) had bought a boat together with another unknown subject (S#2) that was not considered as part of the original investigation. Subject number two was now also under suspicion. The colleagues also told me that there was a picture of the boat on subject number two's desk, which I was able to confirm easily (the ownership was more difficult to confirm).*

i. Work area search

A search of the subject's desk and general work area may identify valuable lifestyle and other information. Are there any documents that show directorships or places where funds were spent on lifestyle? *Two examples refer of where very valuable other (non-lifestyle) information was in the subject's desk:*

- *One example included a signed copy of the policy that the subject had just transgressed, which was located in the bottom drawer of the subject's desk.*
- *In another example, we found the subject's notebook that he used for his work notes/ meeting minutes. This provided information of knowledge of aspects pertinent to the investigation.*

Please ensure that you comply with the rules and/or expectation of privacy and that you abide by the company policies and local laws.

j. Bank accounts

The following is a list of bank accounts that you may need to obtain records of:

- Cheque accounts
- Revolving credit
- Personal loan accounts
- Savings account

- Credit cards
- Bond/mortgage account
- Loan accounts
- Investment accounts
- Vehicle financing records.

j. Social media and internet

Another growing area of public domain information is the internet and social media. More and more people are becoming comfortable with placing information about themselves on the internet. While older people like me struggle to come to terms with this trend, social media is a valuable source of information. Conduct a trawl of social media to identify information about the subject's:

- Hobbies and habits
- Friends, family, associations and loyalties
- General lifestyle
- Ethics and morals.

Once you have identified a company, an individual, a property, a name, etc in relation to a subject, conduct a normal internet search of the identified aspect. You will be surprised at how much information is on the internet.

Furthermore, for example, once you have identified a particular company and located its website, you may identify other pertinent information such as contact details, physical and postal addresses, client references, financial information, etc.

It is also advisable for you to extend your lifestyle audit to conduct the aforementioned public domain searches of companies and other individuals that your lifestyle audit has identified as being associated with the subject.

An example refers in which I found an electronic Christmas card that the subject (suspected of running his own business in conflict to the company) had sent. Who do you send Christmas cards to? Friends, family and clients. After a half-hour internet search, I had much valuable information about all of the companies associated with the subject. I was able to contact them and they confirmed his private business association with them.

6.9. TEMPLATE

The lifestyle audit reference table attached as Annexure 6.5 provides a list of prompts that you may consider using to perform a high-level lifestyle audit. Specify relevant input information on a case-by-case basis.

6.10. DETAILED LIFESTYLE AUDIT

6.10.1. Introduction

A detailed lifestyle audit is an in-depth analysis of all of the known incomes and expenditures of a subject to determine if the subject's declared and/or proven/known sources of income are sufficient to fund the subject's lifestyle. In accounting terms: are the incomes greater than the expenses?

Detailed lifestyle audits represent quite an exciting part of an investigation. This analysis frequently proves that a subject was involved in an undeclared activity from which they were funding their lifestyle. Detailed lifestyle audit results are frequently used in quite a few high-profile fraud and corruption cases that are flaunted in the media.

Detailed lifestyle audits are not difficult to perform. The trick is to identify and obtain all information required and then to summarise, analyse and interpret the information. Sound simple enough? Let us see.

6.10.2. Estimates

In the absence of actual information, you can include an estimate. You should however clearly state which figures are actual figures and which are estimates. You should also clearly show what the basis of your estimate was and the calculation used to arrive at the figure/s. The idea is that your assumptions should be defendable and anyone reading them should concur with your logic.

If possible, get the subject of the lifestyle audit to give their estimate of the amount or quantity of the area being tested. Subjects tend to err on the side of underestimating. This may count in your favour when comparing their estimate to defendable trends or to actual data later. This will bring the subject's credibility into question if the subject's estimate is clearly understated. It may also provide you with an opportunity (at the time of confrontation about the conflicting estimates) to convince them that now is a good time to cooperate and to make full declarations. Intentionally skewed estimates by the subject in interviews may also give you an indication of their planned defences/excuses, which will allow you time to prepare blocks/rebuttal questions to be used in hearings or criminal matters. If on the other hand, they give an accurate basis, then there is less chance of the estimate being contested.

Try, as far as possible, to use more than one defendable basis to arrive at an estimate and compare the various bases to show the comparative accuracy of your bases. If possible compare your estimate against related criteria to demonstrate the accuracy of your estimate. The following are two general data verification examples where an independent basis was used to verify data.

- *In the first example, the contract manager and the site agent of a large construction site had alleged that the reinforcing steel for an entire floor's concrete decking was misplaced. Replacement steel was ordered. A whistle-blower advised us that the two subjects had hired specialised cutting equipment at the company's expense to cut up the initial steel. The subjects also used company paid employees to cut up the steel and to drive it to nearby scrapyards in company paid vehicles. While the loss to the company was the cost of the replacement steel, the cost of the hired equipment, the labour cost and the vehicle costs, I wanted to determine how much the two subjects had obtained from the sale of the steel. I first went to the quantity surveyor on the job to determine the tonnage of steel on the initial and second invoices. I then spoke to the employees who had driven the steel to the scrapyards and who had handed the cash proceeds to the two subjects. I also obtained the satellite tracking records for the vehicles used. I did not have an actual figure of scrap proceeds, so I made use of estimates. I then calculated, using three methods, the estimated tonnage of steel scrapped, based on the steel mill's invoiced tonnage, employees' recollections and the vehicle tracking records of stops at the coordinates of known scrap merchants. I then multiplied the tonnage by the known scrap value per kilogram. I described this logic and showed my calculations in my affidavit on the matter. All three estimates were within a negligible margin of each other and I was comfortable that my estimates were accurate. From a lifestyle point of view, witnesses said that the two main suspects had gone on expensive hunting trips after the steel had been scrapped.*

- *In the second example: I was trying to verify the time and attendance of employees in an apparent wages fraud. The employees had been doing work at a client's secure premises. All employees were scanned in and out of the premises. I obtained the scanned attendance records from the client. The client's premises were many kilometres out of town and the employees had been transported to and from the client's premises in company vehicles. I then also obtained the satellite tracking records of the vehicles used to transport the employees on those days. I could verify that the vehicles were scanned in and out of the gates by the client at times that corresponded to the satellite tracking records. I checked these records to the wage summary sheets captured into the payroll system. I also interviewed the employees individually and asked them who had been on site and who had not. I was then able to focus on the employees who had been paid for a day's work, but who were not on the client's premises.*
- *In a third example: The subject was obtaining cash kickbacks from a supplier. He and his wife drove expensive vehicles with above-average fuel consumption. His fuel utilisation on the declared bank account was negligible. I compared his vehicle's fuel consumption against the manufacturer's specification listed on their website. I had a colleague measure the distance to and from work from his house and I got him to estimate the number of fuel tanks his wife used in a month (this matched my wife's consumption). You could also use figures from the Automobile Association (AA) on average consumption figures. I was able to prove that he had to have been funding his fuel from elsewhere than his declared bank account.*

The idea is to try to use independent data, as this is defendable. Always attach the independent information in support of your estimate. This will create credibility of your assumptions. The previous examples refer.

Lastly, you should list the impact of the estimate on the lifestyle audit of the subject/s. Declare what the limitations of the estimates are. If there is a margin of error, then show the upper and lower scenarios. Do not try to hide potential inaccuracies. This may be used to discredit your evidence. Finally, remember our rule: 'Queensbury (fairness) rules apply.'

6.10.3. Privacy

Ensure that you obtain all information legally. Legal information is information that was obtained:

- By court order
- From the public domain
- Directly from the subject voluntarily
- From a source, not in the public domain, that you are entitled to search (eg personnel records).

You do not need a subject's consent to conduct a lifestyle audit of public domain information. Consent and/or knowledge of the lifestyle audit by the subject may assist you later in your investigation, as it may make them nervous and force them to concede more easily or make a mistake. Lifestyle audits are very invasive for subjects. As far as possible, commence by obtaining the subject's consent and/or cooperation. The subject will go through emotional ups and downs during the process. You may need to remind them throughout that they are doing the right thing by volunteering information.

6.10.4. Completeness of data

As far as possible obtain all the data first that you require and then interpret it. There is a chance that if you question each data element in too much detail upfront, you may frighten off the subject. If the subject gets cold feet and ceases to provide you with all relevant information, you may be unable to complete a meaningful lifestyle audit.

As per our rule, 'the best time to do something is immediately', let the subject sign a consent form and/or bundle them into a car immediately and go and get the records that you need from their bank, house, office, etc. Do not wait for them to bring them to you, as they do not always return and then you will have lost your window of opportunity. Consent forms are useful as they can be submitted later in your own time once the subject leaves the interview.

If the subject volunteers bank accounts, then turn your laptop towards them and ask them to log on and download the statements. Subjects typically memorise their log-on credentials and should be able to assist you immediately. Banks typically however only retain a limited number of months of transactional history (six months) online. Take what you can get immediately and then take the subject to the bank to obtain the additional outstanding archived records.

The best information is that which was volunteered by the subject, as it will not be disputed. Your interpretation may be disputed, but the information can never be disputed, as they gave it to you.

6.10.5. Motivation

Never force a subject to give you information, as this would be duress. Strongly encourage them. Thank them profusely (to build rapport and to keep them convinced that they are doing the right thing). Ask them if they want to assist you in proving their innocence. Tell them that you know that the lifestyle review is difficult for them, but that they are doing the right thing.

6.10.6. Verification

As far as possible, verify data against actual records. Ensure that records were not already manipulated (physically or electronically) before being given to you.

As a rule, accept all records. Do not decline anything. If subjects are dishonest about what they submit to you then this will assist you when you bring their dishonesty to the attention of a judge or the labour tribunal commissioner. As far as possible, try to verify the records whose integrity you are unsure of. PDF files can generally not be manipulated. There are PDF-format reading programs. These programs will allow a subject to manipulate the record in another format and then to resave the manipulated record in PDF again. It is also possible that the subject may have manipulated a record before saving it themselves in a PDF format and submitting it to you. Ensure therefore that you can verify the source of the information. Alternatively, try to be present when data and records are retrieved.

PDF files do not allow for sorting and easy data analysis of many records. Try (if you are planning to conduct analyses of many lines of data) to obtain the information in both an Excel and a PDF format.

Once you have the records, ensure that there are no obvious signs of manipulation. Next, ensure the completeness of the records submitted to you. Completeness may be in the form of page numbers, numerical record numbers or chronological sequence. Foot and cross-check totals to ensure that numbers carry over.

Subjects will frequently submit the records that they know are clean and leave out the ones that they are concerned about. Subjects will frequently blame the banks or the people who gave them the records or say that they were unable to retrieve or find the missing ones.

Original records are always best. Certified copies may be a good alternative. Try as far as possible to compare the copies to the originals yourself. Alternatively, phone the commissioner of oaths who verified the records and satisfy yourself that they are sufficiently independent of the subject and/or applied their mind diligently to certifying the documents.

Record:

- The exact range of data and records received
- From whom you received them
- Date, time and place received
- Sequence numbers, page numbers and date or time range
- Witnesses who were present at the time of handover
- How and where you have secured the records and who had access to this area.

Make copies (physical and electronic) of the documents, records and data received. Never work on the originals. Chapter 5 on data analytics also refers here in terms of electronic information.

6.10.7. Matching principle

As the accounting principle states, you will also need to match incomes with expenses within specific periods. A subject may refer broadly to income that they received. When they received it may be vital to your analyses. For example, if a subject received an income in period X2, then these funds could not have been used to fund lifestyle expenses in period X1, prior to being received. Be careful of general assertions by subjects. Lock them down to specific periods in the detailed analysis phase.

You may want to plot incomes and expenses on a timeline or in chronological columns in a spreadsheet to visualise timeline conflicts.

6.10.8. Interpretation

It is one thing to have the income and expenditure information of a subject. The difficult part is making intelligent sense of it. What does this information tell you about the subject's income and by default, what does it tell you about the sources of that income? Does their known/declared income support their lifestyle or must there have been other income?

Annexure 6.5 provides detailed interpretations of possible lifestyle indicators.

The following are elements that you may wish to concentrate on in a detailed lifestyle audit:

- *Undeclared incomes*

  Identify deposits from unknown, unanticipated or undeclared sources. These may be direct deposits or electronic fund transfers (EFTs) to the account. These may be indicative of:
  - Kickbacks
  - Undeclared earnings, showing where their time was spent instead of serving the organisation and/or corrupt relationships and the loyalties at play
  - Misappropriated funds that were taken by the subject/s
  - Legitimate sources of funds, for example prizes, trust funds, inheritance, etc.

  Denote the details of the source of EFTs into their bank account as this may be required subsequently to verify the payer thereof.

- *Transfers to and from accounts*

  Identify transfers to and from other bank accounts/beneficiaries. Determine if there is anything suspicious about this source or destination of the funds. Does it highlight an unknown relationship or additional areas to be investigated? This may identify:
  - The people who are making payments (legitimate or illegitimate) to the subject - in this way additional lifestyle funding can be explained
  - The co-conspirators with whom the subject is sharing illicit funds
  - Previously unknown areas of financial strain for the subject
  - The areas against which funds were applied or accounts in which funds have been hidden in.

  Other accounts held by the subject. Request to see the details of these accounts as well. Alternatively, list them for possible subpoena by the investigating officer.

- *Absent expenses*

  Identify (mostly by placing yourself in the subject's position by anticipating the expenses that you expect to see based on your knowledge of their lifestyle) those expenses which are conspicuous by their absence. Every individual has to have certain basic expenses in their life. If these are not visible, it does not mean that the expenses were not incurred; it normally means that it is not visible and was funded in an unknown (legitimate or illegitimate) manner.

As an example: I conducted a lifestyle review in which the individual did not have any school fees (with two young children), no municipal utility bills (he owned a house), very little for groceries (they were a family of four), excessive takeaway foods (luxuries compared to daily food) and almost no fuel (with two vehicles). All financed assets (bonds, a personal loan used for an overseas trip and two vehicles) were clearly processed against his main account. It was unclear how his normal day-to-day lifestyle was funded.

Be careful not to only look for the obvious expenses. Also, ensure that you look for the indirect expenses that may support the direct expenses. For example:

- Internet connection fees for electronic devices
- School transportation (bus) costs for a private school
- School uniforms, stationery, extramural activities, textbooks, etc
- Fuel, oil, tyres, servicing and maintenance costs for a vehicle
- Costs to play a round of golf and drinks afterwards, not just annual course membership fees
- Sports clothes and related activities for a particular interest.

Common expense examples to be considered include:

- Mortgage repayments
- Residence rental
- Vehicle finance
- Medical insurance and day-to-day bills
- Retirement funding
- Schooling and university
- Short-term insurance
- Long-term/life assurance
- Food
- Entertainment (restaurants, casinos, etc)
- Satellite TV subscriptions
- Landlines, cellular contracts and internet connections
- Sporting activities and club memberships (golf)
- Hobbies (horses, racing, etc)
- Clothing
- Personal grooming (hair and nails)
- Travel (daily commute and long-haul trips)
- Vacations
- Family gifts
- Jewellery.

- *Under-financed expenses*

The most obvious trend we are looking for is if the person's expenses exceed their income. This means that their expenses were underfinanced when compared to their declared income. The fact that they are standing in front of you in reasonably good health (not starving) means that the gap must have been made up from somewhere else. Remember our rule: 'If it seems too good to be true, then it probably is.' The subject will be unable to explain their apparent under-financing of expenses because there is not a logical reason, other than to admit that they have been receiving undeclared income (most likely illicit funds). They will offer all kinds of excuses and even be highly forgetful, not without due reason.

- *Over-financed expenses*

If, on the other hand, after all the expenses were financed, the subject has excess income, try to understand where the excess income is being invested/ applied? Try to establish if it is possible/within the subject's means of declared income to be able to have this sort of income remaining over. What expenses are missing for a typical person in this situation?

- *Cash funds*

If the subject declares that he has a stash of cash 'under his mattress', try to get the subject to commit to:

  - How much cash he has currently
  - How much it was before he started spending
  - The source of this cash
  - How the cash has been/is applied
  - Who knows about the cash.

Try as far as possible to corroborate the purported source of the cash. Do not be concerned if the subject's purported source seems far-fetched. The idea is to get them to commit to an answer and then to catch them out with logic later, proving that their lifestyle was funded from illicit sources. Examples of places cash could have been obtained from include:

  - Personal loans (from family or friends)
  - Private saving schemes (staff members sometimes embark on a savings scheme at work in which they each get a month to take the proceeds)
  - Casino winnings
  - Birthday gifts
  - Private business (from 'moonlighting')
  - Sale of an item of value (pawn shops, to private individuals).

6.10.9. Assets

List all of the subject's assets, equipment, furnishings, livestock, etc and understand the total value of assets owned. Also, understand over what period they were procured. Substantiate the purchase dates with invoices, serial numbers, model types, the visual age of the item, etc.

If they say that the assets belong to someone else, denote the details for later confirmation.

Understand how the assets were financed (cash or debt). Assets do not just appear; someone has to pay for them. Also understand if any income was generated from these assets (rental income, charter fees, used to provide services, etc) and/or if any of them were subsequently sold and what happened to the funds.

If the subject was receiving another form of income over and above their salary (for example rental income from an additional property owned), understand if the subject declared this for income tax purposes. Substantiate the subject's assertions against actual documentation (eg listed on an actual income tax return).

Summarise the cash flows (in and out) over the period of review associated with all the known assets, equipment, etc in a spreadsheet similar to the example 'overall lifestyle funding template' shown below (see Annexure 6.2 attached hereto).

6.10.10. Special interest transactions and records

In a particular example of a detailed lifestyle audit example, the subject declared that he had funded part of his lifestyle from reimbursements that he had received from the medical aid for extensive medical procedures that his son had undergone (mentioned previously). The subject also tried to play on my sympathies concerning the trauma that his son and the general family endured during the procedures. I could clearly see on the transactional history of the subject's bank account that amounts had been paid into his account from the medical aid. I could, therefore, substantiate the receipt.

The problem was that there were no medical expenses associated with the reimbursement. A medical aid/insurance company will only reimburse you for the actual expenses that you have or still need to incur. Clearly, there was a reimbursement. How and where had he funded these expenses? Had he paid in cash? If so, then this accounted for a portion of the cash drawn from his account. This meant that this cash was not used for other living costs like food. In this case, there was overwhelming evidence that the subject was living beyond his salary. While not required in this circumstance, I could have requested the investigating officer to subpoena the doctor's payment records.

In the aforementioned example, we demonstrate that there may be multiple sources from which to source and/or substantiate incomes and expenditures in a detailed lifestyle audit. Try, as far as possible, to substantiate all figures used in the detailed lifestyle audit against actual, independent and defendable documents and information. Examples of sources of such records include:

- Utility bills/municipality monthly accounts
- Share dealing transactions from the stock exchange
- Retail store monthly statements of account
- Medical aid transaction records or doctor's accounts
- School/university/college monthly statements of account
- Bank account statements
- Company records (payslips)
- Court orders (alimony, garnishee orders).

6.10.11. Information collation

Plot all information, as you receive it, in a spreadsheet. Annexure 6.2 attached hereto provides an example of an 'overall lifestyle funding template'. Where figures are made up of multiple figures, it may be more sensible and easier to read if you only record one figure per period in the summary sheet. This single figure should be referenced to and supported by separately detailed spreadsheets.

6.10.12. Cash

Cash is a slightly tricky topic and one which is frequently used as an excuse by subjects to explain how they funded items not recorded. Cash utilisation will in most circumstances require a separate detailed analysis.

Let us assume that you have conducted a detailed analysis of the subject's lifestyle. You will know that you have to conduct a detailed analysis of cash if:

- You identify cash deposits and withdrawals in the subject's bank account, or
- The subject tells you (or the person giving you information about the subject) about the subject's use of cash.

It is not the number or the size of the cash deposits or withdrawals that alone determine the need to conduct a detailed cash analysis. It is rather what the purported use of the cash was. How complex is the purported use? You will need to determine if the purported use of cash is within their lifestyle or not. In order to be able to conclude on the lifestyle audit, you need to see all incomes and all expenditures together in some form or other to be able to determine if their total income can support their total expenditure. Cash incomes and cash expenditures are one of the forms of funding that need to be considered in the lifestyle audit.

As a general rule, you should always summarise the cash usage. Presumption is dangerous; fact is better. Remember the rule: 'The devil is in the detail.' You will frequently only see the trend once you have summarised the cash and plotted the information on a graph or conducted some form of analysis. So, do not decide not to do it based purely on a visual assessment. Conduct the analysis and you will be surprised what trends float to the top.

Subjects will, in response to questions about anticipated expenditure (eg utility bills, school fees, fuel costs, etc) that is not listed in their bank account, frequently say that they paid for that specific item in cash. They do this as they believe that cash cannot be tracked. It is as if they think that if they paid for an item in cash, no one will question it, as there is no receipt. What subjects fail to see is that they normally only have one source of declared income, being their salary. The cash needed to come from somewhere, being their declared sources of income.

Annexure 6.3 provides a 'cash utilisation template' that you may use to summarise the subject's cash utilisation. Summarise the cash incomes and expenditure in the same categories (eg food, takeaways, clothing, etc), as with any other aspect of their lifestyle (eg bank transfer, credit card expense, etc). This will help you (as per the above) when you put all the types of expenditure and funding sources into one overall analysis.

Capture as much detail as possible, even to a transactional level. The number of transactions may also be important, for example:

- Comparing the number of cash transactions to the times/date that the transaction was expected to have been performed
- Comparing the number of cash transactions to another payment method in a particular category.

The dates, times, weekdays and monthly positioning of payments may therefore be useful as well.

6.10.13. Action list

As part of collating the information, you may already have noticed interesting indicators, hypotheses or further action points. Denote these as you identify them, to ensure that you cover all options and that you do not forget an important element. Annexure 6.4 provides an example of a table that you could use for this purpose.

This may seem a little over the top, but when you have to testify, this can count in your favour. You will need to say what you did and why you did it. Remember the rule: 'He with the most paperwork wins.' In this case, it is not the existence of the paperwork that helps you to 'win'. It is rather the fact that you can refresh your memory closer to the time:

- Recall a long time after the fact what you did. Legal matters can be highly protracted matters lasting long after investigations have been completed.
- Clearly demonstrate what you did.
- Support your conclusions with a clearly demonstrated thought pattern.

Documenting in this manner will also provide you with a list of action points to prioritise. You will also use this when you compile reports and affidavits of the investigation.

6.10.14. Analysis

The whole purpose of collecting all the information is to put you in the best possible position to be able to conduct meaningful analyses. The meaningful analyses, in turn, form the basis of sound conclusions and evidence to indicate if the subject is or is not living within their declared means. The broad inference is that if the person did not obtain their income from known sources, that they must have obtained it from corrupt sources.

Knowing what to analyse and how to conduct the analysis is the trick. Each subject's lifestyle will be slightly different from the next. There are however some common factors to consider, including:

- Deposits listed that are not from known and/or legitimate sources. These may be a direct indicator that the subject received illegitimate/undeclared income.
- Obviously absent expenses. These indicate that the person must have been funding these required, but unlisted expenses, somewhere else and probably illegitimately.
- Payments to strange people or legal entities. Do not just take the subject's word for it; substantiate it. For example, as I found in one of my investigations: the Blue Lizard Lounge is the name that appears on a person's credit card statement when they transact at a particular, notorious strip club.
- Payments that show habits (casinos, horses, collectable items, luxury items, brothels, etc) or how/where their income is spent (eg assets, medical bills, etc). This will indicate a lifestyle which is out of kilter with their income and not one that can be normally associated with a person in that bracket. This implies that their more expensive lifestyle must have been funded illegitimately.

Conduct your analysis per income/pay-period (monthly, weekly, etc). List all incomes and expenditures within those periods. Calculate any variance (over/under-funded lifestyle) per period.

This will be the first and most basic lifestyle analysis that you will be performing. If there is an excess of funds available at the pay-period end, determine if:

- This is reasonable? Can a person in the subject's situation (family, age, economic bracket, etc) live reasonably and still have all this money over at the end of the month? Look a little deeper and try to identify expenses that you expect to see that are not listed (school fees, utility bills, telephone accounts).
- How was the excess applied? Again, is this reasonable?
- Where is it now compared to the time of the misconduct?

Scan the declared incomes and expenditures and determine if there is anything missing or if normal trends are being maintained for a person in the subject's situation. If you are not able to relate to the subject (because of age, family size, country, etc) ask your colleagues in a similar situation/size family what they spend. If you are older and no longer have babies or if you are a high earner, you may not be in touch with a person in a similar situation. Try to include as many people as possible that are in a similar 'declared' lifestyle bracket as the subject in your benchmark. Then summarise the benchmark estimates given and calculate an average. Use this as your benchmark to determine a baseline against which to compare the subject's lifestyle.

Subjects normally (but not always) pay for much of their financed (legitimate) expenses (bond, cars, etc) via their bank account. This is the kind of fixed expenditure that you are expecting to see. This always seems as if this is an attempt to maintain the appearance that they are living a 'normal' life. Remember the rules, 'people always do and say things for a reason' and 'forensics is all about psychology and not about fact'. So then, ask yourself: what is the psychology/behaviour pattern that the subject is trying to tell you about their bank account?

Subjects use the income that they do not declare to fund their more luxurious expenses/lifestyle. Again, I believe that they do this for a reason. I believe that they ensure in this way that all declared/above-board incomes and some of the expenses are put through their account so that they appear to be normal. They then put the rest of their (non-defendable) lifestyle expenses through an account in which they have their illegitimate income to avoid their declared bank account. They cannot put all expenses (normal and exorbitant lifestyle) through their declared bank account, as this may cause their legitimate account to go into an overdraft/under-funded situation. They mostly also do not want their illegitimate income going into their declared account for fear of detection.

6.10.15. Examples

Some examples of analyses are listed below. The figures used are arbitrary figures but relate to an actual case (mentioned previously as one of our examples).

In the first table below, the subject's 'take-away' expenses seemed higher than normal. The take-away costs were in contrast to his grocery expenses, which were too low for a family of four. Many of us will be able to relate to just how expensive it is to keep a family afloat and that eating out (to that degree) is a luxury. It, therefore, seemed strange that the subject could afford to eat out so often. This was also in tough economic times.

EXAMPLE: GROCERY TO TAKE-AWAY FOOD ANALYSIS						
No	**Date range**	**Grocery Amount**	**Take-away Amount**	**Grocery Count**	**Take-away Count**	**% Takeaways to Groceries**
1	Month 1	R 0.00	R 55.80	-	1	5580000%
2	Month 2	R 591.82	R 97.40	2.0	1	16%
3	Month 3	R 1 514.83	R 134.00	2.0	2	9%
4	Month 4	R 1 911.67	R 761.84	3.0	3	40%
5	Month 5	R 369.92	R -	2.0	-	0%
6	Month 6	R 586.73	R 67.30	2.0	1	11%
7	Month 7	R 1 162.90	R 617.39	1.0	3	53%
8	Month 8	R 727.88	R 234.80	3.0	2	32%
9	Month 9	R 1 832.30	R 273.90	3.0	3	15%
10	Month 10	R 273.56	R 109.95	1.0	1	40%
11	Month 11	R 836.29	R 288.30	4.0	1	34%
12	Month 12	R 417.40	R 73.90	1.0	1	18%
	TOTALS	R10 225.30	R2 714.58	24	19	27%

Figure 6.1 *Grocery to take-away analysis table*

As discussed previously, when the subject was asked to explain how he managed this, he said that his father-in-law frequently purchased groceries for them and that his wife and he lived close to his in-laws and that they ate there frequently. I thanked him for his declaration and said that his father-in-law would now need to testify to this effect. I asked the subject if his father-in-law would be happy to do this. The subject resigned! I put this into my affidavit that I handed in to the authorities.

The graph below illustrates the same expenditure over time (his monthly pay periods).

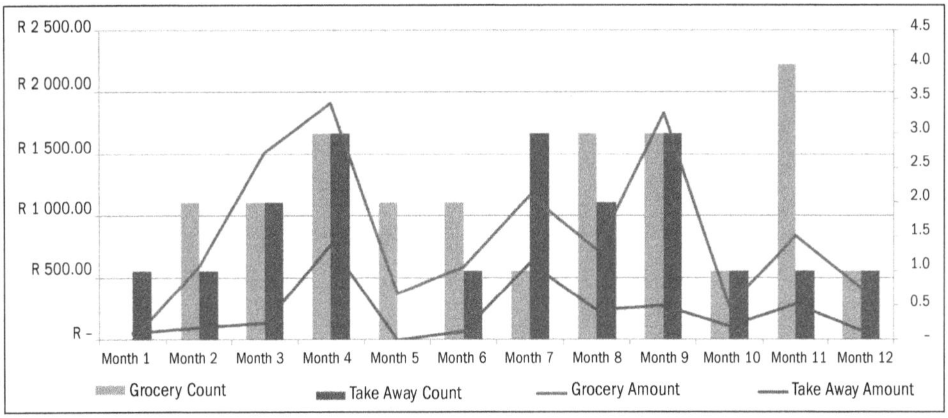

Figure 6.2 *Take-away to grocery expenditure graph*

In the next example, the subject and his wife both had fairly expensive vehicles. These vehicles had larger engine capacities resulting in above-average fuel consumptions. The subject's wife did not work. Analysis of the subject's expenditure indicated that the subject spent far too little on fuel. The subject should have used about 50 litres of fuel in his own vehicle every week or at least every two weeks if he was driving a little. I presumed that his wife should be filling up once to twice a month for low-level in-town driving.

I had one of my colleagues drive from the office to the subject's house so that we could establish the correct distance. I then went onto the Automobile Association's website and the specific vehicle manufacturer's website to determine the vehicles' consumption. The fuel expenditure did not even match his normal driving to work and back, never mind his vacations and non-work driving.

When I asked the subject for an explanation, he said that his wife worked 'unofficially' in her family's business and that his wife paid for the fuel with the money that she earned. I thanked the subject for his declarations and said that I would then be subpoenaing the family's bank records and that they would need to testify to this fact. I also said that I would need to hand the family business over to the revenue authorities, as his wife's family were not withholding the required income taxes on the wife's earnings. The subject said that the wife did not declare this income for tax purposes.

Furthermore, I noted that there was a disproportionate number of toll fees on his account. I was also aware, as per the subject's own admission, that he liked to go to casinos to gamble. The toll plazas that were paid for via his declared bank account were all en-route to casinos. These casinos were all a significant distance out of town. What this meant was that the subject's driving was not limited to in-town driving, as per our initial analysis. If he was doing long-distance driving and going through toll plazas, he must have been travelling far and consuming much more fuel than was visible on his declared bank account. This data was used to prove that the subject was not showing how he funded his petrol expenditure.

EXAMPLE: FUEL AND TOLL PLAZA ANALYSIS				
Time period	**Fuel Total**	**Fuel Count**	**Toll Total**	**Toll Count**
Month 1	R 400.05	2	R -	0
Month 2	R -	0	R -	0
Month 3	R 700.08	2	R -	0
Month 4	R -	0	R -	0
Month 5	R 500.03	1	R -	0
Month 6	R 1 931.77	5	R 62.00	2
Month 7	R -	0	R 20.00	2
Month 8	R 741.83	0	R 580.49	7
Month 9	R -	0	R -	0
Month 10	R -	0	R -	0
Month 11	R 400.01	1	R 117.50	4
Month 12	R 300.02	1	R -	0
Total per category	R 4 973.79	12	R 799.99	15

Figure 6.3 *Fuel and toll plaza analysis table*

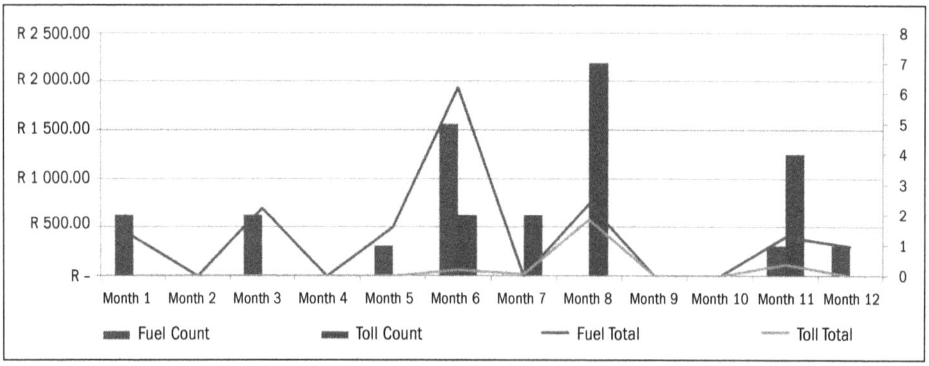

Figure 6.4 *Fuel and toll plaza expenditure graph*

Annexure 6.1
Lifestyle audit permission form

The ABC organisation would like to have the ability to conduct checks on prospective or current employees.

I ______________________________ (full name as per ID) with ID number ______________________________ do hereby give the ABC organisation permission to conduct the following checks on me. I understand that the organisation has full discretion if and when it wants to conduct such checks.

Please indicate your permission against each of the following:

No	Check to be conducted	Permission granted (Yes/No)	Reasons if No
1	Criminal check		
2	Credit check		
3	Reference check		
4	Experience		
5	Qualifications		
6	Directorships		
7	Property held		

Further to my permission I would like to make the following declarations:

Candidate/employee	For the organisation	Witness
(___/___/___)	(___/___/___)	(___/___/___)
______________ (Place)	______________ (Place)	______________ (Place)

Annexure 6.2
Overall lifestyle funding template

OVERALL LIFESTYLE FUNDING TEMPLATE												
	Period 1	Period 2	Period 3	Period 4	Period 5	Period 6	Period 7	Period 8	Period 9	Period 10	Period 11	Period 12
Income												
Salary												
Bonus												
Cash deposits												
Transfers from A Person												
Interest received												
Transfer from Other Own Account												
Sub-total Income												
Expenditure												
Mortgage repayment												
Credit Card payments												
Vehicle hire purchase												
Vehicle insurance												
Groceries												
Clothing												
House maintenance												
Entertainment												
Fuel												
Take-aways												
Restaurants												
Jewellery												
Utilities												
Municipal rates and taxes												
School fees' Education												
Mobile phones												
Data Contracts												
Medical Insurance												
Life Assurance												
Household Insurance												
Personal Loan repayments												
Transfers to own accounts												
Transfers to AN Other												
Sub-total Expenditure												

Net Income/expenditure position												

Annexure 6.3
Cash utilisation template

CASH UTLIZATION TEMPLATE					
	Income			Expenditure	Total cash utilized in period
Date	Cash deposits	Undeposited cash received	Total Cash received	Cash Withdrawal	
Period 1					
Period 2	A	B	A + B = C	D	C + D = E
Period 3					
Period 4					
Period 5					
Period 6					
Period 7					
Period 8					
Period 9					
Period 10					
Period 11					
Period 12					
TOTALS					

	Declaration of cash application								Difference to be explained	
Date	Cellular and data	Fuel	Medical	Take-aways	School fees	Municipal account	Other	Total declared cash expenditure		Explanation given
Period 1										
Period 2								7	E-F=G	
Period 3										
Period 4										
Period 5										
Period 6										
Period 7										
Period 8										
Period 9										
Period 10										
Period 11										
Period 12										
TOTALS										

Annexure 6.4
Detailed lifestyle review follow-up and conclusion table

Detailed lifestyle review follow-up and conclusion table			
No	**Description of item noted for follow-up**	**Follow-up action required**	**Conclusion after follow-up was completed.**
1			
2			
3			
4			
5			

Annexure 6.5
Lifestyle audit reference table

No	Area	Prompt	Discussion/interpretation	Conclusion	Source
a.	**Credit facilities**	List the credit facilities that the subject has access to. As far as possible, legally obtain hard and/or soft copies of these accounts. Some examples include: • Fixed property mortgage bond accounts • Movable property and/or vehicle finance accounts • Personal loans, overdraft facilities, revolving credit, etc • Credit cards • Retail credit facilities • Staff loans, advances, IOUs, staff debtors, etc • Loans against pension, provident funds, etc. Determine per enquiry with the subject if they have any unsecured loans with: • Family and friends • 'Loan sharks'.	It is normal for people to have a certain amount of debt. The amount of debt that a person has will also follow a pattern depending on the person's place in life and on the situation that they find themselves in: • Just starting off in their career • Fixed cycles of needing to replace items • Normal expansion/upgrades (new children, education requirements, renovations, etc) • Scaling down - retirement/in response to a particular situation (illness, business failure, etc). Too much debt can be an indication of a problem, as can too little debt. Look for examples where subjects have no or little debt and try to understand how they are financing their debt-free lifestyle. For example, it may be suspicious if a young person owns a house and a car and is starting a family, but does not have any debt.	• Summarise all debt (capital) and monthly instalments (including interest) for detailed analysis. • List the dates that the facilities were obtained. • Try to see the original sale documents for instalment sale type deals, as monthly statements do not typically show deposits given. The source of deposit funding may need to be verified. • Determine if the subject can afford to service all this debt. • How did the subject qualify for all this debt? Did they have to give sizable deposits? • Was surety provided? If so in what form and by whom? • How were these financed? • How much disposable money do they have left each month after the servicing of their debt? Can they survive at their lifestyle on the remaining funds?	• Public domain websites • Interviews with the subject and others • Volunteered documents and statements • Subpoenaed documents • Employee files (employment reference letters submitted to financial institutions) • Searches of electronic devices.

No	Area	Prompt	Discussion/interpretation	Conclusion	Source
		Please specify the: ▪ Total amount of the credit facility available ▪ Current/ outstanding balance ▪ Repayment terms ▪ Monthly repayment amount/s ▪ Account numbers.	Some religions do not allow for traditional debt financing by institutions. ▪ What you need to decide is if the amount of debt: ▪ Can be supported/financed by their normal/known income ▪ Is in line with their position in life ▪ Is an indication that they are living beyond their means or that they are under financial pressure. If they have a lot of debt, how are they financing their normal lifestyle and more importantly their pleasures and indulgences? Remember our rule: 'It normally involves sex, drugs, gambling or some form of vice.'		
b.	**Credit history**	Specify any previous or current occurrences of the following against the subject: ▪ Default credit judgments ▪ Garnishee orders ▪ Alimony payments ▪ Child support payments ▪ Sequestration or liquidation orders.	Excessive credit judgments may be an indicator that the subject is living beyond their financial means or that they are under financial pressure. A single default judgment against a person may not be an indicator of financial pressure. Try to see credit judgements in the context of the person's life: ▪ Were they just young and inexperienced at the time? ▪ Were they going through an abnormal situation (retrenchment, divorce, etc)?	Summarise these in one document. Consider: ▪ The number of judgments ▪ In conjunction with the number of credit applications ▪ The quantum of the repayments ▪ The duration over which they have applied ▪ Determine if they can afford these repayments and/or if they can survive on the remaining funds after they have honoured the debt repayments.	▪ Public domain websites ▪ Interviews with the subject and others ▪ Volunteered documents and statements ▪ Subpoenaed documents ▪ Employee files in terms of garnishee orders on file ▪ Searches of electronic devices.

No	Area	Prompt	Discussion/interpretation	Conclusion	Source
c.	**Solvency**	Has the subject or any of the subject's immediate family or any of their businesses ever been sequestrated or liquidated? Has the subject or the subject's spouse/partner ever: ▪ Been sequestrated? ▪ Received debt counselling? ▪ Been placed under administration or curatorship? Are any of these matters pending?	If the subject or the subject's family have any liquidity/solvency problems or the subject's family or their businesses are under administration, then this may be an indication of financial pressure. Determine if this places pressure on the subject's legitimate income sources and forces the subject to supplement their income from illegitimate sources. While the subject may not be the party directly affected, they might have to provide funding to a family member, which in turn puts pressure on the subject.	Summarise any solvency issues and try to understand the direct impact of these on the subject's financial position (need to support family members).	▪ Interviews with the subject and/or others ▪ Public domain checks ▪ Subpoenaed records ▪ Personnel files ▪ Searches of electronic devices.
d.	**Sureties and guarantees**	Has the subject or the subject's spouse/partner signed any sureties or issued any guarantees?	What is the reason for the surety? Does this indicate business interests? Does this indicate that they are being required to step in to assist a family member who is in trouble? What financial pressure (if any) does this put on the subject? Does this put pressure on the subject's legitimate sources of income and force them to supplement this income from illegitimate sources?	Summarise any solvency issues and try to understand the direct impact of these on the subject's financial position (need to support family members).	▪ Interviews with the subject and others ▪ Personnel files ▪ Subpoenaed records ▪ Searches of electronic devices.

No	Area	Prompt	Discussion/interpretation	Conclusion	Source
e.	**Criminal history & profile**	Does the subject have a criminal record or are there any matters that are currently pending or under investigation? Has the subject or the subject's spouse/partner ever been: ▪ Arrested in connection with any matter (listed in their police profile)? ▪ Investigated by any of the country's authorities (police services, border control, customs)? Please specify.	Each person has two sets of records with the police, being: ▪ Criminal records (convictions) handed down by a judge. ▪ A police profile of all matters linked to the individual (arrests and release, etc). Only police officers have access to people's profiles. The investigating officer (IO) will sometimes share this information with you or you may become aware of it as a result of your dealings with the police investigating team or the prosecution. You also have to see any criminal record in context. Is this a general way of life or was it a mistake they made many years ago as a youngster for an unrelated matter?	Consider: ▪ The number of convictions ▪ The types of crimes ▪ Incidents implicated in (profile) ▪ Seriousness of the crimes ▪ Relation of the conviction to the current accusations/ ethics of the subject.	▪ Authorised criminal checks ▪ The investigating officer or prosecutor ▪ Interviews with the subject or others ▪ Employee files ▪ Searches of electronic devices.

No	Area	Prompt	Discussion/interpretation	Conclusion	Source
f.	**Revenue/ tax authorities**	Specify the subject's tax number and the revenue office under which the subject falls. Specify the type of taxpayer that the subject currently is and has been in the past (provisional/normal). This may indicate directorships held or other sources of income (rental, commissions, etc) not covered by normal income tax withheld by the organisation. Has the subject ever had to pay any form of penalty or interest to the revenue authorities for any type of tax? Are there any such matters currently pending against the subject? Specify the tax types that the subject has had to pay and/or is currently paying to the revenue authorities.	You may be required to report the individual to the revenue authorities in the event of tax evasion. You may need to subpoena tax records. You may also be able to check if their taxes are all paid (speaks to general integrity of individual). What does their tax history tell you about their declared known income? Are they telling you that they have X income, but only paying tax on Y income? Alternatively do their tax records show other undeclared sources of income (for example a registered business)? Can the subject afford to fund their lifestyle on this income? The tax records are independent and defendable records of income that can be used in subsequent proceedings against the subject.	- Does the subject have a history of not paying taxes (ethics/financial pressure)? - Does the subject have a large unsettled debt with the revenue authorities?	- Interview with the subject and others - Tax authorities - Searches of electronic devices - Subpoenaed records - Personnel files.

No	Area	Prompt	Discussion/interpretation	Conclusion	Source
g.	**Civil claims**	Specify any civil claims currently or previously against the subject or the subject's spouse/partner or immediate family (children, parents, etc). Understand the: ■ Nature of the claim ■ Quantum of the claim ■ Period applicable ■ Outstanding amounts ■ Parties involved.	Civil claims may be an indication of financial pressure on the subject, which may put pressure on the subject's legitimate sources of income and force them to supplement this income from illegitimate sources. The financial effect of a civil claim will be the quantum of the claim as well as the costs of litigation. The claim might indicate undeclared business relationships. The nature of the civil claims may also tell you more about the subject and the type of person they are in so far as what they are inclined to have done (in the context of your investigation) based on actual claims against them.	■ Understand the nature of the claim. ■ Who is suing whom? ■ Summarise all claims and understand the impact of these on the subject's legitimate/ known financial income.	■ Interviews with the subject and/or others ■ Personnel files ■ Searches of electronic devices ■ Subpoenaed records.
h.	**Identity number/s**	Specify all identity numbers (ID) that the subject and/or the subject's spouse/partner and/ or children have had/currently have. These may be used later to conduct public domain searches.	Older subjects may have more than one ID number. Examples of this occur when ID documents and/or the numbering system changes. The numbers are supposed to be linked, but this does not always occur. Valuable information (eg criminal records) may be listed under one ID number and not the other. If the subject is aware of this, then they will use their 'clean' ID number to avoid knowledge of any restrictions listed against the other.	List all ID numbers and summarise all information linked to both in one table. Conduct public domain searches as required.	■ Interviews with the subject and/or others ■ Personnel files ■ Public domain searches.

No	Area	Prompt	Discussion/interpretation	Conclusion	Source
i.	**Passport/s**	How many passports does the subject or the subject's spouse/partner hold? Some countries allow citizens to hold multiple passports for the same country (for travel visa requirements, hand one passport in, use the other) or for different countries (dual citizenship). Please specify the nationality and passport number of each. Do they enjoy any specific diplomatic rights?	This may indicate: ▪ That the subject is a flight risk of fleeing the country without the possibility of consequence ▪ Specific reporting requirements to foreign territories of the actions of their citizens ▪ A need to treat such citizens in a particular manner (for example US citizens) ▪ Possible future trade restrictions to the company from local or foreign territories due to the actions of the subject ▪ Difficulty to track their movements if they are not local ▪ Difficulty to obtain information about the subject's lifestyle if the information is held in another country ▪ A possible place that they could have moved funds offshore to ▪ An opportunity if you are looking for an easier manner to terminate the employee's contract in the face of prima facie evidence without resistance from the subject.	List all passports held by the subject and their immediate family.	▪ Interviews with the subject and/or others ▪ Personnel files ▪ Public domain searches.

No	Area	Prompt	Discussion/interpretation	Conclusion	Source
			The subject's local residence permit may be dependent on the company providing them with a letter of recommendation or being accountable for their costs and/or actions. In such cases, the company can say that in the light of the actual or serious allegations of misconduct the company will not be renewing their residence permit and they will be required to leave the country. In challenging geographies where successful criminal convictions are unlikely, tell the subject that the company will always abide by the local laws and that it is the company's intention to report the matter to the local authorities. The onus is then on the subject to decide if they are going to take their chances with the local authorities. This is normally a daunting prospect to expatriate workers who do not want to be delayed exiting a foreign country without the support of the company. They are normally quick to resign and leave by their own means within days.		

No	Area	Prompt	Discussion/interpretation	Conclusion	Source
j.	**Citizenship**	Please specify in which country the subject, the subject's spouse/partner, children and parents were born. The previous point related to actual passports held refers. The person may not hold a passport from their country of origin, but may still enjoy some rights from this country. Alternatively, this may indicate places of financial pressure (requirement to send funds overseas) or places to hide funds. Please specify the citizenships that the subject or the subject's spouse/partner holds/has held in the past.	This may indicate: ▪ That the subject is a flight risk of fleeing the country without consequence ▪ Particular reporting requirements ▪ A need to handle certain citizens in a particular manner ▪ Possible trade restrictions as a consequence to the company ▪ Difficulty to track their movements if they are not local ▪ A possible place that they could have moved funds offshore to ▪ An opportunity to get the subject to resign, as discussed under the aforementioned point on passports held.	List the countries the subject and the subject's spouse/partner and parents were born. Understand what influence this could have on your investigation.	▪ Interviews with the subject and/or others ▪ Personnel files ▪ Public domain searches.

No	Area	Prompt	Discussion/interpretation	Conclusion	Source
k.	**Address/es**	Please specify all previous and current residential addresses. Please specify any post office boxes that the subject or the subject's spouse/partner currently has or has rented in the past.	It is safe to assume that it is not normal to move residence a lot. It is usual for a person to change residence at key intervals: ▪ Change of job ▪ Change of status (promotion) ▪ Change of marital status ▪ Change of children (additional or departing) ▪ Completion of education ▪ Leaving parental house ▪ Family trauma. A highly unstable history of regular residence moves may be an indication of financial strain or other problems. An abnormal number of moves may also justify the need for additional funds. Moves cost money and must be financed. The impact of these should be considered if a detailed lifestyle review is performed, as described below. *An example refers where the subject kept moving to evade rental payment and the other debt collectors that were trying to trace him. A phone call to some of the rental agencies listed in the public domain search provided me with a lot of information about the subject's history of avoiding paying rental.* *Also, consider if the subject is moving to get away from adverse people or circumstance.*	List all addresses.	▪ Interviews with the subject and/or others ▪ Personnel files ▪ Public domain searches.

No	Area	Prompt	Discussion/interpretation	Conclusion	Source
I.	**Fixed property**	What fixed property does the subject, the subject's spouse/partner and/or children currently own or have they previously owned? Please specify the type of ownership and usage rights. Try to obtain a value of the properties and an indication of how they were financed. Understand the periods that properties were held. Does this mean that they receive rental income or they have to fund the purchase? How do they do this (debt, cash)? What were/are the sources of these funds?	Information about a subject's fixed property could give indications of: • Sources from which to recover misappropriated funds. • Places where the misappropriated funds could have been applied. This in so far as illicit funds could have been used to acquire properties or used to reduce debt finance on their own legitimate properties. • Finance vehicles through which illicit money was laundered. A subject may want to create the appearance that the funds that they have are from a legitimate source. For example: if they gave a sizable deposit and only financed a reduced portion of the actual purchase price, then their net cash position will be higher on the sale of the property. People may accept that they made a sizable 'profit' on the sale of their property. If the subject makes it public knowledge (general office conversation) that they buy and sell properties in their private capacity, then people may be more inclined to feel that the source of the subject's above-average income is from 'legitimate' property investments.	• The number of times that the subject has applied for credit (listed on public domain credit checks) may be an indication that they are under financial pressure. • The size of the bond taken against the property may be an indication of financial pressure. • Analyse transactional history if you are able to legally obtain bank statements. • Look for deposits and inter-account transfers.	• Interviews with the subject and/or others. • Personnel files • Public domain searches • Subpoenaed records • Records volunteered by the subject • Independent property valuator • Building council/ municipal records of building plans • Local estate agent's records (general property values) • Physical inspection of properties.

No	Area	Prompt	Discussion/interpretation	Conclusion	Source
			Another example is that the subject receives a kickback from a supplier and pays it into his mortgage bond. The subject then makes a withdrawal from their mortgage and can, therefore, show people that he is drawing the funds out of my mortgage account, so it is 'legitimate'/their own funds that they are utilising. ▪ Signs of living beyond their known income means. ▪ Signs of financial pressure due to high debt to finance the properties. The following are indicators that the subject is less likely to be a flight risk: ▪ Existence of fixed property. ▪ History of staying a long time in one residence. ▪ If the subject has children and if the subject's children have been in the same school for a long time. They are less likely to uproot them at short notice. ▪ The existence of pets may also prevent the subject/subject's family from uprooting quickly. ▪ The type of position of employment/business interests that the subject or the subject's spouse holds. How easily will they give their career up to flee to protect the subject? The spouse's assets may also be attached in some circumstances to recover misappropriated funds.	▪ Banks also keep scanned copies of every document and have detailed transactional history. Analysis of this information may indicate: ❏ Key transaction dates. ❏ Who physically paid the funds in or performed an electronic transfer. ▪ This information will be vital in the detailed lifestyle analysis. A subject may also not have paid any illicit funds into these accounts. This will put pressure on their disposable income and it may be an indication that they are financing their lifestyle from an unknown source.	

No	Area	Prompt	Discussion/interpretation	Conclusion	Source
			Spend some time to understand the improvements that were made to the properties. A subject may have purchased a property that is within their financial means (evidenced by the debt to finance the original purchase), but they might not be able to justify the actual value of the property due to improvements (kitchen and bathroom upgrades, swimming pools, paving, garden walls, additions to the building, rework of old sections, etc). Not all property is registered with the deeds office. Some may be held by a company or a property syndicate. Some holiday houses are only governed by a usufruct contract. Try to understand from people what the subject's habits are (camping on the weekends) or look for photos on their desks. This may indicate properties held if they frequent one place.		

No	Area	Prompt	Discussion/interpretation	Conclusion	Source
m.	**Vehicles, equipment, furniture, appliances, sporting equipment and other movable assets**	Please specify all vehicles that the subject, the subject's spouse/partner or children have owned/currently own. Please specify any large capital equipment owned as well. List at least all recently acquired (within the period of the fraud) and expensive furniture and appliances. Try to understand values of the items and dates acquired. Understand and verify any special terms of use. Vehicles include: trucks, cars, motorcycles, trailers, tractors, caravans, boats, etc.	Some of these assets (like vehicles) may have been financed. Others may have been paid for without finance. Both financed and non-financed assets impact on the subject's financial position and ultimately on their disposable income. The number and value of assets owned by a subject may be an indication of: ▪ Financial pressure on disposable income to finance these assets. ▪ Sources where illicit funds were applied. ▪ A place from where funds can be recovered. ▪ Places where funds were laundered (see fixed asset discussion above). ▪ Who paid money into the account (they may, therefore, have knowledge of the illicit funds) or who performed the electronic funds transfer. Does the subject or the subject's spouse/partner own or have the use of a boat? Boats are generally not listed on any public domain databases. The trailer used to transport the boat may be registered as a vehicle. If you identify a trailer registered, try to understand what type of trailer it is and if you should naturally deduce that the subject also has a boat or motorcycles to go on it. You will need to establish on which dam or in which port the vessel is registered to verify ownership. Each boat carries a number of the dam on which it is registered. Caravans may also not necessarily be registered and may be located on private property. If they are transported by road they will need to be registered.	▪ As discussed under 'fixed property' above, you will need to analyse the detailed transactional history to determine if illicit funds were used to finance assets. ▪ This information will be vital in a detailed lifestyle audit.	▪ Interviews with the subject and/or others ▪ Personnel files (loan applications, employment and earning confirmation letters, garnishee orders, etc) ▪ Public domain checks ▪ Subpoenaed records ▪ Workspace searches ▪ Photos ▪ Volunteered records from the subject ▪ Searches of electronic devices.

No	Area	Prompt	Discussion/interpretation	Conclusion	Source
n.	**Animals and livestock**	Please specify all animals and livestock owned by the subject or the subject's spouse/partner. Some subjects like to own farms. This can be a status symbol or a personal dream of theirs. Does the subject have to assist in funding a family-held farm? Has the subject or the subject's spouse/partner ever owned (directly, indirectly or in syndicate) a racehorse? Please obtain the particulars.	May indicate: - Places where the illicit funds could have been applied. - A place from which to recover misappropriated funds (asset forfeiture/ court orders). Racehorses are always an interesting element. They are an indication of a certain type of person, being a gambler whose habits need to be financed. They are also an indication of a need for a lot of funding if owned by a person. Identifying that the subject owns a horse is challenging. Look for photos or interview colleagues and friends of the subject. Subjects may be reluctant to volunteer such information. Horses are not registered by the owner. Each horse is registered according to bloodline. The national horse racing association will have information on the horses registered in that country. Each horse has a passport that lists its bloodline. You will need to have the horse's name. The horse racing association will then be able to give you the owner's name.	- Summarise costs associated and understand how they were financed and what impact this had on disposable income for normal living expenses. - Does the subject have associated habits (gambling)? Subjects are normally quick to brag about winnings. Winnings imply that they had to spend money to gamble. Gamblers normally lose more than they win.	- Interviews with the subject and/ or others - Breeders' association records - Personnel files - Workspace searches - Electronic device searches - Public domain searches (farms owned) - Directors of companies (may be a racehorse ownership syndicate).

No	Area	Prompt	Discussion/interpretation	Conclusion	Source
			You may have a challenge if the horse is registered in another country. The following costs may be associated with a racehorse: ▪ Cost of the animal ▪ Stud fees ▪ Stabling fees ▪ Vet fees ▪ Feed ▪ Training ▪ Transport (to events, training, vets, etc) ▪ Gambling debt. There is a high number of subjects (compared to normal people) who have something to do with horses. Regard any subject who has something to do with race-horses as a person with a high propensity to fall foul of the law.		

No	Area	Prompt	Discussion/interpretation	Conclusion	Source
o.	**Partnerships, memberships and directorships**	Please specify all partnerships, memberships (closed corporations) and directorships (listed and private companies) that the subject, the subject's spouse/ partner or children have held/ currently hold.	Information of directorships, etc may be an indication of: • Privately owned companies through which business can be routed (procurement fraud, conflicts of interest, etc). • Financial pressure if the companies are experiencing financial difficulty. • Entities against which the organisation could lodge a claim to recoup fraudulent losses. • Organisations whose records can be subpoenaed for investigation purposes. Be mindful that companies are juristic people and can, in turn, own companies. The initial company identified may not be the actual company doing business with the company that has suffered the loss. Continue to search until the full ownership structure has been identified.	• Determine if the company/ies have been used for goods and services by the company that employs the subject (search on company name or 'trading as' name). • Analyse the transactions with this company to identify fraud. • Individuals do not always have records, but organisations usually have records. These records may be a source of evidence of wrongdoing.	• Public domain searches • Interviews with the subject and/ or others • Subpoenaed records • Company letterheads typically list directors' names • Social media searches • Workplace searches • Electronic device searches.

No	Area	Prompt	Discussion/interpretation	Conclusion	Source
p.	**Trusts**	Please specify any current or previous trusts that the subject or the subject's spouse/partner administer.	Trusts may be used to: ▪ Hide assets ▪ Hide ownership of companies ▪ Limit liability. All newly registered trusts in South Africa now need to be centrally registered on the web-based Integrated Case Management System (ICMS). The system was still in pilot in 2013. A web-portal allows for online searches. The system is not always up to date though. Existing trusts were not centrally registered and can only be traced at the local Master's office at which they were registered. You will need to have the trust's name to enable you to conduct a manual search on the trust's name at the Master's office.	▪ Identify trusts held by the subject or the subject's family. ▪ Understand what the trusts hold/purpose of the trust is. ▪ Determine if fraudulent transactions have been performed via these trusts. ▪ Has the organisation performed business with these trusts? ▪ Determine if the subject paid all taxes. ▪ You can also look for trusts to which funds have been transferred out of the subject's bank account. Determine why these payments have been made and who the members of the trust are.	▪ Public domain searches ▪ Interviews with the subject and/or others ▪ Subpoenaed records ▪ Company or trust letterheads typically list directors' names.

No	Area	Prompt	Discussion/interpretation	Conclusion	Source
q.	**Business interests**	Specify all private business interests held or engaged in by the subject or the subject's spouse/partner or the direct family members of the subject during the subject's tenure with the group. List percentage ownership and value of ownership where possible. List all companies in which the subject or the subject's spouse/partner has held or currently holds shares or any form of business interest. List the number and value of the shares as well. Specify all forms of income that the subject or the subject's spouse/partner receives, eg any form of rental income, dividends, salary, commission, royalties, interests, capital growth, discounts, preferential pricing, etc. Does the subject or the subject's spouse/partner hold any patent rights, intellectual property, etc?	Information concerning business interests may be an indication of: ▪ A conflict of interest ▪ Areas where procurement fraud could have occurred ▪ Places against which recoveries can be made ▪ Source of information (records, people to talk to, etc).	Determine if the aggrieved company (victim) has had any business dealings with any of the organisations with which the subject holds an interest. Analyse the dealings to determine if misconduct has occurred.	▪ Interviews with the subject and/or others ▪ Personnel records ▪ Subpoenaed records ▪ Public domain searches ▪ Physical work area searches ▪ Letterheads ▪ Professional and/or trade associations.

No	Area	Prompt	Discussion/interpretation	Conclusion	Source
r.	**Cronyism**	Is the subject politically connected? Does the subject express strong one-party political views? Is the subject a known member of a political party? Who are the subject's friends?	While cronyism is not limited to politicians, it is very prevalent in politics. Subjects may be extending favour to their friends. Subjects with strong political connections are frequently inclined to provide business to and or receive business from political associates. This is very prevalent in government institutions especially where procurement and tenders are dealt with. Dealing with political parties or people with government influence may be subject to anti-bribery restrictions. Establish what local and international laws are with regards to dealing with government officials in the context of organisation transactions.	Try to understand if the organisation has done business with the political party members. Understand if due process was followed. Understand who the subject's friends are and determine if the organisation has done business with them.	▪ Interviews with the subject and/ or others ▪ Social media searches ▪ E-mail searches.

No	Area	Prompt	Discussion/interpretation	Conclusion	Source
s.	**Power of attorney**	Does the subject or the subject's spouse/partner hold any general powers of attorney (POA) or does anyone hold any powers of attorney over the subject?	A POA could be an indication of another person who may have fallen prey to fraud, being the giver of the POA or the holder of the POA. It could also indicate that the subject is not in a position to run their own affairs.	If suitable, contact the parties involved in the POA and determine the reason for the POA. Understand if they have fallen prey to fraud or if there have been any suspicious behaviours that they have noticed.	▪ Interviews with the subject and/or others.
t.	**Investments**	Specify all shares, debentures, stock, interest-bearing investments, etc held by the subject, the subject's spouse/partner or children and immediate family, as relevant. Specify all investment policies, retirement annuities, unit trusts, fixed investments, shares, syndicates, etc held by the subject, the subject's spouse/partner and/or their children. Determine if the subject has issued any loans to any friends or family. Does the subject or the subject's spouse/partner own or have the right to time-share (shared holiday apartments or property syndicate) or similar arrangements? Does the subject or the subject's spouse/partner own any offshore investments? Specify the history (value, periods applicable and income received) of these investments.	Investments may represent: ▪ Places where misappropriated funds could be hidden ▪ Places from which to recover funds ▪ Conflicts of interest ▪ Explanations for how the subject's lifestyle is funded.	List the investments and analyse for misconduct. What was the source of the funding of the investments and is it within the subject's means to be in a position to afford such investments? Compare the investments over the suspected period of the misconduct. Independently value the investments and determine if claims can be instituted against them.	▪ Interviews with the subject and/or others ▪ Personnel files ▪ Public domain searches ▪ Volunteered records ▪ Subpoenaed records ▪ Work area searches ▪ Electronic device searches.

No	Area	Prompt	Discussion/interpretation	Conclusion	Source
u.	**Memberships**	Specify all current and previous memberships of: ▪ Clubs ▪ Sport clubs ▪ Professional bodies ▪ Societies ▪ Alumnae.	Memberships may provide knowledge of: ▪ People to be interviewed about the subject ▪ People who could have a corrupt relationship with the subject (cronyism) ▪ Potential places where misappropriated funds could have been applied ▪ Bodies to which professional misconduct may need to be reported (for example: the law society, Institute of Chartered Accountants, engineers' guild, etc). It is also common for subjects to misrepresent their qualifications. While not always directly attributable to the fraud under investigation, the qualifications may need to be verified. This may provide insights into the general ethics of the subject.	List all memberships and analyse for potential information as per adjacent discussion.	▪ Interviews with the subject and/ or others ▪ Work area searches ▪ Subpoenaed records ▪ Electronic device searches ▪ Social media searches ▪ Direct contact with institutions ▪ Original document verification.

No	Area	Prompt	Discussion/interpretation	Conclusion	Source
v.	**Employment**	Specify the subject or the subject's spouse/partner's employment history.	An employment history may provide knowledge of: - People and/or companies to interview about the subject - The type of person the subject is - The history of prior offences - Places against which civil recovery claims can be lodged (pension funds, garnishee orders) - Loyalties at play - Potential conflicts of interests - Potential misrepresentation of employment history. Job-hopping around a lot may be an indication of a person who: - Is unqualified to perform tasks - Has a history of performance issues - Is a recurring offender of misconduct.	List all employers. Contact old employers if practical in terms of the investigation. Privacy restrictions may be applicable. Be aware of slanderous accusations. Determine if there were any dealings with these companies during the subject's tenure and the nature of these dealings. Determine if the person was guilty of misconduct at these previous employers (they are typically repeat offenders). If so, what methods did they employ, as this may give insights into current methods employed.	- Personnel files - Interviews with the subject and/or others - Electronic device searches - Workspace searches - Subpoenaed record - Public domain searches - Social media searches.

No	Area	Prompt	Discussion/interpretation	Conclusion	Source
w.	**Marital status**	What is the subject or the subject's spouse/partner's current marital status? How long has the subject and/or the subject's spouse/partner been married/in a common-law union/tribal union/religious union? How would you describe the subject's marriage to date? Please specify how many times the subject or the subject's spouse/partner has been married. Identify potential pressures in the current/previous relationships.	Being married or not married itself will not be a guarantee of anything in terms of a fraud indicator. Knowledge of the subject's marital history will provide information concerning: ▪ The stability of the subject ▪ People (partners) who can be interviewed for information ▪ People and/or assets against which civil claims can be lodged ▪ Signs of financial pressure if the subject is paying (high) maintenance.	List all marriages on a timeline. Analyse them for signs of potential pressure. List any alimony payments made and over which periods.	▪ Personnel files ▪ Interviews with the subject and/or others ▪ Electronic device searches ▪ Workspace searches ▪ Subpoenaed records ▪ Social media searches ▪ Public domain searches.
x.	**Dependants**	Please specify all dependants that the subject or the subject's spouse/partner has or any other person the subject or the subject's spouse/partner is currently taking care of including: ▪ Blood children (full or half) ▪ Children from previous relationships ▪ Adopted children ▪ Parents ▪ Other family or friends.	The list of dependants may provide information concerning: ▪ Financial pressure that the subject is under ▪ People to interview about the subject ▪ Places/people that may be holding assets (knowingly or unknowingly) on behalf of the subject ▪ People against whom claims can be lodged.	List all dependants and estimate the effect on lifestyle costs of these dependants. Retain this information for use in the detailed lifestyle audit and/or interviews.	▪ Personnel files ▪ Interviews with the subject and/or others ▪ Electronic device searches ▪ Workspace searches ▪ Subpoenaed records ▪ Public domain searches ▪ Social media searches.

No	Area	Prompt	Discussion/interpretation	Conclusion	Source
y.	**Society**	Does the subject or the subject's spouse/partner support any charitable societies? What volunteer/community work do they do? This is going to seem like an unlikely item to include in a lifestyle audit.	In two examples, the subjects spent a lot of the illicitly obtained funds on charity work and/or the church. In neither of the cases was the giving of the funds to the charities the main application of the funds nor the motive for misappropriating the funds. It was my unscientific opinion at the time that the subjects gave the funds to these causes as they: - Derived some sort of respect from doing these 'good deeds'. Subjects are typically lonely (despite frequently being in the company of people) and have an above-average need to be liked and/or respected. - Were acutely aware of their misdeeds and somehow felt that the misdeeds were 'less wrong' if they also gave part of the proceeds to a good cause. As discussed under the chapter on interviewing, no one wants to be associated with wrongdoing. People (good and bad) try to distance themselves from wrongdoing and/or present a front that they are 'good'. The active involvement and/or sponsoring of charitable activities may let them feel that they are not really a bad person. The identification of charities may represent: - People to be interviewed regarding the subject - Areas of financial pressure on the subject - Places against which recoveries can be launched - Loyalties at play. For example: in another matter, the subjects were all members of the same church or Freemason society, etc. This was a case of cronyism.	In discussions try to establish if the subject is involved in charitable activities and to what degree.	- Interviews with the subject and/or others - Electronic device searches - Workspace searches - Social media searches.

No	Area	Prompt	Discussion/interpretation	Conclusion	Source
z.	**Education**	Please specify the schools that the subjects' dependants/children attend. Please specify the subject or the subject's spouse/partner's educational qualifications. Please specify any tertiary education that the subject or the subject's spouse/partner are currently engaged in.	Information about a subject's educational background may give you background information on the type of person you are dealing with. This may be of use when profiling a subject. Remember that the typical fraudster is intelligent and frequently well educated (the chapter on interviewing refers with regards to the typical personality traits of a fraudster). In another example, one of my more senior colleagues (and a well-respected member of the local IIA chapter) had amongst other things faked some of his professional designations. It is always sad to see a professional fall foul of the law. It may also be an indication of financial pressure that the subject is under, especially if the subject's dependants are at expensive private schools. Educational backgrounds may also be an indication of loyalties if subjects went to the same institutions. An example refers, when the FD of a multinational organisation called me in and demanded (at the very early stage of the investigation) if the subject was guilty, as he went to school with him and he needed to know. Private school and specific prestigious university alumnae tend to look after each other long after they have completed their education just because they attended the same institution (the so-called 'old boys' club').	List all schools, universities, etc attended by the subject or subject's family. Understand the financial impact of the fees and extramural activities on the subject. List all educational qualifications of the subject (these can frequently be verified online). Determine if there are any obvious loyalties at play or if there have been direct (potentially fraudulent/corrupt) dealings with old colleagues.	▪ Interviews with the subject and/or others ▪ Personnel files ▪ Public domain searches ▪ Electronic device searches ▪ Workspace searches ▪ Subpoenaed records ▪ Social media searches.

No	Area	Prompt	Discussion/interpretation	Conclusion	Source
aa.	**Hobbies and interests**	Please describe the subject or the subject's spouse/partner and family's hobbies and interests. What does the subject or the subject's spouse/partner do for fun, to relax, etc? Hobbies and leisure activities are luxuries and can be a drain on discretionary funds. Not all leisure activities are that ethical either. Our rule that 'it always involves sex, drugs, gambling or some other form of vice' refers.	Information on the subject's hobbies may provide information concerning: ▪ Places where funds were misappropriated to ▪ Assets against which a civil claim can be lodged ▪ People to interview about the subject ▪ Speak to the general ethics of the subject.	List all hobbies and private interests of the subject and subject's immediate family. Determine if these are within their known lifestyle. Understand what the activities tell us about the subject's ethics (for example the frequenting of brothels).	▪ Interviews with the subject and/or others ▪ Personnel files ▪ Public domain searches ▪ Electronic device searches ▪ Workspace searches (including photos) ▪ Subpoenaed records (transaction history) ▪ Social media searches.
bb.	**Leisure activities**	Please describe how frequently the subject or the subject's spouse/partner makes use of the following in their private capacity: ▪ Holidays away/activities ▪ Hotels ▪ Restaurants ▪ Bars/pubs ▪ Clubs ▪ Casinos ▪ Brothels, strip clubs, 'revue' bars etc ▪ Theatres, cinemas, etc.	Information about leisure activities may be an indication of: ▪ Financial pressure that the subject may be under ▪ Places where misappropriated funds may have been applied ▪ Financial transactional history to be used in subsequent detailed lifestyle audits ▪ Activities that could have been enjoyed by the subject as bribes ▪ The type of person we are dealing with. The frequenting of brothels and strip clubs seems to be a consistent theme with male subjects. This speaks to their general ethics and the vices that they need to fund.	List all leisure activities that the subject/subject's family were engaged in over the period of the misconduct. Understand the financial implication of the leisure activity and from where it was funded. Understand what these say about the subject's ethics.	▪ Interviews with the subject and/or others ▪ Personnel files ▪ Public domain searches ▪ Electronic device searches ▪ Workspace searches ▪ Subpoenaed records ▪ Social media searches.

No	Area	Prompt	Discussion/interpretation	Conclusion	Source
cc.	**Private telephones and/or electronic devices**	Please specify all phones and/or electronics held by the subject or the subject's spouse/partner and their family/dependents. Electronic devices include, but are not limited to: ▪ Telephones ▪ Tablets, iPads, PDAs ▪ Personal computers ▪ MP3 players/recorders ▪ Memory sticks, external hard drives, etc ▪ Cameras ▪ Smartwatches.	Information about privately owned and/or funded electronic devices may be an indication of: ▪ Financial pressure that the subject is under (electronic devices are frequently a status symbol. Some fraudsters seem to like to surround themselves with status and glossy items. These devices can be expensive. They may also require connectivity costs). ▪ Places where illicitly obtained funds were applied. ▪ An abuse of power if these were funded directly by the organisation. ▪ Assets/telephone equipment that was given to the subject in a corrupt relationship. ▪ Telephone/data/browsing records that may need to be subpoenaed to prove relations or that list banking history (texts to the phone by the banking institution). ▪ Devices that need to be searched for information.	List all the electronic devices owned by and/or funded by the subject. Determine: ▪ The financial impact of these devices ▪ The devices that need to be searched ▪ If the detailed telephone financial records or call history need to be subpoenaed.	▪ Interviews with the subject and/or others ▪ Personnel files ▪ Public domain searches ▪ Electronic device searches ▪ Workspace searches ▪ Subpoenaed records ▪ Subject-volunteered device searches.

No	Area	Prompt	Discussion/interpretation	Conclusion	Source
dd.	**Working relationships**	Has the subject or the subject's spouse/ partner or family had any relationships (friendship, romantic, business, family, religious, etc) with any person in the group or person who provides goods or services to the group or who makes use of the group's services? Please specify. Relevant relationships can be with: ▪ Senior staff members ▪ Junior staff members ▪ Suppliers, clients and business partners of the organisation. Relationships are more difficult to detect if people have any of the following in common: ▪ Family ties ▪ Tribe, clan, neighbourhood, country, etc ▪ Previous work backgrounds ▪ School or university ▪ Religious background ▪ Sexual persuasion ▪ Gang ▪ Political party support ▪ Sports or other club membership (the proverbial 'old boys' club') ▪ Business grouping (for example a 'brotherhood' or the Freemasons).	Knowledge of the subject's relationships may give you information about: ▪ The type of person they are and their ethical values (having affairs/ propensity to commit misdeeds) ▪ Stability of the subject ▪ Loyalties that may be at play ▪ Financial pressure (divorces are expensive and mistresses even more) ▪ Places/people where corrupt relationships could have existed ▪ People who can be interviewed in respect of the subject ▪ Potential conflicts of interest. While it is perfectly normal to appoint people whom you trust because of previous good working experiences with them, the unfair favouritism of such people represents a problem. It is often very difficult (especially for an 'outside' investigator) to identify these relationships. It is best to try to identify these underlying relationships and loyalties while interviewing other people about the subject/s. This may indicate loyalties and other subjects potentially involved in a scheme.	▪ List the relationships and understand the implication of these on the subject as a person or on their financial situation. ▪ Were any of these relationships corrupt? ▪ Did the organisation ever trade with any of these people/ organisations? ▪ Were the required conflict of interest declarations made at the time? ▪ Are these relationships common knowledge and what do others think about them?	▪ Interviews with the subject and/ or others ▪ Personnel files ▪ Observation ▪ Telephone records ▪ Subpoenaed records ▪ Workspace searches ▪ Electronic device searches ▪ Social media searches.

No	Area	Prompt	Discussion/interpretation	Conclusion	Source
			Numerous examples refer where one influential employee recruited staff members they knew from another previous background. These staff members then proceeded to collude to circumvent controls and defraud the organisation. These were as blatant as the fact that the staff members came from the same church group, tribe, suburb, country background or political party.		
ee.	**Absenteeism**	Please describe the subject's work attendance.	Work attendance history may be an indication of: • The type of person the subject is • The times that they have access to assets/ business premises and therefore the opportunity to perform the misdeed • The times that they were not at the work place and during which they had the opportunity to perform their misdeeds outside of the organisation. Subjects typically do not take leave as they need to be at work constantly to maintain their scheme and prevent detection. It is frequently when they are absent that their scheme is detected. *An example refers where the pressure of what the subject had done just became too much and the subject could not keep rolling the funds to keep his scheme afloat.* *The subject absconded and the fraud was identified.* Some subjects are also frequently 'duckers and divers'. They avoid work and can seem incompetent or lazy. Others rarely take off as they need to ensure that their schemes are kept alive and that they keep prying eyes away. Many publicised examples and my own experiences refer of schemes that were detected when the subject was no longer at work.	Analyse personnel records. Understand who is always absent without due reason. Understand those in a position to perpetrate fraud and whom never/rarely take off.	• Interviews with the subject and/or others • Personnel files • Access records.

No	Area	Prompt	Discussion/interpretation	Conclusion	Source
ff.	**Work relations and general performance**	Has the subject ever been in or is the subject currently the subject of an internal disciplinary procedure? What is the subject's history of internal counselling/hearings? Understand the nature of the hearings in relation to the current matter and the general ethics and make-up of the person. What is the subject's work performance like? Do they get on well with their colleagues and peers? Are they well respected? Are they well trusted and in a position to influence matters?	This may assist us to understand what type of person we are dealing with. People who perpetrate fraud do not only 'cheat' in one way (stealing). They may also evade their work responsibilities and have overall poor work performance. In other cases, they put up a front of always being a good worker. Once you scratch, you find that the actual performance is a little different than the outwardly projected picture. Poor work performance may be an indication that the subject is applying their time and effort whilst at work to non-work (and potentially fraudulent) activities. Aggressive, defensive behaviour is one manner that people keep others away from what they are doing to avoid detection/ criticism.	Formulate a picture of how the subject is with friends, junior colleagues and senior colleagues. Understand what this tells you about their propensity to have been involved in the matter at hand.	■ Interviews with the subject and/or others ■ Personnel files ■ Electronic device searches ■ Workspace searches.

No	Area	Prompt	Discussion/interpretation	Conclusion	Source
gg.	**Losses/ trauma**	Has the subject or the subject's family undergone or been exposed to any trauma in the last few years? Please specify.	Traumas often put great financial pressure on people. There may be bills to pay for medical costs, legal costs, replacement of assets, etc. This also speaks to the subject's stability and/or general state of mind. Our rule refers: 'I have never met a Robin Hood yet.' To the same degree, I have never come across anyone who has perpetrated a fraud solely due to some mental or physical trauma that they have endured. What is more relevant is that legitimate expenses erode a person's disposable income that may have been used to fund their vices. The desire for the vice will remain and may even be stronger in difficult times. The vice will need to be funded from another means if legitimate income sources have been exhausted.	Formulate a picture of the subject and determine if this is expected to place pressure on their lifestyle or if it has actually impacted their ability to fund their lifestyle. Use this information later in the detailed lifestyle analysis of the subject's expenditure and income.	▪ Interview with the subject and/ or others ▪ Personnel files ▪ Electronic device searches ▪ Workspace searches ▪ Volunteered records.

No	Area	Prompt	Discussion/interpretation	Conclusion	Source
hh.	**General health, medical conditions, disabilities, chronic illnesses, mental health and addictions**	Does the subject or any of the subject's family suffer from any health impediments? Is the subject or any of the subject's family on chronic medication or subject to special medical treatment? Has the subject ever been to rehab or had mental instability problems?	As with trauma discussed above, poor health can result in a lot of financial pressure. Again, this can erode their disposable income and their vices may need to be funded elsewhere. *An example refers where the subject told me about a medical problem that his son had had. It was my suspicion that he told me this in an attempt to soften me up. This helped me however later, as there were no/disproportionately few medical bills. This was one of the contributing factors indicating that his lifestyle was funded by other means.*	Form a picture of the subject and the subject's family's medical situation and try to understand if this adds financial or emotional pressure.	- Interview with the subject and/or others - Personnel files - Electronic device searches - Workspace searches - Subpoenaed records - Social media searches - Volunteered records.
ii.	**Receipts, favours, gains, fortuitous gains, prizes, etc.**	Has the subject or the subject's family ever inherited money or assets, won prizes or been given any items of value, property, investments, etc? Have any policies, retirement annuities or fixed-term investments ever been paid out to the subject?	Information of this nature may give insights into places from which the subject's lifestyle could have been funded. A detailed analysis of an underfunded lifestyle may determine the quantum of the shortfall, which could be potentially matched to the known loss incurred by the company to determine if the entire fraud has been identified.	Determine, in the preparation of a detailed lifestyle calculation, if the subject's lifestyle is over or underfunded. Identify the alleged and actual sources of the income. Determine if all income has been from legitimate sources.	- Interview with the subject and/or others - Personnel files - Electronic device searches - Workspace searches - Subpoenaed records - Volunteered records - Direct verification with outside institutions.

No	Area	Prompt	Discussion/interpretation	Conclusion	Source
		Has the subject or any direct family member ever received any special discounts, favours or gains or similar from any other person who is within the group or who provides goods and services to the group, or who receives goods or services from the group? Some organisations allow their staff members to purchase items for private use from the organisation's suppliers. This concession is normally subject to strict policy and approval.	Understanding this information may assist to identify: ▪ Legitimate sources from which their lifestyle could have been funded ▪ Dishonest assertions about how their lifestyle was funded ▪ That there is a variance between what the subject is alleging was their income and what their lifestyle suggests ▪ Places against which recovery claims can be instituted. The lesson is to ensure that you have some form of proof of these assertions. Subjects also try to legitimise to their colleagues and friends where they obtained the money from or how they are able to afford their lifestyle. You will find that they typically take an actual situation and embellish on it to ensure that it is believable to the listener. In the examples below, the 'players' in the subject's story were real people who frequently were in similar roles. The roles were just not as profitable as alleged.		

No	Area	Prompt	Discussion/interpretation	Conclusion	Source
			The following examples refer when subjects made similar allegations to me: ▪ *The subject said that his father-in-law was a wealthy businessman of a successful business (raw meat chicken reseller) with many trucks. The subject said that his father-in-law sponsored many things for the subject and the subject's wife. The subject said that he was frequently embarrassed by his father-in-law's generosity, but his in-laws had a very close relationship with their daughter (the subject's wife). The in-laws had a nice house on the outside and this seemed plausible initially. It later emerged in my investigation (based on transactions running through the subject's bank account) that the father-in-law did not have his own bank account and that the subject frequently had to pay the chicken farm on his behalf. A successful businessman without his own bank account was not believable. In reality, his father-in-law was a common hawker who bought and sold chickens (on a cash-basis) to people out of the back of his van (not a fleet of trucks). I thanked the subject for the declaration and asked him if he was comfortable that his in-laws now needed to testify to confirm his allegations of how his lifestyle was funded. I also told him that I trusted that his in-laws' taxes were in order and that they could prove to the tax authorities that they had declared all their cash income. The subject resigned telephonically the next day.*		

No	Area	Prompt	Discussion/interpretation	Conclusion	Source
			▪ *In another instance, a subject alleged that his wife was a high-earning accountant in a 'big business'. The subject frequently drove new cars and alleged that his father-in-law was 'in the car business' and lent him the vehicles. In reality, the wife was an unskilled bookkeeper in a single branch of a retail tyre franchise and the subject was hiring vehicles on at the company's expense.* ▪ *In another case, I was profiling a group of financial staff members to identify who the perpetrator/s could have been. One lady had previously told her colleagues that she had won a sizable cash prize from the bank. When I heard this, I was immediately suspicious and I called the bank to verify her allegation. In this case, the bank verified that she had in fact received the prize, as part of a national marketing campaign. The lady sitting opposite this initial subject turned out to be the actual perpetrator of the fraud.* The lesson is that a person cannot know in advance if a subject's allegations are truthful or not. It is therefore prudent and necessary to validate all assertions.		

CHAPTER 7

SUBSEQUENT ACTIONS

7.1. CHAPTER OVERVIEW AND INTRODUCTION

There are a finite number of actions that can occur in reaction to fraud incidents. These include initiating criminal action so as to punish perpetrators, embarking on a civil claim to recover losses, engaging in a labour action to discipline transgressors, reporting (discussed in Chapter 8) and the bolstering of internal controls (discussed to some degree in Chapter 1 on strategic fraud risk management) to mitigate future fraud risks. In this chapter, we will discuss the principles of criminal, civil and labour matters.

The purpose of this book is to provide practical guidance on fraud matters. In terms of this practical guidance, this chapter is not intended to provide a list of all applicable laws and regulations that may have a bearing on a fraud matter. It is also not intended to give detailed insights into the interpretation of laws and on complex legal debates. It is merely designed to give a practical overview of some relevant points and considerations when embarking on such matters. Please supplement your knowledge with specialised legal knowledge and/or consult subject matter experts, as required.

A further constraint is that international organisations can be more challenging than national organisations in so far as they operate in multiple jurisdictions. It is difficult to be au fait with the individual laws within multiple jurisdictions at the same time, especially if you are not from a legal background and/or if this is not your primary daily focus. This does not have to be so daunting though. While you will naturally have stronger experience in your home base country, you will quickly see that very similar principles apply in different countries. Always check your understanding with a relevant legal expert for each location and situation that you find yourself in and build on your knowledge base.

The primary goal of this chapter is therefore firstly to develop an appreciation for what these principles are and, secondly, how to apply them.

7.1.1. Legal avenues

There are three legal avenues which can be pursued around a fraudulent matter that we are going to discuss. Each of these is pursued in a different tribunal with different aspects being argued. The three matters are independent of each other and can occur simultaneously or at their own time. The three matters are:

- *Criminal case*
  The parties involved in a criminal case are the state versus an individual/group of individuals. Criminal cases must be proved 'beyond a reasonable doubt'. This is done in a criminal court (magisterial, regional or high court).

- *Civil case*

The parties involved in a civil matter are the complainant versus a defendant. The complainant and defendant can be any two legal entities or persons against each other. You are required to prove the 'quantum' (amount or value) and the 'merit' (is there sound basis to your claim) of a civil case. This can be done in a civil court (magisterial, regional or high court).

- *Labour case*

This involves mostly the organisation versus an employee of the organisation or vice versa. You are required to prove your case on a 'balance of probability'. This can be done at: internal labour tribunals, labour courts or special external labour tribunals (for example the Commission for Conciliation, Mediation and Arbitration (CCMA), discussed later.

7.1.2. List of laws

The following is a quick reference guide of some of the laws that may have a bearing on fraud cases in South Africa and abroad:

The purpose of understanding these Acts and rules is to ensure that:

- Investigations do not transgress these rules
- To identify where individuals' rights (as victims) have been violated
- To gather evidence against perpetrators of transgressions.

Legal areas relating to fraud cases include the common law of the country, the law of contract, the law of agency, and anti-trust and competition law. King III and King IV for ethical leadership and good corporate governance will also have a bearing on fraud cases. Specific legislation includes:

South Africa:

- Basic Conditions of Employment Act 75 of 1997
- Companies Act 71 of 2008
- Constitution of the Republic of South Africa 108 of 1996
- Consumer Protection Act 68 of 2008
- Criminal Procedure Act 51 of 1977
- Customs and Excise Act 91 of 1964
- Electronic Communications and Transactions Act 25 of 2002
- Financial Intelligence Centre Act 38 of 2001
- Human Rights Commission Act 54 of 1994
- Investigation of Serious Economic Offences Amendment Act 46 of 1995
- Labour Relations Act 66 of 1995
- Law of Evidence Amendment Act 45 of 1988
- National Credit Act 34 of 2005
- Occupational Health and Safety Act 85 of 1993, as amended
- Prevention and Combating of Corrupt Activities Act 12 of 2004
- Prevention of Organised Crime Act 121 of 1998
- Prevention of Organised Crime Amendment Act 24 of 1999
- Prevention of Organised Crime Second Amendment Act 38 of 1999

- Promotion of Access to Information Act 2 of 2000
- Promotion of Access to Information Amendment Act 54 of 2002
- Protection of Personal Information Act 4 of 2013
- Regulation of Interception of Communications and Provision of Communication-related Information Act 70 of 2002
- Securities Services Act 36 of 2004
- South African Reserve Bank Act 90 of 1989
- Taxation Laws Amendment Act 22 of 2012

United Kingdom:

- Bribery Act 2010
- Proceeds of Crime Act 2002

United States:

- Foreign Corrupt Practices Act (FCPA) of 1977
- Sarbanes-Oxley Act (SOX) of 2002

7.2. FOREIGN-BASED CONSIDERATIONS

7.2.1. Introduction

As discussed before, the multi-national nature of organisations today requires the consideration of many laws and regulations. The US, Europe and the UK are three common areas of trade. It is wise therefore to have a working understanding of some of their fraud and corruption-related international laws. For example, in the US, the organisation in which you are conducting work for may have foreign legislation compliance issues if:

- Information passes through or is saved in the US
- A US citizen is involved and/or is on board a ship
- A ship flies a US flag
- Goods are travelling to or from the US
- The organisation is dealing with a US-based company
- An organisation is listed on the US stock exchange
- Contracts/dealings with countries/entities are on the US banned list
- Trading in goods listed by the US in their banned list
- There are any dealings with the US government or agencies.

The implications of transgressing EU, UK or US laws can be very onerous. For example a company listed on the US stock exchange may for example pay a bribe in Africa, but be sued in the US for this act even though the act was not perpetrated in the US. Ensure that you consult legal experts on cross-country legal issues.

7.3. CRIMINAL CASES

7.3.1. Introduction

The purpose of this section is to give you an overview of the typical process followed in a criminal matter.

7.3.2. Reporting requirement

Certain matters (based on the type of crime and/or the seriousness thereof) may require immediate reporting to the police/authorities (local or international). For example, in South Africa, section 34 of the of the Prevention and Combating of Corrupt Activities Act requires: '[a]ny person who holds a position of authority and who knows or ought reasonably to have known or suspected that any other person has committed...' an offence as defined by the Act to report such knowledge or suspicion to the directorate of Priority Crime Investigations. Failure to do so would make the person guilty of an offence and they may be subject to harsh punishment. The US has similar requirements for corruption-type matters.

This is of course both a great help and a burden to fraud investigators. It is a great help when management does not want to register a particular matter. In these cases, shrug your shoulders and say to management that you unfortunately have no choice and that you are sure that they do not want to be imprisoned for not reporting the matter. This tends to have the desired effect, with management asking you to report it, but not to do anything further.

On the other hand, the Act provides that matters need to be reported immediately. This is of course not practical, as you rarely have all the facts to be in a position to know if the matter is serious or not when the matter first comes to your attention. If you do not have the facts, then there is even less chance that the police will be able to get to the bottom of a matter related specifically to your industry, which they do not have knowledge and understanding of.

It is acceptable to perform your investigation first and even sometimes to conduct the internal hearings (normally quicker than criminal matters) before registering the criminal case. This is done to ensure that you hand all pertinent facts over to the police and prosecution. In this manner, the prosecution is better positioned to evaluate if additional work needs to be conducted. You will obtain the best response from the prosecution and the investigating officer (IO) when you give them all the facts on a 'silver platter'.

As a rule, do not delay the reporting of criminal matters. Conduct a sufficient (defendable) investigation to know if there is basis for reporting or not. You will also tend to develop good relations with local police officers over time. Have a meeting with them and take the matter under their advisement. Ensure that you minute the discussion and send them a copy of the outcome of the meeting. There is definite merit in establishing whether the matter that you are dealing with needs to be registered and with which body.

7.3.3. Reporting

The opening of a criminal case is a relatively simple activity. It merely involves going to a police station and providing a very simple affidavit (called an A1). The police officer will ask a few clarifying questions and then open the docket. Most charge office constables have no or very little experience in fraud matters. Some (for this very reason) will send you directly to the detectives to register the case if they have detectives on the premises. This is good as you can then get to speak directly to the detectives who are going to handle your matter.

The general rule is that you should register the criminal case at the nearest police station in the physical area where the crime occurred. The most important is to register the case. Thereafter the police frequently transfer the matter to a more appropriate investigating unit (like the specialised commercial crimes unit). With serious crimes, there may very well be a central directorate through which you can register the matter and they will then redirect it to the investigation team they deem suitable. Different countries have different reporting methods. External forensic consulting firms have a lot of experience with this. Discuss the registration of the matter with your consultants.

The most important point is to ensure that you get the reference number when you register the case. You will receive the case number later. The case numbers of cases registered may be texted directly to your mobile. These numbers are vital for follow-up, all future correspondence and to prove that you have registered the matter. Ensure that you supply copies of all your detailed affidavits (some already obtained for the internal labour hearings) with all necessary evidence attached as annexures at the same time that you register the criminal case/lay the criminal charge. This will enable the investigating officer to be in the best position to decide on how to proceed with the matter.

7.3.4. Parties to a criminal matter

The following parties may be involved in a criminal matter:

- *Investigating officer*

  The investigating officer (known as the 'IO') is the person who conducts investigations on behalf of the state. The IO will normally have the rank of 'detective'. See point 7.3.6 below.

- *Station commander or commanding officer*

  The commanding officer (OC) is the most senior police officer at the police station at which the fraud case is registered. The commanding officer is the person who allocates investigations to detectives. The OC can ensure that:

  - A good IO is allocated to a matter.
  - Cases are prioritised if not enjoying sufficient attention.

  Do not run unnecessarily to the OC, as this may have a negative effect. Only use them as required. These are senior and busy people. Ensure that you are respectful when you approach them. Asking for their assistance is preferred to telling them what to do.

  The OC may very well want to be involved/have knowledge of high profile matters under their command. A collaborative approach is best.

- *Police commissioner*

It may be necessary to bring lethargic or undesirable investigations to the attention of the regional or national police commissioner to ensure that they get the desired attention. A matter will be brought to the police commissioner's attention via a formally drafted letter to the commissioner. Only make use of this course of action in exceptional cases.

- *Judge*

The judge is the person in charge of the court in which the matter is heard. The judge is also the person who pronounces judgment (see point 7.3.19 below) and hands down the sentence. See point 7.3.21 below.

- *Jury*

Juries are only applicable in those jurisdictions that make use of a jury system (like the USA). A jury is a group of normal, everyday people who are selected by the prosecution and defence team to listen to the matter and to give a verdict upon completion.

- *Victim*

The victim is the legal entity (person, people, trust or organisation) that has been or could potentially have been prejudiced by the fraud. The state (represented by the prosecutor) carries the victim's case.

- *Accused/defendant*

The accused is the person or the group of people who stands accused of specific charges in relation to the fraud matter.

- *Defence counsel*

Accused parties are not normally au fait with the intricacies of criminal proceedings. They are therefore normally represented in court by a lawyer. Representation in court is a basic right of all accused parties (the discussion on Miranda rights in Chapter 4 on interviewing refers). While not recommended, an accused can decline the right to be represented in court and elect to represent themselves. The state will appoint a lawyer to represent the accused if they cannot afford legal counsel. Not all legal counsel is equally senior enough. An accused needs to be represented by an advocate or senior counsel if in the high court or a more senior court.

- *Prosecutor*

The state puts laws in place in the form of Acts to define the 'rules' of a country. Contravention of these laws will normally be a criminal offence. In a criminal matter, it is the state versus the accused. The state represents the public's interests. The prosecutor is the person who leads the state's case against the accused. See point 7.3.8 below.

- *Senior prosecutor*

The senior prosecutor is the person who allocates cases to different prosecutors. See point 7.3.7 below.

- *Clerk of the court*

The clerk of the court is the person who makes all administrative arrangements on behalf of the court. The clerk does not attend court cases. The clerk of the court maintains the court role of which cases appear when, and in which courts.

- *Witnesses*

Witnesses are the people who are subpoenaed to give evidence and testify in court.

- *Expert witnesses*

These are special witnesses who are experts in their fields and are called to give special testimonies in the field. The court cannot be expected to have knowledge of all fields and so relies on experts to advise it.

- *A translator*

A translator may be required in instances where one or more of the parties involved in the court proceedings is unable to fluently converse in the tongue in which the proceedings are being conducted.

- *Stenographer*

Verbatim transcripts of court proceedings are made for future reference. A stenographer is a person who makes the transcript. A special machine is used to capture the transcripts, and recordings are normally also taken to supplement missed text. In the absence of a stenographer, the judge is required to take verbatim minutes of the proceedings. Court transcripts are public domain documents unless special circumstances apply.

- *Bailiff*

The bailiff is a police officer who stands in the courtroom. The bailiff's duties include:

  - Instructing the occupants of the entire courtroom to stand when the judge enters or leaves the courtroom
  - Ensuring that order is maintained in the courtroom
  - Bringing accused parties in and out of the courtroom from the holding cells.

- *Police officers*

Police officers may be required to chaperone an incarcerated prisoner to the court from prison and in and out of the courtroom from holding cells in the court precinct.

- *Observers*

Observers are normally allowed to observe proceedings in the public gallery. Observers may be disallowed throughout or for sections of the trial. Examples include where the identity of victims and/or witnesses needs to be protected (for example, when children are involved). Observers may not interfere with the proceedings and may be removed if they do. A person cannot observe the proceedings (others' testimonies) before they have testified themselves. Examples of observers include:

  - The victim, once they have testified
  - Witnesses who have already testified
  - Family or friends of the accused or defendant
  - Generally interested members of the public
  - Members of the media
  - Legal students.

Some of these parties are discussed in more detail below.

7.3.5. Type of court

There are different types of courts that exist for different purposes. The purpose could entail the seriousness of the crime or the type of matter being heard. Examples of courts include:

- *Magistrate's court*
  magistrates' courts are the lowest level courts and hear the least serious or less complicated matters.
- *Regional court*
  Regional courts hear matters more serious than those heard in magistrate's courts. Regional courts hear matters:
    - Of lower value fraud
    - Where the case is simpler
    - Where the evidence presented consists only of bank statements.
- *High court*
  High courts hear:
    - Very serious matters
    - Complex matters
    - High-value matters.
- *Supreme Court of Appeal*
  The defence or the prosecution may appeal a matter in a higher court if they are dissatisfied with the ruling handed down or sentence given by the judge. The Supreme Court of Appeal hears appeals from the high court.
- *Constitutional Court*
  The Constitutional Court is the highest court in the country and is the final place that a matter may be appealed. Matters are not retried on the facts of the case but seen against the party's constitutional rights.
- *Special purpose courts*
  Examples of special purpose courts include:
    - Small claims court
    - Specialised commercial crime court
    - Family court
    - Tax courts.

7.3.6. Investigating officer

An investigating officer (IO) will be assigned to the case by the commanding officer. The next step after registering the case is for you to meet with IO. In most countries, the police are overworked and they rarely have the business skills, experience and insights to be able to conduct a large-scale fraud investigation in a corporate organisation. This is just due to a lack of exposure to their work. More experienced police officers will have some exposure to different industries, but not to the same level of detail as a person working in those organisations.

It is therefore normally dependent on you, as the fraud investigator, to drive the process and obtain the evidence. This is good, as you have a degree of control over the outcome. The best results are achieved when a relationship is built with the IO. You will frequently be given the IO's name and contact number when the case number is given to you. It is recommended that you contact them a week or two after registering the case and arrange to meet them. Maintain a friendly and cooperative attitude. Be keen to volunteer to do things on their behalf and inquire what the next steps are and what you can do to expedite the process.

In a particular large fraud case, the matter was given to the 'specialised commercial crime unit'. It may have been more apt to have called them the 'slow crime unit' and the IO was certainly in no hurry to do anything. I had performed an extensive investigation and obtained 45 witness affidavits. In the meantime, I also established where the subject lived, where his children went to school, where his wife worked, who he socialised with and who his girlfriend was. Despite this, no arrests were made. I travelled to our regional office, borrowed the boss's car and drove to the IO. I then requested him to go with me and I took him to the subject's wife's place of work. She then told us where the husband worked and on the way there he phoned us and requested us not to come to his place of work and arranged to meet us at a nearby police station. All of a sudden there was momentum and the matter progressed.

7.3.7. Senior prosecutor

Once the IO is convinced that all the obvious investigative work has been done, the next step involves determining what needs to be done to ensure that the matter can be prosecuted.

Start by going with the IO to the senior prosecutor. The senior prosecutor is the person who allocates cases to the various prosecutors. The first goal is to try to ensure that a 'good' prosecutor is assigned to your matter. The IO will know who the good prosecutors are. You will have to depend on the IO to request the senior prosecutor to assign the case to a particular prosecutor. This does not always work, however. Do not get too hung up on who the prosecutor is as they frequently change in the initial stages of cases. The initially assigned prosecutor may not be the final prosecutor who takes the matter to trial. They may only do the initial appearances. *In the aforementioned IO example, I had three IOs, four prosecutors and a different judge every time the matter went to court, except for the trial itself. That is the reality of the legal system in many countries.*

The next step is to establish if the prosecution has everything that they require to prosecute.

This may be decided by the senior prosecutor or it may (in most cases) be decided by the assigned prosecutor who evaluates the evidence on hand. Prosecutors are measured on their performance, like any other business person. Prosecutors will, therefore, be reluctant to take on matters in which they will not be successful.

7.3.8. Prosecutor

Once you know who the prosecutor is, arrange to meet with them. Now, as a word of warning, all of these people (the IO, senior prosecutor, prosecutor and the clerk of the court) are busy people and they do not like outside people coming in and telling them what to do or 'bossing them around'.

You will need to balance persistence and cooperation to ensure that you do not irritate them and have the opposite effect resulting in them de-prioritising your matter.

Remember that in a criminal case it is the state versus the individual. Even though the organisation suffered the loss, it is the state that prosecutes people and not private legal entities (some exceptions apply, but are not relevant for this explanation). The prosecutor is the person who represents the state in criminal cases.

In some ways, this becomes the 'broken telephone' game. The challenge with the broken telephone game is that the message becomes increasingly skewed the further down the chain/line it travels. To make things worse the prosecutor and the IO also do not always read all facts available in the case and certainly not in the early stages of the matter. You as the investigator may, or you may feel that you are, the only person who knows and understands the case. Part of your challenge is to have to repeatedly ensure that everyone (IO and prosecutor) are au fait with the facts, without you getting irritated. Do not fight this, as it is futile and this is just the way it is. Ensure rather that you are aware of these limitations and be prepared to drive the process to ensure that there is a fair and favourable outcome.

The prosecutor will either ask you as the investigator or the IO to obtain additional requirements. These may include subpoenaed phone records, additional affidavits or amendments to existing affidavits. Setting date milestones are important to drive the process. Once the prosecutor has given the green light, the next stages can occur.

7.3.9. Warning letter

Once the state has decided to prosecute, the subject needs to be informed that there is a criminal case pending against them. This is done by requesting the subject to physically come to the police station, where the IO issues them with a formal warning letter. This is a standard police form with custom fields and not a full custom drafted letter. No evidence is presented to the subject at this point. The IO reads the letter to them and then asks them a few questions to ensure that the subject understands the seriousness of the matter at hand. The letter is just a warning letter and it may not have all the charges in their final form yet. In the worst case (if the subject absconds and/or refuses to cooperate) a warrant of arrest for the subject can be issued. This is seen as an extreme measure as putting someone in jail (albeit temporarily) may be a death sentence in itself.

7.3.10. Charge sheet

The prosecutor then needs to draw up the charge sheet. The charge sheet is a very detailed document specifying the exact charges. For example: 'Fraud in so far as on XX/VV/ZZ you made a payment of ZAR XXX.XX to ABC company.' The charge sheet is worded in legal language to avoid debates.

The judge will give their judgment per charge upon completion of the trial. For example: 'On charge one, guilty, on charge two, etc.' All proceedings, therefore, need to support this and run in the sequence of the charges. Each charge will dictate what needs to be proven and the type of evidence required (for example: to prove the movement of funds, a witness's testimony, etc).

7.3.11. Evidence file

In the same way, the evidence must support the charges. The prosecutor should, therefore, set up an evidence file(s). The evidence file runs in the sequence of the charges and gives each piece of evidence per charge. It is a good idea to volunteer to assist the prosecutor to set this file up, as you (as the investigator) are normally the most knowledgeable about the case and its facts. A good prosecutor would be au fait with the facts of the case and not require assistance. More complicated matters may require cooperation though.

The evidence file is used in court when each charge and its evidence is being debated. See Annexure 7.1 attached hereto for an evidence file summary template. The prosecutor will, at a glance, be able to assess if they have sufficient evidence per charge and/or what else is required.

7.3.12. Witness schedule

In the same way, and as far as possible, the witnesses need to be called per charge. This may not be possible if the same witness is going to testify on multiple charges. The prosecutor therefore also needs to draw up a witness schedule. The witness schedule is like the evidence file for people/witnesses. The witness schedule should include a short description of the evidence anticipated per witness.

See Annexure 7.2 attached hereto for an example of a witness schedule. Again, the prosecutor will, in this way, be able to determine if they have all witnesses per charge.

7.3.13. First appearances

Most (non-legal) people are keen to get the trial underway to know if the accused is guilty or innocent. People are however not always realistic about how quickly this can occur. There are many practical steps that need to be completed before a trial can commence. People often comment in frustration about the fact that an accused has appeared X number of times in a matter and that the matter keeps being postponed, implying that the prosecution is incompetent. The first appearances are not the trial and have a specific purpose. All court proceedings need to be fair to ensure that due consideration is given to all aspects.

First appearances are to ensure that:

- The person knows that they are being charged.
- The person has an opportunity to enter a plea.
- The need to incarcerate a person or release them on their own recognisance can be considered.
- Bail can be set, as appropriate.
- Requests for postponements can be heard. These must be supported by adequate reasons.
- Requests for information can be made.
- The need for any additional assessments can be heard (for example psychological assessments).

- Requests for legal assistance can be considered if the accused is unable to afford legal representation.
- Concerns about the proceedings can be heard from both the prosecution and the defence.
- An actual trial date is set.

Aside from the practical considerations leading up to a trial, the unfortunate reality is that unscrupulous defence attorneys often use 'standard tactics' to delay proceedings. The more a matter is delayed, the less likely success (conviction) becomes, as witnesses forget, die, etc. These sorts of delays can continue for a long time, delaying matters for months or even years.

Some standard defence delay tactics include:

- They did not receive all the information yet and are therefore not ready.
- They need additional time to prepare.
- Their client is sick and is unable to attend court proceedings. The matter, therefore, needs to be postponed.
- Their client has not paid them and they can therefore no longer represent them.
- There is a conflict of interest and they can no longer represent their client. An alternative defence needs to be appointed.
- The accused can no longer afford private legal counsel and the accused wishes to apply for legal aid.
- Once legal aid arrives, legal aid asks for more time to allow legal aid to prepare.
- Once legal aid is up to speed, the accused may say that they no longer like their legal representative and they want another representative.
- In exceptional cases, the accused says that they want to defend themselves.

The opposite extreme is also applicable. There have been numerous examples around the world of high-profile cases where the prosecution has tried to 'steamroller' the proceedings. This is also incorrect and not in the spirit of things.

Meet with the prosecution shortly before the first appearances and try to predict the delay tactics of the defence team. Ask the prosecutor how such tactics can be countered. There is a lot of merit in placing questions and requests on record in the court during the first appearances. This will block/limit delay tactics and create a reference point for later in the event that an excuse is used again, which was already placed on record.

As per the above, anticipate with the prosecutor the type of excuses and postponements which could be used, and plan accordingly. The prosecutor can then put certain aspects on record in the first appearances to head off the delays before they occur. You can only do so much, though, and you should also accept that some delays and postponements are inevitable.

7.3.14. Bail

Not everyone who stands accused of a matter needs to be incarcerated until trial. This is because:

- The jails would be full of people awaiting trial and there are not enough jails available.
- Not all accused people are a risk to society if they remain free until the trial.

- Jail can be dangerous and spending any time in jail could result in serious physical or psychological damage to people.
- Not all people are flight risks and there may not be a need to prevent a person from absconding.
- People need time to be allowed to prepare their defence.

Most accused parties are remanded to their own recognisance subject to certain conditions, including:

- Being under house-arrest and/or
- Reporting to their local police station X times per week and/or
- Wearing a tracking bracelet and/or
- Handing in their passport and/or
- Not going within Y distance of a harbour or an airport and/or
- Payment of a bail amount.

People often comment on the fact that a person's bail was set extremely low for a serious offence. Remember, bail is not a punishment. Bail is just a financial incentive to motivate people to turn up for trial, as bail is repayable if the person does not default on their appearances.

The awarding of bail and the amount of bail is influenced by:

- The seriousness of the crime
- If the person is a danger to themselves or to society
- If they have committed the crime or another serious crime before
- If the person is a flight risk
- Anything that the person has said which may lead to court to believe they should not be released
- The interests of society
- Previous precedent.

The cases we are dealing with are fraud cases. We are not dealing with murder and rape. Generally, a person (an accused) who has a family and a home/assets and who has been living in the same area for a long time is not deemed to be a flight risk. The court will, in initial proceedings, hear arguments for and against bail for the accused. The judge will set bail at an amount in accordance with guidelines and the accused will have to pay the money within a fixed period.

7.3.15. Preparing witnesses

Testifying can be a daunting task. Giving guidance to witnesses as to what they can expect in court can be beneficial. Preparing witnesses is a delicate task. You do not want to (or appear to) influence/school the witnesses. If witnesses need preparing, it is best if a person independent of the trial prepares the witness to know what to expect and what the general decorum in the court is. At no time should answers be prepared for questions.

You will recall from previous chapters that locking witness recollections down in affidavits (Chapter 8 on reporting also refers for more detail on this) is a preferred approach. The goals of this approach are achieved when the witness is preparing for trial. Witnesses are encouraged to:

- Read their affidavits to refresh their memory
- Always be 100% open and honest
- Openly say if they do not know something.

Tell witnesses that they are not on trial and as such, they should relax. They should just answer the questions posed to them in the best manner that they can. Ask witnesses (especially if they were close to the accused or if they were potentially implicated in the misconduct) if there is anything that the accused could use against them. Encourage them to tell you upfront so as to avoid surprises later and to help aspects to be managed in advance. Failure to do so may result in the defence team using undeclared facts to discredit the witness.

Part of the management of these sorts of issues may include them declaring in their (witness) affidavit, where context can be given, why they did what they did (for example in good faith) and to say that in hindsight they now realise that this was not the correct thing to have done. This could break the power of the accused using this against them.

An example refers of where a witness was reluctant to testify. It eventually came out that the reason for his reluctance was that the accused had given him some of the stolen goods. The witness was told to declare this to his seniors and to say that he had accepted the goods in good faith at the time (which he firmly believed), but that subsequent events and the accused's later behaviour made him suspicious about the source of the goods and the legality of the accused's actions.

7.3.16. Pre-trial conference

Pre-trial conferences are sometimes held in chambers to iron out specific aspects before the trial. The matters that are discussed and agreed in the pre-trial conference are not matters that need to be argued in court. They can be as simple as putting on record that the defence team has received all the required documents. A pre-trial conference is done to ensure that minor/easy to resolve matters are dealt with before the trial to prevent the trial being slowed down with less important aspects. Pre-trial matters are placed on record.

7.3.17. Trial

The trial is the court proceedings where the facts of the case are debated against the evidence presented and testimonies given. This is the real meat of the court proceedings and the stuff that we see in movies. You are encouraged to meet with the prosecutor to understand the logic of what they are going to try to prove and which arguments they are going to use. In this manner, you can see if there is anything that you can support them with. As stated previously you, as the investigator, will most likely have the most intimate knowledge of the matter.

For the greater part (and other than general and regular follow-up), there is not much that can be done by a person outside of the court. A good, cooperative relationship with the prosecutors will be of great assistance and while you cannot directly influence the court proceedings, you can have knowledge of what is happening and why. This helps dispel fears and creates confidence in what is occurring.

7.3.18. Special orders

While less applicable to fraud cases, a judge could give specific orders, for example that an accused is sent for psychiatric assessment. The judge will also advise the defence when the accused needs to return to court. Feedback will need to be given to the court by a suitably qualified person who carried out the court's orders (for example a doctor who assessed the accused).

7.3.19. Judgment

At the end of the trial, the judge adjourns the matter for judgment. The judge goes away and deliberates over the matter. This could be days or months for complex matters. The judge will typically inform the court in advance when they should return for him to give his judgment. The judge will give himself sufficient time to contemplate all aspects.

The judge uses legal principles to guide his decisions and it is not left to overall feelings. On judgment day, the judge will give judgment on each individual charge. The judge will summarise aspects discussed and the arguments for and against the charge. For example: 'In the first count of fraud, ... I find the defendant guilty/not guilty.' Judgment is not an all-or-nothing scenario. The accused may be found:

- Guilty on all charges
- Guilty on some charges and not guilty on others
- Not guilty on all charges.

The judge will then inform the court when they need to return for sentencing, as required.

7.3.20. Mitigation and aggravation

At this point, the accused knows their fate, as previously told to them when judgment was handed down. They know that they have been pronounced guilty on certain or all charges. It is now about what punishment they will receive. Before the judge hands down sentence, he hears statements in mitigation (normally by the defence team) and statements in aggravation (normally by the prosecution team). The prosecution may request victims to give statements in aggravation. The judge takes these arguments into account when determining the sentence.

7.3.21. Sentencing

Remember that while we may be angry about what the person did, the punishment needs to suit the crime. It goes without saying that a person found guilty of stealing USD 10 000 once should not receive the same punishment as a person who stole USD 10 million of pensioners' money over many years. Courts typically have sentencing guidelines and these may include minimum sentences that a judge must hand down in the event of finding a person guilty of such an offence. This is to ensure fairness and consistency.

Judges consider the following factors when determining sentence:

- Seriousness/consequences of the crime
- Value of the crime
- Number of counts of fraud committed per charge (speaks to the person's intentions)
- Period over which the crime was committed – was the crime committed over a long period of time (premeditated) or was it a once-off opportunity that the person misguidedly chose to do?
- If restitution has been made
- If the person cooperated with the investigation
- If the person showed remorse for their actions
- If the person was credible on the stand
- Sentencing guidelines/precedent
- Degree of trust expected of the person; for example, there is a higher expectation of trust from a financial director than a financial clerk
- Number of and type of victims
- Previous sentences
- Interests of society.

Sentence is given per charge. Sentencing could include any combination of the following:

- *Jail time*

The purpose of jail time is to remove a person from society for a prescribed period. Part of the idea of jail punishment is that the person is denied (part) of their civil rights. The fact that we continue to have crimes committed would seem to favour the argument that the pure denial of civil rights is insufficient to discourage people from committing crimes. Jails are notoriously frightening places and this, combined with the shame associated with being found guilty, would seem to be a stronger deterrent. A person can receive multiple jail sentences for different charges. Jail time can be served concurrently for different charges if the judge so decides.

- *A suspended sentence*

A suspended sentence means that the sentence does not need to be physically served unless the person is found guilty of the same or another serious crime within a prescribed period. For example, a judge may inform the accused that they are receiving a suspended sentence of three years, which is suspended for five years. If the person is found guilty of reoffending within the prescribed period (five years in the above example), then the original sentence (three years in this example) is added to the new sentence. The person will also not receive a suspended sentence again and they will be compelled to serve the time.

- *House arrest*

House arrest is like a jail sentence served at the guilty person's house. House arrest comes with restrictions. The person serving the sentence may not move about freely and may have to obtain special permission to go to the doctor or attend religious gatherings. The person may have to report to their local police station at prescribed intervals. The person may be required to wear a tracking device.

- *Communal service*

The guilty person may be required, as part of their sentence, to perform some sort of work for the society in which they live. Community service could entail many different services to the public. The idea is that the person should repay society for their misdeeds. They do this by doing some work in the community. Examples include:

  - Cleaning police stations
  - Cleaning streets
  - Working with state-run facilities for quadriplegics/paraplegics/etc.

- *Repayment of misappropriated funds*

The purpose of repaying the misappropriated funds is to place the victim (individual or legal entity/company) back in the original position that they were prior to the fraud. It would be counterproductive to allow a guilty person to retain the funds they misappropriated. The accused may see serving a short jail term as an easy sacrifice to obtain the funds.

- *Payment of costs*

Ordering a person to pay for litigation costs is not normally something that is done by a criminal court. Aggrieved parties normally need to initiate a civil claim to recover costs from guilty persons. A court may order one party to pay the other party's legal costs.

- *Being sequestrated (individual) or liquidated (company)*

A person may be sequestrated and a company may be liquidated if they are found guilty of an offence and not deemed to be able to administer their own affairs. A curator is appointed by the court to administer the financial affairs of the individual/company thereafter. A person can apply for rehabilitation and for the sequestration to be lifted after a certain period and/or if the original funds owing were repaid.

- *Enrolling in a mandatory rehabilitation programme*

The rehabilitation programme may not necessarily be related to the fraud committed and may have more bearing on the person's general lifestyle. Examples of rehabilitation programmes include:

  - Drug rehabilitation
  - Anger management
  - Debt counselling/credit management.

In most cases, guilt on charges will have the consequence that the person will receive a criminal record. This means that their record held centrally by the country's police force will be updated to reflect that the court has found the person guilty of specific charges. This will happen irrespective of the type of sentence received by the person.

Try to insist (in negotiations/plea bargains) that the person at least gets a criminal record for their actions. Broadly speaking, you should be less concerned if they serve ten years or receive a suspended sentence. The criminal record will follow them for the rest of their life (see expungement, discussed below). This is a sentence in itself. Some consequences of having a criminal record include:

  - People with criminal records cannot be directors of listed companies.
  - A person may be prevented from receiving a travel visa if they have a criminal record.
  - A person's criminal record may be checked at the time of application for employment. They may be declined for employment.

As a general rule, a person can only be excluded from employment if their criminal record has a bearing on their ability to perform their job. For example, a person convicted of fraud will most likely be unsuitable to work with money. The question is if a criminal record will ever be acceptable from an employment point of view? Two examples come to mind (discussed elsewhere in this book as well) where it did not matter:

- *A young man was employed as a junior buyer. He worked well. The organisation later introduced (upon my recommendation) proactive lifestyle searches of key personnel to identify high-risk personnel (Chapter 6 on lifestyle audits refers). It turned out that the young man had obtained a criminal record for assault when he was even younger. He had started his working career as a security guard. He assaulted someone in the course of his duties. It was not ideal, but understandable that a young inexperienced person in a high-risk/stressed environment may make such a mistake. No further action was taken after discussion with the individual. He continued to work well and eventually left the company for another more senior buying position.*
- *The second was the CEO of a group of companies. He would frequently joke with me (in my capacity as the auditor dealing with many fraud cases) and ask me if I was aware that he, in fact, had a criminal record. He too had received his criminal record when he was a young student. In his case it was for taking under-sized lobster out of the sea. This was hardly an issue when it came to his ability to run a sizable organisation very successfully.*

Remember, however, that it takes time for people's criminal records to be updated. It is therefore wise to ask the person being checked if there are any criminal matters pending against them.

It is also wise to have them sign a declaration to this effect. In this way, they can always be referred back to their declaration in the event that it is found that they were not truthful in their declaration.

It is possible to have a criminal record expunged. Again, you may be asking why the courts would want to do this, as it seems a little counterproductive (handing down sentence on the one hand and expunging on the other). Well, it comes down to what is deemed to be fair. It would not be fair to hold a person accountable for some menial criminal aspect that they did in error when they were very young. The example of the CEO above refers. Expungement is, however, a long and formal process, which is subject to strict criteria.

An example comes to mind of an individual who applied for employment. He declared that he had a criminal record, but advised the company that this was in the process of being expunged, as 'he had obtained this in the course of conducting volunteer police duties'. He proceeded to provide the company with a falsified cleared criminal record. My enquiries led to the identification of the falsified clearance certificate and a criminal case was opened against him. He had also not obtained his record in the carrying out of his police reservist duties as purported.

7.3.22. Appeals

Unfortunately, humans are fallible and while not all will agree, judges are human too. Not all decisions taken by judges will therefore necessarily be the right decisions. The legal system, in acknowledgement of this, has designed a mechanism by which to appeal decisions that are apparently incorrect. It should also be noted that various aspects of the decision can be appealed, including, but not limited to:

- The decision as to guilt or innocence
- The basis of guilt, for example 'manslaughter' or 'culpable homicide' versus 'murder' in a murder case
- The penalty handed down.

Both the defence (more commonly) and the prosecution could appeal a decision. Decisions are appealed because:

- The judge did not apply their mind to the facts of the matter.
- The decision was not within precedent.
- The decision was based on an unfair procedural process.
- The party appealing the decision does not feel the decision was fair.
- The party appealing the decision would like a more lenient or less lenient decision.

The appealing of matters seems to be a fairly standard practice these days. On the surface, a lot of these appeals seem unjustified. Many may even be ratified by the Supreme Court of Appeal. It is not possible to comment as to whether this increased propensity to appeal decisions is based on:

- A general 'ducking and diving' attitude of society and a brazen, last-ditch attempt by the guilty to try to wriggle out of the decision or to be perceived as 'innocent' by their contemporaries
- Lawyers wanting to make a name for themselves and/or money out of clients
- An indication of the quality of the legal system causing the apparent unfairness

The fact of the matter is that it happens frequently. The idea is not to take it personally, but to try to pre-empt possible factors that could lead to an appeal situation and endeavour to prevent these from occurring, through:

- Placing certain aspects on record in court that could be disputed/used later
- Use of suitably qualified and experienced 'experts' (a relative topic)
- Sound evidence/witness testimony.

An appeal is escalated to the next level of court. If a party is dissatisfied with the decision of a court they can appeal the decision in the next level of court. In theory, they can keep doing this until they get to the highest level court. The highest court in the country is the Constitutional Court. Decisions taken by the Constitutional Court are final and there are no further manners to appeal a decision taken by the Constitutional Court.

7.4. CIVIL CASES

7.4.1. Introduction

In most fraud cases, the organisation will have suffered some form of loss or have been prejudiced in some manner. The organisation will want to claim restitution for this loss. Losses incurred may include:

- Direct losses resulting from misappropriation of funds/assets
- Damages suffered as a result
- Penalties and/or fines
- Investigation costs
- Litigation costs to pursue the subjects
- Litigation costs to defend the organisation
- Loss of income
- Reemployment costs
- Reputational damage.

Restitution is the act of placing the aggrieved party back (or as close as possible) in the same position or situation they were before they were prejudiced. Restitution is either made voluntarily by the subject (in full or in part) or involuntary by way of an instruction (normally from a court of law). Recovery of financial loss is the most common means of restitution that we will deal with. Returning of assets may be another manner.

7.4.2. Recoveries

a. General

Recovering of costs, misappropriated funds, assets, information, intellectual property, etc forms such an important element of the work that we do that it warrants detailed discussion.

Recovery is important for both the aggrieved party and the transgressor. It is fairly obvious that the aggrieved party will want to be placed in a similar situation as they were before they were the victim of the crime. The following may be some of the ways in which the aggrieved party may seek recoveries from the transgressor:

- Having as much (if not all) of the misappropriated funds as possible repaid immediately or committing to instalment repayment
- Paying for investigation costs
- Covering legal fees
- Paying for lost income
- Paying for repair costs/damages
- Returning assets, records, patents, proprietary information, etc
- Destroying files, moulds, counterfeit goods, rerouting contracts and businesses, etc
- Signing restraints of trade and confidentiality agreements (to prevent further losses)
- Making of apologies, make media statements, etc (to regain public image)
- Destroying electronic copies of documents, etc to which they were not entitled.

Recoveries are also good for the transgressors in so far as transgressors:

- Get to demonstrate their remorse and willingness to cooperate (this may be seen in mitigation when the sentence is handed down)
- May also find this a method of redeeming themselves to their family, friends, and peers
- May be able to deal with feelings of guilt. Repayment may assist the transgressor to deal with these feeling (the discussion on the fraudster's personality in the chapter on interviewing refers).

Remember that you cannot recover more funds than were originally taken despite costs and/or losses incurred by the company as a result of the fraud. A court may award damages over and above the recovered loss. You are therefore compelled (despite how unfair it may seem) to pay the balance of any additional funds (that is to say over and above the original fraud or court order) back to the transgressor. In a simplified example: let us presume that the transgressor misappropriated USD 100 000. The transgressor's house is sold for USD 150 000. You would be compelled to give the transgressor the USD 50 000 over the original loss.

b. Discussion

The following are potential areas of financial recovery:

- *Repaying the remaining funds (if any)/returning the assets that were misappropriated*
This is easily achieved. You simply ask the transgressor if they have anything remaining. You then tell them that it is in their best interest to cooperate and to show restitution. The existence of funds may be volunteered by the subject or have been determined during your investigation or as a result of subpoenaed records. Repayment may be voluntary or by order of the court. Public domain checks (of property, businesses, etc) or banking trawls can detect unknown places where funds may be hidden. The fraudster may have acquired assets with the misappropriated funds. These can be sold to recoup costs.

- *Signing over pension money*
The fraudster may very well be an employee of the company that they have defrauded. The fraudster may have built up a pension/provident/retirement annuity-type saving via the company. Retirement funds are normally not readily accessible to people and may be fully intact despite the subject's financial circumstances. Invariably fraudsters have spent part or all of their ill-gotten gains. The fraudster may be willing to voluntarily sign over all or part of their pension as part of the recovery. Strict rules apply to pension funds, however. Take this step under the advisement of legal counsel. Pension funds are separate legal entities to the employer organisations. The employer organisation has no legal right to instruct the pension fund to pay any money out. As a general rule, it will always be lawful if the person voluntarily signs over their pension to the company. A court may also order that the person pays their pension over to the company.

- *Selling assets*
Let us say that the subject used the organisation's funds directly on an online gambling site and lost all funds. The subject may have other assets/funds (from other sources) that can be used to repay the losses. Examples include their residence, vehicles, furniture, livestock, etc. The fraudster may voluntarily sell assets to defray costs and/or to repay the original loss incurred as a result of the fraud. A court may also give the order for assets to be sold to cover costs. Some countries also have asset forfeiture legislation that empowers the government to seize assets and funds from fraudulent/illegal activities. International laws may also prevail over citizens of different countries. Again, you will have to be careful when a transgressor sells assets. The transgressor cannot sell assets that are given as surety to someone else. Assets may also not be sold if other creditors (for example financing institutions) have first right to a share of the proceeds or if the asset is owned by someone else. A court may order the company to repay the money that was received from the fraudster in such circumstances.

The company cannot try to make sure that it gets its money first at the expense of the other (preferential) creditors. Such behaviour may result in penalties against the company. This may happen whether or not the company was aware of the other creditors. The safest would always be to take the matter under the advisement of legal counsel.

- *Freezing assets*

Banks and/or other organisations may be willing to temporarily freeze assets if you can demonstrate that a crime has been perpetrated until a court order can be obtained. It is important to build a relationship with the company's bankers to ensure cooperation in such circumstances. In some cases, the bank may require the company to sign an agreement limiting the bank's liability. *I have used this very successfully in the past to get banks to freeze funds that were clearly transferred from the company to the subject. This prevents further loss of funds until the matter can be resolved.*

- *Loaning money*

The transgressor may take out a loan to repay the funds.

- *Signing an acknowledgement of debt*

As a rule, always get the person to sign an acknowledgement of debt. This may be seen as an admission of guilt. It may also lock the person down to repayment before they have a chance to change their mind. It may also be easier to obtain a civil claim on the strength of the signed acknowledgement of debt.

- *Issuing a receipt*

Issue them with some form of written receipt for what was repaid. This builds rapport with the transgressor and it makes the repayment more 'official'. Do not accept partial payments 'made in full and final settlement' or payments without the right to enact civil or criminal proceedings. Tell subjects that the company will be pressing charges, but that the repayment may be seen in mitigation.

- *Asset forfeiture*

Certain countries allow for the assets of a suspected fraudster to be seized even before a criminal case has been heard. These assets are typically held in trust until the criminal matter has been heard. Strict legislation normally governs these trusts.

- *Civil claims*

A company always has a right to institute a civil claim against a transgressor. Civil claims may be an expensive exercise. Remember the rule: 'Principles are for rich people.' It may be a business decision to walk away from the claim to avoid spending more money than can be claimed/recovered. Be mindful of the usefulness of a civil claim as well. If the person has no money, then it may not be worthwhile to obtain a civil claim. However, the law of prescription may allow civil claims to be in place for a long time and the company may have the right to claim such funds many years after the incident once the person has built up funds. The other aspect is that a civil claim is a black mark against a person, which will always be visible when the person undergoes a credit check. A poor credit history may be a form of 'punishment' due to the limitations that come with a poor credit history. The details of the civil claim may not always be visible to the party conducting the check and the transgressor may be able to give a plausible excuse as to why they were given a poor credit history. For example, they were young and did not know how to manage money or they lost their job and could not help but to default on their payments. An unsuspecting person may believe this. Civil claims are generally quicker and easier to obtain (based on quantum and merit as opposed to beyond reasonable doubt) than criminal claims. Civil judgments may assist in criminal cases.

- *Labour courts and/or tribunals*

Labour courts or labour tribunals may also order that an employee repays losses and/or costs.

- *Staff debtors and/or staff loans*

The company may have a policy of allowing employees to purchase items through the company on credit or take out staff loans. The company may consider putting the amount owed by the employee to staff debtors if the employee is going to remain in employment and pay the debt off. Alternatively, it is also easier to make use of other funds due to the employee (accumulated holiday pay, annual bonuses, remuneration, etc) to offset amounts owing if all funds owing have been captured to a staff debtor's account when paying the final pay on termination. Again, consider the prescripts of legislation concerning the awarding of loans.

- *Third-party claims*

A bank or an agent of the company may have acted outside of the company's mandate to it in the fraud case. The company may be able to claim the losses incurred back from the third party in those circumstances. For example, the company may have instructed the bank to only pay negotiable instruments if signed by two authorised signatories. The bank may have to cover the losses of such fraudulent payments if these are clearly beyond their mandate (for example only one authorised signatory).

- *Family or friends*

A family member (parent or spouse) may be willing to stand in for the financial damages of the subject. If the subject is married in community of property, you might be able to obtain a court order to recover the damages from the spouse.

7.4.3. Prevention

Court proceedings are time-consuming and expensive. As far as possible, therefore, try to do as much as possible in advance to prevent the need to go to a labour or a civil court.

As discussed elsewhere, tell subjects that it is important that they 1) cooperate with the investigation, 2) show remorse for what they have done and 3) relevant to this discussion, show restitution by repaying the funds. As was discussed in Chapter 4 on interviews, ensure that you have an acknowledgement of debt form with you for willing subjects to sign at the time of their interview. The longer you leave it after the interview, the less likely they are to sign it.

If subjects are unwilling to cooperate or if they are unable to repay the funds because they have spent the misappropriated funds, the organisation may have to embark on a civil suit to obtain a court order to force the subjects to reimburse the organisation now or in the future.

7.4.4. Parties to a civil matter

The following parties may be involved in a civil matter:

- *Judge*

The judge is the person who:

  - Presides over the court proceedings
  - Listens to and considers all arguments made
  - Gives judgment
  - Awards damages.

- *Complainant*

This is the person who initiates the suit against the respondent, the person with the 'complaint'. The complainant is the person who needs to prove the quantum (amount) and merit (that they have a valid basis) of their claim.

- *Respondent*

The respondent is the person who needs to respond to the complainant's claim by providing a defence or counter arguments/claims against them. This is the person 'responding' to the 'complaint'.

- *Legal counsel*

The complainant and respondent are normally represented by legal counsel. The parties can also elect to represent themselves. This will frequently be the case in smaller, special purpose courts, like the small claims court.

- *Clerk of the court*

The clerk of the court is the person who makes all administrative arrangements on behalf of the court. The clerk does not attend court cases. The clerk of the court maintains the court role.

- *Witnesses*

Witnesses are the people who are subpoenaed to give evidence and testify in court.

- *Expert witnesses*

These are special witnesses who are experts in their fields and are called to give special testimonies in their field.

- *Stenographer*

Verbatim transcripts of court proceedings are made for future reference. A stenographer is a person who makes the transcript. In the absence of a stenographer, the judge is required to take verbatim minutes of the proceedings.

- *A translator*

A translator may be required in instances where one or more of the parties involved in the court proceedings is unable to fluently converse in the tongue in which the proceedings are being conducted.

- *Observers*

Observers are normally allowed to observe proceedings in the public gallery. Observers may not interfere with the proceedings and may be removed if they do. A person cannot observe the proceedings (others' testimonies) before they have testified themselves (to prevent prejudicing themselves). Examples of observers include:

  - Witnesses who have already testified
  - Family or friends of the complainant or respondent
  - Generally interested members of the public
  - Members of the media
  - Legal students.

7.4.5. Legal counsel

The use of legal counsel is imperative. Ensure that you make use of legal counsel who has experience in the matter and/or industry that you are dealing with. Avoid using organisation lawyers that have been out of practice for a long time. Tiptoeing around internal organisational politics in terms of whom to use may, however, be more difficult.

The nature of a lawyer is mostly to believe that they can pursue and win all matters. While a strong self-belief is admirable, it may be detrimental (cost and time-wise) to the organisation. Tread carefully. Legal counsel is generally costly and a 'business decision' may need to be taken if it is worth pursuing. Sometimes the message sent to the organisation, because the matter is being pursued, justifies the cost. Remember our rule: 'Principles are for rich people'. Investigators do not like to hear this, but at the end of the day we are working for businesses and the anticipated benefits need to be weighed up against the costs.

7.4.6. Practicalities

Criminal courts rarely award damages. In most cases, a civil case will have to be pursued to recoup losses. The good news is that civil matters are mostly quicker and easier to prove than criminal matters. In this manner, the organisation will obtain justice more quickly. A criminal conviction can also not be guaranteed. A civil/default/credit judgment against an individual will be some form of 'record' against them. A small comfort perhaps?

Civil matters (normally concluded prior to criminal cases) may also be seen in aggravation in criminal matters and can, therefore, be of assistance in criminal cases.

Ensure that you initiate a civil matter as soon as possible, as the law of prescription will give the organisation a few years within which to claim the funds. The law of prescription commences from the time that you are aware of the matter and not once you have completed the matter. You should exercise the organisation's right to claim (not necessarily obtain judgment) as soon as possible to prevent the organisation losing the legal right to claim.

Retain all correspondence with the subject in which the organisation exercised its right to claim. This will help you later when they try to dismiss your claim by saying that the organisation did not exercise its right to the claim at all or in time.

To illustrate the point: One of my clients did not listen to me and nearly missed the prescription period within which to lodge a civil claim. My correspondence to the subject laying claim to the misappropriated funds over the period of the investigation did, however, show that 'we' had tried to lay claim to the funds and the court allowed the claim. A default judgment was issued against the subject and, the last I heard, the subject's assets were being attached, by the sheriff of the court.

7.4.7. Proof

To be successful in a civil case, the organisation will have to prove the 'quantum' and 'merit' of the matter. 'Quantum' is the value of the claim. The value is the loss and may include:

- Direct losses resulting from misappropriation of funds/assets
- Damages
- Penalties and/or fines
- Investigation costs
- Litigation costs to pursue the subjects
- Litigation costs to defend the organisation
- Loss of income
- Reemployment costs.

The court will, in the event of a ruling in the organisation's favour, decided based on the merit of the case, what part of the amount claimed to award. 'Merit' is that the organisation's claim has basis. The organisation will have to show that their arguments have basis.

7.4.8. Judgment

After hearing both arguments for and against, the court will make a ruling. A default judgment will be handed down in the event the defendant does not turn up to defend the matter. It is commonplace that a fraud accused does not turn up to defend a civil judgment related to a fraud case that they are implicated in.

7.4.9. Repayment

Upon awarding of the judgment against the person, the court may specify:

- That the person's assets are to be attached by the sheriff of the court. Such assets are typically sold by public auction and the proceeds given to the aggrieved party. It would be unlawful for an organisation to 'collect' a subject's assets. Only a court can instruct the sheriff of the court to attach a person's assets.
- That the person's pension can be used to repay the funds.
- Repayment terms which the person must comply with to repay the funds. A garnishee order may be issued to instruct the person's employer to deduct the repayment amount before their net salary is paid to them. The organisation will have a fixed period (years) in which to exercise their right to claim the debt.

7.4.10. Credit record

The reality is that many subjects will be unable to repay the funds. A criminal record may also be difficult or time-consuming to obtain. A civil judgment is relatively quick and easy to obtain.

A civil judgment sits against a person's name. This affects their credit rating and their ability to obtain future finance. It may also affect their ability to obtain employment. The civil judgment will remain against the person's name even after they have repaid the funds. In the overall scheme of things, therefore, a bad credit rating is a type of 'sentence' albeit low-key.

7.4.11. Rescindment

All is however not 'doom and gloom' for a person who has a civil judgment against their name. They can apply to have the judgment rescinded. Rescindment entails repaying the money owed as well as paying an administrative fee. The person's record will then be cleared of the 'credit' judgment.

7.5. LABOUR CASES

7.5.1. Introduction

Fraud investigators have little direct control and influence over criminal proceedings. Fraud investigators, on the other hand, will spend a fair amount of their time ensuring (directly or indirectly) that guilty parties are disciplined within the organisations that they work and that an appropriate sanction is handed down. We will, therefore, spend a fair amount of time in this chapter understanding how labour matters are handled both internally and externally to an organisation.

7.5.2. Parties to a labour case

The following parties may be involved in a labour tribunal:

- *Chairperson*

  The chairperson is the person who:
  - Presides over the internal labour tribunal and ensures that all procedures are complied with
  - Hears all arguments for and against the charges levied against the accused
  - Makes a ruling per charge
  - Recommends to management an appropriate sanction for the accused as required.

- *Company representative*

  This is the person who leads the organisation's case and presents arguments to prove the accused's guilt.

- *Accused*

  This is the person who stands accused of the charges before the labour tribunal.

- *Employee representation*

Employees are normally entitled to be represented by a fellow employee. Most organisations do not allow for external representation of employees. Simple matters become significantly more complicated as soon as you allow an employee to bring their own external legal counsel into an internal hearing. It is not a requirement of fairness to allow external representation. In fact, it may be unfair towards the organisation to allow an employee to have external legal representation while the organisation does not.

In one matter, the chairperson allowed external representation, as the basis of the charges involved complicated legal arguments on double jeopardy, and it was not reasonable to expect an employee to be aware of these. The organisations accepted this and did not oppose it in the interests of fairness.

The employee is more than welcome to spend their own time preparing counter arguments with their lawyer in their private time. Their lawyer can instruct them on how to approach the matter, but not attend the proceedings. Employee representation can also be done at labour tribunals external to the organisation.

- *Legal counsel*

Once a matter goes to an external labour tribunal (like labour court) the parties may be represented by their own legal counsel. This will be important as case law may need to be referred to and complex legal arguments may be debated.

- *Witnesses*

Witnesses are the people who are subpoenaed to give evidence and testify in court.

- *Expert witnesses*

These are special witnesses who are experts in their fields and are called to give special testimonies in their fields.

- *Minute-taker/stenographer*

Verbatim transcripts of court proceedings are made for future reference. A stenographer is a person who makes the transcript. In the absence of a stenographer, the judge is required to take verbatim minutes of the proceedings.

- *A translator*

A translator may be required in instances where one or more of the parties involved in the court proceedings is unable to fluently converse in the tongue in which the proceedings are being conducted.

7.5.3. Labour tribunals

Labour cases will mostly be handled internal to the organisation or mostly internally initially before going external. Some internally handled labour matters are however not handled to the satisfaction of one of the parties (employer or employee) and may be taken to labour tribunals external to the organisation. Alternatively, an employee may, based on a perception of having been treated unfairly, elect to go directly to an external labour tribunal without going through an internal labour tribunal. Examples of different formats of labour tribunals include:

- *Internal organisational labour tribunals*

Internal labour tribunals are primarily chaired by management-level staff members who are independent of the business area/function from where the accused originates. As discussed later, it is wise to make use of an external chairperson to preside over trickier matters. This is due to the fact that an internal chairperson may be perceived as being biased. External chairpersons may also be more experienced to navigate the trickier procedural or substantive aspects. This will result in a greater probability that the results will be more acceptable to all parties concerned/undisputed.

- *Bargaining counsels*

Some industries have their own bargaining counsels to represent the interests of the industry. Employees and employer organisations may be required to join these industry-governing organisations. Some of these industry bodies require employee members and member organisations to take disputes through their own industry-specific labour tribunals first. There would still be recourse for employees or employers to dispute unsatisfactory tribunal outcomes in another external labour tribunal (like a labour court). Some examples include the Building Industrial Bargaining Council and the Clothing and Textile Bargaining Council.

- *Private arbitrators*

Some employment contracts make provision for compulsory arbitration by a body of professional external arbitrators, in the event of a dispute. This has both good and bad aspects to it. It is 'good', as it forces a result and holds both parties to one method of handling disputes. On the other hand, it is 'bad', as the private arbitrators may not give the result desired by both parties and both parties may be contractually bound by the outcome. The idea is that only important matters will be disputed and also that it forces fairness as a result of the independence of the arbitrators.

- *Special purpose labour tribunals*

Taking a matter through a labour court can be expensive and the process can be highly protracted. To avoid this and to make access to labour dispute resolution more freely available, some countries set up special purpose labour tribunals. In South Africa, the Commission for Conciliation, Mediation and Arbitration (CCMA) refers as such an example. These tribunals specialise in the conciliation and mediation of disputes. There is typically no cost to raise a matter at such a tribunal and matters are heard relatively quickly. The tribunals are designed to speed up the process and to make it more accessible to all employees.

- *Labour courts*

Labour courts are the highest 'tribunal' at which a labour matter can be heard. Either employee or employer can take a matter to the labour court. Taking a matter through the labour courts can, however, be an expensive and a highly protracted route to follow. Remember our rule: 'Principles are for rich people.' It might be a more practical solution to settle before the cost and resource involvement exceed the benefits.

7.5.4. Fairness

As discussed previously, labour cases only need to be proven 'on a balance of probability'. It is imperative though, in trying to prove this, that all proceedings need to be 'substantively' and 'procedurally' fair. Failure to do both of these may result in:

- *An incorrect outcome*
An incorrect outcome may be unfair to the employee and/or employer. As a result, the parties may need to accept an outcome that is incorrect, such as keeping a dishonest employee employed or being unfairly dismissed.
- *Legitimate matters being challenged*
Procedural or substantive unfairness may provide an opportunity for unscrupulous people (mostly the employees, but could also be an employer) to exploit these faults to unfairly evade the consequences.
- *Inefficiencies*
Excessive time and resources may need to be spent to resolve the matter if there are appeals or if the matter is escalated to an external labour tribunal.

'Substantively fair', means that sufficient and accurate evidence (physical or testimony) has been brought to prove (on a balance of probability) the guilt or innocence of the accused on each of the charges levied against them. 'Procedurally fair', means that all applicable processes and procedures have been followed in a manner that is completely fair to all involved.

7.5.5. Process

The disciplinary process is described in detailed practical terms in the Annexures that follow. A short discussion is held on the key elements in the discussion of each document below.

It is ideal if the person who conducted the investigation is the person who initiates the organisation's case. The downside is that this may lead to tying up investigators; it does however result in the best continuity of thought and a high success ratio. Of course investigators would also need to be au fait with structuring labour cases. This is a skill that can be learnt fairly quickly. Alternatively, the investigator can be called as an expert witness.

7.5.6. Document templates

The following document templates have been included below to serve as examples to guide you:

- *Internal disciplinary policy (Annexure 7.3)*
Each organisation should have an internal disciplinary policy. The internal disciplinary policy describes the purpose, principles and scope of the organisation's disciplinary code. It also lists the rules and standards for the application of the disciplinary procedure. You are strongly recommended to read this example policy, as it highlights in practical terms important elements that need to be borne in mind.

- *Disciplinary procedure (Annexure 7.4)*

The disciplinary procedure is important to define, as it describes for all parties concerned the procedure for formal counselling sessions and disciplinary hearings. The procedure also lists possible sanctions and validity periods for different types of misconduct. Finally, it sets out the appeal and arbitration process if required.

- *Guidelines for the chairperson (Annexure 7.5)*

The guidelines for the chairperson are a practical set of instructions. Not all chairpersons are created equal, or at least not all are equally qualified and/or experienced. These guidelines take the guesswork out of the correct procedures. As fraud investigators, we tend to be preoccupied with the substantive nature of the evidence that we are going to present. We tend to forget that 50% of a labour case lies in the procedural fairness thereof. Procedural fairness is 'low-hanging fruit' and easy to achieve. We should 'never' (as far as is within our control) be procedurally unfair. This is as we always want to be ethically correct (our rule promoting the idea of the 'Queensbury rules' of fairness refers) and also because we want to do everything in our power to present a strong case and not weaken our case before we start. The initiator of the organisation's case should, therefore, be completely au fait with these practical steps to ensure that the correct arguments are presented at the right time and that the organisation's case is procedurally fair.

- *Letter of suspension (Annexure 7.6)*

Suspension done prior to a disciplinary hearing is not a punishment. Suspension places the subject on administrative leave to allow an investigation to proceed without influence and to consider the impact on the morale of the subject of the investigation if they were to remain at their place of work while the investigation was ongoing. The subject is on full pay while on suspension. Remember suspension is not a punishment at this time and we cannot prejudge the outcome. The big questions are always 'when', 'if' and for 'how long' to suspend a person from work if they are subject to a disciplinary process. The answers are not clear but err heavily on the side of 'yes, you should suspend'. 'How long', is easier to address. The length of the suspension should basically be the time that it takes to conduct the investigation and to hold the hearing. There are however periods of reasonability that apply. While no fixed prescribed periods exist, the organisation cannot unduly delay the holding of the hearing under the guise of a protracted investigation. This would be procedurally unfair and unethical. The organisation needs to be able to defend the length of the investigation if questioned. The 'when' is also fairly clear. Suspend the person as soon as it becomes clear that they are involved to a degree (as described below) that warrants a hearing in the short-term. The unclear part ('if') relates to the:

  - Seriousness of the misconduct. Fraud is always serious and depending on the person's involvement will probably always necessitate the suspension of the subjects.
  - The subject's ability (directly or indirectly) to influence the investigation. Subjects typically have a strong emotional control over their fellow employees. Do not underestimate the power of the subject to get others to do things on their behalf. As per our previous discussions, a white-collar criminal is a psychopath and they are charismatic. They like to 'divide and rule' (management and employees) and prey on people whom they can influence. They also typically (despite instructions to the contrary) try to contact someone in the organisation three times on a 'fishing

expedition'. An honest and obedient person would abide by their instructions not to contact people.

Subjects are (while guilt has not yet been proven at this stage), on the basis that they are the subject of an investigation, dishonest to some degree. Contacting people 'secretly' is a continuation of their misconduct and a typical behaviour which they demonstrate. It is as if they are trying to establish what the organisation knows before going into the hearing so that they can prepare their defence. They will typically do this three times: The first occasion is typically dressed up as them 'just making contact'. This is done in the hope that their 'loyal' friends will tell them something. The second is normally a little more direct. They spend a lot of time 'pleading the victim' and trying to rally emotional support for themselves, without offering factual reasons why they are not guilty. The third is normally a 'last-ditch' attempt to see if their contact has changed their mind or may have heard something.

Try to anticipate who they are most likely to contact. Go to these people in advance and tell them not to refuse the call/contact. Request them to advise you if they are contacted and to remember what they are asked. Instruct them not to give away anything important. This is a difficult situation for people to be in and your best attempts cannot guarantee that the person being contacted will react in the correct manner. When, however, the contact session happens as you have predicted, it creates a lot of credibility with the people who remain behind for the organisation's case and what you are doing. Do not chastise the people whom they contact. Use it to find out which questions they are asking, as this may give away their counter-arguments, allowing you an opportunity to prepare a suitable response in advance.

It may also be a manner in which the organisation can 'unofficially' get information back to the subject without directly contacting them. For example: if the contact tells the subject that they have heard that the organisation has a bulletproof case, then there is a chance that the subject might decide to resign, which makes everyone's lives easier. A 'long shot' perhaps, but you may have success in maintaining this unofficial channel.

In exceptional cases when the subject is trying to influence witnesses (more than just a fishing expedition) you may use their attempt to influence people against them in a hearing (subject to proof). You may only want to consider using this if the subject is clearly being unethical/acting against direct instructions.

- As discussed in Chapter 4 on interviewing, people have a far greater freedom to talk once the subject is offsite. This is a strange psychological behaviour perhaps. Be aware of it and use it to your advantage.
- The moral of the subject. Our rule of 'Queensbury rules apply' refers. Despite how serious the subject's misconduct may have been, we need to treat them with respect. It is not pleasant for them to have to sit in the work environment and to know that everyone is looking at them. These sentiments may be met by unsympathetic responses.

Try to establish the subject's emotional state and history. There is always a chance that an emotionally distraught subject could do some harm to themselves (suicide being the worst case) or others. Offer the proverbial olive branch to the subject, saying that they can talk to an HR professional if they require or to a professional at the organisation's expense. Most subjects are however extremely selfish and driven by self-preservation, so suicide is not normally an option. On the other hand, you do not want to take a chance and nor do you want to give them an emotional lever to use against you/the organisation. Talk to a professional and proceed cautiously. Do not get involved in psychological matters. Give the employee the option to go themselves to a professional. This is a matter between the employee and a professional.

- The morale of the employees remaining behind. It can be demoralising for the general employees to see a person who is suspected of misconduct still in the workplace, as:
  i. They were possibly friends and may be angry based on the presumption of guilt.
  ii. There may be a perception that they are being treated unfairly. After all: 'Out of sight is out of mind.'
- The message that the organisation wants to send to the rest of the organisation (that the organisation takes misconduct very seriously and acts vigilantly).

Issue the letter of suspension in a face-to-face meeting with the subject. Before issuing the letter ask the subject if there are any reasons while they feel that they should not be suspended. Listen to any reasons offered. You do not need to accept their reasons. Do not argue with them about their reasons. You are advised to:

i. Decide in advance if you are going to suspend the subject.
ii. Listen to their reasons and quietly affirm your initial plan to yourself.
iii. Thank them for their thoughts and do not enter into a debate.
vi. Say to them that the organisation takes these matters very seriously and that the organisation is of the opinion that it will be in the best interests of all parties concerned if they are placed on administrative leave until the hearing can be held.

Get them to sign for receipt of the letter as well as a witness. Retain the original signed copy and let the subject have their own copy. Some subjects are reluctant to sign, as they feel it may be tantamount to an admission of guilt. Say to them (if not already specified in the letter) that they are welcome to write next to their signature that they are signing for receipt of the letter and not to indicate their agreement with the process or as an admission of guilt. If they do not want to sign at all, have a witness sign in front of the subject that the letter was issued, but that they declined to sign for it. This can be used to rebut arguments of procedural unfairness later.

Upon issuance of the letter of suspension, emphasise (also specified in the letter) that they are not to have any contact with any employees whatsoever. They may also not access the organisation's computer network, premises or property. Appoint one senior person whom they may contact if they wish to discuss anything or if they require access. Explain that failure to comply with these instructions may be seen in a very serious light. Be sure to also obtain their contact details and the physical address where they will be. Ensure that they write these down themselves in their writing (preferably in the letter of suspension with all the conditions specified) and require them to inform you if these change. In this manner, if you are unable to contact them leading up to a hearing, they cannot say that the organisation was procedurally unfair as the onus was upon them to supply the correct and up-to-date contact details.

Emphasise to suspended subjects that they must remember that they are on administrative leave. Administrative leave is not the same as annual leave. They are still to make themselves available to the organisation should the organisation require it during their suspension.

Be sure to suspend their network access and obtain all keys and access cards. You may need to restart their devices to enact the revocation of computer access rights. Consult your IT team as to how to proceed. It would be wise to also obtain all the employee's electronic devices. Examination of these may be required as part of the investigation. Subjects could use these to destroy evidence or be malicious. Also, ensure that their duties have been handed over to other responsible employees.

- *Notification to attend a hearing (Annexure 7.7)*

Conducting an investigation or even the suspending of a person is not a guarantee that there will (at the end of the investigation) be grounds to a hold a disciplinary hearing with the person. Prior to an investigation, it is not possible to know if there will be charges levied against the subject and, if so, what those eventual charges will be. Most employees would hopefully be shocked to receive a notification to attend a hearing. It will hopefully be the first time that the employee is receiving such a letter. Employees may, therefore, be a little confused about how to react and what to do. The notification to attend a hearing is, therefore, a very important document, which has multiple purposes, including:

- To formally (procedurally fairly) inform the person that a hearing will be held
- To state the specific charges that are levied against them
- To tell them what their rights are in terms of the hearing
- To inform them where and when they are required to appear.

The charges should read like a criminal charge sheet. This is because you would need to give the person sufficient understanding of exactly what it is they are being charged with to allow them to know what to prepare to defend. Our rule of 'Queensbury rules of fairness apply' refers. The charges are not a secret once notified. We do not always (depending on the country concerned) need to provide evidence in advance. The chairperson will ask the accused at the start of the hearing if they were notified of the hearing within the prescribed time frame and if they know and understand the charges levied against them.

Accused parties should not confuse 'understanding the charges' and 'knowing prior to the hearing what the evidence is against them'. They will frequently reply to the chairperson that they do not understand why the charges are being levied against them, as they are innocent.

Different countries have different labour laws with the regard to conducting disciplinary hearings. In East African countries like Tanzania and Kenya, for example, a 'causal effect' letter is issued. The accused is given a fixed period in which to respond in writing to the charges levied in the letter. The letter also provides what evidence is available. Consult a local labour lawyer to ensure that you follow the correct procedures. As an example, a charge could read:

- 'dereliction of duties, in so far as you failed to reconcile the MM monthly bank statement, as per your job description and to identify the unauthorised payments'
- or 'abuse of power, in so far as you used your company credit card on dd/mm/yy to pay for private hotel expenses for non-business related reasons'
- or 'failure to comply with company policy in so far as you did not notify the MD of the missing YY assets, as required by the use of company assets policy'.

This is sufficient detail to let the person know exactly what they are being charged with.

It is suggested when choosing a charge that you read the sanction tables provided in the 'guidelines to the chairperson' below. This will give you an idea of possible charges to formulate.

The philosophy is to try to think of all charges, not just the obvious one. What are all the other related matters? Did they disobey a policy? Were they negligent? The reason for including all possible charges is twofold: first, you want to be as complete as possible and ensure that you charge them for all misconduct, and second, you will be lucky if you are able to prove all charges. In most cases, you will only be able to successfully prove two-thirds of the charges.

Remember, charges are specific and you need to prove specific things for different charges. You do not want to hang your hope on one charge only. What happens if you are unable to prove the required aspects for that one charge? You will have lost your entire case.

You want to give yourself alternatives. For example: 'dereliction of duty in so far as >>>, alternatively noncompliance to company policy, in so far as >>>'.

On the other hand, you do not want to go too far to get to a stage of what is known as 'charge splitting'. This is where the same charge is actually given multiple times under multiple descriptions of the same facts.

Most of the charges listed in the sanction table below are, subject to the sufficiency of your evidence, easy to prove. As a rule, however, do not charge an internal employee with fraud. Not unless the person confesses and/or the proof is very sound. Fraud is a charge that carries with it clear criminal connotations. As soon as you introduce this in a labour case, you tend to shift the focus of proof from a 'balance of probability' to 'beyond reasonable doubt'. Fraud also implies intent and you may need to prove the movement of funds to the benefit of the accused. If you were to charge the employee with fraud in a labour case, then ensure that you have good alternative charges, as well. It is normally easier to prove that the employee did not comply with company policy with grave financial consequences to the organisation.

- *Opening statements (Annexure 7.8)*

The company initiates the case in a hearing and as such, the company leads in all matters. The accused is given an opportunity at each phase to reply or cross-examine, as required. Both the company and the accused employee make opening statements. The company commences and then the accused follows with their opening statement. It is best to put everything in the hearing in writing. This also allows you to prepare exactly what you want to say in advance (sometimes with the help of external legal counsel). Read the opening statement, thereby ensuring that it is presented in full and that it goes on record exactly as it was prepared. Upon completion, give a copy to the chairperson and the accused. Continue to give copies of all relevant documents to the chairperson and accused as you proceed. In this manner, the chairperson of the labour tribunal can put a 'pack' together of all the relevant sections of the hearing for future deliberation. Our rule of 'he with the most paperwork wins' comes to mind. People often do not understand why it is necessary to have an opening statement. Opening statements are exactly what the term suggests. They are the initial introductory statements to the chairperson. Remember that the chairperson has not been involved in the matter at all and this is the first time that they are hearing about the matter. If the chairperson was involved, they may need to recuse themselves as chairperson on the basis of potential bias.

As per the example of organisation opening statements attached below, the opening statements give a very short synopsis of what occurred and why a hearing is being held. There are no arguments made or evidence presented during the opening statements.

An example of an opening statement from the company's side includes: 'A routine scheduled internal audit of the ABC Company's bank reconciliation process identified unexplained discrepancies. The subsequent investigation of these anomalies has identified serious misconduct and the company has subsequently embarked upon this disciplinary process.'

The opening statement also informs the tribunal who the organisation plans to call as their witnesses. The accused will then have an opportunity to make their opening statements. The accused however typically uses this opportunity to:

- Provide emotional arguments as to why they are such a good employee and why they should not be charged
- Put on record that they object to how they have been treated
- Or that they should be entitled to have external legal representation
- Or that they have not been given access to all evidence in advance
- Or that the time to prepare was inadequate (despite this not being required).

The chairperson would then need to address any concerns before proceeding. For example:

- 'Mr X, your character and person are not on trial here and as such are not brought into question. I, therefore, note your concerns and we will move on to hear what specific evidences the organisation has to present on the charges that were listed at the commencement of this tribunal.'
- 'Ms Y, you have acknowledged receiving the notification of the hearing three days in advance. You have also acknowledged that, while you do not necessarily agree with it, you understand the nature of the charges that the company has levied against you. There is no requirement for the organisation to present its evidence to you in advance. It is also the normal labour process that the company presents its evidence at such a tribunal as today. As such I note your concern as to insufficient time to prepare and I move to proceed to hear the company's case.'
- 'Ms Z, it is not company policy to allow for external representation for internal matters. There are also, based on the opening statements made, no complex legal arguments anticipated that could prejudice your right to a fair hearing. I also note that you have declined an employee representative and that you choose to represent yourself internally. We will now move to hear the company's case. Mr J, please call your first witness.'

One of my favourite examples of an opening statement comes to mind: This was a case against an employee with 20 odd years of employment with the group. The employee was notoriously difficult and even the bosses were scared of him. I walked in and laid down four lever arch files of evidence. I then proceeded to read a very legalistic opening statement that I had prepared in advance with the help of a specialist labour law firm.

The employee, on the other hand, walked in and placed a bible on the table and nothing else. When it came to his turn to make an opening statement, he proceeded to tell the tribunal that he had had a dream leading up to the hearing in which he saw an apparition of two men clad in brilliant white clothes (it sounds like I have heard this story before in another more reverent setting). He then went on to say that the two men had referred him to a particular Psalm, which he proceeded to read to the tribunal. The Psalm came down to the fact that he should not fear his enemies, as they will be eternally damned!

I recall all in the tribunal looking around awestruck by this very different approach. Fortunately for my 'eternal damnation', the organisation later agreed to give him a generous severance (despite his misconduct) and I was 'off the hook'. This does, however, put a whole new spin on the concept of 'external' representation. You meet all types!

- *Questions (Annexure 7.9)*

The questioning of witnesses and/or the accused is the real meat of the hearing. As strange as it seems, accused employees typically do not change their defences or excuses in a hearing. They stick to the original excuses that they offered in the interviews that were held with them, despite being caught out. You cannot bargain on this though. Plan your questions therefore as if the person is going to offer new excuses. The logic of structuring the questions is identical to the structuring of normal interview questions. See Chapter 4 on interviewing for more detail. The difference is in that the accused listens to all the witnesses' questions and answers, gets an opportunity to cross-examine the witnesses and then is questioned by the organisation's initiator after all witnesses have testified.

The sequence of calling witnesses and the sequence of questions become imperative. You do not have to give your questions to the chairperson or the accused at any time. You ask the questions and that is all.

Structure your questions in the sequence of the witnesses to be called. Again, I do not like to leave anything to chance. As far as possible, obtain affidavits from all witnesses in advance. In the hearing, request the witness to give their name for the record. Then ask them to state their position in the organisation, length of service and to give a brief description of their duties. Then ask them to confirm that this is their affidavit. Give a copy of their affidavit after their confirmation to the chairperson and the accused. Then request the witness to read specific sections of their affidavit into evidence in the order that you require. In between sections you might stop them and ask questions related to their statement. Witnesses are, in this manner, much more relaxed, as they know what they are going to say and they are not nervous about saying the wrong thing as they are reading a prepared statement.

The accused then has an opportunity to cross-examine the company's witness. The chairperson will make corrections and request clarification as things proceed. For example: the organisation may not ask leading questions of its own witnesses.

You would generally not make use of affidavits for expert witnesses. Expert witnesses all tend to be handwriting experts or polygraph specialists.

- *Accused questioning*

You will have had the opportunity to place plenty of advance 'blocks' (see Chapter 4 on interviews for an explanation) in front of the accused. Your questions should now be primarily aimed at catching the accused's dishonesty out and proving your case. It is very rare that you will obtain a confession in a hearing. It is not really the forum for it. What sometimes happens however is, when things are clearly starting to pile up against the accused, that the chairperson goes 'off the record' to inform the accused that things at this point are not looking good and asks them if they require a few minutes to consider their options. This frequently results in a resignation, which is, of course, easier for everyone.

- *Accused defence*

The organisation will rest its case after the accused questioning and the accused gets an opportunity to proceed with their defence. The accused may also call witnesses or proceed to question the investigator (frequently the initiator of the organisation's case). The accused will question their witnesses first and then the company will have an opportunity to cross-examine the accused witnesses. The chairperson may also have some clarifying questions for the witnesses.

- *Closing statements (Annexure 7.10)*

The purpose of closing statements is not the last chance to say something that you may have forgotten. Closing statements are the conclusion of each party's case. Closing statements are a summary of what was presented and said. Both the employee and the employer make closing statements. Nothing new can be introduced (arguments or evidence); it is rather the summation of what has gone before.

The closing statements are made in the sequence of the charges levied against the accused. This is done to guide the chairperson to reach a verdict on each charge. For example:

On the charge of dereliction of duty, Mr X has acknowledged that it was part of his normal duties to conduct a monthly bank reconciliation (the purpose of this statement is to say that there was a 'rule'). *The company has also shown that Mr X performed these duties for all months prior to the irregular payments* (the purpose of this statement is to say that he had knowledge of the 'rule'). *Mr X could not give this tribunal a plausible reason why he did not perform the bank reconciliations for the two months when the irregular payments were made. Mr X could furthermore not explain why he told his supervisor Ms S that he had mistakenly shredded the reconciliations for M1 and M2. It is therefore the company's submission that Mr X purposefully neglected his duties for months M1 and M2 and that he intentionally concealed this from the organisation, thereby denying the organisation an opportunity to detect and/or prevent the fraudulent payments resulting in a loss of >>> to the organisation.* Thereafter, the company makes some parting statements. It is recommended to say that the position of trust has been broken down and that the organisation cannot continue with a normal employee/employer relationship.

- *Chairperson's findings*

The chairperson will deliberate for a few days upon completion of the hearing as to the guilt or innocence of the accused on each charge.

The hearing is reconvened at a time set by the chairperson. The chairperson will give a verbal summary of the arguments and give their findings. The chairperson will also say if they feel that the company has been remiss in any of its actions. The chairperson can also make recommendations that the organisation must comply with. The chairperson later commits their findings to writing and gives them to the company.

The chairperson then normally requests that the tribunal reconvenes for sanction to be handed down. This can be after a short break or in a few days. It is wise to maintain momentum though.

- *Statements in aggravation/mitigation (Annexure 7.11)*

Statements in aggravation or mitigation are given by the employer and employee prior to the chairperson's sanction. The innocence/guilt of the employee is now known and it now comes down to the sanction that will be given. Ensure that you put your statements in writing. You will in most cases give a statement in aggravation and request a severe punishment. Commence your statement by giving a short summary of the charges and relate the severity of these to the following aspects:

- Seniority of the employee (more senior, the more trusted, the better they should have known and the more trust placed in them)
- Number of counts of misconduct (the more counts, the more severe as they kept on doing it, it was not just a once-off mistake)
- Period over which the misconduct was perpetrated (as above, the longer the period, the more severe, as their actions are premeditated and this was not just an opportunistic occurrence)
- Others involved (speaks to premeditation and the corrupting of multiple people)
- Severity of the misconduct (the more severe, the greater the prejudice suffered by the organisation)
- Consequences/losses suffered to the organisation and others (to suppliers, colleagues, customers, etc; the greater the loss the more severe the sanction needs to be)
- Costs of investigation (time, resources, etc)
- Emotional damage
- Cooperation given
- Restitution shown
- Remorse demonstrated
- The trust relationship going forward.

Where the employee has cooperated and/or been remorseful and/or was clearly misused, you may give a statement in mitigation. The 'Queensbury rules of fairness' refer. It is unusual for an organisation to give statements in mitigation of employees who have perpetrated crimes against it though. The employee traditionally gives a statement in mitigation in which they motivate why they should not have a severe punishment. Their statement is normally around their length of service and their character.

- *Notification of outcome of hearing (Annexure 7.12)*

The chairperson does not have any decision-making powers within the organisation with regards to the actual action taken against an employee. While the chairperson's findings carry a lot of weight, the organisation has the final call. The chairperson makes a recommendation to the organisation. The organisation considers the chairperson's recommendation and then decides whether to accept or reject it.

The organisation then issues the employee with a letter to formally inform them if the organisation agrees or disagrees with the chairperson's recommendation and what the employee's punishment is.

- *Appeal form (Annexure 7.13)*

The employee has a right to appeal the outcome of the hearing if they are dissatisfied. The organisation should allow for an internal appeal process. Alternatively, the employee can go directly to an external labour tribunal to lodge an appeal.

- *Written warning (Annexure 7.14)*

A warning letter is retained on the employee's file for a fixed period. If the employee reoffends within the period, a more severe punishment may be handed down. Previous offences may be used in subsequent hearings even though the fixed period has expired. If used in a subsequent hearing, the employee may argue that they served their time and that the punishment was only for a fixed period. As an extreme example: if an employee was negligent in their first year of employment and then is found guilty of negligence ten years later, it would not be reasonable to introduce the first occurrence in aggravation of the second. It is true that the employee has served their punishment, but it may be possible to show (perhaps in future statements of aggravation) that the employee is a habitual offender. For example: an employee offends once a year and has a warning letter placed on their file, which is valid for six months. The employee is strictly speaking outside their sanction period if they reoffend after eight months. This could help in imposing a more severe punishment for the new hearing.

- *Final written warning (Annexure 7.15)*

The attached letter refers as an example of a final written warning. A final written warning just means that the employee has no further chances within the prescribed period.

- *Letter of demotion (Annexure 7.16)*

The attached letter refers as an example of a letter of demotion. An employee will only be demoted in exceptional cases, for example if they have shown that they are unable to carry out their duties. Consult local labour laws that govern demotion, as this may be onerous to do.

- *Letter of dismissal (Annexure 7.17)*

The attached letter refers as an example of a letter of dismissal. If the organisation decides to dismiss the employee, then this decision is put in writing to the employee.

7.5.7. Subsequent actions

The hard part for seasoned investigators to remember (when they are so focused on proving their cases) is that the purpose of internal disciplinary procedures is to focus on the guidance and rehabilitation of an employee so as to discourage and correct undesirable behaviour in a constructive manner. The focus is not on punitive action. Now, when it comes to fraud, the only guidance suggested is guiding the employee to the closest door. If a person has been found guilty of fraud, then it is highly unlikely that the organisation could continue a relationship with them.

Depending on the person's involvement there may be some action that the accused is required to carry out or a period they are required to serve. A senior independent person should be assigned the responsibility to oversee that the sanction is carried out.

Ensure that all the required reporting of the outcome of the hearing is conducted. Chapter 8 on reporting refers. Also, ensure that personnel files are updated to reflect all elements of the disciplinary process and all people involved.

Annexure 7.1
Evidence per charge summary

Charge	Evidence			
1	Bank statement 1	Affidavit 2 & 3		
2				
3				
4				

Annexure 7.2
Witness per charge summary

	Witness			
Charge	**#1 A Jones**	**#2 J Smith**	**#3 J Sprat**	**#4 T Nigel**
1	Short description of evidence	Description	Etc.	
2	Description	N/A		
3	N/A			
4	Description			

Annexure 7.3
Internal disciplinary policy example

1. Internal disciplinary policy – example

1.1. Purpose

The purpose of the code and procedure is to provide an outline of the standard rules of conduct so as to ensure sound labour/management relations that will:

- Achieve fairness and consistency in the application of employee disciplinary measures in a prompt manner.
- Act as a guideline to assist management with decision-making in respect of disciplinary measures. It must, however, be emphasised that the circumstances of each case will be considered on their own merits and may, therefore, require a deviation from the procedure.
- Provide employees with an accessible reference for the application of discipline that is easily understood.

1.2 Principles

The code is based on the following principles that must be observed at all times:

- The application of discipline is a right and a responsibility of line management.
- The company reserves the right to institute disciplinary proceedings against an employee for an offence, subject to the employee's right to a fair hearing.
- Disciplinary action should not be taken lightly and the responsibility for initiating action is consequently reserved for company management representatives of the appropriate responsibility and seniority.
- The managing director (title to be altered to suit the organisation in question) should be kept informed of:
  - More serious offences and cases
  - Cases where the accused is a senior member of staff
  - Where the outcome of the hearing could be 'dismissal'.
- Disciplinary steps are instituted in order to obtain the cooperation of all employees within the work place, and to protect the interests of both the employee and the employer in the process of dealing with unacceptable behaviour.
- In exercising discipline, the primary aims are to focus on the guidance and rehabilitation of an employee so as to discourage and correct undesirable behaviour in a constructive manner. The aim is not intended to be on the enforcement of punitive action. However, where necessary, punishment must be used as a legitimate deterrent to the maintenance of discipline.
- The organisation reserves the right, in certain circumstances that demand it, to impose the most severe punishment on an employee without following the principles of corrective and progressive discipline.
- The application of discipline must, at all times, be lawful, just, fair and consistent.
- An employee is expected to maintain acceptable standards of conduct in accordance with the employee's contract, job requirements and the company's rules.

1.3. Scope

This code and procedure apply to all employees (permanent and contractual/term) irrespective of the position they hold. These rules are not intended to be an exhaustive list of disciplinary offences or categories.

1.4. Code, rules and standards

1.4.1. General

The A.N. OTHER ORGANISATION group of companies subscribes to a Code of Conduct, which serves as a guideline containing a list of potential misconduct.

Disciplinary measures must, at all times, be procedurally as well as substantively fair:

- Procedural fairness requires compliance with the disciplinary procedure.
- Substantive fairness requires a fair and valid reason and a justifiable disciplinary sanction in accordance with the nature and circumstances of the relevant misconduct.

The A.N. OTHER ORGANISATION group recognises that, in the course of day-to-day work activities, a manager/supervisor may have occasion to comment informally upon an employee's conduct or performance or counsel the employee in regard to behaviour. The steps taken by the manager/supervisor will depend on the severity of the conduct.

1.4.2. Incapacity

The 'Code of Good Practice: Dismissal' contained in Schedule 8 of the Labour Relations Act (LRA), relates to discipline relating to misconduct. The code also provides guidelines on how to deal with a situation where an employee is unable to perform their duties due to incapacity.

1.4.3. Desertions

Any employee who is unable to attend work must inform their department head. The company will regard an employee to have absconded from duty if they have been absent from work without informing their immediate superior for 5 days or more. The company:

- Must contact the employee by registered post and enquire about their whereabouts.
- May terminate the contract of employment for desertion if there is no response from the employee.
- Must consider all plausible excuses for the employee's absence (eg in jail, ill, etc).
- Must, in the event of a plausible excuse, wait for them to return to work before conducting an investigation.
- Is entitled to terminate the employee's services, 14 working days from the date of posting the registered letter, if they hear nothing from the employee.

It is not company policy to pay out notice pay in the case of desertion. Deserting employees will, however, be paid out all other money owed to them.

1.4.4. Industrial action

Participation in an illegal strike constitutes misconduct and may invoke the provisions of this policy.

1.4.5. Probation

The company may require a prospective employee to serve a period of probation before their employment is confirmed.

During this period the employee should be given reasonable evaluation and instruction so as to assist the employee to render suitable performance.

The company may either decide to extend the probation period or dismiss the employee should the employee's performance be unsatisfactory.

The employee may only be dismissed after they have been informed that their performance does not meet the required standard and after they have been invited to make representations.

1.5. Application of the disciplinary procedure

1.5.1. Enquiry

A.N. OTHER ORGANISATION will endeavour to conduct a disciplinary enquiry within two weeks after the alleged misconduct has been brought to the attention of HR, management or any other delegated party, taking into consideration that the employee must be given at least 48 hours' notice to prepare for his/her case. These periods may be extended depending on the circumstances of the investigation and the seriousness of the offence.

1.5.2. Suspension

1.5.2.1. General

An employee may be suspended from work in one of three circumstances:

- Intoxication
- To allow an investigation into alleged misconduct to progress
- As a form of punishment (discussed below).

The suspension of an employee may only occur upon the recommendation of the local managing director. The managing director may elect to consult with the group CEO where the allegation involves a senior member of staff or where the allegation is of a serious nature. The formal hearing that follows the investigation should be scheduled within at least a month from the date of suspension unless the commencement thereof is prevented by circumstances beyond A.N. OTHER ORGANISATION's control.

1.5.3. Suspension as a form of punishment

Employees may be suspended, as a form of punishment resulting from a disciplinary action.

1.5.4. Suspension without pay

Under certain circumstances, such as when an employee is not fit for work due to intoxication (drugs or alcohol) the employee will be sent home immediately. The decision will be taken by a Director. The employee will in such cases receive no pay for the remainder of the period of his/her absence from work.

1.5.5. Suspension pending an enquiry

The employee accused of the alleged misconduct may, at the discretion of the company, be suspended with remuneration pending the outcome of an enquiry. As such a provisional suspension is not a disciplinary action. The employee is only provisionally suspended with a view to enable the company to conduct a full enquiry.

An employee may be suspended if the:

- Alleged misconduct is of such a nature that the employee's attendance at work holds potential risks; or if
- Employee's presence in his/her position will prejudice or obstruct any investigation.

1.5.6. Disciplinary intervention

At the completion of the enquiry, the company may depending on the severity of the misconduct, elect to embark on a formal counselling session or to call a formal hearing. Formal sanction will result in either event, if the employee is found to be guilty of any part of the alleged misconduct.

1.5.7. Rights

The employee enjoys the following rights:

- If a hearing is to be embarked on, the employee must receive written notification of the disciplinary hearing including details pertaining to the:
  - Alleged misconduct/the charges
  - Date that the hearing is to be held
  - Time and place where the hearing will take place.
- The employee must be given the opportunity to:
  - Request further particulars with regard to the alleged misconduct
  - State his/her case
  - Lead evidence
  - Call witnesses
  - Cross question witnesses led by the company representative/initiator during the hearing.
- The employee has the right to be assisted by a co-worker from A.N. OTHER ORGANISATION. No external representation will be entertained.
- The initiator may, at any time before the hearing, withdraw a charge of misconduct in writing.
- If an employee refuses or intentionally fails to attend a disciplinary hearing, the case may be heard in his/her absence. This usually takes place on the second occasion that the hearing is convened.
- The fact that an employee has been charged, convicted or acquitted of an offence by a court of law shall not preclude A.N. OTHER ORGANISATION from taking any steps in terms of this Code and Procedure.

1.5.8. Disciplinary hearings

- A formal disciplinary enquiry/hearing shall be convened:
  - To consider the facts around alleged misconduct that may lead to the disciplinary action being instituted against an employee; or
  - To hear an appeal against written warnings or final warnings that emanated out of a counselling session.
- In certain cases where there is more than one accused in a linked case, the chairperson may elect to hold one joint hearing for all of the accused simultaneously. The accused will however still be charged individually. A joint hearing will only be considered because it is more practical to have one hearing, than individual hearings. The following include examples of conditions where this may be done:
  - The accused were co-conspirators.
  - The actions of the accused were inextricably linked.
  - The misconduct and/or modus operandi are identical.
  - The witnesses and evidence (allegation and defence) are identical for each of the accused.
  - The accused all give their permission to hold a joint hearing.
  - The accused's right to privacy is not infringed upon.
  - The joint hearing does not distract in any way from the individual's right to a fair proceeding.

- The independent chairperson makes a recommendation with regards to the finding and sanction. The accused is verbally informed of the outcome.
- The chairperson's finding and recommendation are forwarded to the relevant managing director for consideration and/or ratification. The relevant managing director is not bound to accept the chairperson's recommendation.
- The accused is informed in writing of the company's decision.

Annexure 7.4
Internal disciplinary procedure example

2. Disciplinary procedure

2.1. Introduction

The following guidelines may be used entirely or in part by the company during a disciplinary procedure. The application of this guideline will be determined on a case-by-case basis. A disciplinary procedure may take the form of a counselling session or a hearing.

2.2. Procedure for a counselling session

As far as possible and in the spirit of progressive sanctions, the first step in a disciplinary action is to embark on formal counselling. As such a counselling session is normally held before a disciplinary hearing is held. The company may, however, depending on the seriousness of the offence, elect to deviate from the rule of applying progressive sanctions and progress immediately to a hearing.

A counselling session is typically chaired by an internal person, who in most cases will be the employee's immediate superior. Formal notification of the counselling session must be issued to the employee at least two (2) days before the counselling session is due to take place.

The following are the steps to be followed during a formal counselling session:

- The company person leading the counselling session notes the purpose of the session.
- The company brings the unsatisfactory conduct to the employee's attention.
- The reasons for the misconduct are determined and discussed.
- The parties seek to agree on how to remedy the conduct. The remedy may include a form sanction if applicable.
- The parties agree on the time frame over which the intervention will apply and when a measurement will be taken again to determine if the intervention has remedied the misconduct.
- Take the necessary steps to implement the agreed course of action.

The proceedings must be minuted/recorded and the employee must receive a written outcome of the session. A copy of all documents used during the counselling session must be kept on the employee's file.

2.3. Procedure for a disciplinary hearing

A formal hearing may be held in those circumstances in which the misconduct is serious.

- The letters notifying the employee of the charges (charge sheet) against them and/or of suspension are to be issued at least two (2) days prior to the hearing.
- The company is to compile a pack of the hearing documentation for the chairperson, the accused and for witnesses as relevant. The chairperson will use this pack to lead the proceedings. The following documents should be in the pack:
  - The charge sheet or notification of the hearing
  - Letter of suspension (if applicable)
  - Place for opening statements
  - The company's evidence.

- All other documents will be included as required during the hearing. All documents and/or pages should be numbered sequentially by the chairperson, as is his/her individual preference. The following are examples of what may be included in the pack as the hearing progresses:
  - Evidence from the accused
  - Closing statements
  - Chairperson's findings
  - Statements in aggravation and/or mitigation
  - Chairperson's recommendation
  - Hearing minutes.

The following steps may be followed during a disciplinary hearing:

- The chairperson introduces all parties present to the employee and clarifies their respective roles.
- The chairperson ensures that the employee understands the charges and reaffirms his/her rights.
- The chairperson requests the company to make its opening statement.
- The employee now has the opportunity to answer to the alleged charge/s, as stated by pleading guilty or not guilty.
- If the employee pleads 'not guilty' to all or any of the charges against them, they have the opportunity to make an opening statement. If the employee denies guilt the chairperson proceeds to the next step. If the employee admits guilt the chairperson proceeds to the following step.
- The initiator leads evidence (see below for details how to lead evidence) in order to prove the alleged charge of misconduct. The employee has the opportunity to question the evidence and to submit his/her evidence and call witnesses in his/her defence.
- The disciplinary chairperson considers the evidence and makes a finding whether the employee is guilty or not guilty. Only after the person has been found guilty will the decision be made regarding the applicable sanction.
- The decision of the chairperson is communicated to the employee. The employee must, if found guilty, be given the opportunity to raise mitigating factors. The initiator also has the opportunity to raise aggravating circumstances. The chairperson then informs the employee of the applicable sanction. The chairperson also informs the employee that he/she has the right to appeal against either/both the procedural and substantive matters of the case and that the appeal form must be submitted to Human Resources, in writing within five days of receipt of the findings of the disciplinary hearing.

Leading of evidence. When leading evidence, the initiator should:

- Restrict themselves to asking questions only:
  - The company may not ask leading questions to the company's witnesses
  - The company may ask leading questions to the accused and/or the witnesses of the accused
- Be mindful not to make statements
- Not use hostile witnesses (witnesses 'forced/instructed' to give evidence or 'perceived' not to be independent)
- Prepare all the necessary documentation to be submitted at the hearing
- Prepare closing arguments based on evidence led
- Keep in mind previous offences by accused (if any)
- Be mindful not to generalise
- Always treat the parties with respect.

2.3.1. Chairperson's decision

The chairperson of the formal disciplinary hearing may find, in his opinion, the employee guilty on all or part of the charges against the employee. The chairperson will then make a recommendation to the company to impose some form of penal action.

The company has the right to accept or reject the decision of the chairperson. In some circumstances, the company may reject the decision of the chairperson and impose a less or a more severe punishment.

The chairperson's opinion:

- Is subject to consideration and/or ratification by the managing director/CEO or any other delegated senior person
- Must be made in writing to the employee by Human Resources or another delegated company representative.

2.4. Record-keeping

- Disciplinary action will be treated as confidential.
- All disciplinary reports of formal disciplinary inquiries must be retained.
- A copy of the disciplinary hearing finding and any related disciplinary documentation must be sent to Human Resources Services for record-keeping purposes.
- A copy of the sanction must be held in the employee's file.
- Save where proceedings are recorded, the hearing shall be minuted.
- Written outcome of the hearing shall be given to the employee (with reason/s for the decision) within thirty-six (36) hours of the hearing. The employee shall be advised on the same document of his right to appeal in accordance with the provisions, which appear hereinafter. The employee shall not have a right to appeal if the company appoints an independent practitioner to chair the hearing.

2.5. Disciplinary sanctions and validity period

In those circumstances in which the outcome of the counselling session or the hearing was that some form of penal action should be brought against the employee, the company may elect to impose one of the following sanctions:

- Verbal warning
- Written warning
- Final warning
- Suspension
- Demotion
- Dismissal.

2.6. Verbal warning

In the event of a minor misconduct, the appropriate person may give a verbal warning.

A verbal warning is typically associated with disciplinary interventions that precede a formal hearing. A verbal warning can only be issued subject to the completion of a fair procedure. In most cases, a verbal warning will stem out of a formal counselling session.

The employee must, after the verbal warning was given, receive written notification (with a copy to Human Resources for placement on the employee's file) of the warning. This warning is normally valid for 3 months.

2.7. Written warning

If a verbal warning fails to correct an employee's conduct or if the conduct warrants a written warning without a prior verbal warning, the appropriate person to exercise discipline may give the employee a written warning. A written warning may stem out of a formal counselling session or be the sanction of a full disciplinary hearing.

The following provisions apply to written warnings:

- The written warning must be noted on the appropriate form (see annexure attached hereto).
- A copy of the written warning must be given to the employee, who must acknowledge receipt (evidenced by their signature thereto). If the employee refuses to acknowledge receipt, the person issuing the written warning must hand the written warning to the employee in the presence of another employee and note the refusal to acknowledge receipt of the written warning.
- The written warning must be forwarded to Human Resources for noting and is to be filed in the employee's personnel file.
- Written warnings remain (at the recommendation of the chairperson and ratification by the company) valid for a period of between three (3) months and six (6) months.
- If during the six-month period disciplinary sanction is taken against the employee again, the written warning will be taken into account in deciding on an appropriate sanction.

2.8. Final warning

- A final written warning will only stem out of a disciplinary hearing.
- In certain circumstances, it may be appropriate for a final warning to be given without previous written warnings. These circumstances include where the:
  - Employee has had one or more written warnings still within their period of validity
  - Employee demonstrates a history of unacceptable behaviour
  - Seriousness of the offence requires it.
- The appropriate person to exercise the discipline may give the employee a final warning of any misconduct.
- The final warning must be noted on the appropriate form (see annexure attached hereto).
- A copy of the final written warning must be given to the employee, who must acknowledge receipt. If the employee refuses to acknowledge receipt, the person issuing the final written warning must hand it to the employee in the presence of another employee and note the refusal to acknowledge receipt of the final written warning.
- The signed copy of the final written warning must be forwarded to Human Resources for noting and it is to be filed in the employee's personnel file.
- Final written warnings remain (at the recommendation of the chairperson and ratification by the company) valid for a period of between six (6) months and twelve (12) months.
- If during the twelve-month period disciplinary action is taken against the employee again, the final written warning will be taken into account in deciding on an appropriate sanction.

2.9. Suspension without pay (as a disciplinary sanction)

This is a disciplinary sanction, which would need to be agreed to by the employee as an alternative to dismissal. The actual period of the suspension (as recommended by the chairperson) will be determined by the relevant managing director or disciplinary committee, as applicable. Suspension without pay may be tricky. Consult with local labour experts before imposing such a sanction.

2.10. Demotion

In certain instances, the company may elect to demote the employee. The following should be considered in determining if a demotion is an appropriate sanction to apply:

- The nature and seriousness of the offence
- Demotion coupled with a decrease in remuneration
- Demotion as an alternative to dismissal
- Demotions remain (at the recommendation of the chairperson and ratification by the company) valid for a period of 18 months. Should the employee be found guilty (in a hearing) of a similar offence within this period, he/she may be dismissed.

2.11. Dismissal

2.11.1. Recommendation

If the employee already has had a valid final warning or if the seriousness of the misconduct justifies more drastic disciplinary action, the chairperson may recommend that the employee is dismissed.

Dismissal may be with notice or without/summarily. The company may, in the event of 'dismissal with notice', elect to pay the employee the prescribed notice without the employee actually returning to work.

In either event, the date of termination will be the last official working day, being the date of summary dismissal or the last day of the notice period.

2.11.2. Dismissal for absconding

In the case of an employee absconding from duty and not being present at the first hearing convened, a letter must be issued to them notifying them that their services have been terminated from the company.

2.12. Appeals

2.12.1. Appeal conditions

The employee does not have the right to an internal appeal if the hearing was chaired by an independent chairperson.

Alternatively, an appeal hearing may be heard if any of the following conditions apply:

- The hearing was not chaired by an outside independent chairperson.
- If it can be shown that the disciplinary procedures were not adhered to.
- If new evidence or witnesses are available that may materially influence the decision of the hearing.
- If he/she is of the opinion that the disciplinary sanction taken was unfair or was too harsh in the light of the mitigating circumstances.
- If there is a gross misdirection on the part of the disciplinary committee in respect of the facts or law.

2.12.2. Appeal procedure

- The employee must submit a completed appeal form to Human Resources and/or their superior within five working days of receiving the outcome of the disciplinary hearing.
- The company reserves the right to uphold the sanction if an appeal is not received in terms of this policy.
- The company also reserves the right to apply a harsher sanction should the chairperson of the appeal believe this is suitable.
- The appeal must be chaired by:
  - The managing director or
  - A senior member of staff (independent of the matter heard in the hearing) appointed by the managing director or
- Any external party appointed by the company.
- Human Resources must forward all relevant documentation to the appeal chairperson.
- In the case of the CEO or executive management appealing a case, the applicant may refer the matter to the CCMA within the legally prescribed time frame if he/she is dissatisfied with the outcome of the hearing committee.
- The appeal must be conducted according to the procedures for disciplinary hearings.
- Where no new evidence is presented and the appeal is based on the disciplinary sanction, the appeal hearing may call the employee, his/her representative and the initiator to explain any uncertainties.
- It is not necessary to re-hear all the statements. A decision can be based on the documentation and minutes/recordings of the original hearing.
- The appeal should normally be conducted within 10 working days from receiving the written appeal. The decision must be communicated in writing by Human Resources to the employee.
- The appeal is treated as confidential.
- All appeals must be minuted/recorded.
- A copy of the appeal response and any related documentation must be sent to Human Resources for record purposes.
- The decision of the appeal hearing is subject to ratification by the CEO and is to be regarded as final
- The employee may refer the matter to an outside independent body, as applicable, within the legally prescribed time frame if he/she is dissatisfied with the outcome of the appeal.

2.13. Arbitration

Arbitration may only occur in terms of either:

- The contract of employment. The specific contract of employment may specify that arbitration must be referred to either:
  - TOKISA (example of a South African private arbitration organisation).
  - Bargaining council (applicable in certain industries).
- Mutual agreement between the employee and employer.

2.14. The employee has the right to go to the Council for Conciliation, Mediation and Arbitration (CCMA) in the absence of a requirement to refer the matter to a specific body, as per above.

2.15. Incapacity

Incapacity and/or poor work performance due to incapacity/ill health or injury is to be dealt with in accordance with the Labour Relations Act of 1995.

Annexure 7.5
Guidelines for chairperson example

3. Guidelines for chairperson

3.1. Introduction

The following framework may be used by the chairperson as a guide during a hearing. Hearings will, for the greater part, be chaired by an independent chairperson, who will be a labour specialist. As such the chairperson will abide by the prescripts of the relevant laws and regulations and the company's framework (while in accordance with the law) will not be applicable.

3.2. Hearing

With reference to the hearing at hand, record the following information:

Hearing date	:	
Place of hearing	:	
Time of hearing	:	
Accused employee's name	:	
Accused employee's number	:	
National/Region/branch office	:	

3.3. Description of alleged misconduct

The following is a salient description of the misconduct (please refer to charge sheet/notification of hearing if it is sufficiently descriptive):

3.4. ATTENDEES

The following parties are in attendance at the hearing:

Chairperson and/or disciplinary committee members	:	
Initiator/person leading the company's case	:	
Company witnesses	:	
Employee	:	
Employee's representative	:	
Employee witnesses	:	
Translator	:	
Minute-taker	:	

3.5. PROCEDURAL REQUIREMENTS

3.5.1. The chairperson briefly explains the disciplinary hearing procedure to all present, namely:

3.5.1.1. The purpose of the hearing.

3.5.1.2. The roles of the parties present.

3.5.1.3. The following employee rights:

3.5.1.3.1. The right to an interpreter (if applicable).

3.5.1.3.2. The right to representation.

3.5.1.3.3. The right to call witnesses.

3.5.1.3.4. The right to cross-question.

3.5.1.3.5. The right to appeal.

3.5.1.3.6. The right to timely notification.

NOTE: Should no representative be required it is advisable to record this in writing and have this acknowledged by the accused employee.

3.5.2. The chairperson reads the alleged misconduct, as stated in the notification of disciplinary hearing to the employee, and ensures that the person understands both the nature and seriousness of the misconduct.

3.5.3. The chairperson asks the employee to state his/her plea for each item of misconduct:

NO	CHARGE	PLEA
		GUILTY/ NOT GUILTY
		GUILTY/ NOT GUILTY
		GUILTY/ NOT GUILTY
		GUILTY/ NOT GUILTY

3.5.4. In the event of a 'guilty' plea, the chairperson has a duty to:
   3.5.4.1. Understand exactly what the accused is admitting guilt to.
   3.5.4.2. Ensure that the accused employee understands the severity of a 'guilty' plea.

3.5.5. Should the employee plead 'guilty' proceed with the hearing to the heading which reads 'MITIGATION'.

3.5.6. Should the employee plead 'not guilty' all evidence needs to be heard according to the following procedure:

3.5.7. In the event of a 'not guilty' plea, the chairperson leads the proceedings of the hearing according to the following stages:

- The chair asks the initiator to present the company's case. The chair makes comprehensive notes of all that is said/a recording. The chair may elect to make use of a dedicated minute-taker to record the proceedings. The chair will nevertheless still take cursory notes of important points to ponder on or that will need to be taken into consideration later in the proceedings. All recordings of hearings need to be reduced to paper and the initiator and the accused employee need to agree that the transcription is a true reflection of the actual hearing. The initiator will present:
  - Calculations
  - Documentary evidence
  - Photos, video and/or audio material.
- The initiator calls company witnesses and questions them. Interviewers may only ask their witnesses questions. They may not make statements or draw conclusions.
- The accused employee/representative is afforded the opportunity to cross-question the evidence presented and/or cross-question the company witnesses.
- The accused employee then leads evidence and/or calls witnesses.
- The initiator is then allowed to cross-question the accused employee's evidence presented to cross-question the accused employee's witnesses.
- The chair then allows the initiator to give closing arguments.
- Thereafter the chair allows the accused employee to present closing arguments.

3.6. Finding and motivation

3.6.1. The hearing is then typically adjourned for the chairperson to reflect on the merits of the case and the evidence presented. The chair will normally define a re-adjournment date before the hearing is concluded for the day. Only in exceptional cases, where the facts overwhelmingly point to a definite conclusion (guilty or non-guilty), will the chair give his conclusion immediately.

3.6.2. The chairperson must denote his findings and his reasons for reaching these conclusions below:

3.7. Mitigation

3.7.1. At re-adjournment, the chair requests the accused employee to state any mitigating factors in the case.

3.7.2. The following is a summary of the mitigation presented for consideration:

3.8. Aggravation

3.8.1. The chair then requests the initiator to present factors to be taken into account in aggravation when handing down his opinion.

3.8.2. The following aggravating circumstances were presented:

3.9. Substantive fairness

3.9.1. Before deciding on the appropriate sanction it is necessary for the chair to consider the following:

3.9.1.1. Custom and practice at A.N. OTHER ORGANISATION.

3.9.1.2. The seriousness of the transgressions (extent of damages/cost impact on the organisation).

3.9.1.3. Extenuating circumstances (factors that may have led to the misconduct being committed: provocation, incorrect procedures, custom and practice).

3.9.1.4. Aggravating circumstances: seniority of employee, intent, premeditation, self-gain, deviousness and repeatedly having committed similar misconducts.

3.9.1.5. Mitigating circumstances: age, length of service, attendance record, remorse shown.

3.9.1.6. Employee's personal record: valid disciplinary interventions (during the last 6 months), attendance history, work performance, comment from their supervisor.

3.9.1.7. Precedent – what precedent will be set for future from this decision.

3.9.1.8. Action taken in previous cases of this nature.

3.9.1.9. Alternatives to dismissal.

3.10. Outcome

3.10.1. After hearing the mitigating and aggravating circumstances, the chair verbally gives the outcome of the hearing and makes his recommendation to the company in terms of his sanction (see below).

3.10.2. The chairperson's opinion may either be wholly or partially in favour of the employee or the company.

3.10.3. The following is the chair's opinion and recommended sanction:

3.10.4. Assuming that the chair's decision was wholly or partially against the employee, the chair notifies the employee of his/her right to appeal the decision.

3.10.5. The chair then finalises a notification of the disciplinary hearing's outcome and arranges to have it distributed to all parties present at the hearing (excluding witnesses).

3.11. Sanction

3.11.1. The company reduces the chair's decision to writing and forwards this to the employee.

3.11.2. The company then has an opportunity to consider the chair's recommendation and to adopt or decline the chair's recommendation.

3.11.3. The company puts its chosen course of action in writing to the accused employee.

3.11.4. Copies of all hearing and associated documents are sent to HR for filing on the accused employee's file.

3.12. Introduction

These sanctions do not represent an exhaustive list. The sanctions should be decided on a case-by-case basis.

Please note that any misconduct in categories 2 and 3 may be recognised as gross misconduct and be dealt with as a very serious form of misconduct.

Category 1

VERY SERIOUS OFFENCE	First Offence
Grossly offensive behaviour	Dismissal
Gross dereliction of duties (negligence/incapacity)	Dismissal
Gross negligence	Dismissal
Actual assault/threat of assault/being in possession of dangerous weapons	Dismissal
Unauthorised possession of A.N. OTHER ORGANISATION property	Dismissal
Theft, fraud, bribery, disclosure of confidential information	Dismissal
Gross dishonesty	Dismissal
Sexual harassment	Dismissal
Gross insubordination	Dismissal
Bringing A.N. OTHER ORGANISATION's name into disrepute	Dismissal
Malicious damage to A.N. OTHER ORGANISATION property or property of fellow employees	Dismissal
Unauthorised and/or un-communicated absence from work for a period of more than one week (five working days absent without leave {AWOL})	Dismissal
Unfair discrimination	Dismissal
Unauthorised use of A.N. OTHER ORGANISATION property	Dismissal
Refusal to work (group)	Dismissal
Gross failure to comply with fire, health and/or safety regulations	Dismissal

Category 2

SERIOUS OFFENCE	First Offence	Second Offence
Insubordination	Final written warning	Dismissal
Unauthorised use of A.N. OTHER ORGANISATION labour/material to work under any circumstances	Final written warning	Dismissal
Unauthorised private work during working hours	Final written warning	Dismissal
Dishonesty	Final written warning	Dismissal
Dereliction of duty	Final written warning	Dismissal
Being under the influence of liquor during working hours (breathalyzer result of 0,05 or higher)	Final written warning	Dismissal
Being under the influence of/misuse of substances (illegal/legal)	Final written warning	Dismissal
Failure to comply with fire, health and/or safety regulations	Final written warning	Dismissal
Unauthorised absence for longer than two days without a reasonable excuse or doctor's certificate	Final written warning	Dismissal
Refusal to carry out an authorised instruction in respect of normal work practice not involving abnormal physical risk, and also not in conflict with any other instruction	Final written warning	Dismissal

Category 3

MODERATE OFFENCE	First Offence	Second Offence	Third Offence	Fourth Offence	Fifth Offence
Absenteeism without informing the relevant person	Corrective counselling	Verbal warning	Written warning	Final written warning	Dismissal
Unauthorised absence from workplace whilst on duty	Corrective counselling	Verbal warning	Written warning	Final written warning	Dismissal
Swearing and/or abusive language/gestures	Corrective counselling	Verbal warning	Written warning	Final written warning	Dismissal
Habitual absence of one to two days without a reasonable excuse or producing a doctor's certificate	Corrective counselling	Verbal warning	Written warning	Final written warning	Dismissal
Poor timekeeping (habitual late coming/leaving work early/extended breaks	Corrective counselling	Verbal warning	Written warning	Final written warning	Dismissal
Poor work performance/ incapacity	Corrective counselling	Verbal warning	Written warning	Final written warning	Dismissal
Health and Safety contraventions	Written site warning	Written site warning	Written warning	Final written warning	Dismissal

Annexure 7.6
Letter of suspension

Letter of suspension

Ref # ....

dd Mmmm 20yy
Employee name
C/o A.N. Other organisation
Address

Dear Sir/Madam

ADMINISTRATIVE LEAVE

You are hereby advised not to attend work with immediate effect until further notice. The Company is currently investigating an alleged serious charge of misconduct against you.

You will be paid in full during this period, however you must provide contactable telephone numbers as well as ensuring that your address on record is up to date, in order that the Company can contact you.

If the Company intends to lay charges against you in terms of its Disciplinary Policy, these will be conveyed to you either by hand or by registered post in due course.

FOR: A.N. OTHER ORGANISATION

Yours sincerely

Human Resources

CC:

Annexure 7.7
Notification to attend a hearing

Notification to attend a hearing

Ref # ....

dd Mm 20yy
Employee name
C/o A.N. Other organisation
Address

Dear Sir/Madam

NOTICE TO ATTEND DISCIPLINARY HEARING

This letter serves to confirm that in accordance with A.N. OTHER ORGANISATION's staff disciplinary procedure and code, a disciplinary hearing is scheduled to take place on __date__ at ___time_____ in the company's offices in __________. Your presence is required at the hearing to answer to charges that are forwarded by (initiator's name) who will be leading evidence on the company's behalf. The charges against you are as follows:

1	
2	
3	

The hearing will be chaired by (chairperson's name).

I wish to take this opportunity to remind you of the following:

- You have the right to be represented by a fellow employee of your choice.
- It is your responsibility to establish who your representative will be (should you require one) and to make contact with that person as soon as possible in order to prepare your case before the disciplinary hearing.
- You have the right to call your own witnesses.
- You have the right to cross-question the company's witnesses at the disciplinary hearing.
- Please make the necessary arrangements to ensure that your witnesses are present on the day of the hearing. You may advise your manager in order that the necessary arrangements are made for them to be present.
- At the proceedings, you will be granted the opportunity to plead guilty/not guilty, state your case, call witnesses, cross-question and make closing arguments.
- Furthermore, you may be expected to present mitigation should you be found guilty of any of the aforementioned misconduct.
- The hearing will be conducted in English. Should you require an interpreter, kindly inform the writer of this letter at least one working day before the disciplinary hearing, as stated in this notification.
- You have the right to appeal the decision taken at the hearing by lodging an appeal within five (5) days of being informed of the outcome of the disciplinary hearing and/or disciplinary action. The notice of appeal is to be submitted to Human Resources in writing, setting out in detail the grounds and reason for appeal.

If you fail to attend these proceedings the company reserves the right to proceed. You should advise your manager at least two (2) working days prior to the hearing for a postponement should you be unable to attend for any valid reason. The company will only consider one postponement.

A.N. OTHER ORGANISATION's Staff Disciplinary Procedure and Code is attached to this notification. Please feel free to contact me prior to the disciplinary hearing should you have any questions requiring clarity.

FOR: A.N. OTHER ORGANISATION

Yours sincerely

Human Resources

CC: (Disciplinary Committee)
(Initiator)

Annexure 7.8
Opening statements

Opening statement

Hearing of	:	Employee's name
Brought on by	:	Company initiator's name
Charges	:	As per hearing notification
Date, time & place	:	>>h00, dd MM 20>>, A.N. Other Organisation's offices.

Short description of misconduct >>>.

The company has consequently embarked on this disciplinary action.

The company will call the following witness and lead evidence to prove the charges levied in this matter:

Witness's name	

Statement made by:

______________________	dd/MM/20>>
Initiator's name Title	at A.N. Other Organisation's offices

Annexure 7.9
Hearing questions

Hearing questions

The following questioning may be referred to in the aforementioned hearing:

1. PLEA

How do you plea?

- **Guilty** – Please give details of yours and others involvement, or
- **Not guilty** – Initiator to call witnesses.

2. WITNESS QUESTIONING

2.1	WITNESS NAME #1	
2.1.1.	▪ What is your position at the company? ▪ How long have you been with the company? ▪ What do your duties include?	
2.1.2.	Specific questions relating to the misconduct	
2.1.3.		
2.1.4.		
2.1.5.		
	Accused's right to cross-examine	
	Cross-examination	
	Initiator's right to clarify	
	Clarifying questions	

2.2.	WITNESS NAME #2	
2.2.1.	▪ What is your position at the company? ▪ How long have you been with the company? ▪ What are your responsibilities at the company?	
2.2.2.	Specific questions relating to the misconduct	
2.2.3.		
2.2.4.		
2.2.5.		
	Accused's right to cross-examine	
	Cross-examination	
	Initiator's right to clarify	
	Clarifying questions	

2.3.	WITNESS NAME #3	
2.3.1.	■ What is your position at the company? ■ How long have you been with the company? ■ What are your responsibilities at the company?	
2.3.2.	Specific questions relating to the misconduct	
2.3.3.		
2.3.4.		
2.3.5.		
	Accused's right to cross-examine	
	Cross-examination	
	Initiator's right to clarify	
	Clarifying questions	

2.4.	WITNESS NAME #4	
2.4.1.	■ What is your position at the company? ■ How long have you been with the company? ■ What are your responsibilities at the company?	
2.4.2.	Specific questions relating to the misconduct	
2.4.3.		
2.4.4.		
2.4.5.		
	Accused's right to cross-examine	
	Cross-examination	
	Initiator's right to clarify	
	Clarifying questions	

2.5.	WITNESS NAME #5	
2.5.1.	▪ What is your position at the company? ▪ How long have you been with the company? ▪ What are your responsibilities at the company?	
2.5.2.	Specific questions relating to the misconduct	
2.5.3.	Etc.	
2.5.4.	Etc.	
2.5.5.	Etc.	
	Accused's right to cross-examine	
	Cross-examination	
	Initiator's right to clarify	
	Clarifying questions	

3. ACCUSED QUESTIONING

3.1.		Name	
3.1.1.		▪ How long have you been with the company? ▪ What do you do?	
3.1.2.		Specific questions relating to the misconduct	
3.1.3.		Etc.	
3.1.4.		Etc.	
3.1.5.		Etc.	
3.1.6.		Etc.	
3.1.7.		Etc.	
	3.1.7.1.	Etc.	
	3.1.7.2.	Etc.	
	3.1.7.3.	Etc.	
	3.1.7.4.	Etc.	

Annexure 7.10
Closing statements

Closing statements

Hearing of	:	Accused's name
Brought on by	:	Initiator's name on behalf of A.N. Other Organisation.
Charges	:	>>>>
Date, time & place	:	tth00, weekday, dd/MM/20>>, A.N. Other Organisation Offices, >>>.

A. With reference to the disciplinary h]earing that was held with Mr >>> (hereafter referred to as >>>>) on the charges of >>>> at A.N. Other Organisation's offices on dd/MM/20>> at tth00, the company would like to make the following closing statements:

1. >>>>>Charge>>>>
On the charge of >>>>:
These aforementioned factors are not plausible and the balance of probability is that >>>>>. It is therefore the opinion of the company that >>> has been >>>>.

2. >>>>>Charge>>>>
On the alternate charge of >>>:
It is therefore concluded that >>>>>.

B. The company would like to conclude that >>> has been proven to be:

- >>>
- >>>

The company is devastated by the behaviour demonstrated by >>>. The trust that the company had in >>> has been irreparably damaged.

The company requests that the chairperson take these factors into consideration when making his ruling.

The company would also like to take this opportunity to thank the chairperson for presiding over the proceedings.

Statement made by:

______________________________	dd/MM/20>>
Initiator's name Title	at A.N. Other Organisation's Offices

Annexure 7.11
Statements in aggravation

Statements in aggravation

Hearing of	:	Accused's name
Brought on by	:	Initiator's name on behalf of A.N. Other Organisation.
Charges	:	>>>>
Date, time & place	:	tth00, weekday, dd MM 20>>, A.N. Other Organisation's Offices.

With reference to the hearing of >>>, the company would like to bring the following aggravating factors to the attention of the chairperson in consideration of his ruling:

1. The company has brought arguments proving >>>>.
2. >>>>
3. The company has a 'zero tolerance' stance on crime and cannot associate itself with those associated with criminal activity.
4. The company has initiated criminal proceedings. The company has already and will be compelled to spend a lot of time and money to bring the perpetrators of these crimes to justice, with very little prospect of any recoverability of its losses and costs.
5. The outcome of this case is imperative in sending a strong message to existing and/or future perpetrators of crime.

The company, therefore, seeks the harshest outcome of this hearing and the company consequently requests that >>> be summarily dismissed.

Statement made by:

____________________	dd/MM/20>>
Initiator's name Title	at A.N. Other Organisation's Offices

Annexure 7.12
Notification of outcome of hearing

Notification of outcome of hearing

Ref # ....
dd Mm 20yy
Employee name
C/o A.N. Other Organisation
Address

Dear (employee's name) ____

OUTCOME OF DISCIPLINARY HEARING – dd Mm 20yy

The chairperson has verbally advised you on dd Mm 20yy of his decision, as to the outcome of the hearing that was held. The chairperson's decision was to find you guilty/not guilty of the/the first/all of the charges brought against you and he has recommended to the company that you receive a warning/ final written warning/be summarily dismissed, effective dd Mm 20yy.

The company is currently contemplating the chairperson's decision to .../summarily dismiss you.

You will be informed in due course of the company's decision to adopt/decline the chairperson's decision.

FOR: A.N. OTHER ORGANISATION

Yours sincerely

Human Resources

CC:
- Disciplinary Committee
- Initiator
- Employee
- Employee's representative
- Employee files

Annexure 7.13
Appeal form

Appeal form

NAME OF EMPLOYEE APPEALING	:	
EMPLOYEE NUMBER	:	
DESIGNATION	:	
DATE OF ORIGINAL DISCIPLINARY INTERVENTION	:	
CHAIRPERSON OF ORIGINAL DISCIPLINARY INTERVENTION	:	

REASON FOR APPEAL

Please provide full details of why you wish to appeal the disciplinary sanction:

SUGGESTED OUTCOME

Please describe the outcome that you seek to accomplish:

ADDITIONAL EVIDENCE

Please list and attach all new evidence/statements attached hereto:

APPEAL LODGED BY

SIGNED	DATE
______________________ (Appellant)	
______________________ (Appellant's representative)	

COMMITTEE'S FINDING

The following is the appeal committee's finding:

APPEAL HEARD BY

SIGNED	DATE
______________________ (Chairperson of appeal committee)	
______________________ (Member #1 of appeal committee)	
______________________ (Member #2 of appeal committee)	
______________________ (Member #3 of appeal committee)	

APPEAL COMMITTEE'S OUTCOME

ACCEPT OUTCOME:		DO NOT ACCEPT OUTCOME:	

COMMITTEE'S SANCTION

The following is the appeal committee's sanction:

FOR: A.N. OTHER ORGANISATION

Human Resources

CC:
- Original disciplinary committee
- Appeal committee
- Initiator
- Employee
- Employee's representative
- Employee files

Annexure 7.14
Written warning

Written warning

Ref # ....

dd Mm 20yy
Employee name
C/o A.N. Other Organisation
Address

Dear(nameofemployee)____

WRITTEN WARNING

This letter serves as a written warning in terms of A.N. OTHER ORGANISATION's staff disciplinary procedure and code. The purpose of this warning is to correct errant behaviour. If you engage in further misconduct, the written warning may be taken into account in determining a more serious sanction.

The written warning will be placed on your personnel file. The warning remains valid for 3/6 (three/six) months from today.

Should you wish to appeal against the decision taken, please forward your appeal to human resources within 5 (five) working days of receipt of this warning.

NATURE

The following is a summary of the misconduct/charge/s that has/have been proven:

AGREED ACTION

The following is a summary of the agreed plan of action to obviate repeat of misconduct:

ACKNOWLEDGEMENT

SIGNED	DATE
______________________ (Employee)	
______________________ (Employee's representative)	
______________________ (Employee's manager/supervisor)	

FOR: A.N. OTHER ORGANISATION

Yours sincerely

Human Resources

CC:
- Disciplinary Committee
- Initiator
- Employee
- Employee's representative
- Employee files

Annexure 7.15
Final Written warning

Final written warning

Ref # ....

dd Mm 20yy
Employee name
C/o A.N. Other Organisation
Address

Dear (name of employee) ____________________

FINAL WRITTEN WARNING

Dear (name of employee) ____________________

This letter serves as a final written warning in terms of A.N. OTHER ORGANISATION's staff disciplinary procedure and code. The purpose of this warning is to correct errant behaviour. If you engage in further misconduct, the written warning may be taken into account in determining a more serious sanction.

The written warning will be placed on your personnel file. The warning remains valid for 6/12 (six/twelve) months from today.

Should you wish to appeal against the decision taken, please forward your appeal to human resources within 5 (five) working days of receipt of this warning.

NATURE

The following is a summary of the misconduct/charge/s that has/have been proven:

AGREED ACTION

The following is a summary of the agreed plan of action to obviate repeat of misconduct:

ACKNOWLEDGEMENT

SIGNED	DATE
______________________ (Employee)	
______________________ (Employee's representative)	
______________________ (Employee's manager/supervisor)	

FOR: A.N. OTHER ORGANISATION

Yours sincerely

Human Resources

CC:
- Disciplinary Committee
- Initiator
- Employee
- Employee's representative
- Employee files

Annexure 7.16
Letter of demotion

Letter of demotion

Ref # ....

dd Mm 20yy
Employee name
C/o A.N. Other organisation
Address

Dear (name of employee) ______________________________

LETTER OF DEMOTION

This letter serves to notify you in terms of A.N. OTHER ORGANISATION's staff disciplinary procedure and code that you have been demoted to the position of ______________________. The effective date of your demotion is ________________. In this new position you will report to ________________ and your duties are as per the attached job description (see annexure A).

Should you wish to appeal against the decision taken, please forward your appeal to human resources within 5 (five) working days of receipt of this warning.

NATURE

The following is a summary of the misconduct/charge/s that has/have been proven:

AGREED ACTION

The following is a summary of additionally agreed action to obviate repeat of misconduct:

ACKNOWLEDGEMENT

SIGNED	DATE
____________________ (Employee)	
____________________ (Employee's representative)	
____________________ (Employee's manager/supervisor)	

FOR: A.N. OTHER ORGANISATION

Yours sincerely

Human Resources

CC:
- Disciplinary Committee
- Initiator
- Employee
- Employee's representative
- Employee files

Annexure 7.17
Letter of dismissal

Letter of dismissal

Ref # ....

dd Mm 20yy
Employee name
C/o A.N. Other Organisation
Address

Dear (employee's name)____

OUTCOME OF DISCIPLINARY HEARING – dd Mm 20yy

Management has considered the recommendation of the chairperson, of which you have been verbally advised and which will be forwarded to you once reduced to writing. Accordingly, we hereby confirm that we agree with the chairperson's decision to summarily dismiss you, effective dd Mm 20yy.

In terms of the Labour Relations Act of 1995 as amended, any dispute in this matter may be referred to the >>> Industrial Bargaining Council within 30 days of today's date.

Your wages, up to and including the dd[th] of Mm 20yy, less any monies that you may owe the company, will be ready for collection dd Mm 20yy.

Also, be advised that you may contact our wage department to make arrangements to obtain your UIF card (U.I.19).

FOR: A.N. OTHER ORGANISATION

Yours sincerely

Human Resources

CC:
- Disciplinary Committee
- Initiator
- Employee
- Employee's representative
- Employee files

CHAPTER 8

REPORTING

8.1. CHAPTER OVERVIEW AND INTRODUCTION

The reporting of your work is the most important part of the investigation/your work. This is because, for the greater part, the report is the only 'product' that you deliver to your 'client' and/or to other parties. You may have performed a technically brilliant investigation, but it will all be in vain if you are unable to carry your findings and conclusions across well to the reader/user of your report.

In this chapter, we are going to discuss all 'reporting' aspects, as opposed to discussing investigation reports only. Reporting is seen therefore as the broader communication of any aspects of your work. We discuss the types and purposes of reports and the various parties who could be reported to. We also discuss typical sections and some practical 'do's and don'ts' to a full report. Lastly, we discuss the valuable use of affidavits in the wider reporting arena.

8.1.1. Purpose of reporting

Too many people dive straight into detailed report drafting upon completion of an investigation. This is definitely not the correct approach. The cliché suggests that 'only fools rush in'. Remember our rule: 'Plan, plan and plan'.

As the investigation unfolds, start to visualise the 'end-game'. Start to think about all the parties that you may need to report to and the message that you want to convey to each of them respectively. Gather information accordingly. Similarly, when leading a forensic function, think about all the parties you have to and/or should report to and design mechanisms to collate the data that you require (discussed later) to conduct such reporting.

Commence therefore by understanding who you are reporting to and the purpose of your reporting. The 'who' will most likely define the purpose of the report. For example, is this a high-level report to the audit committee or is it the basis of your detailed testimony? As you can well imagine, the purpose of your reporting will define your approach.

As highlighted in Chapter 3 on conducting the investigation, the following include some of the purposes of reporting:

- *To inform*
  To inform the reader of what has transpired, who was involved, how they did what they did, why it occurred, accountabilities, etc. The degree of detail may vary significantly depending on the recipient of the report.

- *To obtain action*
  To recommend remedial action, bolstering of controls, additional work, etc.

- *To request assistance/action*

To request guidance, legal opinion, involvement in, additional resources, postponement, assistance to resolve a bottleneck, etc.

- *To prove a matter*

To serve to summarise the detailed facts of the case, the investigation steps, the investigation logic, the chain of evidence, conclusions, comparisons, subsequent actions, testimonies, etc.

- *To give evidence*

Very similar to the aforementioned point, but this time limited to the work, views and testimony of the author of the report.

- *To deter*

To make an example, to educate recipients, to discourage them from acts of misconduct, etc.

8.1.2. Report recipients

The possible parties to whom we may be reporting may include:

- *Criminal matters*

Detailed reporting via affidavits, oral testimony, expert opinion reports and conclusions: The first use of this type of report is to open a criminal case with the police. This is a very important action and should be the aim of all investigations. Chapter 7 on subsequent actions (discussion on legal aspects) sets forth a detailed discussion. The purpose of opening a case is to get the authorities to do something about the matter that you are dealing with. Reports used in criminal matters can also be used to summarise evidence, methods, the chain of evidence or to present testimony.

- *Authorities*

Detailed reporting via affidavits, oral testimony or a written report: There may be a legal or a moral obligation to report matters to the authorities. Examples of authorities and specialised police units include:

  - Narcotics police officers/units
  - Tax and revenue authorities
  - Border and customs units
  - Environmental officers
  - Military
  - EU union, USA and British anti-bribery and anti-corruption units.

Establish which authorities are relevant to your investigation and what the reporting requirements are. Take the reporting to these authorities under advisement of legal counsel if required to ensure that you do not make any incorrect statements that may inadvertently incriminate the organisation/prejudice the organisation's legal position.

- *Audit committee*

High-level overall oral summaries or written reports and/or statistics: The audit committee is normally an important client, especially if you are working for an in-house forensic function.

There are normally formally structured reporting protocols in place for reporting to the audit committee. The audit committee is typically interested to know:

- High-level statistics and trends
- What the amount of the loss was
- If a senior/trusted employee perpetrated misconduct
- What the chance is of:
    - Criminal conviction
    - Determining the full extent of the fraud
    - Recovery/possibility of and the amount to be recovered
    - Dismissal of internal employees
- If the organisation is guilty of any misconduct
- What the organisation is doing to prevent recurrence.

- *Board and senior management*

High-level overall oral summaries or written reports and/or statistics. Individually written summary reports: While the audit committee is a working committee of the board, you may be required to report separately or in greater detail to the board. The audit committee is made up of independent non-executive board members. The executive board members (who are involved with the running of the organisation) may require greater detail. The organisation's internal reporting conventions would need to be established and complied with.

- *Management*

Medium-level of detailed oral and written reports: Management is responsible for the day-to-day running of the organisation and will need to have greater detail on the matter, as they will need to take action.

- *The general organisation*

Salient and sanitised gist only. Verbal reports, e-mail notifications and fraud newsletters: People in the organisation themselves may need to be informed of the outcome of serious matters. This may entail a specific communication from management or it may be done via a periodic fraud newsletter. Facts will need to be sanitised.

- *Specific colleagues affected by the matter*

Salient and sanitised gist only. Verbal report only: Conduct any such discussions with the support of HR or a suitably qualified counsellor. People who remain behind sit with all kinds of emotions including:

- Empathy/pity for the subject/s of the investigation.
- Support for the subject or the organisation. This tends to be an 'either/or' scenario and not both at the same time.
- Guilt and remorse because they were somehow involved and/or did not act to prevent/report the matter.
- Anger at the subject or organisation.

Such reporting, despite what the subject did, needs to be factual, free of emotion and respectful. It is advisable to err on the side of giving less detail rather than too much. Please also bear in mind that legal processes may still be ongoing and you do not want to be defeating the ends of justice. Facts will need to be sanitised. Inform the people to whom you are reporting that:

- The matter is sub-judice and that you are not permitted to provide more detail.
- You need to respect people's privacy and that you cannot make all facts publicly known. If they persist, ask them how they would want the organisation to act if they were the subject of such an investigation and if they would want the details of their misdeeds generally distributed.

- *Shareholders, owners, holding companies and subsidiaries lower down*

High-level overall oral summaries or written reports and/or statistics. Some individual oral or written progress reports may be required throughout: shareholders and holding companies may need to be informed of the outcome of serious matters. This may be done via the organisation's own reporting channels or you may be requested to do it.

- *Key clients, business parties, key suppliers and other parties*

High-level oral reports: As with shareholders and owners, the key parties that the organisation deals with may need to be updated on the outcome of matters. This will be especially true if the matter affects the business that is being conducted with these parties. Alternatively, it may be to give an update of the organisation's overall standing. Facts will need to be sanitised.

- *The stock exchange*

High-level written reports. Determine what the specific stock exchange's reporting requirements are. Ensure that you take the reporting under the advisement of suitable people such as legal counsel and professional accountants.

- *Financing institutions*

High-level oral reporting: The institution that is providing funding may require reporting to as well. Even if there is no formal reporting requirement, it may be good practice to inform them of the occurrences and what the organisation has done about it. This will contribute to building a relationship of trust. The matter may also have a bearing on the financial stability or good standing of the organisation. Banks tend to be conservative and sensitive to their public image. A bank will generally not want to be seen to be supporting an unethical organisation.

- *Insurance houses*

Medium-level detail, as defined by the specific insurance house. Initially oral, then written: Insurance houses will need to be informed of all matters for which the organisation intends lodging a claim. Some insurance policies require that the organisation reports all matters to them and not only the ones that the organisation is going to lodge a claim for. This is done for statistical reasons. Obtain the relevant insurance policy and determine the reporting requirements. Let the organisation's insurance officer do the reporting or pass the report by the organisation's communication experts.

- *External parties and/or the press*

Salient and sanitised gist of the matter only. Oral or written press releases: Informing of internal matters to external parties should be the exception. If it must be done, it must be well planned and handled by those people in the organisation authorised to communicate to the public. As far as possible a statement should be prepared and approved in advance by the senior organisation leadership. The message to be communicated should be role-played and practised. Facts will need to be sanitised. Examples of external parties include:

- The general public
- Specific private individuals affected by the matter
- Landlords or properties that the organisation is renting
- Private security companies.

In one small incident, a painter had climbed up scaffolding during lunchtime and tried to gain access to an apartment in the block that the company was painting. I gave feedback to the apartment owner after the matter had been handed over to the police and they were dealing with the culprit. Now, the owner was understandably disturbed and I was met with an emotional response. I listened empathetically to the owner and I calmly explained the facts at hand and what had been done. She was significantly calm by the time I left. The company received a compliment for the manner in which we had handled the matter. This was important, as the company did a lot of work in the area and one of the company owners lived in the area.

- *Industry and professional bodies*

High-level oral, written reports or statements: There is an element of trust associated with professionals. Failure to uphold the ethics of the industry may be a poor reflection of the whole industry and brings everyone down. It is therefore important to report misconduct of members to the responsible professional body to allow them the take any actions they deem necessary. Please also bear in mind that you cannot make any declarations if the subject has not yet been found guilty. The punishment also needs to suit the crime. Barring a person for life may not be the fairest option. Examples of industry bodies to be contacted include:

- The Institute of Chartered Accountants
- The Institute of Internal Auditors
- The Association of Certified Fraud Examiners
- The Information Systems Audit and Control Association
- Bar/law society
- Estate agents' board
- Medical societies
- Engineers' boards.

- *Internal audit*

Medium- to high-detail oral or written reports: Internal audit should be aware of all fraud matters, as they evaluate the internal controls. Auditors try, through various analyses, to identify high-risk areas. The area in which the matter occurred may represent a higher risk area for inclusion in an audit cycle. You may also wish to direct internal audit to conduct an immediate evaluation of the internal controls in the business processes around the matter. Internal audit would be able to make recommendations to bolster controls to prevent and/or detect future occurrences. Alternatively, internal audit may need to avoid an area in which a current investigation is ongoing to allow the investigation to continue uninterrupted.

- *External audit*

Medium to high level of detail of oral or written reports: External audit will also need to be aware of all material matters that may affect their audit procedures and opinion. You are advised to sit with external audit at year-end and give them a list of all matters dealt with. They request details of the matters they deem important. I have never experienced any interference by external audit. They typically offer their forensic services (may be a conflict of interest as they cannot conduct the external audit and provide consulting services). They mostly just increase their substantive testing in the affected area.

- *Third-parties, suppliers, clients, etc*
  Salient sanitised gist of the matter only. Oral, written letters, press statements: While organisations do not like airing their dirty laundry, it may be required to meet with suppliers to define a way forward if they were affected by the matter. These parties may also have been the employer of one of the offending parties. Alternatively, your organisation may have employed the subject who affected them. Facts will need to be sanitised.

As discussed, the purpose and the intended recipient of the report will define the level of detail and the type of report that you will draft. Too many fraud investigators try to serve too many masters in one report. This may please some and displease others. Alternatively, each reader may not relate to an element of the report and therefore not feel that the report is a good report. In this way, you rarely end up satisfying anyone.

Please also bear in mind that the actual recipient of the report and the intended recipient may differ. You will draft your report for a particular audience and you will (normally) formally circulate your report to the intended recipient/s. While you may have influence, you have little or no control over the subsequent full or partial circulation and/or formal or informal communication of its contents.

Remember our rule 'Be careful who you share what information with.'

It is therefore important to formally define the purpose of your report and the intended audience in the introductory section. In this way, 'expectations' can be more successfully managed. You will then also be able to refer people to the purpose when they say that the report does not satisfy their requirements. Be sure to also list limitations of the work and any disclaimers required.

Furthermore, you should only ever say or write things that you are comfortable being read by a wider audience. Comfortable means true and defendable. This is vital. Reports' wider communication rarely conforms to the intended degree of confidentiality and/or the intended restricted audience.

8.1.3. Reporting types

At the highest level, all forms of communication concerning a matter can be considered as reporting. All communication should, therefore, be well planned and treated with due care and professionalism. Matters may be reported in the following manners:

- *Informal oral*
  This is the type of reporting that you would do when you walk into someone's office without an appointment or where you bump into them en-route and give them a quick update of what has happened and the status of the investigation. The purpose of this type of reporting is to provide a quick update. You could also arrange to accidentally meet with someone and use this to your advantage to communicate an important message to a particular party. There may

be some planning to your informal report, but it often tends to be impromptu. The facts and figures reported also tend to be high-level and sanitised. The problem with oral reporting is that there is no record of what you said. You are advised to make notes of such reporting for future reference.

I recall a particular learning in this regard. I stopped at the washroom on my way to the boardroom of a company where I worked for the standard 'Friday drinks'. One of the regional operations managers was leaving the washroom and stopped to ask me about the results of a particular (substantive) audit that we were performing at the time. This was an area on which business units' and leaders' performance was measured and consequently enjoyed more than its fair share of attention. People were always trying to get early insights into the results. I did not want to completely dismiss him but knew that I could not divulge results at this premature stage. I said something along the lines that everything was going fine and off he went.

When I walked into the boardroom everyone was staring at me. I looked around to understand what was going on, and the group MD said: 'I hear Craig says that the results are looking good.' Now, you must understand that no results were allowed to be released before reporting to and sign-off from the group MD. The MD looked at me with daggers out. The results were far from being complete and I had thought that I had communicated that the process of substantiating the results was progressing well. I felt completely betrayed by the operations manager. Even if I had given him a confidential insight into the results (which I had not) he should have kept it to himself.

The moral of the story is that you have no control over anything that you tell people. The more emotionally connected people are to the topic the 'worse'/more unpredictable the reaction is that you can expect. Speak (report) therefore with caution.

- *Formal oral*

On occasion, you will be asked to formally address a gathering to update them. In these cases, you may make use of a formal PowerPoint presentation. You may also leave a written report with the attendees after your update. The facts and figures will also tend to be high-level and in summary, but in more specific detail than an informal oral meeting. There will be a fair amount of thought and planning into what you would like to say. Also, decide in advance how much detail you will give in response to questions.

- *Oral testimony*

You may be called to testify in a labour or a criminal matter. In such a case, you can prepare by refreshing your memory of how the investigation transpired. You may also read your affidavit to remind yourself of what was declared. You may have an opportunity to be briefed by the prosecutor or person carrying the organisation's case in terms of the line of questioning that they intend to follow. This may be dangerous and potentially unfair witness coaching though. There is therefore limited preparation that you can conduct in advance.

- *Detailed affidavit*

You are strongly advised to draft affidavits for most matters. Affidavits are wonderful instruments. They secure the evidence (people's memories) – our first rule. They help you to structure what you want to say and to 'deliver' the information in the sequence that you require to illustrate your point/support your conclusions. Have your witnesses (in internal labour matters) prepare affidavits in advance. Then request them to read those sections of the affidavit that you want into evidence. In this manner, everything that you want goes into evidence in the sequence that you want, without the witness getting nervous. This method has received a lot of praise from labour commissioners who chair tribunals.

- *Informal written*

On occasion, you may send an e-mail update to a senior manager to keep them posted on the status of a particular matter. This is important in the building of a trust relationship with management. This type of correspondence is generally short but needs to be well thought out to ensure that the true picture is communicated, without too much detail. Please remember that you have no control over the e-mail trail thereafter and you should only put the level of detail in the e-mail which you would be comfortable being communicated to a wider audience. Alternatively, management may draft or request you to draft an e-mail communication on their behalf to update the organisation. Even if you draft the e-mail, it is better if these types of communications come from management as:

  - Management is the custodians of the control and have the responsibility for fraud investigation.
  - The organisation needs to see that fraud is taken seriously by the highest levels of management.

- *High-level report*

With reporting, you always need to consider who your audience is and what kind of things they want to know. High-level reports are normally directed at senior people in the organisation. Senior people are busy people. They do not have the time or the need to wade through detail. They just want to be informed; they do not want you to prove your entire case to them. They pay people to do this for them. They want you, as the expert, to cut to the chase and tell them what is going on and what has been done to resolve the matter. A high-level report gives account therefore of the most important aspects of the matter without going into unnecessary detail, including:

  - The actual or estimated financial value of the loss
  - If any recoveries have been made
  - Who was involved
  - What action has been taken against them
  - The salient reasons why the situation occurred
  - What has been done and what still needs to be done
  - Sometimes the cost of the investigation. This can cause an emotional response though, as management does not like 'throwing good money after bad'.

Reports are discussed in more detail below.

- *Detailed written report*

Detailed reports are overplayed and/or not always used for the correct reasons. Detailed affidavits are the best mechanism to use to convey detail. The detailed affidavit is the document that provides the evidence to arrive at conclusions. A detailed report is aimed at the people who are going to act on the issues being reported. They therefore only require the detail that they need to act. You do not therefore always need to provide all detailed evidence and to prove all your opinions. A detailed report can include multiple people's inputs and even hearsay.

The purpose of an affidavit is to give a detailed account of what the deponent of the affidavit has seen and/or done. The reader of the affidavit must, after reading it, arrive at the same conclusion as the author. The problem with detailed affidavits is firstly that they are detailed and secondly that the facts will most likely be spread over a number of documents/affidavits. The investigator's affidavit may very well tie all aspects together, but not always.

A detailed report fits into an in-between stage, between a detailed affidavit and a high-level report. The detailed report pulls all the individual aspects of the investigation together and spends sufficient time on the issues to ensure that the reader can act in the most informed way.

The problem with a detailed report is again that it is not made under oath and is most times not submitted as evidence. Many detailed reports written by external audit/big four type consulting companies have carefully worded disclaimers and usage limitation clauses. The subsequent use of such reports is therefore severely limited. Why issue a report with a disclaimer? If you issue a report, you must be prepared to stand by it. If the company pays for a report, they want to be able to use it. Why pay for something that you cannot use? Ensure that you clarify the subsequent use of reports by external firms before you contract with them to conduct the investigation.

The other difference and use of a detailed report is to list actions required afterwards and other issues also identified in the investigation. The detailed affidavit is very much focused on the issue that the deponent is testifying to. It is not the purpose of an affidavit to make recommendations. A detailed report can include other issues required to be brought to management's attention.

Both a detailed report and an affidavit have their place. There is however frequently an element of duplication (with affidavits) when drafting a detailed report. Keep your audience of both documents in mind when drafting the documents.

Reports are discussed in more detail below.

- *Fraud statistics and trends*

Fraud statistics may be reported to audit committees, boards of directors, senior organisation leadership and the general organisation. Fraud statistics and trends may be:

  - Generally informative to a wider, less responsible audience
  - Specifically, informative to those who hold a direct responsibility for organisation performance, internal controls and fraud
  - Given in support of a request for resources or to motivate an organisational change or need to partner with an external service provider
  - Used as part of educational material.

- *Fraud newsletter*

A fraud newsletter serves multiple purposes, including:

  - To inform the organisation as a whole of the outcome of a matter/s
  - To educate staff members
  - To act as a deterrent for would-be perpetrators of misconduct.

8.1.4. Reporting strategy

It is wise to define a general reporting strategy for the fraud investigation function. This strategy should cover:

- The broad typical reports that should be issued (discussed above)
- To whom they should be issued
- When they should be issued
- The purpose of the various reports
- Exception handling.

This strategy should be approved by the authority to which the fraud investigation function reports and communicated to all relevant stakeholders. The following is an example of a fraud reporting structure:

- *Audit committee*

  At each audit committee meeting, including:
    - Fraud statistics
    - Salient overview of investigations (one to two sentences per investigation)
    - Specific detailed reports in support of key investigations only for their reference.

- *Organisation-wide*

  Could be quarterly, including:
    - Fraud newsletter
    - Specific formal communication/announcement.

- *Specific business unit/company/geographic area/functional unit*

  Could be monthly or quarterly, including:
    - Summary statistics
    - All detailed reports of the investigations specific to their responsibility.

- *Investigation-specific*

  Within X days of completion of the report including detailed reports to the senior responsible leaders.

8.1.5. Concepts

The following are some general concepts to be borne in mind when drafting reports:

- The purpose of a report is defined by the audience of the report.
- The report should tell a **story**. It should take the reader on a journey, at the end of which the reader should arrive at the same conclusion as the author.
- The report should **stand alone**. The report (including annexures) should not require any supplementary explanation. Anyone (such as the audit committee) reading the report with no background to the investigation/review/audit or the field should be able to understand the report and get the message the author is trying to carry. If it requires further explanation, then it is inadequate.
- The purpose of a traditional report is to report. It is not to provide all evidence available in a matter or to prove opinions, assertions and conclusions. This is the purpose of affidavits.

- The report should be **simple** and easy to understand. Use plain English. Do not try to be too 'fancy' in your wording. The 'message' of the report is typically lost and grammatical errors are frequently made as soon as the author tries to be too 'fancy'.
- Avoid **jargon, industry-specific language and acronyms**. Jargon typically has a meaning to you as an investigator or as an auditor, but rarely to anyone else. The audit committee (however experienced they may be) will most likely not attach the same academic meaning to the jargon as you attach to it. It can be very frustrating to a reader if they have to keep stopping to understand the sentence.
- The acid test is that **anyone outside** of the organisation should be able to pick up the report and read it and understand it without explanation.
- Sentences should be **short**.
- Only have **one concept**/issue/message per sentence. This will avoid important issues dropping between the cracks or receiving less attention than less important aspects in the same sentence.
- Your report should have a **formal** tone. 'Formal' can still be simple and uncomplicated.
- Avoid using colloquialisms or **vernacular**.
- Your report must always be **professional** in all aspects.
- The report must be **factual**.
- State **limitations** in advance. If an area remains untested, then clearly state that it has not been tested. Also, mention which dependencies may be affected by this.
- The report should be free of **hearsay**. This is less important for a report but very important for an affidavit.
- The report should be free of **emotion**.
- The report should not be **slanderous**.
- The report should be **grammatically** sound.
- Only include those aspects in a report (even with supposedly limited circulation) that you are prepared to defend in the public/a wider domain.

8.1.6. Never

Never try to:

- Cover up wrongdoing
- Protect people/parties
- Purposefully exclude information from the report; if it must be excluded, say that it is being excluded and give a reason why
- Provide excuses for why something happened. It is management's purpose to explain why something happened.

You, as the author of the report, are there to report the complete (relevant to the purpose and audience), unemotional facts. It is up to the reader to interpret the facts and how to use the facts.

8.1.7. Practical advice

The following are some practical steps that may assist you when drafting a report:

- Do not commence the report by jumping straight in and starting to write immediately. Stop, plan, then write. Even the most accomplished report writer should slow themselves down and plan. The report, themes, concepts, messages and findings will take shape by themselves once you have designed the direction.
- Commence by putting all concepts down on paper/a whiteboard. You do not want too much detail, just individual points. Mind-maps are very useful for this purpose. Look for common themes, areas of duplication and omissions. Coming out of this you should have a list of or the structure of the points of discussion.
- Think about your original investigation's purpose, hypothesis and/or audit objective. Talk to your hypothesis or objectives: Were they achieved or not? How does the finding impact on the investigation/audit objective? What is the risk to the organisation?
- Write down, as part of your planning, the one or two things that you want to tell the reader. Once the report has been written, refer back to your list of things you planned to say and determine if these were carried across adequately in the report.
- When you are determining what you want to say, think about which aspects are the most important to the audience. What are the things that they want to hear about (the things that keep them awake at night). For example, '... that all revenue was received completely and accurately'. Steer away from academic audit categorisations and speak to the real things that the reader wants to hear.
- Picture the report recipient (for example: the audit committee) standing in front of you. What are the things you want to tell them and what are the things they want to hear? Write the report as if you are having a conversation with them and ensure that you tell them the things that they want to know.
- When you think about the message you would like to tell the reader, ensure that you apply this to the overall general message of the report/summary/conclusion, as well as to the message per detailed finding.
- Try to anticipate what management's comments (if any) will be and how management can 'get around' a valid finding. Amend your wording and provide figures and actual examples to block excuses and to prevent emotional defensiveness.
- Once you have completed the report, get an independent person to read it and to tell you if they understood it and/or what they think the report was about.
- Your report needs to contain certain standard sections (eg background, conclusion, significant findings, etc). These sections may differ from organisation to organisation. Determine what these are and run through to ensure that you tick all the boxes.
- Check your report for basic grammatical accuracy and general rules:
    - Write in the active voice and not in the passive voice.
    - Check your use of 'is' and 'are'. It is the 'subject' of the sentence (singular or plural) that determines the use of 'is' or 'are'.
    - Check your use of 'a' and 'an'. 'An' is used in front of a vowel 'sounding' word.

- The following should be considered when using abbreviations:
    - The purpose of abbreviations is to reduce long, unnecessary clutter in sentences. The idea is to establish a concept/meaning associated with an abbreviation to avoid long, complex sentences.
    - Write the abbreviation in brackets after the full written term the first time that the term is used. Thereafter you only need to use the abbreviation. For example: Association of Certified Fraud Examiners (ACFE); thereafter 'the ACFE'....
    - Be consistent and do not switch between the full term and the abbreviation throughout the text.
    - Certain words (for example: dates, numbers) should never be abbreviated. This is considered sloppy/lazy/unprofessional report writing. Do not use 'Feb 20X1'. Rather write 'February 20X1'.

- The following should be borne in mind when using numbers:
  - Write numbers (integers) one to ten out as words.
  - Numbers 11 and above are written as numbers. Dates, time, percentages, street addresses, decimals and numbers as part of the document (eg chapter, section, etc) are exceptions and are always written as numbers.
  - Choose one form to write in for those sentences that have both numbers 'less than' and 'greater than ten' in the same sentence.
  - Do not put two numbers next to each other, for example: 50 50s. Use 50 fifties.
  - Avoid commencing a sentence with a number. Dates are an exception.
  - Money is always written as a number.
  - Use a comma to separate groups of three numbers (eg 1,000,000.00).
  - Hyphenate numbers greater than 20 if using at the beginning of a sentence (eg 'Twenty-nine').
- Simplify specific words. For example: 'not available' should be written as 'unavailable'.
- Do not use 'double negatives'. For example: 'I am not feeling bad' should be 'I am feeling good'. 'We didn't see nothing' should be 'We saw nothing'.
- Use 'white space' between paragraphs and logical breaks in the report. The spacing in the report should allow for natural breaks between paragraphs containing separate concepts being discussed, to make it easier on the reader's eye. Avoid writing one long continuous 'sea' of words.
- Do not start sentences with 'however', 'although' and 'therefore'.
- Reframe from unnecessary padding and/or redundancy. For example: 'It was determined during our tests that ....' It goes without saying that your findings were determined during your tests. Rather use: 'We determined that ....'

8.1.8. Other concepts

Other concepts to be borne in mind when drafting reports include the following:

- As a general rule, there should be a direct relationship between findings, risks and recommendations. For every finding, there should be a risk/effect and a recommendation.

One risk may relate to more than one finding. One recommendation may also satisfy more than one finding. Do not raise recommendations for which you have not raised a finding.

- Do not presume that the report is correct in terms of this. Formally sit and run through the report to check that there are a risk and a recommendation for each finding.
- You should only discuss significant findings and matters in the conclusion that were raised in the detailed appendix. Do not raise matters in the summary that were not raised in the detailed section (new findings).
- Your conclusion should speak to/describe any ratings given. Ratings vary from company to company and could include:
    - High, medium and low
    - Catastrophic, significant, important and housekeeping
    - Etc.

8.2. REPORT FORMAT EXAMPLES

8.2.1. Introduction

There are many different report types that can be used, as defined by the purpose of the report, the intended audience, format, style and the level of detail. The different paragraphs that may be considered for inclusion in a report, as defined by the report's purpose, are discussed below.

8.2.2. Planning

As discussed throughout, the purpose of a report is to report. Many people forget this very basic fact. It seems as if they want to write long stories and provide all possible information available in their report, regardless of the purpose and/or audience. This may not be relevant or required for the given audience.

The start of any report is the planning of the report. Resist the temptation to dive in and start typing. Plan the whole report before you write. Thereafter, the writing becomes like an easy 'paint-by-numbers' exercise, filling in the details on a strong frame. Of course, good writing techniques can 'colour' the words, but knowing which 'colour' to put where is most important.

Commence your planning by defining who you are reporting to and what they want to know. Then list the issues/findings. You may also consider listing some of the traditional paragraphs that you typically include in the report for that purpose on a planning 'mind-map'.

As stated before, make use of a mind-map to do your planning, as it enables you to see all the facts that you have and what you have to report, at one glance. It is then easier to visualise the report in front of you. Lists of points do not facilitate this easily. It is too easy to get lost in a 'sea' of words. You may also make use of 'post-it notes' to list all issues and aspects to be taken into account. These can then be shifted around on a whiteboard until you obtain an optimal grouping.

The moral of the story is not to favour one form of planning above another. The moral is to promote planning of reports. You need to find the method that suits your aptitude. Some people relate to mind-maps and find them very effective.

It is strongly recommended that you discuss your report planning with your colleagues who assisted you on the matter or who are skilled in report writing. They will have different insights and they may also recall issues to be reported that you may have left out.

In a similar manner, have a colleague who had nothing to do with the investigation read your report after drafting. As mentioned before, this is the acid test to see if someone reading the report 'cold' will understand and follow what you are saying.

8.2.3. Mind-map example

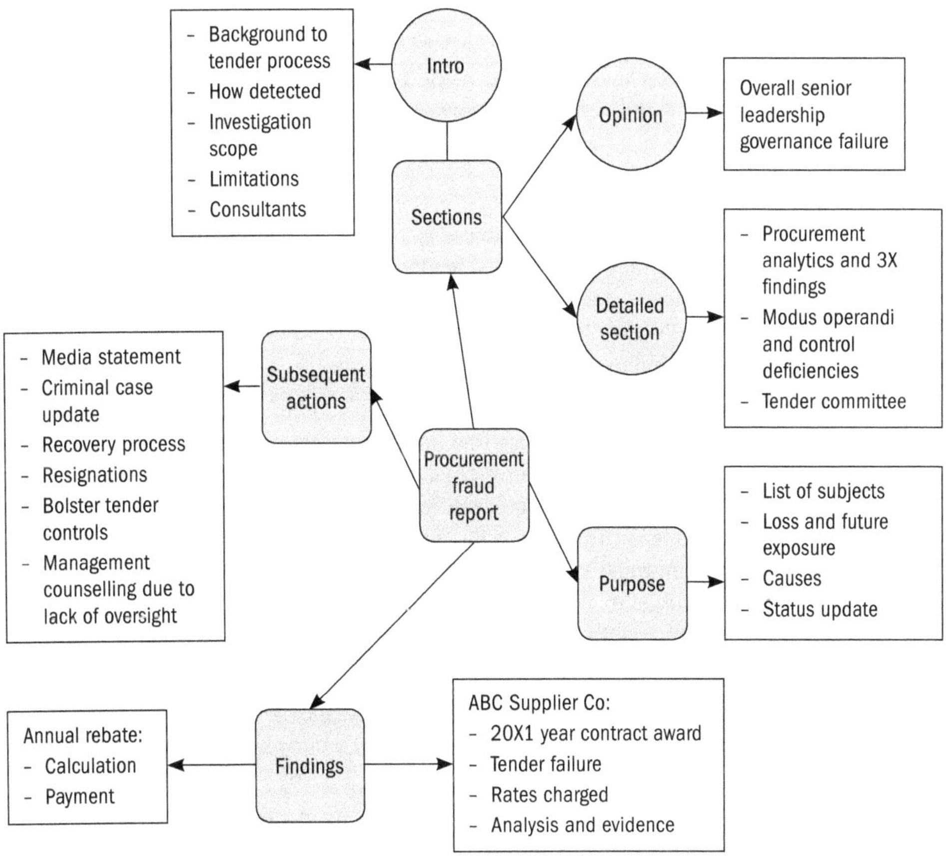

8.2.4. Paragraphs

We will only be discussing a detailed report format in this section. This is as the detailed report will represent most of what you could use in a report. Please tailor the discussion to suit your individual reporting requirements, by excluding paragraphs not relevant to the purpose of your specific report.

The following are examples of standard sections that you may consider including in your report:

- *Structure*

Consider making use of the following sections for a full detailed report:

  - Directors' summary
  - Executive summary
  - Detailed findings
  - Annexures.

As far as possible, avoid duplication between the various sections of the report. The directors' summary is really the report. The other sections are all appendices that support it and build on what has already been said.

Do not have a section/a paragraph in a report just for the sake of having it. The section must serve a purpose and you should not have it just to 'tick a box'. The reader will pick this up very quickly and become irritated and disinterested with your report if you have unnecessary sections.

A. Directors' summary

The first section that you may want to use is the directors' summary. The logic for this is that the most important section to the reader should be first. At the end of the day, the reader wants to know what the outcome of the investigation is. They do not want to wait and especially senior leaders do not want to wait. Once they know, they can decide if they want to read further.

This is the highest level of the report and it is intended to be read by the directors of listed companies. These are people who have neither the time nor the interest to read the detail. It is important then for you to get straight to the essence of what you want to tell them. More importantly, you need to tell them what they want to know. Picture the reader of the report (director, audit committee, etc) standing in front of you. What are the things they would ask you? If you were talking directly to them without a report, what would the things be that you would tell them? Write these down in your report.

I recall in one organisation in which I worked where the chairman of the board used to ask me for one paragraph per report. It takes skill to reduce a full 60-page report (of four geographic locations with two facilities per location and an element of head office work as well) down to a single paragraph of around six lines and to still get the message across.

It is only necessary to make use of two paragraphs in the directors' summary, as directors only enquire about what the outcome (conclusion) was and what the purpose of the investigation was. If you tell them what the outcome was, they are less interested in the purpose. The one supposes the other.

- *Conclusion*

As discussed previously start, as a general rule, with what the reader wants to know. The conclusion is the paragraph where you do this. The reader can then decide after reading the conclusion if they want to read further to obtain more detail. It should also be easy for the reader to navigate from the conclusion straight to those sections that they want to read in greater detail if they only want to read specific details. The conclusion is the outcome. It is an 'end result' and it is not 'everything leading up to an end result'. Only inform the readers/ directors therefore of what the outcome was. Directors do not have the time to sit and think and conclude. This is what they pay you to do. They want you to tell them what you found and what it means. They want to know if they can sleep at night or if they should pace up and down.

Directors also do not want to know about problems; they want to know about solutions. A forensic report tends to be a negative report, as it is really only highlighting problems. As far as possible, try to report positively. Try to identify solutions or encourage management to initiate remedial action prior to issuance of your report. This way you can say: 'I found this ... and management is already doing that ...'. The directors will then say: 'Okay, we don't like what happened, but we are pleased that you (management) have resolved it or are well on your way to resolving it.'

Most importantly, directors do not like surprises. Directors pay people like you to warn them of things in advance and to sort out problems for them. It is vital that they see that they can trust you to do this. Trust is built over time. Trust matures over a two- to three-year period, so be realistic about how long you need to work at this. Trust can be broken in one event too, so do not rest on your laurels. You need to consistently show them over time that you can be trusted to keep them informed of the most important issues and that you are sorting out issues before they ask you to do it.

Do not inundate them with trivia. Just give them the essence. Pretend that you are making a quick call to a friend to inform them of the matter that you are reporting. What would you say in that conversation? Only write this down. And write it in the same simple way that you would tell your friend. Report authors try to be too fancy. Talking to a friend is easy and we can all relate to it. It is also non-threatening. Think of it in this way and then it will be easy.

In terms of the trust relationship, you may also want to consider verbally informing directors of important matters before waiting to issue a formal report. This is all part of reporting. You may even refer to the verbal report/updates in your written report.

Reports take a long time and are issued long after the fact. Directors can be embarrassed, in-between the event being investigated and the formal report being issued, if they are asked about an important matter that they have no knowledge of. You do not want to be the one who should have informed them. Rather be the one they know they can trust to always keep them abreast of the most important aspects.

- *Background, objectives and/or purpose*

The objective and purpose of an investigation is really a description of the problem. For example: 'An analysis of the working capital conducted by the financial manager in January X1 highlighted Y million of funds that could not be accounted for. The purpose of this report is to discuss the findings of an investigation into the unaccounted-for funds.'

That sort of a 'purpose' is quite high-level and to the point. This is ideal for readers who do not want or need to know more detail.

The purpose covers both the 'what' and the 'why'; what was investigated and why was it investigated.

Alternatively, you may wish to highlight specific aspects that were considered in the investigation. For example: 'An analysis of the working capital conducted by the financial manager in January X1 highlighted Y million of funds that could not be accounted for. The purpose of this report is to communicate the findings of an investigation that was subsequently embarked upon to determine:

- The full extent of the financial loss
- All those who were involved in the fraud
- The methods employed to misappropriate the funds
- Manners to bolster the internal controls to prevent recurrence
- Remedial action that can be undertaken.'

This sort of a purpose is used when you need to highlight specific aspects of what was looked at. It may be required when you are aware that the reader will want to know about specific aspects of the matter or investigation.

More detail may also be useful in creating credibility to demonstrate that the investigation was complete. The communication of the purpose may also be educational in nature to the reader. Over time you may consider giving a more salient purpose as the reader becomes more au fait with investigations.

The purpose also serves as a record of what was done and why. The recollection of events, reasons and rationale diminish over time. A well-crafted purpose may be successful in preserving some of this.

Some of the specific reasons for conducting the investigation may include matters of law. For example: 'The purpose of this investigation was to comply with regulation X of Act Y 20X3. Section X of the Y Act requires that .... Failure to report such matters may result in a sentence of not less than five years.'

B. Executive summary

The next section that you may wish to make use of for a detailed report is the executive summary section. In this section, we give a little more detail about what was done and about the findings.

Try not to duplicate what you have already said in the directors' summary section. The directors' summary and the executive summary are not 'either/or'. They build on one another. Someone should be able to read both sections and not feel that their time is being wasted as they are reading what they already know.

The executive summary serves to provide a summary to a particular audience of people who do not want to read the entire detailed report, but who require more than the conclusion.

The executive summary differs from the director's summary, in so far as the conclusions (contained in the director's summary) 'tell' the reader what they should think/what your opinion is. The executive summary does not really conclude overall. It merely summarises the key aspects/findings. The executive summary may list a potential risk or actual exposure. The executive summary will give the reader sufficient detail of what was performed and concluded. The reader can then decide if they wish to read specific detailed sections to obtain a greater understanding. If you find that you are saying the same things in the conclusion and the executive summary, then do away with one of them.

The executive summary can be sequenced in accordance with the priority of findings or in the sequence of the detailed report. The executive summary should, regardless of the chosen sequence, provide the reader with an easy indication of the relevant importance of findings. This can be indicated by a scale such as:

- High, medium or low
- Catastrophic, significant, important or housekeeping
- Smiley face, neutral face or sad face
- Red, orange, yellow, green or blue
- Etc.

The executive summary should also provide the reader with a user-friendly and quick reference to where the findings are discussed in detail.

Overall then, the:

- Directors' summary is in the sequence of the objectives of the investigation – the things that the directors want to know.
- Executive summary is in the sequence of the findings. The most important findings are summarised first and the less significant findings last or not at all or statistically only.

- *Timing*

The timing described in a report discusses the high-level investigation timeline. Only give as much detail as is relevant to the reader to complete the picture for the reader. To help you understand what may be relevant to the reader, consider, as per our previous conversations on the same, that there may be many different readers of forensic reports.

Managers frequently ask why the investigation took so long. They ask this normally because they do not have an understanding of what is involved in investigations. An explanation as to the timing of the investigation can, therefore, be relevant or required to contextualise the timeline of events. Do not go overboard to impress them with the nitty-gritty of what you have done. The purpose of listing the timeline of events is not to get you an increase for a job well done. Consider if discussing the timing of the investigation is really necessary.

- *Scope and coverage*

The 'scope' and the 'purpose' described in a report support each other. You have already raised the purpose of the report, so determine if it is necessary to raise the scope as well. You may want to provide a bit of background as to what the problem was (purpose) and then link this to the discussion of what the scope of the investigation was.

The scope is important as it contextualises what is being done and what is not. Each reader of the report will have their own expectation of what should have been done/included in the scope of the investigation. You cannot satisfy all people's expectations, but you can go a long way toward managing their expectations.

Peoples' expectations are normally linked to their organisational responsibilities and degree of interaction with the matter at hand. People who are not privy to the details of an investigation react from an emotional point of view and not from a position of fact. While you may not be able to divulge all the facts in your report, try to at least describe the broad areas of scope to ensure that the reader understands that their areas of concern were covered or why they were not. You may even mention why a particular area, while investigated, has been excluded from the report, by saying, for example, that it is 'sub judice' (under judgment) or that management denied you access to certain records or that the evidence was destroyed, etc. It may also be necessary for you to describe why certain elements were included in the investigation. This should be at a salient level only.

The scope described in the report can also pertain to the period of transactions covered and why. This is not the same as the investigative timeline, as described previously. This is particularly to be clear about what was included and why. For example: 'The ABC forensic service company was contracted to investigate all accounts payable transactions in the X2 financial year, as the subject of the review only commenced employment in year X2.'

The scope not only describes what was included but also what was excluded from the investigation. Again, this is to manage expectations and to ensure that the reader understands the true context of the findings and conclusions. It is about being open and transparent. You do not want the reader to be under a misguided impression that an element of work was included in the scope if this cannot be supported by the actual work that was performed. Audit committee members and senior management may just naturally assume that the investigation was all-encompassing when it was only a partial investigation or highly focused or restricted due to limitations.

The limitation of scope could be contained in its own paragraph with its own heading or form part of the general scope paragraph.

- *Methodology*

The methodology is a description of what was done in the investigation. Examples of methodology include:

- Interviews
- Data analytics
- Imaging of machines
- Document analysis
- Search and seizure.

This can be a prime example of an unnecessary paragraph. Only describe therefore the methodology followed if:

- It is radically different from any other matter investigated by you; do not bore the reader with the same things over and over again.
- It adds to the credibility of what was done.
- The reader of the report will want to know.
- The directors could be questioned about the methods used. You do not want them to appear as if they do not know what is going on.
- You are still in the early stages of 'educating' people on what it is that you do and why.

- It has a bearing on what was done and what was not done (managing expectations - also see purpose, objectives, scope and limitations).

For example: 'The investigation methodology was limited to a desktop analysis of documents available. No system walkthroughs or subject interviews were conducted. The purpose was to determine if there was a basis for further, more detailed investigation.'

- *Investigative team*

It may also be a good idea to list the team members involved in the investigation. Consider listing the team members':

- Names
- Responsibilities (for example IT forensics, legal advice, handwriting specialist, forensic accountant, etc)
- Capacity (for example quality assurance, senior investigator, etc)
- Company employed by (multiple companies may have been engaged during the assignment).

These details may also be listed in the letter of appointment. Listing the investigative team may:

- Create credibility for the integrity of the investigation conducted if the team is perceived to be sufficiently senior, independent and/or experienced
- Put into context the resources (and any constraints) available in the investigation
- Give credit where credit is due and foster relationships where a diverse team was used
- Give exposure of the individual team members to the senior leadership of the organisation
- Be the only means by which to acknowledge people's or departments' or functions' efforts and inputs into the investigation. This is really about giving credit where credit is due.

Be selective about the use of this paragraph. You may also consider adding it as an annexure to the report.

Unless the report is that of an expert witness, do not list the investigative team's credentials at this stage of the report. In sticking with the theme of providing what the reader wants to know as a priority, listing credentials at this stage clutters the report with unnecessary details. If required to be listed, refer the reader to an annexure where they can read the team's credentials if they require. Credentials are discussed later in more detail.

Whistle-blowers should never be mentioned in this section. In fact, a whistle-blower's name should, as a general rule, never be mentioned in a report. Exceptions to this (where mentioning the whistle-blower's name elsewhere in the report may be justified) may include where the whistle-blower has given you express permission to do so or where the whistle-blower has made their revelation of the truth in the public domain.

- *Statement of confidentiality*

It is also fairly standard to include a statement to the effect that this report:

- Is confidential
- Is only intended for the sight and use of the listed recipients
- Should be returned to the company in the event that it is not in the possession of one of the listed recipients.

The legal enforcement of such a statement is unclear if a person other than one of the listed recipients was in possession of the report. It is, however, better to include a statement on confidentiality so as to have a basis through which to hold people who circulate or make use of confidential reports accountable.

- *Disclaimers*

It is also fairly standard practice to list a disclaimer in the report to prevent there being any repercussions to the author of the report or the author's company. This sort of statement is fairly common practice in big accounting firms. The author of the report thereby expressly distances themselves from any improper use of the report.

Lawyers will have long debates about the enforceability of such a disclaimer. It is safer to include it than to exclude it and then require it later.

As a general rule, do not write anything in a report that you cannot defend in a public arena if it was to come into the public domain.

As mentioned previously, there is a fundamental question around the big accounting firm disclaimers that preclude/limit their reports being used in subsequent actions. Ensure that you determine the usability of the report prior to contracting with the firm. There is no purpose in paying for a report that cannot be used for the purposes that you intend.

C. *Detailed findings*

This is the section in which the detailed findings of your investigation are listed. There are two possible ways in which to sequence the findings listed, namely:

- Sorted in accordance with the risk/relative importance of the finding to the organisation. This approach is suitable for a summary report in which you are just communicating the outcomes. There should be no or little requirement to demonstrate what was done over the entire investigation. You may elect to describe how you arrived at the conclusion of the individual findings though.
- Following the flow of the investigation and building the findings as the investigation progressed. As a general rule, you want to take the reader on a journey, at the end of which they must arrive at the same conclusion that you arrived at. This approach is suitable for detailed reports of which it is necessary for you to convince the reader of your conclusions, based on your investigation.

Define who the audience of the report is and then define the best structure to communicate your message. You may also elect to structure your report with the formal paragraphs presented below or alternatively, you may only elect to ensure that the body of the report contains these detailed elements.

The first method of formally defining paragraphs with headings depicting the purpose of the paragraph (for example: effect of fraud) is preferred. The first method is typical of an audit report but is preferred because:

- It focuses the reader on what you are talking about.
- It forces you as the author to think about each of these aspects and to ensure that you include something on each of them. In the absence of formal headed paragraphs, it is too easy to leave an important element of the report out.

- *Investigation steps*

The purpose of your report/the report audience will define which of the two methods (the investigative course or a list of findings) you use. For example, if the purpose of the report is to present detailed evidence and to lead the reader to the same conclusion that you reached, it is recommended to follow the detailed description of investigation steps and the findings per step.

The flow of the 'investigation structure' to the report would require subheadings to break the report up into logical chunks for the reader. The discussion under point 8.3 below about the preferred use of affidavits to present detailed evidence refers. You may also elect to give a less detailed description of the investigation steps followed and then to have another (more detailed) paragraph (described below) with detailed findings.

- *Summary of findings*

The 'investigation step reporting structure' results in many findings being scattered all over the body of the report. While what you want to say and what you have said may be perfectly clear in your head, readers may find it difficult to keep track of everything that has been said. It is therefore strongly recommended that you provide the reader with short summaries per section/investigation step to ensure that they 'keep up with you'.

- *Conclusion per investigation step*

It is also recommended that you conclude per investigative step to ensure that you are leading the reader to the same overall conclusion that you reached. Make use of a formal heading to tell the reader that this is a conclusion of, for example 'the detailed lifestyle audit'. You may also consider combining the summary of findings and conclusion per investigation step into one paragraph.

- *Specific findings*

If on the other hand, the purpose of the report is to just present findings, then you may tend to group the findings per issue. For example: let us assume that there were two areas in which the specific fraud was perpetrated. Commence with a short introductory statement to inform the reader that there were two broad areas of misconduct under this matter. Let us presume that these were a manipulation of inventory records and the collusion with customers to fraudulently reduce the amounts payable to the organisation. You may use two main headings ('inventory manipulation' and 'revenue reduction' in our example) in the detailed finding discussion section. Within each of these sections, you could then give further headings and/or raise specific detailed findings based on the findings of the investigation.

Contemplate the need for finding summaries and conclusions (as described above) per fraud finding section to make the report easy for the reader to follow.

- *Standard*

In some cases, you may elect to list the 'required standard', law or policy and procedure. This is done to enable the reader to compare the actual behaviour to the required behaviour. Do not overplay this though. Only use it if required and if it adds to the report. Do not include it just for the sake of including it, as it will be quickly perceived as unnecessary or bureaucratic by the reader.

This approach may work well in a disciplinary hearing where the policy said, for example: 'No outside private business interests may be held.' You should also attach the actual policy as an annexure in support of the rule. This will assist in comparing the actual behaviour to the policy. Alternatively, it will help in a hearing to have the policy and procedure close at hand per section.

- *Cause*

Similar to the standard, it may be required to include the cause/reason why the incident was allowed to occur. Enquiring what the cause was is a frequent (and understandable) question by organisational leadership. Again, do not overplay this. Only include the cause if it is necessary and adds something that was unknown to the reader. A lack of training, control breakdowns, control circumvention, etc may be too generic and not really add value.

- *Risk/effect*

The risk and the effect of what was found are vital to the reader. While it may seem strange, the reader of a report (bearing in mind that they are frequently senior people detached from detail) may not always intuitively know what to 'think'/conclude about a statement/finding. This may be abundantly clear to you, as you will have the entire case laid out in your head. This will, mostly, be the first time that the reader is getting an overview of what has happened. It will therefore be up to you, as the author, to tell the reader what to think. Your statement of the risk and/or known effect will inform the reader to what extent to be concerned about what they are reading. It will be important to ensure that there is a risk/effect for each finding raised. This relationship may be one-to-one, many-to-one or one-to-many. Consciously check that you have a risk/effect for each finding raised.

You may struggle to convince an audience of what needs to be done to prevent what could go wrong. On the other hand, you will rarely struggle to convince organisation leadership of what they need to do if you can inform the reader what has already happened. Spending money to cover potential risks can be a hard sell. Convincing someone based on what has already gone wrong is a lot easier. Crafting a well-worded statement of risk/effect could be key to your reporting goals.

- *Conclusion*

You may elect to conclude per point or, as stated earlier, per investigation step. In this case, the conclusion is specific to the point being discussed and is more detailed and specific than the overall report conclusion mentioned in the directors' summary. It focuses the reader on what they should feel with regards to that specific point/issue being covered. This may be an important step to guide the reader in a lengthy report to the same overall conclusion that you reached. As with the risk/effect, ensure that you conclude on all elements raised as findings and all risks/effects raised.

- *Recommendation*

You may also elect to list recommendations in your report:

  - Of remedial action required
  - To bolster controls to prevent recurrence
  - Any other action steps.

Ensure that your recommendations cover all findings, risks and/or effects. Recommendations should be practical, cost-effective and measurable.

Take care however not to confuse reports. It is therefore advised to report separately on the control weaknesses that gave rise to the misconduct and/or of the control improvements required to prevent future recurrence. The purpose of the report refers, but you need to keep the fraud investigation/forensic elements in one report and the control deficiencies in another, as:

- The reports serve different purposes.
- The control action items will need to be followed up later to ensure that they are implemented. It is easier to follow up on them if they are all contained in one control report.
- The case may be currently subject to a criminal case or labour matter (called 'sub-judice'). Elements of the investigation and specific facts of the case may be confidential until the conclusion of these legal proceedings. A separate report will allow you to focus on the control concerns in the meantime.
- General confidentiality concerns may be applicable to protect the rights of the subject, witnesses and investigators. The users of the control deficiency side may not be required to know the investigative facts as well.
- Your investigation report may be shared with a criminal court or a labour tribunal. In that case, you will probably not want to highlight the poor state of controls to the subject of the investigation. Subjects could use this against you and plead that the organisation's controls were in such a poor state that they are in fact the victim and not the organisation.

- *Management comment*

While less applicable to forensic reports, it may be appropriate to obtain management's comments on the findings and/or on the monthly recommendations. This may be required to:

- Obtain management's formal input on the incidents to prevent comebacks
- Obtain management's formal commitment to implementing the recommendations
- Give confidence to the reader (audit committee, senior executive other than management) that the matter is being taken seriously by those entrusted with the running of the organisation.

Management's comments should:

- Cover all elements of the findings/recommendations
- Be realistic, tangible, achievable and measurable
- Be concise and to the point
- Resist making excuses and passing blame
- Assign responsibility for corrective action
- Clearly define timelines and/or achievement milestones.

As a rule, you should never edit management's comments. It is imperative to cut and paste management's comments verbatim into the report. The reasons for this include to:

- Prevent interpretation and/or translation errors. You should even leave grammatical errors as is.
- Ensure that management's true view is reflected completely and accurately in the report.

- Prevent management coming back after the final report has been issued and changing what they have committed to.
- Prevent being blamed by management for amending what they have committed to/ said or taking it out of context. If they say it, there can be no debate.

It is most beneficial to have a meeting with management after receiving their comments. Thank them for their comments and discuss each of them individually to determine if they satisfy the issue, are sufficiently concise, etc. Management is typically fearful of reprisal. Their fears are allayed if they see that you are trying to help them report in a positive manner. Request management to furnish you with their revised comments.

Over and above the formal written comments to the report, it is also wise to ensure that you formalise all conversations with management that you have related to the investigated matters. This is because you want to prevent management turning around afterwards to say that they did not say/commit to something. Develop the habit of sending them a mail after such conversations (or referring to the conversation in another mail) in which you thank them for the discussion and in which you say that you just want to confirm that the following points were discussed and the following was the agreed action.

Ensure that management answers each finding/recommendation. If, in the process of your investigation, management makes some comment on the aspects that you are going to report on, then include these in the draft report. Do not include emotional statements or comments made in passing. These types of management comments are only included in the draft report and management still has the opportunity to edit them if they disagree with the comments. The good thing about this approach is that you have an opportunity to record what they have said and there is a better chance that they will accept these as their final comments. The danger of this approach is that you may:

- Embarrass or expose someone, as they might not want others to know what their opinion is
- Be 'putting words' in management's mouth
- Lead them and prevent them from making their own more complete/applicable comment.

Ignoring management's prior comments, as a rule, the report must first be discussed with management before releasing. You may consider including the salient points discussed in the report debriefing meeting and then circulate the report to management for final agreement of the wording.

Alternatively, request management to provide you with their formal written comment within an agreed period. Clarify any comments made after the report debriefing meeting which are not in accordance with the discussions that were held or which do not satisfy the criteria (for example: measurable, responsibility assigned, etc).

Ensure that you always define the time with management by which they need to provide their comments. You will develop a standard period (for example one week) for management comments after working with them over time. Do not make the period too long, as people forget what they said and you will spend your time chasing up management comments. Ensure that you give yourself sufficient time as there may be further refinement of management comments required. The period in which you need to issue your final report to senior executives will dictate these reporting milestones.

There is also a 'shock factor' once a report has been drafted, despite previous discussions on the same points. It is as if the issues look different to management once committed to paper. Alternatively, the report may be a manner of formalising an issue and this may be the first time that management considers the real ramifications. Do not be surprised therefore if management reacts differently once they see the final report.

- *Agreed actions*

Again, while less applicable to forensic reports, some organisations like to only include agreed actions. Agreed actions replace the recommendations and management comments.

This is not a preferred approach, as:

- You cannot show the build-up to the final comments and actions
- It is not to say that management agrees with all recommendations
- The agreed actions tend to lose the valuable detail of the recommendations.

Agreed actions are good, however, as they provide points of agreement/solutions.

- *Investigator's closing comments*

As far as possible your first aim should be to achieve management's agreement to a report's output, where relevant. Notwithstanding this philosophy, and while not ideal, you may still reach a stage when you, as the investigator, and management reach a deadlock. This may be on an individual point or concerning the entire investigation.

Management's reluctance to action matters may speak to their:

- Potential guilt, negligence or involvement
- Avoidance of accountability due to them not preventing the matter/s in the first place
- Disagreement with the findings
- Disagreement with the practicality or requirement to implement the recommendations.

Try to examine what you are saying and determine if you need to rephrase anything. As per our rule, you as the investigator have a responsibility to the truth. You need to try (as much as is reasonable) to get your view across. In principle, the investigator should have the final say to the party that mandated them to investigate the matter. Include therefore any final comments that are required to further explain or contextualise management's comments. You may wish to expressly state that consensus could not be reached on a particular point.

D. Supporting documents

Your report is now essentially finished. The next section contains any supporting documents and additional information which was referred to in the body of the report, but which could not be accommodated in the body of the report.

- *Index of annexures*

It is most practical for the reader (if you have many annexures), to list these in a table at the front of the annexures. Information for consideration of inclusion in the annexure index includes:

- Annexure number
- Annexure name/description
- Page numbers (from/to) where the annexure can be located.

- *Supporting documents*

Supporting documents that were referred to in the body of the report should be attached here. As a rule, if you refer to a piece of evidence in your report, it should be attached in support. Not all documents referred to will be required as evidence. This will need to be determined on a case-by-case basis. Examples of supporting documents include:

  - Invoices, delivery notes, receipts, etc
  - Transaction listings/registers/etc
  - Supporting reports
  - Examples to demonstrate issues
  - Diagrams
  - Contracts
  - E-mail correspondence
  - Statements
  - Affidavits
  - Transcripts
  - Minutes
  - Notice of resignation/termination
  - Admission of guilt
  - Photographs.

- *Detailed calculations and analyses*

Calculations frequently need to be made in reports. These may be too long to include in the body of the report and they can be included as an annexure and referenced in the body of the report. Examples of detailed calculations include:

  - Calculations of losses
  - Recalculation and/or comparison of actual events to what should have happened
  - Calculations of rates
  - Detailed data analytics
  - Lifestyle audit analyses.

- *Other information*

Specific reference material may also be required in support of the body of the report. This sort of reference material is more general in nature (not seen as evidence), but still required to support assertions in the report. Examples of such reference material include:

  - Industry trends, rates, etc
  - Excerpts of regulations
  - Press releases.

- *Credentials*

As referred to previously (under point 8.2.4.B on the investigative team), you may be required to establish yourself as an expert witness/expert or to list the investigative team's credentials. If you work for a consulting firm, you would typically only list the investigative team's credentials in your proposal to the client. While this is good for obtaining the work, the credentials do not follow the report. If it is necessary for the reader of the report to evaluate if the investigation team was duly qualified and experienced to conduct the investigation, then it will be necessary to list the investigative team's credentials in the report. Not all readers will be interested in reading the credentials. Also, once read, the reader will typically not want to refer to them again. They may, however, want to refer back to the findings, actions and recommendations.

Refer the reader therefore at the beginning of the report to an annexure where the detailed credentials can be read if required. Be selective in the use of this section though, as report readers rarely find value in it. The specifying of credentials should not be a monument to the investigation team.

- *Glossary of terms*

It is sometimes helpful to include a glossary of terms used in the report. This will enable the reader to refer to these terms if they are unfamiliar with them. The glossary of terms is not a dictionary. It is a list of industry-specific terms that may not be known to a wider audience. A glossary of terms will be used when there are numerous terms to define. Footnotes can also be used in the body of the report if there are only a few terms that require explanation.

8.3. AFFIDAVITS

8.3.1. Introduction

As discussed previously, affidavits are tremendously useful. It is therefore imperative to ensure that they are drafted correctly.

8.3.2. Responsibility

Spend time planning who needs to draft affidavits and what you want to achieve with each affidavit. Drafting of affidavits is not a common skill set. It is recommended that you give a lot of guidance and assistance to people required to draft an affidavit.

Giving too much assistance presents the danger of your case being seen to be a 'complainant driven' case. A criminal matter needs to be seen to be driven from the police services' side. The reality is that it is rarely reasonable to expect a police officer to understand and therefore independently investigate complex commercial crimes as:

- They rarely have a commercial background and/or commercial education
- They do not understand/have exposure to the industries/fields in which we operate
- They do not have insights into how the organisation is structured and the systems and procedures that we follow.

They have other skills, but not the skills that we are looking for by default of their specific training and experience.

Deponents are also typically slow in providing affidavits. This partly because:

- Drafting of affidavits is not something that they are used to.
- It is far more difficult to get out of having said something which is committed to paper than it is to get out of a verbal statement.
- An affidavit is made under oath and untrue statements may carry serious repercussions.

- They are fearful of possible repercussions from the subjects or anyone who feels that they or the organisation have been put in a bad light as a result of the matter.
- They avoid being involved to avoid having to testify.
- They may be directly or indirectly implicated and therefore are reluctant to put this in writing.

You should draft most affidavits on behalf of individuals. It is just much easier and you are sure that it gets done and that it is done in a manner that ensures that the correct aspects are discussed. Spend a lot of time with the witnesses to understand the facts at hand. Provide them with a first draft and work through it with them to cover the obvious missing or incorrectly understood elements. Make all the changes requested by the deponent, as at the end of the day the deponent needs to be happy with the affidavit before signing.

The 'witness schedule' (discussed in Chapter 7 on subsequent actions) provides a matrix of charges and who will testify on each. The witness schedule may be a good source to identify:

- Who needs to provide an affidavit
- What each party is to testify about
- Which aspects they need to include in their affidavit.

As a general rule, all people making allegations and providing relevant information should provide an affidavit to confirm that this is what they witnessed/was said.

8.3.3. Hearsay

Hearsay concerns events that were relayed to another party, which you did not witness yourself but which you have been told.

When you testify in court, you are sworn in to tell the truth. In this way, you can be held accountable if you do not tell the truth. The court requires you to testify to what you did, saw or heard 'first hand'. The court cannot hold another person accountable if they have not sworn to tell the truth. The court should, therefore, subpoena that person to appear themselves to testify to the facts that they are aware of or as to what they told you if this is important to the case. As a general rule do not use hearsay in affidavits.

You may still use hearsay when you are trying to explain why you did something. Some examples include:

- 'Mr A informed me that Mr B could not have been involved, as Mr B was not present at work on the day of the loss of the asset. I therefore requested a printout of the building access records (see annexure ...2, attached hereto) from the security manager, Mr C. My analysis of the access records revealed that Mr B entered the building on ...date... at ...time... and departed again at ...time....'
- 'Mr X said to me that .... While I am unable to confirm Mrs X's assertion, I, therefore, decided to....'

8.3.4. Opinions and conclusions

As a general rule, the judge is the only person who should draw conclusions. Refrain therefore from providing your opinions and conclusions. These are after all just your views and not a statement of fact.

The judge uses legal principles to arrive at conclusions. Judges and courts are however not schooled in all aspects that are brought before them. Courts, therefore, make use of experts to guide them. These people are referred to as expert witnesses or subject matter experts. Courts normally firstly establish if the person is, in fact, an expert in their field. Examples of experts include:

- Digital forensic experts
- Computer specialists
- Handwriting experts
- Doctors
- Accountants
- Engineers
- Scientists
- Pathologists
- Aviation specialists
- Arson specialists
- Ballistic experts
- Fingerprint experts
- Etc.

Ensure that any experts you make use of establish their credentials in the early stages of their affidavit. You, as the investigator, may also need to establish yourself as an expert.

You should (as an investigator) include a standard summarised paragraph of your experience and qualifications.

All opinions and conclusions should be supported by evidence, logic and/or established principles to explain their basis to the court.

8.3.5. General guidance

The discussion below refers to some of the typical paragraphs that you may consider including in an affidavit, as appropriate, and the general affidavit template below (see annexure 8.1 attached hereto) refers in this regard. Draft your own general affidavit template that you can use as a base. You can then adapt the template to include or exclude elements, as you are exposed to different types of cases and to suit your local laws.

a. Header and footer

Make use of headers and footers in your affidavits. The purpose of headers and footers is to facilitate navigation of the affidavit. It tells the reader what document they are looking at (deponent's name) and where they are in the document (page number) and helps them to jump to other sections in the document with relative ease.

A full affidavit with annexures can be a considerable document. You just need to drop one of these documents (without clear page links) to appreciate the benefits of good header/ footer information.

The affidavit template attached refers as an example. Typical information to be contained in the header section of an affidavit could include:

- *Name of the deponent*

This should be the deponent's full names as per their identity document/passport.

- *Multiple affidavits*

Deponents may issue multiple affidavits in a matter, being the main affidavit and supplementary affidavits. It may be important to inform the reader which affidavit this is for the deponent in the matter at hand. This can be denoted by, for example: this the first (1st) or the second (2nd) affidavit by this deponent in this matter. It sometimes occurs that additional information comes to light after an initial affidavit has been drafted and it may be necessary for a deponent to issue a supplementary or additional affidavit. This will be particularly relevant to the investigator of the matter. The investigator may issue an initial affidavit to open a criminal matter. They may then issue a second affidavit with the bulk of the information identified in their investigation. A subsequent/third affidavit may be required in the event that additional material facts come to light after the second detailed affidavit was issued.

- *Unique deponent identifying number*

It will be necessary to uniquely identify the deponent so that the reader will be able to associate one person with the affidavit. A unique identifying number is an official number and not just any number like an employee number, which is unknown to a wider audience like the police. Examples of unique identifying numbers include:

  - Identity numbers
  - Passport numbers
  - Social security numbers.

- *Matter in which the affidavit is made*

This is a short description of what the purpose of this affidavit is. For example: 'Affidavit by A.N. Other in the Joe Blogs matter.'

- *Section*

There are only two sections that should be differentiated in the header section of an affidavit, being the body of the affidavit and the annexures.

- *Page number*

You need to make the affidavit as easy to read and as easy to navigate as possible for the reader. Page numbers are vital for ease of navigation. Make use of the 'page X of Y pages' format. Word processing packages can automatically number pages.

- *Date*

This is the date that the deponent completes and normally signs the affidavit as well. The reason for this is because the deponent may have many draft versions of the affidavit. It is important to ensure that the final version is dated correctly. The date is contained in the body of the affidavit where the deponent signs, but this is not visible to the reader on other pages.

As an acid test, ask yourself how easy it would be for someone with no knowledge of the affidavit to put the affidavit and all annexures back together into its logical sequence without any assistance if two or three affidavits or unrelated documents are dropped on the floor.

b. Preamble

The preamble of the affidavit gives a background of who the deponent is, including:

- The deponent's names
- How the deponent can be identified (for example identity or passport number)
- The deponent's employer and job title
- Duration of the deponent's employment with the organisation
- How and where the deponent can be contacted.

The preamble also says that the deponent is authorised to provide the affidavit in the event that the deponent is testifying on the organisation's behalf. The preamble lastly mentions that the deponent is providing the affidavit of their own free will.

c. Purpose

The purpose of the affidavit is quite important, as it sketches the reasons for drafting the affidavit. An affidavit may, depending on the intended recipient, serve different purposes. The affidavit will have the information in it that suits its purpose. It is important for the reader of the affidavit to understand the purpose so that they can establish if the affidavit serves the purpose that they are reading the affidavit for. Some illustrative examples of affidavit purposes include:

- 'The purpose of this affidavit is to comply with the reporting requirements of Act XYZ.'
- 'The purpose of this affidavit is to open a criminal case so that the police services can investigate the alleged fraudulent payment of funds to the ABC company.'
- 'The purpose of this affidavit is to summarise the deponent's testimony in the Joe Blogs internal disciplinary hearing to be held >>>.'

The purpose may be used to inform the reader that there has been more than one affidavit issued by the deponent in the matter. It can also tell the reader which affidavit by the deponent this one is. State if this affidavit is the first or a subsequent affidavit for the deponent. Also, describe what the purpose of each affidavit was. An example includes:

Affidavit sequence	Affidavit date	Affidavit purpose
First	23 March 20X1	To register a criminal case with the police services.
Second	05 May 20X1	To describe the initial investigation process, facts identified, conclusions reached and actions taken.
Third	16 September 20X1	To document additional information requested by the prosecutor.

d. Legal entities

List, in a table, all the legal entities (natural persons and juristic persons) that you refer to in the affidavit. It is important to do this very early in the affidavit before you start to use the entities' names so that the reader will know who is being referred to, as early as possible.

Explain in the table the entities' relevance to the case and provide a shortened name by which they are referred to in the affidavit.

This list may seem long and unnecessary, but it provides context and background to the reader when they read a name. It also provides a single place in the affidavit for the reader to seek clarity in the event that they are unsure of who the person or juristic person is that is being referred to in the affidavit. Affidavit readers find a lot of value in this.

e. Credentials

As discussed above under the paragraph on 'opinions and conclusions', it may be required to list the credentials of yourself or an expert. You may elect to refer the reader to an annexure to the affidavit if the credentials are long and/or if you feel that they are distracting from the essence of the affidavit.

The expert's credentials need to show that they are an expert in their field and should, therefore, be restricted to the relevant credentials to demonstrate this. Credentials to list may include:

- *Educational background:*
    - Tertiary education
    - Postgraduate education
    - Professional qualifications (for example certified fraud examiner)
    - Short courses attended (show relevance and currency of continuing education)
    - Seminars attended.

- *Relevant working experience*

Consider including any of the following aspects:

- Organisations worked for
- Duration of employment
- Job title in organisation
- Roles or responsibilities.
- Specific/relevant experience in these roles
- Industry types worked in.

- *Memberships*

Consider including all relevant professional and/or industry-specific memberships, for example the Association of Certified Fraud Examiners.

- *Books and articles written*

Consider including any books and articles authored by the expert that are relevant to establish them as an expert.

- *Cases investigated:*
    - May include the number of cases investigated, but less likely.
    - May include the type or category of cases investigated.

- *Testimony given*

List all or a summary of criminal and civil courts, labour tribunals, etc where the deponent has given evidence.

- *Conference presentations delivered*

Consider listing industry-relevant conference presentations delivered.

- *General*

Consider if there are any other roles or responsibilities that the expert holds that may establish credibility. For example, being a commissioner of oaths, chairman of a professional body, part-time relevant lecturer, etc.

An example of the wording that you may use to describe your own credentials includes:

1. I was the person who conducted and/or had the primary coordinating responsibility for the investigation into the ABC 20X2 allegations.
    - 1.1. As such it is important to demonstrate my knowledge and experience to investigate these matters in the event that I am required to testify as an expert witness.
    - 1.2. A summary of my forensic investigative experience and auditing qualifications is attached as Annexure CGB 1 attached hereto.

f. Background

Next, give a background to the matter at hand. This includes how the matter came to the deponent's attention and the chosen course of action in response. It should be very short and just serve to sketch the background.

g. Statement

Next, commence with the actual statement of facts that the deponent wishes to carry across to the reader. You may elect to have numerous sub-paragraphs. Try to break the statement into logical groups. The paragraphs should flow logically and the reader should not need to jump around to find different disjointed facts/sections.

- *Style*

The general style of an affidavit is to state the bare facts and what the deponent has seen or been told even to the point of being too obvious and then to leave it up to the reader to conclude. For example: 'I do not know why cheque number 1234 (see annexure ...1 attached hereto) to the value of USD 10,000.00 would be in the name of Mrs Smith. Mrs Smith is the wife of the ABC Company's chief accountant. The ABC Company does not have a contract with Mrs Smith and I could not find any legal obligation that the ABC Company has to pay Mrs Smith this amount or any other amount.'

You do not say: 'I found cheque number 1234 (see annexure ...1 attached hereto) to the value of USD 10,000.00 fraudulently made out to the wife of the chief accountant.' The reader of your affidavit or the judge who is listening to your oral testimony must conclude if the cheque payment was fraudulent or not.

- *Prediction*

As far as possible, try to anticipate counter-arguments to your testimony or the witnesses' testimonies, which are encapsulated in the affidavit. This is very similar to the approach used in the structuring of interview questions. Remember that the reader of the affidavit may not have the opportunity to clarify what the deponent of the affidavit has written. The affidavit needs to be able to stand alone and guide the reader to the facts required to reach the correct conclusion. Try to think therefore of which excuses can be given and then think which evidence the deponent needs to present in advance to counter/block these excuses. Add testimony/facts to prevent these arguments being used. This will save a lot of time and effort to disprove assertions afterwards.

- *Names*

Use a person's first and family name in the affidavit throughout. This ensures a more formal tone of the affidavit and it reduces the possibility of confusion as to whom you are referring to. Also, use the person's name and do not refer to them as 'he', 'she' or 'they'. Confusion can also arise when there is more than one person with the same name.

First-time readers find this style of writing uncomfortable. The affidavit is a factual and formal document and you will, therefore, sacrifice ease of reading to ensure that the facts are portrayed correctly. As an example: 'I asked Mr John Smith to tell me if he was aware of the payment to YYZ company to the value of USD 10,000.00 on 10 March 2015. Mr John Smith said that he was unaware of it, as his creditors' staff members dealt with all such payments. I then showed Mr John Smith an e-mail (see annexure ...3 attached hereto), etc.' A person frequently has to deal with family or common family names in an affidavit. You can therefore not just refer to Mr Smith, as there may be two Mr Smiths in the matter. *An example refers of an affidavit I drafted on behalf of a deponent. There were four brothers (all with the same surname) covered in the affidavit. The confusion was reduced by the affidavit section: 'list of legal entities discussed in this document' and the full use of the brothers' names.*

- *Facts*

Do not leave anything to chance or to the interpretation of the reader of the affidavit. Ensure that you always state clearly which events and items you are referring to.

For example: 'I showed electronic payment voucher number 1234, dated 20 June 2015, to the value of USD 3,578.00 (see annexure ...3, attached hereto), to Mr Rob Banks.'

Again, this style can seem unnecessarily cumbersome, but it reduces any confusion as to what the deponent is referring to.

- *Documents*

Affidavits can be long documents. While the flow of the affidavit should always be logical and easy to read, the reader of an affidavit will invariably not have the same detailed knowledge of the subjects/facts in the affidavit, as the deponent. Part of this knowledge is what is written and part is what is in documents and other information sources referred to/used in the affidavit.

As a rule, you should only refer to documents that you have attached to your affidavit. In this manner, the reader can refer to the document and ensure that they have a complete picture of what you are referring to. It also reduces any confusion as to which document the deponent is referring to.

Documents are attached as annexures at the end of the affidavit. Ensure that you refer the reader to the relevant annexure each time that you mention the document. This may occur multiple times, but you should maintain the discipline throughout. This way the reader knows exactly which document you are referring to and can refer to it as required. For example: 'I obtained invoice number 227788 (attached as annexure CGB 3 hereto), from Mrs Jane Osborne.' Then later in the affidavit: 'I recalculated the amounts charged on invoice number 227788 (attached as annexure CGB3 hereto), by multiplying the number of goods invoiced with the unit price.' And then again later: 'The unit prices listed on invoice number 227788 (attached as annexure CGB3 hereto) did not correspond to the unit prices contained in the DDD computer system price master file (see annexure CGB4 attached hereto).' This may seem a bit over the top, but it removes any confusion and it creates a degree of formality to the affidavit, which in turn creates credibility.

If you have attached the full version of a relevant document as an annexure to an affidavit, then you may cut and paste relevant sections that you are discussing into the specific paragraphs. You will still refer to the full document in the main body of the affidavit. In this way, you are able to refer the reader to specific areas of the document being discussed. This is particularly useful if the attached document is long or if it is important to focus on very specific sentences/ areas of the document. Please also refer to the discussion below on 'annexures', which covers some practical considerations on the use of documents in affidavits.

- *Numbering*

For the greater part, almost every sentence should be numbered. Again, this may seem over the top, but it allows for easy reference to specific areas of the affidavit. Try to group similar facts and concepts together under one group of numbers in the affidavit. Try, even in the same paragraph, to break the paragraph into easy pieces for the reader by using newly numbered sub-points. The example affidavit below refers.

h. Specific paragraphs

You may also wish to provide headings for specific subparagraphs that inform the reader what a section in the affidavit covers. These may be sections of your investigation. They may also be separate observations of a witness deponent. For example:

- Lifestyle audit
- Cash book analysis
- Work responsibilities.

The purpose of such headings is to make it easier for the reader to navigate the affidavit. The groupings should be necessary to break the affidavit into logical areas.

i. Declaration

The declaration is a very important paragraph to include, as it 'locks' the deponent down and clearly states that they are not concealing any other relevant facts. While a deponent may still elect to withhold information or lie, as part of their affidavit, it provides you with a distinct point of reference to refer them once their actual actions have been identified.

It also provides an opportunity, at the time of drafting or signing the affidavit, for you to ask the deponent if there are any additional facts that they need to declare. This is a so-to-say last chance for them to make declarations.

An example of the wording of such a declaration includes:

1. Other than the declarations made in this document I can say that:
    1.1. I do not have any further knowledge of any other material facts or wrongdoings related to this case.
    1.2. I do not know anyone else who is involved or that may have knowledge of involvement in this case.
    1.3. I did not partake in or assist anyone in any manner to perpetrate the wrongdoings in this case.
    1.4. I did not derive any benefit in any form from the wrongdoings in this case.

j. Conclusion

The elements contained in the conclusion section, as per the affidavit example below (see Annexure 8.1 attached hereto), are those aspects that are required to 'legally' make this an affidavit. These aspects will be prescribed by the individual country's laws in which you operate. Determine therefore what the specific legal requirements are that you need to comply with in the countries in which you operate.

The major difference between a statement and an affidavit is the fact that an affidavit is made under oath. A deponent can be held accountable and be subject to some form of penalty if they are found to have knowingly made a false declaration in an affidavit submitted in a court. Lying under oath is perjury and carries strict penalties.

Lying and/or the misrepresentation of facts in a statement is always wrong and is seen in a serious light. The providing of information under oath is seen as an important matter and failure to provide all information correctly under oath is seen in even more of a serious light than plain lying on a statement.

As discussed previously, use affidavits in internal organisation disciplinary hearings as well. While an employer is not a court, lying and/or the misrepresentation of facts may also be seen in a serious light by an employer. Employees have a duty to tell the truth and failure to do so may invoke disciplinary action.

k. Commissioner of oaths

Different countries require affidavits to be signed by different parties to 'legitimise' the affidavit. In South Africa, an affidavit must be signed in the presence of a commissioner of oaths. Certain people may, by virtue of their profession or qualifications, be automatically admitted as a commissioner of oaths. Some examples include:

- Professional accountants (chartered accountants)
- Police officers
- Judges
- Lawyers.

Alternatively, anyone who has been appointed as a commissioner of oaths under the Justices of the Peace and Commissioners of Oaths Act 16 of 1963 may act in this capacity.

A commissioner of oaths cannot commission their own documents. These must be commissioned by an independent person. Each page of the affidavit (including every page of all annexures) should be initialled by the deponent and the commissioner of oaths.

Only the page with the commissioning paragraph on it must be signed in full by both the commissioner of oaths and the deponent.

The commissioner of oaths should read the paragraph aloud to the deponent before signing, and ask the deponent to swear. Thereafter both parties sign the declaration to evidence the declaration. An example of the paragraph in which the affidavit is commissioned includes:

I certify that:

I. the Deponent acknowledged to me that:
   A. he knows and understands the contents of this declaration;
   B. he has no objection to taking the prescribed oath;
   C. he considers the prescribed oath to be binding on his conscience.

II. the Deponent thereafter uttered the words, 'I swear that the contents of this declaration are true, so help me God'.

III. the Deponent signed this declaration in my presence at Cape Town on dd Mm 20yy.

____

COMMISSIONER OF OATHS

I. Annexures

This section continues from the paragraph on documents above. As discussed previously you need, as far as is practical, to include any document that you refer to in your affidavit as an annexure. To make things worse, you need to include the original document. If an original document is unavailable, then you need to include a copy with an explanation as to why the original is not included. If there is no original nor copy available, then the deponent needs to provide testimony concerning the document. There is, therefore, a diminishing reliance on documents in the absence of an original document.

Do not submit the original signed copies of the affidavits and the original annexure documents to the police services/the court immediately. Documents have a 'reputation' for disappearing. Missing evidence could materially affect your case. Give the affidavit recipient a working copy of the relevant documents in the meantime and only bring the original documents in on the day before the trial. Ensure that the receiving party signs to acknowledge receipt of the original documents. Still, maintain your own copies of all documents for reference/query purposes.

It may also be a good idea to have a list of annexures that are attached to the affidavit at the start of the annexure section of your affidavit. This will provide one reference point for the reader to navigate the annexures. An example of such a list follows:

Annexure number	Affidavit pages	Document name	Relevance to affidavit
CGB1	... to ...	Invoice number 227788	
CGB2			
Etc...			

One document may tend to blur into itself if you have many documents attached as annexures. You will, therefore, need to make it easy for the reader to know where a document starts and ends. In terms of this, you may also want to separate documents with a blank page or a heading-type page. Decide on a logical convention to number annexures. Your numbering system should be simple.

8.3.6. Example

Below (see Annexure 8.1 attached hereto) is an example of an affidavit template which may be used.

Annexure 8.1
Affidavit example

Affidavit number 1	by NAME AS PER ID DOC	_ _ /Month/ 20_ _
ID # >>>>>>>>	In the >>>>> matter	Page 1 of 10

Preamble

1. I, the undersigned, >> (full names as per ID/passport)>>>, do hereby state in English and under oath that:

1.1. I am an adult male with >> (country name)>> ID Number >>>.

1.2. I am employed by >>>.
- 1.2.1. I am employed as the >>>.
- 1.2.2. I have been employed by >>> in this capacity since -- >>> ----.
- 1.2.3. My office is situated at >>>>.

1.3. I am contactable at:
- 1.3.1. >>>@>>>.com (work - e-mail).
- 1.3.2. +27 (0)21 --- ---- (work - switchboard).
- 1.3.3. +27 (0)21 --- ---- (work - direct landline).
- 1.3.4. +27 (0) ------- (work - cellular).

1.4. I am authorised to give this affidavit by virtue of my capacity as the >>>>.

1.5. I depose to this affidavit by my own free will.

Purpose

2. The purpose of this affidavit is to give an account of the events surrounding the alleged ...

2.1. ......

3. Legal entities

The following are the legal entities mentioned in this document:

No	Name	ID No/Company registration No	Hereafter referred to as/known as	Case relevance
				The subject of the investigation.
	XYZ Company			
	JKH Supplier			
	The South African Police Services	N/A	SAPS	The South African Police Services.
	ABC Bank	N/A	SARS	
	Mr Super Sleuth	123456...	Sleuth	Lead investigator and deponent of this affidavit.

Credentials

4. I hold the following qualifications and professional designations:

 4.1.

5. My experience includes....

 5.1.

Background

6. >>>>.

 6.1.

Statement

7. >>>>

 7.1.

 7.2.

 7.3.

Declaration

8. Other than the declarations made in this document I can say that:

 8.1. I do not have any further knowledge of any other material facts or wrongdoings related to this case.

 8.2. I do not know anyone else who is involved or that may have knowledge of involvement in this case.

 8.3. I did not partake in or assist anyone in any manner to perpetrate the wrongdoings in this case.

 8.4. I did not derive any benefit in any form from the wrongdoings in this case.

Conclusion

9. I know and understand the contents of this affidavit.
10. I have no objection to taking the prescribed oath.
11. I consider the prescribed oath to be binding on my conscience.

____

Name

I certify that:

IV. the Deponent acknowledged to me that:

   A. he knows and understands the contents of this declaration;

   B. he has no objection to taking the prescribed oath;

   C. he considers the prescribed oath to be binding on his conscience.

V. the Deponent thereafter uttered the words, 'I swear that the contents of this declaration are true, so help me God'.

VI. the Deponent signed this declaration in my presence at Cape Town on dd Mm 20yy.

____

COMMISSIONER OF OATHS

Annexure 8.A1
Affidavit example

Annexure A1 to Affidavit number 1	**by >>>**	**_ _/Month/ 20_ _**
ID # >>>	In the >>> Matter	Page 8 of 10

CHAPTER 9

FRAUD EXAMPLES

9.1. CHAPTER OVERVIEW AND INTRODUCTION

It is important, regardless of whether a fraudulent activity has been identified or if the existence of fraud is being tested for, for the investigator to know what to look for and who should be looked at. The 'who' is discussed in Chapter 3 on conducting the investigation and Chapter 4 on interviewing. We consider the 'what' in this chapter. The 'what' in this case is inextricably tied to the 'how'.

Let us go back to the introduction of this book. What would the seasoned fraud investigator who was retiring have done? An experienced fraud investigator would intuitively know from experience:

- 'Where' to look to find fraud
- The methods by which frauds are perpetrated in a particular situation
- The signs to look for
- How to investigate each type of fraud
- How to prove the fraud.

This chapter is designed to be a reference chapter. You may either read the entire chapter or reference a specific section, as required. We discuss 'what you are going to be looking for' in each of the typical frauds described here, 'why you are looking for it' and some pointers on 'how to find it'. Before long you will see a pattern developing of how to approach frauds.

Your investigation will be easier if you know what possibilities to consider in particular situations/areas. It is very dangerous to confine your thoughts to only what was initially identified or even to what your experience covers. A fraudster is rarely going to volunteer exactly what they have done. Even if they do admit to something, you cannot be sure that they are declaring everything. They may have used multiple modus operandi to defraud the organisation. Remember the rule: 'Whatever they admit to or whatever you find initially, multiply it by three and that is what they have taken.' You are, as the investigator, going to have to identify the extent of the fraudulent activity.

Fraudsters tend however to stick to one or two related modus operandi, although there are many cases where the subjects perpetrate fraud in every area of the business that they touch. While these are less common, you will not know the scope of what you are dealing with at the onset of your investigation and you will need to keep an open mind and consider the full gambit.

In this section of the book, we discuss a framework of possibilities that may guide you during your investigation. The idea of the framework is to provide a checklist that could be a checklist (albeit in thought only) to ensure that most of the possibilities have been considered. Many of the approaches proposed for detecting and proving the fraud are common. There will, therefore, be a fair amount of repetition of these methods throughout the list.

9.1.1. Categories

The Association of Certified Fraud Examiners (ACFE) has a very complete fraud category tree (see the diagram below) that clearly shows the categorisation of different types of fraud. The ACFE's has extremely comprehensive literature on fraud. You are strongly encouraged to refer to the ACFE's resources on a regular basis.

The premise of this book is based on the belief that people learn better and are better equipped to deal with real situations when they are armed with practical learning. You are therefore encouraged to spend most of your time understanding practical examples of fraud that you may encounter and little or no time of the theoretical categorisation of fraud.

When criminal or labour charges are drafted or when a civil suit is contemplated, it is important for the person drafting the charges to know how the irregularity is categorised in terms of the law. This is important for the purposes of formulating the charges and knowing what must be proven in a court of law/labour tribunal in terms of the specific charge. The categorisation of various frauds that we use as fraud investigators may also be very different from the legal categorisation of the misconduct into charges. You will, therefore, need to have a good appreciation of both frauds and legal charges.

As per the diagram below, the ACFE's fraud tree (http://www.acfe.com/fraud-tree.aspx) highlights three categories of fraud, being:

- *Asset misappropriation*

  The theft or unauthorised use of assets (assets being an accounting definition).

- *Corruption*

  Any corrupt practice, such as paying kickbacks or soliciting bribes.

- *Fraudulent statements*

  The fraudulent misstatement of a financial statement or other record.

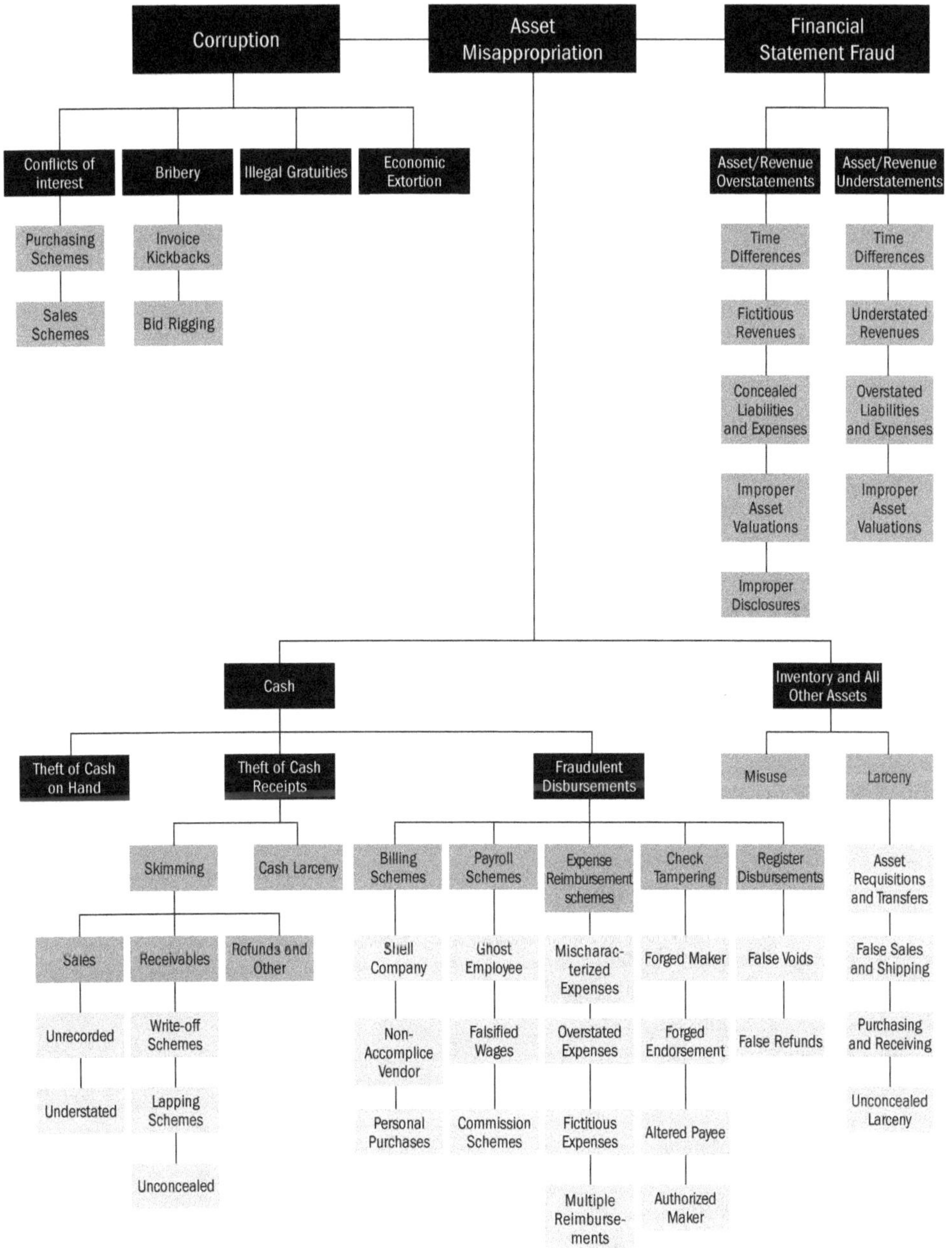

Figure 9.1 *The ACFE's Fraud Tree*

This provides a good high-level categorisation of fraud. Examples of fraud are discussed according to the following structure in this chapter:

Section A – More common fraud types

- Payments
- Procurement
- Types of procurement frauds
    - Front companies
    - Corrupt relationships with suppliers
    - Tender fraud, bid rigging and bid rotation
- Contract fraud
    - Substandard materials/services or subcontractors used in contracts
    - Rates/prices
- Investments
- Unentitled discounts, denying entitled discounts and/or preferential pricing
    - Suppliers
    - Clients
- Unfair extended credit terms
- Overpayments
- Exploitation of staff discounts/privilege and/or access to knowledge
- Payroll
    - Key field amendments
    - Fictitious employees
    - Pay rate changes
    - Fictitious hours
    - Status changes
    - Staff loans
    - Unentitled benefits
    - Payroll tax evasion
    - Fraudulent incomes
    - Fraudulent deductions
    - Commission fraud
- HR fraud
- Journals

Financial statement fraud

Section B – Balance sheet

- Owners' equity/share capital
- Debentures
- Retained earnings
- Long-term/short-term loans
- Accruals
- Provisions

- Contingent liabilities/assets
- Current liabilities
- Tax liabilities
- Fixed assets, buildings, plant and equipment, vehicles, capital items, assets being built
- Decommission and abandonment decisions
- Land and buildings
- Building assets
- Depreciation/wear and tear
- Current assets
- Bank/cash
- Stock/materials/stationery/work in progress/finished goods
- Deposits paid/received
- Prepaid expenses paid or received
- Retentions
- Debtors/accounts receivable
- Bad debt provisions
- Intellectual property, trademarks, copyrights, pate3nts, intangible assets
- Notes to the financial statements
- Corporate governance statements
- Directors' emoluments

Section C – Income statement

- Sales/turnover
- Purchases, prime costs and/or cost of sales
- Subcontractors
- Contract accounts/job accounts
- Expense accounts, overhead charges
- Other income
- Labour costs, salaries, wages, commissions, etc
- Loss/gain on sale of assets
- Asset revaluation/impairment
- GL transactions
- Gross profit
- Net profit
- Petty cash
- Exchange gains
- Extraordinary items
- Dividends

Other interesting fraud schemes

- Share incentive schemes
- Snagging/rework
- Accounting policies
- Structural changes
- Operating systems and financial systems

- Budgets/estimates/forecasting
- Management accounts
- Masterfile updates
- Deal brokering
- Insider trading
- Trusts
- Deceased estates

9.2. KEY CONCEPTS

Before we can progress, we need to understand the broad concepts of fraud and related activities. For this reason, we need to consider definitions of these concepts. Let us begin by looking at some important definitions and clarifications to guide us to the categories of fraudulent and generally corrupt behaviour. These concepts can be kept in the back of your mind when considering fraud examples. They can also start to form the link to criminal-type charges, as they are more about the wrongdoing and less about the example. The concepts include:

- *Fraud*

The ACFE quotes *Black's Law Dictionary*'s definition of fraud, being: 'A knowing misrepresentation of the truth or concealment of a material fact to induce another to act to his or her detriment' (Bryan Garner, ed., *Black's Law Dictionary.* 8th Ed. (2004), s.v., 'fraud.').

- *Corruption*

The World Bank's definition of corruption is: 'the abuse of public office for private gain' (www.tinyurl.com/pdwhgk9).

- *Conflict of interest*

The Organisation for Economic Co-operation and Development states: 'Conflict of interest occurs when an individual or a corporation (either private or governmental) is in a position to exploit his or their own professional or official capacity in some way for personal or corporate benefit.' (www. stats.oecd.org).

- *Bribery*

Bribery involves offering, giving, receiving, or soliciting anything of value to influence an official act or business decision (www.acfe.com/uploadedFiles/ACFE/bc/01-Introduction.pdf).

- *Kickbacks*

Kickbacks are improper, undisclosed payments made to obtain favourable treatment (www.acfe.com/uploadedFiles/ACFE.../bc/01-Introduction.pdf).

- *Illegal gratuities*

Illegal gratuities are something of value given to another party to reward a decision after it has been made, rather than to influence it before the decision is made (www.acfe.com/uploadedFiles/ACFE.../bc/01-Introduction.pdf).

- *Theft*

Asset misappropriation schemes include both the theft of company assets, such as cash, and the misuse and theft of company assets, such as using a company car for a personal trip.

The asset misappropriation schemes to be discussed here are cash schemes and misuse of noncash assets, such as inventory and all other assets (www.acfe.com/Fraud-Trial-2011-Chapter-Excerpt.pdf).

- *Embezzlement*

Embezzlement is a particular kind of fraud that is distinguished from larceny, and it is committed not by the act of deception, but by a breaching of one's fiduciary responsibility. The difference centres on the legal custody of the article stolen. A larcenist takes something from its rightful owner without ever having had legal custody of it himself; the embezzler, on the other hand, has been given legal custody of the article for a period of time or specific purpose and has instead assumed full and sole custody. Embezzlement exceeds the originally authorised custody agreement (www.acfe.com/Fraud-Trial-2011-Chapter-Excerpt.pdf).

- *Larceny*

Larceny refers to what is more widely called theft, and it is defined as wrongfully depriving someone of their possessions with the intent to steal. If the taking is by stealth or force, the act is larceny. If the taking is by guile or deception, false representation, or concealment of crucial information, the act is fraud, false pretences, or larceny by trick. The deception may be designed to cause others to act or may be part of concealing one's own actions (www.acfe.com/Fraud-Trial-2011-Chapter-Excerpt.pdf).

- *Robbery*

The felonious taking of the property of another from his or her person or in his or her immediate presence, against his or her will, by violence or intimidation (www.dictionary.com).

- *Espionage*

The act or practice of spying. The use of spies by a government to discover the military and political secrets of other nations. The use of spies by a corporation or the like to acquire the plans, technical knowledge, etc, of a competitor: industrial espionage (www.dictionary.com).

- *Misappropriation*

Misappropriation is the intentional, illegal use of the property, funds, or ideas of another person for an unauthorised purpose (www.acfe.com/fraudtrial-2013chapter-20excerpt.pdf). To put to a wrong use. To apply wrongfully or dishonestly, as funds entrusted to one's care (www.dictionary.com).

- *Fraudulent disbursements*

Fraudulent disbursements are the most common form of asset misappropriation, and they occur when an employee uses his position of employment to cause a payment for some inappropriate purpose. Fraudulent disbursements are on-book fraud schemes, meaning that cash (cheques) leaves the entity fraudulently, but it is recorded in the books and thus an audit trail exists (www.acfe.com/article.aspx?id=436). Fraudulent disbursement schemes are broken down into the following types:

  - Cheque tampering
  - Register disbursement schemes
  - Billing schemes
  - Expense reimbursement schemes
  - Payroll schemes.

- *Misrepresentation*

To represent incorrectly, improperly, or falsely. To represent in an unsatisfactory manner (www.dictionary.com).

- *Extortion*

Economic extortion is present when an employee or official, through the wrongful use of actual or threatened force or fear, demands money or some other consideration to make a particular business decision (www.acfe.com/uploadedFiles/ACFE/bc/01-Introduction.pdf).

- *Forgery*

The crime of falsely making or altering a writing by which the legal rights or obligations of another person are apparently affected; simulated signing of another person's name to any such writing whether or not it is also the forger's name; the production of a spurious work that is claimed to be genuine, as a coin, a painting, a work of art, a writing, an invention or an artefact (www.dictionary.com).

- *Identity theft*

Identity theft, as defined by the FTC, 'occurs when someone uses your personally identifying information, like your name, Social Security number, or credit card number, to commit fraud or other crimes' (www.acfe.com/article.aspx?id=436).

- *Theft of intellectual property*

Intellectual property (IP) is any product or idea that is protected by the law from unauthorised use by others. IP can be comprised of patents, copyrights, trademarks or trade secrets. It involves stealing someone's ideas or inventions, things that are often intangible (www.acfe.com/fraud-examiner.aspx?id=4294985057).

- *Counterfeiting*

Counterfeiting of goods involves the manufacture and distribution of an inferior good using stolen IP with the intent to sell a cheaper version of the brand name product without the owner's permission (www.acfe.com/fraud-examiner. aspx?id=4294985057).

- *Money laundering*

Money-laundering operations are designed to take the proceeds of illegal activity, such as profits from fraud, and disguise the existence, source or application of those funds so the proceeds appear to come from a legitimate source. In short, 'dirty money' is made to appear clean. Once illegal money has been laundered, the perpetrator is able to spend or invest the illicit income in legitimate assets (www.acfe.com/products.aspx?id=2838).

9.3. THE VICTIM

In any fraud matter, there are one or more parties that are prejudiced in some or other manner. This may be in the form of prejudice, a financial loss or a loss of an opportunity, etc. Who the victim is will differ from case to case and may be any one or combination of parties. Some examples of possible victim parties and prejudices suffered include:

- *Company*

In most cases, the company will be the victim and suffer some sort of direct or indirect loss. Assets can be misappropriated, unnecessary costs incurred, business opportunities (and potential future earnings) may be lost, brand damage done, fines and penalties incurred, etc.

- *Supplier*

In some cases, the victim can be a supplier to the company. This may be in cases where the supplier is being forced against their will to, for example, pay a bribe to a procurement officer. While 'forced against their will' is a relative and debatable concept, let us not debate that here. Let us just acknowledge that the supplier can suffer some form of loss. In other cases, the supplier may be blissfully unaware that they have been prejudiced in the process. The company may not be overpaying for goods/services or suffering a loss/being prejudiced. The supplier may be the one who is being prejudiced.

- *Company's client*

Similar in some ways to a supplier suffering a loss, the victim may be a client of the company. The client may end up paying additionally for the company's products or be prejudiced due to not receiving what they require and needing to source from alternative suppliers.

- *A competitor*

Competitors to the company may have been unfairly denied the opportunity to engage in business, as a result of a fraudulent activity within the company.

- *The bank/financial institutions/financing houses*

Financial institutions lend companies money to facilitate the company's growth/sustain existing business. Financial institutions are (mostly) businesses as well. They consider the relative risks of their transactions and embark on transactions in anticipation of profit. Even government agencies or companies incorporated not for gain for the purpose of developing business need to minimise costs and successfully fulfil their mandates. Financial losses will also impact on their ability to do this. Financial institutions frequently mitigate the risks of loss on the surety of assets ceded to them. Financial institutions may incur the loss of the funds lent to the company and/or not be in a position to recoup losses if the ceded assets are no longer available to them or not worth what was anticipated.

- *Investors and/or shareholders*

Investors may not be obtaining the returns that they were entitled to. They, as with financial institutions, may, in addition, lose the capital that they have invested in good faith or have to pay unnecessary penalties, costs, etc.

- *The staff members of the company*

There is frequently a direct impact on staff members if a company does not make the profits that they should. Fraud has a direct impact on a company's bottom line. Staff costs are frequently one of the first places that companies consider to reduce costs in less profitable times. This is because an increase in revenue is less controllable to a company than costs are. A significant fraud may materially impact the company's profitability and necessitate that other measures be taken (for example reducing costs) in an attempt to increase profitability. A reduction in costs may be of total remuneration bills, additional staff members, incentives, profit shares, etc. Companies are less likely to pay bonuses in times of low profit. Staff members may also not be given increases. On the other hand, frauds may have entailed the fraudulent manipulation of bonus/incentive recognition criteria. Fraudulent staff members may have manipulated the bonus recognition criteria to such a degree that other staff members may have been unlawfully deprived of a bonus/remuneration/incentive payment that they were entitled to. Alternatively, the company may need to retrench staff members as a result of having suffered a significant financial loss as the result of a fraud. Retrenched staff members would need to seek alternative employment and be out of pocket for the duration of time until they are able to be put back in a position similar to when they were gainfully employed.

- *The government or other public organisation*

Government agencies may have been deprived of taxes if these were misappropriated. Alternatively, reduced profits normally reduce taxable income, which would equate to reduced taxes payable. The accounting treatment of unnatural losses may not be tax deductible and in the extreme, the company may need to close its doors if it is unable to recover from the financial losses resulting from the fraud. This would, in turn, mean that the government agencies would no longer receive taxes and dues.

9.4. EXAMPLES

The examples of frauds listed below can be used as prompts:

- When conducting an investigation in a particular area, which has been hit by fraud, to assist you in determining the areas of actual fraud, the extent of the fraud or to identify the existence of fraud.
- To be used as potential areas of exposure when conducting proactive fraud identification and prevention.

The list is by no means an exhaustive list. You can supplement your knowledge of examples within the categories, as your practical exposure requires. Different industries may have more or less of a particular type of fraud. Your knowledge of fraud examples will increase as you are exposed to more industries and each time you are involved in more investigations.

There is no particular academic accuracy to the categorisation used in this book. The categorisation is merely a grouping to make it easier to understand the examples and to facilitate discussion.

Before we delve into the detail, let us go back to our rules. The most relevant rule to this section of the book is: 'Follow the money.' Consider this during your investigation and answer the following questions:

- How could they possibly be getting a financial benefit in this situation?
- What other corrupt benefit could they or their nominees be deriving in this situation?
- Why would they want /what is motivating them to be party to something fraudulent or corrupt?

The examples have been grouped in functional areas so as to assist you when confronted with a specific situation.

Section A – More common fraud types

9.4.1. Payments

Discussion

Payment-type frauds are very common. This is because a lot of frauds are perpetrated with the purpose of obtaining funds that the subject/s would ordinarily not be entitled to.

Payment-type frauds really cover any fraudulent payment of funds. We will be discussing various types of fraud examples that involve payments in this section (eg creditor payments, payroll payments, etc). The generic nature of payment-type frauds is discussed in this paragraph from an introductory point of view.

As discussed elsewhere in this book, fraudsters typically utilise legitimate means to conduct their frauds. This because:

- They know and understand how the processes that they work with function.
- They know what the control deficiencies are and how to exploit them.
- It is less likely for people to suspect fraud if the fraudulent transaction appears to be the same as any normal transaction and does not stand out.

For example: I am responsible for making creditor payments on behalf of the company. I make a few fraudulent payments to myself and I apply the payments to a cost centre in which many similar payments occur on a daily basis to prevent detection.

Payments reflect the actual flow of money out of the organisation. The obligation to make a payment is carried in the balance sheet as a liability. The effect (contra entry) of having made a payment (credit to the bank) may be reflected in the balance sheet as:

- An increase in fixed assets (debit) in the balance sheet
- A reduction of cash in the balance sheet
- A reduction of a liability in the balance sheet
- An increase is current assets in the balance sheet in the form of a prepayment which was made.

Other financial statements that may reflect the effect of a payment include:

- In the trading section of the profit and loss (purchases paid - Debit)
- As an expense (debit) in the profit and loss
- As a negative flow of cash in the cash flow statement.

It is important to consider both sides of the double entry when discussing payments, purchases, profits, assets and liabilities later.

Observations/tips to identify and prove

This is just a general introduction to payment-type frauds and specific examples are discussed later in greater detail.

Remember the rule: 'Follow the money.' Follow the transactions through from start to finish, from the time that the transaction was captured on an operating system (if relevant), all the way to the interface to the financial system (where the payment is recorded) and to the actual payment (normally some form of external bank record).

In most cases, the flow of money will be out of the organisation.

Specific details are discussed below.

9.4.2. Procurement

Discussion

One of my early forensic mentors used to say that he guarantees that if he comes into your company, he will find fraud. He used to say that you do not even have to pay him until he finds it. Then he used to tell me that the first place he will go is to the procurement function, as, in his words, 'there is no such thing as an honest buyer'. That may seem a little harsh, but I have to say that this has also been my consistent experience during my career.

This standpoint has put me in difficult situations with colleagues (in the function) and friends (who work in the function or who have family members who work in a procurement function). In my experience, it is only the degree and/or type of irregular behaviour that differs.

In one company where I worked, the senior procurement officers were indignant at the implications stemming from our standard fraud risk questions in a routine audit. Upon closer inspection, no elaborate kickback schemes were identified, but the buyers were all found to be manipulating and overstating their actual performance against their targets/KPIs. The senior management did not see this misrepresentation as fraud. Perhaps their 'willful blindness' had something to do with the fact that they, in turn, were measured by their seniors on the cumulative KPIs of the procurement staff members. The KPI attainment was also the reason for the procurement function's existence. One of our rules comes to mind: 'People always do and say things for a reason.' I think we have an idea of management's reasons in this example!

In another company, buyers were enjoying undeclared supplier-sponsored weekends away at expensive hotels.

If I think about it quickly, then I will have to conclude that the majority of cases that I have had to deal with have, in the wider sense, been 'procurement/corruption-related' cases. These are also the most difficult to prove, as they are normally clandestine. I would, therefore, encourage you to pay particular attention to any learnings that you can acquire on procurement fraud.

To illustrate my mentor's point about there not being any honest buyers, let me share one of my favourite forensic experiences. I was working as the Head of Audit for a multinational (let us call them company A), when the same mentor as mentioned above contacted me on my mobile to say that he and his colleague were at another multinational (company B) in the same industry where they had identified fraud. They identified that an employee of A (let us call him 'Jack') was fronting a company that had been providing services to B for sizable amounts. Jack's uncle was a director of B and was responsible for signing off on the deals that ensured that Jack got the work. Jack was, in turn, subcontracting the actual work and taking a sizeable markup. The spoils were being shared.

I told my mentor that I was not in office at the moment, but that I would contact my colleague to arrange an interview. I contacted one of my colleagues and said to him: 'You know Jack who sits down the corridor? Well I have just been contacted ...' and I proceeded to relay the story to him. My colleague called Jack in and proceeded to read him the riot act saying that we knew what he was up to and he had better confess. Jack then proceeded to confess to something completely different. As it turns out, there were two people with the name Jack: one with the first name Jack (eg Jack Jones) and the other with the surname Jack (eg John Jack). The confusion was confounded by the fact that they worked in similar functions in different companies within the group.

So, what did we do? Well, we thanked the incorrect Jack for his admissions and said to him that by the way he was the wrong Jack, but that he was suspended in any case. We then called in the correct Jack and he confessed quickly.

So, what is the moral of the story? No, not that we should do away with all buyers forthwith. Rather that procurement is an area highly susceptible to fraud and corruption. While I know I will take criticism for this 'general rule', I am confident that we will all agree that procurement is an area prone to fraud and corruption. For this reason then, it is an area that you would do well to understand how to investigate.

Building on my mentor's hypotheses: if you are going to apply the 80:20 rule, then concentrate your prevention and detection efforts (20%) on procurement to obtain the most benefits (80%) for the least effort.

Procurement can be reflected in the profit and loss as purchases or as expenses paid. It can be reflected in the balance sheet in terms of assets acquired or accrued expenses or prepayments.

Observations/tips to identify and prove

Interview staff and suppliers alike.

Understand the company's 'procurement' and 'conflict of interest' policies and compare these to the actual behaviour under review. Examples of specific processes that may need to be abided by include: the three-quote system, tender process, procurement committee, framework agreements, preferential suppliers, etc. Was any of the actual behaviour in contravention of these policies? Obtain explanations for deviations (the chapter on interviewing refers). Understand in how many other cases the deviations occur or if it is just for the supplier/s in question. If so, try to understand why this deviation is not applicable to other suppliers as well. Buyers will normally try to convince you with all sorts of weak arguments that the particular supplier has a service differentiation or that it is about loyalty, etc.

In one case, a subject tried to convince me that the reason why he used a particular transport company was because their trucks were processed quicker through a particular service point resulting in value added to the end customer. A whistle-blower had already told me that the trucking company was bribing gate officials. I asked the subject how the trucking company was able to achieve the quicker turnaround as surely all the different trucking companies all had to stand in the same queue. He was unable to answer me.

Understand local and international legal requirements and compare behaviour to it. Cartels and price-fixing may be occurring. *I recall another example when, as an auditor, I had performed a value-add analysis of procurement for a particular company. The results quickly highlighted that one product (core to the industry that the company operated in) was the highest percentage of procurement spend. I agreed with the group MD that we should approach the top five suppliers and negotiate rebates and preferential prices in accordance with actual volumes given to them in the coming year. To my shock, none of the suppliers moved one inch! The MD tried to convince me not to try to apply the rebate model in their particular industry, as it was unlike other industries where I had experience of it being very successful. I reluctantly accepted defeat and withdrew. About a year later the newspapers printed headlines of a pricing cartel that had been uncovered between the suppliers that we had approached. While I was unable to obtain the preferential prices for the company, I consoled myself that I knew that this was a valid reason why none of the suppliers budged one inch in their pricing strategy for the anticipated dedicated volumes.*

Perform analytical reviews of goods and service volumes and prices. Compare trends to previous periods, across suppliers and within a single supplier. Obtain explanations for procurement peaks and valleys. Try to talk to people independent of the procurement people. Obtain their input as to what they think the prices should be. I recall numerous examples when I showed actual invoices to cost centre owners only to be told that the prices were 3 to 10 times higher than what the man in the street can obtain the articles for, let alone what a company with high volumes should be paying for the same articles.

Obtain comparative quotes (as if you are a small enterprise, not large) and compare these to the actual price paid. If you, as an unidentified individual, are getting better prices than a big corporate with high volumes, then there is something wrong.

Continuing with the aforementioned example, we would often just phone the suppliers and request a price for the items. On other occasions, we had an independent contractor phone for quotes or the cost centre/expense owner himself. This is a very simple test, but one that speaks volumes. As far as possible, have the supplier e-mail or fax the quote to you, as you may need it as evidence. You may need to use an e-mail address that would not attract attention for this. If the corrupt supplier sees the company name, he may contact the procurement officer to clarify why a different person in the company is requesting prices. Many prices are also freely available on the internet. Print or save comparisons obtained.

Compare contractual terms to standard terms or to other contracts. Obtain 'explanations', as to why the suspected corrupt supplier is enjoying different terms/conditions. This could be the inclusion of special clauses or the removal of other standard clauses. What benefit could they derive from this? Try to understand how this favours the supplier above others.

Compare the supplier's actual performance to the contractual terms/company policy to identify deviations. Why is the supplier not being taken to task on poor delivery, if any?

Is there consistent and fair measurement of all service providers? What do rival companies say?

Conduct lifestyle audits (subjects internal to the organisation and external) to:

- Profile potential subjects
- Identify subjects whose lifestyles appear to have been financed from sources other than known/declared income sources (assets, credit applications, default judgments, etc)
- Identify conflicts of interest (business/personal) and/or undeclared interests (directorships, etc).

9.4.3. Types of procurement frauds

Discussion

Procurement-type frauds are very important and it will be beneficial to spend a bit of time to understand the types of frauds associated with procurement.

Observations/tips to identify and prove

I will refer to the aforementioned methods in summary when discussing how to identify procurement frauds listed below.

a. Front companies

Discussion

Front companies are something that I have had to deal with on quite a few matters in many different companies that I worked for.

In explanation, the subject or the subject's associates set up a new company or use an existing company via which they route company business. Now, the company that they set up rarely provides actual goods or services. In most cases, they subcontract or pass the actual work onto actual service providers. The sole purpose of the company is to obtain a share of the transaction in addition to the market-related price. The amount paid to the front company is also normally significantly higher than the market rate for the same goods/services. In this way, the real supplier and the intermediary company are both happy as they each receive a cut.

It is normal business practice for buyers to make use of agencies via which they route the business. The fraudulent use of such agencies can be particularly difficult to prevent and detect in big international businesses, especially when buyers set up companies in countries that they travel to, in order to procure goods. You, in the company's home country, may not have ready access to public domain information in the supplier's country.

The logical question to ask when agencies are used is why they do not just go directly to the supplier/manufacturer. What service is the agency providing that the supplier/manufacturer cannot? In most instances where fraud is suspected, you will not get a valid reason.

The front company is a manner by which the subject can separate themselves from the business and not be directly and/or easily identified as being party to the transactions.

The company will rarely have any other clients. Your company/client will typically be the only customer.

Establish what the supplier selection process was and if this was complied with for the front company in question. Once a supplier has been set up on the preferred suppliers list it is easier for fraudsters to ensure that they get used. The non-compliance with the supplier selection process may give you valuable information to be used in an internal labour case. As a general rule, proving fraud in a labour case can be difficult and procedural breaches are easier to prove. The non-compliance with the supplier selection process may also identify other negligent or involved parties that did not exercise due care.

Observations/tips to identify and prove

Try to identify addresses and telephone numbers that correspond to staff members' numbers. Obtain these from a review of actual documents (invoices, orders, etc), electronic searches, work area searches, etc.

Perform public domain company searches both ways on:

- Key staff members to see if they are directors of any companies
- A selection of companies providing services to your client's company to see who the real owners of the company are.

Conduct lifestyle audits to:

- Profile potential subjects
- Identify subjects whose lifestyles appear to have been financed from sources other than known/declared income sources (assets, credit applications, default judgments, etc)
- Identify conflicts of interest (business/personal) and/or undeclared interests (directorships, etc).

The company does not even have to be a real company. *In one matter we dealt with our checks with the respective country's registrar of companies revealed that the company was never registered and was in fact only a company on paper.* The subject may very well plead that he was unaware that the company was not registered. You could use this to understand why the subject did not perform the required due diligence on the supplier to identify this.

Conduct e-mail searches and general correspondence searches. *In two more recent cases, our e-mail searches of the subjects' company mailbox showed how the subjects were drafting documents on behalf of the company providing the service and/or giving guidance on how to respond to the company.*

Conduct searches of the subject's physical work environment/desk/workspace. Mirror computers and conduct searches of files saved and/or deleted.

Try to establish how many other clients the 'front company' has. *In another recent case, an evaluation of the front company's bank account revealed that only one payment was being made at each month-end from the normal service provider to the front company's bank account. There were no other deposits into the account.* This would most likely mean that the front company was established for the sole purpose of passing the company's business through. *In another example, the subject said in defence that the company was aware that the suspect company was very small and that the company was trying to help the supplier build his business. I asked the subject if he had approval for this and if he had any other examples of where the company had done this for other suppliers. The subject could not provide valid explanations.*

Talk to people in the market/industry/company to understand what they know about the company in question. How is their behaviour and is it well known and established in the industry? Is it known to be ethical or underhanded?

In another matter, the company MD was using his friend's agency to import goods when the company had teams of buyers procuring goods for resale. The agency did not have any special import rights nor did it provide any special service to the company. The company would have saved money if they had sourced the goods directly from the suppliers. I later established from other staff members that the MD's son worked for the agency. This was no coincidence. It was in fact a matter of favours being given for favours. This MD made a habit of this sort of behaviour and another of his friend's guesthouses was used extensively for visiting executives.

Conduct a price analysis. *In one matter, the manufacturer came to us and reported that our buying executive was routing the purchase of the manufacturer's product via an agency that was in turn selling it on to our company. The manufacturer said that he was not losing anything as he was being paid his normal price, but that it was not right that the agent and the buying executive were doing this. In this case, the subject was in fact only marking each unit up by ZAR 60 cents. ZAR 60 cents might not seem like a lot, but over the volumes that we were talking about it amounted to around ZAR 120K per quarter.*

b. Corrupt relationships with suppliers

Discussion

Corrupt relationships with suppliers will be the most common type of procurement fraud that you will have to deal with. This is probably because it is one of the more easily orchestrated procurement frauds. All it entails is some form of corrupt 'agreement' between a company official and an outside supplier. The hallmark of this type of fraud (as compared to many other types) is that it takes at least two to tango in this wicked dance. The key issue is therefore that there must be at least two parties to the fraud. You would need (to some degree) to include both parties in an investigation. If the supplier was paying a bribe, then they most likely took the 'easy path' and will want to plead that they were forced to pay the money. They could have opted to say no and lose the business or alternatively report the corrupt official, but they chose not to.

You should decide if the supplier willingly participated in the corrupt relationship or not. The buyer may have pressurised the supplier to pay a kickback in order to obtain/retain the business. Alternatively, the supplier may have corrupted the buyer.

c. Tender fraud, bid rigging and bid rotation

Discussion

A tender or bidding process is designed to allow the organisation that is putting out the tender to solicit prices and proposals in response to specific requirements. The nature of a tender/bidding process is that certain generic criteria are published to all prospective applicants and that prospective bidders submit a bid in response. The idea is that the company should receive bids in line with market trends, as none of the bidders has any insights into the company's pricing strategy and/or that all bidders are equal and that none have an unfair advantage over the other bidders.

Bidders may collude with a company official who has knowledge of the bidding criteria or who has the power to influence the awarding of the tender to unfairly advantage the bidder.

This could mean that the bidder obtains the tender despite any one or a combination of the following aspects:

- Being more expensive than the other bidders
- Not having the required experience/expertise to conduct the work
- Not having the required guarantees, insurance cover, cash flow, etc to cover for uncertain eventualities
- Not being able to or intending to deliver at all or to the required quality
- Not performing the work themselves and merely using a subcontractor
- Not being able to fulfil contractual requirements subsequent to being awarded the contract
- Not fulfilling the minimum bid entry requirements.

A group of bidders could also collude, unbeknown to the company, to:

- Rotate the bids so that they each have a turn over a period of time to 'win' a bid
- Overprice bids and share the ill-gotten gains
- Agree on a minimum price below which none of the pricing cartels will go.

Auctions are designed to use public (or concealed) bidding to solicit the best bid on an item. Colluding parties may agree in advance to underbid if they are somehow able to control/anticipate the bidding.

Observations/tips to identify and prove

Perform analytical reviews to identify trends of bid winners and/or pricing trends.

Obtain independent quotes and compare these to the tendered prices. Look for:

- Similarities between otherwise purportedly competitive bids
- Information submitted as part of a bid/tender, which should not have been known to outside parties
- Similarities across the range of bids and/or trends submitted by purportedly independent parties.

Look for the relative success of one bidder in relation to others (one party always winning may be too coincidental). Include the trend of the closeness of the bidder's price to the company's predefined budget. If it is consistently close, then it may be as a result of inside information.

Interview staff and/or suppliers.

Conduct lifestyle audits to:

- Profile potential subjects
- Identify subjects whose lifestyles appear to have been financed from sources other than known/declared income sources (assets, credit applications, default judgments, etc)
- Identify conflicts of interest (business/personal) and/or undeclared interests (directorships, etc).

Conduct e-mail searches and general correspondence reviews. Conduct searches of the subject's general workspace and desk. Examine documents. Mirror hard drives and other company-owned electronic devices and search files saved and/or deleted.

Examine the tender/bid process to ensure that:

- Controls and procedures were adequate
- Controls and procedures were followed
- It was impartial and that the criteria were maintained
- Deviations are investigated.

Examine the dates and times that bids were submitted:

- Bids submitted after the cut of time/date
- Bids submitted directly after key correspondence with a subject
- Bids that were submitted just after key information was made available
- Winning bids or bids that were too close to the organisation's budgeted price, that was submitted right at the end of the tender process (indicating that they waited to find out what the other tenders bid)
- Purportedly competitive bids that were submitted too close together
- If a complex bid was submitted shortly after the tender was made public, it may indicate that the bidder had prior knowledge of the criteria and/or tender.
- If the winning bid/lowest price bid always comes in just after the last bidder submitted their bid, it may indicate that the bidder was being fed information from an internal party.

Search work areas, documents and computer files.

E-mail searches can be very helpful to highlight:

- The source/who the internal colluding party is
- The recipient (outside colluding party)
- The times that information was sent/received
- Correspondence at key times/dates
- The price received
- The information shared
- The number of times corresponded.

In one case, our analysis of e-mail correspondence showed two bids coming in for one supplier. The first bid came in just after the tender process had closed and at a price significantly below the lowest bidder. Then a few minutes later a new e-mail came in with a revised price just below the lowest bidder.

9.4.4. Contract fraud

Discussion

The fraudulent and/or corrupt awarding of contracts/procurement was discussed previously and refers to contract fraud as well. The following examples refer:

a. Substandard materials/services or sub-contractors used in contracts

Discussion

In large contracts (such as construction contracts or big supply contracts), corrupt parties may collude with company officials to:

- Overprice goods and services. The company thereby pays higher prices and the supplier unfairly enjoys increased revenues. Corrupt company officials may also receive kickbacks and/or share in profits from supplier companies in which they have undeclared interests.
- In some cases, the price, quality and terms may be market-related, but the corrupt relationship ensures that the particular supplier obtains the business at the expense of the other bidders.
- Enjoy preferential payment terms. For example, suppliers may, unfairly to the company:
    - Not be required to give discounts or rebates
    - Reduce payment periods (for example, from 30 days to 7 days. The company will lose the cash flow benefit).
- By-pass procurement procedures/controls.
- Be granted contracts for which they do not actually qualify. Some contracts require that suppliers have:
    - Specific insurances
    - Cash facilities
    - Experience
    - Partnerships
    - Corporate social development programmes to develop local, disadvantaged citizens.
- Supply substandard goods or services. This results in mechanical failure, lost productivity due to production interruptions, customer complaints and injury.

Observations/tips to identify and prove

Analyse contractual terms for absent terms or for non-enforcement of clauses. Compare this to other contracts and to other suppliers.

Conduct lifestyle audits to:

- Profile potential subjects
- Identify subjects whose lifestyles appear to have been financed from sources other than known/declared income sources (assets, credit applications, default judgments, etc)
- Identify conflicts of interest (business/personal) and/or undeclared interests (directorships, etc).

Conduct e-mail searches and general business related correspondence reviews to identify correspondence proving corrupt relationships.

Conduct searches of the subject's general workspace and/or desk to identify evidence of corrupt activities.

Mirror hard drives and other company-owned electronic devices and search files saved and/or deleted to identify documents, correspondence, calculations and images that may identify corrupt activity.

Interview staff members, suppliers, bidders, etc and understand:

- Who is the most likely to be involved and why
- Who are friends and who are enemies and why
- Where you must look and what you are looking for.

Conduct polygraph tests and combine these with interviews of subjects. Make use of other documentary evidence in the interviews.

Understand and document the business process, document and information flow and understand the existing controls. Understand via interviews and analysis of information and documents what actually transpired and obtain explanations for deviations.

Conduct analytical reviews of costs and revenues and operational information.

b. Rates/prices

Discussion

Many costs and/or incomes are based on a unit of volume multiplied by a rate per unit of volume. Units of volume could include:

- Stock/raw material units
- Time units, such as labour hours or machine hours, etc
- Cubic metres, square metres, running/linear metres, etc
- Volume/capacity/litres.

Fraudsters may fraudulently amend prices and/or rates by:

- Amending the pricing master files
- Under-charging/reducing rates
- Increasing rates charged.

Rates may be fraudulent in so far as the payee has to unfairly pay:

- A reduced price thereby disadvantaging the seller
- An increased amount thereby disadvantaging the buyer. This may be done just to obtain increased funds and/or to receive a kickback/share of the increased funds. The organisation may receive the full amount normally due or not.

I recall one case when a corrupt subcontractor (painter) contacted me to say that he had been 'forced' to pay the construction site contract manager a portion of the fee that the company was paying the subcontractor. He had purportedly told the contract manager that he could no longer *afford to pay the kickback amount of ZAR 10/m^2, but that he could only pay ZAR 5/m^2. The contract manager had then given the work to another painting subcontractor who was allegedly prepared to pay him the larger kickback. The subcontractor was now angry that he had lost the work and wanted to know if I could force the contract manager to give the work back to him.*

The whistle-blowing subcontractor was not terribly sophisticated and he did not realise in his rage that he was implicating himself. While I was totally dumbfounded by the request, I do not 'discriminate' and I take my information from wherever I can get it.

The contract manager purportedly used to tell the subcontractors what the client's bill rate for the work was (for example ZAR 45/m^2). He would then say to them they can have the work, but they need to pay him ZAR 10/m^2 of the rate for getting the work. In this example, the subcontractor took ZAR 35/m^2.

The company paid the subcontractors directly to avoid such extortion. The subcontractors were, as said before, not sophisticated people and like to work with cash. The contract manager was not perturbed by the company's control. He was so brazen that he would accompany the subcontractors to the bank and stand next to them at the tellers and take 'his share' right in front of the bank officials.

I obtained an affidavit from the bank staff members to support this. I also photographed him going in and out of the bank. Video footage of him at the teller receiving his cut may have been better but would need to have been subpoenaed. I did not deem this to be necessary in this case.

Upon confrontation, the contract manager gave me the excuse that he frequently lent the subcontractors money and this was the only way that he could ensure that he was repaid.

Another amusing part of the story was that when I phoned the contract manager over lunchtime to set up a meeting, I could clearly hear the sound of casino machines in the background. Remember the rule: 'It is always about sex, drugs or gambling.'

The nearest casino was about 200 km from the rural-based construction site. The company was paying his fuel bills and this was in work time. Vehicle tracking records were unfortunately not available on his vehicle and the casino declined to give me gate video footage.

In this case, I did not have sufficient evidence to charge the contract manager. He was transferred to a smaller contract and his contract was not renewed upon completion of the job (taking the path of least resistance).

Observations/tips to identify and prove

Interview staff members, subcontractors, suppliers, etc. Conduct analytical reviews of rates/prices. Independently obtain your own comparative prices.

Conduct lifestyle audits to:

- Profile potential subjects
- Identify subjects whose lifestyles appear to have been financed from sources other than known/declared income sources (assets, credit applications, default judgments, etc)
- Identify conflicts of interest (business/personal) and/or undeclared interests (directorships, etc).

Conduct e-mail searches and general business related correspondence reviews to identify correspondence proving corrupt relationships. Conduct searches of the subject's general workspace and/or desk to identify evidence of corrupt activities. Mirror hard drives and other company-owned electronic devices and search files saved and/or deleted to identify documents, correspondence, calculations and images that may identify corrupt activity.

Substantiate payment records to ensure that payment reached the correct person (in full) and/or that they were not endorsed.

9.4.5. Investments

Discussion

Investment frauds are fairly commonplace and numerous high profile cases have caught the media's attention over the years. Investment frauds can occur in numerous manners and the following examples refer:

- The fraudster shows potential investors false projected or purported actual returns on a particular investment. Victims are lured in and invest in the scheme only to lose their money and never see any of the promised returns.
- Fraudsters could take all of the investor's money without investing it at all.
- The fraudsters could also only pay a portion of the return back to the investor and retain the balance. While the fraudster may be entitled to a reasonable fee or commission, the amount withheld in this case is far beyond what is deemed reasonable, allowed in terms of regulatory bodies or contractually agreed to.
- Fraudsters may promise investors that they will be investing in one type of investment (eg a specific company's shares, blue chip companies only, lower risk companies only, etc) and then in reality (unbeknown to the investor) invest in another scheme. This may expose the investor to undue/un-agreed risks or lower returns.
- The fraudster may just mislead prospective investors about their own abilities or the size of their brokerage firm. This will again expose the investor to undue risks that were not agreed upon up front.
- Fraudsters may require potential investors to pay an administration fee up front, without delivering the required service.
- Fraudsters may promise the investor the use of rights/assets that they are not entitled to.

Investment frauds could be in:

- Equities
- Cash
- Bond markets
- Loans
- Property
- Partnership/business share
- Tangible assets (vehicles, boats, etc)

- Artworks
- Rights (intellectual, brands, mining, patents, copyrights, etc)
- Minerals, precious metals, precious stones, etc.

Investments are carried in the balance sheet.

Observations/tips to identify and prove

Confirm that all legislation has been complied with. Confirm ownership of the investment. Does the subject actually own and/or have the legal rights to the investment? Independently value the investment. What is the investment really worth? Try as far as possible to make use of an independent expert on the type of investment. Such an expert may be able to testify and/or create credibility to the value given. Also, try to compare the investment to more than one source to substantiate the value appraised.

Confirm that the investment company/individual is legally registered and/or qualified to invest money in accordance with the banking and/or relevant country's laws.

Check that the investment is a legal scheme. For example, Ponzi and pyramid schemes are illegal in most countries.

Interview subjects, staff members, investors and subject matter experts. This is one of those areas where the credibility of a subject matter expert may contribute to your investigation.

Conduct lifestyle audits to:

- Profile potential subjects
- Identify subjects whose lifestyles appear to have been financed from sources other than known/declared income sources (assets, credit applications, default judgments, etc)
- Identify conflicts of interest (business/personal) and/or undeclared interests (directorships, etc).

Follow the flow of funds to its destination (it may be through multiple bank accounts and/or legal entities). Apply logic and/or the assumptions of the scheme. Remember the rule: 'If it is too good to be true, then it generally is.' Substantiate actual returns and results. Ensure that the returns were actually paid to the benefactors and that they did not just repay them later. Conduct analytical reviews of the investment portfolio to similar products on the market. Investment trends should run more or less in unison with the market leaders.

Conduct e-mail searches and general business related correspondence reviews to identify correspondence proving corrupt relationships. Conduct searches of the subject's general workspace and/or desk to identify evidence of corrupt activities. Mirror hard drives and other company-owned electronic devices and search files saved and/or deleted to identify documents, correspondence, calculations and images that may identify corrupt activity.

9.4.6. Unentitled discounts, denying entitled discounts and/or preferential pricing

Discussion

a. Suppliers

When the company is paying suppliers, the suppliers are frequently prepared to offer discounts in lieu of:

- Achieving greater sales volumes
- Being paid quicker/before contracted payment terms become prescribed
- To build longer-term relationships with clients
- To secure business, which may otherwise not have been secured.

Corrupt employees may collude with suppliers to pay them before credit terms fall due, with or without the entitled discount. Alternatively, the agreed preferential pricing may not be given.

b. Clients

When clients pay the company – Companies typically empower their sales and/or finance staff members to act on the company's behalf within a specific mandate/tolerances/limits. This may be for credit terms or pricing of products and services.

Corrupt clients may pay sales staff members a kickback for a discount given or extended payment terms received beyond what they are entitled to. The sales staff members may give prices to clients not entitled to them.

While the company may still be paid in full for the service/products, the company may be receiving less money if these unauthorised/invalid/unentitled terms were given. The company may also be exposed to undue risks.

The effect of fraudulent discounts can be seen in:

- Purchases and liabilities (suppliers – when the organisation is paying)
- Sales and debtors (clients – where the organisation is selling)
- Profits in so far as the effect of fraudulent transactions that affect sales and purchases may affect profits as well.

Observations/tips to identify and prove

Obtain sales contracts and/or standard terms and conditions and compare these to the actual rates, discounts and terms.

Conduct lifestyle audits to:

- Profile potential subjects
- Identify subjects whose lifestyles appear to have been financed from sources other than known/declared income sources (assets, credit applications, default judgments, etc)
- Identify conflicts of interest (business/personal) and/or undeclared interests (directorships, etc).

Interview subjects: staff members, competitors, etc. Conduct analytical reviews. Identify who performed the suspect transactions.

Conduct e-mail searches and general business related correspondence reviews to identify correspondence proving corrupt relationships. Conduct searches of the subject's general workspace and/or desk to identify evidence of corrupt activities. Mirror hard drives and other company-owned electronic devices and search files saved and/or deleted to identify documents, correspondence, calculations and images that may identify corrupt activity.

9.4.7. Unfairly extended credit terms

Discussion

In the same light as discounts, corrupt staff members may collude with a client to give the particular client credit terms beyond contractually agreed terms. While the client may be paying the full amount outstanding, the company will be receiving their money later. The company loses interest and there will be a negative impact on cash flow. The company will have been prejudiced.

The same may be applicable for suppliers of goods and services to the company. The supplier may collude with a corrupt employee to pay before the debt is due and/or not give the required discount for early payment.

The effect of credit terms will mostly be reflected in the assets (debtors) or liabilities (creditors) within the balance sheet depending on whether the company is receiving or giving discounts.

Observations/tips to identify and prove

Compare actual credit terms given to client/supplier contracts. In most cases, companies have overall contracts that apply to a fixed period. An electronic analysis of days' credit could easily be compared to the overall contract terms. Determine what the standard terms are and what negotiated terms are. Also, determine the authorisations required to deviate from standard terms.

Interview key staff, suppliers and subjects. Conduct analytical reviews to identify 'problem' suppliers/ clients. It is unlikely that the corrupt employee will collude with all or most of the suppliers/clients. Compare actual behaviour/patterns of subjects to other general clients/suppliers.

Conduct lifestyle audits to:

- Profile potential subjects
- Identify subjects whose lifestyles appear to have been financed from sources other than known/declared income sources (assets, credit applications, default judgments, etc)
- Identify conflicts of interest (business/personal) and/or undeclared interests (directorships, etc).

Conduct e-mail searches and general business related correspondence reviews to identify correspondence proving corrupt relationships. Conduct searches of the subject's general workspace and/or desk to identify evidence of corrupt activities. Mirror hard drives and other company owned electronic devices and search files saved and/or deleted to identify documents, correspondence, calculations and images that may identify corrupt activity.

9.4.8. Overpayments

Discussion

In this case, staff members overpay a supplier. If the supplier is a colluding party to the scheme, the supplier then 'repays' the overpayment in their books and shares the overpayment with the corrupt employee. Alternatively, if the supplier is not party to the fraud, the employee furnishes the supplier with a fraudulent bank account into which the refund should be paid.

The following example refers: In one case, the company's accounts receivables were managed centrally. The company had set up separate debtor accounts for each of its branches in which the same customer did business with them. Many of the branch debtor accounts had become disused, as some of the suppliers moved away from paying per branch. They were now making a single payment to the central head office debtors' account and not to the individual branch debtor accounts. The application of the funds was segregated from the other debtor functions. In this particular case, the debtors' clerk used to advise the receipt team to incorrectly apply the central funds to one of the disused debtor accounts for the customer.

The debtors' clerk had previously instructed the master file team (based on forged proof of bank details) to amend the client's bank details on the disused branch debtors' accounts to his own bank account details. He would then go to his supervisor and show how there had been an overpayment to a debtor's branch account. He requested his supervisor to approve a refund (unbeknown to the fraudulent bank account), as there was a credit balance in the disused account. The accounts were for high value and high-volume clients and the debtors' clerk was able to roll receipts to ensure that the clients' balances were not aged too badly. When the stress got too much for him, he resigned and the scheme was uncovered, but not until the company was defrauded of a sizable amount.

Observations/tips to identify and prove

Interview staff members, clients, subjects, etc.

Conduct lifestyle audits to:

- Profile potential subjects
- Identify subjects whose lifestyles appear to have been financed from sources other than known/declared income sources (assets, credit applications, default judgments, etc)
- Identify conflicts of interest (business/personal) and/or undeclared interests (directorships, etc).

Conduct e-mail searches and general business related correspondence reviews to identify correspondence proving corrupt relationships. Conduct searches of the subject's general workspace and/or desk to identify evidence of corrupt activities. Mirror hard drives and other company-owned electronic devices and search files saved and/or deleted to identify documents, correspondence, calculations and images that may identify corrupt activity.

Substantiate debtors' balances/conduct a debtors' certification. Substantiate refund payments for the period under review. Independently verify bank account details. Check supplier bank details electronically to staff members' bank details listed on the payroll.

9.4.9. Exploitation of staff discounts/ privilege and/or access to knowledge

Discussion

Some companies allow their staff members to purchase directly from their suppliers. This is subject to special conditions and/or approvals. This may or may not include buying on the company's account and using the company to fund (albeit temporarily) their private expenses. If not approved, this could prejudice the company's cash flow and cost of financed capital.

The payment on behalf of a staff member may attract fringe benefit taxes. The company could be subject to penalties if corrupt staff members circumvent this process/do not pay the required taxes.

In some countries, the payment on behalf of the staff member may also constitute a loan. Special laws may be applicable to staff loans and companies may incur penalties if they are seen to be acting as financial institutions, without the required authorisations.

Private expenditure will not qualify for the same tax concessions that the company expenditure is normally entitled to. Exploitation of this may, therefore, put the company at risk of penalties from the tax authorities.

Unfairly enjoying preferential pricing: pricing may be a privileged agreement between a supplier and the company (competitive advantage) and not something freely available to the public at large. The supplier may suspend the preferential agreements if they feel that the company is abusing this privilege.

One case comes to mind when the driver of a vehicle was buying excess stock and selling it privately for his own business interests and in direct competition (albeit on a small scale) to his employer. Luckily, in this case, the supplier did not find out and the employee was disciplined without the contract being cancelled.

In a similar light to the preferential pricing, it may be possible for corrupt employees to abuse the information that they are privy to with regards to a particular supplier/client.

Observations/tips to identify and prove

Try to understand what benefits the subject/s derived from the alleged corrupt scheme. Conduct interviews with suppliers, clients, staff members, subjects, family members and colleagues. Match payment details to employee records in the payroll files. Conduct analytical reviews.

Conduct lifestyle audits to:

- Profile potential subjects
- Identify subjects whose lifestyles appear to have been financed from sources other than known/declared income sources (assets, credit applications, default judgments, etc)
- Identify conflicts of interest (business/personal) and/or undeclared interests (directorships, etc).

Conduct e-mail searches and general business related correspondence reviews to identify correspondence proving corrupt relationships. Conduct searches of the subject's general workspace and/or desk to identify evidence of corrupt activities. Mirror hard drives and other company-owned electronic devices and search files saved and/or deleted to identify documents, correspondence, calculations and images that may identify corrupt activity. Substantiate actual payments. Compare payments to contractual terms/laws and regulations.

9.4.10. Payroll

Discussion

Payroll frauds were more commonplace a few years ago. Since then payroll systems have become quite sophisticated with embedded controls.

Payroll systems are frequently standalone systems or modules of a larger financial system. This has its advantages, including being segregated from the main financial system, but not being bound by the same more restrictive limitations that a financial system may have. A payroll system is essentially an 'operating system' and consequently has a lot of transactional and other data. So, they have more than just financial transactional data.

Disadvantages include that a separate system typically has fewer 'eyes' on it. Only summary entries are passed through to the financial system and it is difficult for financial staff members to understand the movement of payroll transactions month-on-month.

Payrolls can be administered in-house or be outsourced or be a combination of both. There are numerous attractions to outsourced payrolls. Outsourced payrolls imply specialisation of skill and economies of scale and segregation. You would be wise to consider that outsourcing normally comes at a cost premium and they tend to be bureaus doing as they are told. Outsourced payrolls are normally measured on productivity-type KPIs and not on control KPIs or on end-to-end business process KPIs. As a result, they may be keener to process a transaction just to ensure that their productivity-based KPIs reflect that they are processing all transactions and processing them within a prescribed period. *I have seen numerous examples where fraudsters are still able to manage their schemes remotely by giving instructions to transitional, low-cost, KPI-driven offshored offices, while management comforts themselves that they are keeping costs down. My tone may suggest where my bias lies. I am an auditor and I like control, so I tend to prefer in-house functions.*

As a rule, payrolls of salaried staff members are less prone to fraud. This is because there tend to be fewer salaried staff members than wage-earning staff members. Consequently, there are more eyes on fewer people, which normally means that fraud is less likely to be perpetrated if there is a higher chance of being discovered.

I also believe that management is generally more cost-conscious these days and they have more information at their disposal to monitor trends. There tends, therefore, to be more regular and in-depth control of department costs.

When 'salaried' fraud is perpetrated though, it tends to be of a higher value per case.

I have noted in general that there tends to be more movement (engagements and terminations) of wage-earning staff members than salaried staff members. Variations (erroneous or fraudulent) are consequently more difficult to detect and there is not a constant baseline to compare to. There also tends to be a higher number of waged staff members and it may be easier to conceal fraud in higher numbers of staff.

Payroll frauds can be perpetrated by:

- Management wanting to hide expenditure or over- or understate expenses, evade tax payments, etc
- Payroll staff members who have access to the systems and who are able to process payments
- Salaried employees themselves by misstating information
- Management in charge of staff members and/or cost centres, to keep terminated employees on the payroll or to add ghost employees to the payroll, etc
- Outside people. There are a few rare examples of where outsiders have gained physical access to payroll environments. A friend or partner would need to give them access to the environment. There they would need access to systems. The advent of web-based systems provides an easier accessible method to perpetrate this.
- Outsourced companies, as with in-house payroll staff members
- Banks processing payment transactions
- External companies, such as medical or pension companies, debt collectors, etc.

Observations/tips to identify and prove

The positive aspect is that payroll environments are restricted (physically, computer systems and documents) from general access. There is less opportunity for people to perpetrate fraud in this environment. There is also an expectation that there should be more control in a payroll environment. It also means that when fraud has been perpetrated, there are fewer people to focus on.

Payroll environments also typically require much documentation and approval by many managers, etc. This means that there is a transactional and approval trail and that it is easier to obtain documentary evidence and to prove accountability.

In a similar light, there are normally well-defined transactions by which to process payroll transactions. This means more control and it also means that it is easier to identify who performed the transaction and exactly what happened and where the money went.

Conduct lifestyle audits to:

- Profile potential subjects
- Identify subjects whose lifestyles appear to have been financed from sources other than known/declared income sources (assets, credit applications, default judgments, etc)
- Identify conflicts of interest (business/personal) and/or undeclared interests (directorships, etc).

a. Key field amendments

Discussion

The fraudulent amendment of key fields on the payroll system can be a means by which fraud is perpetrated.

The invalid amendment of bank records is one such example how a payment can be made to an unentitled party. Further examples of these are discussed below.

Observations/tips to identify and prove

If you are embarking on a proactive fraud identification method, then one method is to identify the key fields within the payroll system, which if invalidly amended could result in fraud. Obtain an independent extract of these amendments and substantiate them. Specific examples are discussed below.

b. Fictitious employees

Discussion

Fictitious employees are typically referred to as 'ghost' employees and are employees who do not exist and/or to whom the company has no contractual obligation of remuneration. The ghost employee has been set up on the payroll and they are being paid despite not having performed any contractually payable work for the company and/or do not exist in reality.

Some or all of the fictitious employee's details may be legitimate. Fraudsters may make use of some legitimate details in an attempt to portray the fictitious employee as a legitimate employee.

Examples of fictitious employees include:

- Setting up a new employee on the payroll (new engagement) who does not exist at all
- Duplicating an existing employee on the payroll
- Failing to terminate an employee on the payroll on their actual date of termination. The terminated employee's bank details are then typically fraudulently altered to the subject's bank details. Alternatively, the terminated employee shares the ill-gotten funds with a colluding employee still within the company.

Observations/tips to identify and prove

One of the most trusted methods of detecting ghost employees is to note that ghost employees generally do not make use of health/medical, pensions or other benefits. They also do not pay tax. The corrupt employee will normally only receive the basic pay portion of the ghost employee. Check to see which employees do not have such benefits or do not pay tax.

External institutions (to whom benefits are paid, eg pension funds) may require some other verification which the subject may want to avoid for fear of detection.

It will be very difficult for or unlikely that a fraudster will set up a fictitious employee as a tax-paying individual. The fraudster may very well make use of a false number just to complete a required field or they may make use of someone else's genuine tax number.

Check for legitimate:

- Identity numbers - these normally have some form of parity digit check built into them.
- Tax numbers - these can normally be verified on a government website. In addition check for duplicate tax numbers as you would check for duplicate bank numbers. There should never be an example of a duplicate tax number for the same period.
- Addresses - check electronically for duplicate address criteria (see below). There are also places were postal codes can be downloaded and used to check against those listed in the system.

Check for duplicate bank accounts and/or address and telephone details on the payroll system. This is an exercise which is easily done with the help of data analytics software, which will have standard functionality to conduct duplicate tests of uploaded files.

Ensure that you conduct the check across all payrolls relevant. *In one company where I worked, they had in excess of five payrolls (eg company A, company B, salaried staff members, waged staff members and executives). They were luckily all on the same payroll program and all fields pulled into my audit file were identical. I obtained extracts of each and combined them all into one large file (over 30 000 lines) on which I conducted my tests. In this case, I identified five 'duplicate' bank accounts for employees. All were subsequently verified (sisters, boyfriend and girlfriend, etc) and there was no fraud detected. The data analytical test helped me identify potential duplicate bank accounts, which was not possible to do visually across different payrolls.*

Physically verify the existence of all staff members. If there are geographic challenges or the numbers of staff members are prohibitive, then concentrate on the highest risk areas first or enlist the help of independent parties (not the management responsible for the cost centre or the payroll staff members themselves).

Another manner to verify if staff members physically exist is to verify payroll records against other independent records, eg building access records, computer system log-on files, driver logs, site records, parking records, permits, store booking records, such as the booking out of equipment or personal protective clothing, etc.

Hold verification discussions with colleagues, supervisors and management. Some of the people you interview may, however, be the perpetrators of the crime. Promote the use of a whistle-blower line through which staff members can report irregularities.

Conduct analytical reviews of:

- Payments over time (peaks and valleys)
- Benefits to pay
- Average cost per employee
- Monthly movement (number and value) of staff members over time.

Conduct lifestyle audits to:

- Profile potential subjects
- Identify subjects whose lifestyles appear to have been financed from sources other than known/declared income sources (assets, credit applications, default judgments, etc)
- Identify conflicts of interest (business/personal) and/or undeclared interests (directorships, etc).

Identify who requested for the employee to be created or amended or who performed the transaction on the payroll system. Check if there is anything unusual about the person who did this (eg it is not part of their normal responsibilities).

Analyse the updates of all key fields (eg bank detail fields) to determine if these are valid or not. Conduct e-mail searches and general business related correspondence reviews to identify correspondence proving corrupt relationships. Conduct searches of the subject's general workspace and/or desk to identify evidence of corrupt activities. Mirror hard drives and other company-owned electronic devices and search files saved and/or deleted to identify documents, correspondence, calculations and images that may identify corrupt activity.

c. Pay rate changes

Discussion

Pay rate changes are also a relatively easy method to perpetrate payroll fraud on a smaller/ individual scale. The subject increases the employee's pay rate (normally per hour rate or day rate). This may be done as a once-off transaction or it may be done as part of a scheduled annual pay rate change process.

Observations/tips to identify and prove

Electronically extract all pay rates per employee. Also, ensure that you extract the field that differentiates between the pay rates (eg job grade). Compare the full file of all employees' pay rates to an independent file of pay rates.

Conduct lifestyle audits to:

- Profile potential subjects
- Identify subjects whose lifestyles appear to have been financed from sources other than known/declared income sources (assets, credit applications, default judgments, etc)
- Identify conflicts of interest (business/personal) and/or undeclared interests (directorships, etc).

Interview staff members and subjects. Leave staff members with a whistle-blowing mechanism. Review the actual approved annual pay rate sheets. If these are correct, review these against the actual rates on the system (to ensure that they were captured correctly). Analyse who performed the rate change and when it was performed. Determine if there is anything unusual about the person who performed it (eg they do not normally deal with those employees) or the time that it was done (eg is an annual process only).

Identify what the rule is for pay rate changes. If the rule only applies to a certain number of employees for a particular period (eg mid-year reviews or ad hoc promotions) then obtain an independent extract of all employees who had pay rate changes in the period under review and substantiate these.

Conduct e-mail searches and general business related correspondence reviews to identify correspondence proving corrupt relationships. Conduct searches of the subject's general workspace and/or desk to identify evidence of corrupt activities. Mirror hard drives and other company-owned electronic devices and search files saved and/or deleted to identify documents, correspondence, calculations and images that may identify corrupt activity.

d. Fictitious hours

Discussion

Employees themselves or their supervisors or colluding payroll staff members could fraudulently increase the number of hours/days worked. This level of fraud is normally limited to specific individuals (as opposed to groups of people) and would most likely not be material compared to the company's turnover.

Observations/tips to identify and prove

Verify the days/hours claimed on the payroll system against the actual completed timesheets or attendance registers or access records. These may be general department attendance registers or per job sheets.

If possible verify against independent records as well. *One matter comes to mind which I investigated in a service-type company. I contacted the client for whom we were rendering the service and informed them that I was conducting a standard audit. I asked them if they would be willing to supply me with their own company's access records for our staff members for the period of the job. The client was more than willing to assist. I also obtained vehicle tracking records. The client access records and vehicle tracking records matched and were therefore proven to be credible and reliable as evidence. These did not however match the number of days claimed to have been worked on the payroll system.*

Conduct e-mail searches and general business related correspondence reviews to identify correspondence proving corrupt relationships. Conduct searches of the subject's general workspace and/or desk to identify evidence of corrupt activities. Mirror hard drives and other company owned electronic devices and search files saved and/or deleted to identify documents, correspondence, calculations and images that may identify corrupt activity.

Conduct lifestyle audits to:

- Profile potential subjects
- Identify subjects whose lifestyles appear to have been financed from sources other than known/declared income sources (assets, credit applications, default judgments, etc)
- Identify conflicts of interest (business/personal) and/or undeclared interests (directorships, etc).

e. Status changes

Discussion

Companies make use of job grades or the like to depict an employee's relative status in the organisation. Companies tend to use standard systems (eg the 'Patterson' job grading system).

Job grade and/or status level determines pay rates, bonus entitlements, share schemes, eligibility for promotion, etc.

If payroll staff members or managers or employees fraudulently amend an employee's status (position, job title) on the payroll system, this may result in the employee being eligible for promotions, larger bonuses, etc.

Status changes occur as an ad hoc transaction (eg a person being promoted at any time within the year) or it may be part of an annual grade increase/status change process.

Observations/tips to identify and prove

Check the actual status levels as reflected on the payroll system against the actual approved status change sheets that were circulated to the responsible managers.

Analyse who performed the status change and when it was performed. Determine if there is anything unusual about the person who performed it (eg they do not normally deal with those employees) or the time that it was done (eg if it is an annual process only).

Substantiate all status changes tested against the required formal authorisation. Status changes are normally summarised on a status change sheet per payroll. There may be multiple versions of the status sheets leading up to the final version. No unauthorised changes should be made to these after approval.

Interview staff members and subjects. Conduct analytical reviews to identify out of trend statuses.

Conduct lifestyle audits to:

- Profile potential subjects
- Identify subjects whose lifestyles appear to have been financed from sources other than known/declared income sources (assets, credit applications, default judgments, etc)
- Identify conflicts of interest (business/personal) and/or undeclared interests (directorships, etc).

Conduct e-mail searches and general business related correspondence reviews to identify correspondence proving corrupt relationships. Conduct searches of the subject's general workspace and/or desk to identify evidence of corrupt activities. Mirror hard drives and other company owned electronic devices and search files saved and/or deleted to identify documents, correspondence, calculations and images that may identify corrupt activity.

f. Staff loans

Discussion

Many companies have a policy of allowing staff members to borrow money. Some of these loan schemes are administered internally. Others are outsourced to financial institutions with the organisation just referring the employee to the financial institution. The company has generally already negotiated easier credit policies or favourable general terms for all employees.

Loans can be for any number of reasons, including:

- A straight loan to assist an employee to finance a private expense
- A secured loan, eg on the strength of their pension fund
- Staff purchases for company products or supplier products
- Private expenses eg incurred on a business trip
- Excessive expenses, eg private phone calls on a company phone
- Outstanding amounts for errors, overpayments made by the company
- Uncompleted obligations to the company (eg study schemes)
- Pure study loans
- Damages, eg the employee incurs a traffic fine in a company vehicle for which they are liable
- Shortages, eg some companies hold their staff members personally liable for cash shortages in the till.

Not all 'loans' are real loans. For example:

- Cash advances given to employees are often recorded against an employee's name until they bring back the supporting expense documents and unused funds.
- A company may pay for an employee's studies on the condition that they work a fixed period of time. The study expenses may be held against the employee's name and expensed as the obligation is met.

There are two elements applicable to loans, being the:

- Awarding of loans - may be awarded to an employee who is not entitled to receive a loan or for an amount above what they are entitled to.
- Repayment of loans - the loans may never be repaid.

A couple of examples of fraud cases come to mind:

- *We were told as part of interviewing staff members in a fraud investigation that the local company MD (subject of a wider fraud investigation) had been 'granted' a loan, but that he had never made any repayments against the loan. The nature of this business was also that the expatriate staff members typically worked two to three years in a position before moving to another position or moving completely out of the group. There was a good chance that the MD had planned never to repay the outstanding loan before exiting the group. The authorisation of the loan was outside of the MD's powers and the non-repayment was outside of company policy. The MD was implicated in numerous other fraudulent activities and chose to resign and leave the country before we could report the matter to the local authorities.*
- *In this case the company had legitimately negotiated preferential lending for its low-earning staff members from a micro-lender. In this way, the company was able to assist its staff members, but without the administrative burden. Repayment was done via the payroll and the micro-lender was guaranteed its payment before the employee was paid. The payroll clerk embarked on two frauds. Firstly, she started her own illegal lending scheme to non-qualifying employees over and above the legitimate scheme. She took a fee from them for this 'service'. She then also misappropriated some of the repaid funds and rolled the repayment of other employees to cover the misappropriated funds. The scheme was found out as a result of complaining employees.*

Observations/tips to identify and prove

Identify the loan rules and compare actual loans granted against these. Loans should be granted to relatively few employees and it may be practical to conduct a 100% check of all loans granted as per the payroll system depending on the organisation's size. Check the following:

- Do the employees qualify for the loan?
- Was the amount granted appropriate and approved?
- Was the interest rate correct?
- Were the correct taxes applied?
- Was the loan authorised correctly?
- Is repayment made according to the terms and company policy?

- Is the loan scheme legal in terms of the local country's laws?
- Were all procedures followed (eg loan contracts signed, credit checks performed to determine affordability, etc)?

Interview staff members and subjects and managers charged with approval. The example of the MD's loan case refers. Conduct analytical reviews to identify out of trend loans.

Conduct lifestyle audits to:

- Profile potential subjects
- Identify subjects whose lifestyles appear to have been financed from sources other than known/declared income sources (assets, credit applications, default judgments, etc)
- Identify conflicts of interest (business/personal) and/or undeclared interests (directorships, etc).

Check to see if there is anything unusual about the person requesting, approving and 'receiving' the loan. Check also if there is something unusual about the timing of the granting of the loan (eg at bonus time when everyone is expected to be 'cash-flush' and repaying old loans and not incurring new ones).

Follow the payment of the loaned funds from the company to the recipient to ensure that the correct person received the funds. *In the payroll clerk's example, the employees were relatively unsophisticated and they did not keep track of the many loans that they had had and where they stood in terms of repayments. They were used to seeing loan deductions on their payslips.*

Fraudsters are also quick to say that money taken was actually a loan from the company. Check the circumstances, substantiate the approval, the amount, etc against other 'legitimate' loans to identify differences.

Another case comes to mind. Before I give the background, let me start with a question. If an employee takes petty cash on the Friday and puts the exact amount back in the petty cash box on a Monday, has fraud been perpetrated?

The answer is yes, definitely. I normally start to explain this by asking people if their car was taken without their permission on the Friday and then returned to them by the police on the Monday, has a crime been committed against them? The unequivocal reply is yes! Well, this is very similar. The unauthorised use of company assets (vehicles, cash, etc) is fraud or theft in the least. In some countries, there is case law to support this.

Some factors to consider in this case are:

- Did the person act outside of their authorisation?
- Was the company placed at any risk of loss?
- Did the company suffer any loss (non-repayment, damages, interest lost, transaction fee, etc)?
- Was the act within policy?
- How does this purported loan compare to other legitimate loans?
- Was the person entitled to it?
- What was the precedent?
- Would they have repaid it if their act was not identified?

- How many times before have they done this (this speaks to intent, not that they were allowed to do it because they had got away with it before)?

Conduct e-mail searches and general business related correspondence reviews to identify correspondence proving corrupt relationships. Conduct searches of the subject's general workspace and/or desk to identify evidence of corrupt activities. Mirror hard drives and other company-owned electronic devices and search files saved and/or deleted to identify documents, correspondence, calculations and images that may identify corrupt activity.

g. Unentitled benefits

Discussion

Similar to irregular status changes, managers, supervisors, employees or payroll staff members may fraudulently request and/or process transactions on the payroll system to grant unentitled benefits to an employee.

A special type of benefit that may occur will be those that are paid during retrenchments. The country's law may be to pay one-week severance per completed year. Company policy may be to pay two weeks per year for non-executives and three weeks for executives. Check in this example what actual benefit was received by the employee.

Observations/tips to identify and prove

Determine the company policies for all benefits. Identify all benefit field updates within the period under review and substantiate these to the rules and supporting documents.

Determine if there was anything unusual about the person requesting, authorising or performing the benefit update. Determine if there is anything unusual about the period updated as well.

Conduct interviews with staff members and subjects.

Conduct lifestyle audits to:

- Profile potential subjects
- Identify subjects whose lifestyles appear to have been financed from sources other than known/declared income sources (assets, credit applications, default judgments, etc)
- Identify conflicts of interest (business/personal) and/or undeclared interests (directorships, etc).

Conduct analytical reviews, including:

- Benefits per employee over time
- Benefits to other payments and income over time.

Conduct e-mail searches and general business related correspondence reviews to identify correspondence proving corrupt relationships. Conduct searches of the subject's general workspace and/or desk to identify evidence of corrupt activities. Mirror hard drives and other company-owned electronic devices and search files saved and/or deleted to identify documents, correspondence, calculations and images that may identify corrupt activity.

h. Payroll tax evasion

Discussion

Tax is a grudge payment for anyone. Employers may want to pay lower taxes over to the authorities in an attempt to reduce 'costs'/increase 'income'. The tax authorities typically (unlike normal creditors) rely on a company's declaration of what is owed to them. It may only be tax inspections that expose incorrect tax declarations.

Management and/or employees may also want to fraudulently reduce their personal tax liabilities. They may fraudulently alter their tax liability.

Taxes may be reduced by:

- Not including all income for tax calculation
- Claiming invalid deductions
- Using invalid rates (eg those applicable to lower earning employees)
- Invalid calculations.

In one case, the financial manager was misappropriating funds (credit to the bank) and booking the debit to the tax liability account. The books balanced and no one was the wiser.

Observations/tips to identify and prove

Determine applicable taxes and understand the basis of calculation. Substantiate questionable subjects' personal taxes. Substantiate the company's liabilities and payments.

Follow total tax liabilities according to the respective systems through to the actual payment to ensure that they were paid completely, accurately and on time. Identify any manual journals or other transactions that amend the liability. Conduct analytical reviews.

Conduct lifestyle audits to:

- Profile potential subjects
- Identify subjects whose lifestyles appear to have been financed from sources other than known/declared income sources (assets, credit applications, default judgments, etc)
- Identify conflicts of interest (business/personal) and/or undeclared interests (directorships, etc).

Interview staff members and subjects. Conduct e-mail searches and general business related correspondence reviews to identify correspondence proving corrupt relationships. Conduct searches of the subject's general workspace and/or desk to identify evidence of corrupt activities. Mirror hard drives and other company-owned electronic devices and search files saved and/or deleted to identify documents, correspondence, calculations and images that may identify corrupt activity.

i. Fraudulent incomes

Discussion

Fraudulent incomes could be due to the aforementioned rate changes, volume changes, benefit changes or status changes. Incomes could also be added by some other means directly (income codes, payroll transaction or manually) to an employee's remuneration. The latter will depend on the individual payroll's functionality and sophistication.

Examples of incomes include:

- Salary
- Wages
- Bonuses
- Commissions
- Profit shares.

Observations/tips to identify and prove

Determine which incomes the subject is entitled to. Independently obtain the payroll transactional history of the subject and substantiate all incomes received by them. Try to obtain as much data as is available and go back as far as possible. Interview managers, supervisors, employees and subjects.

Conduct lifestyle audits to:

- Profile potential subjects
- Identify subjects whose lifestyles appear to have been financed from sources other than known/declared income sources (assets, credit applications, default judgments, etc)
- Identify conflicts of interest (business/personal) and/or undeclared interests (directorships, etc).

Conduct analytical reviews. Identify who processed and approved the fraudulent incomes for the employee. Conduct e-mail searches and general business related correspondence reviews to identify correspondence proving corrupt relationships. Conduct searches of the subject's general workspace and/or desk to identify evidence of corrupt activities. Mirror hard drives and other company-owned electronic devices and search files saved and/or deleted to identify documents, correspondence, calculations and images that may identify corrupt activity.

j. Fraudulent deductions

Discussion - Fraudulent deductions can take many forms, including:

- Companies deducting/withholding funds from employees that they are not entitled to or which they may not legally do in that manner.
- Employees not making specific/any/the full deductions that they are required to make.
- Making deductions at incorrect rates.
- Employees making deductions for benefits that they are not entitled to.
- External companies (such as debt collectors) claiming fraudulent deductions (in total or over what is due).

Examples of deductions include:

- Pension/retirement funding
- Medical scheme payments
- Loans
- Taxes.

While it is academically the employee's responsibility to ensure that their remuneration and deductions are correct, there is an obligation on the employer to ensure that everything reasonable is done to ensure that deductions are correct.

One example comes to mind where the company was paying a garnishee order to a debt collector. This is not an example of employee fraud. It is an example of negligence on the company's part. The company did not put the full amount owing on the payroll system (like a loan) and they kept paying over the monthly instalment expecting the debt collector to advise when the full amount had been recovered from the employee. In this case, the company had significantly overpaid the debt collector. I advised them in future to treat the garnishee order on the payroll system like a loan paid to a third party. In this manner, the system would automatically suspend payment once the amount was repaid.

Observations/tips to identify and prove

Determine which deductions the subject is entitled to and for how much. Independently obtain the payroll transactional history of the subject and substantiate all deductions paid by them. Try to obtain as much data as is available and go back as far as possible. Interview managers, supervisors, employees and subjects.

Conduct lifestyle audits to:

- Profile potential subjects
- Identify subjects whose lifestyles appear to have been financed from sources other than known/declared income sources (assets, credit applications, default judgments, etc)
- Identify conflicts of interest (business/personal) and/or undeclared interests (directorships, etc).

Conduct analytical reviews. Identify who processed and approved the fraudulent deductions for the employee. Conduct e-mail searches and general business related correspondence reviews to identify correspondence proving corrupt relationships. Conduct searches of the subject's general workspace and/or desk to identify evidence of corrupt activities. Mirror hard drives and other company-owned electronic devices and search files saved and/or deleted to identify documents, correspondence, calculations and images that may identify corrupt activity.

k. Commissions frauds

Discussion

Commissions are one type of income mentioned above. Companies pay commissions to incentivise agents/employees to secure business on their behalf.

Commission fraud could take the form of:

- Commission being claimed that the subject is not entitled to at all. As an example, insurance brokers claiming commission on policies never sold.
- Commission earned by in-house employees when commission is only paid to external independent salespeople. For example, a customer service agent sitting at a desk may not be entitled to commission as customers walk in themselves. An external agent that

goes from door to door may be entitled to commission, as they are going out and getting the business. In this example, the in-house customer service agent writes up the walk-in-trade as if they have concluded the sale door-to-door.
- Paying commission not according to the commission scales.
- Having to pay a portion of commission as a 'finder's fee'/facilitation/kickback for getting the business.

In certain industries, it is normal practice for anyone referring business to receive a finder's fee. This is however transparent and according to known scales.

Observations/tips to identify and prove

Understand the organisation's commission rules or policies and procedures. Recalculate and substantiate commission payments against the rules.

Conduct lifestyle audits to:

- Profile potential subjects
- Identify subjects whose lifestyles appear to have been financed from sources other than known/declared income sources (assets, credit applications, default judgments, etc)
- Identify conflicts of interest (business/personal) and/or undeclared interests (directorships, etc).

Conduct analytical reviews, including:

- Commissions per employee over time
- Commissions in relation to sales of production volumes.

Identify who processed and approved the fraudulent commission payments. Conduct e-mail searches and general business related correspondence reviews to identify correspondence proving corrupt relationships. Conduct searches of the subject's general workspace and/or desk to identify evidence of corrupt activities. Mirror hard drives and other company-owned electronic devices and search files saved and/or deleted to identify documents, correspondence, calculations and images that may identify corrupt activity.

9.4.11. HR fraud

Discussion

Payroll is the transactional side and HR is the qualitative side of dealing with employees.

HR activities may include:

- Recruitments
- Terminations
- Training and development
- Industrial relations and conflict resolution
- Union negotiations
- Policy setting.

Candidates may in a recruitment campaign:

- Falsify their qualifications or experience.
- Give fictitious references.
- Inflate current emoluments when applying for a job in the hope that the new company will give them a fixed markup on their current purported cost-to-company. I had an auditor applying for a job with me many years ago do this. Needless to say, we withdrew our offer quickly. There is no sense appointing a person who has demonstrated dishonesty even before being employed.
- Not declare or falsify criminal records. In one example, a clear criminal record was a requirement for travel visa purposes for the job. The candidate falsified his clearance certificate and we opened a criminal case and let the police deal with the individual.
- Not declaring illness in situations where health is a job prerequisite.

Other HR frauds include:

- Favouritism, cronyism, nepotism in recruitment or when promotions are done
- Coaching of candidates in advance of selection criteria
- Favouritism when training and benefits are awarded
- Applying different standards to different employees
- Overlooking/not declaring/expunging previous performance factors (hearings, etc) or destroying of such records
- Unfair awarding of incentive schemes to employees not qualifying
- Unfair dismissal of an internal labour tribunal matter
- Unfair/inconsistent sanctions handed down in labour tribunal of employees. 'Unfair' in this case is not a matter of legal opinion. It is the actual and intentional unfair action.
- Failure to record the true reasons for an employee leaving on the payroll system. The employee is then reemployed in another company in the group some time later.

Observations/tips to identify and prove

HR matters mostly need to be handled on a case-by-case basis. For the greater part, we as investigators would not get involved in pure 'HR' matters. Investigators would only get involved where the allegation is fraudulent in nature.

For the action in question:

- Determine if the act could have been fraudulent.
- Identify the rules and compare the actual actions to the standard.

Interview staff and subjects. Try to determine trends, practice and precedents. Determine if there is anything strange about the person that made the HR amendment? Are they authorised to do this? Is it part of what they normally do?

Conduct lifestyle audits to:

- Profile potential subjects
- Identify subjects whose lifestyles appear to have been financed from sources other than known/declared income sources (assets, credit applications, default judgments, etc)

- Identify conflicts of interest (business/personal) and/or undeclared interests (directorships, etc).

Conduct e-mail searches and general business related correspondence reviews to identify correspondence proving corrupt relationships. Conduct searches of the subject's general workspace and/or desk to identify evidence of corrupt activities. Mirror hard drives and other company-owned electronic devices and search files saved and/or deleted to identify documents, correspondence, calculations and images that may identify corrupt activity.

9.4.12. Journals

Discussion

Manual journals are high-risk transactions as they give the author of the journal the ability to move about in the accounting system and process transactions without standard accounting constraints. Automated and/or standard transactions imply a standard or anticipated set of rules. It is less likely that fraudulent transactions are performed via standard or automated transactions. Manual journals are discussed here as they are frequently the method through which fraudulent transactions are processed and/or hidden.

I have observed that many fraudulent transactions are performed via manual journals. You are strongly advised to regard manual journals with caution.

Manual journals can be used for many reasons including:

- To process month-end transactions
- To process once-off transactions not defined within the financial system
- For corrections that cannot be processed via standard system transactions (eg customer credit notes)
- Intercompany journals/transactions.

Numerous examples come to mind:

- *A finance clerk was making fraudulent cheque payments to herself. These were appearing as reconciling items on the bank statement. She was able to manipulate the bank reconciliation for a while. She then started to post the payments to general ledger accounts (sales) where she thought they would not be detected. As it turned out she was unaware of a reconciliation that the manager performed on the sales account. The corresponding credit was to the bank account. The sales reconciliation did not balance and the manager, upon closer inspection, found it most unusual to see all the debits to the sales account. He then called me to help him understand. I easily identified the fraud.*
- *In another instance, fraudulent employees were accruing for non-existent income. A simple substantiation of the accruals by my colleague showed that there was no basis whatsoever for the income accruals. He later obtained admissions and evidence to prove that income was being artificially inflated to cover misappropriation of funds and for performance bonus reasons.*

Observations/tips to identify and prove

As an investigator, you should expect to see certain controls in place to mitigate the higher risks associated with them. Their absence may imply reason for concern. Good practice controls over manual journals include:

- Pre-numbered files of sequentially filled journals
- Pre-approval of journals prior to posting
- Suspension of journals on the accounting system, pending online approval if the system allows for journals to be captured prior to a manual authorisation
- Defence files of documents in support of journals
- Monthly or weekly system printouts of all manual journals processed in the period, placed on the front of the defence file
- Managerial completeness and validity check of supporting documents in the defence file against the printout of manual journals processed in the period
- Periodic audit of a sample of journals
- External audit review of key manual journals.

When investigating manual journals:

- Obtain a printout of all manual journals (normally identified by a system indicator) processed on the system in the period under review.
- Check that documents adequately support each journal.
- Identify the normal reasons for using manual journals.
- Compare the actual reasons for journals against the normal reasons why they should have been used.
- Identify the policy and procedure for manual journals.
- Identify journals that were processed outside of the policy guidelines.
- Identify journals processed after the event.
- Identify unapproved journals.
- Look for trends (type, reason, accounts, suppliers, clients, employee processing, period, etc) and exceptional transactions.
- Conduct analytical reviews.
- Identify and substantiate all journal entries between unusual general ledger accounts.

Interview staff members, subjects, journal approvers and external auditors.

Conduct lifestyle audits to:

- Profile potential subjects
- Identify subjects whose lifestyles appear to have been financed from sources other than known/declared income sources (assets, credit applications, default judgments, etc)
- Identify conflicts of interest (business/personal) and/or undeclared interests (directorships, etc).

Conduct e-mail searches and general business related correspondence reviews to identify correspondence proving corrupt relationships. Conduct searches of the subject's general workspace and/or desk to identify evidence of corrupt activities. Mirror hard drives and other company-owned electronic devices and search files saved and/or deleted to identify documents, correspondence, calculations and images that may identify corrupt activity.

9.4.13. Financial statement fraud

Discussion

Financial misstatement frauds are less common, but when they occur they normally amount to sizable amounts. Understanding the 'why' and the 'who' may provide you with valuable insights during your investigation.

Those who will perpetrate financial misstatement fraud may include:

- Shareholders and/or owners
- Holding companies
- Directors and/or senior management
- Prospective buyers/investors
- Financial institutions
- Creditors
- Tender boards.

To begin to understand financial statement fraud, you have to appreciate what financial statements are used for. Financial statements give a 'picture-in-time' view of (mostly) the financial position of an organisation. Try to consider who would have wanted to project a better picture (or in some cases a worse picture) of the financial position of the company.

Why they may want to do this could include:

- To obtain finance by presenting a financially stronger picture
- Not to be dismissed for poor financial performance
- Contracts may be terminated/not renewed based on the relative financial position
- To avoid review by showing a better trend/financial level
- To obtain bonuses/commissions
- To allow certain contracts to commence.

Fraud can be demonstrated in one of two ways on financial statements:

- The first is the purposeful misstatement of figures and other information for a fraudulent purpose. It may be for the purpose to conceal another fraud or to portray a different picture than reality. This may just be the incorrect statement of information and figures without the actual processing of transactions through the financial system. For example, let us say that the assets are actually worth USD 100. I then simply record that the assets are worth USD 1000 in the financial statements. No transactions performed and no connection to the actual underlying financial records, just a pure printing of a value. Alternatively, financial transactions may be processed for the sole purpose of misstating the financial statements. For example, a fraudster has processed many fraudulent payments. The fraudster now puts fraudulent entries through in the financial records, for example: crediting the bank and debiting accrued expenses in the balance sheet.
- The second is that the effect of another fraud scheme may be seen in the financial statements. For example, I sold a fixed asset without permission and at below the market price to a colluding external party. The fixed asset is no longer in the balance sheet and the receipt is not carried in the bank account. This is not financial statement fraud. The

financial statements are just one of the company records in which we can see the effects of the fraud. The purpose was not to misstate the financial statements. I may need to misstate the financial statements by some or other means to conceal my fraud, but my initial intent was the unlawful sale of the asset.

The intention is what defines if it is financial misstatement fraud or not. The discussion below will be a combination of both situations.

Financial misstatement fraud can occur in almost any aspect of the financial statements. We therefore basically need to consider every aspect of the financial statements, as per below.

Periods of higher risk of fraud in this area may include:

- When migrating legacy data to new/ERP systems
- Purchase of/merger with/sale of a company/division/brand
- At the time when funding/financing is being sought
- At a time when a significant deal is to go through
- When profits are significantly down and/or in tough trading conditions
- When management/executives are highly incentivised based on profit performance.

Observations/tips to identify and prove

As a general rule, it is advisable to consider what the corresponding entry was or should have been.

Specific examples are discussed below.

Section B - Balance sheet

Discussion

One trick I have learnt is to work through the figures in the balance sheet and to look for out of trend figures or for things that you are not expecting to see or that are conspicuous by their absence.

9.4.14. Owners' equity/share capital

Discussion

A misstatement of owner's equity could conceal ownership ratios and distort earning (dividends, profit share, etc) sharing.

This can be done by:

- Purely misstating the actual numbers of shares or the value without any further transactions or link to the underlying records.
- Issuing more shares for sale to some members and excluding others. This would change the ownership ratio.
- Selling shares without permission (reducing ownership) and/or without giving first option to existing shareholders, as may be required.

In one matter I dealt with, one of the major owners of a group of companies was concerned that his co-owners may have amended the company shareholdings without his permission to reduce his rightful share and to diminish his voting ability. My client was responsible for the international business, while the co-owners were responsible for the local business. I checked some 54 companies at the registered auditors and all ownership was confirmed as being in order and un-amended.

Your tests should verify:

- All classes of shares
- The number of shares in total
- The ratio of issued shares between shareholders. Have more shares been issued thereby affecting the ownership of the company?

Observations/tips to identify and prove

Go the registered external auditors/accounting officer/company lawyers and obtain the articles of association or shareholder agreements. Obtain the registered ownership certificates. For listed companies, obtain a shareholder register from the stock exchange. You may require permission from the company for this.

Checked the audited financial statements against the shareholding certificates. This will verify the total shareholding. Where available verify the individual ownership listed with the individuals themselves.

Conduct lifestyle audits to:

- Profile potential subjects
- Identify subjects whose lifestyles appear to have been financed from sources other than known/declared income sources (assets, credit applications, default judgments, etc)
- Identify conflicts of interest (business/personal) and/or undeclared interests (directorships, etc).

9.4.15. Debentures

Discussion

Debentures are a type of loan. The company sells a tradable financial instrument and guarantees a fixed return. At the end of the period, the company may/will buy the financial instrument back at the face value of the debenture. Determine the individual debenture requirements applicable to the instrument that you are dealing with. Debenture holders do not normally have any voting rights. They also do not have any earning rights over the debentures listed earning (interest-based). It is therefore unlikely that there will be any manipulation of these. The correctness, completeness and timing of the income payments should be confirmed as applicable. The over or understating of the company's liability may be a risk.

Observations/tips to identify and prove

Confirm the total issued debentures. Confirm the validity, completeness, accuracy and timing of all payments. Independently verify the number of debentures held and issued. Check board meeting minutes and annual general meeting minutes.

Conduct lifestyle audits to:

- Profile potential subjects
- Identify subjects whose lifestyles appear to have been financed from sources other than known/declared income sources (assets, credit applications, default judgments, etc)
- Identify conflicts of interest (business/personal) and/or undeclared interests (directorships, etc).

9.4.16. Retained earnings

Discussion

Companies exist largely to earn profits. Companies sometimes choose to retain some of a year's earnings for a future project or for current cash flow reasons (not to make payments now). Companies must show shareholders what they have retained and what they still need to pay out. If the company is in difficulty and there is no cash, then there is no possibility of paying the retained earnings. There is no guarantee that retained earnings will ever be paid.

Retained earnings could be general (just earnings retained and not paid) or retained for a specific reason (such as a certain loss or expense anticipated in the future).

High retained earnings would be an indication that the company has been profitable in the past.

Consider the possible benefit from fraud on retained earnings:

- Understating – to hide the actual higher retained earnings for some other intended use.
- Overstating – To hide the actual lower value so as to portray a better picture.
- Payment – payment against the retained earnings, but not at all or only partially to the shareholders. The payment may also not be for an authorised use.

Observations/tips to identify and prove

Independently verify the value of retained earnings against this year's final earning figures and last year's audited financial statements.

Conduct lifestyle audits to:

- Profile potential subjects
- Identify subjects whose lifestyles appear to have been financed from sources other than known/declared income sources (assets, credit applications, default judgments, etc)
- Identify conflicts of interest (business/personal) and/or undeclared interests (directorships, etc).

9.4.17. Long-term/short-term loans

Discussion

Loans made could be between the company and:

- External financial institutions
- Private companies/individuals
- Suppliers/customers
- Employees/the owners themselves
- Other companies in the same group, as the company with the loan.

Loans can be for various periods and the repayment of the loans may be done in various manners, including:

- Instalments (monthly, weekly, quarterly, fixed intervals, milestone-driven, etc)
- Fixed payment (at end of contractual period)
- Asset swap
- Share of business
- Just a credit facility (overdraft, revolving credit, etc) that the individual/company can use.

Loans can be secured or unsecured. Secured loans would have some form of guarantee. The guarantee may be the surety of an asset (which the lending party will receive in the event the borrowing party defaults on the loan) or that someone/company undertakes to cover the loan in the event of defaulting on the loan.

The less 'fixed' and secured the loan is, the more chance there is for manipulation. Loans should be regarded with a fair amount of scepticism when it comes to fraud matters.

Loans can be made to the company by a party or by the company to another party.

- If the loan is made by the company then it may form part of the investments in the balance sheet and/or income in the income statement. Alternatively, it may be part of accounts receivable if lending is the nature of the business.
- If the loan is made to the company it will be carried in the balance sheet under liabilities (long-term or short-term/current depending on the nature of the loan).

Again, consider the possible benefit to perpetrators of fraud on loans. For loans made to the company:

- Understatement - to hide unauthorised loans or to present a better picture than the actual picture.
- Overstatement - To show a poorer picture. This may be done to discourage buyers or to devalue a company for cheaper purchase.
- Lawfulness - to hide an unlawful act/loan.
- Obtaining a loan for which the company does not qualify (through some fraudulent misrepresentation by the company or together with a colluding party).

For loans made by the company:

- Overstatement - to portray a financially stronger position in terms of income due to the company.
- Understatement - to hide unauthorised loans or to devalue the company for easy/ cheaper takeover. Alternatively, to avoid liabilities.
- Lawfulness - to hide unlawful acts/loans
- The giving of loans to parties that do not qualify.

Bank loans to the company will normally be used to finance cash-shortfalls or specific items. These normally run in trend with other items/financial records. For example: an asset was acquired and the loan was obtained to finance it (assets went up, loans went up and cash went in and out). Alternatively, purchases are made and the overdraft increases. Customers pay when terms are due and the overdraft reduces. Patterns outside of the purpose of the loan may need to be investigated.

Intercompany loans do not necessarily run in trend with other items in the same company (eg Co. 'A'). This is because another company (eg Co. 'B') in the group may require shortfall funding. The extraordinary funding requirements of Co. B do not necessarily run in trend with Co. A, which is being analysed. Intercompany transactions may need to be made on the strength of an invoice.

Observations/tips to identify and prove

List all:

- Bank loan accounts including bank accounts with credit facilities
- Intercompany loan accounts
- Loans with any other company or individual.

Obtain the loan agreement and understand the purpose of the loan and the terms and conditions thereof. Test to see that the loan is lawful and/or enforceable. Test to see that all transactions and actions around to loan were in accordance with the purpose and terms.

Ensure that the surety of the loan actually exists and that the surety will pass legally in the event of default. Substantiate all information supplied in the loan process and ensure that it is correct, complete, lawful and supplied within the prescribed period.

Obtain the company authorisation hierarchy and ensure that approvers acted within their limits. Check for loan splitting. For example, if the authorisation limit is, say, 100, then two loans of 50 each are made use of to avoid/circumvent the limit. This may avoid attention or require less onerous/easier approval. There is a notorious case in the media where the bank's staff gave loans to customers who did not qualify by breaking the one loan into smaller loans. This gave more than normal business to the bank but placed undue risk on the bank of defaulting clients. The staff alleged that they did not receive personal benefit.

Trends in terms of who is approving loans or the time and/or day of approval may have significance. Obtain a detailed transactional/payment history. Create or substantiate the full amortisation of the loan from inception to termination. Verify the completeness, accuracy and timeliness of interest accumulated and paid/received. Substantiate instalment/capital amounts.

Independently verify that the owner of the loan is really the owner of the loan or that the company is the owner of the loan. This may be for income or cost purposes. If the company does not hold the right to the loan, then the company's income may not be guaranteed/may be overstated.

Alternatively, ensure that the company really received the capital of the loan registered against their name. You want, if relevant, to identify employees using the company to cover their own personal loans.

In one matter we dealt with, the staff told us in an interview about another fraud, that the MD had made a loan from the company and that he had never repaid it. The loan was purportedly 'secured' on the strength of his retirement benefit. The company, however, had no legal right to the MD's retirement benefit and the loan was never repaid when he left. The MD was also using the company to make payments on behalf of his wife's business. It was never determined if the full amounts were received for all payments paid on her behalf.

Follow all payments through to independent, defendable bank records. Check these against both party's financial records. Interview whistle-blowers, staff members, family and subjects.

Try to identify any other significant events that occurred close to the loan-granting/receiving:

- That may have influenced the receipt
- That may have been the reason for needing the loan
- That seem out of trend and are coincidentally close to the loan
- That are large transactions
- Changes in ownership
- Changes in lifestyle
- Changes in behaviour.

Conduct analytical reviews and consider:

- Value
- Timing
- Who approved
- Customer.

Conduct lifestyle audits to:

- Profile potential subjects
- Identify subjects whose lifestyles appear to have been financed from sources other than known/declared income sources (assets, credit applications, default judgments, etc)
- Identify conflicts of interest (business/personal) and/or undeclared interests (directorships, etc).

Conduct e-mail searches and general business related correspondence reviews to identify correspondence proving corrupt relationships. Conduct searches of the subject's general workspace and/or desk to identify evidence of corrupt activities. Mirror hard drives and other company-owned electronic devices and search files saved and/or deleted to identify documents, correspondence, calculations and images that may identify corrupt activity.

9.4.18. Accruals

Discussion

Accruals are one of those areas that you should regard with a high degree of professional scepticism. This has been a common area of fraud that I have seen.

Accruals can be for future costs or for future incomes. Accruals are for transactions in which the legal liability has already transferred, but for which the physical transaction has not occurred yet.

Accounting principles ('matching concept') require incomes and expenditures to be matched and recorded in the period in which they actually occurred. This is an important concept to ensure that the accounting records correctly reflect the actual value and timing of transactions. It will also ensure that the true number of credit days are reflected (the example below refers).

Let us assume that the income/funds of a particular transaction is/are due and payable (liable) in this accounting period. In this illustration, the funds will, due to a practical reason, only physically pass to the company in a following (may not be the next period) accounting period. The income should be recorded in the first period to ensure that the first period reflects the transactions that took place during that time and not in the following accounting period when the funds physically flow.

As an example: A branch office of the company sells goods to a customer on the 28th of accounting book month 1 (BM1). The goods were delivered and the customer has signed the delivery note on the 28th of BM1. The documentation is being sent by the branch to the head office where in this case all accounting documents are processed. The documents will only arrive on the 1st of BM2 and they will only be captured into the system on the 3rd of BM2.

The company needs to record the sale's transaction in BM1 to ensure that BM1's profit is correctly reflected. Practically speaking the transaction can only be physically captured in BM2. If the transaction was captured as having occurred in BM2, then BM1's profit would be understated and BM2's profit would be overstated.

So what the company does is that it contacts all its branches and establishes what the final invoice and/or delivery document numbers were that were issued on or before the final day of the month (the 31st of BM1 in this case). The head office accounting staff members then capture an accrual for the value of the sale in BM1. BM1's profit is now complete and accurate.

On the 1st day of BM2, they reverse all accruals pertaining to previous accounting periods. The actual transaction is captured on the 3rd of BM2 with a transaction date of 28 BM1 and a captured date of 3 BM2. BM2's profit is now also correct and complete as it had a negative (reversal of the accrual) and a positive transaction (capturing of the invoice) which equates to zero.

If the customer pays on 30 days, then the customer would need to pay by the 28th of BM2. If the transaction had been incorrectly only captured as the 3rd of BM2, then the customer would only have needed to have paid on the 3rd of BM3. So, in our example the credit terms will also be correct.

There is a high degree of certainty about transactions that need to be accrued for. As per the aforementioned example the accrual process needs to occur to ensure that the accounting records are in line with the actual transactions.

When the actual payment occurs (in 30 days' time in our example) is not at question here. It is when the legal liability transferred and when this transaction will actually be recorded.

Now, if you think about the volumes that companies deal with on a daily basis, the accrual process can quickly become a complicated matter. The uncertain nature of an accrual provides an opportunity for abuse.

I hear some of you saying, but what is the issue as the accrual is reversed and therefore it has no affect. This is untrue. It has a temporary effect which may be what is desired. So, try to understand the benefit of fraudulent accruals to the perpetrators. Some examples include:

- To overstate income
- To understate costs
- To serve as a place to hide untoward transactions
- To influence KPIs and/or bonuses.

From my own experience, I can caution you to regard accruals that have a 'positive' effect on profits with scepticism. Determine what the basis for the accrual is and that it is an actual (not optimistic or imaginary) expectation of what profits could be.

Observations/tips to identify and prove

The comfort is that accruals are normally clearly recorded as such. The sheer volume of transactions may make the thorough review of all accruals impractical though. Obtain an extract of all accruals processed in the system for the period under review. Identify the purpose of the accruals and substantiate the completeness and accuracy of the accruals. Accruals are carried in the balance sheet. Review the balance sheet and substantiate accruals as required. Try to identify if there is a significant event or dependability on the accounts in which accruals are processed. For example, the monthly profit figures are the figures against which the management is measured for their KPIs or on which their bonuses are calculated. Try to understand how manipulation of the accruals on these accounts could benefit the perpetrators.

In one significant matter that we dealt with, the MD was instructing his branch CFOs to manipulate the income and expenditure accruals to 'positively' influence the profit figures. Significant bonuses were paid on these figures. The wider group also was unaware that the business in those areas was actually not profitable in its current form and they were effectively denied the opportunity to remedy to the situation. This went on for many years and cost the group millions.

Conduct analytical reviews of transaction trends. Remember that if the perpetrators have been doing this for some time, that the baseline trend will already be skewed. Compare profit, income and cost details to other data (volumes, orders, invoices, etc) to determine if there is a relationship. Conduct interviews with whistle-blowers, staff members, friends, family and subjects.

Conduct lifestyle audits to:

- Profile potential subjects
- Identify subjects whose lifestyles appear to have been financed from sources other than known/declared income sources (assets, credit applications, default judgments, etc)
- Identify conflicts of interest (business/personal) and/or undeclared interests (directorships, etc).

Conduct e-mail searches and general business related correspondence reviews to identify correspondence proving corrupt relationships. Conduct searches of the subject's general workspace and/or desk to identify evidence of corrupt activities. Mirror hard drives and other company-owned electronic devices and search files saved and/or deleted to identify documents, correspondence, calculations and images that may identify corrupt activity.

9.4.19. Provisions

Discussion

Provisions are similar to accruals. The difference with provisions is that there is a degree of uncertainty to the transaction. For accruals, the transaction had legally occurred and the amount was certain. It was only the timing of the processing of the transaction was unknown.

In the case of provisions, the amount may or may not be known. The main consideration is that the certainty of occurrence of the transaction is unknown. This is because the nature of a provision is for an uncertain event and therefore may be difficult to prove/measure/substantiate totally. Accounting principles require companies to be conservative. Companies therefore provide for these events (costs in this case) by 'putting aside' a portion of their profits in the event that this uncertain event was to materialise.

Commence by determining (through interviews and/or a balance sheet review) if there were any large provisions (eg provision for bad debts, tax, etc) that were created or adjusted (up or down) in the period under review. Movements in provisions should be seen as movements in profits. For example, if the profit before provisions was ZAR 10 and the provision increased by ZAR 2 in the period, then some of the profit must have been used to create the provision. The profit after provisions was therefore ZAR 8. Ignoring any valid reason/s for the increase in the provision, the ZAR 8 profit should be seen together with the ZAR 2 increased provision to determine the profit before changes (ZAR 10).

As an illustration: assuming that all things are even, debtors will increase proportionately (assuming unchanged payment terms) as turnover increases. If debtors increase, then the provision for bad debts will increase proportionately. There should be a linear relationship between profit, turnover, debtors and the bad debt provision. Now, if the bad debt provision percentage was increased, then the linear relationship will change. There will also be a greater reduction in profits, as more profits will be set aside for the provision.

Provisions could be made for 'costs' or income. As stated before, accounting principles require that companies are conservative. Companies therefore provide for all probable costs/liabilities and refrain from providing for income/turnover unless there is a high degree of certainty. Most of the provisions that you encounter will therefore be for cost/liability items.

Both the creation of and the release of provisions needs to be checked. Provisions are normally restricted to accounting staff members and management. A fraud on provisions would therefore be perpetrated by and/or to the benefit of this group of people. It is therefore important to understand how they could have 'benefited' from the provision movement. Remember our rule: 'People always do and say things for a reason.' In this case, establish what their motive was.

Observations/tips to identify and prove

Provisions are balance sheet accounts. Review the balance sheet and/or obtain an extract of all provisions processed/carried in the period under review. Understand the nature of the provision/s and determine the basis of the calculation/s. Ensure that this basis is sound.

Substantiate the accuracy and completeness of the provision/s. Obtain explanations for deviations from the basis of the provisions. Conduct analytical reviews. Conduct interviews with company accountants, financial directors, external and internal auditors, whistle-blowers, staff members, subjects, family and friends.

Conduct lifestyle audits to:

- Profile potential subjects
- Identify subjects whose lifestyles appear to have been financed from sources other than known/declared income sources (assets, credit applications, default judgments, etc)
- Identify conflicts of interest (business/personal) and/or undeclared interests (directorships, etc).

Conduct e-mail searches and general business related correspondence reviews to identify correspondence proving corrupt relationships. Conduct searches of the subject's general workspace and/or desk to identify evidence of corrupt activities. Mirror hard drives and other company-owned electronic devices and search files saved and/or deleted to identify documents, correspondence, calculations and images that may identify corrupt activity.

9.4.20. Contingent liabilities/assets

Discussion

Contingencies are for some or other future event that is fairly certain and for which the legal obligation has not yet passed.

The difference between accruals, provisions and contingencies is the degree of certainty. With accruals, the legal obligation has passed to the receiving party, but the transaction has not been processed yet. With provisions, there is a high degree of certainty that the event may occur. There is a diminishing chance that contingencies will occur.

No transaction is processed for a contingency. Only the nature of the contingency is described in the notes to the financial statements.

The purpose of listing contingencies in the notes to the financial statements is to ensure that reporting is 'conservative' in so far as the reader of the financial statements is made aware that there is a probability of a future adverse event.

Examples of contingencies include:

- Actual or probable lawsuits
- The obligation to rehabilitate a piece of land in the future after a mining operation.

Contingent liabilities may intentionally not be declared and in so doing fraudulently misrepresent the true financial 'picture' of the legal entity to the reader of the financial statements. Alternatively, contingencies may be intentionally overstated in an attempt to misrepresent the legal entity's actual financial position as poorer than it actually is. This may be done at a time that the company is going to be purchased (to ensure that it is acquired below its true value) or to prevent a company from obtaining a contract that they are bidding for.

Observations/tips to identify and prove

Determine through interviews and/or a review of the balance sheet if there were any contingencies. Understand the nature of the contingencies.

We would typically interview the company lawyers (list of litigation) and external auditors independently and determine if there are any future events for which a contingency needs to be raised.

Obtain a written undertaking from management as to the nature and extent of contingencies. Where possible, substantiate the accuracy and/or completeness of the contingency/ies. Obtain explanations for deviations from the basis of assumption of the contingency.

Conduct analytical reviews. Conduct interviews with company accountants, financial directors, external and internal auditors, whistle-blowers, staff members, subjects, family and friends.

Conduct lifestyle audits to:

- Profile potential subjects
- Identify subjects whose lifestyles appear to have been financed from sources other than known/declared income sources (assets, credit applications, default judgments, etc)
- Identify conflicts of interest (business/personal) and/or undeclared interests (directorships, etc).

Conduct e-mail searches and general business related correspondence reviews to identify correspondence proving corrupt relationships. Conduct searches of the subject's general workspace and/or desk to identify evidence of corrupt activities. Mirror hard drives and other company-owned electronic devices and search files saved and/or deleted to identify documents, correspondence, calculations and images that may identify corrupt activity.

9.4.21. Current liabilities

Discussion

Current liabilities are any contractual obligations that the organisation still has to pay to another party in the short- to medium-term (not years). Some examples of current liabilities include:

- Trade creditors (items such as stock that are purchased for the company's trade purposes)
- Expense creditors (items procured for the general administration of the organisation)
- Subcontractors (people/entities from which the organisation procures services for the organisation's trade)
- Pre-payments made to the company before the company has completed its obligation
- Tax liabilities (discussed separately below).

For these items we have to consider:

- Should there have been a liability?
- Is the liability fair-valued?
- If the amounts carried in the balance sheet for them are an accurate reflection of the transaction/s.
- Any amounts actually paid for them.
- The corresponding entry (debit) to the liability.

For example, in the latter case, let us presume that the company is procuring stock for resale from a creditor. The liability (credit balance) is carried in the balance sheet. The corresponding entry is a debit to the stock account (an asset). Stock that has been applied in the course of the business is 'moved' to the trading account and is reflected in the profit/loss figure. There may, therefore, be a linear relationship between the liability and the corresponding entries.

What benefit could be derived from fraudulent misstatement of liabilities:

- Understatement of liabilities to present a better financial picture than reality to:
  - Obtain finance
  - Persuade a buyer to purchase the company
  - Present a better picture for KPIs/bonus reasons, etc.
- To overstate liabilities to present a poorer picture than reality to:
  - Discourage potential buyers
  - Undervalue the company to allow for the taking over of the company at a reduced value
  - Disqualify the company from deals or finance so that a competitor obtains the business, etc.

Observations/tips to identify and prove

Obtain the balance sheet and determine how the current liabilities are made up (categories). Understand the nature of each liability category. Ensure that these make sense. Check actual liabilities against any applicable contracts or source documents (purchase orders, quotes, invoices, etc).

Conduct interviews with company accountants, financial directors, external and internal auditors, whistle-blowers, staff members, subjects, family and friends. Conduct analytical reviews.

Conduct lifestyle audits to:

- Profile potential subjects
- Identify subjects whose lifestyles appear to have been financed from sources other than known/declared income sources (assets, credit applications, default judgments, etc)
- Identify conflicts of interest (business/personal) and/or undeclared interests (directorships, etc).

Conduct e-mail searches and general business related correspondence reviews to identify correspondence proving corrupt relationships. Conduct searches of the subject's general workspace and/or desk to identify evidence of corrupt activities. Mirror hard drives and other company-owned electronic devices and search files saved and/or deleted to identify documents, correspondence, calculations and images that may identify corrupt activity.

Substantiate the completeness and accuracy of all liabilities under scrutiny. Determine if:

- Amounts are complete and accurate
- Contractual terms were complied with
- Applicable discounts received
- Rebates correct/complete
- Correctly authorised
- Adequately supported by source documents
- Reflected in the correct period.

9.4.22. Tax liabilities

Discussion

There are many different tax types that could be applicable to the organisations in which you and/or the subjects under investigation work.

I suppose that the most likely tax fraud scenario is that of tax evasion. Tax avoidance is the legal avoiding of paying too much tax. Tax avoidance involves a full and accurate declaration of all applicable facts. Tax evasion is, on the other hand, the intentional non-payment of taxes that are legally due and payable to the authorities.

The taxman is an interesting creditor in so far as he is mostly unaware of the tax liability that the organisation has against him. The taxman therefore in most cases (unlike a normal creditor) does not come asking for his money.

Subjects could, therefore:

- Fraudulently reduce the actual tax liability. This may be done by pure calculation misstatements or misdeclarations.
- Fraudulently pay a portion (say 20) of the correctly calculated tax liability (say 100) to a party that is not entitled to the taxman's revenue. The balance (80) is paid to the taxman

and the total payment appears to be correct in the accounting records (being 100). Paperwork sent to the taxman to support the 80 would also need to be manipulated.

The contra entry of fraudulent transactions (debits or credits) could be posted against tax accounts. This may be difficult to detect amidst high transactional volumes. For example if I make a fraudulent payment (credit to the bank account) to myself, then I need a general ledger account against which to post the debit.

Example of taxes include:

- Corporate income tax
- Dividends tax
- Personal income tax (eg PAYE & SITE)
- Transfer duties
- Donations tax
- Secondary tax on companies (STC)
- Value Added Tax (VAT)
- General Sales Tax (GST)
- Capital Gains Tax (CGT)
- Estate duty
- Import and export customs and excise duties (mis-declarations/non-declaration)
- Various levies (skills development levy (SDL), Unemployment Insurance Fund (UIF), fuel levy, etc)
- Retirement Funds Tax (RFT)
- Air passenger tax
- Diamond Export Levy
- Mineral and petroleum royalties
- Stamp duty
- Securities Transfer Tax
- Uncertificated Securities Tax.

Not only are there different tax types, but there are different tax individuals liable for the taxes and who pay the taxes. Some examples include:

- Companies
- Juristic bodies/legal entities
- Individuals (provisional taxpayers, normal taxpayers)
- Trusts
- Employers (paying on behalf of employees)
- Retailers.

Different countries have different tax laws and there may be special agreements between countries (tax treaties, double taxation agreements, etc).

Accountants pride themselves on all kinds of schemes to reduce tax liabilities (tax avoidance). The line between legal and illegal avoidance, however, frequently becomes blurred. It is perfectly normal for there to be varying opinions as to the plausibility of schemes, especially when precedent has not been set or legislation is not clearly defined. So what is allowable and what may not be accepted by the tax authorities once tested may be unknown.

What we are talking about here is the purposeful and fraudulent evasion of tax (in full or partially). Alternatively, it may be the purposeful delay in paying taxes (for cash flow reasons, to represent a more favourable reporting position, etc).

Taxes may be paid at different times of the year (eg monthly, quarterly or annually). The time of payment may, therefore, have a direct bearing on cash flow in the period paid. Sudden changes in cash flow trends may indicate differing payment patterns.

Observations/tips to identify and prove

Establish the different tax types applicable to the entity and understand the nature of each. Focus your attention on those that are suspicious/financially material.

Understand the different bases of taxes applicable to the organisation. Substantiate them through recalculation and ensure that they have been calculated completely and accurately. Try to check tax liabilities for independent systems (sales or purchasing systems listing VAT). Consult a tax subject matter expert, as applicable.

Conduct interviews with company accountants, financial directors, external and internal auditors, whistle-blowers, staff members, subjects, family and friends. Request management to sign declarations as to the complete and accurate calculation and/or payment of tax liabilities. Conduct analytical reviews.

Conduct lifestyle audits to:

- Profile potential subjects
- Identify subjects whose lifestyles appear to have been financed from sources other than known/declared income sources (assets, credit applications, default judgments, etc)
- Identify conflicts of interest (business/personal) and/or undeclared interests (directorships, etc).

Conduct e-mail searches and general business related correspondence reviews to identify correspondence proving corrupt relationships. Conduct searches of the subject's general workspace and/or desk to identify evidence of corrupt activities. Mirror hard drives and other company-owned electronic devices and search files saved and/or deleted to identify documents, correspondence, calculations and images that may identify corrupt activity.

9.4.23. Fixed assets, buildings, plant and equipment, vehicles, capital items, assets being built, etc.

Discussion

This section should be read together with the 'gain/loss on the sale of an asset' and 'revaluation/impairments of assets' sections discussed in the income statement section later.

The types of assets that we are referring to here are larger/more material assets. These could be movable or immovable assets. Fraud perpetrated with regards to these types of assets may include:

- Misappropriation of the assets.
- Use of the assets for self-gain/private business purposes/not for the purposes of the company's business/unauthorised use/usage outside of company policy, etc.
- Assets that do not belong to the company or that are not within the company's right to use, may be used and applied in the company's business and records.
- The value of assets may be misstated or valued incorrectly for aforementioned reasons and/or to allow staff members to acquire company assets at reduced rates upon the sale thereof.
- Not recording the asset/s at all (in the balance sheet, in an asset register, etc) or recording them at a later/earlier point in time. Budget may only be available in another period, but management wants to secure the asset and therefore physically acquires the asset and hides it until the budget becomes available.
- Not depreciating assets/revaluing assets according to accounting policies and/or international standards for the purpose of affecting profits (overstating or understating). There may be tax ramifications/penalties/interest payable if the fraud resulted in the non-payment of all taxes ordinarily due on profits.
- Use of company assets as collateral where not entitled to do so. Check who holds the title deeds to the assets.
- Assets may be miscategorised to avoid paying duties, needing to have special permits, needing special treatment (eg hazardous goods), to avoid restrictions and because of a need to make declarations and/or keep records. Dual purpose (military/commercial) products refer in terms of US foreign trade controls.
- The source or destination of the assets may also be misstated to avoid trade restrictions.

The purpose of misstating assets in the accounting records could be to:

- Conceal misappropriated assets.
- Overvalue assets to present a more favourable financial picture to shareholders, investors, bankers, auditors, etc.
- Undervalue assets to present a poorer financial picture for example to prevent the sale of the company, prevent a company from obtaining contracts, reduce the purchase price of the company at acquisition, etc.
- Obtain tax rebates otherwise not entitled to (eg capital allowances).
- To hide a fraudulent contra-entry, by booking it against the assets.

Assets may be procured in cash or financed on terms (30 days, 60 days, 60 months, etc). The fraud may also relate to and/or affect the financing of the assets.

Another frequent area of abuse is the disposal of decommissioned, disused or damaged company assets. Employees may abuse the scrapping or sale of assets purportedly damaged, assets at the end of their useful life (like company vehicles), disused/discontinued assets, etc. I have frequently seen examples of when:

- People not entitled to assets have acquired assets.
- People have not abided by company policy and/or prevented others from acquiring the assets and/or have not given others the equal chance to also bid on/acquire the assets.

- People have sold the assets immediately on acquiring them. While this may be within their fair right, it might also not be a condition of sale and it may put the company in jeopardy/at risk with their suppliers or clients to whom goods are normally sold.
- Assets are written off in the company's records and then sold for scrap, with the funds being given to an employee and not to the company. The company's records balance, as there was no expectation to receive the income.
- The proceeds from the sale of scrapped assets are fraudulently applied in the company to cover other costs.

The fraudulent use of scrapped assets or 'end-of-life' assets is a common area of abuse, as these assets do not typically enjoy the same degree of control as normal assets do. The assets will also 'not be missed' by anyone and detection is less likely or more easily explained.

The use of these funds/proceeds from the sale of an asset, as 'slush funds' to pay for parties and other unauthorised expenditure, is commonplace. Somehow employees seem to feel entitled to the assets and they feel that it is not stealing if they use the funds for office parties. They ignore that the company should have received the funds and had a right to determine how best to apply the funds.

Observations/tips to identify and prove

Check accounting records (asset register, general ledger and balance sheet) to determine if there were any material movements (increase or decrease) in assets for the period? If there has been an unexplained decrease in the cash position, this may contribute to an explanation as to where some of the cash went if the asset was paid for in cash. Alternatively, the contra entry for the procurement of an asset could have been to creditors or loans if the asset was procured on terms. The liabilities would have increased to fund the assets.

Understand the company policy with regards to:

- The authorisation hierarchy. Who may authorise the acquisition or disposal of assets?
- Depreciation rates and periods.
- Tax wear and tear rates.
- The type of assets that the company holds and/or uses in the course of normal business.

Follow transactions through from the bank (bank statements - independent or cash book - consider the integrity of information) to determine if the corresponding entry (to the credit to the bank account) is a debit to an asset account. Alternatively, the sale of an asset would require a debit to the bank and a credit to the 'sale of asset' account. Determine if these were authorised, treated correctly in terms of policy, accurate and complete.

Obtain and review contracts to determine rights, obligations, valuation, terms, etc. Compare the contractual terms to the actual usage and assets. Obtain explanations for variances.

Use an independent expert to determine the true value of the assets and/or compare the assets' book value to market trends/industry standards/company benchmarks.

In some companies, assets may be charged directly to a job or a contract. Obtain the contract accounts or job costings and identify sales and acquisitions of assets. Determine if these have been treated correctly. These contracts can be financially material and assets can 'get lost' in the total contract price. Management tends to look at the overall job profitability and not at the detail. It is easy for contract managers to hide unauthorised acquisitions or sales of assets in this way.

Conduct lifestyle audits to:

- Profile potential subjects
- Identify subjects whose lifestyles appear to have been financed from sources other than known/declared income sources (assets, credit applications, default judgments, etc)
- Identify conflicts of interest (business/personal) and/or undeclared interests (directorships, etc).

Interview staff members, family and friends, maintenance staff members, suppliers of the assets, etc. Obtain declarations from management.

Conduct e-mail searches and general business related correspondence reviews to identify correspondence proving corrupt relationships. Conduct searches of the subject's general workspace and/or desk to identify evidence of corrupt activities. Mirror hard drives and other company-owned electronic devices and search files saved and/or deleted to identify documents, correspondence, calculations and images that may identify corrupt activity.

Conduct analytical reviews of assets to each other or assets to fuel, maintenance, licence fees, etc. Identify who had/s access to assets and/or records and/or the ability to use assets and/or alter records/conceal the fraud.

The accounting records will not always be the best source of information through which to determine if assets are being used for non-company purposes. Examine:

- Maintenance records (excessive maintenance, unknown maintenance, etc); private maintenance booked to company expenses
- Asset registers/lists
- Access registers
- Licence records
- Physical asset counts/verification on site
- Video footage
- Interviews
- Records of actual usage (vehicle gauges) compared to operating/job costing records to where usage is charged/recovered
- Fuel/energy records
- Man hours used/mileage meters, kilowatt hours, units produced, tons lifted, etc
- Analytical reviews
- Comparison of industry trends/other similar company assets.

Obtain company policy on the sale/scrapping/disposal of assets. Identify how the funds derived from the sales of assets are supposed to be applied. Identify scrapped assets (cash book, sale of asset accounts and/or asset registers) and determine if these were according to policy.

Examples come to mind of cases that I worked on when asset managers in two different companies were using company funds to pay for the licences and spare parts of their own private vehicles:

In the first case, a physical verification of vehicle licences procured to actual vehicles identified the variance. The subjects confessed to procuring the licences for their own privately owned vehicles at the company's expense while they were doing the annual licences of the company's vehicles.

In the second case, an analytical review of spare parts identified the need for additional review. Not all spare parts could be matched to actual vehicles (on vehicle's make). The subject confessed on confrontation to procuring vehicle spares for his private vehicle at company expense.

9.4.24. Decommissioning and abandonment decisions

Discussion

Most assets have a useful life. Certain assets may have decommissioning and abandonment requirements at the end of their useful life. Examples of assets where this is applicable include end-of-life/disused mines and oil rigs. There is normally a contractual obligation for the owner of the asset to restore the site where the asset is and/or return the asset in a restored state. There may be environmental, reputational and legislative (fines, imprisonment, etc) repercussions to non-compliance.

Fraud schemes may include:

- Not carrying out all or part of the contractual obligations to restore the asset and misrepresenting what was done
- Fraudulently claiming (reimbursement from a third party, as relevant) for work not performed or at un-agreed rates
- Claiming tax deductions and/or benefits for work not performed
- Substandard completion of abandonment work
- Bribery and/or paying people off to ignore penalties, abandonment requirements, etc
- Subsequent sale of land/assets to another party misrepresenting the work completed or non-disclosure of contractual requirements or hazards
- Booking unrelated expenses to abandonment costs
- Booking abandonment costs to unrelated projects
- Irregular awarding of procurement contracts to those appointed to conduct the decommissioning work. This may include inflated prices, inflated quantities, mis-categorisation of work categories (skewed towards more expensive work), substandard work and awarding of work to friends and family. Kickbacks may be applicable.
- There may be a scrap value to the decommissioned parts. The sale of scrap may be understated in total, misappropriated, reduced rates paid, incorrect quantities paid, etc. Kickbacks may be applicable.
- There may also be a second-hand value to the onward sale of the asset. The assets may be undervalued and sold to a colluding third-party. Kickbacks may be applicable. Proceeds may also be misappropriated or applied to other unrelated projects and cost centres.

Observations/tips to identify and prove

Review contracts to establish obligations. Comparison of contractual obligations to actual work performed. A subject matter expert may be required. Review of meeting minutes and board packs.

Substantiation of expenses claimed. E-mail searches to identify complicit parties and knowledge of misconduct.

Conduct searches of the subject's general workspace and/or desk to identify evidence of corrupt activities. Mirror hard drives and other company-owned electronic devices and search files saved and/or deleted to identify documents, correspondence, calculations and images that may identify corrupt activity. Expert assessment of quality and quantity of work performed.

9.4.25. Land and buildings

Discussion

Land and buildings are a type of asset. These may be kept the same or refurbished after a period of time to increase their value and/or the use of the asset. Land and buildings can just be premises at which the organisation conducts its business or they could be used to generate income (rental income). The income derived from the asset should, therefore, increase as well.

Examples of land and building fraud schemes include:

- Selling assets without permission
- Selling to unauthorised persons
- Under- or over-valuing land and buildings
- Claiming unentitled tax deductions or incentives
- Non-recording of land and buildings
- Using assets for private/non-business purposes
- Using assets/land/building for disallowed purposes.

Observations/tips to identify and prove

Review meeting minutes. Identify sales, acquisitions etc. Follow these through to ensure that all were carried out lawfully and in line with the agreement. Obtain the authorisation hierarchy and determine who has the authority to do what with land and buildings. Compare actual behaviour to the authorisation hierarchy.

Obtain title deeds to determine ownership. Obtain contracts to review rights and obligations. Obtain plans from municipalities to determine property additions and ensure that these were authorised and recorded correctly.

Identify any special property restrictions (for example no processing of industrial waste, no mining, etc) and determine if the organisation is using the land correctly.

Determine through discussion with town planning departments if any major events will be occurring (for example, building of highways through the organisation's property, changing of land or water rights, etc).

Conduct lifestyle audits to:

- Profile potential subjects
- Identify subjects whose lifestyles appear to have been financed from sources other than known/declared income sources (assets, credit applications, default judgments, etc)
- Identify conflicts of interest (business/personal) and/or undeclared interests (directorships, etc).

Conduct e-mail searches. Conduct searches of the subject's general workspace and/or desk to identify evidence of corrupt activities. Mirror hard drives and other company-owned electronic devices and search files saved and/or deleted to identify documents, correspondence, calculations and images that may identify corrupt activity. Analytical reviews of cost spent, value of property, etc. Substantiation of costs and capitalised amounts. Obtain independent valuation of land and buildings.

Comparison of actual usage data to accounting recording data. Was the asset in use earlier than recorded or later? Reviewing contracts to identify special clauses, rights and obligations. Asset ownership verification.

9.4.26. Building assets

Discussion

While a category of fixed assets, this area warrants specific discussion. In some industries like mining, aeronautical, petrochemical, etc, organisations build assets for use in the production of income. These assets are large (normally physically and financially material) and capital in nature. They may take years to build and many cost millions. Software-building or installations can also be treated in this manner. All costs associated with the asset are capitalised and not expensed until the asset is complete. The costs are held in the balance sheet and depreciated in line with the organisation's accounting policies.

If a built asset is 'complete', this means that ownership has transferred and/or the asset has been placed into production. Once the asset is in use it is depreciated or revalued as required. Depreciation of the asset moves the cost from the assets in the balance sheet to the profit and loss (P&L).

Building of assets could also include the partial building or repairing of an asset. This might be a scheduled part of the use of the asset (for example aircraft propellers need to be replaced after a predefined usage). Alternatively, it could be a capital repair or an expansion or extension or repurposing of the asset (for example a brownfield development).

Potential asset-building fraud schemes include:

- Booking too few costs to capital. Costs are directly expensed (hitting the profit and loss directly).
- Too many costs are capitalised. Not all costs related to the build need to be capitalised. Some can be expensed.
- Booking unrelated expenses to the project. For example: from unrelated assets that may be underperforming, in an attempt to hide costs/underperformance.

- Change in accounting policy at a key time in order to derive an effect on profits.
- Purporting to comply with requirements in order to obtain special grants or tax incentives.

Observations/tips to identify and prove

Review senior management/board meeting minutes. Review contracts to determine what must be done and when. Review the authorisation hierarchy to determine the authorisations applicable. Review accounting policies to determine if this is correct and if actual behaviour was aligned. Substantiate amounts claimed, capitalised or expensed. Conduct e-mail searches.

Conduct lifestyle audits to:

- Profile potential subjects
- Identify subjects whose lifestyles appear to have been financed from sources other than known/declared income sources (assets, credit applications, default judgments, etc)
- Identify conflicts of interest (business/personal) and/or undeclared interests (directorships, etc).

Conduct searches of the subject's general workspace and/or desk to identify evidence of corrupt activities. Mirror hard drives and other company-owned electronic devices and search files saved and/or deleted to identify documents, correspondence, calculations and images that may identify corrupt activity.

9.4.27. Depreciation/wear and tear

Discussion

Companies purchase assets. Simplistically:

- Most times, companies cannot afford financially to absorb/write the entire cost of the asset off in one year, so they spread it over a period that they can 'afford'. Assets are written off against profits in the income statement. 'Afford' in this instance means the impact to profits and not the payment of the asset. The payment of the asset is separate and may have been financed or paid in cash.
- Assets are frequently procured for the production of income and assets are 'used' in this way for a number of years. The company would, therefore, want to write off the cost of the asset over the 'useful life' (income-producing life) of the asset to ensure that the cost of the asset is applied in the same period as the income that it is generating. The matching of costs and incomes creates a more realistic view of profits in a period.
- Assets' value typically reduces over time. Accounting principles require companies to value assets in their books (balance sheet) at their actual value and not the original procured value. This ensures that the company portrays a realistic view of its financial position. This may require revaluing the assets on an annual basis (discussed later).

'Depreciation' is the accounting reduction of the value of the asset against profits. Based on the aforementioned, companies determine rates and/or periods over which they want to depreciate their assets. Companies have different rates and periods for different classes of assets.

'Wear and tear' is logically the same as depreciation. The difference is that depreciation is the rate and/or period that the company wants to write off their assets. Wear and tear is the rate and/or period that the 'tax man' (revenue authority) allows companies to write assets off over. Depreciation periods are typically longer (effect on profits less over a longer period) than wear and tear periods which are normally shorter (reducing taxable income initially with no tax effect after the period has ended) in comparison.

In essence, companies have to maintain two sets of accounting records, one for the revenue authorities to calculate tax (at wear and tear rates) and one for itself to calculate profit (at depreciation rates). In theory, the asset will eventually reduce to nil value in both scenarios. Alternatively, the asset is sold and both values come together at that time.

So over time there will be no difference between depreciation and wear and tear. In the interim, companies sit with 'timing differences'. The timing differences are recorded as 'deferred tax' (assets or liabilities depending on which way they fall).

This is all well and good from an accounting point of view, but what does it mean to us from a fraud point of view? To honest accountants, nothing; but to fraudsters it represents an opportunity.

The good thing for fraud investigators is that depreciation is typically well documented in accounting policy and wear and tear are contained in law. This gives fraud investigators a good comparative base against which to compare actual behaviour.

This is also an area perfectly suited to using data analytics to test the entire population and not just individual items.

The benefit to fraudsters for manipulating depreciation or wear and tear may include:

- To affect profits (increase or decrease depending on motive to show a better or poorer financial position)
- To hide another unrelated fraud
- To evade taxes.

Observations/tips to identify and prove

Understand depreciation accounting policies and wear and tear rules. Compare these to actual depreciation and/or wear and tear and obtain explanations for variances.

Conduct interviews with company accountants, financial directors, external and internal auditors, whistle-blowers, any other relevant staff members, subjects, family and friends. Request management to sign declarations as to the complete and accurate calculation and/or payment of the item. Conduct analytical reviews.

Conduct lifestyle audits to:

- Profile potential subjects
- Identify subjects whose lifestyles appear to have been financed from sources other than known/declared income sources (assets, credit applications, default judgments, etc)
- Identify conflicts of interest (business/personal) and/or undeclared interests (directorships, etc).

Conduct data analytics to recalculate all depreciation and/or wear and tear and compare the recalculated amounts to actual amounts. Conduct e-mail searches and general business related correspondence reviews to identify correspondence proving corrupt relationships. Conduct searches of the subject's general workspace and/or desk to identify evidence of corrupt activities. Mirror hard drives and other company-owned electronic devices and search files saved and/or deleted to identify documents, correspondence, calculations and images that may identify corrupt activity.

9.4.28. Current assets

Discussion

Examples of current assets include:

- Accounts receivable
- Bank and cash
- Stock
- Finished goods and 'work-in-progress'
- Materials
- Prepaid expense and deposits.

These are all discussed separately below.

Observations/tips to identify and prove

These are all discussed separately below.

9.4.29. Bank/cash

Discussion

Bank and/or cash should be the simplest area of accounting records. The bank is really just a record of what was paid to the company, what was paid out by the company and the balance of what is remaining to the company or owed by the company, as relevant.

The company's bank records should match the records (bank statements) of financial institutions holding the company's funds. This presents the fraud investigator an opportunity to independently verify the integrity of the company's records against a defendable source.

The good thing is that all actual payments and receipts have to be recorded in the bank's records at some or other time. They may be excluded from the company's records, but they have to reflect on the bank's records. A large portion of frauds has to do with the fraudulent movement of funds (income or payments). This means that there will be a record at the bank of what actually transpired. While this represents an opportunity for fraud investigators, as per above, fraudsters are aware of this as well and employ many creative means to defeat this challenge and prevent their schemes from being identified.

In this section, we are concerned about the effect of fraud schemes on the company's bank. While not relevant here, please also bear in mind that the bank accounts of subjects can be a valuable source of information and/or evidence too. This is discussed in other sections of this book.

A company does not always know exactly when a payment will be received or when a payee will physically cash/receive a payment from the company. While the bank's records are independent and defendable, there may very well be timing differences between when transactions are recorded in either the company's records or on the bank statement. The company, therefore, maintains its own bank record of what it is aware of. The company then conducts a process of comparing and explaining the differences between its records and the records of the financial institution that performs the company's banking. This process is known as a 'bank reconciliation'. A 'reconciliation' is, as the word implies, a 'bringing together' of two figures.

Bank reconciliations are to my mind the most important control in an organisation. Bank reconciliations are 'detective' in nature, but nevertheless very important, as they tell us when a discrepancy has occurred and quantify the discrepancy.

Bank reconciliations will only 'detect' what has cleared the bank, without being recorded in the company's books.

I recall one example when the dumbstruck financial manager was explaining to me that one of his staff members had made fraudulent payments. My first response was to say that either the fraudulent payments must have been booked to another account or they must be unreconciled in the bank reconciliation. The financial manager said the latter was impossible, as he personally signed off the bank reconciliation. I asked him to bring me the bank reconciliation. I looked at the bank reconciliation and on the surface, the purported company's balance and the bank's balance were reconciled and I could see that the financial manager had signed it. I asked him if he had checked the arithmetic of the reconciliation before signing it. His response was that no he had not, as the reconciliation was a printout from the 'system'. I added it up in front of him and proved that the bank reconciliation was in fact manipulated and did not reconcile. He asked me how this was possible. I then did a 'screen dump' from the bank system into Excel and showed him how the bank reconciliation had been manipulated in Excel.

In another example, staff members in a branch retail store were making fraudulent refunds to themselves, without putting the corresponding entries through. The head office accounting staff members thought that the retail store staff members had just forgotten to post the required entries and they posted the entries at the head office when the refunds appeared as unreconciled without investigating.

In both of these examples, the subjects had processed payments through the bank, without processing corresponding entries in the company's records. The bank reconciliation, if performed properly, would have 'detected' the fraudulent payments.

Fraud manifesting itself in bank records could therefore include:

- Fraudulent payments out of the company's bank account
- Fraudulent amounts 'paid' to the company. This would be an entry in the company's records to purport that a payment had been made. Alternatively, it may have been a misapplied actual payment (the discussion on receivables refers).
- A pure misstatement of funds that did not exist or an understatement of funds that do exist.

What fraudsters do to prevent being detected is to:

- 'Roll' actual amounts between accounts (see receivables)
- Process a fictitious entry in the company's records to ensure that the amount 'reconciles'
- Manipulate the bank reconciliation to appear to reconcile (previous example refers)
- Alter/misrepresent the bank statement to appear as if the entry was not processed or that the balance is different from the actual balance
- Fail to perform the bank reconciliation
- 'Lose' the bank reconciliation after it was performed or not show it to anyone
- Create so much 'confusion' around the bank reconciliation that no one understands it or can identify the unreconciled amounts
- Alter or omit actual legitimate amounts in the reconciliation to 'force' the bank reconciliation to balance
- Process entries in the company's books in advance to ensure that the balances reconcile in total, albeit not necessarily per item
- Advise the bank that payments were not company authorised payments and that the payment is for the bank's account.

Observations/tips to identify and prove

List all month-end bank balances (look at the trial balance) for the period under review. Analyse actual bank statements to identify unusual transactions per criteria defined as suspicious. Analyse the cashbook to identify any unusual transactions per criteria defined as suspicious. Confirm balances in the general ledger to the cashbook and/or financial statements.

Recalculate bank reconciliations. Be careful if unreconciled amounts are swept into a suspense account. *I consulted at an organisation which had a high volume of unknown transactions. I could not believe that the bank reconciliation balanced perfectly every month with no aged reconciling items. I established that the cashbook clerk was moving all unreconciled entries to a growing suspense account, which was not being actioned.*

Suspicious transactions include transactions that are:

- Unsupported by sufficient supporting documents
- Not within company policy or procedures, contractual guidelines, the ambit of the law, etc
- Outside of tolerances
- Outside of the applicable period
- Not approved at all or by an authorised person
- Payments to unknown persons or for unknown reasons
- Entries posted to non-fitting GL accounts, contracts, cost centres, etc.

Conduct lifestyle audits to:

- Profile potential subjects
- Identify subjects whose lifestyles appear to have been financed from sources other than known/declared income sources (assets, credit applications, default judgments, etc)
- Identify conflicts of interest (business/personal) and/or undeclared interests (directorships, etc).

Conduct e-mail searches and general business related correspondence reviews to identify correspondence proving corrupt relationships. Conduct searches of the subject's general workspace and/or desk to identify evidence of corrupt activities. Mirror hard drives and other company-owned electronic devices and search files saved and/or deleted to identify documents, correspondence, calculations and images that may identify corrupt activity.

Conduct interviews with company accountants, financial directors, external and internal auditors, whistle-blowers, any other relevant staff members, subjects, family and friends. Request management to sign declarations as to the complete and accurate calculation and/or payment of the item. Conduct analytical reviews.

9.4.30. Stock/materials/stationery/work in progress (WIP)/finished goods

Discussion

Stock, materials, stationery, work in progress and finished goods (the final finished goods that the company has manufactured for sale) can fall prey to the same fraud schemes as any other asset. They may be:

- Misappropriated
- Used for self-gain/private business purposes/not for the purposes of the company's business/unauthorised use/usage outside of company policy, etc
- Used, but without belonging to the company or not within the company's right to use or apply in the company's business and records
- Incorrectly valued (over or under) for aforementioned reasons and/or to allow staff members to acquire company assets at reduced rates upon the sale thereof or to present a more favourable financial picture
- Unrecorded (in the balance sheet, in an asset register, etc) or recorded at a later/earlier point in time (budget may only be available in another period, but management wants to secure the asset and therefore physically acquires the asset and hides it until the budget becomes available)
- Used as collateral where not entitled to do so
- Unrecorded or miscategorised to avoid paying duties (production of alcohol, tobacco, etc), needing to have special permits, needing special treatment (eg hazardous goods), to avoid restrictions and a need to make declarations and/or keep records (dual purpose (military/commercial) products refer in terms of US foreign trade controls)
- The source or destination of the items may be misstated to avoid trade restrictions
- Incorrect composition of goods
- Mix/yield frauds (recording incorrect yields)
- Quality misrepresentations (to be graded higher than actual)
- Over- or under-statements of stock value or volume
- Unit price discrepancies.

The purpose of misstating assets in the accounting records could be to:

- Conceal misappropriated assets
- Overvalue assets to present a more favourable financial picture to shareholders, investors, bankers, auditors, etc

- Undervalue assets to present a poorer financial picture for example to prevent the sale of the company, prevent a company from obtaining contracts, reduce the purchase price of the company at acquisition, etc
- Obtain tax rebates otherwise not entitled to (eg special allowances, duties payable, etc)
- Hide a fraudulent contra-entry by booking it against the assets.

Assets may be procured in cash or financed on terms (30 days, 60 days, etc). The fraud may also relate to and/or affect the financing of the assets.

Another frequent area of abuse is the disposal of decommissioned, disused or damaged company assets. Employees may abuse the scrapping or sale of assets purportedly damaged, assets at the end of their useful life, disused/discontinued assets, etc. I have frequently seen examples of when:

- People not entitled to assets have acquired assets.
- People have not abided by company policy and/or prevented others to acquire the assets and/or have not given others the free chance to also bid on/acquire the assets.
- People have sold the assets immediately on acquiring them. While this may be within their fair right, it might also not be a condition of sale and it may put the company in jeopardy/at risk with their suppliers or clients to whom goods are normally sold.
- Assets are written off in the company's records and then sold for scrap, the funds given to an employee and not to the company. The company's records balance as there was no expectation to receive the income.

As discussed under fixed assets, the fraudulent use of scrapped assets or 'end-of-life' assets is a common area of abuse, as these assets do not typically enjoy the same degree of control as normal assets do. The assets will also 'not be missed' by anyone and detection is less likely or more easily explained.

The use of these funds as 'slush funds' to pay for parties and other unauthorised expenditure is commonplace. Somehow employees seem to feel entitled to the assets and they feel that it is not stealing if they use the funds for office parties. They ignore that the company should have received the funds and had a right to determine how best to apply the funds.

Observations/tips to identify and prove

Identify the:

- Types of stock (materials, WIP, finished goods)
- Location of items
- Quantities of items
- Systems on which they are recorded
- Controls (stock counts, physical release, etc)
- Policies and procedures around stock handling.

Understand the:

- Stock keeping procedures and safeguards; test to see if these have been complied with
- Recording methods

- Accounting treatment and valuation of stock (LIFO, FIFO); check actual treatment against policy
- Check if the treatment is in line with IFRS.

Substantiate a sample of stock/material transactions to the appropriate general ledger accounts and stock records. Review production records (WIP and finished goods) to general ledger accounts for completeness.

Conduct lifestyle audits to:

- Profile potential subjects
- Identify subjects whose lifestyles appear to have been financed from sources other than known/declare income sources (assets, credit applications, default judgments, etc)
- Identify conflicts of interest (business/personal) and/or undeclared interests (directorships, etc).

Conduct interviews with company accountants, financial directors, external and internal auditors, whistle-blowers, any other relevant staff members, subjects, family and friends. Request management to sign declarations as to the complete and accurate calculation and/or payment of the item.

Conduct analytical reviews. Expected yield figures will be helpful to determine if the required amount of material has resulted in the correct amount of finished goods. Conduct physical verification of assets (stock counts).

Conduct e-mail searches and general business related correspondence reviews to identify correspondence proving corrupt relationships. Conduct searches of the subject's general workspace and/or desk to identify evidence of corrupt activities. Mirror hard drives and other company-owned electronic devices and search files saved and/or deleted to identify documents, correspondence, calculations and images that may identify corrupt activity.

9.4.31. Deposits paid/received

Discussion

Deposits are used:

- As collateral to discourage the non-return of an asset and/or to minimise the financial loss of an asset (equipment, tools, vehicle rental, gas bottles, etc)
- To cover potential repair/damages (eg for apartment rentals)
- To 'secure' work (shows you are serious if you provide a deposit)
- To reserve the right to use equipment
- As a first instalment.

Deposits are frequently forgotten about. This happens especially in companies where deposits are frequently used and/or when deposits are held over a protracted period and/or where there are many layers of management. For example, in the construction industry, the company must pay utility deposits, deposits to hire equipment, deposits to secure orders, etc. Construction contracts can extend over years and deposits are made at various stages over the life of the project. In this time people come and go and there may be various foremen and site agents on site. The value of individual deposits is also normally insignificant to the overall construction value and will not be missed.

Corrupt staff may have the 'forgotten' deposits refunded to themselves and not back to the company. In a similar fashion, the company may receive deposits on behalf of customers. Customers may also forget about their deposits. Subjects may request the repayment of the deposit to themselves and not to the client.

Deposits should be carried in the balance sheet as a prepayment/asset.

Observations/tips to identify and prove

Understand the organisation policy and procedures over deposits. Obtain a list of all deposits paid or held. Analyse the ageing of deposits held. Understand what happens to deposits paid to the company not claimed. For example, after one year transferred to a suspense account, after three years transferred to profits, etc. Check actual behaviour against policy.

Substantiate deposit refunds to ensure that they were authorised and made to the correct recipient. Compare bank accounts refunded to, to personnel records. Data analytic tools are helpful for this.

Conduct lifestyle audits to:

- Profile potential subjects
- Identify subjects whose lifestyles appear to have been financed from sources other than known/declared income sources (assets, credit applications, default judgments, etc)
- Identify conflicts of interest (business/personal) and/or undeclared interests (directorships, etc)

Conduct interviews with company accountants, financial directors, external and internal auditors, whistle-blowers, any other relevant staff members, subjects, family and friends. Request management to sign declarations as to the complete and accurate calculation and/or payment of the item.

Conduct analytical reviews. Conduct e-mail searches and general business related correspondence reviews to identify correspondence proving corrupt relationships. Conduct searches of the subject's general workspace and/or desk to identify evidence of corrupt activities. Mirror hard drives and other company-owned electronic devices and search files saved and/or deleted to identify documents, correspondence, calculations and images that may identify corrupt activity.

9.4.32. Prepaid expenses paid or received

Discussion

The company may either make prepayments or receive prepayments, as described below. Prepaid expenses may include:

- Deposits (as discussed previously)
- Advance payments; payments may need to be made in instalments in advance before the next stage of a contract can commence
- Overpayments
- Customer credits.

Prepayments are owed to the customer/debtor by the company receiving/having the funds until they are repaid or until the liability becomes due and payable. The liability becomes due and payable when delivery transfers or once a contractual stage has been reached. For example, in a contract in which an asset is being manufactured for a customer, the customer may be required to make advanced payments at predetermined stages before the next stage can commence. While the money has been paid in advance, the contractual stage has not been completed yet. That portion of the liability will only become due and payable upon completion. The prepayment can only be netted off against the liability at that stage.

Fraudulent use of prepayments may include:

- Prepayments sometimes become forgotten about for various reasons. Fraudsters may pay these forgotten amounts to themselves. The liability is cleared in the balance sheet and the party to whom the money was actually owed is none the wiser as they were unaware of the funds.
- Prepayments may also be applied to another customer's balance to fraudulently reduce their balance.
- The prepayment (credit balance – held as a liability in the balance sheet) may be the contra entry to another unrelated fraudulent (debit) transaction. The prepayment account may just be an easy account against which to capture the corresponding entry.

Observations/tips to identify and prove

Obtain a listing of all prepaid expenses. Understand organisation policy and procedure with regards to pre-payments. Substantiate all prepayments to ensure that they are valid. Substantiate the contra entry of the prepayment as required. Obtain a transaction listing of all repayments or application of prepayments to a debtors' balance. Substantiate the repayments/applications to ensure that these are valid and correct.

Conduct lifestyle audits to:

- Profile potential subjects
- Identify subjects whose lifestyles appear to have been financed from sources other than known/declared income sources (assets, credit applications, default judgments, etc)
- Identify conflicts of interest (business/personal) and/or undeclared interests (directorships, etc).

Conduct interviews with company accountants, financial directors, external and internal auditors, whistle-blowers, any other relevant staff members, subjects, family and friends. Request management to sign declarations as to the complete and accurate calculation and/or payment of the item. Conduct analytical reviews.

Conduct e-mail searches and general business related correspondence reviews to identify correspondence proving corrupt relationships. Conduct searches of the subject's general workspace and/or desk to identify evidence of corrupt activities. Mirror hard drives and other company owned electronic devices and search files saved and/or deleted to identify documents, correspondence, calculations and images that may identify corrupt activity.

9.4.33. Retentions

Discussion

Retentions are amounts that a customer holds back on paying to ensure that snagging and/or aftersales service is rendered as agreed/required.

The retention amount is not just an amount that the customer does not feel like paying and then says that the amount is being withheld as a retention. The retention amount is an amount that is contractually agreed at the commencement of the contract. The period of retention is the period (days or months) for which the retention funds will be withheld to see if any snagging/repairs/aftersales service needs to occur. The retention amount is paid to the contractor/supplier thereafter. The retention period is also contractually agreed.

Various industries (for example the construction industry) develop 'norms' as to what retention amount and period is deemed to be fair for both the party conducting the work and the party paying for the work. These norms are not law and can be negotiated. Specific countries, government contracts and special and/or hazardous goods may have prescribed amounts and periods.

In construction companies, retentions can become complicated. The client may withhold a retention amount against the construction company. The construction company may, in turn, withhold retentions against subcontractors that conducted work on the site. Both are subject to the same fraud risks.

Retentions carry similar risks to deposits, as they can be forgotten about. Risks include:

- Forgotten about/unclaimed retentions may be fraudulently paid to corrupt staff members themselves.
- I have heard about unethical companies that refuse to pay contractors retention amounts not due to any contractual reason. This is typically done when the contracting party is less sophisticated and/or does not have the means to fight this contractually. While some dress this up as a contractual dispute, I say it is fraud if done knowingly to fraudulently prejudice the other party.
- Contractors could collude with corrupt staff members to repay retentions before the retention period has prescribed and/or for an amount that they are not entitled to.

If a subcontractor does not claim the retention held against them, then the company normally does not volunteer to repay it to them. They keep the money and pay it into a suspense account (in accordance with accounting prescripts) after a while (normally one year) and keep it there until the prescription period (could be three years) on the amount lapses. If the subcontractor does not exercise their right to claim the amount within the prescription/contractual period they write the amount back to profits.

I recall raising this issue with the FD of a construction company and telling him that the non-advising of subcontractors of retentions due to them was unethical. I said that this was especially exploitative in nature, as some of the subcontractors were not sophisticated businessmen with administrative departments to assist them. They were frequently tradesmen living from hand to mouth.

Needless to say, my idealistic suggestions fell on deaf ears and the company patted themselves on the back for their increased profits.

Observations/tips to identify and prove

Obtain a listing of all retentions held. Substantiate these to ensure that they are valid and correct. Determine contractual and organisation policy and procedure on retentions. Compare actual behaviour to it. Obtain a transaction listing of all retentions paid and substantiate the payment to ensure that it was valid/to a contractually valid party. Data analytics can be employed to compare payment bank details to employee bank details on the payroll. Obtain contracts and ensure that the retentions (amount and period) are within contractual terms. Check if the retention is within industry norms and if there are any special legal requirements.

Conduct lifestyle audits to:

- Profile potential subjects
- Identify subjects whose lifestyles appear to have been financed from sources other than known/declared income sources (assets, credit applications, default judgments, etc)
- Identify conflicts of interest (business/personal) and/or undeclared interests (directorships, etc).

Conduct interviews with company accountants, financial directors, external and internal auditors, whistle-blowers, any other relevant staff members, subjects, family and friends. Request management to sign declarations as to the complete and accurate calculation and/or payment of the item. Conduct analytical reviews.

Conduct e-mail searches and general business related correspondence reviews to identify correspondence proving corrupt relationships. Conduct searches of the subject's general workspace and/or desk to identify evidence of corrupt activities. Mirror hard drives and other company-owned electronic devices and search files saved and/or deleted to identify documents, correspondence, calculations and images that may identify corrupt activity.

9.4.34. Debtors/accounts receivable

Discussion

Companies are in the business of selling goods and/or services to customers. Companies frequently allow customers to accept goods and services on credit and to pay for them after delivery has taken place. They do this to ensure that they sell their products/services. Customers are typically analysed and given a financial limit up to which they can procure on credit. The repayment period and any other charges (for example interest, administration fees, etc) are normally also specified in a contract signed with the customer. This is in line with the company's risk appetite. Companies revisit the credit terms of customers and amend them (increase or decrease) from time to time based on the customer's credit performance and procurement history.

So the total amount of trade debtors represents the debts that a company incurs in the course of carrying out its trade. This is an important distinction to make, as any other money owed to the company (not in the course of its trade) is, therefore, a loan of sorts and not trade debtors.

The balance of the debtors in the general ledger is the amount of money owed to the company by customers. The general ledger balance may be updated on a daily basis. It is mostly up to date on a monthly basis after the 'month-end' has been finalised. Companies go through a series of processes to close the books off at the end of a month so that they have a complete and accurate view of the financial position at that month end. The previous conversations concerning accruals refer. This will vary from company to company.

The balance of debtors at year-end (or any other financial reporting period) is carried in the balance sheet. This balance will be the balance of the debtors at the date of drafting the financial statements (frequently annually). Companies work with a double entry accounting system. Now, if debtors are balances incurred in the course of carrying out trade, then the corresponding entry to the debtor (being a debit) is 'sales' (being a credit). This as 'sales' represents the amount of 'trade' carried on by a company within a period. Sales are reflected in the trading section of the income statement.

Each of these can be seen in isolation, but it will be more meaningful to understand the interrelationship of all aspects related to debtors. In line with this logic, debtors and cash should really be seen together in relation to sales. For example:

- If turnover is constant and cash is increasing, then debtors should decrease, as the debtors are paying the company.
- Similarly, if turnover is constant and cash is decreasing, then we may expect the debtors' balance to increase if all else remains the same and cash was not spent on another activity.

Companies frequently sub-divide their debtors into 'classes' to enable them to manage different groupings of debtors. As an example, let us assume that a company trades with the government and the general public. The government is a reliable debtor and will not default on its payments. Governments are however frequently slow payers and normally enjoy extended credit terms that companies are prepared to entertain to obtain lucrative contracts. Let us assume that the government has 120 days' credit terms and that the public in this example has 30 days' standard credit terms. Now if the company was to analyse the ageing of all its debtors in total, it may reflect that the average age of its debtors is, say, 100 days. In terms of the general public, this would be of concern.

The company's analysis would be much more meaningful if it was able to see its debtors in two groups (classes). The analysis of each class of debtor would give a realistic picture of how well the debtors are paying their debts. When analysing debtors therefore, try to understand if there are different types/classes of debtors that the company trades with.

Now, frauds with debtors can be perpetrated from the company's side or from the debtor's side. Debtor related frauds can also be perpetrated when the transaction is performed or when the payment is made.

The following are some of the potential areas of fraud concerning debtors:

- Recording debtor transactions that did not occur, thereby unfairly increasing the debtors' balance. This will increase the asset value of a company (debtors are current assets). This may be done by processing actual debtor transactions or posting a journal.
- Debtor accrual transactions may be an easy vehicle by which to temporarily inflate a debtors' balance.

- A simple misstatement of a debtors' balance in the financial statements without any actual entries being passed is also a highly likely method to 'increase' debtors.
- Recording debtor transactions at incorrect amounts and/or products and quantities.
- Not recording all debtor transactions. This may be done to reduce the actual assets recorded by the company and effectively devaluing it or in collusion with the debtor to reduce the debtor's liability.
- Recording debtor transactions against another valid debtor that did not incur the liability. The actual debtor will have the goods, but not have to pay the liability.
- The giving of terms and conditions to which the debtor is not entitled, including:
  - Discounts
  - Credit terms (days)
  - Amount of credit/threshold
  - Rates
  - Interest charged
  - Other fees normally payable
  - Preferential pricing
  - Non-enforcement of policies (eg collections, interest, etc)
  - Non-enforcement of actual or standard contractual terms.
- Conducting business with debtors that are not within company policy or against which trade or legal restrictions exist.
- Intentional accounting period 'cut-off' errors and/or misstatements to ensure that debtors' balances are processed in a different accounting period than when they actually occurred. This is done to inflate or reduce a particular period's debtors' balance.
- An entry/journal (debit or credit) to a debtor's account may just be the corresponding side of another fraudulent transaction. The debtor's account may just be a convenient place to post the other side of the entry. For example, a credit to the bank may be debited to a debtor. While such an entry is not the normal way to process a bank payment, it may be the only method that a fraudster has to hide a fraudulent entry. Understand therefore both sides of the accounting entry identified.
- Debtor payments can be paid to an entity/a person/an account to which they are not supposed to be paid. Fraudsters supply debtors with fraudulent bank details for them to pay into.
- Application of payments to incorrect accounts/debtors. This may be done as a pure fraud to benefit one debtor or it may be a method of rolling payments to prevent the misappropriation of debtor payments being detected.
- Fraudulent refunds. Fraudsters may pay refunds to themselves and not to the customer to which they are due.
- Fraudulent processing of credit notes and/or waivers that the customer is not entitled to.
- A lot of organisations have an operating system on which the company's operations are processed. The transactions per customer are interfaced to the debtors' module of the financial system on a monthly basis. A fraudulent waiver may therefore occur on the operating system before interface or on the financial system after interface.
- Closing/'resolving' of disputes to the company's prejudice.
- Not signing a contract at all or excluding certain terms from a particular contract, to the detriment of the company.

- Not conducting a credit check on all customers and exposing the company to undue credit risk.
- Unaccounted for debtor payments in the entity's bank account (for example tuition fees at a university with thousands of students) may be written to a suspense account until they can be identified and allocated. As discussed under suspense accounts, fraudsters may misappropriate funds out of the suspense account. Funds in a suspense account are typically not missed after misappropriation.

The following examples of actual cases refer:

- I have experienced numerous cases where debtors' clerks forwarded their personal bank details to customers. Customers proceeded to make payments to these accounts. The debtors' clerks then typically have to keep rolling payments received from another debtor into the account of the debtor who made the payment. This is a 'zero-sum game' and their crime eventually catches up with the fraudster, as they take more money out of the system than they can roll between debtors. They eventually end up getting caught.
- In a similar light, there are numerous syndicates (that operate external to the company) that will take a chance and forward letters to all of a company's customers advising them of a purported change of banking details. The customers then make payments to the fraudulent bank account.
- In one matter discussed already, some customers had branch accounts. The customers later made all payments into one main branch account only. The fraudulent debtors' clerk applied legitimate payments to the unused branch accounts ensuring that these were in credit. The debtors' clerk was then in a position to motivate to his supervisor to approve 'refunds' for the purported credits into his own account that he had arranged to have set up on the system.
- A family member of a debtors' clerk was fronting a company. Suppliers owed the company large sums of money (say 500). Customers would pay a reduced sum to the front company (say 250), as agreed with the fraudulent debtors' clerk. The debtors' clerk would pay an even greater reduced amount to the company (say 90). The debtors' clerk and the family member shared the remaining amount (160 in this example). The debtors' clerk would then write off the customer's outstanding balance in the company's books (410 in this example).

Observations/tips to identify and prove

Conduct lifestyle audits to:

- Profile potential subjects
- Identify subjects whose lifestyles appear to have been financed from sources other than known/declared income sources (assets, credit applications, default judgments, etc)
- Identify conflicts of interest (business/personal) and/or undeclared interests (directorships, etc).

Substantiate:

- All debtor transactions under review/that are suspicious; determine if these are for the correct customer, rates, period, amounts, etc

- Credit notes
- Bad debts
- Refunds
- Discounts
- Interest charged (to see that it was charged and/or charged at the correct rate).

Check banking details communicated to customers. Conduct a debtors' certification. Understand what the normal authorities are in relation to debtors. Check actual transactions to identify deviations from given authorities. Understand organisational policy and procedures of how, when and by whom debtors are normally processed. Identify actual deviations to these.

Obtain the debtor contracts and ensure that:

- They are approved
- They are in line with company policy/standard terms
- Terms have been enforced.

Conduct interviews with company accountants, financial directors, external and internal auditors, whistle-blowers, any other relevant staff members, subjects, family and friends. Request management to sign declarations as to the complete and accurate calculation and/or payment of the item.

Conduct e-mail searches and general business related correspondence reviews to identify correspondence proving corrupt relationships. Conduct searches of the subject's general workspace and/or desk to identify evidence of corrupt activities. Mirror hard drives and other company-owned electronic devices and search files saved and/or deleted to identify documents, correspondence, calculations and images that may identify corrupt activity.

Try to understand if there have been any material changes in the classes of debtors. Determine if the ageing and/or mix changed within a period.

Conduct analytical reviews, including:

- Individual debtors to themselves
- One debtor to another
- Classes of debtors over time
- Debtors to sales and cash
- Debtors to sales and stock.

Substantiate the debtors' balance in the balance sheet to the general ledger and/or debtors' system.

9.4.35. Bad debt provisions

Discussion

Bad debt provisions go hand in hand with debtors. There is a direct relationship between debtors and bad debt provisions. Bad debt provisions were discussed previously under provisions.

Observations/tips to identify and prove

Discussed under provisions previously.

9.4.36. Intellectual property, trademarks, copyrights, patents and intangible assets

Discussion

Organisations and individuals have ideas and spend time and money to develop these ideas. At a certain point, these ideas become the property of the individual/organisation. The use of these ideas is therefore at the organisation/individual's discretion.

Examples of intellectual rights include:

- Literary works
- Works of art
- Music or film rights
- Copyrights
- Trademarks
- Patents
- Research
- Specialised programmes
- Teaching aids.

For example, this book and its contents are my intellectual property. No one may take any part of it and sell it or portray it as their work. I think this is quite easy to understand. Things become a little more difficult in an organisational context.

Intellectual property is not a tangible thing. If I take your company car and use it for my own benefit it is easy to understand what I have done wrong. If on the other hand I take your organisation's words and use them, this may not be so easy to identify. Furthermore, the exact point at which my words and ideas become my intellectual property is also not that easy to understand. The infringement of the rights may be by an individual, a group of people or a legal entity (organisation). It is for these reasons that theft of intellectual property is very difficult to prove, as you have to prove the owner's unique privilege and how they have been deprived by the act.

A practical example comes to mind of theft of intellectual property. A company that I worked for had paid an inordinate amount of money to be 'ISO' (International Organization for Standardization) rated. The cost was both the cost to put everything in place and for the annual certification. The certification gave the company a distinct competitive advantage. The international head office of the group holding company was situated in the same building as one of the branch offices. The national manager responsible for this area had made use of two staff members in this branch office to assist him to set everything up for the certification. They had basically done all the hard work and developed all the required programmes.

The national manager had his own consulting business prior to joining the group. Unbeknown to the company, the national manager had never discontinued his own business. He maintained a national portfolio of clients by flying around the country at the company's expense, purportedly for the company's business. The national manager was also rarely in the local office, despite the fact that he held a national responsibility for the group and the branch staff members held the local responsibilities.

A tip-off to the group MD unravelled his empire. Our investigation showed that he was purporting to be ISO certified to his clients. He was also selling the company programmes as his own to his clients. He chose to resign in the face of the plethora of charges. Evidence accumulated included:

- *ISO grading standards*
- *An estimate of costs to obtain the grading*
- *An affidavit from the group MD summarising the subject's responsibilities and what the ISO grading entailed*
- *Affidavits from the local staff members comparing the private business material and the material that they drafted for the group*
- *Interviews with the subject's clients, family and friends*
- *Written undertakings from the subject's client base that they will refrain from using the material and that they will destroy all material supplied to them.*

The subject signed an undertaking to refrain from using the company's property and to destroy all such material. While the subject had already proven to be dishonest, the undertaking did provide the company with a sound basis to act in the event that the subject continued to make use of the company's material. An effective civil claim was not deemed to be cost effective and therefore not undertaken.

The subject was also reported to the relevant industry body to be defrocked and to the tax authorities for tax evasion. No criminal matter was opened, as it was thought to be too difficult to prove in this case. It was also part of the conditions of the undertaking signed by the subject and the company.

Observations/tips to identify and prove

Intellectual rights are a specialised area of law. Obtain expert advice first.

Determine if any intellectual rights have been registered anywhere or if they are defined in a contract anywhere. Obtain the legal documents and:

- Understand the jurisdictional limitations of these documents
- Determine if any laws are applicable
- Compare the disputed use of the rights to the legal requirements.

Obtain the opinions of the purported owner of the rights and the subject who used the rights. As a simple step, but a vital one, determine what their logic is and what they want. Determine if precedent exists for the use of such rights. For example: songwriters, musicians, etc. Understand the similarities between what the subject has used the purported owner's material for. For example: are the words used in the same way in two books? A simple electronic document comparison can assist with this. Also, check who the original author of the document was under the properties of the document.

Understand how the intellectual rights have been used, how the subject unfairly benefitted from the use thereof, and how the owner of the rights has been unfairly prejudiced. Define the type of intellectual property and understand what it is that makes the intellectual property unique.

Conduct lifestyle audits to:

- Profile potential subjects
- Identify subjects whose lifestyles appear to have been financed from sources other than known/declared income sources (assets, credit applications, default judgments, etc)
- Identify conflicts of interest (business/personal) and/or undeclared interests (directorships, etc).

Conduct interviews with company accountants, financial directors, external and internal auditors, whistle-blowers, any other relevant staff members, subjects, family and friends. Request management to sign declarations as to the complete and accurate calculation and/or payment of the item. Conduct analytical reviews.

Conduct e-mail searches and general business related correspondence reviews to identify correspondence proving corrupt relationships. Conduct searches of the subject's general workspace and/or desk to identify evidence of corrupt activities. Mirror hard drives and other company-owned electronic devices and search files saved and/or deleted to identify documents, correspondence, calculations and images that may identify corrupt activity.

9.4.37. Notes to the financial statements

Discussion

The notes to the financial statements are formal undertakings by management that the readers of the financial statements rely upon for their accuracy. The importance of notes to the financial statements have increased in the last few years, with more and more emphasis on the notes to provide much-needed insights into the financial numbers contained in the financial statements.

The reason for the fraudulent use of notes to the financial statements is simply to misrepresent the actual picture that the financial statements should provide, to the reader of the financial statements.

Observations/tips to identify and prove

Read the notes and determine if these fairly represent the true picture to reader in the financial statements. International financial reporting standards can be highly tricky and represent a specialised area. The use of an up-to-date independent expert is advised. Determine if the financial statements were subject to audit. If so, interview the auditor and understand the reliance that can be placed on the testing conducted by the auditor as well as the auditor's skills in this area. Compare the notes under dispute to International Financial Reporting Standards (IFRS) and/or company policy.

Conduct lifestyle audits to:

- Profile potential subjects
- Identify subjects whose lifestyles appear to have been financed from sources other than known/declared income sources (assets, credit applications, default judgments, etc)
- Identify conflicts of interest (business/personal) and/or undeclared interests (directorships, etc).

Conduct interviews with company accountants, financial directors, external and internal auditors, whistle-blowers, any other relevant staff members, subjects, family and friends. Request management to sign declarations as to the complete and accurate calculation and/or payment of the item. Conduct analytical reviews.

Conduct e-mail searches and general business related correspondence reviews to identify correspondence proving corrupt relationships. Conduct searches of the subject's general workspace and/or desk to identify evidence of corrupt activities. Mirror hard drives and other company-owned electronic devices and search files saved and/or deleted to identify documents, correspondence, calculations and images that may identify corrupt activity.

9.4.38. Corporate governance statements

Discussion

Notes to the financial statements give further explanation of the figures in the financial statements. Corporate governance statements give the reader of the financial statements insights into the governance policies and practices. It has become increasingly important for companies to portray a good corporate governance image to the readers of the financial statements and the public at large.

Companies' equity value can be influenced by the investor public's perception of the company's corporate governance.

Directors and management may be incentivised by the increase in equity value. Alternatively, they may be measured by the general perception that the company holds in the marketplace. Deals may be dependent on a good perception in the market. Management and/or directors may, therefore, feel pressurised to fraudulently misstate the company's actual corporate governance position.

Observations/tips to identify and prove

Obtain a copy of the company's financial statement pack and determine if the corporate governance statements are a true reflection of the company's position. Vet all assertions against actual independent evidence (not just opinion).

Determine if any independent or other vetting (such as by an external agency or by the external auditors) was performed on the company's corporate governance statements. Interview these parties and determine:

- Their suitability (qualifications)
- Their experience
- Their independence and objectivity
- The actual vetting conducted.

Determine if:

- The corporate governance statements are measured and publicised
- The corporate governance statements are a dependency on business licences, contracts, concessions, etc.

Conduct lifestyle audits to:

- Profile potential subjects
- Identify subjects whose lifestyles appear to have been financed from sources other than known/declared income sources (assets, credit applications, default judgments, etc)
- Identify conflicts of interest (business/personal) and/or undeclared interests (directorships, etc).

Conduct interviews with company accountants, financial directors, external and internal auditors, whistle-blowers, any other relevant staff members, subjects, family and friends. Request management to sign declarations as to the complete and accurate calculation and/or payment of the item.

Conduct e-mail searches and general business related correspondence reviews to identify correspondence proving corrupt relationships. Conduct searches of the subject's general workspace and/or desk to identify evidence of corrupt activities. Mirror hard drives and other company-owned electronic devices and search files saved and/or deleted to identify documents, correspondence, calculations and images that may identify corrupt activity.

9.4.39. Directors' emoluments

Discussion

Directors' emoluments may need to be summarised and declared in the company's annual financial statements. These declarations will need to be complete and accurate, as with all other areas of the financial statements.

Public perception as to the fairness of the emoluments can impact on how the company is perceived in the market. Corrupt officials may not want to show the true directors' emoluments as:

- Public perception may regard the emoluments as excessive
- They may not be authorised (may require approval at an AGM)
- The emoluments may indicate a potential or accurate conflict of interest.

Corrupt officials may refrain from declaring all or part of the directors' emoluments.

Observations/tips to identify and prove

Substantiate the director's emoluments in the financial statements to the actual payroll records and vice versa. Determine if these were the only emoluments. Look for traditional emoluments in the payroll and test to see who the real recipient of the emoluments was. It may be that the actual emoluments are recorded in the payroll and other company records, but that they have just been excluded from the financial statements. Look at actual tax records paid by the company and ensure that all directors' emoluments taxed were reflected completely and accurately on the financial statements. Understand the nature of the emoluments and determine if the summary declaration (even if correct in value) gives a true reflection of the emoluments.

The highest risk is not the emoluments recorded on the executive payroll. The highest risk is other payments that are made outside of the payroll on behalf of directors. Some examples include:

- Security for directors' residences
- Hotel and other accommodation
- Flights and travel
- Tuition (look at expatriate contracts)
- Entertainment.

Determine if the directors were entitled to the emoluments and/or if they were authorised (eg special share deals, etc). Determine what director emolument declarations need to be made and compare these to the actual declarations. Determine what industry-specific norms dictate and compare these to actual declarations made. Examine board packs and/or board remuneration committee minutes to identify emoluments and amendments. Determine if the directors' emolument statements were audited. Interview the external auditors and establish the degree of reliance that can be placed on the testing that was conducted.

Conduct lifestyle audits to:

- Profile potential subjects
- Identify subjects whose lifestyles appear to have been financed from sources other than known/declared income sources (assets, credit applications, default judgments, etc)
- Identify conflicts of interest (business/personal) and/or undeclared interests (directorships, etc).

Conduct interviews with company accountants, financial directors, external and internal auditors, whistle-blowers, any other relevant staff members, subjects, family and friends. Request management to sign declarations as to the complete and accurate calculation and/or payment of the item.

Conduct analytical reviews of:

- Directors over time
- Directors to each other
- Emoluments declared to taxable emoluments.

Conduct e-mail searches and general business related correspondence reviews to identify correspondence proving corrupt relationships. Conduct searches of the subject's general workspace and/or desk to identify evidence of corrupt activities. Mirror hard drives and other company-owned electronic devices and search files saved and/or deleted to identify documents, correspondence, calculations and images that may identify corrupt activity.

Section C – Income statement

Discussion

The income statement is one of the statutory financial statements. The income statement provides a summary of incomes and expenditures in the period for which the income statement was produced.

No balances are carried in the income statement.

Observations/tips to identify and prove

See individual income statement accounts discussed in this chapter.

9.4.40. Trading account

Discussion

The trading account is where the financial aspects specific to the company's trading are summarised. It typically contains all items directly related to sales and purchases. The company's gross profit is determined in the trading account.

Fraudulent manipulation of the trading account may:

- Increase or decrease the gross profit
- Be the corresponding entry of another unrelated fraudulent transaction. The trading account and or the accounts that make up the trading account may represent an easy place to book a fraudulent contra entry.

Observations/tips to identify and prove

Substantiate the individual numbers making up the trading account. Conduct interviews with company accountants, financial directors, external and internal auditors, whistle-blowers, any other relevant staff members, subjects, family and friends. Request management to sign declarations as to the complete and accurate calculation and/or payment of the item. Conduct analytical reviews.

Conduct e-mail searches and general business related correspondence reviews to identify correspondence proving corrupt relationships. Conduct searches of the subject's general workspace and/or desk to identify evidence of corrupt activities. Mirror hard drives and other company-owned electronic devices and search files saved and/or deleted to identify documents, correspondence, calculations and images that may identify corrupt activity.

Conduct lifestyle audits to:

- Profile potential subjects
- Identify subjects whose lifestyles appear to have been financed from sources other than known/declared income sources (assets, credit applications, default judgments, etc)
- Identify conflicts of interest (business/personal) and/or undeclared interests (directorships, etc).

9.4.41. Sales/turnover

Discussion

As discussed under debtors (balance sheet), sales have a direct relationship with debtors and/or cash. Sales may also have a direct analytical relationship to purchases and stock. The discussions on these individual items refer as well. Sales are therefore a common benchmark which can be used in trend analyses against which to compare other items.

The following include some of the benefits and/or motivation for fraudsters to manipulate sales:

- To misrepresent that the company is doing better than it actually is, so as to:
    - Obtain finance for which the company would not qualify based on the actual performance
    - Avoid scrutiny by investors/shareholders/holding companies/management/auditors/tax authorities
    - Receive incentives (bonuses) and/or emoluments (commissions) based on sales/performance
    - Receive better pricing, discounts or rebates reserved for a higher value or volume of sales
    - Be applicable for contracts (above a specified turnover)
    - Ensure the sale/merger of the company.
- To misrepresent that the company is not doing as well as it actually is, so as to:
    - Prevent the sale of the company
    - Avoid obtaining finance and/or to prevent obtaining specific contracts, normally to advantage another party
    - Avoid having to pay incentives and/or royalties and/or turnover rental and/or profit share to employees/agents/intellectual property right holders/landlords/business partners
    - Devalue the sales value of a company/purchase price thereof
    - Tax avoidance (tax is paid in net profit, but the reduction of sales will have an eventual effect to reduce net profit/increase net loss)
    - Avoid having to comply with laws and regulations applicable to companies greater than a particular size/sales volume.

Sales figures may not always be manipulated. They may be a reflection of the actual picture. For example, low turnover could be an indication that:

- The company is just not getting the business. Analysis of sales trends to other indicators, as mentioned above, will determine if further investigation is warranted.
- An internal fraudster is redirecting business that should be coming to the company to their own business or to a colluding party (such as a competitor).
- Sales are not being recorded at all. This could be as a result of invoices not being issued or unrecorded retail sales at a point of sale.
- Recorded sales are being credited. Stock is invoiced and delivered to a customer. The customer is credited and the stock is never returned.
- A high value of trade discounts is being given.
- Sales agents are giving customers lower rates/prices than they should.

Alternatively, high turnover could be an indication that:

- The company is doing well and actually achieving the sales.
- Fictitious sales are being created and/or recorded.
- High sales and low cash and/or debtors could be an indication that cash is being stolen or debtors are not being recorded.

In some organisations (like construction companies) customers hold a retention against the organisation for a contractually agreed period. The purpose of this retention is to protect the customer in the event that there are problems with the work performed by the organisation. The retention serves as a financial incentive for the organisation to return and correct their faulty work. The organisation would at least forfeit their retention if they did not return to correct their work. Other sanctions may also apply, such as: reputational damage, civil lawsuits and reporting of the organisation to industry bodies. Different organisations may record sales and any retentions differently. The work is strictly speaking complete and the organisation (depending on accounting policies) has the right to record the full cost of the contract as sales in their books. The problem is that part of the sale (retention) is not guaranteed yet and may not pass in full to the organisation, as the client may withhold part of the retention amount as a breach of contract. Income can only be recorded once the liability has passed. The liability of the retention has not passed.

Your analysis of sales does not have to relate perfectly to accounting policies depending on the purpose of your test. You may want to include the 'full' picture of sales including retentions. Sales retentions may, therefore, need to be taken into account in your analysis, as turnover/sales may be recorded in the organisation's books net of client retentions held against the organisation. Sales will otherwise appear to be lower than 'actual'. Establish during your preliminary investigation how to treat sales retentions.

Sales can be manipulated by altering:

- Unit prices
- Volumes sold
- Discounts given
- Waivers authorised
- High number of returned items accepted
- Yields
- Stock availability (to prevent sales occurring, by not having product available)
- The total sales value (unit price multiplied by unit volume)
- Periods to which sales pertain
- The recording of transactions.

The sales process frequently commences with clients requesting bids. Internal fraudsters may prevent certain requests for bids from being brought to the company's attention. The accuracy of the sales estimates and quotes may also be questionable. *In one company I was in, the management at one stage considered if their estimator was perhaps in cahoots with the competition, as the company never seemed to be successful with their bids.*

In sport, we have had many examples of where sports stars 'throw a game' for the purposes of a winning bet that they have placed with a 'bookie'. In business, the person calculating the company's sales quotes and estimates is a powerful person. They can, if corrupt and if they collude with a competitor, ensure that the company does not win bids. The probability of a company estimator colluding with a competitor may increase in an industry with few competitors. This was discussed under bid rigging, but warrants mentioning here again due to the sales cycle and potential effect on sales.

The following controls may mitigate estimation fraud risks:

- Estimates drafted by more than one person at a time. Colluding parties will have to corrupt more than one person. This is not unlikely, just more difficult. Alleged FIFA bid rigging refers as an example where this still occurred.
- Alternating estimation duties/client responsibilities. This will prevent long and strong relationships and/or loyalties being misused for the client's purposes.
- The establishment of strong independent controls over checking estimates before bid submission.
- Incentivising estimators for successful bids obtained. This may be limited as fraudulent estimators may be making more from bid rigging than from company incentives.
- Remunerating estimators well.
- Maintaining fair employer/employee relations, policies and procedures.
- Obtaining references before appointing estimators.
- Maintaining a policy of periodically screening estimators and/or other high-risk employees. The discussion on lifestyle checks refers.

Where sales agents have the discretion to award contracts to clients based on negotiations, sales agents may collude with clients to give the clients pricing that they should not be entitled to receive. Compensating controls to prevent/identify this include:

- Incentivising sales agents
- Remunerating sales agents well
- Maintaining fair employee practices
- Conducting screening of sales agents prior to employment and periodically whilst employed
- Conducting lifestyle reviews (to show employees under financial pressure and/or direct relationships with colluding parties)
- Setting budgets and measuring actual performance against these
- Comparing sales agents to each other
- Establishing healthy competitiveness between agents
- Conducting spot checks
- Setting tolerances outside of which a sales agent needs to seek approval
- Having standard price lists.

The absence of these controls may raise suspicion and/or be a good place to commence an investigation.

Observations/tips to identify and prove

Analyse the sales process and identify controls/areas of fraud weakness. Investigate the identified fraud weakness areas in greater detail to understand if fraud actually occurred.

Observe actual behaviours (current) and/or test behaviours found in documentary evidence (historic) to policies and procedures. Deviations to established policy may be an indication of areas where fraud may have occurred.

Substantiate sales invoices and/or transactions for completeness, accuracy and validity. Review supporting documents and relevant correspondence.

You may need to enlist the assistance of a specialist in more complex industries to test sales. Examples include:

- Chemical engineers
- Quantity surveyors (construction and civil contracts)
- Actuaries and/or chartered accountants (financial transactions).

Conduct lifestyle audits to:

- Profile potential subjects
- Identify subjects whose lifestyles appear to have been financed from sources other than known/declared income sources (assets, credit applications, default judgements, etc)
- Identify conflicts of interest (business/personal) and/or undeclared interests (directorships, etc).

Conduct interviews with company accountants, financial directors, external and internal auditors, whistle-blowers, any other relevant staff members, subjects, family and friends. Request management to sign declarations as to the complete and accurate calculation and/or payment of the item.

Obtain contracts and identify areas of fraud weakness in the contracts. Compare actual sales/behaviours to the contractual requirements.

Conduct e-mail searches and general business related correspondence reviews to identify correspondence proving corrupt relationships. Conduct searches of the subject's general workspace and/or desk to identify evidence of corrupt activities. Mirror hard drives and other company-owned electronic devices and search files saved and/or deleted to identify documents, correspondence, calculations and images that may identify corrupt activity.

Conduct analytical reviews:

- Sales to sales over time
- Sales to cash and/or debtors
- Sales to purchases
- Sales to stock
- Sales to operational/manufacturing volumes
- Sales to industry trends
- Trends of estimators who submit bids
- Trends of competitors who win bids; try to establish if there is a trend to certain competitors winning bids
- Bid pricing trends (winners and losers).

Try to compare sales trends to independent sources related to sales. High or low activity in these areas may be an indication of fraudulent activity. Examples include:

- Obtain the company's marketing plan and sales representatives' call records. Compare these to sales trends to establish if there is a relationship.
- Obtain production records, materials used and/or procured.
- Obtain finished stock records.
- Obtain delivery records and/or vehicle usage figures/courier company billing.

9.4.42. Purchases, prime costs and/or cost of sales

Discussion

These costs were mentioned previously under the trading account section. The trading account is where the gross profit is calculated, as the difference between the sales and purchases or prime costs. We discuss these costs in greater detail in this section.

'Cost of sales' is the costs that can be directly attributed to the finished goods that were sold in the accounting period for which the cost of sales is being calculated.

The cost of sales is calculated as the cost of finished goods on hand (opening stock) at the start of the accounting period for which the cost of sales is being calculated plus the cost to manufacture/acquire the finished goods within the specific accounting period, less the cost of finished goods not sold (closing stock) in the period and carried over to the next accounting period. No overhead costs (selling costs, rental, etc) are included in the cost of sales. Cost of sales is a term used in manufacturing industries and retail industries. It is not typically a term that is used in service-type industries. Another way of describing the cost of sales is to say that they are the costs incurred in order to derive sales (in a previous or the current period).

Purchases are part of the manufacturing/acquisition costs and are included in the stock figures and in the cost of the goods sold in the month. The point that I am trying to make is therefore that a fraud in purchases may affect the opening and closing finished goods stock figures, as well as the cost of the goods sold in the period. Materials purchased may be first taken into stock or alternatively applied directly to the production process. Also, bear in mind that the corresponding entry to purchases is normally creditors (purchases on terms) or bank (cash purchases).

Prime costs are those costs that are directly attributable to the manufacturing of goods. These are the direct labour costs (ie labour working on the production and not the cost of, for example, office administration staff members) and material costs directly attributable to the manufacturing (for example, body parts in a vehicle). Overhead costs are not included therefore.

The motive for manipulating purchases and/or prime costs can, therefore, be to influence gross profit. Manipulation can also just be the plain manipulation of the individual elements of purchases or prime costs.

Possible types of fraudulent manipulation of purchases and/or other prime costs include:

- Not recording all costs to avoid scrutiny and/or to prevent cost overruns being detected.
- Recording too many costs to reduce gross profit. A reduction in gross profit will portray a poorer financial picture. Possible reasons for wanting to reduce gross profit include:
  - This may make the sale/merger of the company less attractive. Would-be buyers may be discouraged from purchasing the company.

  - Alternatively, to devalue the sales value of a company, enabling buyers to acquire the company below its true value.
  - It may also cause the company to be less suitable to obtain finance or be eligible to bid for certain size contracts. Such behaviour may be aimed at harming the company or benefitting a competitor.
  - Tax avoidance. Taxes are paid as a per cent of profits. Low profits mean low taxes.
  - Avoiding paying royalties, profit-based rentals, profit share, bonuses, commissions, etc.
- Recording too many costs so as to increase creditors.
- Posting other (non-prime costs) costs to purchases in an attempt to hide the other costs.
- The debit to the purchases account may be the contra entry to another unrelated fraudulent transaction. For example, you find a debit to purchase. The credit side of this entry could be a credit to the bank account for a fraudulent payment. The purchases account may just be a convenient account in which to 'hide' the fraudulent entry.
- Recording of costs in the incorrect accounting period, region, job, customer, etc.

An example comes to mind where two senior company employees were colluding with a corrupt company. The corrupt company was the supplier of fuel. The corrupt employees were making payments to the supplier for purported trucking services rendered. The supplier was the supplier of fuel and not of trucking services. Remember our rule: 'It is always the people who are the closest.' The corrupt employees had access to set up suppliers and to approve payments. They did not have ready access to the operating system. They, therefore, used the means that they had access to, by which to misappropriate funds. The first suspicion was that the supplier was purportedly rendering a service outside of their normal trade. The contract with the supplier only made provision for the supply of materials. A comparison of the operational records would show no such operational trucking activity could be linked to that supplier.

As discussed under sales, purchases and prime costs have an analytical relationship to many other items, including:

- Sales values and volumes
- Gross profit
- Work in progress and finished goods stock figures
- Materials and stock figures
- Production volumes
- Orders
- Trade creditors and/or cash.

The processing of credit notes is very important. There needs to be proper approval of credit notes. The risk of the credit note is that I can reverse a legitimate invoice and process a higher invoice and get a kickback from the supplier. I can also move the invoice to another cost centre where I believe it is less likely to be identified.

An example comes to mind of where a depot office was between the outside gate and the depot housing all stock. Depot staff members used to generate an invoice, which was used to get stock out of the depot. The invoice charged an arbitrary existing client. Security would carefully check the stock to the invoice and load it into a vehicle outside the gate. The staff members would then come back into the depot office and pass a credit note to reverse the charge to the arbitrary customer.

The controls required over credit notes/transaction cancellation include:

- Sequential numbering of credit notes
- Pre-approval of credit notes prior to processing
- Access rights and privileges to only allow restricted staff members to process credit notes
- Proper segregation of duties
- System blocks to suspend credit notes captured to the system subject to release by an authorised person
- A printout of all credit notes processed in a book month and placed on the front of a defence file with the batches of approved credit notes. A senior independent person should conduct spot checks to ensure that all credit notes were valid and authorised.

Special mention must be made here of the need to have the standard 'three-way match' of purchase orders (PO) to good receipt notes (GR) to invoices (IR). There may be many practical reasons why there is a low financial value mismatch. It is acceptable to have a tolerance below which there will be an automatic match. This is due to the fact that it may not be practical to investigate every difference and it may be more cost efficient to just process the differences. This will depend on the company's risk appetite.

The need for the three-way match is driven by the fact that you do not want the company to pay for goods and services not received/misappropriated. Suppliers also may send goods not ordered (type or quantity) or charge another amount than agreed at the time of order (innocently or intentionally). The three-way match identifies and prevents this.

The placing of an official company order will legally bind the company to purchase and pay for the item. The company is liable to pay once ownership transfers (normally on delivery). A purchase order (PO) on its own/without delivery does not create a liability. Only POs with GRs (on the financial system) for which the IR has not been received yet create a liability. Companies must accrue for these POs with GRs to ensure that liabilities are recorded completely.

If the IR is processed with no PO (straight expense payment), then there was no chance that the IR could have been accrued if it fell over an accounting period. Accruals may be understated for all these cases.

The PO serves as a financial and a quantity 'limit' on the transactions albeit after the fact when the invoice is received from the customer. In the absence of a PO, there is no way to know that the company overspent on a particular item/service. The company should have a process to approve additional work/costs over and above the initially approved expense.

The PO should also not be processed for a nominal amount. Opening a PO for say 1 dollar just to have a PO and then later processing the actual higher amount is completely against the three-way match control principle.

The three-way match is one issue. Segregation of duties is the other important consideration. There may very well have been a three-way match, but all these documents may have been fraudulently processed by the same person. Obtain therefore an electronic dump/printout of the staff members who captured/created the PO/GR/IRs on the system. Identify and investigate actual segregation of duty (SOD) conflicts that occurred, by substantiating the transaction in question.

Where there is no PO, check to see if this practice was consistent for each vendor:

- Never had a PO for that customer
- Making use of a PO on some occasions and not others
- This needs to be defined in a guideline.

Observations/tips to identify and prove

Understand how the purchasing process works:

- Analyse the end-to-end purchasing process for fraud vulnerabilities.
- Identify the rules, policies and procedures that apply to purchases.
- Test purchases/costs against these rules and policies and procedures to see if these 'rules' have been applied consistently/in a non-fraudulent manner.
- Determine which discounts and special deals are applicable (eg free stock, annual purchases, volume rebates from suppliers, etc.
- Understand how purchases are recorded and/or conducted (per job, geography, category, etc).
- Obtain explanations for deviations.

Substantiate purchase figures against supporting documents and predefined criteria that may deem purchase transactions as 'suspicious' for:

- Accuracy
- Completeness
- Validity and/or authorisation.

Valid purchase documents may include:

- Purchase requisitions
- Purchase orders (for trade creditors, not always for expense creditors)
- Quotes and calculations
- Invoices
- Credit notes
- Supplier contracts
- Delivery notes
- Payment requisitions
- Honoured cheques returned by the bank/electronic funds transfer (EFT) proof
- Requests for proposals
- Tender bid documentation.

Check financial payments to operational records to see if the payments were for goods and services actually received. In this instance, we are more concerned with operational volume records than with the proof of delivery itself, as it can be forged. We are concerned about operational or production volumes. For example, what was the factory producing and how does this compare to the POD? Could the factory have produced this amount given the low volume on the POD? Alternatively, should there be large quantities of materials in stock given the low production volumes?

Obtain supplier contracts and understand the terms and conditions so as to determine if:

- The clauses and conditions are fair/in line with the company's risk profile and/or normal contracts and/or not 'fraudulent' in nature against predefined criteria
- The contract was appropriately approved (person, date and amount)
- All addendums and/or alterations are attached and were duly approved
- All contractual obligations were fulfilled
- There is a pattern to exceptions (certain suppliers, particular staff members, specific products, etc).

In another example, the subject used to book fraudulent payments that she made to herself to a rubble cartage contractor's account to 'hide' payments. Rubble cartage costs were a prime cost of the construction sites. Rubble cartage did however not follow the same strict controls as other more significant prime costs (eg concrete, construction labour, etc) did. They were, therefore, a convenient place to hide the fraudulent payments. She got away with her scam until a vigilant contract manager spotted out of trend rubble cartage costs on his site.

Understand what the authorisation hierarchy specifies in terms of purchases and/or prime cost authorisation. Determine if authorisations were carried out in accordance with the authorisation hierarchy.

Understand who normally deals (records, approves and processes) with these types of costs and when they are normally incurred, dependencies as well as when they are processed. Look for purchases that were conducted outside of these norms.

Conduct e-mail searches and general business related correspondence reviews to identify correspondence proving corrupt relationships. Conduct searches of the subject's general workspace and/or desk to identify evidence of corrupt activities. Mirror hard drives and other company-owned electronic devices and search files saved and/or deleted to identify documents, correspondence, calculations and images that may identify corrupt activity.

Conduct lifestyle audits to:

- Profile potential subjects
- Identify subjects whose lifestyles appear to have been financed from sources other than known/declared income sources (assets, credit applications, default judgments, etc)
- Identify conflicts of interest (business/personal) and/or undeclared interests (directorships, etc).

Conduct interviews with company accountants, financial directors, external and internal auditors, whistle-blowers, any other relevant staff members, subjects, family and friends. Request management to sign declarations as to the complete and accurate calculation and/or payment of the items.

Conduct analytical reviews:

- Purchases to purchases
- Purchases per job, region, etc
- Purchases to contract value or sales
- Purchases over time
- Purchases to stock values
- Number of credit notes per supplier.

Obtain and investigate the following reports:

- IR processed without PO (standalone invoices/no accrual). Risk of no authorisation. Risk of duplicate payments.
- IR processed without GR (no delivery confirmation).
- Mismatch between PO/GR/IR.

9.4.43. Subcontractors

Discussion

Subcontractors are a specific type of creditor from which the company subcontracts work to perform on its behalf. Companies do this as it may not be practical for a company to retain every type of expertise required for its business. The company may also be unable to keep workers productive in seasonal trends. The use of subcontractors may be used to keep the company's overheads low during times of demand peaks and troughs. Companies may also not be able to maintain the specialised knowledge of a person/subcontractor dedicated to the specific field. Subcontractor firms can, therefore, possess specialised skills or expertise.

Payments to subcontractors may be made up of materials supplied and a labour portion or service provided. Subcontractors can, therefore, be 'supply and fit' subcontractors (the subcontractor provides materials and labour) or 'labour only'-type subcontractors (the subcontractor only provides labour and the company provides materials).

Subcontractor costs will be part of the prime costs discussed previously and the risks associated with prime costs refer. Also see the discussion on trade creditors, as many similar risks may apply.

The use of subcontractors is common in many industries, such as:

- Construction (the construction company will make use of bricklayers, lift technicians, electricians, air conditioning technicians, plumbers, painters, carpenters, etc)
- The wider information systems industry
- The film industry
- Farming (crop pickers, etc)
- Manufacturing (the use of labour broker firms that supply labour).

The risks of fraud with subcontractors may include the same risks that we have already discussed under other fraud schemes. Some examples include:

- Procurement-type fraud
- Trade creditors-type fraud
- Prime cost related fraud
- Gross profit-type fraud.

The type of fraud with subcontractors could therefore include:

- Rate/price discrepancies (overcharging or using a rate for a more expensive type of work)
- Volume discrepancies (paying for hours not worked)
- The giving of work to parties not qualified/authorised/certified to conduct the work

- Awarding unrequired work to a subcontractor/s for a kickback, cronyism, nepotism, etc
- Contractual risks, as a result of signing contracts with clauses that put the company at risk
- Subcontractors who are unable to complete work resulting in re-work, loss of productivity costs, duplication of costs, etc
- Paying for substandard work resulting in rework costs, loss of image with customers, etc
- Incorrect allocation of costs between subcontractors. Applying one subcontractor's costs to another subcontractor to avoid scrutiny of the initial subcontractor's costs.

Observations/tips to identify and prove

Determine the different categories or types of subcontractors. Understand the basis of payment of subcontractors. Some examples of payment bases include:

- Milestones achieved
- Rates per:
    - Units completed
    - Machine hours
    - Man hours
    - Days worked (known as 'day rates')
    - Running meters
    - Square metres
    - Cubic metres
    - Etc
- Number of workers.

Substantiate the payment of the subcontractors under review. Ensure that the payments were duly authorised and adequately supported by documents. Determine how subcontractors' work is signed off (production manager, quantity surveyor, etc). The signing off of the work performed is in effect a 'delivery note' or a 'proof of delivery' or the 'approval of the expense'. The payment of the expense and subsequent approval of the payment will follow later.

Understand the basis of subcontractor selection. Determine if this process was followed for the awarding of the subcontractor under review.

Obtain the contracts/SLAs that govern the relationship and determine if:

- They are fair
- They are enforced
- They are within the company's normal practice.

Conduct lifestyle audits to:

- Profile potential subjects
- Identify subjects whose lifestyles appear to have been financed from sources other than known/declared income sources (assets, credit applications, default judgments, etc)
- Identify conflicts of interest (business/personal) and/or undeclared interests (directorships, etc).

Obtain conflict of interest declarations and determine if:

- These were approved
- They result in an actual conflict
- It is any of the jobs or subcontractors that you are investigating.

Conduct interviews with company accountants, financial directors, external and internal auditors, whistle-blowers, any other relevant staff members, subjects, family and friends. Request management to sign declarations as to the complete and accurate calculation and/or payment of the item.

Conduct e-mail searches and general business related correspondence reviews to identify correspondence proving corrupt relationships. Conduct searches of the subject's general workspace and/or desk to identify evidence of corrupt activities. Mirror hard drives and other company-owned electronic devices and search files saved and/or deleted to identify documents, correspondence, calculations and images that may identify corrupt activity. Conduct analytical reviews.

One subcontractor red flag that I was taught to watch out for is subcontractors who work across trades and/or in multiple fields/disciplines. As an example: if a construction subcontractor does the electrical work, the ceiling installation and the site cleaning then you should regard this as suspicious. This is not always the case, as some trades complement each other and it may be common practice for subcontractors to perform more than one service (for example, plumbing and electrical). The risk is that the subcontractor is not performing the work themselves and they may, in turn, be subcontracting it at greater expense to the organisation. This represents both a commercial risk and a fraudulent risk. From a fraudulent point of view, the construction site manager may be the actual owner of the subcontracting firm. He would subcontract the work to actual subcontractors and charge the work at a premium to the organisation without adding any value to the organisation and to the financial detriment of the organisation. Quality of work may also be of concern.

In one related matter that I dealt with, a construction site contract manager was subcontracting various items of work to his own company. The contract manager was charging the company the standard rates and he was not overcharging. It is unknown if there would have been room for negotiation if another subcontractor had obtained the work. The contract manager had not declared the fact that he had a private company nor that he was awarding work to himself. It is also unlikely that he would have been objective to any quality issues or to the actual need to conduct all the work.

9.4.44. Contract accounts/job accounts

Discussion

Contract accounts are used to group all of the financial transactions specific to one contract. This account may be an actual general ledger account or it may be a management account in the management accounting system. The contract account may consist of a main account with sub-accounts per contract.

The benefits of having one view per contract are self-evident and may include:

- A view per contract of profit or loss and a basis for management reporting
- An ability to highlight under/over performing contracts
- Offering a focused ability to drill down and analyse contract performance.

The downsides of a contract view include:

- A potential inability to quickly compare relative contract performance
- A potential inability to view performance at a macro level (sales and/or prime costs).

Contract accounts are used in various types of businesses including:

- Construction (buildings, civil work, etc)
- Manufacturing (normally capital assets such as aircraft, etc)
- Service contracts (providing a specific number of hours/work in a fixed period).

There is normally at least one operational-type person who has control over the contract. There may even be a contract accountant designated to the contract depending on the size of the contract. There may also be specialist resources (for example quantity surveyors) that monitor and control the contract/specific elements of the contract. One/numerous resources may be dedicated to a single contract or the resource may work across a specific number of contracts as a shared resource.

The contract manager mostly is responsible for the approval of the 'expenses' on the contract. A separate finance team may be responsible for the approval of the 'payment' of these expenses.

A contract account is really just an accumulation of costs and revenues. Contract accounts are therefore subject to the same risks already discussed under the individual elements making up the account, including:

- Sales/turnover
- Purchases
- Prime costs
- Procurement risks
- Labour cost risks
- Quality risks
- Performance/degree completion risks
- Contract management team incentive risks.

The contract manager has a lot of power and the normal risks of fraud shift from a centralised business to a specific contract. The most important controls include:

- Detailed operating and financial data
- Visibility and analysis
- Defined budgets
- Defined deliverables
- Consistent action/enforcement
- The correct performance measures
- Defined policies and procedures
- Whistle-blower facilities.

Incentives can be a high-risk area, as they typically drive the incorrect behaviour in so far as people may do what is required to obtain the incentive, but without consideration for the overall accuracy/wellbeing of the contract. This risk is higher for:

- Highly technical contracts (difficult to understand what is really happening)
- Very large contracts (easy to hide fraud)
- High demand contracts (people may be prepared to sacrifice control just to get the contract/work done)
- Contracts where there is poor visibility of figures
- Contracts that are not clearly defined
- Contracts that carry high incentives/penalties.

Fraud on contract accounts could include:

- Booking unrelated costs to a contract
- Booking unauthorised costs to a contract
- Not booking costs at all
- Misstating milestone achievement
- Rate, volume frauds
- Collusion with staff, suppliers or subcontractors.

Controls to mitigate contract account fraud include:

- Strong budgets, bills of quantities and contract specifications
- Having frequent independent review of contracts
- Putting strong contracts in place
- Segregating contract account and approval duties.

Observations/tips to identify and prove

Identify all contract accounts. Understand the basis of contract accounting. Compare actual accounting to established policies and procedures.

Obtain the legal contracts that govern the contract and test to establish if all terms and conditions have been complied with.

Substantiate the individual elements making up the contract account:

- Adequately supported by documents
- Proof of delivery
- Rates in line with the contract
- Duly approved.

Conduct lifestyle audits to:

- Profile potential subjects
- Identify subjects whose lifestyles appear to have been financed from sources other than known/declared income sources (assets, credit applications, default judgments, etc)
- Identify conflicts of interest (business/personal) and/or undeclared interests (directorships, etc).

Conduct interviews with company accountants, financial directors, external and internal auditors, whistle-blowers, any other relevant staff members, subjects, family and friends. Request management to sign declarations as to the complete and accurate calculation and/or payment of the item.

Conduct analytical reviews:

- Contract to contract
- Industry benchmarks
- Individual elements of the contract to themselves.

9.4.45. Expense accounts, overhead charges

Discussion

These are all of the overhead-type expenses (ie not trading account-type expenses/prime costs) in the business. So, they are expenses that are not directly attributable to the trade of the company. The overhead expenses are deducted from gross profit to derive the net profit. Expenses can be repetitive or once off-type payments. Some examples include:

- Office rental
- Office staff salaries (not production staff members)
- Stationery costs
- IT costs.

Expenses are an area where money and goods change hands. Expenses are therefore a common area of abuse.

Expenses are recorded as debits to the general ledger expense account with the contra entry being a credit to the bank (cash) or to a creditor (terms).

Fraud risks include:

- Payment of private expenses
- Overstatement/understatement of expenses
- Incorrect quality received
- Special type of goods not declared/treated correctly (for example hazardous goods)
- Procuring from disallowed/illegal suppliers/contractually disallowed suppliers
- Failure to comply with contractual obligations
- Contravention of laws and regulations
- Approval of expenses that are not allowed in terms of company policy
- Expenses not required
- Non-approval of expenses that have been paid. This could include
    - The payment of an expense even though approval was declined
    - The payment of an expense without seeking approval at all
    - The approval of an expense beyond the approver's approval limits
- Fraudulent/duplicate claiming of expenses in order to receive a fraudulent refund. The company pays the creditor twice. The fraudulent staff member gives a non-company bank account into which the refund should be paid.

- Booking of expenses to incorrect accounts, cost centres, period, jobs, etc.
- Overstatement/understatement of cost accruals.
- Obtaining a kickback from the supplier for expenses incurred.
- Fronting of a company. The staff member sets up their own company. Services and goods are still procured from the normal suppliers. The fraudulent staff member however routes the business via his own company and takes a fee/markup.
- Nepotism or cronyism.
- All the contract and procurement risks discussed previously refer as well.

The following are controls that mitigate the risk of expense frauds:

- Requiring pre-approval of a purchase requisition before a purchase order (PO) can be opened
- Having a prior approved purchase order (PO)
- Using a three-quote system
- Only using pre-approved suppliers
- Having framework agreements with suppliers
- Having some form of proof of delivery, such as a goods received/delivery note (GR)
- Using a three-way match between PO/GR/IR
- Having budgets and monitoring actual spend against budgets
- Having audits and other random independent checks
- Segregation of duties of key responsibilities (ordering, expense approval, payment approval, receipt of goods, raising of the GR, processing of the transactions on the general ledger
- Supplier account reconciliations (not always performed for expense creditors; normally only done for trade creditors)
- System enforced controls
- Exception reports of non-compliance (timely payment, three-way match, late approval, etc)
- A clear and communicated authorisation hierarchy.

Observations/tips to identify and prove

Identify the company expense policy and procedures and test actual behaviour against this. Obtain explanations for deviations.

Substantiate payments against supporting documents and determine:

- If it was within policy
- Approved
- Allowed
- Required
- Actually delivered
- The correct quality
- Within contractual obligations
- Recorded correctly
- Segregation of duties was maintained
- Correctly accrued if required
- From an authorised/legitimate supplier
- The amounts and quantities agree to the supporting documents.

Sort expense payments in the cashbook and check for duplicate payments:

- Per supplier
- Per month
- Per invoice number (IR)
- Per account type
- Per job/cost centre.

Conduct lifestyle audits to:

- Profile potential subjects
- Identify subjects whose lifestyles appear to have been financed from sources other than known/declared income sources (assets, credit applications, default judgments, etc)
- Identify conflicts of interest (business/personal) and/or undeclared interests (directorships, etc).

Conduct interviews with company accountants, financial directors, external and internal auditors, whistle-blowers, any other relevant staff members, subjects, family and friends. Request management to sign declarations as to the complete and accurate calculation and/or payment of the item.

Conduct e-mail searches and general business related correspondence reviews to identify correspondence proving corrupt relationships. Conduct searches of the subject's general workspace and/or desk to identify evidence of corrupt activities. Mirror hard drives and other company-owned electronic devices and search files saved and/or deleted to identify documents, correspondence, calculations and images that may identify corrupt activity.

Conduct analytical reviews:

- Expenses to themselves over time
- Expenses to other related expenses or indicators.

I recall one matter that I dealt with. The employee was running his own IT service company and routing all company business through it. We identified numerous amounts of compelling evidence in this matter. One analytical review conducted in this matter is a good example: printer costs were identified to be very high. The examination determined that the costs were for printer cartridges and paper. We established that the printers in question were identical and were all dedicated to the company's customer service desk. The company only used one manufacturer's printer (a common IT brand name). The cartridges on the invoice were also purportedly for this manufacturer's cartridges. I performed the following checks:

- *I 'Googled' the printer cartridge model and manufacturer and established the expected number of print pages per cartridges. I multiplied this against the number of printer cartridges to obtain the theoretical number of single-page prints made.*
- *I also obtained a summary of the actual number of transactions performed per customer service agent and multiplied this by the number of pages required to be printed per transaction (being five). This gave me the actual number of pages printed.*
- *Lastly, I established the number of pages purportedly procured as per the invoices. There was no opening and closing stock of paper and this was, therefore, another measure of the number of pages purportedly actually used in the period.*

Comparison of the three measures identified that there were significant deviations of purportedly used and actually used. We were unable to use the printers' internal tallies of prints conducted, as we did not have a starting figure. As it turned out, the analytical review highlighted significant deviations.

9.4.46. Other income

Discussion

Companies basically have two types of income, being:

- Trading income, which is derived from the conduct of the company's main trade (this is called turnover or sales
- Any other income obtained, which does not stem from the company's main business.

Examples of other income include:

- Non-trade rental income
- Profit on the sale of assets
- Royalties
- Investment income (interest, dividends, etc).

Other income is recorded as a credit in the specific general ledger income account. The corresponding debit is to the bank account, a debtor or a loan account.

Other income can be manipulated by fraudulently increasing the income so as to:

- Make the income received appear to be better than it actually was
- Avoid scrutiny
- Obtain finance
- Obtain work/be eligible to tender on more significant work
- Obtain incentives or remuneration
- Hide the misappropriation of all/part of the other income.

Income can be fraudulently made to appear less in an attempt to show a poorer financial picture so as to:

- Hide misappropriated income
- Prevent obtaining finance
- Reduce the sale value of an entity
- Prevent having to pay incentives, royalties, etc.

The credit to the income account may also just be a convenient place to put the contra entry of another unrelated fraudulent debit.

Observations/tips to identify and prove

Determine all types of other income. Understand company policy and procedure with regards to these. Compare actual behaviour to policies and procedures. Substantiate all other income.

Conduct lifestyle audits to:

- Profile potential subjects
- Identify subjects whose lifestyles appear to have been financed from sources other than known/declared income sources (assets, credit applications, default judgments, etc)
- Identify conflicts of interest (business/personal) and/or undeclared interests (directorships, etc).

Conduct interviews with company accountants, financial directors, external and internal auditors, whistle-blowers, any other relevant staff members, subjects, family and friends. Request management to sign declarations as to the complete and accurate calculation and/or payment of the item.

Conduct e-mail searches and general business related correspondence reviews to identify correspondence proving corrupt relationships. Conduct searches of the subject's general workspace and/or desk to identify evidence of corrupt activities. Mirror hard drives and other company-owned electronic devices and search files saved and/or deleted to identify documents, correspondence, calculations and images that may identify corrupt activity. Conduct analytical reviews.

9.4.47. Labour costs, salaries, wages, commissions, etc.

Discussion

Under the payroll section, we discussed the detail behind some of these amounts. We concentrated on the payroll environment and the more transactional type frauds in this environment. Under this section, we are more concerned by the general ledger side of these emoluments and how frauds can be perpetrated in relation to particular contracts, jobs or cost centres.

Direct labour costs are included in prime costs. Indirect labour (eg supervision costs) will (unless related to a specific contract, etc) be an overhead-type expense.

Frauds can be perpetrated by:

- Recording costs in another cost centre, account, contract, accounting period, etc.
- Fraudulent journal entries may be used to manipulate costs.
- Fraudulent manual calculations may be used to manipulate labour costs before being captured.
- Not declaring all/understating these costs.
- Overstating/understating of labour costs.
- Rate or hour variances to result in over or under costs.
- The debit to the labour account could just be the contra entry of another unrelated fraudulent transaction.
- Giving instruction to the payroll department to process fraudulent transactions.

Observations/tips to identify and prove

Determine the types of labour costs in the period under review. Understand company policy and procedure with regards to these. Compare actual behaviour to policies and procedures.

Determine high-risk labour types/contracts, etc. Concentrate your efforts on the high-risk labour types unless you are aware of fraud in a specific type of labour. Establish if there were any salary/labour cost increases in the period. Substantiate labour calculations and payments.

Conduct lifestyle audits to:

- Profile potential subjects
- Identify subjects whose lifestyles appear to have been financed from sources other than known/declared income sources (assets, credit applications, default judgments, etc)
- Identify conflicts of interest (business/personal) and/or undeclared interests (directorships, etc).

Conduct interviews with company accountants, financial directors, external and internal auditors, whistle-blowers, any other relevant staff members, subjects, family and friends. Request management to sign declarations as to the complete and accurate calculation and/or payment of the item.

Conduct e-mail searches and general business related correspondence reviews to identify correspondence proving corrupt relationships. Conduct searches of the subject's general workspace and/or desk to identify evidence of corrupt activities. Mirror hard drives and other company-owned electronic devices and search files saved and/or deleted to identify documents, correspondence, calculations and images that may identify corrupt activity. Conduct analytical reviews.

9.4.48. Loss/gain on sale of assets

Discussion

This section should be read together with the discussion on assets under the balance sheet section. When an organisation purchases an asset, it records the asset in its books at the purchase price. The organisation then depreciates the asset over the useful life of the asset. The organisation may, in the normal course of its business, decide to sell the asset at a later stage. The market value of the asset at the time of sale of the asset may be more or less than the book value. For example: an asset was purchased for 100 and depreciated to 50 over two years before being sold for 80. The company, therefore, made a profit/gain on the sale of the asset of 30, being the difference between the sale price (80) and the book value (50).

Fraudsters may manipulate the loss or gain on the sale of an asset to:

- Fraudulently increase the profit/gain at the time of sale so as to:
  - Make the sale appear to be better than it was for performance review reasons.
  - Hide the misappropriation of all or part of the proceeds of the asset. For example if the known market value of a sold asset is 100 and the subject misappropriates 20, the subject would need to record the sale at 100 in the books to avoid detection.
- Fraudulently reduce the profit/gain on the sale of the asset so as to:
  - Make the sale appear less successful than it was.
  - Hide the misappropriation of all or part of the proceeds of the asset. As per our previous example, if the market value of the asset was unknown, the subject may just need to record the sale of the asset at the reduced amount net of the misappropriated portion.

- Fraudulently reduce the loss on the sale so as to:
    - Make the sale appear to have been better than it actually was for performance review reasons.
    - Make the loss seem less than it actually was to hide the fact that the subject or the subject's accomplices acquired the asset at a loss/below market value.
- Fraudulently increase the loss on the sale of the asset so as to:
    - Make the sale of the asset appear to be less favourable to hide successes or avoid scrutiny of incorrect sales.
- The loss may also serve as a:
    - Distraction from another fraudulent transaction that the subject does not want people to notice. The subject will stir up a lot of dust around the loss of the sale of the asset and keep people's attention focused on it in the hope that they do not look at other more serious issues.
    - The loss on the sale of asset account may be a convenient place to hide another unrelated fraudulent transaction. People are expecting to have a loss in this account, so a slightly greater loss may be unquestioned.
    - The loss of sale of asset account may be a convenient place to hide the fraudulent portion of the asset sale.

Observations/tips to identify and prove

Obtain a list of all assets sold in the period under review. Independently verify the sale of assets:

- In the fixed asset register
- Through physical verification
- In the general ledger
- Reductions in the balance sheet (assets, accumulated depreciation)
- Receipts in the bank account.

Substantiate the sale of the asset against supporting documents. Independently verify the market value of such assets. The use of an expert valuator may be required. Determine who purchased the asset/s. Determine if the sale was within company policy (for example that assets are sold after X years or that assets are only scrapped, etc. Determine if all relevant special regulations were complied with (for example hazardous goods). Determine if the sale was authorised and by whom. Check if this is commensurate with the organisational hierarchy.

Conduct lifestyle audits to:

- Profile potential subjects
- Identify subjects whose lifestyles appear to have been financed from sources other than known/declared income sources (assets, credit applications, default judgments, etc).
- Identify conflicts of interest (business/personal) and/or undeclared interests (directorships, etc).

Conduct interviews with company accountants, financial directors, external and internal auditors, whistle-blowers, any other relevant staff members, subjects, family and friends. Request management to sign declarations as to the complete and accurate calculation and/or payment of the item.

Conduct e-mail searches and general business related correspondence reviews to identify correspondence proving corrupt relationships. Conduct searches of the subject's general workspace and/or desk to identify evidence of corrupt activities. Mirror hard drives and other company-owned electronic devices and search files saved and/or deleted to identify documents, correspondence, calculations and images that may identify corrupt activity. Conduct analytical reviews.

9.4.49. Asset revaluation/impairment

Discussion

This section should be read together with the discussion on assets under the balance sheet section.

Revaluation (increase in value) and impairments (reduction in value) are movements in the asset's recorded value. Organisations are, in terms of international accounting standards, required to record assets at their true value. Depreciation in accordance with the organisation's accounting policies may be insufficient to value the asset at the true value (up or down). Organisations therefore annually consider if their assets are fairly valued and adjust the values accordingly.

Asset revaluations and impairments are made against current profits or against previous periods' profits that have been provisioned one side for such events. The motive for the fraudulent manipulation of revaluations/impairments may be driven by the anticipated effect of the revaluation/impairment on the profit/provision figures.

Revaluations may be subject to opinion and may, therefore, represent a unique opportunity for fraudsters to manipulate the situation to their advantage without necessarily being detected or able to be directly proven to be fraudulent.

There may be a variety of fraudulent reasons to increase and decrease the value of assets. Increased value will result in the asset/s appearing to be more valuable than they actually are and present a more favourable financial position. This may be done in order to:

Secure loans and/or investments

- Make the organisation's financial position appear to be better
- Make assets appear more valuable during a potential sale
- Avoid scrutiny
- Obtain bonuses/incentives
- Hide other unrelated fraudulent transactions.

Reductions in value will, in turn, present a less favourable picture. This may be done in an attempt to:

- Acquire a business or asset/s at a reduced price
- Hide other fraudulent transactions.

Observations/tips to identify and prove

Identify all assets revalued/impaired within the period under review:

- Movements in balance sheet asset values
- Revaluation transactions in the general ledger
- Movements in relevant provision accounts
- In consultation with the external auditors.

Substantiate the revaluation/impairment. Understand the company policy and international accounting standards relevant to asset revaluation/impairments. Determine if revaluations/impairments occurred within policy and reporting requirements. Independently verify the market value of such assets. The use of an expert valuator may be required. Interview the external auditors and/or obtain written undertaking from the auditors that they are comfortable with the revaluations/impairments. Physically verify that assets exist and that they are in the organisation's name.

Conduct lifestyle audits to:

- Profile potential subjects
- Identify subjects whose lifestyles appear to have been financed from sources other than known/declared income sources (assets, credit applications, default judgments, etc)
- Identify conflicts of interest (business/personal) and/or undeclared interests (directorships, etc).

Conduct interviews with company accountants, financial directors, external and internal auditors, whistle-blowers, any other relevant staff members, subjects, family and friends. Request management to sign declarations as to the complete and accurate calculation and/or payment of the item.

Conduct e-mail searches and general business related correspondence reviews to identify correspondence proving corrupt relationships. Conduct searches of the subject's general workspace and/or desk to identify evidence of corrupt activities. Mirror hard drives and other company-owned electronic devices and search files saved and/or deleted to identify documents, correspondence, calculations and images that may identify corrupt activity. Conduct analytical reviews.

9.4.50. General ledger transactions

Discussion

The general ledger is the place where the 'nuts and bolts'/daily financial accounting transactions are processed. General ledger transactions could be income or expense related. Try, when reviewing transactions posted in the general ledger, to understand both sides of the entry before concluding on the 'correctness' of the entry. One side of the entry may appear perfectly normal, but the combination of the entries may seem strange. *In one example that I dealt with, the subject put a debit to wages and a credit to sales. While it is perfectly normal to have debits to wages and credits to sales, there is no accounting logic to support entries directly between these two accounts. In this particular case, there were numerous such 'strange' entries. The entries were a desperate attempt by the subject to conceal fraudulent transactions.*

Keep in mind that the corresponding entry to a seemingly normal debit on an account may very well be a credit to the bank account, being a payment. Fraudulent payments need to be posted somewhere to prevent them from being identified as unreconciling entries in a bank reconciliation.

You will also need to understand what the nature is of the transactions that are normally posted to that account.

Observations/tips to identify and prove

Compare the actual entries to:

- International accounting standards and/or generally accepted accounting practice, as applicable
- Company policy and procedure
- Applicable laws and regulations
- General logic.

Ask yourself if it is normal to have transactions:

- Between those two general ledger accounts
- For those legal entities/business units
- Performed by those people
- Within that period
- Authorised by those people
- With or without supporting documents.

Independently determine:

- The correct value of the transaction/s
- The completeness of the transaction/s
- The timeliness of the transaction/s.

Conduct interviews with company accountants, financial directors, external and internal auditors, whistle-blowers, any other relevant staff members, subjects, family and friends. Request management to sign declarations as to the complete and accurate calculation and/or payment of the item.

Conduct e-mail searches and general business related correspondence reviews to identify correspondence proving corrupt relationships. Conduct searches of the subject's general workspace and/or desk to identify evidence of corrupt activities. Mirror hard drives and other company-owned electronic devices and search files saved and/or deleted to identify documents, correspondence, calculations and images that may identify corrupt activity.

Conduct lifestyle audits to:

- Profile potential subjects
- Identify subjects whose lifestyles appear to have been financed from sources other than known/declared income sources (assets, credit applications, default judgments, etc)
- Identify conflicts of interest (business/personal) and/or undeclared interests (directorships, etc).

Conduct analytical reviews.

9.4.51. Gross profit

Gross profit can be recorded per:

- Legal entity
- Job

- Product
- Trade area
- Business unit, etc

Discussion

This section should be read together with the previous discussion on the trading account. Under the trading account section, we discussed all the individual trading account entries that could affect the gross profit. Here we are concerned about the gross profit figure itself, which may be shown in a financial ledger or in the management accounts.

Understand the business model used, for example:

- Does the organisation target low gross profit and high turnover (for example in a supermarket)?
- Higher gross profit and reduced volume of transactions (for example in an exotic car dealership or an estate agent).

It is normal business practice for an organisation to cut gross profits in order to derive business/ obtain contracts. Reductions in gross profit must, therefore, be understood in terms of the period in which the organisation is trading, the business model, the specific client, etc.

The fraudulent increasing in the gross profit could:

- Make the organisation's financial position appear to be better than it actually is
- Be used to:
    - Avoid scrutiny
    - Unfairly obtain bonuses and incentives
    - Make the purchase of the organisation appear more favourable to the unknown buyer
    - Obtain finance
    - Win bids
    - Be eligible for work above the organisation's actual financial position.

The fraudulent decrease in the gross profit could:

- Make the organisation appear less favourable to:
    - Unfairly reduce the sale value of the organisation
    - Avoid winning business (in collusion with a competitor/to get vengeance, etc)
    - Prevent obtaining finance.

Gross profit may be manipulated by:

- Putting entries through (trading account level transactions) the general ledger.
- Physically recording another figure to what is in the general ledger.

Observations/tips to identify and prove

Understand the process for determining gross profit in the organisation and the business model (profit versus volume) used.

Conduct interviews with company accountants, financial directors, external and internal auditors, whistle-blowers, any other relevant staff members, subjects, family and friends. Request management to sign declarations as to the complete and accurate calculation and/or payment of the item.

Conduct e-mail searches and general business related correspondence reviews to identify correspondence proving corrupt relationships. Conduct searches of the subject's general workspace and/or desk to identify evidence of corrupt activities. Mirror hard drives and other company-owned electronic devices and search files saved and/or deleted to identify documents, correspondence, calculations and images that may identify corrupt activity.

Conduct analytical reviews:

- Gross profit over time
- Gross profit to turnover
- Gross profit to operational volumes
- Gross profit to net profit.

Conduct lifestyle audits to:

- Profile potential subjects
- Identify subjects whose lifestyles appear to have been financed from sources other than known/declared income sources (assets, credit applications, default judgments, etc)
- Identify conflicts of interest (business/personal) and/or undeclared interests (directorships, etc).

9.4.52. Net profit

Discussion

The net profit is the amount of gross profit that remains after all overheads have been deducted and other income (not trading income) added. Net profit is before extraordinary items, tax and profit share have been taken into account.

Out of trend net profit may be an indication of:

- Trading account-level problems, the effect of which is being manifested in the net profit
- Overhead expense related misconduct
- Direct manipulation of the net profit figure.

The fraudulent increasing in the net profit could:

- Make the organisation's financial position appear to be better than it actually is
- Be used to:
    - Avoid scrutiny
    - Unfairly obtain bonuses and incentives
    - Make the purchase of the organisation appear more favourable to the unknown buyer
    - Obtain finance
    - Win bids
    - Be eligible for work above the organisation's actual financial position.

The fraudulent decrease in the net profit could:

- Make the organisation appear less favourable to:
    - Unfairly reduce the sale value of the organisation
    - Avoid winning business (in collusion with a competitor/to get vengeance, etc)
    - Prevent obtaining finance
    - Prevent having to pay incentives to staff members.

Net profit may be manipulated by:

- Putting entries through (expenses or incomes) the general ledger
- Physically recording another figure to what is in the general ledger.

Observations/tips to identify and prove

Substantiate the net profit from the general ledger to the financial statements.

Conduct interviews with company accountants, financial directors, external and internal auditors, whistle-blowers, any other relevant staff members, subjects, family and friends. Request management to sign declarations as to the complete and accurate calculation and/or payment of the item.

Conduct e-mail searches and general business related correspondence reviews to identify correspondence proving corrupt relationships. Conduct searches of the subject's general workspace and/or desk to identify evidence of corrupt activities. Mirror hard drives and other company-owned electronic devices and search files saved and/or deleted to identify documents, correspondence, calculations and images that may identify corrupt activity. Conduct analytical reviews.

Conduct lifestyle audits to:

- Profile potential subjects
- Identify subjects whose lifestyles appear to have been financed from sources other than known/declared income sources (assets, credit applications, default judgments, etc)
- Identify conflicts of interest (business/personal) and/or undeclared interests (directorships, etc).

9.4.53. Petty cash

Discussion

Most organisations do not work with physical cash at all or to a large degree. While some of their income may be received in the form of cash (for example: a retail outlet), the organisation would bank the cash and pay their creditors and staff members via cheques and/or electronic transfers.

Organisations typically keep a small amount of cash in a locked 'purpose made' metal box for financially materially low expenses. Examples of these expenses include: cleaning materials for the office, a replacement padlock for a door, a small tin of touch-up paint, etc.

The manner in which petty cash works is for the organisation to withdraw a fixed amount of cash (for example 5,000.00). Staff members may either spend their own cash and request a reimbursement for expenses incurred on behalf of the company or request an advance with which to fund the company expenses. Petty cash expenses need to be approved by an authorised person just like normal company expenses. The signing of the invoice may suffice or in more sophisticated companies a formal petty cash approval and allocation form may need to be completed.

Once the cash on hand has reduced to a particular level (for example from the aforementioned 5,000.00 to 300.00), the petty cash clerk would attach all till slips and invoices of expenses paid (4,700.00 in our example) to a summary sheet (of all petty cash incomes and expenses in the period) and present this to the accountant for authorisation to replenish the petty cash balance back to the original level (5,000.00 in our example).

A petty cash reimbursement is not limited by financial period and can take place whenever the cash runs low, provided that the company has the funds available. A reimbursement may therefore occur more than once in a month or every so many months, as the reimbursement need requires.

The physical balance of cash on hand should be checked every time a reimbursement is done, or at least every month, by a senior person who is independent of the petty cash function.

The reimbursement verification only entails checking that the slips attached match the reimbursement amount. The full petty cash verification entails checking the opening cash balance less the expenses in the box (not yet reimbursed) and plus any income or replenishment of the physical cash on hand. The conducting of unannounced surprise petty cash verifications is highly recommended.

No petty cash should ever 'leave' the petty cash box without being exchanged by a slip for the exact amount removed. If a staff member requests an advance (for example 500.00), then they should sign a petty cash advance form to evidence that they have taken 500 worth of money. The signed advance form should be captured in the petty cash register (-500.00) and retained as supporting evidence. The staff member will later return with change (say 50.00) and a slip for the expense (say 450.00). The change (50.00) should be replaced in the petty cash box and the full amount of the advance should be captured as an income (+500). The actual expense (for example -450.00.00) should be captured as an expense and the supporting slip retained. The net effect is that the physical cash on hand will balance with the theoretical cash on hand per the petty cash register.

If on the other hand, a staff member has used their own cash, they present the approved slip/invoice to the petty cash clerk. The petty cash clerk gives the staff member the required amount of cash and captures the expense in the petty cash register. The slip is retained in support of the payment.

Petty cash, while of low financial materiality, has been a common area of fraudulent abuse in companies in my experience. I believe that this is because petty cash is not always well controlled and it is not seen as important.

No 'IOUs' are to be allowed at all. It is a common incident for staff members responsible for the petty cash to 'fund' their lifestyles from the petty cash box and repay it later. This would be an unauthorised use of company funds, no matter how insignificant.

It should also be noted that staff members may say upon detection of an IOU that they were merely borrowing the money and that they were going to replace it at a later stage. It is difficult to know if this is the actual case or if this is an excuse to cover for misappropriated cash that was detected.

In one matter referred to in this book, we caught a lady who was reimbursing staff members via an electronic payment and duplicating the claim form and paying herself the cash equivalent from petty cash as well. This was identified during a surprise petty cash verification by us as the auditors.

Another interesting behaviour in the case was that the fraudulent petty cash clerk always used to request the financial manager (FM) to sign the petty cash reimbursement just before he was going home. Now you must understand that a person could set their watch by the FM's going home times. He did not like being held back at work and would not pay the reimbursements the desired level of attention.

In another matter, the lady concerned was required to put scrap proceeds into the petty cash box. She was, however, keeping these for herself and not recording any receipt. The operations manager could recall that there should have been proceeds captured for the sale of scrap. The lady confessed to misappropriating the funds upon confrontation.

Observations/tips to identify and prove

Conduct a surprise verification of the petty cash on hand. Arrive unannounced and request to count the cash. Do not allow the staff member to make an excuse and request that you return later, as they may need to replace IOUs or complete the petty cash register. Commence by counting the cash in front of them. Never take it out of their sight. Get them to sign that the cash counted is correct. Then give the cash back to them for safekeeping. Then go to the detail of the transactions. Check that all incomes and expenses are supported by adequate approved documents (invoices, till slips or cash advance forms).

Determine what company policy is on petty cash expenses. Ensure that all expenses were within policy and that they were authorised by the appropriate person. Also, ensure that all petty cash float reimbursements were authorised.

Speak to various people and try to understand the nature of expenses and incomes that are processed through petty cash. Try to identify which incomes (for example scrap sale proceeds) were received/due in the period under review. Check to see that these were receipted completely and accurately. Vouch the petty cash amounts to the cash book and/or general ledger.

Conduct interviews with company accountants, financial directors, external and internal auditors, whistle-blowers, any other relevant staff members, subjects, family and friends. Request management to sign declarations as to the complete and accurate calculation and/or payment of the item. Conduct analytical reviews.

Conduct lifestyle audits to:

- Profile potential subjects
- Identify subjects whose lifestyles appear to have been financed from sources other than known/declared income sources (assets, credit applications, default judgments, etc)
- Identify conflicts of interest (business/personal) and/or undeclared interests (directorships, etc).

9.4.54. Exchange gains and losses

Discussion

Organisations deal with multiple currencies. Physical cash may be used or electronic transactions may be conducted. This frequently results in differences between the values of the two currencies between the time that the transactions were performed and when the amounts were processed in the company's bank accounts and/or records.

Companies need to record the difference as an exchange loss or gain. Such differences may be material on large transactions. The booking of an exchange gain or loss may present a fraudster with the opportunity to hide an unauthorised transaction or to utilise an amount to cover another transaction.

Observations/tips to identify and prove

- Determine which transactions attract exchange differences.
- Identify all exchange gains/losses booked in the period under review.
- Check that all exchange differences that needed to be booked were in fact booked.
- Substantiate the exchange differences.
- Independently verify the exchange rates used to banking sites or independent reliable internet sites.

Identify regulations, company policy and accounting reporting requirements with regards to exchange differences. Test to see that transactions were processed within the precepts of these requirements. Conduct analytical reviews

Conduct e-mail searches and general business related correspondence reviews to identify correspondence proving corrupt relationships. Conduct searches of the subject's general workspace and/or desk to identify evidence of corrupt activities. Mirror hard drives and other company-owned electronic devices and search files saved and/or deleted to identify documents, correspondence, calculations and images that may identify corrupt activity.

Conduct lifestyle audits to:

- Profile potential subjects
- Identify subjects whose lifestyles appear to have been financed from sources other than known/declared income sources (assets, credit applications, default judgments, etc)
- Identify conflicts of interest (business/personal) and/or undeclared interests (directorships, etc).

9.4.55. Extraordinary items

Discussion

Extraordinary items are transactions that occur which are not within the organisation's normal business and/or which are unlikely to reoccur.

Examples include:

- Insurance claims
- Legal fees
- Theft or fire damage
- Tax penalties.

Extraordinary items must be recorded completely, but separately to show what the organisation's profits would have been without the item and what they are after the item. Extraordinary items may represent an opportunity for fraudsters to hide all kinds of other evils. Extraordinary items may reflect badly on management and they may be less than reluctant to highlight these as items.

Observations/tips to identify and prove

Speak to various people and try to determine if anything unusual occurred within the period under review. Determine if these activities are to be categorised as extraordinary items. Check to see that all extraordinary items were duly recorded.

Substantiate all extraordinary items to adequately approved and supporting documents. Identify company policy and international accounting reporting requirements with regards to extraordinary items. Determine if there are any regulatory or tax regulations that apply specifically to these items. Test to see that transactions were processed within the precepts of these requirements.

Determine authorisation requirements and test to see that all extraordinary items were correctly authorised. Interview the external auditors and ensure that they are happy with the treatment of the items.

Conduct e-mail searches and general business related correspondence reviews to identify correspondence proving corrupt relationships. Conduct searches of the subject's general workspace and/or desk to identify evidence of corrupt activities. Mirror hard drives and other company owned electronic devices and search files saved and/or deleted to identify documents, correspondence, calculations and images that may identify corrupt activity.

Conduct lifestyle audits to:

- Profile potential subjects
- Identify subjects whose lifestyles appear to have been financed from sources other than known/declared income sources (assets, credit applications, default judgments, etc)
- Identify conflicts of interest (business/personal) and/or undeclared interests (directorships, etc).

9.4.56. Dividends

Discussion

Companies have investors. Investors invest in a company primarily to receive a share of the profits and/or to achieve capital growth on their investment. The investors' share of the company's profits will be dependent on their degree of investment and their type or class of investment.

A share of profits is paid to investors in the form of a dividend. A company does however not always pay out a dividend. There first needs to be a profit to distribute and second there needs to be cash in the bank to fund the payment. Companies may also wish to put some of the profits away to provide for another future event (provisions).

Dividend fraud may include the following types of fraudulent activity:

- Excessive dividends may be paid over and above what should be paid or could be paid out.
- Dividends may be unfairly retained and not all dividends due and payable may be paid out.
- Dividends may not be paid out in the correct ratios.
- Dividends may not be paid to the people who qualify for payments.
- Profits may be unfairly reduced prior to dividend calculation resulting in underpayment of dividends.

In one matter that I dealt with, there was a group of (private) companies with an unnecessarily complicated structure. At the top of this structure, there were shareholder companies. Then there was a holding company which held the individual operating companies and various property companies.

I was contracted to look at the holding company. The holding company was intended to be a vehicle through which to pay the major shareholders and to ensure that ownership ratios were maintained correctly. The individual operating companies were generally well controlled with a lot of eyes on their performance. The colluding partners had total control over the non-operating companies. They were paying fraudulent amounts (supported by invoices) to themselves out of the holding company and/or property companies. In this manner, they were able to reduce the profits on which dividends were to be paid out of the holding company. The colluding parties then also received their reduced share of the dividends over and above the fraudulent payments they had already received. The shareholder that they were defrauding only received a reduced dividend payment, which appeared to be correct. I unfortunately never got to complete my investigation, as the other shareholders restricted me from obtaining the required information. The matter remained unresolved. Some years later one of the financial managers contacted me to say that some of the colluding shareholders' shenanigans were unearthed and a management buyout was in process.

Observations/tips to identify and prove

- Understand the dividend policies and procedures.
- Review shareholder agreements.
- Verify shareholding ratios to independent records (stock exchange, external auditors, other public records, bank records, etc).
- Check board meeting minutes and annual general meeting minutes.

Substantiate all dividends paid. Conduct interviews with company accountants, financial directors, external and internal auditors, whistle-blowers, any other relevant staff members, subjects, family and friends. Request management to sign declarations as to the complete and accurate calculation and/or payment of the item.

Conduct e-mail searches and general business related correspondence reviews to identify correspondence proving corrupt relationships. Conduct searches of the subject's general workspace and/or desk to identify evidence of corrupt activities. Mirror hard drives and other company-owned electronic devices and search files saved and/or deleted to identify documents, correspondence, calculations and images that may identify corrupt activity. Conduct analytical reviews.

Conduct lifestyle audits to:

- Profile potential subjects
- Identify subjects whose lifestyles appear to have been financed from sources other than known/declared income sources (assets, credit applications, default judgments, etc)
- Identify conflicts of interest (business/personal) and/or undeclared interests (directorships, etc).

Section D - Other interesting fraud schemes

9.4.57. Share incentive schemes

Discussion

Companies sometimes give key managers a share of and/or shares in the business. This is done to incentivise and motivate the employee by giving them a sense of ownership and to encourage profit maximisation. The idea is that a person receiving the shares and will be motivated to work harder and/or smarter in order to obtain dividends and/or capital growth and/or influence.

Share incentive schemes may be actual shares that are being issued. Alternatively, the company may issue share options.

Share options give the employee the right to the actual shares subject to certain conditions (for example partial payment or growing the business by X%, etc) at some future date.

Phantom share schemes are also sometimes used when the organisation cannot issue actual shares. The organisation devises a scheme of 'notional' shares which are awarded to key managers subject to satisfying certain conditions. This type of a scheme is really a bonus incentive scheme and not a share incentive scheme.

The following are examples of frauds that could occur with share incentive schemes:

- Employees being included in the scheme who should not be included in the scheme
- Employees receiving a type of shares that they are not entitled to
- Employees receiving a number of shares that they are not entitled to
- Employers who unfairly withhold shares from employees rightfully entitled to receive the shares
- Terms of share schemes not applied correctly
- Managers manipulating KPIs in order to derive short-term benefits to qualify for the shares.

Observations/tips to identify and prove

- Determine if the company has share incentive schemes. If so understand the scheme rules.
- Understand who was eligible to receive shares during the period under review. Substantiate the share scheme.
- Understand the authorisations required and determine if these were correctly applied.

Conduct interviews with company accountants, financial directors, external and internal auditors, whistle-blowers, any other relevant staff members, subjects, family and friends. Request management to sign declarations as to the complete and accurate calculation and/or payment of the item.

Conduct e-mail searches and general business related correspondence reviews to identify correspondence proving corrupt relationships. Conduct searches of the subject's general workspace and/or desk to identify evidence of corrupt activities. Mirror hard drives and other company-owned electronic devices and search files saved and/or deleted to identify documents, correspondence, calculations and images that may identify corrupt activity. Conduct analytical reviews.

Conduct lifestyle audits to:

- Profile potential subjects
- Identify subjects whose lifestyles appear to have been financed from sources other than known/declared income sources (assets, credit applications, default judgments, etc)
- Identify conflicts of interest (business/personal) and/or undeclared interests (directorships, etc).

9.4.58. Snagging/rework

Discussion

This section should be read together with the discussion on retentions. Our discussion on retentions concerned the amount retained in the balance sheet for retentions. In this section, we are discussing the amounts expensed in the profit and loss for rework that was completed.

It is commonplace in certain industries (for example: construction) for the client to retain a standard/agreed portion of money to cover breakages or poor workmanship.

Snagging or rework may also be contractually applicable in situations where a guarantee was given.

While the company may have allocated a portion of funds for rework, it may be difficult to ring-fence/determine the exact amount that will be spent on re-work. The inability to determine the exact amount to be spent on rework represents an opportunity for abuse.

Examples of snagging/rework fraud schemes include:

- Not booking all costs of rework/snagging and booking these elsewhere
- Booking too many costs and/or other costs not applicable to the project/job/cost centre (this may be to hide unrelated costs or it may be to 'make use' of an unutilised provision of rework on one job to smooth/hide costs of another job)
- Booking costs to another project/job/incorrect cost centre
- Booking costs in a different period
- Booking all costs, but not showing the breakdown of costs and/or allocating work into different/incorrect cost types
- Processing rework not authorised at all or not authorised by the correct person.

All of this provides an inability to see the true state of a job/project and denies the organisation the opportunity to optimise jobs/projects and/or hold people accountable.

Motives for manipulating snagging/rework may include to:

- Show a higher profit/project success in one job or across jobs
- Avoid scrutiny of those responsible for project delivery
- Ensure that incentives are received by employees
- Avoid paying incentives by employers
- Use the snagging costs to hide other unrelated inefficiencies due to the inability to ring-fence the exact value.

Observations/tips to identify and prove

Understand the organisation's policy and practice on rework and snagging:

- When is a job regarded as closed?
- When is profit recognised?
- What effect does rework have on current and prior period profits?

Understand who may authorise rework. Substantiate rework/snagging to ensure that it was:

- Accurate and complete
- Valid and authorised
- Booked to the correct period, job, work/expense classification, etc
- Processed in time
- Supported by adequate source documents.

Conduct interviews with company accountants, financial directors, external and internal auditors, whistle-blowers, any other relevant staff members, subjects, family and friends. Request management to sign declarations as to the complete and accurate calculation and/or payment of the item.

Conduct e-mail searches and general business related correspondence reviews to identify correspondence proving corrupt relationships. Conduct searches of the subject's general workspace and/or desk to identify evidence of corrupt activities. Mirror hard drives and other company-owned electronic devices and search files saved and/or deleted to identify documents, correspondence, calculations and images that may identify corrupt activity. Conduct analytical reviews.

Conduct lifestyle audits to:

- Profile potential subjects
- Identify subjects whose lifestyles appear to have been financed from sources other than known/declared income sources (assets, credit applications, default judgments, etc).
- Identify conflicts of interest (business/personal) and/or undeclared interests (directorships, etc).

9.4.59. Accounting policies

Discussion

Companies define the manners in which they want to treat their accounting transactions. This ensures uniformity, transparency, acceptability and predictability. Company accounting policies are normally variants/more specific versions of international accounting standards.

A change in an accounting policy can have an effect (albeit temporary) on profits. Companies should not make changes to policies to suit themselves and/or just to derive a short-term effect on profits. They should maintain consistent and correct policies.

Observations/tips to identify and prove

Obtain a copy of company accounting policies. Check to see that these are reasonable and in line with international standards.

Determine if there were any changes in accounting policy in the period under review. Examples include:

- Depreciation rates/periods
- Asset revaluation/s.

Understand the effect of the changes (for example on profits). Understand all other events that occurred close to the time that the accounting policy changes were made. Determine if the changes can be justified. Interview the external auditors and ensure that they are comfortable with the policy changes.

Ensure that these policy changes:

- Were authorised
- Communicated to the board
- Specified in the financial statements
- Known and signed off by the external auditors.

In general, ensure that company accounting policies were applied consistently and correctly. Conduct interviews with company accountants, financial directors, external and internal auditors, whistle-blowers, any other relevant staff members, subjects, family and friends. Request management to sign declarations as to the complete and accurate calculation and/or payment of the item.

Conduct e-mail searches and general business related correspondence reviews to identify correspondence proving corrupt relationships. Conduct searches of the subject's general workspace and/or desk to identify evidence of corrupt activities. Mirror hard drives and other company-owned electronic devices and search files saved and/or deleted to identify documents, correspondence, calculations and images that may identify corrupt activity. Conduct analytical reviews.

Conduct lifestyle audits to:

- Profile potential subjects
- Identify subjects whose lifestyles appear to have been financed from sources other than known/declared income sources (assets, credit applications, default judgments, etc)
- Identify conflicts of interest (business/personal) and/or undeclared interests (directorships, etc).

9.4.60. Structural changes

Discussion

Structural changes refer to organisational structural changes. Examples include:

- Organisational structures (for example: centralised, matrix, divisional, branches, regional offices, etc)
- Reporting line changes
- Geographic/regional changes
- New functions being established or being done away with and/or merged
- Product portfolio changes
- Sales of/divestment in companies, divisions, brands, products, etc
- Investment in any of the above.

Such changes may represent an opportunity for fraudsters to:

- Hide irregular transactions
- Not report all information.

Observations/tips to identify and prove

Determine if there were any structural changes in the period under review. Understand the implication of the structural change on:

- Profits
- Costs
- Revenue
- Reporting information/lines/times/etc
- Control and monitoring.

Conduct interviews with company accountants, financial directors, external and internal auditors, whistle-blowers, any other relevant staff members, subjects, family and friends. Request management to sign declarations as to the complete and accurate calculation and/or payment of the item.

Conduct e-mail searches and general business related correspondence reviews to identify correspondence proving corrupt relationships. Conduct searches of the subject's general workspace and/or desk to identify evidence of corrupt activities. Mirror hard drives and other company-owned electronic devices and search files saved and/or deleted to identify documents, correspondence, calculations and images that may identify corrupt activity. Conduct analytical reviews.

Conduct lifestyle audits to:

- Profile potential subjects
- Identify subjects whose lifestyles appear to have been financed from sources other than known/declared income sources (assets, credit applications, default judgments, etc)
- Identify conflicts of interest (business/personal) and/or undeclared interests (directorships, etc).

9.4.61. Operating systems and financial systems

Discussion

Companies make use of a combination of operating systems and financial systems. Financial systems have been around a lot longer than operating systems. Before the advent of operating systems (or strong operating systems), the financial system had to serve both purposes of providing financial information and management information. Consequently, the financial system was typically required to perform beyond its original intention. This resulted in inefficiencies (from laborious and cumbersome information capturing and reporting methods) and the information seldom reached the full desired level. The advent of ERP systems has resulted in strong integrated systems with powerful information for those companies that make use of them. Today operating systems have a wealth of information and financial systems pass summary transactions.

The importance of this discussion is to note that less sophisticated systems provide more room for manipulation and/or fraud. The need for reconciling and/or compensating controls is important in the absence of adequate system functionality.

Another reason to discuss operating and financial systems is that these systems provide a wealth of information to be used as a comparative base and/or in analytical reviews.

An experience comes to mind where the local company FD and the Group FD resisted the implementation of a more powerful ERP system. I would like to refer us back to our rule: 'People always do and say things for a reason.' In this case, it was the conclusion of the ERP implementation team that the two FDs (despite the organisation's need for a more powerful system) wanted to retain their ability to manipulate the figures. The new system did not allow this and they blocked the implementation until the system implementation was eventually abandoned. They successfully managed to blame the system and all others involved for the failed implementation.

Observations/tips to identify and prove

Understand the systems that the organisation has and what their dependency and purposes are. Understand the nature of the business that the organisation is involved in. Reconcile the operating system to the financial system. Allow for cut off differences if the two have different reporting periods.

Conduct interviews with company accountants, financial directors, external and internal auditors, whistle-blowers, any other relevant staff members, subjects, family and friends. Request management to sign declarations as to the complete and accurate calculation and/or payment of the item.

Conduct e-mail searches and general business related correspondence reviews to identify correspondence proving corrupt relationships. Conduct searches of the subject's general workspace and/or desk to identify evidence of corrupt activities. Mirror hard drives and other company-owned electronic devices and search files saved and/or deleted to identify documents, correspondence, calculations and images that may identify corrupt activity. Conduct analytical reviews.

Conduct lifestyle audits to:

- Profile potential subjects
- Identify subjects whose lifestyles appear to have been financed from sources other than known/declared income sources (assets, credit applications, default judgments, etc)
- Identify conflicts of interest (business/personal) and/or undeclared interests (directorships, etc).

9.4.62. Budgets/estimates/forecasting

Discussion

In order to plan, organisations try to predict future costs and incomes. This helps organisations to know where to concentrate efforts. The plans are then used as a benchmark against which to measure actual performance.

Budgets/forecasts become less accurate:

- The further into the future they look
- The more unknown the process is. Highly repetitive, mature and well-established processes are predictable. Estimating greenfield/new build-type work is challenging.

Motivations for fraudulent manipulation of budgets include:

- Unfairly increasing the budget figures to:
    - Hide inefficiencies/discrepancies
    - Avoid scrutiny
    - Receive incentives by employees
    - Be able to incur unauthorised expenditure.
- Unfairly reducing budget figures to:
    - Prevent/block expenditure/projects
    - Avoid paying incentives by employers.

A weak budget process would entail marking up last year's expenditure by a fixed percentage/amount.

A strong budget process:

- Would break down expenditure into all elements and anticipate actual performance in the coming year
- Is logical and sufficiently detailed to support figures.
- Can be supported by independent trends.

Observations/tips to identify and prove

Understand the budget process.

Understand what decisions are based on the budget process (investment decisions). Understand if there is a retrospective analysis of the accuracy of the budget to the actual performance.

Substantiate budgets and test to see that they are in line with policy.

Understand which authorisations are required for budgets and budget overages. Check to see that this has been complied with consistently.

Conduct interviews with company accountants, financial directors, external and internal auditors, whistle-blowers, any other relevant staff members, subjects, family and friends. Request management to sign declarations as to the complete and accurate calculation and/or payment of the item.

Conduct e-mail searches and general business related correspondence reviews to identify correspondence proving corrupt relationships. Conduct searches of the subject's general workspace and/or desk to identify evidence of corrupt activities. Mirror hard drives and other company-owned electronic devices and search files saved and/or deleted to identify documents, correspondence, calculations and images that may identify corrupt activity. Conduct analytical reviews.

Conduct lifestyle audits to:

- Profile potential subjects
- Identify subjects whose lifestyles appear to have been financed from sources other than known/declared income sources (assets, credit applications, default judgments, etc).
- Identify conflicts of interest (business/personal) and/or undeclared interests (directorships, etc).

9.4.63. Management accounts

Discussion

Broadly speaking organisations make use of financial accounts and management accounts:

- Financial accounts stem from the general ledger transactions and include the annual reports which are mainly intended for shareholders and external stakeholders. Financial accounts are not in sufficient detail nor sufficiently current to provide the information required for the day-to-day running of the business. Financial accounts may also only be up to date at one point in time (for example monthly).
- Management accounts could include any summarised accounting and non-accounting information, including the:
    - Balance sheet
    - Actual cash flow status and forecasted cash flow
    - Income statement
    - Sales revenue generated to date compared to budget
    - Amount of orders confirmed and those pending confirmation
    - State of the accounts payable
    - State of the accounts receivable
    - Outstanding debts
    - Raw material balances and future forecasts
    - Finished goods inventory current balance on hand and future usage forecasts
    - Trend charts, variance analysis and other statistics.
- Management accounts are prepared and presented on a monthly, fortnightly or weekly basis.
- Management accounts are specifically intended for internal use by the organisation's management.
- The objective of management accounts is to provide timely and key financial and statistical information required by managers to make day-to-day and short-term decisions.
- Management accounts are unaudited.

Management accounts typically have different cut-off dates to the financial accounts. There will, therefore, be timing differences between the management account figures and the financial ledgers/system.

Fraud involving management accounts is concerned with misrepresenting information. The motives for misrepresentation may include:

- To show a more favourable position than actual

- Hiding inefficiencies/discrepancies/fraud
- Avoiding scrutiny
- Receiving performance-based incentives by employees
- Being able to incur unauthorised expenditure.

Observations/tips to identify and prove

- Understand how the organisation's management accounts process works.
- Understand who uses the management accounts and for which reason.
- Understand the data sources of the information used in the management accounts.
- Substantiate the management accounts.
- Understand the checks and authorisations involved in management accounts.

Conduct e-mail searches and general business related correspondence reviews to identify correspondence proving corrupt relationships. Conduct searches of the subject's general workspace and/or desk to identify evidence of corrupt activities. Mirror hard drives and other company-owned electronic devices and search files saved and/or deleted to identify documents, correspondence, calculations and images that may identify corrupt activity.

Conduct lifestyle audits to:

- Profile potential subjects
- Identify subjects whose lifestyles appear to have been financed from sources other than known/declared income sources (assets, credit applications, default judgments, etc)
- Identify conflicts of interest (business/personal) and/or undeclared interests (directorships, etc).
- Conduct analytical reviews.

9.4.64. Master file updates

Discussion

Master files are included in many of the aforementioned items discussed. It is important to understand the effect of a potential fraud in the context of these individual items. Fraudulent changes to master files are however important enough to warrant a separate discussion here.

There are essentially two types of electronic data, being transactional data and master data. Transactional data is a list of the individual transactions that occurred. A program may read from a master file (for example customer details and prices) when creating transactional data (for example sales files). Transactional data may be used as an input to a master file later.

Some examples of master file data include:

- Supplier data
- Customer data
- Employee payroll data
- Pricing/tariff data files
- Stock, materials, etc
- Fixed asset register.

Master file changes should be made on the strength of an instruction from an authorised person to make the change. Master file changes should be pre-approved and/or trigger a suspended status on the system requiring system authorisation before being made live.

As a control principle, the person making the master file change should not have the system access to authorise master file updates, process transactions and/or perform reconciliations. It is best if system transactions are divided into 'input', 'view' and 'approve'. If a person has the ability to input, then they should not have the ability to approve transactions/the input. A person who has 'read' access has the lowest form of access. They can view information required for their work, but they do not have the access to input data or approve transactions.

Organisations frequently require their staff members to bring a master file change to a manager for approval before being made. The risk is that the amendment may be made without bringing it to the manager for approval. Alternatively, a change different from what was approved may be made. It is therefore best practice to generate an independent list of all master file changes made within a period. The list should be filed in the front of a defence file of all approved master file changes. A senior independent person should review the list to ensure that all master file updates are adequately supported by documents, were approved and/or are valid.

Fraudulent master file changes may include:

- Amending rates
- Amending banking details
- Adding or removing people from the database
- Deleting or amending key information fields.

Invalid master file changes may be made by:

- The subjects themselves
- By colluding with another to make the changes
- By instructing a normal/uninvolved party to make the changes purporting them to be legitimate.

Observations/tips to identify and prove

- Understand the types of master files that exist and where they are kept (systems, servers, programs, geographic offices, companies, etc).
- Understand the master file amendment and authorisation processes.
- Understand the source of data to create/update the master files.
- Understand which systems and processes use the master files and for which purpose. Understand the key fields in the master file.

Obtain an independent list of the access that users have to the system under review. Identify conflicts. Consider cross-system and/or cross-module conflicts as well if applicable:

- Operating to financial system
- Payroll to financial system
- Stock system to financial system.

Obtain an independent transaction log of all master file changes (specifying user) made in the period. Substantiate the updates:

- To ensure that they are valid and authorised
- That they weren't made and approved by the same person
- That they were made completely and correctly
- That they were made within the correct period
- Against supporting documents.

Conduct e-mail searches and general business related correspondence reviews to identify correspondence proving corrupt relationships. Conduct searches of the subject's general workspace and/or desk to identify evidence of corrupt activities. Mirror hard drives and other company-owned electronic devices and search files saved and/or deleted to identify documents, correspondence, calculations and images that may identify corrupt activity.

Conduct lifestyle audits to:

- Profile potential subjects
- Identify subjects whose lifestyles appear to have been financed from sources other than known/declared income sources (assets, credit applications, default judgments, etc)
- Identify conflicts of interest (business/personal) and/or undeclared interests (directorships, etc).

9.4.65. Deal brokering

Discussion

Organisations sometimes make use of a broker of sorts to set up a deal, negotiate and/or contract on the organisation's behalf. They do this as:

- They do not have access to the markets/clients that the broker has
- They do not have the required expertise
- They want to be anonymous (to prevent influencing the price/deal).

Deal brokering is really subject to the same risks as procurement fraud. Brokers may:

- Take kickbacks
- Demand a share of the business
- Have undeclared conflicts of interests
- Collude with the seller or buyer to unduly influence the deal
- Hide important facts about the products, regulations, parties, etc.

One war story comes to mind of a company that required specialised business licences (one per branch) to trade. Obtaining new licences was regulated to protect the market and more difficult than acquiring existing businesses with the licences. The company, therefore, decided to acquire as many existing businesses needed to obtain their trade licences and in so doing could dominate the market with a greater number of outlets.

The company aggressively pursued this strategy and was prepared to pay premiums for businesses, just to get the licences. Their plan was to move the licence to one of their own/more successful branches.

The company made use of an individual to broker the deals to buy the smaller businesses up. The individual however conspired with the existing business owners to inflate the business purchase prices and to share the proceeds.

The story does not end there. Legislation changed subsequently leaving the company unable to simply transfer licences. A transfer was to be treated like a new application. The businesses that had been purchased were not necessarily purchased due to their high profitability. In reality, many of the businesses were struggling to keep their head above water.

The company, therefore, decided (subsequent to the change in legislation) to sell the less profitable businesses. The individual that brokered the inflated deals was requested to sell the struggling businesses.

The individual concerned could not believe his luck. He then conspired again with the original business owners (many of whom were retained by the company to run the branches) to repurchase their business at a cost below the value of the stock. The individual received a fee from the business owner for the reduced purchase price.

Observations/tips to identify and prove

- Understand if brokers are used for any of the company's business.
- Understand the nature of the brokerage agreement. Substantiate the deals against contracts and supporting documents.
- Obtain explanations for variations to the contract.
- Understand the authorisations required for the deals and/or to engage the services of the broker.
- Understand the monitoring, governance and oversight of the deals. Management may be driven more by achieving the strategy and less on ensuring sound controls/good governance.

In what kind of industry or geographic region does the company operate? Establish if this is an industry/area in which this sort of behaviour is common practice. Independently value the deal done by the broker and determine if it was fairly valued. Conduct public domain checks of the broker, the clients and key organisational leadership. Vet the broker's qualifications and experience.

Conduct interviews with company accountants, financial directors, external and internal auditors, whistle-blowers, any other relevant staff members, subjects, family and friends. Benchmark similar deals to the deals under review.

Request management to sign declarations as to the complete and accurate calculation and/or payment of the item.

Conduct e-mail searches and general business related correspondence reviews to identify correspondence proving corrupt relationships. Conduct searches of the subject's general workspace and/or desk to identify evidence of corrupt activities. Mirror hard drives and other company-owned electronic devices and search files saved and/or deleted to identify documents, correspondence, calculations and images that may identify corrupt activity.

Conduct lifestyle audits to:

- Profile potential subjects
- Identify subjects whose lifestyles appear to have been financed from sources other than known/declared income sources (assets, credit applications, default judgments, etc)
- Identify conflicts of interest (business/personal) and/or undeclared interests (directorships, etc).

Conduct analytical reviews.

9.4.66. Insider trading

Discussion

Insider trading is essentially the use of privileged information (not in the public domain at that point) for the unfair benefit of the person using it. Insider trading normally refers to the buying or selling of shares at key times based on such information. This is an unfair (fraudulent) practice, as it benefits one person (group) without others having the same opportunity.

I received a phone call from the company secretary of a company where I worked. The company secretary said that the chairman of the board and the group CEO had been accused of insider trading and they wanted me to get an external audit firm to prove that they were innocent. My first reaction was to say, well, that would depend on whether they had done it or not. I made use of an independent firm of external auditors. Their conclusion was that it will always seem as if the group CEO and the chairman are guilty of insider trading as they have access to all the company's financial information.

Let me give you a little more information and you can be the judge: The two subjects sold many shares mid-December. In January, they released a cautionary to the market to say that the company's profits were not expected to be high, as business was down. In February, the financials were published and the share price dropped through the floor.

The company did not have a policy to restrict trading in the company's shares within a prescribed period before the release of the annual financial statements.

I was not involved in the investigation, but to me, it smelled very bad. I later became aware of numerous other unethical behaviours and misconduct that the two subjects had been involved in. I am therefore of the opinion that they were most likely guilty of insider trading, as they had been involved in other self-enriching practices and demonstrated morally barren behaviour.

Observations/tips to identify and prove

Understand who the shareholders are/which key individuals/staff members hold shares and how many they hold/held. Understand the periods of restriction (before release of financials, a big deal, etc) and any other key dates. Obtain independent confirmation from the stock exchange of share trades in the period. Understand the share trading restrictions.

Check company share trust/share option scheme rules and registers for sales of shares by employees. Understand which events took place around the share trades which could have influenced the share price. Identify who had access to this information. Compare this to actual trades. Understand the benefit derived to the subjects from the trades at that point as opposed to others without the knowledge.

Conduct interviews with company accountants, financial directors, external and internal auditors, whistle-blowers, any other relevant staff members, subjects, family and friends. Request management to sign declarations as to the complete and accurate calculation and/or payment of the item.

Conduct e-mail searches and general business related correspondence reviews to identify correspondence proving corrupt relationships. Conduct searches of the subject's general workspace and/or desk to identify evidence of corrupt activities. Mirror hard drives and other company-owned electronic devices and search files saved and/or deleted to identify documents, correspondence, calculations and images that may identify corrupt activity.

Conduct analytical reviews. Conduct lifestyle audits to:

- Profile potential subjects
- Identify subjects whose lifestyles appear to have been financed from sources other than known/declared income sources (assets, credit applications, default judgments, etc)
- Identify conflicts of interest (business/personal) and/or undeclared interests (directorships, etc).

9.4.67. Trusts

Discussion

Trusts are legal entities designed to provide protection. They are established to hold funds, investments, assets, etc for specific reasons as defined in the trusts' founding documents. People frequently establish family trusts to hold joint family interests. This may make the subsequent sale of the trusts' assets easier as a transfer of the ownership of the trust can just occur.

Trusts may also be used in the normal course of a person's life for estate planning purposes. This is because the assets (say a residence) can be held by the trust and not by the person who is planning their estate. When a person dies, all assets in their name form part of their estate and may be subject to tax. Assets already removed from an individual's name and placed in a trust will not form part of the individual's estate. The individual can be a member of the trust and in so doing still maintain control of the assets. Their membership of the trust could then be transferred to their bequeathed upon their death. There may, therefore, be tax benefits to structuring trusts in this manner.

Trusts are also frequently used by lawyers to hold funds temporarily on behalf of another party until certain conditions have been met. Trusts are governed by legislation and trustees have very specific responsibilities in terms of the law.

The problem with trusts is that the trustees have sole authority to conduct the trust in the manner that they see fit. This may be in contradiction with the rules of the trust and all legislation. The details of trusts/trust transactions are also not visible to all beneficiaries, the authorities, etc. The ability to conceal misconduct makes trusts attractive legal entities for fraudsters.

Trustees may:

- Misappropriate funds/assets from the trust
- Not apply funds in accordance with the rules of the trust
- Not make all declarations as required
- Not pay the required taxes and duties
- Portray a different financial position as actually is
- Use the trust to obscure/hide the true ownership of the trust or the real reason for having the trust.

Benefactors may:

- Hide funds/assets in this manner to avoid paying taxes and duties or to unfairly prejudice another party
- Not pay all taxes and duties as required.

Observations/tips to identify and prove

Trust registration details are public domain details as with companies. If not available online, go to the registrar's office and obtain a copy of the registration details. You will need to know the specific trust's name and registered office though.

Determine:

- Who the trustees are
- Who the trust beneficiaries are
- What their responsibilities entailed
- The purpose of the trust
- The rules applicable to the trust
- When last there was any activity on the trust
- What records are available on the trust's activities.

Obtain declarations from trustees and beneficiaries as to the actual transactions performed. Obtain the rules of the trust. Conduct lifestyle reviews of trustees and trust beneficiaries.

Ensure that:

- All financial records accurately and completely reflect the financial position of the trust.
- All major fund movements in and out of the trust can be substantiated. Check against actual records and against the actual bank statements.
- The rules of the trust have been complied with by comparing actual financial records and behaviours to the trust rules.
- The funds/assets of the trust have been applied in line with the rules of the trust and no one else has benefited unfairly from the trust.
- All taxes have been paid completely, accurately and on time.

Conduct analytical reviews where relevant.

9.4.68. Deceased estates

Discussion

When a person dies, their assets, liabilities, properties and bank accounts are frozen until the executor of the estate can determine:

- The true size and makeup (assets and liabilities) of the estate
- What the person's last will and testament was
- Who the creditors are
- Who the benefactors of the estate are.

Executors of the estate may even hold funds, investments, properties and other assets, etc in a trust until the estate can be wound up. The discussion on trusts refers.

This is done to ensure that:

- All taxes and/or duties payable to the authorities are paid correctly
- Any amounts owing to creditors prior to the person's death are paid before the estate is wound up and all assets divided/cash paid out
- All payments and division of the estate are done in line with the person's last will and testament.

People's deaths are associated with a lot of emotion, including:

- Remorse, regret for not having done something while the person was alive
- Sadness and loss on the passing of the person
- Feelings of jealousy and greed
- Feelings of entitlement/that they should have received all of the specific items or a greater share of an item that actually received more
- Feelings that the actual beneficiary of an item does not really deserve it and someone else would have
- Feelings that the executors have been unfair, fraudulent, not dealt with the estate in line with the person's last will and testament.

Again, a big contributing factor is either the person's own perception of what they should have received or of what happened. It could also be the lack of general insight (mostly for good reason) that outsiders have of the winding up of the estate.

The concealed nature of the winding up of an estate is also an attractive feeding ground for fraudsters. Part of the problem is also that not everything that needs to be 'dealt with' is listed. The winding up of deceased estates is strictly controlled by legislation. The executor of the estate gets a fee (based on a scale, which is governed by law). Failure to notify all concerned so that less claims need to be paid out.

I assisted in the investigation of the fraudulent winding up of a deceased estate. In this case, the deceased had built up a successful factory. The deceased got the widow (not a strong person) to sign a general power of attorney. The deceased's brother then got his colluding firm of accountants to be the executors of the estate. He transferred the factory into his own name, despite it being bequeathed to the widow. The rest of the estate was minuscule. The executors charged the widow an exorbitant fee for winding up the estate. The executors said, upon confrontation, that the factory was insolvent and therefore not an asset in the estate. Many listed companies are technically insolvent (assets and liabilities equal to zero). This was not a valid manner to exclude the factory. The factory was trading as a going concern for a few years and had many orders on the books, a high turnover and many debtors. The other mistake that the executors made was to 'confuse' the concept of management and ownership. They said that the brother was doing the widow a favour to take on the running of the factory. She derived no benefit whatsoever subsequent to the passing of her husband. The entire stock exchange is based on the principle that the owners (shareholders) and management of companies are separate. In truth, the widow would most likely have asked the brother to assist with the running of the business. She would have remunerated him well, but the outright theft of the factory ruined the relationship. The matter is pending civil litigation.

Observations/tips to identify and prove

Obtain:

- The last will and testament if the person
- Documents submitted to the master of the court to ratify the winding up of the estate
- Death notices published as required
- All financial statement and valuations of the assets
- All claims lodged against the estate.

Determine the applicable estate laws and if actual behaviour was aligned.

Ensure:

- That assets were fairly valued
- All creditors were paid correctly
- The beneficiaries received their correct inheritances
- All taxes and duties were paid.

Conduct lifestyle checks on:

- The executors
- The deceased
- The beneficiaries
- People making claims against the estate.

Conduct e-mail searches and general correspondence reviews to identify correspondence proving corrupt relationships. Conduct searches of the subject's general workspace and/or desk to identify evidence of corrupt activities. Mirror hard drives and other company-owned electronic devices and search files saved and/or deleted to identify documents, correspondence, calculations and images that may identify corrupt activity. Determine if the trust account rules were followed. Were all the required taxes paid?

CHAPTER 10

SETTING UP A FORENSIC FUNCTION

10.1. CHAPTER OUTLINE AND INTRODUCTION

The setting up of a forensic function is similar regardless of whether you are setting up a large organisation's forensic function or a relatively small organisation's function. Some difference exists though between setting up an in-house function and an external consultancy/service provider. The setting up of an external forensic consultancy is discussed at the end of this chapter.

In this chapter, we will discuss how to motivate for a forensic function as well as provide some practical tips and templates on the day-to-day running of a forensic function. The purpose of this chapter is to provide you with the basic insights to enable you to set up and manage a forensic function.

10.2. MOTIVATING FOR A FORENSIC FUNCTION

Motivating the need for a fully-fledged in-house forensic function will almost always be a difficult task to conduct. Even motivating the need to commit funds to external consultants for a once-off investigation can be challenging. The motivating of full-time dedicated resources is much more difficult, but certainly not impossible.

An in-house function can be a fully-fledged and staffed function or it can be merely the formalising of the access to the required (external) skills as needed. Perhaps your organisation outsources its internal audit function to service providers on a three-year contract basis. A forensic 'function' can be set up in the same manner. The in-house component may be more of a coordinating role in that situation.

10.2.1. Need

The notion (not necessarily a need yet) of having an in-house forensic function may stem from, amongst other sources:

- New members on the board of directors or senior management who have seen the positive value added by an in-house function in other organisations.
- The aftermath when an organisation has been affected by an actual fraud case.
- Legislation (for example the Companies Act) and/or stock exchange requirements and/or industry requirements and/or governance models (COSO, COCO, King, etc) to have such capability. This capability may not be defined as the need to have a forensic function. It may be defined as the requirement to have an internal audit function.
- Competitive behaviour and/or the need to respond to initiatives taken by competitors.
- The need to demonstrate the existence of the capability so as to qualify for a contract or particular avenue of business (contract or joint venture).

10.2.2. Reaction

Senior management in organisations always seems to have a similar response when the notion of setting up a forensic function is communicated. They:

- Mostly immediately reject the notion
- Give reasons:
  - Why the organisation should not have such a function
  - Why it will not work
  - What can go wrong
  - Why the organisation should not be compared to other organisations that have such functions
  - To support that there is not any fraud really (and therefore no need) or that the current cases are just once-off matters that cannot justify dedicating full-time resources to it
- Prioritise other activities ahead of it, without directly rejecting the notion
- Even once convinced/forced to accept the need, try to restrict the resources allocated to the function and the scope of the function prior to commencement
- Try to control or restrict the functioning once established
- Require the function to report to them/all reports to be 'approved' by them
- In a last desperate attempt, say things such as they do not want to:
  - Be draconian
  - Be bureaucratic
  - Layer in red tape
  - Take the business' responsibility (to investigate fraud) away from them/their subordinates
  - Take on the police's responsibility
  - Open themselves to poor public image
  - Open themselves up to potential lawsuits
  - Arouse suspicion with the authorities and give them reason to come and audit them.

It helps to be aware of these potential responses so that you know what to expect and can prepare counter-arguments.

10.2.3. Stakeholders

Senior management is the organisation's decision-makers. They are the very people to whom the running of the organisation has been entrusted. How then do we convince them of the need? The short answer is: through patience. As the old cliché says: 'Slowly, slowly, catch the monkey.' You need to be realistic about the fact that it is highly unlikely that you are going to obtain approval for ten full-time employees in the department on your first request.

Main board directors are far more open to the idea of having a forensic function than other organisation members. This is most likely as they:

- Do not like surprises
- Do not see investigations as a threat (to themselves or the functions/business units for whom they work), as they are (generally) not responsible for the execution of the business (executive board members do have operational responsibility, though, and the direct support for a forensic function may be less applicable to them)
- Do not have a vested interest in the business areas being investigated (executive directors may be exceptions, as per the previous point)
- Are ultimately responsible for the organisational governance.

Be careful not to underestimate the power (positive or negative) of stakeholders. Conduct a formal exercise in identifying your stakeholders and whether they like you (personality conflicts) and if they are proponents of fraud risk management. Design a strategy to build stronger relationships with them and to gain their legitimate support. Reasons that you may experience stakeholder resistance include:

- Conflicting priorities
- Personality differences
- Lack of understanding
- Fear of losing control, internal politics/power struggle
- Fear that they may be blamed for the fraud occurrence
- Prior experiences
- Different loyalties/networks
- Guilt due to involvement in misconduct themselves.

Some examples to assist you with stakeholder strategy interventions to manage and improve stakeholder relationships include:

- Holding clarifying meetings to understand both sides
- Frequent communication to build transparency and trust
- Inclusion of stakeholders in decisions and processes
- Demonstration of value-add through the satisfaction created by doing something positive for the stakeholder
- Explanation and/or alignment of key performance indicators (KPIs)
- Both sides being compromising and accommodating
- Empathy on both sides
- Education, training and awareness of stakeholders
- Reading, research and formal courses to provide you with stakeholder management skills
- Defining robust fraud risk management processes to eliminate ambiguity and to create confidence
- Building on prior successes
- Making use of the informal organisation/networks by influencing one person to influence another
- Direct intervention of an independent (supportive) third party
- Formal instruction (last option) to enforce policies and procedures
- Disciplinary action to enforce policies and procedures or modify behaviour (exceptional cases only).

10.2.4. Approach

When trying to obtain approval or support for a forensic function, it is not recommended that you go with the 'big bang' approach, as if you are declined you will not have an easy task to try to reintroduce the idea later. As our aforementioned cliché suggests, the way to catch a monkey is slowly. 'Plant the seeds' (ideas) of what you want to achieve with the key stakeholders (management/directors) by communicating the idea only. At this point, you just communicate the notion and then back off immediately. Do not go with too much hard-sell at the time of the introduction of the idea. Just mention principles.

Avoid giving too much detail upfront so as to avoid scaring people off with a complicated idea that seems like a lot of work. When you are coming from a base where a forensic function has not existed before, a whole new function can seem over the top by comparison. Just sell the high-level concept of having forensic capability and then back strategically off till another time. Most people also do not like change and people need time to get used to a new idea.

Then go back a few times over a period of time and 'water' the idea, frequently giving a little more detail and motivating a little more each time. Before long they will start to become comfortable with the idea and more open to trying it/the benefits thereof. You may even have cases where the people with whom you 'planted the seeds', speak to you later as if the original idea was theirs. This is a powerful place to be in if they are convinced by the idea. Say nothing about the fact that the idea was yours to begin with. Lose the battle and win the war.

This approach will vary if there is an immediate need for forensic resources in so far as the time frame of convincing the decision makers will be greatly compressed.

10.2.5. Allies

Notwithstanding the timing, it is recommended to gather allies to support your idea. Work with them and get them to convince the others. Alternatively, quote your allies when convincing a person who is not convinced of the notion. This works well when your ally is a senior/respected member of staff.

If you are required to make a presentation to the board or senior management, ensure that you try to build support for the idea in advance. Do not walk into a meeting/situation where you are unsure which way the participants' support could go. Furthermore, the more people you convince in advance, the fewer people you will have to convince later (possibly at decision time/in a meeting at which approval is required).

Do not, however, rely on their support in the board meeting. People sometimes say one thing to you in person, but say something different in the actual situation when faced with their peers who think differently, provide strong counter-arguments or when there is a very dominant personality in the room who is against the idea.

10.2.6. Timing

A forensic function is a good idea, but you need to be strategic in your approach. Be mindful to choose an appropriate time at which to bring up a new idea. Avoid times when people are busy and having to deal with new issues or pressures (like costs or poor public image). A good idea might be dismissed just because they cannot deal with anything additional at that point.

If you find yourself in that situation, then back off immediately and say that it is not at all important and that you can see that they are very busy and promise to return when things calm down. This way you may develop a rapport with them because you are being sympathetic to the pressures that they are under. You will also be able to refer to your original conversation when you return. You can say for example: '*Joe, you may recall that I mentioned to you at the end of last year that I am increasingly seeing the need to have our own forensic capability. Well, we have just had another case reported to us and I have looked at the numbers. I am confident that we can save a lot of money if we do this ourselves. Not only do we have better knowledge of our own business, but we can employ a person for an entire year and derive much more value out of them for the same cost as employing an external consultant for a single assignment. I would be able to use them for proactive work to detect issues more quickly and even to bolster control deficiencies in advance.*'

10.2.7. Locking down

Try to have the decision to reject or accept the idea minuted. This way you will always be able to refer back to it. Of course, to minute a decision to implement an in-house function does not guarantee that it will happen. Last minute budget constraints and other changes may result in the decision to proceed being overturned. The motive for this, as discussed previously, could be malicious or purely practical.

Main board members do not like to be on record saying that they have rejected the suggestion to improve controls and governance. One approach is to say to the board: 'You are the custodians of the controls. Please tell me how you would be comfortable for me to proceed.' Invariably they say: 'Please go ahead.'

10.2.8. Value

If you can, try to prove value in advance in small ways. Use these wins to motivate why the function will work. Aim at the low-hanging fruit first.

Even once you get the go-ahead, take the time to consolidate and ensure that you prove value before going too big. You can demonstrate value by what you do, for example conducting an investigation, winning a case for the organisation, obtaining recoveries of misappropriated funds or through proactive work to highlight unknown issues, cooperating with the police, etc. It is about success; breeding success.

Another sure-fire way to prove value is to obtain recoveries from a case. This will show that the forensic function is not just about costs, but income too. Businesses like income and dislike costs. You could motivate that it is important to have someone to follow up on recoveries otherwise the organisation will just lose the money.

Compare the costs of getting someone else from outside to conduct the investigation versus having in-house resources. Fortunately for in-house functions, large external consultancies charge a fortune. This increased cost cannot always, if ever, be justified. Costs are however not the only determinant for using or not using an outside consultant. We will discuss situations later, where the use of outside consultants is preferred to in-house resources.

10.2.9. Conclusion

In conclusion: 'Think big, start small!'

10.3. CONSULTANCY

If you have your own consultancy/offer fraud risk services to a variety of clients, it may be wise to differentiate yourself by your 'product' offering. Even if you are a one-man-band, you may have particular skills which set you apart from other fraud practitioners. Your practice should either have the skills or be able to in-source the required skills. Set in-source arrangements/agreements in place with partners.

Try to motivate the need to procure your services to your clients. Signing a retainer agreement will guarantee them a minimum amount of consultancy and allow for the immediate response to fraud losses by implementing fraud prevention and detection tools.

10.4. RESOURCES

Once you know what the forensic function needs to do (strategy) and how it will be performed (procedures), the function will need to be resourced in order to carry out the strategy. Determining the resource requirements entails predicting the amount of time to be spent in each of the defined areas, as well as the skills and equipment required to perform.

10.4.1. Skills

The first step to achieving the fraud strategy is to understand the skills required to carry this out. The skills required to execute the fraud strategy refer to the specific skills, the formal educational backgrounds desired and the level of experience required in the forensic function. A further dimension would entail the degree of seniority in each of these areas. While there is a natural assumption that the people who have been around for a long time or those who are in more senior/managerial positions are the most technically competent, this is not necessarily the case. In larger organisations, you may have the luxury of a number of subject matter technical experts reporting to a manager/team leader. The manager of a diverse team is unlikely to be the most experienced in all fields represented on the team. Furthermore, the more senior the leader, the less their day-to-day tasks involve carrying out the detailed technical aspects of the function they manage. As an example, a chief audit executive (CAE) spends their time building relationships with the senior organisational leadership, ensuring that they (CAE) understand what the board of directors wants, and they set the strategic direction of the function. The CAE will need to be technically competent/have a high appreciation of the aspects being performed, but they do not have to be the best at performing these tasks. The table in Annexure 10.1 attached hereto may be used to summarised skills required.

10.4.2. Generic skills

Skills are the generic competencies required to ensure optimal performance. Examples of the specific skills required may include, but are not limited to:

- *Leadership/ management*

The skills to lead a department and/or team of fraud examiners and other specialists. These include all the general management planning, leading, recruiting, motivating, etc aspects.

- *Investigative*

These are the specific skills to plan, lead, conduct and conclude on an investigation. Each of the steps discussed in the chapter on conducting an investigation requires differing skills. I find that a lot of people charged with investigations do not:

  - Always recognise that an investigation needs to be conducted. Professional insight (a combination of specific skills and experience) is required to know when and what to investigate.
  - Know how to commence or execute an investigation.
  - Conclude on all the aspects of the investigation. The conclusion of an investigation is rarely just the identification and dismissal of a corrupt employee. Many interrelated aspects need to be considered and may warrant action.

- *Interviewing*

As stated previously, I firmly believe that interviewing skills are the most important skill that an investigator needs to have. An investigator may be the most technical accountant or the most experienced lawyer, but will be lost without the ability to effectively interview people. Interviewing touches almost every aspect of an investigation and may be the only method available to unearth the truth in the absence of tangible evidence. Good interviewing skills will also assist an investigator in structuring an investigation, as they will know what they want to achieve in the interview process and they will structure the investigation steps to support this.

- *Business*

This refers to a general knowledge and understanding of how business works. A person with these skills will be able to walk into a work environment in which they have never been and know what to expect in various business processes. While you are not expected to understand the detailed working of all business processes, a sound working knowledge is what is required. For example: Accounts payable is pretty much the same in any organisation. The more experienced you are the greater your ability will be to navigate businesses and business processes that you have never been exposed to. This as you will know which generic aspects you are looking for and therefore how to conduct your investigation.

- *Accounting*

Accounting skill is one specific area of business skills that frequently touches investigations. Most fraud cases have a financial aspect to them. A working knowledge of accountancy is imperative to investigations. I suppose you could get by without it, but you will be missing an important dimension of investigating, as you may be unable to:

  - Follow conversations and key aspects
  - Identify key aspects of the investigation
  - Conclude on all aspects
  - Know how to remedy all aspects.

- *Business process analysis*

At a simplistic level, business process analysis is the ability to identify (and possibly document) business processes and then to 'walk through' them to:

  - Understand how they work
  - Identify their purpose (objective), associated risks and mitigating controls
  - Identify deviations to the processes
  - Design remedies
  - Design tests to compare actual behaviour to policy.

A process view is vital to ensure a complete analysis of a business process. Walking through the process forces the analyser of the process to consider all steps in the process and provides an opportunity to consider all aspects of each of these. It does not matter how experienced I am, I always adopt the process view and walk through the process to ensure that I have considered all aspects. A typical shortcoming I see (probably based on a lack of training) is people who try to analyse systems of control from memory. They may have seen how other systems (like the one under review) work and they try to recall which aspects they should cover. The problem with this approach is that a person's memory is finite and cannot recall everything. Also, no two systems are perfectly alike. It is highly unlikely that they will cover all aspects systematically, so they are already handicapped.

My greatest 'bugbear' is that people have 'favourites' that they refer to and that is all. Favourites include concepts like:

  - Segregation of duty (SOD) conflicts
  - Degree of training (subjective)
  - Existence of standard operating procedures (SOP). If they exist they move on without considering the adequacy of the SOP.

Favourites and memory will only provide a limited analysis of business processes.

- *Reporting*

Your report (all types as discussed in the chapter on reporting) is the most important product of your investigation. If you have an inability to communicate your outcome, then your work will serve no purpose. Reporting refers to both oral and written reporting skills. The chapter on reporting refers.

- *Public speaking*

Public speaking is a life skill. Most people avoid public speaking. It is something that you will have to do from a child (presenting orals at school), through your working career to retirement.

You might as well learn how to master it. This is a principle that my own father highlighted the importance of to me from a young age. My staff members in one organisation where I worked used to hate the fact that I forced them, as part of their development, to do public speaking (presentations at auditing institutes). Afterwards, they thanked me though.

- *Data analytics*

Remember one of our rules: 'The devil is in the detail.' Well, unfortunately, that is true and the 'devil' in this case is data. I consistently find that the longer I look at an aspect, the more issues I identify. One of the 'tools' for looking at data is 'data analytics'. Invariably you will be faced with masses of transactions in a corporate fraud investigation. Data analytics provides the structured method by which to analyse data to understand it and to identify the issues. The chapter on data analytics refers.

- *IT systems*

IT system knowledge is really the same as business process skills. Most things are automated or have a degree of automation. It is therefore imperative that fraud investigators have a working knowledge of IT systems. This knowledge will enable the investigator to:

  - Understand the business processes under review
  - Be able to identify control weaknesses
  - Know where to look for evidence
  - Know how to put preventative and detective controls in place.

- *IT security*

IT security is a specialised subset of IT controls and relates to the authentication of users, software and hardware to IT systems and infrastructure. A working knowledge of IT security is required, to allow you to be in a position to:

  - Ask the right questions
  - Drive the investigation in the correct direction
  - Follow conversations with others on the topic
  - Lead experts assisting in the investigation
  - Occasionally perform detailed testing and identification yourself
  - Know where to find evidence and what evidence you are looking for.

IT security is a specialised skill and it is unlikely that a general investigator will conduct detailed IT security tests. You may however need to work with IT security team members.

- *Legal*

Legal skills are a broad description for a wide array of skills that will be of benefit to a fraud investigator, including but not limited to knowledge of:

  - The criminal justice system
  - Law of contracts
  - The Companies Act
  - Law of evidence
  - The Constitution
  - Labour law.

Legal skills include a working knowledge of:

- The police investigation process
- What a docket entails and the different stages that it goes through
- The court system and processes
- What is required to open a criminal, civil or labour case
- Which evidence needs to be subpoenaed and how to go about it
- Common charges to be levied
- How to write a charge sheet
- How to structure a witness schedule per charge
- How to recover misappropriated funds/assets.

- *Testifying*

This may seem like a strange thing to say, but remember our rule: 'Keep the end-game in mind.' Testifying in a criminal trial or in an internal disciplinary hearing may very well be one of the last steps in an investigation. The ability to know how to testify and what is required to testify will help to set direction in the conduct of the investigation. Testifying is however not a commonly taught skill. In my own case, I have either learnt by physically testifying myself or in the preparatory talks that I have had with prosecutors before a trial. The benefit of good testifying skills include:

- To be able to testify the truth in a manner that does not prejudice the case/obtains the desired result
- To be able to teach others how to testify
- Knowing what evidence to look for/obtain, which will assist in proving the case later.

- *Security*

Security experience and skills relate to the physical security aspects of a matter. It could also entail access controls. Security insights are helpful when gathering evidence/ understanding of what happened. A general understanding of security protocols and general safety when conducting investigations is also helpful to ensure the safeguarding of all involved.

- *Industry- or field-specific*

Depending on the nature of the matter under investigation, industry-specific knowledge may be required to be able to conduct the investigation. Examples of industry-specific knowledge include: engineering, quantity surveying, chemical, financial instruments, etc.

10.4.3. In-house or external

Another big question to consider is whether to have:

- All the required skills within the forensic function or
- The skills within the organisation or
- The skills externally available.

The reality is that all functions (whether in-house or external functions):

- Have budgets and cannot, from a pure cost point of view, justify having all skills in-house. More specialised skills tend to come at a premium. Organisations need to conduct cost-benefit analyses to determine if it is cost efficient to have the required skills in-house.

- May physically not be in a position to attract the prerequisite skills. Smaller organisations may not be as desirable to work for as larger organisations. Alternatively, certain industries attract staff members more easily than others. As an example: Everyone wants to work for a dynamic IT company. Not many people, on the other hand, want to work for an undertaker.
- May not have all the skills, at the required level, available in the market. One organisation that I worked for struggled to attract certain specialised skills to smaller countries where their operations were based and/or in more dangerous environments.
- May be unable to retain specialised/sought-after skills. Professionals tend to be defined and therefore driven by their work. Professionals often want to do what professionals do; that is:
    - Conduct the work that they have specialised in.
    - Specialists may become bored in generalist environments in which they cannot live their professions out.
    - They may want to interact with their contemporaries and therefore need to move to another organisation where more like-minded individuals work and/or where they can obtain the stimulation they require or be recognised for what they do.
    - Not all organisations are equal. Professionals may, therefore, want to work for an organisation where they have more control and influence over the methodologies and standards of work.

External consultancies tend to be able to/need to attract, utilise and retain specialists to serve multiple clients.

The most pragmatic approach is to attempt to have access to the required skills as required. Try to set framework agreements in place with service providers to have access to the required skills.

10.4.4. Business units

The skills we have discussed here pertain to those that the forensic investigators themselves should possess/have access to.

As mentioned before, the business units in conglomerate-type organisations may have some responsibilities for the execution of part of the fraud strategy and/or for conducting investigations. The question then naturally extends to what sort of skills the business units should have and what role the group-level forensic function can play in all this.

Let us start by considering which positions the business units should have. As expected there is no single answer for this and it depends on the individual organisation. Irrespective of the size of the organisation though, there should always be one person in each business unit who holds the responsibility for fraud in that business unit. When I refer to a business unit, I am referring to a separate company or group of companies that form a unit under a holding company. Life assurance companies may have life divisions, short-term insurance divisions, medical insurance divisions, investment divisions, etc. I like to call this person the chief fraud risk officer (CFRO). This is an important and responsible position. It should be at the same level of seniority as the chief operating officer (COO) or the chief information security officer (CISO). The CFRO will most likely report to the chief financial officer (CFO) of the business unit.

Independence is less of an issue for a business unit level CFRO. The business unit will then need to decide how they wish to carry out the group's fraud strategy in their individual business unit. They determine their own structure and number of resources.

The skills that these people hold are really no different to those of the group-level forensic services function. The business units need to ensure that they have the skills that are appropriate for them to carry out their part of the fraud strategy.

The group-level/holding company forensic services can provide guidance and support to the individual business units as to what they need and how to structure their function. The group-level forensic function should also independently assess and report to the group leadership as to the adequacy of the individual business unit's fraud resources and ability to carry out their respective fraud strategies. The group-level forensic function can also provide guidance and recruitment support.

10.4.5. Job matrix

Annexure 10.2 provides an example of a job matrix that can be used to understand some of the generic job skill requirements in a forensic function.

10.5. TIME

10.5.1. Introduction

The scope of what the forensic function is to achieve is defined in the fraud strategy. The contemplation of 'time' is firstly to gain an understanding of how many man-hours are required to execute the entire fraud strategy. It also entails the decision as to how much time to dedicate to the various strategic directions. Lastly, the concept of time entails when particular activities need to be carried out.

At the end of the day, you will need to temper the fraud strategy and/or how much of the fraud strategy can be achieved annually, to suit the resources available.

The use of in-house or outsourced resources will have a direct bearing on the amount of time available for utilisation within the forensic function. The use of an external consultancy will essentially expand the amount of time available (measured in man-hours), by the contracted period/hours.

10.5.2. Skills audit

Forensic skills are not generally or even necessarily available. Different staff members will possess different skills. Commence therefore by conducting an assessment of the type of skills that you have available and where these skills are (in the department, in the wider organisation or in external consulting firms). Then conduct a gap analysis to identify areas of excess skills or areas in which there is a shortage of skills. Use this information to decide how best to address the skills mismatch.

More specifically, the first step of this would be to estimate how long each element of the fraud strategy will take to execute and/or how much time you wish to dedicate to each element. The next step would be to determine which type and how much of each type of resource you have available to carry this strategy out. An example of the output from a skills audit may include these elements, as per Annexure 10.3 attached hereto.

10.5.3. Annual resource requirements

Unfortunately, things change over time. You will, therefore, need to revisit your resource assessment periodically. The template below can be used to determine the duration of annual tasks and the number of full-time employees required to complete the tasks.

The problem with estimates is that estimates are inaccurate. To illustrate this point, if you ask a senior forensic manager to estimate the duration per task that his staff members should take, they will most likely provide an inaccurate high-level assessment; for example: one day for this, two days for that, etc. They will not consider all the smaller tasks that make up the larger task. The reality is that we are all busy all day and we do not have time to spare. Why then are our estimates so inaccurate?

Another factor is that I will have an estimation bias towards the aspects that I am measured on. If a manager is measured on investigation duration, he will be inclined to give himself more time to deliver on his requirement.

Lastly, if you give me a day, I will take a day. If you give me two hours, I will take two hours.

These are not easy factors to compensate for. The trick is, therefore, to make the estimates as realistic as possible to ensure greater accuracy (never total accuracy). Most people could not be bothered and that is their right. If however you are looking for a realistic measurable for KPIs or to motivate additional resources, then you are going to require greater accuracy. Greater accuracy means greater detail.

I normally apply more detail to list all tasks involved in a specific activity. For example, in performing fraud vulnerability, I include planning, drafting of material, request for information, travel to and from the venue, conducting the workshops, reporting, review and follow-up. Now, all of a sudden, a person is forced to recognise that the duration of a fraud vulnerability assessment is not only the time spent in the workshop. The purpose is not to overlook the actual duration of tasks and to have a realistic view of actual time spent.

Annexure 10.4 has an example template of how time estimates can be documented.

At the conclusion of this exercise you will either have determined:

- *Exactly the correct amount of resources utilised*

None required.

- *Unutilised resources:*
    - Rework the strategy to productively utilise the unutilised resources.
    - Potentially change the skills mix of resources in the team/available, by redeploying excessive resources of one type and hiring in or having access to another lacking type of skill. This may not be as easy as implied though.

- *Insufficient resources to execute the fraud strategy:*
    - Hire in the required/missing resources.
    - Set framework agreements in place with external service providers to have access to the required skills.
    - Make arrangements with organisational leadership to have access to in-house resources (exchange programme or a programme of secondment).
    - Amend the fraud strategy to accommodate the lack of sufficient skills.

10.5.4. Annual schedule

Reactive forensic work is not repetitive/predictive work and the actual length of an investigation may be difficult to estimate in advance. It is also impossible to predict the exact number of fraud investigations you may have to deal with in a year. There are however some tasks that can be estimated with greater accuracy than others. The consolation is that duration forecasts become more accurate with more of your own experience and data trends within your function.

Predicting the duration of proactive fraud work can generally be performed with greater accuracy.

While we can acknowledge that time planning in a forensic function is not an exact science, we can say confidently that some planning (albeit rough) is better than no planning at all. So, even though you may be unable to control how long an investigation takes, you will at least have a view of when your timelines are moving out and what is being sacrificed. You will then be in a better position to inform relevant parties and/or to respond in the most applicable manner to minimise the impact of the affected schedule.

I always recommend visually depicting what time is available and what time is not. I find a traditional time schedule the most useful for this. Start therefore with a blank annual planning schedule. Microsoft Excel is an effective tool to use to draft an annual work plan. Then add in the obvious time constraints, such as:

- Weekends
- Public holidays
- Annual leave (where known in advance)
- Training
- Other known activities (for example a known office move, etc).

Next, I like to add in any formal reporting deadlines or any known events, including:

- Audit committee meetings
- Senior organisational leadership feedback meetings
- Fraud newsletter deadlines
- External audits.

Also add in any known or planned work, including:

- Relationship building/regional visits
- Fraud vulnerability assessments
- Proactive data analytic exercises
- Scheduled proactive lifestyle audits.

Lastly, add in your more flexible 'nice-to-haves' that you have in the forensic strategy. While all work performed by a forensic function is important, not all can be rescheduled when for example an investigation takes longer than envisaged. Some examples of 'nice-to-haves' include:

- Training
- Educational campaigns
- Proactive fraud risk assessments.

Over time you will be able to determine annual investigation duration averages and the average number of cases actually dealt with and any seasonal trends (for example: retail theft trends may spike over the festive season or procurement related frauds have the highest probability of occurrence at annual bidding time).

10.5.5. Productive time

While there are 365 days in a year, there are not 365 productive days available in a year. The following is an illustration of how to compute the number of days in a year which can be used productively.

Days in a Year			365
Less	Weekends	-104	
	Public holidays	-14	
	Allowance for Annual Leave	-15	
	Allowance for Sick Leave	-5	
	Training	-5	
Sub-total			-143
Available productive days in a year			**222**

Figure 10.1 *Annual productive day illustration*

Furthermore, while there may be eight hours in a normal working day, it is not to say that you will obtain a full eight hours' productivity out of staff members. It is safest to work on six productive hours in a day.

It is unlikely that an in-house forensic function will make use of time to an hourly level of detail. In-house functions will most likely stop at a daily level. Some in-house functions charge time out to 'client'-cost centres. An hourly level of detail will be required in this case.

External consultancies frequently charge out their time to clients and an hourly level of detail on time will most likely be required.

10.5.6. Forecasts

It would be best to maintain three levels of time forecasting and scheduling detail, namely:

- An annual overview - broad-brush planning
- Quarterly planning
- Assignment-specific planning - greatest detail

10.5.7. Inputs vs outputs

Some managers are very concerned about the times that staff members come and go and the duration that they spend on tasks.

An old sage once taught to take care of the 'outputs' and the 'inputs' will take care of themselves. This is very true and especially when dealing with more senior/experienced professional people. They do not want to be told what to do and they want to be told what the task is and given the rough boundaries in which to move. Then they like to be left alone.

It is not suggested that you throw caution to the wind. Some degree of high-level monitoring of a team's inputs is wise. The greatest emphasis should be on the outputs:

- When the task is delivered
- The quality of the outputs.

A simple functional duration estimating and usage model is, therefore, better than a detailed theoretical model.

10.6. FUNDING

The funding of the forensic function is discussed in detail under the 'budget' section below.

10.7. LOCATION

It is not often that we can choose upfront where our forensic function will be located. With some time (years) and together with other changes in the building, you may be able to request changes to the location where your function is located. Try overall, as far as possible, to select or have your current location changed to ensure that it:

- Is secure, so that no one can break in and destroy sensitive information (this may require the use of monitoring cameras, special locks, special doors, access control, and/or the use of a receptionist)
- Has restricted access even when staff members are working and people do not just wander in and out
- Has a secure storage area
- Has a confidential interview location
- Has an area to conduct planning and/co-coordinating, which could be as simple as a whiteboard (it may however not be possible to remove planning until it is complete)

- Being located on-site or off-site to the general organisation also has its challenges. If you are off-site, then you tend to be cut off and you may miss out on important information, knowledge of occurrences or opportunities to informally build relationships. On-site locations have the obvious challenges of restricting access and not being able to work free from influence or distraction.

10.8. EQUIPMENT

Some equipment requirements that may be required for a forensic function include:

- *Computers*

Laptops, dedicated screens and keyboards.

- *Specialised computer servers*

These may be used to reduce the load on production servers due to the running of large data analytic scripts/programs.

- *Mobile phones*

for basic communication.

- *Recording equipment*

Freeware or proprietary software on your laptop. The recording of matters is discussed in the chapter on interviewing.

- *Specialised software*

Could include data analytic software, e-mail search software, etc.

- *Vehicles/ability to travel*

This could include company vehicles, air ticket budgets, etc.

- *General office equipment*

Including:
  - Desks
  - Chairs
  - Cupboards
  - Shredder
  - Printers.

- *Stationery*

Standard pens, paper, etc.

- *Uniforms*

Generally, I would say, unless it is company policy, avoid wearing uniforms. Try to dress in a professional/big four type manner.

10.9. BUDGET

10.9.1. General

The budget (like the charter) is a method of legitimising the forensic function. This budget may be a fully-fledged standalone budget or it may form part of another budget (for example the internal audit department, a governance function, the finance function, the main board's budget, etc).

It may be difficult to convince a person that the forensic function is a legitimate and standalone function if it does not have its own budget. The establishment of a budget, while offering the obvious limitations, also offers some freedom to manoeuver within the budget. This freedom provides agility to respond to situations without having to run backwards and forwards every five minutes to obtain approval for funds. The constant approval may entail the need to continually justify the need for the forensic function. It also provides an opportunity for those not convinced of the need for a forensic function to restrict the function.

10.9.2. Measurement

Budget also provides an element of measurement that may be utilised in KPI assessments. Many people who do not understand forensics or auditing may try to enforce irrelevant KPIs onto the forensic team. Budget is one form of measurement. The use of KPIs is discussed below.

Investigative costs and the forensic function's general costs may be sensitive and knowledge and access to this information should be limited to senior staff members who are free of any investigations or ability to influence the forensic function.

10.9.3. Approval

The budget should be tabled on at least an annual basis before the audit committee for approval. The head of the forensic function should also provide the audit committee with a view of the function's performance against previously budgeted amounts. The need to have the budget approved by an audit committee revolves around the need for independence and/or objectivity. Independence, in this case, is to avoid any intentional or indirect scope limitations imposed by a reduced budget.

A CFO may be measured on the overall organisation's or finance function's budget. The CFO will, therefore, be inclined to want to reduce the overall budget that he has responsibility for if this is one of his KPIs. The forensic function may provide an easy area for the CFO to reduce his overall budget. The need for proactive areas may be difficult to justify in times of financial pressure. Alternatively, the CFO may not want to approve the additional budget for example for external IT forensics or laptops which he knows will implicate him in a matter under investigation.

Of course what happens, in reality, is that the budget is not debated for the first time at the audit committee. The head of forensics normally reports functionally to a CFO or to the head of internal audit. The forensic budget goes through a few iterations with the CFO before the final budget is tabled before the audit committee. The CFO would restrict the budget at this stage already.

We need to be realistic though. The CFO is charged with financial control and the head of forensics with fraud investigation and anti-fraud programmes. Human nature is that we will invariably have differences of opinion as to the priorities. This does not mean that one is more right than the other. It does mean that someone needs to have the casting vote as to where the priority should fall. We also have to be practical. We work for businesses that do not have access to unlimited funds. We should expect that we will need to compromise on our budget.

The head of forensics should have an open line of communication to the chairman of the audit committee, either directly or via the head of internal audit (depending on the organisational structure).

The audit committee should also ask the head of forensics when the budget is tabled if there are any limitations that should be discussed. The head of forensics should, for example, say that the budget as presented is the budget that was agreed with the CFO. The audit committee should be aware that the areas of the budget that have been excluded include X and Y and the anticipated effect on the work. The audit committee will then have an opportunity to discuss the excluded areas and potentially override the CFO. This will also all be minuted.

You are not advised to do this without informing people of what you are going to do. You are part of the organisation and you need to work with the CFO. You should tell the CFO in advance that you will, as part of the tabling of the budget, also be listing the areas that have been excluded. This can be done in a positive manner. For example: The head of forensics can say that the three-year plan includes a desire to conduct the following activities: A, B & C. We have, however, given the X & Y organisational capital projects, decided to delay these elements. This way the CFO gets an opportunity to prepare and is not caught off-guard. This builds trust. You will have to continue to work with the CFO long after the budget is tabled. You do not want to win the budget battle and lose the forensic support war.

You should also prime the chairman of the audit committee on the budget limitations. In this way, the audit committee can prepare questions to ensure that the restriction is debated in a meaningful manner.

It is ideal that the party to whom the forensic function is reporting or who requested the establishment of the forensic function should approve the budget.

As an example: In one organisation the group FD was against the forensic function, but all the other directors were in favour of it. This resulted in a constant battle with the FD. Fortunately, over time the function naturally reported to the group MD who was very supportive. The Group FD was happy as he was rid of the responsibility of something that he did not believe in. The moral of the story is not to fight things head-on, but to look for practical solutions that suit everyone.

10.9.4. Budgeted costs

Examples of forensic function related costs to be budgeted for may include:

- *Staff remuneration costs (salaries, bonuses, pension plans, medical insurance, etc)*
  These are all the costs normally associated with the remuneration of staff members. Staff members may be permanently employed in a full-time capacity in the forensic function, be temporarily employed or be seconded to the forensic function with a partial charge being allocated to the forensic function.

- *Other operating costs*

These may include rentals, vehicles, subsistence, etc.

- *Training and development of the forensic staff members*

Staff members need to keep up to date and improve their skill levels. Attendance of ACFE training, interviewing skill training, questioned document evaluation skills, etc is one method through which to achieve this.

- *Travel and subsistence*

These are the costs of travel to and from investigations, training, meetings, etc. The costs include the transport (airfares, taxis, trains, etc) and the subsistence costs (meals, drinks, laundry, etc).

- *Equipment*

Equipment cost may include:

  - Computers
  - Mobile phones
  - Cameras
  - Recording equipment
  - Software
  - Vehicles
  - Specialised measuring equipment required in particular industries.

- *External investigation costs*

If the entire forensic function has been contracted out on a fixed period contract basis, it will be easy to budget for the annual contract fee. Please note however that the contract price includes a provision for specific work or a fixed number of hours. This standard fee presumes that everything runs according to plan and it does not include any additional work, which is inevitable. It would be good practice to allow for an additional amount (not visible to the contractor/s) to cover such eventualities.

The fixed fee may include specific proactive assignments and maybe even have an allowance for specific known investigations. The amount and/or allocated hours may be specified in the contract. The hourly rate at which additional work is billed may also be specified.

Be cautious, as contractors typically give preferential rates for specified work because the work is guaranteed (and they can forecast/decide to employ full-time employees) and to secure the business. They then typically charge significantly higher rates for all subsequent work.

An alternative pricing strategy is to put framework agreements in place with a few contractors. This is good for the organisation as different contractors may have different strengths, regional presence and availability. You may even include a volume rebate subject to annual hourly usage.

The frequent ad hoc use of external companies may allow for an element of predictability, which may allow for the budgeting of anticipated consulting costs. Alternatively, an upper limit could be established, based on historical trends, risk appetite or pure budget allocation constraints.

10.9.5. Budgeted incomes

The big question is if there are any incomes to be budgeted for in a forensic function. At the simplest level, this will depend on whether you are in an in-house function or an external consultancy. As an external consultancy, you would be budgeting for incomes as with any other business.

As an in-house function, it may depend on the structure of your internal accounting philosophy. For example, do you have cost and/or income centres and are inter-departmental costs charged out? This charge may be a plain in and an out. You will also need to determine if there is a markup to any internal charges.

In certain types of organisations, it makes perfect sense to ensure that costs are allocated completely to the correct cost centre.

In terms of recoveries, these should be allocated back to the division/company/entity that incurred the initial fraud loss to offset the known losses.

While in some companies it makes sense, as a general rule, the charging out of forensic costs is not always a good thing. Forensics tends largely to be a 'grudge spend'. People do not like 'throwing good money after bad'. They also do not like spending on areas that people do not know exist yet (such as proactive work). This will distract from their ability to spend on the core business on which they are measured.

Management may also resist conducting investigations when they do not want to be hit by the associated costs. Remember they have just lost X amount and now they need to spend Y to investigate what they think they already know (the loss). Management also typically says that they want to have a degree of say in the costs that are going to be charged to them/their cost centres.

It is ideal if management is not given the opportunity to decide if they want to investigate based on internal costs (cost centre charges). The normal running costs should be part of a larger budget (like the finance department's budget or a general charge to the organisational governance costs) and not charged out. After all, these are mostly 'sunk costs'.

This is different for external investigation costs. Investigation-specific costs should be charged to the area in which the matter occurred. This is because they had the responsibility to prevent and detect the matter originally. The controls failed in their area for which they had the responsibility. Confidentiality may be an overriding factor in not doing this though. An independent and senior person should have the casting vote over functions that resist investigations based on costs.

10.10. KEY PERFORMANCE INDICATORS

10.10.1. Introduction

People generally want to know how well something is working. People are also aware that there are both subjective and objective assessments and the tendency is to want to be more objective and to remove 'emotion' from assessments.

Those involved in the detail of an activity may have less of a reason to want to measure things as they are more in tune with the level of performance. Those who are not involved in the detail of an activity and/or who have the responsibility for an area are more inclined to want to have some form of tangible measurement to indicate how things are progressing. This is good and in the right spirit of doing things.

The challenge is that not everything can be measured, or rather that measurement alone may be insufficient. Nevertheless, some degree of measurement is better than none. It is what the 'some measurement' should be that is the question.

10.10.2. Challenge

There is a difference between monitoring trends and measuring people. Perhaps this is where the lines become a bit blurred for some people. There are many trends that should be monitored to ensure that there is early detection if performance is veering off the road and to ensure that behaviours are amended in time and/or that we respond appropriately to ensure a 'desirable' outcome.

On the other hand, to hold people accountable for things that they have no or little control/influence over is meaningless. We therefore need to actively differentiate between the monitoring of trends and the measurement of good and bad performance.

It is typically the people who do not understand what is involved in a forensic investigation who tend to want to enforce arbitrary KPIs. This is just a statement of fact and there is no sense in fighting it. It is our job to educate them and to respond appropriately to ensure that the most meaningful indicators are adopted.

Encouraging people to 'drive the outputs, not the inputs' may also be applicable in this situation. We only need to be concerned when there is a disproportionate number of KPIs and time spent on them as compared to the efforts to drive sound outputs.

You can, as your guide, try to determine if the KPIs referred to are measurable. Also, are they put on the table in every weekly progress meeting or is it something that is not used to drive the daily running of the function? If not, they are not useful KPIs driving what needs to be done.

Look at what behaviours they drive. Do staff members comply with them to be in a position to tick a box or is it something that drives real performance? How do they contribute to the meaningful and correct resolution of performance issues?

10.10.3. Solution

So how then do we strike the balance and ensure meaningful measurement of the functioning of the forensic function? The answer is by choosing (only) a handful of KPIs with an allowance for reasons and the reading of KPIs by senior management with insight and to only be used as a broad trend. Consider the deliverables of the forensic function try to identify one measurable per deliverable.

The following are examples of some KPIs used and a short discussion of the advantages and disadvantages of using such a measurable:

- *Registration days*

The number of days to register a matter on the central system from the time that the matter occurred and/or was first identified. This is not a bad indicator and certainly something that is important to monitor, because if matters are not being registered at all or being registered late, then there is less or no opportunity to respond appropriately and ensure a more favourable outcome.

Please note that the timely registration of matters may not be under the direct control of the forensic function, as the timely registration and/or notification of cases (directly on the system or purely notifying the forensic function) may be a business responsibility and not one of the forensic function. It does represent an important area to remind the business about and/or to follow up with the business, though. The challenge is that the business:

- Has different priorities and may not see the importance of reporting/investigating a matter
- May wish to screen what is reported for fear of reprisal/that the matter may be a poor reflection of the business unit/an individual
- May not have the insights to know that a fraud exists or not initiate an investigation to determine if there is fraud or not, therefore never giving the matter a chance
- May only want to report proven matters. In this manner, they ignore unproven/suspected matters and these never get the opportunity to be understood by someone with the required skills.

The reporting of matters may, therefore, be more of a business KPI than a forensic function measurable in that case. The forensic function has a gate-keeping oversight role however.

- *Investigation days*

Number of days from registering a matter to closing it. This is one of those difficult items. While we need to monitor it, we cannot use a 'one-size-fits-all' approach. This is as not all investigations have the same number of activities involved in them and the length of the same activity may differ from matter to matter.

This is not a good KPI measurable for the forensic function, as it may not be a reflection of 'performance'. It is a good one to watch from an overall trend point of view. If investigations are taking longer on average, then you would need to know why. Is it because:

- The fraud investigator does not have the skills or is performing more slowly?
- The business is not cooperating?
- There are dependencies on other outside parties (banks, suppliers, prosecutors, police, etc), over which there is minimal influence?
- The matter is more complicated than the typical matters that have established the benchmark?

Any good manager will be aware of what is happening with the matters under investigation and the reasons for slower progress. The fraud investigator's leaders may, however, be unaware of the trends and reasons for the trends.

What would be important, if you did want to use this as a KPI, is to have a meaningful baseline. Establishing the baseline would entail listing all possible investigation steps and allocating an average number of days to each. It is not advisable to establish a baseline on only the existing trend as the existing trend may already include inefficiencies or may have been based on investigations which were not carried out taking all steps sufficiently into account. The temptation is there to want to just set the KPI baseline at the historical trend, but then you miss the opportunity to be realistic and to stretch existing practices.

- *Report issue days*

The number of days from completion of the investigation to issuing the final report. This is also quite a good KPI. It ignores the quality of the report and the relative complexity of different matters to document though. Overall this is a useful KPI to monitor.

- *Report length*

The number of pages the final report is. Management tries in some organisations to limit the length of a report to a maximum number of pages. The motive is to ensure that the report author only concentrates on the most important aspects.

While there is an appreciation that management does not want to spend time wading through masses of detail, more often the opposite extreme applies where management is just too lazy and does not want to make the effort to read about the matters that they are responsible for. Of course, this is extreme and we need to strike a balance.

You should only commit to issuing reports at the length that the report needs to be to deliver the correct message. It is unfortunately impossible to define a benchmark of the optimal length of a report. Furthermore, there is no direct relationship between the length of a report and the quality of the report or the type of investigation. There is, however, a lot of merit in ensuring that the report suits the reader's requirements and avoiding clutter. A pure KPI is, in my opinion, not the best method by which to monitor this.

It is better to split the report into a summary and detailed section or even to issue different reports to different audiences, for example: a summary report for directors and senior organisational leadership and a more detailed report for the responsible management. Summary reports are also easier to restrict in length. Report length is therefore not a good KPI.

- *Significant findings*

The number of significant findings versus the total number of findings in the report. Here is another KPI that is not ideal. The idea of this KPI is to try to force fraud investigators or auditors to concentrate on the most important aspects only. This is a great concept, but the incorrect method by which to carry it out.

So if, for example, there are ten findings raised in a report, we need to establish how many of these can be classified as 'significant'. Let us say in this example that eight of the ten are classified as significant. You would then have a KPI score of 80% in that case, which sounds great. This KPI is however fraught with problems.

While the principle remains the same, this KPI ignores that different reports have varying numbers of findings. Mathematically, it is easier to obtain a higher KPI score in a report with fewer findings. So if I only have two findings and one is significant then I will have a 50% KPI score. Alternatively, if I have a report with ten findings I will require five of them to be classified as significant findings to obtain the same 50% KPI score. So what does this drive? Either I get prejudiced for trying to report more things or I report less. Now while I can hear all the intrinsically motivated people saying that they would never do that, I have seen many KPI driven people not responding in this manner.

So it drives the wrong behaviour. In so doing the organisation may be losing out on valuable aspects. It is rather recommended to report less important aspects in a separate memo or label them as 'housekeeping'/low significance in the main report. It is not advisable to lose any aspect. If you have done the work and identified the aspects to be reported, then you might as well report it. Where and how are the only questions and not whether to report or not.

- *Number of investigations*

The number of investigations compared to previous periods. This is not seen as a KPI. The number of investigations registered in a year tells us a couple of things. Every organisation has fraud. No organisation is immune to it. If there are no fraud cases being reported or relatively few cases being reported, then it does not mean that you do not have fraud in the organisation. All it means is that all the cases are not being reported. So a low number of cases is not something to be proud of.

It is normal that there are naturally more fraud cases in the areas where you conduct forensic work, as the people working in those areas are aware of the anti-fraud efforts. When a new case pops up in another area you will move your attention to the new area. The number of matters reported from the initial area slowly diminishes, while the number of matters in the new area increases.

A high number of cases registered means that your fraud awareness campaign is working well and that people are reporting matters that would otherwise have gone unnoticed. This is good, not bad. In conclusion then, try turning this KPI on its head and drive fraud awareness in areas where there is no or little reporting of fraud cases.

Of course, a relatively high number of fraud cases will also point to a weaker control environment and again you are encouraged to analyse the systems of control to identify fraud vulnerabilities for mitigation.

- *Resolution timc*

The length of time for management to resolve reported items. This is a very good aspect to monitor as it will help to understand if future occurrence will be prevented and/or detected. The number of items resolved KPI discussed below also refers.

This KPI unfortunately ignores that different aspects take varying time frames to resolve. A more accurate KPI is to monitor how long after management's committed deadline aspects are resolved.

This KPI is also more of a management KPI and not necessarily restricted to a forensic function KPI. Of course, the forensic function needs to follow up and establish relationships and drive implementation. This is, therefore, more of a trend to monitor than a performance KPI to monitor.

As the timely and/or complete resolution of matters may not be at the full control of the forensic function, so too may the resolution not be at the full control of management. There may be other priorities, budget restrictions or other practical problems that prevent management from resolving the matters. In this case, the forensic function has a responsibility to bring this to the attention of the senior organisational leadership. This may just be to keep the senior leadership abreast of the current position of previously reported risks or it may be to act as an ally with management to influence the senior organisational leadership to assist in the resolution (possibly by approving budget, resources, etc).

Setting up service level agreements (SLAs) with management for periods in which they are to resolve reported matters is also recommended.

- *Resolved items*

Number of unresolved reported items. As above. This KPI differs in so far as it refers to the number of items and not the duration to resolution.

The same limitations are applicable. It is however a good aspect to monitor to ensure the timely intervention in the event of a tardy response.

- *Feedback*

Satisfaction questionnaire/feedback obtained. Some organisations make use of a 'customer satisfaction questionnaire' after an investigation to determine areas of improvement and/or continuation (satisfaction). This KPI refers to both positive and negative feedback. Feedback is always good and can be given formally (for example in response to a questionnaire) or informally based on established relationships.

This KPI is however not a totally reliable measurable, as:

- You do not always receive a response to every satisfaction questionnaire sent out.
- If you do not make use of questionnaires, then you cannot guarantee that all negative or positive feedback will be received in every case.
- People do not always answer questionnaires sincerely/honestly. They sometimes answer in response to the hierarchy and in terms of what they think is wanted and not necessarily what the actual picture is.
- Questionnaires tend to ask the questions to suit the answers that they seek. Questionnaires are not a scientific instrument and may be skewed in terms of the questions and the results by design.
- If you give a tough review, you tend to get sour grapes back.

The select use of questionnaires is recommended in anticipation of each individual situation. The results must also be read and used with insight. 'Score only' type questionnaires are discouraged, as they deny the opportunity for understanding and leave much to the interpretation of scores. Overall this is not a good KPI. It is necessary to invite feedback and to use the results constructively. This does not suggest that you should try to excuse away any feedback received, which some managers do. It is important to read the feedback with insight.

- *Prevention*

The number of frauds prevented. This is not regarded as a KPI measure, as it is impossible to know all matters that have been prevented, mainly due to the concealed nature of frauds. When it does however become known that anti-fraud efforts or sound controls have detected or prevented frauds, this should be reported to senior organisation leadership and/or published to the organisation (for example in a sanitised article).

- *Recoveries*

The amount of funds recovered. Again not a good KPI, but certainly something to encourage and to report to senior organisational leadership and to the general organisation where practical to do so. In fact, the formal consideration of recoveries to be included in the investigation methodology is encouraged. Recoveries should be pursued in all cases where possible, but the forensic function cannot be held accountable where there are no funds to recover or where it is not practical to do so.

- *Costs*

The amount spent on investigations. Investigation costs include direct and indirect costs. Direct costs are easier to measure than indirect costs. Direct costs include:

- Direct financial losses
- External investigator costs
- IT forensic costs
- Data analytic costs
- Litigation costs
- Travel costs
- Computer reprogramming costs (additional controls).

Indirect costs include:

- Internal employees' time spent on investigations and/or corrections
- Cost of additional controls
- Rehiring costs
- Retraining costs
- Set-up costs
- Productivity losses
- Loss of business/customers
- Loss of intellectual capital
- Tarnished name/brand
- General overhead costs (telephones, office rent, etc)
- Internal fraud investigators' salary costs. Investigators work on multiple matters at the same time and it may be difficult to accurately apportion costs to specific matters. Timekeeping records may assist.

The difficulty with investigation costs is to determine a baseline against which to determine if costs are high or low. It is good (to manage service providers and to determine which scope will be covered) if a budget can be established and approved in advance. Perhaps the ability to keep costs within the approved investigation budget is a good measure.

The organisation's ability to afford conducting an investigation is paramount. Different organisations will have different appetites and abilities to conduct investigations.

Direct investigation costs frequently exceed known financial losses resulting from the fraud. This is often done to prove a point and show that the organisation is serious about investigating fraud.

- *Losses*

The size of the financial losses directly attributable to fraud. Fraud investigators should not be held accountable for actual fraud losses or for the prevention of fraud. This is management's responsibility. Management in the retail industry is frequently incentivised to reduce stock 'shrinkage'. Shrinkage is all unknown stock losses and could be attributed to theft and cut-off problems.

This is not a totally bad idea. It can, however, drive the incorrect behaviour though. Management may be inclined to use short-term drivers to reduce shrinkage or even massage numbers to reduce the appearance of shrinkage/losses. The substantiation of the shrinkage results also requires a lot of resources.

Internal auditors in some retail organisations are responsible to independently sign off on the shrinkage numbers. The auditors are also engaged in partnership with management in many anti-shrinkage efforts. This sort of involvement will be industry specific.

10.11. INSOURCED OR OUTSOURCED

The perennial debate is whether to insource the forensic function or to outsource it. It unfortunately depends on the organisation.

The total outsourcing of the forensic function can be expected in organisations where:

- The entire audit function is outsourced
- There is a strong need for independence in investigations
- There is no or little 'real' fraud. The absence of detected fraud may be an indication of poor controls and low fraud awareness.

It is not possible for internal forensic functions to:

- Have access to all the required skills, tools and networks
- Keep up to date with all investigating and legal aspects.

Total outsourcing is not favoured. In fact, in-house forensic functions should outsource as little as possible, as:

- External consultancies can be excessively expensive.
- External consultants are mostly not more skilled than a well-established forensic function.
- They take a long time to understand your business.
- They do not have easy access to or knowledge of internal data.
- There is little knowledge transfer/retention, making the need for consultants a perpetuating cycle.
- They do not have the time or the motive to complete many detailed and subsequent aspects that need to be carried out.
- It is more difficult for them to build internal relationships/trust.

There are many frustrations as an external consultant in so far that you are unable to add additional value to clients, as you only have limited time available to dedicate to them.

Co-sourcing is favoured. Your best experiences will be when the internal function has frequent access to external consultancies. External consultancies are open to sharing, as long as they knew that this was part of the relationship and that they still received some business albeit in the more specialised areas. In this manner the internal function builds its own basic skills quickly, but also has the option to use the external consultancies as a sounding board and for more esoteric skills. The external agencies are also not bogged down with detailed follow-up and investigations.

Please ensure that the outsourcing of the external audit, internal audit and forensic investigation are all awarded to different competing companies. This as:

- External auditors may not be allowed to also offer consulting services
- There is a risk of conflict of interest if the external auditors and/or internal auditors did not detect fraud and now need to investigate a fraud.

Annexure 10.1
Forensic skill table

	Executive	**Managerial**	**Non-managerial**	**Trainee/ intern/ student**	**Administrative**
Education					
Specific skills					
Level of experience					

Annexure 10.2
Skills job matrix

JOB MATRIX

COMPARATIVE AREA	FORENSIC AUDIT MANAGER	SENIOR FORENSIC AUDITOR	FORENSIC AUDITOR	TRAINEE FORENSIC AUDITOR
Post/Job Grade	TBD	TBD	TBD	TBD
No. of staff currently in the area	TBD	TBD	TBD	TBD
No. of staff currently reporting to incumbent	TBD	TBD	0	0
No. of staff reporting to incumbent in future	TBD	TBD	0	0
Incumbent reports to the	Chief Audit Executive	Forensic Audit Manager	Forensic Audit Manager	Forensic Audit Manager
Areas of responsibility	Providing input to the Company-wide risk assessment	Providing input to the Forensic Audit Manager on the Company-wide risk assessment	-	-
	Conducting and Co-ordinating high-level Forensic risk assessments	Assist in conducting and co-ordinating high-level Forensic risk assessments	-	-
	Conducting Business process specific fraud risk assessments	Oversight of and conducting of Business process specific fraud risk assessments	Conducting Business process specific fraud risk assessments	Providing assistance in Business process specific fraud risk assessments
	Annual Forensic Audit and specific audit/investigative planning and scheduling	Assist in drafting the Annual Forensic Audit and specific audit/investigative planning and scheduling	-	-
	High-level annual Forensic Audit and specific resource determination and planning	-	-	-
	Conducting and Co-ordinating Forensic Audit preliminary surveys	Conducting Forensic Audit preliminary surveys	Conducting Forensic Audit preliminary surveys	Providing assistance in conducting Forensic Audit preliminary surveys
	Conducting introductory Forensic Audit meetings	Conducting introductory Forensic Audit meetings	Conducting introductory Forensic Audit meetings	-
	Defining and reviewing Forensic audit/investigative/preventative strategy objectives	Defining Forensic audit/investigative/preventative strategy objectives	-	-
	Setting and reviewing of the scope of the Forensic audit/investigation	Setting of the scope of the Forensic audit/investigation	Setting of the scope of the Forensic audit/investigation	Providing input as to the scope of the Forensic audit/investgation
	Reviewing of and limited documentation of systems of control and business processes	Documenting systems of control and business processes	Documenting systems of control and business processes	Documenting systems of control and business processes
	Review of and limited documenting of program logic	Limited documenting of program logic	Limited documenting of program logic	Limited documenting of program logic
	Review of and limited identifying of application controls (controls within programs)	Identifying of application controls (controls within programs)	Identifying of application controls (controls within programs)	Limited identifying of application controls (controls within programs)
	Review of and limited analysing of systems of Internal control (manual and automated) for fraud risks and control deficiencies	Analysing of systems of Internal control (manual and automated) for risks and control deficiencies	Analysing of systems of Internal control (manual and automated) for risks and control deficiencies	Documenting of systems of control and providing input into their analysis.
	Drafting and review of complex audit/investigative programmes	Drafting of difficult audit/investigative programmes	Drafting of audit/investigative programmes	Executing audit programmes and specific investigation methodologies.
	Review of and limited designing of complex Computer Assisted Audit techniques (CAATS)	Designing of Computer Assisted Audit techniques (CAATS)	Limited designing of Computer Assisted Audit techniques (CAATS)	-

JOB MATRIX				
COMPARATIVE AREA	FORENSIC AUDIT MANAGER	SENIOR FORENSIC AUDITOR	FORENSIC AUDITOR	TRAINEE FORENSIC AUDITOR
Post/Job Grade	TBD	TBD	TBD	TBD
No. of staff currently in the area	TBD	TBD	TBD	TBD
No. of staff currently reporting to incumbent	TBD	TBD	0	0
No. of staff reporting to incumbent in future	TBD	TBD	0	0
Incumbent reports to the	Chief Audit Executive	Forensic Audit Manager	Forensic Audit Manager	Forensic Audit Manager
Areas of responsibility	Providing input to the Company-wide risk assessment	Providing input to the Forensic Audit Manager on the Company-wide risk assessment	-	-
	Conducting and Co-ordinating high-level Forensic risk assessments	Assist in conducting and co-ordinating high-level Forensic risk assessments	-	-
	Conducting Business process specific fraud risk assessments	Oversight of and conducting of Business process specific fraud risk assessments	Conducting Business process specific fraud risk assessments	Providing assistance in Business process specific fraud risk assessments
	Annual Forensic Audit and specific audit/investigative planning and scheduling	Assist in drafting the Annual Forensic Audit and specific audit/investigative planning and scheduling	-	-
	High-level annual Forensic Audit and specific resource determination and planning	-	-	-
	Conducting and Co-ordinating Forensic Audit preliminary surveys	Conducting Forensic Audit preliminary surveys	Conducting Forensic Audit preliminary surveys	Providing assistance in conducting Forensic Audit preliminary surveys
	Conducting introductory Forensic Audit meetings	Conducting introductory Forensic Audit meetings	Conducting introductory Forensic Audit meetings	-
	Defining and reviewing Forensic audit/investigative/preventative strategy objectives	Defining Forensic audit/investigative/preventative strategy objectives	-	-
	Setting and reviewing of the scope of the Forensic audit/investgation	Setting of the scope of the Forensic audit/investgation	Setting of the scope of the Forensic audit/investgation	Providing input as to the scope of the Forensic audit/investgation
	Reviewing of and limited documentation of systems of control and business processes	Documenting systems of control and business processes	Documenting systems of control and business processes	Documenting systems of control and business processes
	Review of and limited documenting of program logic	Limited documenting of program logic	Limited documenting of program logic	Limited documenting of program logic
	Review of and limited identifying of application controls (controls within programs)	Identifying of application controls (controls within programs)	Identifying of application controls (controls within programs)	Limited identifying of application controls (controls within programs)
	Review of and limited analysing of systems of Internal control (manual and automated) for fraud risks and control deficiencies	Analysing of systems of Internal control (manual and automated) for risks and control deficiencies	Analysing of systems of Internal control (manual and automated) for risks and control deficiencies	Documenting of systems of control and providing input into their analysis.
	Drafting and review of complex audit/investigative programmes	Drafting of difficult audit/investigative programmes	Drafting of audit/investigative programmes	Executing audit programmes and specific investigation methodologies
	Review of and limited designing of complex Computer Assisted Audit techniques (CAATS)	Designing of Computer Assisted Audit techniques (CAATS)	Limited designing of Computer Assisted Audit techniques (CAATS)	-

Review of and limited performing data mining exercises	Sound ability to perform data mining exercises	Ability to perform data mining exercises	Introductory ability to perform data mining exercises
Review of and limited performing of analytical reviews	Performing of analytical reviews	Limited performing of analytical reviews	Introductory ability to perform analytical reviews
Review of and limited conducting of Compliance tests	Conducting of and limited review of Compliance tests	Conducting of Compliance tests	Limited conducting of Compliance tests
Review of and limited conducting substantive tests (proving a financial balance)	Conducting of and limited review of Substantive tests	Conducting of Substantive tests	Limited conducting of Substantive tests
Co-ordinating investigations, both centrally and geographically dispersed	Some co-ordinating of investigations, both centrally and geographically dispersed	Some co-ordinating of investigations	-
Discussing of audit/investigation findings during audits/investigations	Discussing of audit/investigation findings during audits/investigations	Discussing of own audit/investigation findings during audits/investigations	Compiling of supporting documents and evidence for own findings
Conducting post-audit/investigation debriefings	Conducting post-audit/investigation debriefings	Conducting of elementry post-audit/investigation debriefings	Attending some post audt/investigation debriefings
Sound ability to draft forensic audit reports	Drafting forensic audit reports	Drafting elementry forensic audit reports	Giving input to own report points
Sound ability to review Forensic Audit/Investigative Reports	Some ability to review forensic audit/Investigative reports	-	-
Discussing reports	Discussing reports	Discussing own sections of reports	Sit in on discussions of reports
Scheduling and performing follow-up audits/investigations	Scheduling and performing follow-up audits/investigations	Executing follow-up audits/investigations	Executing specific follow-up actions
Management and Leadership of Forensic Auditors	Supervisory oversight of auditors and contractors	Oversight of external contractors	-
Management and Leadership of Specialist Auditors per assignment	Supervision of Specialist Auditors per assignment	Some coordination of Specialist Auditors per assignment	-
Liaison with all levels of Auditees	Liaison with all levels of Auditees	Liaison with all levels of Auditees	
Liaison with all levels of Management/Leadership	Liaison with all levels of Management/Leadership	Liaison with all levels of Management/Leadership	Liaison with investigation specific people
Limited liaison with External Auditors	Liaison with External Auditors	Limited liaison with External Auditors	Limited liaison with External Auditors on investigations in which they were involved
Performing complex Ad hoc investigations	Performing difficult Ad hoc investigations	Performing Ad hoc investigations	Performing elementry Ad hoc investigations
Performing Benchmarking exercises	Limited performing Benchmarking exercises	-	-
Conducting "Control Self Assessment" (CSA)assignments/Fraud Vulnerability Assessemnts (FVA)	Conducting CSA/FVA assignments	Assisting in conducting CSA/FVA assignments	Providing administrative support for CSA/FVAs
Sound ability to perform forensic reviews	Ability to perform forensic reviews	Provide limited input to forensic reviews	Some ability to perform forensic reviews
Liaising with the Police/government departments/Security providers and other service providers	Liaising with the Police/government departments/Security providers and other service providers	Limited liaising with the Police/government departments/Security providers and other service providers	Accompaning colleagues to police and governement departments
Sound ability to present evidence at hearings/in court	Sound ability to present evidence at hearings/in court	Sound ability to present evidence at hearings/in court	Introduction to court/hearing proceedings
Co-ordination of drafting of the Fraud/conflict of interest and gift policies	Provide input to the Forensic audit manager on fraud/conflict of interest and gift policies	Knowledge of fraud/conflict of interest and gift policies	Introductory knowledge of fraud/conflict of interest and gift policies
Coordinating and conducting Fraud Awareness campaigns/education	Conducting Fraud Awareness campaigns/education	Assisting in conducting Fraud Awareness campaigns/education	Administrative support in fraud awareness and training campaigns
Assigned as investigator/co-ordinating and maintaining the Tip-Off's line. Generating statistics. Negotiating with service providers	Assigned as investigator/maintaining the Tip-Off's line, maintaining statistics, generating reports	Assigned as investigator/coordinator of cases on the Tip-Off's line	Administrative support on the Tip Off's line
Maintaining/Presenting of fraud/incident statistics	Maintaining fraud/incident statistics	Providing input into/compiling fraud/incident statistics	Administrative support in compiling statistics
Overall design of, maintaining and compiling of the fraud risk register. Use of and reporting of issues/trends	Maintaining and compiling of the fraud risk register	Maintaining and compiling of the fraud risk register	Administrative support of the fraud risk register

Good computer literacy	Good computer literacy	Fair computer literacy	Introductory computer literacy
Sound flowcharting skills	Good flowcharting skills	Fair flowcharting skills	Introductory flowcharting skills
Sound knowledge of forensic skills and tools	Good knowledge of forensic skills and tools	Fair knowledge of forensic skills and tools	Introductory knowledge of forensic skills and tools
Good accounting skills	Fair accounting skills	Basic accounting skills	Basic accounting skills
Sound subject interviewing skills	Good subject interviewing skills	Fair subject interviewing skills	Introductory subject interviewing skills
Sound Internal Auditing skills	Sound Internal Auditing skills	Internal Auditing skills	Introductory Internal Auditing skills
Basic IT Auditing skills	Basic IT Auditing skills	Basic IT Auditing skills	Introductory IT auditing concepts

Skills requirements (Competencies)	Fair general business knowledge	Fair general business knowledge	General business knowledge	Introductory business knowledge
	Sound diagnostic skills	Good diagnostic skills	Fair diagnostic skills	Basic diagnostic skills
	Enquiring mind	Enquiring mind	Enquiring mind	Enquiring mind
	Professionalism	Professionalism	Professionalism	Professionalism
	Assertiveness without being antagonistic	Assertiveness without being antagonistic	Assertiveness without being antagonistic	Assertiveness without being antagonistic
	Sound conflict management abilities	Good conflict management abilities	Fair conflict management abilities	Conflict management awareness
	An ability to work on a variety of dissimilar assignments at the same time	An ability to work on a variety of dissimilar assignments at the same time	An ability to work on a variety of dissimilar assignments at the same time	An ability to work on a variety of dissimilar assignments at the same time
	Sound interpersonal and communication skills	Good interpersonal and communication skills	Fair interpersonal and communication skills	Introductory interpersonal and communication skills
	Sound ability to build relationships and network	Good ability to build relationships and network	Fair ability to build relationships and network	Introductory ability to build relationships and network
	Sound planning and scheduling skills	Good planning and scheduling skills	Fair planning and scheduling skills	Introductory planning and scheduling skills
	Staff interviewing, recruitment and selection skills	-	-	-
	Disciplinary hearing and performance management/evaluation skills	-	-	-
	Budgeting and expense management skills	-	-	-
	Sound coaching, training and mentoring skills	Good coaching, training and mentoring skills	-	-
	Exceptional report writing skills	Sound report writing skills	Good report writing skills	Introductory report writing skills
	Exceptional verbal communication skills	Sound verbal communication skills	Good verbal communication skills	Verbal communication skills
	Exceptional attention to detail	Sound attention to detail	Good attention to detail	Attention to detail
	Sound leadership skills	Good leadership skills	-	-
	Ability to work alone and in/co-ordinate teams	Ability to work alone and in/co-ordinate teams	Ability to work alone and in teams	Ability to work alone and in teams
	Ethically sound and beyond influence	Ethically sound and beyond influence	Ethically sound and beyond influence	Ethically sound and beyond influence
	Ability to work with highly confidential information	Ability to work with highly confidential information	Ability to work with highly confidential information	Ability to work with highly confidential information
	High degree of emotional maturity	High degree of emotional maturity	High degree of emotional maturity	High degree of emotional maturity
Minimum Educational Requirements	Relevant legal, commerce or business qualification	Relevant legal, commerce or business qualification	Relevant legal, commerce or business qualification	Relevant legal, commerce or business qualification
	Either have of studing towards one or more of the following LLB, CFE, CIA or CA	Either have of studing towards one or more of the following LLB, CFE, CIA or CA	Either have of studing towards one or more of the following LLB, CFE, CIA or CA	Either have of studing towards one or more of the following LLB, CFE, CIA or CA
Minimum Experience Requirements	7 to 10 years Forensic Auditing/Investigative experience	5 to 7 years Forensic Auditing/Investigative experience	2 to 3 years Forensic Auditing/Investigative experience	No provious Forensic Auditing/Investigative experience
	5 to 10 years managerial/team leader experience	2 to 3 years team supervisory experience	No managerial/team leader experience	No managerial/team leader experience
	Sound knowledge of Criminal Law and the Judicial Process	A good working knowledge of Criminal Law and the Judicial Process	A fair working knowledge of Criminal Law and the Judicial Process	Introductory knowledge of Criminal Law and the Judicial Process
	Sound exposure to analytical reviews	Good exposure to analytical reviews	Some exposure to analytical reviews	Basic understanding of analytical reviews
	Sound data mining experience	Good data mining experience	Some data mining experience	knowledge ofdata mining concepts
	Sound report writing experience	Sound report writing experience	Good report writing experience	Basic report writing skills
	Sound mentoring experience	Fair mentoring experience	-	-

Annexure 10.3
Skills Audit Template

Staff member's name	Skill type	Level of competence	Location
			In-department
			In-house
			External service provider

Annexure 10.4
Time Estimate Template

Strategic area	No of people involved	frequency per year	Productive resources per year per activity	days per activity	Duration (Days)	Days per year
Annual activities						
Planning					0	
revision of polices and procedures					0	**0**
Key Meetings						
Meeting with key internal role players					0	
External Audit					0	
Legal function					0	
Enterprise Risk Manageemnt					0	
IT function					0	
External Agencies					0	
Outside forensic firms - SLAs					0	**0**
Fraud Reporting						
Key business Leaders					0	
Audit Committee					0	**0**
Proactive work						
Fraud Awareness training and campaigns						
Fraud Vulnerability Assessments						
Proactive lifestyle audits						
Data Analytics	0	0	0		0	**0**
Whistle-blower line						
General Admin					0	
Metrics					0	**0**
Fraud Newsletter						
Drafting					0	
Editing						**0**
Fraud investigations	**Average # of cases per year**		**Days per case per year**			
Own investigations		**% of total cases per year**			**cases**	
Common investigation steps					0	
					0	
					0	
					0	
						0
Outside consultant led investigations		**% of total cases per year**			**cases**	
Common investigation steps					0	
					0	
					0	
					0	
			0		0	**0**
Grand total of estimated productives days per year						**0**
Divided by: Productive days per year per person						**222**
Equals: Number of full time resources required per year						**0**

INDEX

B

Z

www.ingramcontent.com/pod-product-compliance
Lightning Source LLC
LaVergne TN
LVHW060007210926
848481LV00013B/3667
9781485120308